Aristotle on What Emotions Are

OXFORD ARISTOTLE STUDIES

General Editor
Lindsay Judson

PUBLISHED VOLUMES INCLUDE

Doing and Being
An Interpretation of Aristotle's Metaphysics *Theta*
Jonathan Beere

Aristotle on the Sources of the Ethical Life
Sylvia Berryman

Space, Time, Matter, and Form
Essays on Aristotle's Physics
David Bostock

Aristotle on Knowledge and Learning
The Posterior Analytics
David Bronstein

The Undivided Self
Aristotle and the 'Mind-Body Problem'
David Charles

Aristotle and the Eleatic One
Timothy Clarke

Passions and Persuasion in Aristotle's *Rhetoric*
Jamie Dow

Teleology, First Principles, and Scientific Method in Aristotle's Biology
Allan Gotthelf

Aristotle on the Common Sense
Pavel Gregoric

Aristotle on Shame and Learning to Be Good
Marta Jimenez

The Powers of Aristotle's Soul
Thomas Kjeller Johansen

How Aristotle gets by in *Metaphysics Zeta*
Frank A. Lewis

Aristotle on the Apparent Good
Perception, Phantasia, *Thought, and Desire*
Jessica Moss

Priority in Aristotle's *Metaphysics*
Michail Peramatzis

Aristotle's Theory of Bodies
Christian Pfeiffer

Aristotle on What Emotions Are

GILES PEARSON

Great Clarendon Street, Oxford, OX2 6DP,
United Kingdom

Oxford University Press is a department of the University of Oxford.
It furthers the University's objective of excellence in research, scholarship,
and education by publishing worldwide. Oxford is a registered trade mark of
Oxford University Press in the UK and in certain other countries

© Giles Pearson 2024

The moral rights of the author have been asserted

All rights reserved. No part of this publication may be reproduced, stored in
a retrieval system, or transmitted, in any form or by any means, without the
prior permission in writing of Oxford University Press, or as expressly permitted
by law, by licence or under terms agreed with the appropriate reprographics
rights organization. Enquiries concerning reproduction outside the scope of the
above should be sent to the Rights Department, Oxford University Press, at the
address above

You must not circulate this work in any other form
and you must impose this same condition on any acquirer

Published in the United States of America by Oxford University Press
198 Madison Avenue, New York, NY 10016, United States of America

British Library Cataloguing in Publication Data

Data available

Library of Congress Control Number: 2024932376

ISBN 9780198879343

DOI: 10.1093/9780191989292.001.0001

Printed and bound by
CPI Group (UK) Ltd, Croydon, CR0 4YY

Links to third party websites are provided by Oxford in good faith and
for information only. Oxford disclaims any responsibility for the materials
contained in any third party website referenced in this work.

To Monty and Lottie

Contents

Acknowledgements ix
Abbreviations, Translations, Use of Transliteration, and Cross-References xi

Introduction: What This Book Aims to Achieve
(and What It Doesn't). A Map 1

1. Some Key Terminology and Distinctions. The Prospects for an Analysis of Emotions in Terms of Other Intentional States 17

PART I. EMOTIONS AS PLEASURES AND DISTRESSES

2. Emotions as Representational Hedonic States 43

3. Pleasure and Distress as Contributing to the Individuation of Emotion-Types 65

4. Emotions as Hedonic States That Are Formed *in Response to* Intentional States That Apprehend Their Objects 89

5. Emotions and the Account(s) of Pleasure in the *Ethics* 115

PART II. EMOTIONS AND DESIRES

6. Anger (*Orgē*) 137

7. Some Other (Putative) Links between Emotions and Desires 154

8. Appetite (*Epithumia*) 179

PART III. THE MATERIAL DIMENSION OF EMOTIONS AND SOME PROBLEMATIC CASES

9. The Material or Bodily Dimension of Emotions 195

10. Some Problematic Cases and the Supplements in the *EE* Specification of the Emotions 235

PART IV. FURTHER PHILOSOPHICAL CONSIDERATIONS AND A SIGNIFICANT PHILOSOPHICAL ADVANTAGE

11. Contrast with a Contemporary Motivational Theory. Which Representational Role(s) Do Emotions Play?   259

12. Explaining Recalcitrant Emotions with Aristotle   275

Catalogue of Aristotle's Emotions as Representational Pleasures or Distresses   317

Bibliography   345
General Index   359
Index Locorum   372

Acknowledgements

A number of individuals have helped me along the way with this book, to whom I owe considerable thanks. First, I must mention Gisela Striker, who first encouraged me to think about Aristotle on the emotions a very long time ago. Her own insights in her 1996 provide rich pickings. Second, a number of other scholars who (in response to talks I've given or individually) have provided me with important questions or objections, or prompted further development of my ideas; viz. Malcolm Schofield, David Sedley, Geoffrey Lloyd, Sophia Connell, Nick Denyer, James Warren, Frisbee Sheffield, Myrto Hatzimichali, Arif Ahmed, Anthony Everett, Daniel Simão Nascimento, Gabriela Rossi, Lucas Angioni, and Breno Zuppolini. Third, two anonymous readers of this book for OUP provided many helpful queries and objections. Fourth, Peter Momtchiloff and Jamie Mortimer for their calm guidance and support in bringing the book to fruition with OUP. And, fifth, Maureen Pearson for compiling the Index Locorum.

Besides individuals, I have also had important institutional support, most crucially, a University Research Fellowship at my home institution Bristol University for the academic year 2019–20 which enabled me to thrash out the core ideas of this book. I would also like to thank my colleagues in the Philosophy Department for supporting my leave.

I would also like to stress that any advance this book may make on the question of what Aristotle thinks emotions are would not have been possible without the crucial research of some other scholars on Aristotle on the emotions. In particular, I have benefitted significantly from the work of Jamie Dow, Jessica Moss, Anthony Price, and Christof Rapp, as well as Martha Nussbaum, John Cooper, Gisela Striker, and Stephen Leighton. And, of course, W. W. Fortenbaugh set the whole thing going with his pathbreaking work in the early 1970s. Although, ultimately, I disagree with the views advanced by these scholars in key respects, even formulating the position I ascribe to Aristotle would not have been possible without their work.

Finally, I would like to make some thanks of a more personal nature. First, to my parents, and my sister and her family, for their continued love, support, and good humour. Second, to some friends (old Cambridge ones, local Bathonians, and one Hertfordian) for helping me to keep my sanity (although they would doubtless dispute this) over a pint or five. But my biggest debt of gratitude must be reserved for my partner—Olya Simakova—and our two wonderful children—Monty and Lottie—for putting up with me and making my life worth living. I dedicate the book to the kids.

Abbreviations, Translations, Use of Transliteration, and Cross-References

Abbreviations for works of Aristotle

Cael.	De caelo
Cat.	Categoriae
De an.	De anima
De resp.	De respiratione
EE	Ethica Eudemia
Gen. an.	De generatione animalium
Gen. cor.	De generatione et corruptione
Hist. an.	Historia animalium
Insomn.	De insomniis
Int.	De interpretatione
MA	De motu animalium
Mem.	De memoria et reminiscentia
Met.	Metaphysica
MM†	Magna moralia
NE	Ethica Nicomachea
PA	De partibus animalium
Phys.	Physica
Poet.	De arte poetica liber
Pol.	Politica
Pr. an.	Analytica priora
Probl.	Problemata
Rhet.	Rhetorica
SE	De sophisticis elenchis
Sens.	De sensu
Somn.	De somno
Top.	Topica

Other abbreviations

LSJ	Greek-English Lexicon (H. G. Liddell, R. Scott, and H. S. Jones)
OCT	Oxford Classical Texts
ROT	Revised Oxford Translation (J. Barnes 1984)
SVF	Stoicorum veterum fragmenta (H. von Arnim 1903–5)

† Not (in my view) by Aristotle.

Translations

Unless otherwise stated, the translations in this book are based on those listed below, but with many emendations of my own. The emendations are typically unflagged, unless I think something of substance hinges on it.

De an.	Hamlyn (1993)[1]
EE	Inwood and Woolf (2013)
Insomn.	*ROT* (Beare)
Int.	*ROT* (Ackrill)
MA	Morison in Rapp and Primavesi (2020)
Mem.	Sorabji (1972)
Met.	*ROT* (Ross)
NE	Ross (1980, i.e. as revised by Ackrill and Urmson)
PA	Lennox (2001)
Pol.	Reeve (2017)
Rhet.	Reeve (2018)
Top.	*ROT* (Pickard-Cambridge)

References to Aristotle in quotations from other authors

To avoid confusion, I have regularized the abbreviations and reference style (e.g. *NE* VI.13) in quotations of other authors in line with mine above. But I have not regularized British and American English or grammar styles.

Transliteration and use of Greek

This book does not require one to know Greek, but I seek to provide readers with Greek access to information they may want. In the interests of accessibility, I have generally transliterated Greek. But, occasionally, especially with longer passages or phrases, I have provided the original Greek. It should always be clear what I am discussing and the few terms that I use in transliterated but untranslated forms (esp. *phantasia*) will be explained as we go along.

---

[1] Hamlyn's (1992) translation and commentary has now been replaced with Shields' (2016) in the Clarendon Aristotle series. I have consulted the latter and it is invaluable in providing a complete translation and commentary of *De an.* I (which Hamlyn inexcusably omitted most of). But I have to admit I still prefer Hamlyn's translation (primarily on stylistic grounds) and so continue to use that unless otherwise noted.

Cross-references to other parts of the book

I have provided generous cross-references to other parts of the book when this might be helpful. To make these as economical as possible and yet not confusing, I have restricted specific sectional references to numbers only, and placed them in bold; e.g. 'as addressed in **1.4**'. But when I refer to whole chapters, these are not in bold. I abbreviate the Introduction at the start of the book with 'Intro.', e.g. Intro.2, and the Catalogue at the end by 'Cat.', e.g. Cat.7 for shame.

Introduction
What This Book Aims to Achieve (and What It Doesn't). A Map

In this book I argue for an interpretation of what Aristotle thinks occurrent emotions are and point to some philosophical merits of that view. As I understand him, Aristotle holds that emotions are representational pleasures or distresses that are formed in response to other intentional states that apprehend their objects. The precise sense in which I understand 'intentional states' (e.g. belief/judgement, perception), 'objects of emotions' (roughly, what emotions are about) and what I mean by the former 'apprehending' the latter will be explained in Chapter 1.[1] But even my bare formulation of Aristotle's view above is notable in several respects. First, the idea that he thinks that the pleasures or distresses of emotions are representational—directed at objects in the world (or ourselves)—contrasts sharply with accounts that would instead identify emotions with non-representational sensations or feelings.[2] Second, the notion that Aristotle thinks of emotions as pleasurable or distressful *responses* to other intentional states that apprehend their objects provides a fundamental contrast with many contemporary accounts (i.e. accounts of our time), which view emotions as (in part) modes of apprehension or kinds of epistemic state themselves.[3] Third, my characterization is intended to indicate that Aristotle holds that emotions are representational pleasures or distresses *alone*. This means not merely that they do not incorporate (even as a part) the intentional state that apprehends their object, but also that, in direct opposition to motivational accounts of emotions, they are to be distinguished from *desires* or *motivational states*. While emotions interact with desires and motivations in important ways, they are not, on Aristotle's view (as I read

---

[1] Although I might note now that I am using 'apprehend' non-factively (we can have mistaken apprehensions) and am not treating it as restricting us to types of epistemic access. See **1.4**.

[2] I am not the first to claim that Aristotle thinks that the pleasures or distresses of emotions are representational. See esp. Nussbaum (1994: 88, 2001: 64) and Dow (2011: §2, 2015: §9.3). But, as we shall see, my reading will ultimately differ from those of others who have maintained this. Aristotle's representational pleasures or distresses might be closer to what Goldie (2000) calls 'feelings toward', but Goldie distinguishes the latter from pleasures or pains (e.g. 19). Cf. also Gaus (1990: e.g. 64).

[3] A recent exception to this trend is Müller (2017, 2019).

him), *themselves* (even in part) desires or motivations.[4] As I shall examine (**11.3**), the combination of the second and third points, here, means that Aristotle has a novel understanding of the representational *role* that emotions play; namely, neither descriptive, nor prescriptive, but *reactive*.

In the course of this book, besides developing these ideas both textually and philosophically, I shall also explore, *inter alia*, how Aristotle individuates emotion-types; his understanding of the material dimension of emotions; and how his account could potentially provide a novel explanation of recalcitrant emotions (emotions that persist in light of a conflicting judgement), a phenomenon that has proved notoriously problematic for many recent accounts of emotions.

In this Introduction I provide a few preliminary points (**Intro.1**), sketch a key question about Aristotle's account of the emotions that this book does *not* address (and show how answering that question is independent of my project) (**Intro.2**), and outline the contents of the book (**Intro.3**).

1. Some preliminaries

Let me make a few preliminary points. First, I make no apology for employing the Latinate 'emotions' as the term for the phenomena in question (others prefer 'passions' or 'feelings'). Aristotle's word *pathē* can be used in broader or narrower ways.[5] Indeed, even his expression 'affections of the soul' (*ta pathē tēs psuchēs*, *ta tēs psuchēs pathē*: *De an.* I.1.403a3, 16), which may be closer to picking out the category, may also include perception, not just emotions.[6] However, several lists-cum-specifications (*Rhet.* II.1.1378a19–22; *NE* II.5.1105b21–3; *EE* II.2.1220b12–14; all quoted in **2.1**) indicate that he has a category of states in mind that meaningfully corresponds to our 'emotion'. And using 'emotion' facilitates fruitful engagement with germane contemporary discussions. After all, it is not as if our category is unequivocal and uncontested.[7] If the interpretation of Aristotle I provide is plausible, his view will challenge contemporary accounts of emotions, but not in a way that would suggest they are talking about different concepts (which would in fact preclude such a challenge). There will also be

---

[4] Anger (*orgē*) may seem an obvious counter-example to this claim, insofar as it is defined as a 'desire accompanied by a distress' (*Rhet.* II.2.1378a30). But I shall explain how even this fits the analysis in Chapter 6. So too, I address appetite (*epithumia*), which appears on several lists of emotions (see **2.1**), in Chapter 8.

[5] See esp. *Met.* Δ.21; *Cat.* 8.9a36–9b9, 9b28–10a11; Bonitz (1870: *s.v*); Rorty (1984); and Rapp (2002: 543–5).

[6] This is a matter of dispute; see e.g. Burnyeat (1995: 433n.38, 2001: 129–30, 2002: 82n.143) and Caston (2005: 281–5). See also Rapp (2002: 545) and Corcilius (2008: 156–8). Charles (2021: 30–1) proposes that the first formulation at 403a3 picks out a broader set of states (including perception: 403a7) than the second at 403a16, which concerns the emotions specifically. (I shall deal with some other issues that Corcilius raises, e.g. pertaining to desires and difficult cases, in due course.)

[7] For an overview, see e.g. Deonna and Teroni (2012: ch. 2) and de Sousa and Scarantino (2018).

difficulties pertaining to how we carve up various intentional phenomena (about the distinction between emotions and desires, for instance), but these are issues that apply to us no less than to Aristotle.

Second, unless otherwise noted, I am concerned with emotions as occurrent states—emotional episodes—not dispositional states.[8] This fits Aristotle's notion of emotions as states in virtue of which we are moved, rather than disposed (see *NE* II.5.1106a4–5; cf. *EE* II.2.1220b5–6). He does, I should note, on occasion use emotion-terms to refer to dispositional states; e.g. he sometimes uses shame (*aidōs*) to refer to a disposition to experience an occurrent emotion (*EE* III.7.1233b26–9; cf. *NE* II.7.1108a31–5) or mild-manneredness (*praotēs*) as a disposition to experience anger in the right way (*NE* IV.5).[9] And he will refer to *people* who are disposed to undergo certain emotional states e.g. those prone to experience shame (*NE* II.7.1107b32; *EE* III.7.1233b29), or envy (*NE* II.7.1108b3), or indignation (*NE* II.7.1108b3; *EE* III.7.1233b23), or schadenfreude (*NE* II.7.1108b5; *EE* III.7.1233b20–1) or, indeed, courageous people and their vicious counter-parts, who are characterized in terms of dispositions to feel fear and confidence (*NE* III.6–9; *EE* III.1). But these further specifications are clearly compatible with him having a clear-cut notion of emotions as occurrent states, i.e. states which involve some occurrent episode of pleasure or distress, and it is this notion that I am interested in and explore in this book.[10]

Third, it will prove helpful (especially in certain contexts) to have a shorter noun phrase to stand in for the expression 'pleasurable or distressful states'. I shall employ 'hedonic states' for this purpose. Although 'hedonic' obviously strictly speaking refers to pleasure alone (from the Greek, *hēdonē*, pleasure), I shall use it as a convenient shorthand to mark that we are in the domain of pleasure *or* distress.

It is also perhaps worth emphasizing from the start why, besides its intrinsic interest, Aristotle's account of the emotions (as I shall reconstruct it) warrants such detailed study. There are two main reasons for this. First, the rather obvious one that emotions play a significant role in many parts of his thought; for instance, in his ethical works, as underlying virtues of character; in his *Rhetoric*, as bearing on audiences' decisions and verdicts (*kriseis*); in his philosophy of mind, as paradigm states that 'involve the body'; in his *Poetics*, as pertaining to the appropriate response to

---

[8] For contemporary discussion of the distinction between occurrent emotions/emotional episodes and emotional dispositions, see e.g. Pitcher (1965: 331–3); Lyons (1980: 53–7); Deonna and Teroni (2012: 8–9); Tappolet (2016: 3).

[9] Elsewhere shame (*aidōs* or *aischunē*) clearly refers to an occurrent emotion; see esp. *NE* IV.9.1128b10–15 and *Rhet*. II.6. Aristotle's use of mild-manneredness in *NE* IV.5 should be contrasted with *Rhet*. II.3, on which see **10.3** below.

[10] Aristotle seems to have this very distinction in mind in *EE* II.2.1220b12–18. He refers to the dispositional state as a 'quality' (*poiotēs*) and mentions 'being irascible (*orgilos*), stolid (*analgētos*), passionate (*erōtikos*), bashful (*aischuntēlos*), and shameless (*anaischuntos*)'. This is in contrast to the occurrent emotions (*pathē*) he had just cited in the specification quoted in **2.1**.

tragic drama; and in his *Politics* as motivating a change of constitution. Understanding his account of emotions is thereby likely to have a significant bearing on how we should construe his views on a good number of important matters.

Second, there is a more purely philosophical reason. At least insofar as the texts of the era have survived, Aristotle occupies a somewhat privileged position with respect to the philosophical understanding of the emotions in the western tradition. While Plato clearly pre-empted him in some respects (especially in the *Philebus*), in book II of his *Rhetoric* Aristotle seems to have been the first to provide a systematic discussion of various emotions, starting from a definition of what each emotion is. And while the context of this discussion (enabling the orator to engender or abate emotions in an audience) dictates that a general theory is not explicitly propounded, the accounts he provides do appear to rely on such a theory in the background.[11] Hence Aristotle could well be the first—or at least one of the first—in the western tradition to work out a general theory of the emotions and apply it to various particular emotions. In so doing he appears to have operated with an *analysis* of what emotions are in terms of other intentional states (in his case, pleasure and distress), and then distinguished individual emotions in accordance with that general analysis. This is very much the project that many philosophers and psychologists would still view themselves as engaged in until this very day (I consider one recent challenge to it in **1.5**). Furthermore, Aristotle is alive to many of the key issues, e.g. the relation of emotions to beliefs or perceptual states, to desires, to action, to character, and so on. Since he stands at the beginning of such theorizing, and could well be the first, or one of the first, to develop a systematic account of the emotions—and thereby, as it were, carve up the phenomena and investigate the key questions—it will be well to scrutinize his account in detail, even if we end up thinking he got it wrong. But, in fact, as I have indicated, I shall argue that his account of emotions, when properly understood, offers a striking alternative to many contemporary accounts and has a number of philosophical benefits. I explore these further at various points throughout the book (e.g. **1.5, 2.4, 3.3, 3.6, 4.4, 10.9**), but especially in Part IV, where I leave Aristotle exegesis behind and consider the philosophical 'payoff' of his view by

---

[11] There was, we should acknowledge, an older reading according to which the accounts of the emotions found in *Rhet.* II were merely a matter of commonplace opinions that Aristotle had simply gathered together without any commitment to their truth (see Fortenbaugh 1970: 40n.2 for references; cf. also Cooper 1996: 239–42). But at least since Fortenbaugh (1970) this has long been rejected, and rightly so (see also e.g. Nehamas 1992: 295; Nussbaum 1994: 82–3; Sihvola 1996: 110–11; Striker 1996: 286–8; Nieuwenburg 2002: 86–7; Dow 2015: e.g. 144–5, 164n.57). Aristotle's aim in providing accounts of the individual emotions in *Rhet.* II is not to provide the orator with colourful examples to employ in speeches (even if it can double as such). His explicitly stated goal is to enable the orator to engender (*empoiein*: II.1.1378a26; *engignetai*: II.11.1388b29) or abate (*dialuetai*: II.11.1388b29) emotions in the audience, so as to bear on their decisions or verdicts (*kriseis*) (II.1.1378a19–21). But if his accounts of the emotions are to achieve this, they must be *adequate* for the purpose at hand. And that seems to require that in some sense they are *true*, or at least that Aristotle thinks they are.

explaining how it improves over a recent motivational theory of emotions (Chapter 11) and provides a novel and promising account of recalcitrant emotions (Chapter 12).

I shall, as I just have, continue to write of Aristotle's 'account' of what emotions are. I mean by this the theory of emotions that he is applying in providing his accounts of individual emotions in *Rhet*. II. As indicated, this account has to be reconstructed since he nowhere argues for a general account of what emotions are (although he does offer some general specifications). But as we have the theory *being applied* to many individual cases of emotions, the applications create criteria for any plausible interpretation of what the account in question is.[12] Of course, it might be proposed that Aristotle had not really formulated the account explicitly, but just found himself operating with one. But, as we shall see, there is evidence to suggest that this is not in fact the case. At any rate, by Aristotle's 'account' of what emotions are, I mean the general account lying the background that best explains his accounts of the individual emotions.[13]

2. What this book does and does not purport to do

There has been significant dispute about one aspect of Aristotle's account of the emotions that I will *not* address in this book, and it will be well for me to emphasize this and explain why now (in part to prevent disappointment). For some time commentators on Aristotle had been divided between (what we can label) 'judgementalist' and 'perceptualist' readings. According to the former, he holds that objects of emotions must be apprehended by belief or judgement.[14] And, on this view, since objects of emotions must be apprehended by belief or judgement, we must assent that they are the way the belief or judgement presents them.[15] According to the latter, by contrast, he holds that objects of emotions must be apprehended by the perceptual capacity of *phantasia* (roughly, 'perceptual

---

[12] Thus my reconstruction of his view in this case is not simply a matter of interpreting his remarks on emotions that are scattered about across various works; as is the case with his account of desire, for example, which I tried to reconstruct in an earlier book (2012).

[13] I should acknowledge that not everyone is as sanguine as me about the prospects for such an undertaking. Corcilius (2008: 157–8), for instance, insists that the context of the discussion of the emotions in *Rhet*. makes it unsuitable to provide Aristotle's philosophical theory of the emotions. The latter, on his view, could only occur in natural philosophy, but in that context Aristotle is not concerned to distinguish emotions from other affections of the soul (*pathē tēs psuchēs*) (see n.6 above). However, I reject the idea that there is no meaningful analysis of the emotions to be had independently of their analysis in natural philosophy. I argue for this and consider the material or physical dimension of emotions more generally, in Chapter 9 below.

[14] Following current practice in discussions of the emotions, I use 'belief' and 'judgement' interchangeably, even though it may mask some important differences (see e.g. Roberts 1999: 793–4; Cassam 2010).

[15] Judgementalist readings have been advanced by e.g. Fortenbaugh (1975, 2002); Nussbaum (1994: ch. 3); Dow (2009); see also Leighton (1996); Frede (1996) and Knuuttila (2004).

construal').¹⁶ And, on this view, it was stressed that Aristotle emphasizes just this feature of emotions to highlight how they can come apart from, and indeed contradict, our beliefs or judgements.¹⁷ More recently, though, a view has emerged which undermines this simple division. According to a growing consensus, while the perceptualist is right to think that Aristotle holds that objects of emotions are apprehended by *phantasia*, the judgementalist is right to claim that he thinks that we must take a belief-like attitude towards those objects, that is, must affirm or assent that they are as they are presented to us. To distinguish such interpretations from both judgementalist and perceptualist readings, but to reflect the fact that such views still maintain that only *phantasia* ever apprehends objects of emotion, we might dub them 'quasi-perceptualist'.¹⁸

This debate about Aristotle mirrors one that has taken place in current philosophical accounts of the emotions. In contemporary literature there has been a dispute concerning whether emotions are best thought of as (in part) identical to a certain kind of belief or judgement—'judgementalism'—or instead as (in part) identical to perceptual states (or perceptual construals)—'perceptualism'. And, as with the discussions of Aristotle, there have been attempts to reject both these views and instead provide an intermediate option. For instance, it has been proposed that emotions are kinds of passive assent or inclination to assent.¹⁹ To distinguish these latter views from both judgementalism and perceptualism, and yet to flag that they do not share the perceptualist dimension of the quasi-perceptualist readings of Aristotle, we might dub them 'quasi-judgementalist' accounts.²⁰

---

[16] For more on how I understand *phantasia* in this book, see **1.2n.9**.

[17] See especially Cooper (1996) and Striker (1996). For others who have advanced perceptualist readings of Aristotle, see e.g. Sihvola (1996); Achtenberg (2002: ch. 6); and Nieuwenburg (2002).

[18] I have in mind Price (2009, 2011: 113–22); Moss (2012a: ch. 4); and Dow (2014, 2015).

[19] For contemporary accounts of emotions as a type of belief or judgement, see e.g. Bedford (1956–57); Neu (1977, 2000); Solomon (1993: 125–32, 2003); and Nussbaum (2001). Perceptualist views are advanced by e.g. Roberts (1988, 1996, 2003); Tappolet (2000, 2016); Deonna (2006); and Döring (2007, 2009a, 2009b, 2014). (For a different, 'indirect', perceptual view, see Prinz 2004; for the 'direct'/'indirect' contrast, see Deonna and Teroni 2012: ch. 6.) I use the term 'quasi-judgementalist' (on which, see next note) to pick out the views of esp. Helm (2001, 2002, 2009, 2015) (who characterizes emotions as 'passive assents') and Brady (2009) ('inclinations to assent'). In allowing views that only incorporate a belief or judgement as a component of an emotion to count as 'judgementalist', the label can encompass views, such as Marks' (1982), Searle's (1983: 29–36), and Green's (1992: ch. 6), which identify emotions with belief/desire *pairs*. For such views to count as judgementalist, it must still be the case that the particular and evaluative objects of the emotion (see **1.3**) are apprehended by belief.

[20] So long as it is borne in mind that those in this category are not all advancing the same view, this should not overly mislead. Terminology for characterizing this third category is not consistent. D'Arms and Jacobson (2003) use 'quasi-judgmentalism' for any view that still ascribes defining content to the emotion, without committing to a strict judgementalism—this makes perceptualists come out as quasi-judgementalists. Brady (2009: 415) uses 'neojudgementalism' to include perceptualism, as well as Greenspan's propositional thought view, but does not apply it to his own 'inclination to assent' view. Some characterize Roberts' construal account as 'neo-judgmentalist' (e.g. Majeed 2022), whereas I construe it as perceptualist, given Roberts' direct appeal to the perceptual analogy (see e.g. 1996: 153,

This book will not address these debates. This is not because I do not have a take on them. In fact, as I see it, all these views—both the current accounts and the interpretations of Aristotle—share a common assumption that Aristotle rejects. The assumption is that objects of emotions must be apprehended by one and only one intentional state. By contrast, I believe that Aristotle holds that emotions can be about their objects just insofar as those objects are represented by either *phantasia* or belief. Indeed, I think it plausible that he holds that emotions can be about their objects as they are represented by sense-perception, perceptual imaginations, or uncommitted thoughts, no less. And, as this implies, contra judgementalist and quasi-perceptualist readings, I would also resist the idea that he thinks that we must assent that the objects of our emotions are as the emotion presents them (although many emotions will of course involve such assent). Furthermore, I think Aristotle is right to resist the common assumption I have just specified and that rejecting it helps us not merely with regard to understanding our emotional responses to fiction, but also with explaining the existence of certain cases of recalcitrant emotions that mono-state views (as we may call them) cannot.[21]

Establishing this reading, though, is involved and controversial, and requires detailed analysis. Furthermore, it is possible to leave open how we should resolve the above debate while we tackle the question of what Aristotle thinks emotions are. Of course, if one simply *assumes* that emotions are to be identified with the intentional state that apprehends their object (judgement, perception, etc.), the only further question one could have about what emotions are will concern *which* intentional state(s) they should be identified with. But it is precisely this assumption that I believe Aristotle rejects. As already noted, I shall argue that he holds that emotions are hedonic *responses* to such states, not those apprehending states themselves. This means that there is a fundamental debate to be had about what Aristotle thinks emotions are that can remain neutral on the question of which intentional state(s) he believes apprehend objects of emotions. For *however* he thinks we apprehend such objects—whether by judgement, or *phantasia*, or (as I believe) by either (and other states besides)—we can distinguish views that claim that he holds that the emotion is to be (in part) identified with the intentional

---

2003: 75). Döring (2014: 125) uses 'quasi-judgementalism' as I do, i.e. as distinct from both judgementalism and perceptualism, and picking out positions such as Helm's and Brady's.

[21] I argued for an early version of this view in my 2014a. I have a vastly expanded and reworked book-length defence in draft form in my MS. Cf. also Rapp (2002: 570–5, 2022: suppl. b). Sometimes the idea that Aristotle thinks that the intentional state that apprehends the emotion's object must be a perceptual state is thought to follow simply from his appearing to attribute them to the non-rational part of the soul (see e.g. *Pol.* I.5.1254b8; and see Price 2011: 119, Moss 2012a: §4.2, and Dow 2015: §10.3.1). But if, as I argue in this book, emotions are not, even in part, the intentional state that apprehends the object of the emotion, but instead hedonic responses to such states, the attribution of emotions to the non-rational part of the soul could follow simply because emotions are pleasures or distresses, not because of how their objects are apprehended. I discuss this further in my 2014a (192–4) and, at greater length, in my MS.

state that apprehends its object (whichever state(s) those are) from views that maintain that he does not (even in part) identify the apprehending state and the emotion as such.

Now, as it happens, with respect to the interpretation of Aristotle, all commentators accept that there is a further explanatory burden for understanding his account of the emotions, besides ascertaining how he thinks we apprehend their objects. For it is abundantly clear (with at least a core set of emotions) that he holds that emotions have some fundamental connection to pleasure and pain/distress.[22] And, in fact, as we shall see (Chapter 2), it is also clear (with at least a core set of cases) that he thinks emotions are, at least in part, pleasures or pains/distresses themselves. This presents several questions about the hedonic dimension of an Aristotelian emotion relevant for ascertaining what he thinks emotions are; and, again, these are, in my view, best tackled while leaving open the question of precisely which intentional state(s) he thinks apprehend objects of emotions. For example, while remaining neutral on the latter question, we will see (in Chapters 2–4) that some think Aristotle holds that the pleasure or pain/distress of an emotion, on the one hand, and the intentional state that apprehends its object, on the other, form *two different component parts* of an emotion. And some further advance the view that he holds that the pleasure or pain/distress component is a non-representational state (a sensation or feeling) caused by the intentional state that apprehends the object of the emotion, while others insist that the pleasures or pains/distresses are representational states. Again, still others have claimed that he thinks the pleasure or pain/distress of an emotion *just is* (another way of describing) the intentional state that apprehends its object. But, in spite of their fundamental differences, each of these readings assumes that Aristotle holds that the intentional state that apprehends the object of the emotion is at least part of what the emotion itself is. And yet, as noted, it is just this assumption that I think Aristotle rejects. I agree with (and shall further defend: Chapter 2) the view that he holds that the pleasures or pains/distresses of emotions are representational states (and hence that in fact 'distress' is better than 'pain'). On this reading, he thinks that the pleasures or distresses of emotions are *about* or *directed at* objects. And they are so not in the way in which a pain in a stubbed toe might be said (by some, at least) to represent bodily pain in that location.[23] Rather, the pleasures or distresses in question are typically directed outwards at objects (as apprehended) in the world (or, if directed at ourselves, at our place within it). We are distressed *about* the undeserved suffering of another or we take pleasure *in* someone's deserved downfall, for instance. However, as mentioned, on my view (argued for in Chapters 3

---

[22] Although, as we shall consider later (in Part II and Chapter 10), there are some difficult cases, this is clear from his general specifications of emotions, quoted in **2.1**, and from his specifications of a number of particular emotions, as discussed in **2.3**.

[23] See e.g. Crane (1998) and, for discussion, **2.4** below.

and 4), Aristotle does not hold that emotions *are, even in part*, the intentional state that apprehends the object of the emotion (whichever state(s) those are). Instead, he thinks that emotions are representational pleasures or distresses that are formed *in response to* (*in light of*) another intentional state (e.g. a belief or a perceptual state) which apprehends the emotion's object.[24]

Also central for the question of what Aristotle thinks emotions are is the relation he thinks holds between emotions and desires or motivations. In line with motivational theories of emotions, a number of commentators have claimed that he thinks emotions essentially involve desires. But, as we shall see (although this may appear more obvious), we can address this view, no less, independently of the question of which intentional state(s) Aristotle thinks apprehend objects of emotions. Accordingly, in Part II, without taking a stand on the latter matter, I will argue that while Aristotle thinks that emotions bear important relations to desires and motivations and can, e.g., be components of states that also essentially incorporate a desire (as with anger (*orgē*), for Aristotle; see Chapter 6), nonetheless emotions, as representational pleasures or distresses, do not, *as such*, incorporate any desiderative/motivational aspect. Instead, on his view, they are representational pleasures or distresses *alone*.[25]

This gives Aristotle quite a striking view. His account, so construed, contrasts with many contemporary views (and interpretations of Aristotle) that insist that emotions are themselves modes of apprehension or types of epistemic state. Emotions, on my reading of Aristotle, neither *reveal* anything about the world as such (as perceptualists may suggest), nor do they even involve the subject taking the world to be a certain way (as judgementalists may claim). Rather, they manifest us as *responding* to the world, as we have apprehended it by another intentional state. A key advantage of such a view is that the pleasures or distresses of emotions can themselves contribute to the *individuation* of emotion types (see Chapter 3). This means that Aristotle can explain how two people (or one person at different times) can, in principle, experience two different emotions in response to forming the very same intentional state. For instance, someone might form pity (a representational distress) and another schadenfreude (a representational pleasure or joy) in response to the very same intentional state of apprehending

---

[24] The independence of my discussion in this book (concerning what Aristotle thinks emotions are) from the question of which intentional state(s) he thinks apprehend their objects means that someone wedded to e.g. a perceptualist, or quasi-perceptualist, or judgementalist reading of Aristotle (each of which, as it happens, I reject) could still embrace my arguments in this book concerning how he connects the pleasures or distresses of emotions and the intentional state that apprehends their objects. (Equally, someone could maintain that emotions are to be (in part) identified with the intentional state that apprehends their objects (contra this book), but accept my view (not argued here) that more than one intentional state can do the apprehending (such that token emotions could be (in part) identified with different token intentional states).)

[25] It is clear that Aristotle also thinks emotions are material states no less (e.g. *De an.* I.1; *PA* II.4), but I argue in Chapter 9 that this does not undermine his specifying them simply in terms of representational pleasures or distresses alone.

someone as having suffered some undeserved misfortune. Another significant advantage of Aristotle's view, as we shall see in Chapter 12, is that it enables us to explain the irrationality of recalcitrant emotions (when they are irrational), a feature of them that has proved notoriously difficult for other theories of emotions.[26] It is worth stressing, though, that emotions, so construed, are far from epiphenomenal. As hedonic states they can be integral to our forming desires and intentions, and in action. But they are not modes of apprehension or types of epistemic state themselves, as many philosophers think (nor are they desires or motivations). Instead, insofar as they reveal something of significance about us, they reveal it *indirectly*. As manifestations of our basic hedonic dispositions, they indirectly reveal *who we are*.[27]

3. A map of this book

As this is quite a long book, it may prove useful for me to provide a brief sketch of its contents in advance. In Chapter 1 I explain in more detail some terminology and distinctions I have already begun to use and which it will be helpful to employ throughout. In particular, I explain what I mean by 'intentional states apprehending objects of emotion' by unpacking the notions of 'an intentional state' (and its 'content', 'attitude', and 'object') and 'objects of emotion' (formal/evaluative and particular objects), and specifying what I intend by referring to the former 'apprehending' the latter. This conceptual framework is helpful to employ in examining Aristotle's views, but I also provide some reasons for thinking that it may not be anachronistic to use it. Finally, I defend the general idea that it is legitimate to attempt (as Aristotle does) to analyse emotions in terms of other intentional states against a recent objection to this notion found in contemporary discussions.

After this, the book is divided into four parts. In the first part (Chapters 2–5) I argue for my core interpretation of Aristotle's account of emotions as representational pleasures or distresses that are formed in response to intentional states that apprehend their objects. A number of considerations—not least his general specifications of emotions (*Rhet.* II.1.1378a19–22; *NE* II.5.1105b21–3; *EE* II.2.1220b12–14)—suggest that Aristotle holds that emotions have some essential

---

[26] My discussion here is an exception to my remaining neutral on the question of which intentional states apprehend objects of emotions. For in Chapter 12 I show the benefits of combining the view I develop in this book with my preferred answer to that question (as sketched above). I argue that the latter allows us to account for the full range of existence of recalcitrant emotions, while the former enables us to explain their irrationality (when they are irrational). **3.6** will also bear on the debate about which intentional state(s) can apprehend objects of emotion, but independently of the interpretation of Aristotle.

[27] Which is, of course, compatible with them revealing us as conflicted; if, say, an emotion we possess conflicts with our evaluative judgements.

connection to pleasure and pain.[28] In Chapter 2 I first address what he means, in these general specifications, in claiming that emotions 'are accompanied by' (*hepetai*) pleasure or pain. Although a few options are available, I argue that it is at any rate clear from many of Aristotle's definitions of emotions in *Rhet.* II that for at least a good range of cases he thinks that emotions *are* (at least in part) pleasures or pains. But what sort of pleasures or pains? On one view they are non-representational states (sensations or feelings). I resist such a reading and argue that Aristotle is most plausibly construed as holding that the pleasures or pains of emotions are representational states in their own right (and hence that 'distress' is better than 'pain'). I close by considering this feature of his account in light of some contemporary views about pain. The idea that the pleasures or distresses of emotions are intentional is (even) less problematic than the notion that bodily pains can be about their objects (e.g. a stubbed toe about the body) because the pleasures or distresses of emotions are directed at objects in the world (e.g. an occurrent danger, or an undeserved misfortune) or our place in it (e.g. our being disgraced).

If an emotion requires both an intentional state that apprehends its object and a representational pleasure or distress directed at that object, the next question is: what is the relation between those two elements.[29] In Chapter 3 I consider the view advanced by several commentators that he thinks the two are one and the same thing, viz. that the representational pleasure or distress of an emotion is just another way of describing the intentional state that apprehends its object. I resist this reading—which I call 'the Identification view'—on two grounds. First, and most simply, some of Aristotle's specifications of emotions indicate that he thinks the two are separate states. Fear, for instance, is said to be a kind of distress that *arises from* the appearance of danger (*Rhet.* II.5.1382a21–2). Second, I show that the way Aristotle individuates emotions (roughly, by a combination of pleasure/distress and the emotion's evaluative object) dictates that he cannot hold the Identification view. Interestingly, the considerations I adduce here pertaining to the individuation of emotions can be used to construct an argument against current judgementalist and perceptualist views, insofar as they must (minimally) involve extraneous representational *additions*. I sketch this at the end of the chapter.

---

[28] There are some tricky cases to deal with but, as noted, I first investigate (in Part I) the link for the cases which unequivocally do possess the connection. I deal with the tricky cases in Parts II and III.

[29] Once again, it is worth flagging that addressing this is independent of the question of which intentional state(s) can apprehend objects of emotion. As we have seen, commentators have been divided on whether Aristotle holds that objects of emotion must be apprehended by belief/judgement or by perceptual *phantasia*. But *everyone* accepts that he thinks emotions require an intentional state to apprehend their object. Whether that intentional state is a belief/judgement, or a perceptual *phantasia*, or (as I think) can be either of these (or other sorts of apprehension), makes no difference. Each account must face a further question: in what way does the intentional state that apprehends the emotion's object relate to the emotion's pleasure or distress?

If Aristotle does not identify the representational pleasure or distress of an emotion with the intentional state that apprehends its object, the two must remain distinct. But what is the relation between them? And are they two components of an emotion or is the emotion, strictly speaking, to be identified with the pleasure or distress alone?[30] In Chapter 4 I address these questions. I first consider three relations that Aristotle might have had in mind between the pleasure or distress of the emotion and the apprehending intentional state; (mere) concurrence, a causal connection, and an 'in light of' relation. On my view, the latter is most plausible: the representational pleasure or distress of an emotion is formed *in light of* the intentional state that apprehends its object. I next argue that Aristotle's characterizations of a core set of emotions suggests that he holds that emotions are representational pleasures or distresses *alone* and that, strictly speaking, the intentional state that apprehends the object of the emotion is not a component part of it as such, but instead what that emotion is formed *in response to*. If this is right, Aristotle's view contrasts sharply with many contemporary accounts of emotions (and indeed previous interpretations of Aristotle) which hold that emotions are *themselves* perceptual apprehensions, or judgements, of value. Instead, on his view, emotions are hedonic *responses* to apprehensions of value. I explore this further at the end of Chapter 4.

By this point of the book, I have argued that Aristotle thinks emotions are representational pleasures or distresses that are formed in response to intentional states that apprehend their objects. But, of course, Aristotle explicitly discusses pleasure in various places. Thus, we may well wonder how, if at all, his understanding of emotions as pleasures or distresses relates to those discussions. I address this in Chapter 5 in relation to Aristotle's accounts of pleasure in the ethical works.[31] While the pleasures that Aristotle is discussing in his ethical works are pleasures *in* activities (paradigmatically perceiving or thinking), rather than pleasures directed *at* objects (as represented through some intentional state), I nonetheless show that the account of pleasure that we find in *NE* X (and *NE* VII, insofar as the latter is compatible with *NE* X) can be extended to encompass the representational pleasures or distresses of emotions. I also deal with two potential objections to this claim; pertaining to (i) the notion that the same activity entails the same pleasure and (ii) defective pleasures. I close by considering two recent readings of what Aristotle means in claiming that pleasures 'perfect' activities. I suggest that one of these may help provide him with an explanation of the phenomenological or felt dimension of emotions. This completes the first part of the book.

---

[30] Since, as argued in Chapter 2, emotions are, at least in part, pleasures or distresses, there is no third option, viz. that the emotion is to be identified solely with the intentional state that apprehends its object.

[31] I also briefly discuss and put to one side his treatment of pleasure in *Rhet.* I.11.

In Part II (Chapters 6–8) I address Aristotle's understanding of the relation between emotions and desires. To anyone familiar with Aristotle's account of anger (*orgē*), my claim that he holds that emotions are representational pleasures or distresses *alone* will (at the very least) look in need of significant qualification. For, even if anger involves such a distress, Aristotle explicitly defines it, in *Rhet.* II.2, as a *desire* accompanied by pain (or distress) (1378a30). In line with this, a number of commentators have thought that he holds that emotions in general essentially involve a desiderative component. In Part II of the book, I resist this interpretation.

In Chapter 6 I tackle anger head on. I first consider some background texts from Aristotle's *Topics* which suggest that the genus of anger had been a matter of debate in the Academy. In spite of these I argue that it is clear that he holds that anger involves *both* a desire *and* a concurrent distress (and I show that he thinks the distress must remain present if the subject is to count as angry). However, I then demonstrate that this need not undermine the idea that Aristotle thinks that emotions are representational pleasures or distresses alone. So long as he holds that anger essentially incorporates *both* a desire (for revenge or rectification) *and* an emotion (a representational distress directed at a slight), he can, quite legitimately, refer to anger as an emotion (*qua* distress), even if he also thinks it involves a desire (for revenge). In this chapter I also consider a representational *pleasure* he connects to anger (directed at the hope of revenge) and I close by addressing, more generally, why he wants to insist that anger, as such, essentially involves a desire.

While Aristotle's account of anger does not entail that he thinks that emotions themselves involve desires (rather than that there can be states which incorporate both), we might nonetheless think that we should adopt that reading if there were evidence that he thought emotions involve desires more generally. In Chapter 7 I consider what else might be thought to support such a view. I examine (1) the suggestion that in *Rhet.* I.10, in his discussion of motives for action, he treats emotions generally as types of desire; (2) the fact that in some of his definitions of emotions Aristotle refers to them not merely as 'distresses' (*lupai*) but as 'disturbances' (*tarachai*); (3) whether fear's role in courage and its related vices suggests that Aristotle has a motivational understanding of this emotion; and (4) the fact that in *Rhet.* II.4 he appears to define feeling-friendly-towards (*to philein*) as a kind of desire and that, by implication, its contrary, hating (*to misein*), would be such no less. I argue that none of these considerations threatens the idea that Aristotle has a clear-cut notion of emotions as representational pleasures or distresses alone (although the second does perhaps suggest that he *also* has a notion of *fear*, in particular, as motivational). In this chapter I also explore the way desires or desiderative dispositions may be a background condition for certain occurrent emotions. But, overall, while Aristotle palpably holds that desires and emotions link up in various ways and, indeed, that some states, such as anger, can involve both, I uphold my claim that he nonetheless retains a clear distinction between the two.

In Chapter 8 I close the second part of the book by considering the puzzling status of appetite (*epithumia*) for Aristotle's account of the emotions. This appears on several lists of emotions, but it does not receive separate discussion in the catalogue of emotions in *Rhet.* II; and, elsewhere, Aristotle seems to view it as one of his three species of desire (alongside, *thumos* (spirit), and *boulēsis* (rational desire or wish)). I argue that there is good evidence that Aristotle thinks that appetite can count as an emotion in the *Rhetoric* and that we can make sense of this if we envisage him as holding that (at least one category of) appetites can be construed along the lines of anger, viz. as involving both a representational distress and a desire. In appetite's case, the representational distress concerns not a perceived slight, but a perceived lack, discomfort, or bodily pain.

By this point I have argued that Aristotle thinks that emotions are representational pleasures or distresses that are formed in response to an intentional state that apprehends their object and I have distinguished emotions from desires. In Part III (Chapters 9 and 10) I address some further challenges to this account. Aristotle clearly holds that emotions essentially involve a material dimension (see esp. *De an.* I.1 and *PA* II.4). In my view this is compatible with him thinking that emotions can be adequately specified just in terms of representational pleasures or distresses (directed at an apparent instantiation of the emotion's evaluative object). But some have thought that it has more significant implications. It has been argued that he holds that emotions cannot be adequately defined at all without *explicit* reference to their material dimension. In Chapter 9 I resist this. On my view, Aristotle thinks that definitions of emotions as representational pleasures or distresses are extensionally equivalent to definitions that include direct reference to their material dimension and do not mislead or misrepresent. Instead, the material dimension need only be mentioned in certain contexts—in natural science investigations or when it would be explanatorily helpful—but is unnecessary (and even unhelpful) in many other contexts. Emotions essentially possess a material dimension, on Aristotle's view, but it is not necessary to specify this in each legitimate kind of investigation.

In Chapter 10 I consider a few (further) tricky cases for my reading.[32] In particular, I consider (1) what Aristotle intends by defining 'favour' (as in 'giving a favour') in *Rhet.* II.7; (2) his account of confidence in *Rhet.* II.5; and (3) a series of 'opposites' that he specifies for various emotions; e.g. being-mild-mannered (op. anger) and shamelessness (op. shame). I argue that in some of these cases (as with (1)—where Aristotle turns out to discussing 'feeling-grateful-for'—and (2)) Aristotle is most plausibly construed as specifying representational hedonic states, as per my core analysis already provided. But with at least some of the tricky opposites something else seems to be going on. Aristotle instead appears to

---

[32] 'Further' insofar as, by this point, I have already considered (in Part II) anger (Chapter 6), feeling-friendly-towards and hating (7.4), and appetite (Chapter 8).

be characterizing a specific *privation* of some determinate representational pleasure or distress. I also consider this in relation to his general specification of emotions in *EE* II.2, which has a number of supplements not found elsewhere, and suggest, on its basis, that Aristotle might have both narrow and broad notions of 'emotion'. On the narrow notion, which we might call 'emotions proper' (*pathē kuriōs*), emotions pick out representational pleasures or distresses as such (*kath' hauta*). On the broader notion, the category allows in the determinate privations of emotions proper. The account dominating the discussion in this book can then be thought of as specifying emotions *proper*.

In the fourth and final part of the book, I consider (further) the merits of Aristotle's view (so developed) and point to a significant philosophical 'payoff' of my reading.[33] In Chapter 11 I contrast Aristotle's view that emotions just are representational hedonic states with a recent account that takes emotions to be motivational states. I raise some problematic cases for the latter and show that Aristotle's view is better placed to deal with the examples in question. I also show that his account is in a better position than such a view to explain cases in which it appears that two diametrically opposed emotions could prompt the same motivational tendencies (e.g. fear and thrilled panic). I close by sketching how different accounts of emotions link to different representational roles (descriptive, prescriptive) that emotions purportedly play and show how Aristotle's view provides a novel perspective on this matter, viz. that emotions play neither a descriptive nor a prescriptive role as such, but instead what we might call a *reactive* role.

A notorious touchstone in recent discussions of emotions has been how different accounts deal with recalcitrant emotions. In Chapter 12 I argue that Aristotle's view has a significant advantage over accounts that identify emotions with perceptual states, judgements, or quasi-judgements (such as passive assent or inclination to assent). All such views either fail to explain the existence of (all plausible cases of) recalcitrant emotions or fail to account for their irrationality (when they are irrational); even if that irrationality is specified in practical or motivational terms. By contrast, I suggest that Aristotle's view enables him not only to explain the *existence* of the full range of cases that seem possible, but also their *irrationality* (when they are irrational).[34] As my concessive parentheses imply, I do not think that recalcitrant emotions are necessarily irrational. They are so only when the judgement they conflict with is itself rationally formed. I finish the chapter by

---

[33] 'Further' because I have already addressed some philosophical matters at various points earlier in the book: esp. **1.5, 2.4, 3.6, 4.4, 10.9**.

[34] To explain the existence part of this, Aristotle needs to adopt the view I ascribe to him that emotions can be about their objects just insofar as those objects are represented by a variety of intentional states. This is the one point in this current book where I draw on my own particular answer (as developed in my 2014a and MS) to the question of which intentional state(s) can apprehend objects of emotion (see **Intro.2**).

defending this latter claim against those who take rationality simply to be a matter of coherence.

I close the book by providing a Catalogue of Aristotle's various emotions as representational pleasures or distresses. I have twenty-one entries in the hall of fame, although some of these in fact cover more than one emotional state.

Aristotle on What Emotions Are. Giles Pearson, Oxford University Press. © Giles Pearson 2024.
DOI: 10.1093/9780191989292.003.0001

1
Some Key Terminology and Distinctions. The Prospects for an Analysis of Emotions in Terms of Other Intentional States

In this chapter I first set out some key terminology and distinctions concerning intentional states that I will employ in investigating Aristotle's views in this book (pertaining to intentional states, attitudes, contents, and objects) (1.1). The chief reason I use this conceptual framework is because I find it the most fruitful for investigating his ideas and relating them to contemporary discussions. However, as it happens, I do not think that applying the framework significantly distorts his view and, although space prevents a thorough defence of this, I will briefly indicate why we might think he assents to the core ideas (1.2).[1] I then turn to 'objects of emotions' and, following others, distinguish between an emotion's *evaluative* (or 'formal') object and its *particular* object (and the 'target' and 'focus' of the latter) (1.3). I next explain the sense of 'apprehend' I intend when referring to 'intentional states apprehending objects of emotions' (1.4). I close by addressing a recent objection to the very idea of attempting to analyse emotions in terms of other intentional states (as Aristotle does), viz. that such analyses are unable to account for the fact that one person can be afraid of the very same thing that someone else is amused by (1.5).

1.1 Intentional states, attitudes, contents, and objects

It will prove useful in discussing Aristotle's account of emotions to employ some terminology and distinctions drawn from modern treatments of intentional states.[2] In this section I sketch the distinctions I have mind, in the next I discuss them in relation to Aristotle.

---

[1] To be clear: I incline to the view that Aristotle subscribes to the distinctions I employ but (i) I cannot provide a thorough defence of this here (although I will give some indicators) and (ii), even if he did not draw the distinctions in quite the way I develop, I do not believe that it distorts his view to examine it with those distinctions in play.

[2] My account follows Crane (esp. 2009, but see also e.g. 1998, 2001a (ch. 1), 2001b, 2003, 2006, 2013 (esp. ch. 4)), but I take the basic picture (esp. the notion of an 'intentional object') in contemporary discussions to trace back at least to Anscombe (1965). See also e.g. Tye (1995: 94–6).

Intentional states are states that are *about* or *of* something and, on the account I am considering, they concern something *other than* themselves. *What* an intentional state is about, what it concerns, may, in the broadest terms, be called its *intentional object*. Thus, just as belief is about something believed (to obtain), and desire is about something desired, so too fear is about something feared, pity about something pitied, shame about something one feels ashamed of, and so on.[3] In invoking intentional objects, we need to be aware both in what sense they are *intentional* and in what sense they are *objects*. One reason for saying that intentional states are about *intentional* objects, rather than simply about objects, is to flag that the object in question may not exist. I can have a belief about a packet of crisps in my study but, as it happens, my son has eaten them. So too I can have a belief about how many horns unicorns have. Intentional objects are what our intentional states are about, whether or not those objects exist. In what follows, I shall frequently drop the 'intentional', but it should be taken as understood.[4] In addition, the notion that intentional states are about intentional *objects* should not be taken to restrict what sort of thing an intentional object can be, when it exists. My belief that Monty is playing football in the courtyard is about Monty (and a football and a courtyard). But beliefs typically represent states of affairs or events. When I believe that Monty is playing football in the courtyard, and that belief is true, both Monty and the football can be said to be 'objects' (physical or material) represented by my intentional state. But equally we can here think of what is represented as a state of affairs—the state of affairs of Monty playing football in the courtyard. In the sense I intend, intentional 'objects', when they exist, can include physical or material objects, states of affairs, events, or, indeed, anything that can be represented.[5] Furthermore, I am not proposing that what is represented must be specifiable by a proposition or something as structurally complex as a proposition. I can have a thought of a cow, and what represents a cow need not be propositional in form.[6]

---

[3] Given this characterization, an intentional state may incidentally be about itself, viz. when the intentional object is the intentional state itself; e.g. a belief about the intentional state of belief.

[4] Another reason to refer to 'intentional objects' is to mark out that the object is as it is represented by the combination of the intentional state's attitude and content. I come to this below.

[5] For why we should not think of intentional objects that do not exist as forming a kind or category of 'non-existent objects', see Anscombe (1965) and Crane (2001a: §7, 2001b). More generally, as Crane puts it: 'An intentional object is not a kind of object, but rather the intentional object of thought T is what is given in answer to the question 'what is T about?' If this question has an answer, then the thought has an intentional object. If the answer refers to some existent thing, then the intentional object is something real: perhaps an object in the more normal sense—a material or physical object—perhaps a place, or a property or an event. To say that an intentional object is real is to say that the phrase which gives the intentional object has a reference. It is not to say, for example, that one set of things (the set of intentional objects) shares a member with another set of things (the set of real things)' (2001a: 26).

[6] See e.g. Crane (2001a: 112–14); Montague (2007); Grzankowski (2012, 2013, 2016a, 2016b); and contrast e.g. Sinhababu (2015).

If intentional states are *about* something other than themselves—i.e. their 'objects'—what is the intentional state itself? On the model I am embracing, we distinguish between an intentional state's *attitude* (or *mode* or *manner*), on the one hand, and its *content*, on the other.[7] Intentional contents are the complements of intentional attitudes and an intentional state necessarily has both an attitude and a content. We can take different attitudes towards the same content. I might *believe* that Monty will not eat my crisps or *hope* or *desire* that Monty will not eat them. The content of the intentional state is its particular way of presenting the intentional object. It is very important to distinguish the intentional content of a state from its intentional object. The content of an intentional state is a feature of the state itself. It is, in part (i.e. along with the attitude), what is responsible for represent*ing* an intentional object. Whereas the intentional state's object (the intentional object) is what the intentional content (in conjunction with the state's attitude) *represents*.[8] Intentional contents form part of the intentional state, whereas the intentional object does not—the intentional object is what the intentional state is about.

It is also important to stress that the intentional content is not *solely* responsible for representing the intentional object. The intentional object is what the intentional state is about. But the intentional state is composed of *both* its intentional attitude and its intentional content and only *together* do they represent an intentional object. Thus, the intentional attitude contributes to how the intentional object is represented no less than the intentional content. A *belief* that-the-cat-is-on-the-mat represents the cat on the mat as *obtaining*. A *conjecture* that-the-cat-is-on-the-mat represents the cat on the mat as *probable*. A *doubt* that-the-cat-is-on-the-mat represents the cat on the mat as *unlikely*. And so on. Similarly, with fear that-the-dog-will-bite-me: we need *both* the attitude (fearing) *and* the content (that the dog will bite me) to specify the intentional object as a fearful one. The content alone is not automatically fearful: some may, without

---

[7] I will use 'attitude' instead of 'mode'. The former helps avoid confusion with Frege's 'modes of presentation' which are actually part of the content of the state. But I do not take 'attitude' as short for 'propositional attitude' and so restricting us to propositional content. Hence my difference with Crane is merely terminological (see e.g. 2001a: 32). Searle (1983) and Crane (2001a, 2001b, 2003, 2006, 2009, 2013) prefer 'mode'. 'Manner' is used by Chalmers (2004). 'Attitude' preserves the connection to attitudinal theories of emotions; see Deonna and Teroni (2012, 2014, 2015) and Müller (2017).

[8] Crane (2009: 477) notes that the same object could be presented to the mind in different ways even when the same intentional attitude is in play, and so suggests that we could have a difference in intentional content without a difference in the object represented. His example is: 'my bottle of inexpensive champagne could also be thought of as a bottle of inexpensive famous sparkling wine from France'. But it is an interesting question at what point changes in content will effectively entail that a different object is represented. (Note, we cannot appeal to the *actual* object referred to by the intentional state to sort this out, since it may not even exist: the content is part of the way we specify the *intentional* object.) Would we, e.g., be happy to say that the same intentional object—a dog, say—could be picked out by *contradictory* predicates—dangerous/harmless—or must those generate different intentional objects (Crane's case involved complementary predicates)? Note, also, even with Crane's example the change of content will still result in a different intentional *state*, since the latter is specified by an attitude + content pair, and we have a different content.

fear, *want* a dog to bite them for some reason; e.g. police dog handlers on a training session, wearing protective armguards. So too, if Damian is angry with Jamie because Jamie called him a liar, we need both the attitude (being angry) and the content (that Jamie called Damian a liar) to specify the intentional object as one that angers Damian (for Damian might realize that Jamie was joking and not care one jot).

1.2 Applying these distinctions to Aristotle

Bearing the above points in mind will help considerably when we turn to investigate Aristotle's account of the emotions. But it may well be thought that in introducing these distinctions and terminology into a discussion of Aristotle I am open to a charge of anachronism from the very start. Now, of course, the conceptual framework I have sketched could be useful for illuminating Aristotle's views even if he did not draw all the distinctions. But, as it happens, I suspect that he would subscribe to the framework in broad outline or, at least, that to employ it does not significantly distort his views. And while a thorough exploration and defence of this is beyond the scope of this book, I shall at least now provide some basic indicators that Aristotle may in fact subscribe to the core ideas (without using the terminology, obviously).

In *MA* 7 he writes:

> 'I have to drink', says appetite. 'Here's drink', says perception or *phantasia*[9] or thought. (701a32–3; trans. after Nussbaum 1978)

In this passage, the content of an appetite (*epithumia*) is specified by the desire itself asserting that some action is required, and then, in response, the very same information, viz. 'Here's drink', is envisaged as potentially conveyed by either

---

[9] I shall leave '*phantasia*' untranslated. Here and elsewhere it may be thought of as a kind of perceptual envisaging that is not restricted to an occurrent perceptible. Caston (esp. 1996, 1998, 2021) argues extensively that we should resist the idea that *phantasmata* (objects of *phantasia*) are mental images that represent by being viewed. On his view, *phantasmata* simply refer to physical changes in the perceptual system—although such changes can *give rise* to imagistic experiences. He claims that a *phantasma* is 'that *by which* our mental states are directed at objects, without itself being an object of a mental state at all' (2006: 334; his emphasis). But while Aristotle does appear to think of *phantasmata* as physical changes in the perceptual system (e.g. *Mem.* 1.450a10–12, a32–b11), he also clearly thinks of *phantasia* as a capacity or faculty in its own right, *itself* capable of providing its possessor with information (information which may, in fact, be true or false) (contrast Wedin 1988). We see this most clearly in the *MA* 7 passage quoted above and the *NE* VII.6 passage quoted below. (See also Lorenz 2006: 119, 134–6, 192–3 and Schofield 2011: 123–5.) These suggest that *phantasia* represents an intentional object in a distinctive way, one which distinguishes it from perception and thought. In this sense it may be thought as a kind of perceptual envisaging that is not restricted to an occurrent perceptible.

perception, *phantasia*, or thought.¹⁰ Now, perception, *phantasia*, and thought are discriminative capacities (*kritika*; see *MA* 6.700b19–21, *De an.* III.9.432a16), but when those capacities are employed in a particular situation—as here—they result in a particular perception, *phantasia*, or thought.¹¹ We perceive the drink, or have a *phantasia* or thought of the drink. But since the perception, *phantasia*, and thought do not, in this case, differ with respect to their *content* ('Here's drink'), they must differ with respect to their intentional attitude (otherwise they would not differ at all). In each case, that is, the subject must be envisaged to be taking a different intentional attitude (A) towards the same intentional content (C):

Perception (A): Here's drink (C)
Phantasia (A): Here's drink (C)
Thought (A): Here's drink (C)

And since each of the above possesses a different intentional attitude, they each thereby specify a different intentional state (attitude + content combination).

As the foregoing indicates, the same word —'thought', '*phantasia*', or 'perception'— can serve as either marking the intentional state as a whole or its intentional attitude.¹² Although we refer to particular thoughts or perceptions as intentional states, each thought or perception involves taking a distinct attitude (a thinking or perceiving attitude) to the intentional object, and we typically refer to that attitude by the name we employ for the intentional state itself. If you like, we could try to make this more transparent by using verbal forms for the attitude: the belief that there is drink (intentional state) might be said to consist of an intentional attitude, *believing*, and the intentional content, 'Here's drink'. At any rate, the *MA* passage suggests that Aristotle operates with the model of intentional states I have set out.

Here is another example, this time with evaluative content:

reason or *phantasia* informs us that we have been insulted or slighted, and spirit (*thumos*), reasoning as it were that anything like this must be fought against, boils up straightaway; while appetite (*epithumia*), if reason or perception merely says that an object is pleasant, springs to the enjoyment of it. (*NE* VII.6.1149a32–b1)

---

¹⁰ Could not Aristotle mean that they each supply this information in different ways? Of course. But that is a function of their involving different intentional attitudes, not their content (so described) as such. With respect to *that*, at least, each intentional state provides the very same information.

¹¹ Hence Aristotle will talk of *perceivings* or perceptions (*aisthēseis*) and *imaginings* (*phantasiai*) (see e.g. *De an.* III.3.428a12, 429a5, III.10.433a11), and of individual beliefs and thoughts with specifiable contents and as true or false (e.g. *NE* VII.3.1147a24–1147b3, 1147b8–12; *MA* 7; *De an.* III.3.428b4–9; *Met.* Θ.10.1051b2–17).

¹² Or, indeed, the capacity itself, although Aristotle also has other words for those: *aisthētikon*, *phantastikon*, *doxastikon*, *noētikon*, etc.

As with the *MA* passage, reason, *phantasia*, and perception are here capacities that are envisaged to provide us with certain information (where the information is the content of the intentional state). But subjects who have been informed by reason that they have been slighted will possess an intentional state—presumably a belief or judgement (*doxa*)—with that content. Equally, when that information is conveyed by *phantasia*, the subject will have a different intentional state, *a phantasia*. And, once again, since in our example there is no difference between the two intentional states in terms of content, they differ simply in terms of intentional attitude. We have:

Belief (A): that I have been slighted (C)
Phantasia (A): that I have been slighted (C)

And:

Belief (A): that X would be pleasant (C)
Perception (A): that X would be pleasant (C)

And, as with the *MA* passage, each of the above amounts to a different intentional state. For, in spite of their overlapping contents, they possess different intentional attitudes and intentional states are individuated by attitude-content pairings.[13]

What about intentional objects? Greek lends itself to specifying objects of intentional states, since it often forms objectival specifications with a single word. Just as we have *aisthēsis* (perception), *phantasia*, and *noēsis* (thought), so too we have an *aisthēton* (an object of perception), a *phantasma* (an object of *phantasia*), and a *noēton* (an object of thought). Similarly, with desires. We have *orexis* (desire in general) and its species, *epithumia* (appetite) and *boulēsis* (rational desire or wish). And we have *orekta* (objects of desire), *epithumēta* (objects of appetite), and *boulēta* (objects of wish). The same applies with emotions—*pathē*. We can have objects of emotions—*pathēmata*—and objects of particular emotions; e.g. with fear—*phobos*—we have fearful things—*phobera* (e.g. *Rhet.* II.5.1382a28)—and with pity—*eleos*—pitiable things—*eleeina* (e.g. *Rhet.* II.5.1382b26). Of course, Aristotle has other ways of specifying objects besides these singular terms. For instance, he refers to *those things people pity* (*ha eleousin*: *Rhet.* II.8.1386a4), *what we are ashamed about* (*aischunesthai epi...*: *Rhet.* II.6.1383b16), and so on.

---

[13] For further discussion of the *NE* VII.6 passage and, in particular, how we should understand the difference between the desires it attempts to mark, see my 2011.

We get a clear notion of an *intentional* object in Aristotle with his account of the truth of assertions. In *Met.* E.4 he writes:

> truth has the affirmation in the case of what is compounded and the denial in the case of what is divided, and falsity has the contradictory of this apportionment. (1027b20–3)

An affirmation is a statement that affirms something about something, a denial is one that denies something about something (*Int.* 6.17a25–6), and an opposing pair of statements form a contradiction (*Int.* 6.17a33; *Met.* Γ.7.1011b23–9). 'What is compounded' (*to sunkeimonen*) and 'what is divided' (*to diē(i)rēmenon*) pick out the arrangement of the actual things the statement refers to. 'The ball is red' affirms of the ball that it is red; the statement is about the ball and red. When the ball and red are 'compounded', 'the ball is red' is true and 'the ball is not red' is false, and when the ball and red are 'divided', the reverse holds. Aristotle thinks that both the ball and red are things-that-are, namely, a substance and a quality respectively, and when the two are compounded, we are to think of them as forming some kind of unity, whereas when divided, some kind of plurality (see *Met.* Z.12.1037b14–18). But it is with regard to our statements or beliefs *about* such things that we get the notion of an intentional object. For, on Aristotle's view, statements or beliefs about actual things *mirror* the complexity we find in the things themselves. Just as actual things are compounded or divided, so too there is *combination* (*sunthesis*) and *separation* (*diairesis*) of subjects and predicates 'in thought' (*Met.* E.4.1027b18–19, b28–31). And if we combine or separate objects in thought in a way that matches the way things are actually compounded or divided, we have truth; if not, falsity. But in the notion of combining things in thought to specify an object that may or may not match how things are, we have a clear notion of an intentional object in the sense developed.

Similarly, with other intentional states besides thought and belief. Aristotle calls complex (i.e. predicative) perception 'incidental' or 'extrinsic' (*kata sumbebēkos*) (e.g. 'the white thing is the son of Diares': *De an.* II.6.418a21), and he notes that 'about whether the white thing is this thing or another we may be mistaken' (*De an.* III.3.428b21–2). This indicates that the object of perception (an *aisthēton*) in such a case is a complex intentional object that may or may not exist.[14] Consider, also, an example from *Insomn.* 2. When an object is placed

---

[14] Some have claimed that incidental perception is not a case of genuine perception (e.g. Hicks 1907: 430; Block 1960: 94; Kahn 1966: 48, 1995: 367–9) but, as others have noted, that seems to be a mistake (see e.g. Cashdollar 1973: 158–60; Hamlyn 1993: 105; and Caston unpublished)—Aristotle never gives us any reason to think that it is anything other than genuine. Note also that Aristotle claims that with special perceptibles, e.g. seeing red, we cannot be in error (*De an.* II.6.418a11–12, although cp. III.3.428b18–19). We still seem to have an intentional object here, though; it is just that because the intentional object does not involve combination or separation, there is no scope for going wrong. We either perceive red or we do not. Similarly, we might say that my thought of a cow cannot

between two fingers that are crossed, Aristotle claims that we feel the object as two, even though we deny (on the basis of sight) that it is two (460b20-2). The sense of touch, here, represents an intentional object (of two distinct things obtaining) that we know not to obtain. Similarly, with *phantasia*. *Phantasia* can represent the sun as about a foot across even when we believe it to be bigger than the inhabited world (*De an.* III.3.428b3-4; *Insomn.* 2.460b18-20). Once again, the intentional object as represented by *phantasia*—the sun as a foot across—is entertained at the very same time that we know that the *phantasia* misrepresents the object. And Aristotle is happy to call such a misrepresenting 'false' (*pseudē*: *De an.* III.3.428b2) and the conflicting belief or supposition (*doxa* at b5; *hupolēpsis* at b3) 'true' (*alēthē*).[15] We also see a notion of an intentional object in the case of desire (*orexis*). Aristotle tells us that an object of desire—an *orekton*—is able to produce movement in an animal insofar as it is *thought of* or *represented by phantasia* (*tō(i) noēthēnai ē phantasthēnai*: *De an.* III.10.433b11-12). But evidently some specific object of desire need not exist. Hence desires are directed at objects which are represented by some other intentional state, and these objects may or may not exist, i.e. desires are directed at intentional objects.[16] Similarly, with emotions. As we shall see (**1.3**), Aristotle thinks that we can (e.g.) be afraid of things that are not really fearful, but only seem so to us. His ground for holding this is not crucial in this context, but the fact that he holds it indicates that he thinks fear involves representing an intentional object in the sense I have specified: an object may be represented as fearful when it is not in fact so.[17]

Finally, let me note that just as we saw at the start of this section that Aristotle is happy to write of intentional capacities (perception, *phantasia*, thought) as themselves providing us with information (or of desire as making demands on us), so too I shall refer to intentional states as apprehending objects of emotions (where the notion of 'apprehend' will be specified in **1.4**). Let me stress, though,

---

be in error, but my thinking that cows are purple can, if believed or asserted (cf. *Met.* Θ.10). Combination and separation can be necessary for the possibility of error, without being sufficient for it (e.g. unasserted thoughts).

[15] In *De an.* III.8 Aristotle distinguishes *phantasia* from assertion and denial on the ground that 'truth and falsity involve a combination (*sumplokē*) of thoughts (*noēmata*)' (432a10-12). But this must overstate the contrast: as we have seen, he thinks that there can be combination, and hence error and falsity, with both (incidental) perception and *phantasia*. His point must be that assertion and denial *entail* combination, whereas there can be *phantasiai* that do not involve it, just as there can be simple perceptions (as is explicitly claimed for both at *De an.* III.3.428b25-30).

[16] For an alternative view, see Corcilius (2008, 2011).

[17] In the above I have used the fact that an intentional state can represent an object which does not exist to indicate that we must be considering an intentional object. But this does not preclude the possibility of intentional states whose application guarantees success. Aristotle recognizes such states; e.g. the theoretical grasping he mentions in *Met.* Θ.10, where error is not possible (we can only either think the objects in question or not: 1051b30-1052a4), and perception of special perceptibles (see n.14). Similarly, many think that, e.g., knowledge, seeing, noticing, love, and hate are such; see e.g. Crane (2013: 104-6). Such factive states clearly still represent intentional objects; they are mental phenomena that are directed at objects, in the sense specified.

nothing substantial is intended in referring to intentional states as *themselves* doing this. In particular, it should not be taken to imply that intentional states are homunculi: agents that can themselves apprehend things (and then potentially decide what to do with the information or even act in certain ways). All we *need* assume is that *subjects*—human beings or animals—apprehend objects of emotion *with* an intentional state or, in more Aristotelian language, that subjects apprehend intentional objects *by exercising some capacity of their soul*. Thus, following Aristotle, I shall write of perception, for example, as apprehending a dog (say), but all this need amount to is that *I* (the subject) apprehend the dog *with* my perceptual capacities (or when my perceptual capacities are exercised in the relevant way): I, that is, *perceive the dog*. The first formulation can be convenient as a mode of expression, but does not have to mark out psychological capacities as homunculi.[18]

1.3 Aspects of the objects of emotions: the evaluative (or formal) object and the particular object

Let me now turn to objects of emotions. In line with what has been said thus far, it is clear that the *real* objects of our emotions—i.e. what one actually fears, pities, is ashamed of, is angry about—can be anything whatsoever. Indeed, such objects need not even exist, or not under the description we have emotions about them. We can fear monsters under the bed, fictional slime in a horror movie, or objects that are not in fact as we suppose them to be: a bit of fluff as a spider, say, or a malign tumble-dryer that 'deliberately' failed when we needed a key shirt. And so on. But even when we turn our attention to the intentional object of an emotion—where what is feared, pitied, etc., is what one *represents* as fearful, pitiable, etc.—there is still a huge range of possible objects of emotions.[19] Aristotle claims that

---

[18] Aristotle may appear to make a related point in a famous passage in *De an.* I.4: 'we say that the soul is pained and pleased, is confident and afraid and further that it is angry and also that it perceives and thinks... Yet saying that the soul is angry would be like saying that the soul weaves or builds. For it is perhaps [or 'probably': *isōs*] better not to say that the soul pities or learns or thinks, but that the human being does these things with the soul (*tē(i) psuchē(i)*)' (408b1-3, 11-15). Barnes (1971-2: 103) called this the 'celebrated Rylean passage' and took it to be 'preparing' us for the non-substantialist view of the soul he finds elsewhere in *De an.* Shields (1988, 2009: 286-9, 2016: 142-5) resists this, noting, *inter alia*, that Aristotle is more than happy elsewhere to refer to the soul as substance (citing *De an.* II.1.412a19-20; *Met.* Z.11.1037a5) and hence subject (citing *Met.* Z.3.1029a1-2). I cannot consider this further here. All I need is the more modest idea that in referring to perception, etc., as providing us with information, we are not required to think of such capacities as homunculi, themselves capable of receiving information and doing things (cf. Caston 1996, 1998, 2021). But that claim is in turn compatible with the idea that there can still be some sensible notion (to be specified) in which perception, etc., are proper subjects (or bearers) of the intentional objects we apprehend by exercising those capacities (cf. n.9).

[19] It is worth stressing that it is debatable whether all emotions possess a specifiable object. Cf. de Sousa and Scarantino (2018: §4): 'I can be depressed or elated but not depressed or elated about any specific target or fact. These seemingly objectless affective states share many properties with

'what is fearful is not the same for all human beings' (*NE* III.7.1115b7) and that the coward does not just fear more than he should, but *what* he should not (1115b34). Indeed, he even goes on to say that the coward fears *everything* (1116a3)—although that must be an overstatement for emphasis ('he's afraid of the littlest thing!'), for he will distinguish cowardice from 'cowardly brutishness', a state of depravity beyond (or beneath) vice proper: 'the man who is by nature apt to fear everything, even the squeak of a mouse, is cowardly with a brutish cowardice' (*NE* VII.5.1149a7–8).[20] But he clearly thinks that people can fear all manner of things. Similarly, we can be prone to get angry at people or things we should not be angry about, not just more angry than we should about things that do warrant anger (see *NE* IV.5.1126a9–11).[21] Nonetheless, there is, of course, still a sense in which what is fearful for those who fear, or anger-inducing for those who are angry, is represented by them *as* fearful or *as* anger-inducing. While the coward fears things that are fearful to no one else (or only mildly fearful), those things are nonetheless fearful *to the coward* (*tini*) (*EE* III.1.1228b23–4, see also 1229a33–5). So too, while bad-tempered people (*chalepoi*) experience anger at the wrong things, more than is right, and longer than they should (*NE* IV.5.1126a26–8), if their anger is to be intelligible, it requires they construe the objects of their anger as anger-inducing. Indeed, as we shall see in Chapter 12, even when we are afraid of or angry about something that we ourselves judge we should not be afraid of or angry about, there is still a sense in which we must represent the object of the emotion as fearful or anger-inducing.[22] Thus, while many different things can be represented by us as fearful or anger-inducing, in order for these things to be intentional objects of fear or anger respectively, they

---

object-directed emotions, especially with respect to their physiological and motivational aspects, so we may consider them to be emotions without objects. On the other hand, some have suggested that such objectless states are better regarded as moods [citing Frijda 1994; Stephan 2017]. Whether we think of seemingly objectless affective states as emotions or moods, we must decide what kinds of objects they lack. Here two main options are available. The first is to assert that some affective states have neither particular objects nor formal objects. If we think of moods and objectless emotions that way, it becomes hard to explain how such affective states may have conditions of correctness—formal objects being among other things descriptions of what the world must be like for the affective state to be fitting [citing Teroni 2007]. If instead we think of such affective states as having formal objects and conditions of correctness, then their objectlessness is only apparent, because they need to have targets or propositional objects of some kind to which they implicitly ascribe the property defined by the formal object. (For the latter, they cite Goldie 2000 'who thinks moods take the whole world as their object' and C. Price 2006, 'who thinks that moods have generic objects but "watch out" for particular ones'.)

[20] This would be an innate disorder, but apparently someone also feared a 'house-weasel' (*galē*) in consequence of disease (1149a8–9). House-weasels were used in the home to keep mice down. Fearing such a creature would be like us fearing a benign household pet. I provide a detailed discussion of Aristotle's brutish states and conditions in my 2018.

[21] Aristotle is unequivocal in holding that some things do warrant anger; see e.g. *NE* IV.5.1126a4–8. Contrast e.g. Nussbaum (2016).

[22] I shall return to how, in his discussion of the individual emotions in *Rhet*. II, Aristotle indicates that objects of emotions are intentional objects, in Chapter 4.

need to be represented in a way that is distinctive of those emotions (and, indeed, distinctive of each other—so that we can distinguish being afraid of Sue and being angry with her).

In line with the vast majority of current philosophical views, Aristotle thinks that emotions essentially involve representing their objects *evaluatively*. He specifies fear, for example, as concerned with the prospect of a destructive or painful evil occurring to one (*Rhet.* II.5.1382a21–2); and links this to *danger* as the 'sign' of such things (1382a27–32). But representing something as prospectively destructive or painful (dangerous) is representing it as falling under a specific evaluative sortal. Similarly, anger represents an *offence* (literally a belittling or slight: *oligōria*) directed at us by someone unfitted to offend us (*Rhet.* II.2.1378a30–2); shame represents *bad things that bring us into disrepute* (*adoxia*) (*Rhet.* II.6.1383b13–14); pity represents *undeserved destructive or painful bad things happening to another* (*Rhet.* II.8.1385b13–16); and so on. In each case, the object of our emotion is represented evaluatively.[23]

It is customary in the philosophy of the emotions to follow Anthony Kenny (1963) in referring to the evaluative aspect of an object of an emotion as its 'formal object'.[24] Kenny noted (189) that there can be trivial and non-trivial specifications of formal objects. Trivial specifications are along the lines provided above, namely, *fearful, shameful, pitiable,* or *angering*. Non-trivial specifications purport to provide substantial characterizations of the formal objects of the emotions that are both more informative and falsifiable. We have just seen Aristotle's substantial specifications for fear, shame, pity, and anger.[25] Similarly, in contemporary philosophy, *danger* is often cited as the formal object of fear, *offence* of anger. There is an issue here about whether substantive formulations of the formal objects of emotions can individuate them. I shall return to this in Chapter 3.

---

[23] For current purposes it is unimportant whether we accept Aristotle's specifications of these emotions (for a broader notion of fear, bound to negative prospects more generally, see *NE* III.6.1115a10–12). The key claim is that emotions involve representing objects *evaluatively*. This is in part why they *matter* to us: they reflect what we value or *care about*. Equally, we do not need to establish or assume that the evaluative properties represented are, or even can be, 'objective' or 'real'. Evaluative features can present themselves to us (via our intentional states) regardless as to whether they are, e.g., part of the fabric of the universe, or simply projected onto it by us. Aristotle has a view about this, of course. He thinks that values are real and are set, at the physical level, by how the healthy person would find them and, at the ethical level, by the way the virtuous person would find them. For an exploration of Aristotle's evaluative realism, see e.g. Charles (1995).

[24] Deigh (1994) impugned this characterization as 'medieval mumbo jumbo' (835) but, so far as I can see, his objection to Kenny hinged primarily on the fact that the latter thinks that '[t]he description of a formal object of a mental attitude such as an emotion…must contain reference to a belief' (Kenny 1963: 193–4). This marks Kenny out as advancing a judgementalist view, but the notion that emotions have formal objects is not bound to judgementalism, hence contemporary perceptualists typically embrace the idea no less (e.g. Tappolet, Döring). I have no problem with 'formal object', but am equally happy to refer to *the evaluative aspect* of the intentional object of the emotion, or the emotion's *evaluative object*. In the psychological literature, the notion of 'core relational themes' has taken on the same role; see esp. Lazarus (1991: 121–4 and chs. 6–7).

[25] For both types of specification, see e.g. *EE* III.1: 'Generally speaking, fearful things (*phobera*) are what is productive of fear, and that in turn is whatever appears capable of producing pain that is destructive (*phainetai poiētika lupēs phthartikēs*)' (1229a33–5).

Besides having an evaluative (formal) object, emotions also have a particular object.[26] The particular object of an emotion is what the person having the emotion in question represents as manifesting the evaluative object of the emotion. We can distinguish at least two different aspects of the particular object that may be in play in specific emotions, the *target* and the *focus*. The intentional target of an emotion is some person or thing the emotion is directed at. Pat's fear that Fido will bite her is directed at Fido. Fido can be said to be the target of her fear.[27] So too if I boot my tumble-dryer in anger at it failing to dry my shirt, the dryer is the target of my ire. As I am using the term, the 'target' of an emotion is still an aspect of the intentional object, as I have specified the latter, i.e. it is part of what is represented by the intentional state. On this understanding, the target of my belief that Anna Karenina died a tragic death is Anna Karenina, even though I do not believe that Anna Karenina ever existed. As an aspect of the intentional object, the target specifies what the emotion is directed at insofar as it manifests the evaluative or formal object of the emotion in question.[28]

In his discussions of individual emotions in *Rhet*. II, Aristotle typically assumes that the intentional targets of our emotions are *people*.[29] This befits the oratorical context of his discussion because he is there concerned with the effect an emotion might have on changing a person's (the judge's) verdict (*krisis*) about an individual. We are angry with someone who slights us, we feel pity about someone who has suffered some undeserved misfortune, we are ashamed of ourselves for acting

---

[26] Kenny (1963: 189) uses 'material object' rather than 'particular object'.

[27] The infamous 'Fido' was introduced by Patricia Greenspan (1980, 1981, 1988: 17–18) to resist judgementalist theories by providing an example of a fear unresponsive to a contrary judgement.

[28] By contrast, de Sousa (1987: 116) uses 'target' to refer to the *real* object of the emotion if there is one. I find this usage less helpful because I do not want the target to be able to cease to exist without any change in me or my emotional state. Otherwise, my emotion about a bottle of wine I was given can suddenly cease to have a target when, unbeknownst to me, my son inadvertently smashes it with a football. Whereas I want to say that the target of my emotion remains the bottle of wine. This preserves the idea that a target is something that one can aim at, but miss (see Sainsbury 1999: 248). Interestingly, despite referring the reader back to his 1987 discussion of the notion, de Sousa seems to adopt my use in his (and Scarantino's) 2018 (§4): '[t]he target object of an emotion is the specific entity the emotion is about. For example, love can be about Mary, or about Bangkok, or about Homer Simpson and so on. These are all possible targets of love, and *they may be real or imaginary*' (my emphasis). Contrast: 'I might fall in love with a fictional character, say, or—a rather different case—be enraged against somebody who doesn't exist or about something that didn't happen. Such emotions, such as certain fears or hopes, normally *lack targets* even though they have grammatical objects' (de Sousa 1987: 134; my emphasis).

[29] Aristotle divides his discussions of the particular emotions under three heads: 'at what' (*epi poiois*), 'conditions under which' (*pōs diakeimenoi*), and 'at whom' (*tisin*) (II.1.1378a22–6). In the latter he for the most part specifies the sorts of people we might experience the emotion at. E.g. those who have done injustice or who are stronger than us are people we may fear (II.5.1382b10–12, 14–16); those we rival are the kind we might envy (II.10.1388a9–12); and those who speak badly about something we take great pride in are the kind who make us angry (II.2.1379a34–8). The target of shame is of course *ourselves* (or one we feel responsible for: II.6.1383b17–18) and so, interestingly, in this 'at whom' section Aristotle tells us about the kind of person we might be particularly prone to feel shame *in front of* (1384a21–b26) (cp. Dow 2015: 157).

disreputably, and so on. But Aristotle of course thinks that we can have emotions directed at other things besides people. As mentioned, in *NE* he observes that some depraved characters even fear the squeak of mice; and he notes that 'the Celts' do not even fear earthquakes or the resulting tsunami waves, whereas every sane person would (*NE* III.7.1115b24–8).[30] With the latter, the target of our fear would be the tsunami wave itself given its destructive power. So too he claims we can fear disease, poverty, or friendlessness (*NE* III.6.1115a10–11), not just someone's capacity to bring about our death, and these too could be 'targets' of fear, as specified.

Some emotions also have a separate and clearly identifiable intentional *focus*. To take an example of Bennet Helm's (2002: 15–16), one might be angry with someone for smashing a treasured vase with a ball. In this case, the target of one's anger is the person who throws the ball, and one must represent that person as acting under the guise of anger's evaluative object (perhaps the person is taken to manifest *offence* by failing to show due concern for something that is known to be cared about deeply?). But the vase itself seems to be a further feature of the intentional object. It is neither the target, nor the formal object, but instead something that the emotion *focuses* on, the bone of contention, we might say.[31]

As aspects of the particular object of the emotion, the target and (when present) the focus mark out what the person having the emotion represents as manifesting the evaluative or formal object of the emotion.[32] You represent *my* (target) *joking about you* (focus) as offensive (formal object). Helm represents *the person* (target) *smashing his treasured vase* (focus) as offensive (formal object). Pat represents Fido (target) as dangerous (formal object) *insofar as he might bite her* (focus). And so on. We can, then, more simply refer to the evaluative (or formal) object of the emotion, on the one hand, and its particular object, on the other. Both are aspects of the intentional object of the emotion, as I have characterized that.

---

[30] Ross (1980: *ad loc.*) translates 'neither earthquakes nor the waves', but the Greek has earthquake singular (*siesmon*). Crisp (2000: *ad loc.*) renders 'not even an earthquake or rough seas'. But there is reason to think that the earthquake and waves (*kumata*) are connected and that Aristotle means: 'not even an earthquake or the tsunami waves (that result)'; see Sedley (2005), also my 2018 (135).

[31] For an extension of the 'focus' of an emotion to 'a wider *experiential world* that operates as a backdrop to our various experiences, thoughts, and activities', see Ratcliffe (2019: quotation at 256, his emphasis).

[32] de Sousa (1987: 116–17) also distinguishes what he calls a 'motivating aspect', but this will be subsumed by the focus of the emotion except when it does not refer to something that falls within the intentional object (as with de Sousa's case where the focus of the emotion is actually illusory and motivated by some sub- or unconscious feature of the target). That said, I am open to the idea that other aspects of the particular object could be specified (in some cases).

1.4 What I mean in referring to intentional states 'apprehending' objects of emotion

In this book I shall frequently refer to intentional states 'apprehending' objects of emotion. Let me now clarify how I am employing 'apprehend' in this context. 'Apprehend', like 'know' or 'understand', would standardly be understood factively; that is, if I apprehend X, this implies X (if I apprehend the situation, I grasp it or understand it). But of course I do not only wish to consider cases in which emotions are about objects that really are as they are represented to be. Just as Monty may be afraid of a ghost he believes inhabits the kitchen, but there is no such ghost, so too I might be angry with my tumble-dryer for 'deliberately' failing to dry my shirt, when of course it did no such thing. So I am, for convenience, employing 'apprehend' non-factively. Jean Müller (2017) instead understands 'apprehend' factively and then writes of '(mere) apprehensions *as of* value' to account for the error cases (see e.g. 291f.). But to write 'the intentional state that apprehends the object of the emotion or as of apprehends the object of the emotion' throughout the book would not only be too cumbersome, but probably more likely mislead than using 'apprehend' in a non-factive sense. So I shall employ the latter. If it helps, please think of my use as a shorthand for the longer version.

Even given the non-factive use, there are narrower or broader senses in which we might think of an intentional state as 'apprehending' an object. On a narrow notion, one might think that for an intentional state to count as 'apprehending' something it must provide original access to it, that is, be a direct source of the content of the experience (whether accurate or not). On this notion, while perception might be said to apprehend objects, insofar as it reveals (whether accurately or not) the world around us by providing perceptual content, this may not be so with some notions of belief/judgement; for example, when the latter is construed as an assent (or rejection) to already encountered appearances.[33] We might call this restricted notion of 'apprehend' an 'epistemic access' notion and take 'apprehension' in this sense to refer to cases in which the state provides direct access to the object or reveals the content of the experience.

On a broader notion of 'apprehend', by contrast, we might say that for an intentional state to count as 'apprehending' an object (in the non-factive sense), it only has to make a claim that the world (or our place in it) is a certain way, regardless as to whether it provides original access to the content of the experience (in the way perception was construed on the narrow notion). On this notion, even

---

[33] Müller (2017) may have (a factive version of) this notion of 'apprehend' in mind. He claims that the view that emotions are modes of apprehension construes them as 'coming to be aware of value' (282). On this view, Nussbaum's (1994: 321–3) Stoic notion of 'judgement'—as an assent / rejection / or withholding assent / rejection to an already existing appearance that things are such and such—would not count as an apprehension of value, since we are already aware of what we then assent/reject/etc. Whereas on the broader notion of 'apprehend' I go on to sketch, it will.

judgement as assent to a (prior) appearance will count as 'apprehending' its object, since judgement in this sense involves making a claim that the object is a certain way (one judges it to be this way). Likewise, while perception may not include the agential assent of judgement (subjects can themselves reject a perceptual state, as with perceptual illusions), it can still count as making a claim that the world (or our place in it) is a certain way to the extent that it counts as (what Döring calls 2007: 378–9, 2009a: 245) a 'subsystem' that provides 'the appearance of truth'—it presents things as being a certain way even if the *agent* is aware that in the current situation it misleads.[34] We might call this broader notion of 'apprehend' an 'epistemic state' notion and take 'apprehension' in this sense to refer to cases in which the state makes a claim to represent things how they are.[35]

I certainly want at least the broader of these two notions, since when I refer to the intentional state that apprehends the object of emotion I want this to be compatible with both perceptualist and judgementalist views. And, for most of this book, this broader notion of 'apprehend' will be adequate for my purposes. However, ultimately, I want a broader notion of 'apprehend' than even the epistemic state notion. This is because I believe that Aristotle does not even require that objects of emotions have to be apprehended by epistemic states, in the sense specified above (e.g. perceptual states ('appearances as truth') or beliefs/judgements). On my view—although I shall not argue for it here—he also allows that emotions can be about their objects as those objects are represented by perceptual imaginations or uncommitted thoughts, i.e. states that are not even purporting to represent reality. On this view, we could experience fear by, e.g., perceptually imagining some dangerous snake, even if we do not believe we are in danger or even perceive (appearance-as-truth) danger.[36] In such cases, objects of emotions would be apprehended neither in the epistemic access sense, nor in the epistemic state sense.

Nonetheless, there is another sense (a weaker one still) in which non-epistemic states (like perceptual imagination or uncommitted thought) *and* epistemic states (such as perception (appearance-as-truth) and belief/judgement) may count as 'apprehending' their objects. For there is another type of 'achievement' to mark out besides (i) epistemic access or (ii) qualifying as an epistemic state. This can be brought out by noting that it seems perfectly possible for an object of emotion to be represented by more than one intentional state. We might, for example, believe that some snake is dangerous and also perceive it as dangerous. Neither judgementalists nor perceptualists need deny this possibility. Their claim that emotions are to be (in part) identified with evaluative judgements (judgementalism) or

---

[34] Contrast perceptual imagination. More on this contrast in 3.6.
[35] Deonna and Teroni (2012: 53) speak of beliefs/judgements as 'apprehensions of the world' in this way.
[36] I offered some preliminary considerations in favour of this in my 2014a (§§9–10), but argue the case in much more detail in my MS.

evaluative perceptions (perceptualism) is compatible with the idea that other intentional states can also represent objects of emotion. Perceptualists, for instance, do not have to maintain, implausibly, that we cannot represent objects of emotions by belief or judgement (indeed we may often form beliefs in response to our perceptual states). Instead, their claim is that when we have an emotion, we do so *just insofar as* the object of the emotion is represented by perception. This means that if we could somehow take away the perception, but leave the judgement (e.g. cease to see the group of people as threatening, even though we still believe they are), the emotion would disappear. So too, *mutatis mutandis*, for judgementalism. I ultimately want to use 'apprehend' to indicate this sort of success. That is, the statement 'belief apprehends the object of the emotion' entails that when I have an emotion about that object, I do so just insofar as the object is represented by belief, regardless as to whether or not I also represent the object by a perceptual state.[37] On this notion, 'intentional state X apprehends the object of the emotion' means that it is just insofar as the object is represented by X (e.g. perception, *phantasia*, or belief/judgement) that we are having the emotion about it. Our emotion is about the object *as* it is represented by that intentional state. And note that on this use of 'apprehend' we can just as easily refer to perceptual imaginations or uncommitted thoughts as apprehending objects of emotion as we can belief or perception. If we can experience fear about a snake we perceptually imagine, or if merely thinking about a particularly vicious snake can send a shudder down our spine, we can say that our emotion would be about its object just insofar as that object is apprehended by perceptual imagination or non-doxastic thought. The latter intentional states would, therefore, count as 'apprehending' the object of emotion in such cases, in this sense of 'apprehend'. We might call this broadest notion of 'apprehend' a 'specifying' notion and take 'apprehension' in this sense to refer to cases in which the state specifies the object in the way in which we have the emotion about it, when we do.[38]

The specifying notion is all I ultimately want from 'apprehend'. But if you think of 'apprehend' in the (non-factive) epistemic state sense that will, for the vast majority of the book, be no less adequate, since we will primarily be considering cases in which emotions are about their objects as those are represented by epistemic states.

---

[37] I do not mean to rule out the possibility that an emotion could be about its object insofar as that object is represented by two (or more) states or by a combination of two states. But obviously current perceptualists and judgementalists reject this.

[38] Aristotle groups perception, *phantasia*, and thought together, in contrast to desire (*orexis*), as discriminatory capacities (*kritika*: MA 6.700b17–22). If perceptual imagination and non-doxastic thought also count as discriminatory, we would here have a sense in which states can be grouped insofar they can determine or specify content (whereas desires react to content that is provided by a *kritikon*). See also **11.3**. Cf. also the broad notion of thought (*hupolēsis*) at *De an.* III.3.427b24–6, although all the kinds mentioned there (belief, knowledge, and *phronēsis*) seem truth-apt.

Referring to the intentional state that 'apprehends' the object of the emotion in the specifying sense is helpful insofar as it allows me to make terminological space for the response view of emotions that I will argue is Aristotle's. Contemporary perceptualists and judgementalists maintain that the intentional state that apprehends the object of the emotion (a perceptual state or judgement) *is*, at least in part, the emotion.[39] Similarly, with interpretations of Aristotle (insofar as they take a stand on the matter). Both perceptualist and quasi-perceptualist readings (see **Intro.2**) hold that he identifies emotions (at least in part) with perceptual *phantasiai*; whereas judgementalist readings postulate the same for belief or judgement. I reject such views. As I see it, Aristotle thinks that emotions are hedonic *responses* to intentional states that apprehend their objects. At the same time, I will also support those interpretations that claim that Aristotle holds that the pleasures or distresses of emotions are *themselves* representational. They are about or directed at the object of the emotion (e.g. the world or our place in it). Thus, on my reading, Aristotle thinks that emotions are representational pleasures or distresses that are about their objects *as those objects* are apprehended (in the 'specifying' sense) by another intentional state. Using 'apprehend' (rather than e.g. 'represents') in 'the intentional state that apprehends the object of the emotion' thereby allows me to distinguish (i) the representational pleasure or distress of the emotion from (ii) the intentional state that apprehends its object, in line with my reading. Of course, drawing this distinction does not *itself* dictate any specific relation between (i) and (ii). On some views (discussed in Chapter 3), Aristotle thinks that the intentional state that apprehends the object of the emotion (whether judgement, *phantasia*, or perception) *just is* the representational pleasure or distress of the emotion. On such views, the representational pleasures or distresses of emotions are modes of apprehension (indeed, on the views mentioned, not only in the 'specifying' sense, but the epistemic state sense). But drawing the distinction does at least allow us *to formulate the question* of whether the intentional state that apprehends the object of the emotion and the representational pleasure or distress should be (in part) identified. And, as indicated, I shall in fact argue that Aristotle rejects the identification and instead holds that emotions are representational pleasures or distresses that are formed *in response to* other intentional states that apprehend their objects.

1.5 Analysing emotions in terms of other intentional states

If my reading proves correct, Aristotle rejects the notion of many contemporary philosophers (and, indeed, his interpreters) that emotions should be (at least in

---

[39] See **Intro.2n.19** for references.

part) identified with evaluative judgements or perceptual states. Nonetheless, it is worth stressing that his view still shares a key structural *parallel* with such accounts. For, like such accounts, he seeks to analyse emotions in terms of *other intentional states*—it is just that for him we have representational hedonic states, rather than perception or judgement. But just this more general point has recently been challenged. It has been argued that *any* attempt to analyse emotions in terms of other intentional states is doomed to failure from the start. Since this would clearly threaten Aristotle's view, no less than perceptualist or judgementalist accounts, it needs addressing.

Deonna and Teroni propose what they call an 'attitudinal theory of emotions' (2012: ch. 7, 2014, 2015). Operating with the model of intentional states sketched in 1.1—i.e. where each intentional state consists of an intentional attitude and an intentional content—they maintain that what distinguishes individual emotions must be their own distinctive *attitudes*—the attitudes of fear, anger, amusement, for instance—*not* their intentional *contents*.[40] If this were right, it would seem to undermine both perceptualist and judgementalist accounts, as well as Aristotle's. For each of these locates the difference in question (at least in part) in terms of content. Fear involves perceiving something as dangerous, judging that something is dangerous, or (for Aristotle) distress at a danger. Whereas anger involves perceiving some offence, a judgement about an offence, or distress at an offence. But, with each kind of analysis, 'danger' and 'offence', as the (putative) evaluative objects of fear and anger, respectively, are taken to enter into the intentional content. Similarly, with other emotions. And yet, according to Deonna and Teroni:

> If it makes sense to say that what frightens Julianne is what John is amused by—a dog, for instance—then we have reason enough to think that the difference between their two emotions is not to be located at the level of their respective contents. If this difference were located at the level of the content, that would imply that Julianne is frightened by (a specific instance of) dangerousness, whereas John is amused by (a specific instance of) funniness; their respective emotions would then be about different things. (2012: 77)

On this view, in order to preserve the idea that we can have two different emotions about the very same thing, we cannot distinguish emotion-types from each other by reference to their contents—for, if we do, our two emotions will not in fact be about the same thing after all. Indeed, Deonna and Teroni take this to be generalizable to other intentional states besides emotions. If, for instance, it can make sense to say that what John *believes* is what Julienne *doubts*, the difference between their mental states must be to do with the fact that each involves a

---

[40] Prudently, they do not seek to explain emotions in terms of one general attitude, 'emoting' (which would seem a step back) (2012: 78, 2015: 296).

distinct intentional attitude (2012: 77). John believes and Julienne doubts the same content.[41]

Now it is clearly true that when we characterize the intentional state of fear simply as *fear (attitude) that* p *(content)*, the fearfulness of the object represented by the intentional state (its evaluative or formal object), must be specified by the intentional state's *attitude*, rather than its content. For *p* just specifies the particular object of the emotion. However, as I see it, this does not preclude analysing fear in terms of another intentional state (or states), which, via a different attitude-content combination, nonetheless represents the same object. All that is required is that the alternative characterizations—*fear (A) that* p *(C)*, on the one hand, and *the analysing intentional attitude (A) that* p *is dangerous (C)*,[42] on the other— succeed in representing the same object.[43] According to the model of intentional states I am operating with, and which Deonna and Teroni also claim to be using (see e.g. 2015: 296n.5), the object an intentional state represents is a function of both its attitude and content. But it is important to stress that nothing in this model prevents two different attitude + content combinations from representing *the very same* object.[44] Hence, there is nothing in principle that precludes one

---

[41] They express this in terms of such intentional states having different 'correctness conditions'. The 'correctness conditions' of an intentional state are the minimum conditions it needs to meet to be correct. An intentional state's satisfying such conditions just means it matches reality: a *belief that* p satisfies the correctness conditions of belief just in case *p* is true, a *rejection that* p satisfies its correctness conditions just in case *p* is false, and so on. (An intentional state's satisfying its correctness conditions does not make it rational or justified because someone may, e.g., irrationally believe, correctly, that *p* is true in spite of having overwhelming evidence that *p* is false; see Deonna and Teroni 2012: 6–7.) Deonna and Teroni also assume that emotions have correctness conditions (e.g. 2012: 6, 77). As is already implicit, it is unclear to me that emotions *as such* have correctness conditions. If we can form emotions about objects as they are represented by, e.g., a perceptual imagination or daydream (or fictional scenarios more generally), it may sound odd to say that such emotions can be 'assessed as correct or incorrect depending on whether or not they fit the facts' (2012: 6). But this point is not crucial for my current argument.

[42] This specifies the content in the way a judgementalist would characterize it. The perceptualist may prefer '*of* p *as dangerous* (C)'; similarly, Aristotle may prefer '*at* p*'s danger* (C)'.

[43] The natural grammar of our language sometimes directs us to contents, other times to objects. We can fear that Fido will bite us or feel ashamed that Tony has bared his legs in public. But we would generally say that we pity David or David's falling off his bike, not that we pity *that* David fell off his bike (so too we say: we are envious of Bill Gates (with respect to his money), not (?): we envy that Bill Gates has so much money). The difference, here, seems to concern whether our natural grammar has the emotion term pointing to its target—which, as we have seen, is a feature of the intentional object—or a proposition, which will pick out the intentional content that (in part) specifies the object represented. But I do not think anything hinges on this. Pity (A): that David fell of his bike (C), can be taken to represent David's falling of his bike as pitiable, even if we would not naturally use sentences that correspond to the former. The plausibility of an analysis of emotions in terms of other intentional states does not require that we naturally talk about each emotion at the attitude + content level, rather than the object level.

[44] Although Deonna and Teroni claim to follow Crane (2009) with respect to the distinction between attitude and content, they seem to fail to adhere to one of his key points, viz. that what an intentional state represents is a function of both its attitude and content. This is manifest in their sometimes treating 'what a state represents' and 'the state's content' as equivalent; e.g. 'What is represented and the attitude towards it each make their respective contributions' (2015: 299, where 'what is represented' picks up 'content' on 298); also: 'not a matter of what these states represent, i.e., of their content' (2015: 308).

attitude + content combination from providing a sound analysis of another. (Indeed, I shall shortly provide a non-emotional example of just this.) So, as I see it, contemporary perceptualists or judgementalists (and, indeed, Aristotle) should not feel threatened by specifications of emotions in terms of attitude + content, where the attitude is specified by the emotion-type (fear, anger, amusement, etc.).[45] They should simply point out that they are trying to offer an *analysis* of such specifications in terms of more basic states (or at least an analysis that reveals more of the underlying structure of the emotion, or some such).

But what about Deonna and Teroni's claim that such an analysis will inevitably fail to capture the idea that just as different people can believe or doubt the same thing, so too they can fear or be amused by the very same thing? As noted, the analysis of fear that perceptualists and judgementalists (or my Aristotle) seek to offer places some of what was represented by the intentional *attitude* (in the *fear (A) that* p *(C)* formulation Deonna and Teroni prefer) into the intentional *content*. In particular, representing the formal object of the emotion, on such views, ceases to be a function of the attitude and is instead a function of the content. If danger is the formal object of fear, *danger* will enter into the content.[46] And yet, on Deonna and Teroni's view, this means that we cannot say that Julienne can be afraid of what John is amused by. And, if that were the case, it would seem unpalatable.

But *do* such analyses have the consequence that Deonna and Teroni claim? In fact, the parallel with belief and doubt, which they themselves invoked, suggests otherwise. For just as perceptualists, judgementalists, and Aristotle propose to analyse emotions in terms of other intentional states, so too we might analyse

---

[45] Cp. Rossi and Tappolet (2019) who, mistakenly in my view, accept that their perceptualist analysis is incompatible with the general idea of the attitudinal view of analysing emotions in terms of e.g. *fear (A) that* p *(C)*. The general idea is harmless, but it should be contrasted with the specific details of Deonna and Teroni's view—as sketched in the next note—which fill out the idea in a determinate way and, accordingly, need not be accepted by all.

[46] This is what I take Deonna and Teroni to be objecting to. But, of course, they do not just want to stick with *fear (A) that* p *(C)* either—they seek to provide their own analysis. They do so, however, without shifting the responsibility of representing the formal object of the emotion into the content (that remains the job of the attitude), but instead unpacking the attitude. On their view, the attitudes of emotions are 'felt bodily attitudes directed towards the world' (2012: 80), that is, 'states of felt action readiness' (81). 'Fear of the dog is an experience of the dog as dangerous, precisely because it consists in feeling the body's readiness to act so as to diminish the dog's likely impact on it (flight, preemptive attack, etc.)' (81). In effect, Deonna and Teroni seek to analyse emotions in terms of feelings of action readiness, where the specific kind of action readiness provides a non-trivial specification of the formal object of the emotion. Whether or not this is feasible in its own terms, such an approach (or something like it) is not required for us to say that one person can fear the same thing that another is amused by. For, as we shall see, the latter does not preclude an analysis of emotions which involves shifting some of what the emotion represents (the formal object) out of the attitude and into the content. (Deonna and Teroni's particular account will face the difficulties any motivational view faces; see their 2012 (81); Scarantino (2014); and Chapter 11 below. Note, though, Deonna and Teroni think that emotions still have world-to-mind direction of fit (2012: 83), whereas Scarantino does not (2014: 177–8); see **11.3**.)

belief and other related states in terms of the more basic notion of *thought*. Consider:

(1) Thought: that *p* is true
(2) Thought: that *p* is false
(3) Thought: that *p* is probable
(4) Thought: that *p* is unlikely

(1)–(4) purport to represent the *very same objects* as, respectively, the belief that *p*, rejecting that *p*, the conjecture that *p*, and doubting that *p*. The parallel nicely illustrates how a specification of an intentional state in terms of one type of attitude-content combination is compatible with an analysis of that state in terms of a more basic intentional state with a different content. The *belief (A) that* p *(C)* can be analysed by a more basic attitude-content combination if we place some of what was represented by the original attitude (believing) into the intentional content of the analysing intentional state, the *thought (A) that* p *is true (C)*. So too, perceptualists, judgementalists, and Aristotle should maintain of their analyses of emotions.

But this parallel also undermines Deonna and Teroni's claim that such analyses prevent us from saying that we can, e.g., fear and be amused by the same thing. For presumably they would not want to say that (1) above and the *belief that* p are about different intentional objects; nor that (2) above and the *rejection that* p represent different objects; and so on.[47] If so, the analyses in (1) and (2) must be compatible with us saying that we can believe and reject the same thing. For they represent the very same objects as the *belief that* p and the *rejection that* p, respectively.

Now, of course, there is a sense in which (1)–(4) *themselves* represent different objects. (1) represents the object or state of affairs specified by *p* as obtaining, (2) represents it as not obtaining, (3) as probably obtaining, and (4) as unlikely to obtain. But that does not mean that (1) to (4) do not all involve representing the object or state of affairs *specified by* p. Just because *p* is not in the content all-on-its-lonesome in the thoughts specified in (1)–(4) (as it is when it is a complement of belief, conjecture, doubt, or rejection themselves) does not entail that those

---

[47] When Deonna and Teroni claim (in the passage quoted) that it can 'make sense to say that what frightens Julianne is what John is amused by—a dog for instance', they are still referring to the dog under a certain intentional description. On their view, emotions have 'cognitive bases' (judgement, perception, imagination, memory, etc.) which represent the particular intentional object of the emotion in its non-evaluative form (see e.g. 2012: 5, 69, 2015: 300) (only the evaluative aspect is represented by the intentional attitude). They are thus envisaging that the same particular intentional object is specified by a cognitive base, but one person takes an attitude of fear to it, another an attitude of amusement. (In any event, it is hard to see how the idea that we can fear and be amused by the same thing *under two different intentional descriptions* could help support their view over those that put the evaluative aspect of emotions in the intentional content.)

thoughts are not about the *very same* proposition, *p*. Clearly, they are. So too, then, the fact that Julienne can fear that *p* and John be amused at (the very same) *p* does not show that there cannot be an analysis of these emotions in terms of another (more basic) intentional state (perception, judgement, or distress/pleasure), an analysis which places some of the representational work of the original intentional attitudes into the new (analysing) intentional state's content. And what is moved, of course, is the evaluative aspect of the emotion (danger, in the case of fear). '*P*', in the content, specifies the particular object that the intentional state represents. But that particular object is still specified regardless as to what else is added to it by the intentional attitude, or, as with our putative analyses of emotions, what else is placed next to it in the intentional content. Thus, so long as *p* remains in the intentional content *alongside* 'danger', *p* will specify the very same intentional object as it did in the formulation *fearing (A) that* p *(C)*. Just as the *thought that* p *is true* and the *belief that* p are both about the intentional object specified by *p*, so too analyses of *fearing (A) that* p *(C)* in terms of *perceiving/judging (A) that* p *is dangerous (C)* or, as Aristotle would suggest, *distress (A) at* p*'s danger* are still about the intentional object specified by *p*. Deonna and Teroni's argument was therefore spurious.

Deonna and Teroni's formulation of fear in terms of *fearing (A) + content (C)* does help emphasize something important, however. Although specifying fear in such a way does not spell doom for attempts to analyse fear in terms of other intentional states, it does highlight that any putative analysis must plausibly represent *precisely the same intentional objects* as that formulation. This means, first, that the analysis must be able to specify emotions in all their richness and complexity. If, then, either belief or perception are going to be able to represent objects of fear, they must be able to represent objects *as fearful*, and not lose anything in their analysis, and they must be capable of representing not just all the different *types* of emotion we can undergo, but also each possible *token* we can encounter of those types. It is no good if the proposed analysis can only represent certain types of emotions, but not others, or cannot account for each token we can experience of any given type. Equally importantly, second, the *fearing (A) + content (C)* formulation highlights that if an account claims to *identify* emotions with its proposed analysis, it should not *add anything extraneous*. For if the account is intended to provide an analysis of the emotion itself, not some state that is closely related to it, or overlaps with it in some way, it must pick out *only* instances of that emotion.

In this way, the *fearing (A) + content (C)* formulation effectively provides us with two *constraints* on any plausible analysis. First, the analysis must be able to pick out all instances of emotions (it must be sufficient); second, the analysis cannot posit anything extraneous (everything it posits must be necessary). In fact, in Chapter 3 I shall argue that perceptualism and judgementalism fail with respect to the second constraint and do so in a way that then makes them fail with regard to the first constraint no less. Unlike Aristotle's analysis of emotions in terms of representational pleasures or distresses, they each make an unwarranted extraneous addition to the representation (thereby failing the second constraint), one that then means they fail to be able to accommodate the full range of emotions that are possible (thereby failing the first constraint).

Conclusion

In this chapter I first highlighted the basic notion of an intentional state as consisting of an intentional attitude and an intentional content which together represent an intentional object (1.1). I then indicated, in a preliminary way, why it might not be anachronistic to think of Aristotle as operating which such a general model (1.2). I next turned to objects of emotions and distinguished the *evaluative (or formal)* object of an emotion, on the one hand, from its *particular* object, on the other (and, as aspects of the latter, the object's *target* and *focus*) (1.3). I then explained the sense in which I intend us to understand intentional states as 'apprehending' objects of emotion (1.4). I closed by addressing a recent objection to the very idea of offering an analysis of emotions in terms of other (more basic) intentional states. If I am right, such analyses are still very much on the table (1.5).

Aristotle on What Emotions Are. Giles Pearson, Oxford University Press. © Giles Pearson 2024.
DOI: 10.1093/9780191989292.003.0002

PART I
EMOTIONS AS PLEASURES AND DISTRESSES

2
Emotions as Representational Hedonic States

In the first part of this book I develop my view that Aristotle holds that at least a central class of emotions are representational pleasures or distresses (hedonic states) that are formed in response to intentional states that apprehend their objects (in the sense of 'apprehend' specified in **1.4**). As I flagged in **Intro.1**, I use 'hedonic' as a convenient shorthand to cover *both* 'pleasurable' *and* 'painful/distressful', and not, as the term strictly means, just pertaining to pleasure. I first argue that Aristotle thinks that a central category of emotions are, at least in part, pleasures or distresses and also that the pleasures and distresses in question are representational rather than (as has alternatively been proposed) non-representational (and hence that 'distress' is better than 'pain') (Chapter 2). I next argue against views that identify the representational pleasure or distress of the emotion with the intentional state that apprehends its object (Chapter 3). I then resist the idea that the representational pleasure or distress and the intentional state that apprehends the object of the emotion form two distinct components of the emotion. Instead, on my reading, Aristotle holds that emotions are representational pleasures or distresses alone and are formed in response to (or, as I shall argue, 'in light of') the intentional state that apprehends the object of the emotion (Chapter 4). I close by arguing that this account of emotions as representational hedonic states is compatible with the account(s) of pleasure we find in Aristotle's ethical works (Chapter 5).

In this chapter I begin (**2.1**) by considering what Aristotle means when he claims that emotions 'are accompanied by' (*hepetai*) pleasure or pain, as he does in several lists-cum-specifications. I consider various ways this may be understood (and note some problematic cases) but, ultimately, end up with the notion that Aristotle thinks that (at least very many) emotions *just are* (at least in part) pleasures or pains. If this is right, we next need to consider what sort of pleasures and pains he has in mind. On one view they are non-representational states (sensations or feelings). I resist such a reading (**2.2**) and suggest that Aristotle is more plausibly construed as holding that the pleasures or pains of emotions are themselves representational states, directed at their objects (**2.3**). I close the chapter by considering this dimension of Aristotle's account in light of some contemporary views about pain (**2.4**).

Let me add a note about 'pain' and 'pleasure' at the start. For the time being in this chapter I shall write of *pain* (*lupē*) in connection with the emotions. *Lupē* can refer to bodily pain or (mental) distress. Ultimately, as we shall see, the latter will prove more appropriate. But initially—to avoid prejudicing against interpretations I shall shortly address—I will stick with 'pain'. Also, interestingly, although in his general specifications of the emotions Aristotle refers to *pleasure* (*hēdonē*), he will sometimes characterize certain emotions in terms of *feeling joy* (*chairein*). I return to this at the end of the chapter but, again, for now will simply stick with 'pleasure'.

2.1 What does Aristotle mean in claiming that emotions 'are accompanied by' (*hepetai*) pleasure and pain?

Aristotle connects emotions to pleasure and pain in several general specifications. In *Rhet*. II.1 he writes:

> The emotions (*ta pathē*) are those things owing to which people, by undergoing change, differ in their judgements (*kriseis*), and which are accompanied by (*hepetai*) pain and pleasure—for example, anger (*orgē*), pity (*eleos*), fear (*phobos*) and other such things, and their contraries (*kai ta toutois enantia*). (1378a19–22)

We find the same connection specified in the ethical works. In *NE* II.5 he notes:

> By emotions (*pathē*) I mean appetite (*epithumia*), anger (*orgē*), fear (*phobos*), confidence (*tharsos*), envy (*phthonos*), joy (*chara*), feeling-friendly (*philia*), hatred (*misos*), longing (*pothos*), emulation (*zēlos*), pity (*eleos*), and in general those things which are accompanied by (*hepetai*) pleasure or pain. (1105b21–3)

Again, in *EE* II.2 he formulates the link as follows:

> By emotions (*pathē*) I mean things like spirit (*thumos*), fear (*phobos*), shame (*aidōs*), appetite (*epithumia*), in general things that for the most part (*epi to polu*) are accompanied by (*hepetai*) perceptible pleasure or pain in their own right (*kath' hauta*). (1220b12–14)

There are several thorny questions about the detail of these specifications, some of which will be more tractable later on.[1] But let me start by considering what

---

[1] I discuss the 'in general' (*holōs*) in the *NE* and *EE* specifications later on in this section, but more detailed discussion of the further qualifications in the *EE* specification ('for the most part' (*epi to polu*), 'perceptible', and 'in their own right' (*kath' hauta*)) will have to wait until **10.8** (although I do

Aristotle means in claiming that emotions 'are accompanied by' (*hepetai*) pleasure or pain.

The Greek verb *hepetai* takes the dative. A (nominative) *hepetai* B (dative) means: *A accompanies / follows / is implied by / etc. B* or, equivalently, *B (dative) is accompanied by / is followed by / implies / etc. A (nominative)*. In our passages we are told that pleasure or pain (or 'pain and pleasure') (nominative) *hepetai* the emotions (dative: *hois*, 'those things' = the emotions) or (following the word order of the Greek) that the emotions (dative) *hepetai* pleasure or pain (nominative). So we can say that pleasure or pain *accompany / follow / are implied by* the emotions or, equivalently, that the emotions *are accompanied by / are followed by / imply* pleasure or pain. Aristotle's claim that emotions (dative) *hepetai* pleasure or pain (nominative) has attracted considerable attention in the literature.[2] Part of the issue, as already indicated, is that *hepetai* can be used in quite a few ways, some of which would indicate a loose connection, others something very tight. As Anthony Price notes, *hepetai* 'could signify a subsequent state, but may well signify a current aspect, essential or accidental' (2011: 115). Hence anything from 'follows', 'attends', 'accompanies', 'is entailed by', or 'is implied by' can seem appropriate.[3] But the matter is not quite as open-ended as this. As Jamie Dow points out (2015: 147–8), while *hepetai* can be used, like 'follows', simply to indicate that one thing comes after another (at e.g. *NE* III.2.1111b5, VIII.1.1155a3, X.1.1172a19; *Cael.* II.7.289a11, III.4.302b11), it more commonly indicates that where you find one thing, you also find something else. This usage may, perhaps, sometimes simply indicate a contingent generalization (Dow cites *Rhet.* II.16.1390b32 as a possible case: 'the sorts of character (nominative) that *hepetai* wealth (dative) are on the surface for all to see'), but more often it indicates that something by its very nature implies something else. We see the latter commonly in the logical works, where *hepesthai* can be synonymous with *akolouthein* (and mean '(logically) entails'; see e.g. *Pr. an.* I.27.43b3, 17–19, 22, 29–31) or *huparchein tini* (and mean '(logically) belongs'; e.g. *Pr. an.* II.2.54b31, II.3.56a27, 29). But we also see it elsewhere; for example, in *NE* when Aristotle claims that 'giving (dative) implies (*hepetai*) doing good and doing what is noble (nominative)' (IV.1.1120a14,

---

consider a possible meaning of 'in their own right' (*kath' hauta*) later in this section and mention one possible understanding of the 'perceptible' in 2.2). I shall not here pick up on the link between emotions and changes in 'judgement' (*krisis* = decision or verdict; see e.g. *Rhet.* I.3.1358b3–5, 9–10, I.13.1374b19–21) in the *Rhet.* specification. For more discussion, see e.g. Leighton (1996: 206–17) and Rapp (2002: 575–83).

[2] See e.g. Leighton (1996: part 2); Cooper (1996: 244–6); Striker (1996: 288–93); Fortenbaugh (2002: 106ff.); Rapp (2002: 548, 550, 2013: 35–8); Price (2011: 114–15); Moss (2012a: 80–1n.26); Dow (2015: 147–50). Already in ancient times the term seems to have attracted attention. The author of *MM* glosses it with *parakolouthein* ('to follow beside') (I.7.1186a13); cf. also Aspasius (Heylbut 1889): 42.27ff.

[3] Reeve uses 'entail' in both his translations of *NE* (2014) and *Rhet.* (2018). Irwin (1985) translates 'implies' in several places in his translation of the *NE* (e.g. 1120a14, a26, b32); Ross (1980) has 'implies' in the first of these, 'accompanies' in the last two. For more passages, see Bonitz (1870: s.v.).

cf. 1120b32, 34), and in *De an*. III.3 when he claims that 'belief (dative) entails (*hepetai*) conviction (nominative) (for it is not possible to believe things without being convinced of them)' (428a19–21).

Importantly, as Dow also flags (so too Frede 1996: 282n.25), Aristotle explicitly draws attention to the different ways *hepetai* can be used in *Rhet*. itself. He writes:

> [We say that that is a greater good than this] also whenever this (nominative) would *hepētai* that (dative), but not that (nominative) this (dative) (and it *hepētai* either (i) simultaneously (*tō(i) hama*), (ii) subsequently (*tō(i) ephexēs*), or (iii) potentially (*tē(i) dunamei*) (all dative)), since the use of the latter is already contained in the former. (i) Living (nominative) *hepetai* being healthy (dative), but not vice versa, and does so simultaneously (*hama*); (ii) scientific knowledge (*to epistasthai*; also 'understanding', 'knowing') (nominative) [*hepetai*] learning (*tō(i) manthanein*) (dative) and does so subsequently (*husteron*); and (iii) stealing (nominative) [*hepetai*] violating a holy place (dative) and does so potentially (for someone violating a holy place might also steal from it). (I.7.1363b28–33; numerals added)[4]

Let us consider these three possible significations of *hepetai* in relation to the emotions. Dow dismisses the 'potential' use without explanation. I agree we should reject this reading but think it worthwhile briefly spelling out why. On this signification, pleasure or pain (nominative) *hepetai* the emotions (dative) in the same way that stealing (nominative) *hepetai* violating a holy place (dative). As Aristotle notes, stealing *hepetai* violating a holy place in the sense that someone violating a holy place might also steal from it. There is, that is, the potential for the latter to occur when the former does. The implication for the emotions, on this signification, would be that pleasure or pain would *hepetai* the emotions insofar as it is possible that when we have an emotion, pleasure or pain might also (contingently) occur. The problem with this reading is that it seems *too weak*. With the *NE* and *EE* specifications the link to pleasure or pain is the *sole* feature that Aristotle invokes to group the emotions and is that by which he specifies what he means by *pathē*. 'By the emotions, *I mean* (*legō*)…those things (dative) which *hepetai* pleasure or pain (nominative)'. If this merely meant: 'By the emotions I mean those things which *might happen to go along with* pleasure or pain', the specification would not seem tight enough. Aristotle needs a feature that will group the states he has mentioned, not one that might drop in and out. Indeed, we might note that before his *NE* II.5 specification he had already claimed in *NE* II.3 that *every* emotion (*panti pathei*) (dative) *hepetai* pleasure and pain (nominative) (1104b14–15).[5]

---

[4] Cf. also *Top*. III.2.117a5–15.
[5] I shall return to this passage shortly, as it also asserts the same about actions (*praxeis*).

What about the other two significations of *hepetai*; the 'subsequent' and 'simultaneous' uses? Dow claims that Aristotle's examples *with both of these* suggest that the connection signalled by *hepetai* 'is between two things one of which is part of the essence of the other' (2015: 148). He writes:

> Being alive is part of the essence of being healthy, since being healthy is *a way of being alive*. Likewise, one has not learned unless one subsequently understands (or "knows")—it is essential to learning that it is the achieving of a state of *having learned*, indeed, of understanding. (148; Dow's emphases)

He goes on to suggest, though, that this feature of the examples cannot 'mandate' a particular interpretation of *hepetai* in the *Rhet.* II.1 specification. On his view, all that is *directly asserted* by that use is 'nothing less than concurrence', even if the passage as least prompts the idea that Aristotle 'is more likely to have in mind a tighter connection such as that pain or pleasure is essential to being a passion' (148).

I think Dow is too quick with the subsequent usage. It is surely questionable that it is essential to learning that it is the achievement of understanding. That might be the *goal* of learning, but presumably we still want to say that people count as learning things *before* they have achieved understanding (hence learning does not simply co-occur with understanding). After all, understanding something might involve learning a number of different things. One does not understand French or calculus, for example, by learning one French word or one function. We might rather say that learning *results in* understanding, assuming all goes well.[6] In any event, it is, I suggest, much more likely that Aristotle is here specifying a *temporal* notion of *hepetai* which does not entail concurrence. Understanding follows learning in the sense that it *results from* learning (if all goes well). Indeed, this is presumably why Aristotle gives this as an example of the *subsequent* (*ephexēs*, *husteron*) use of *hepetai*, where the Greek terms often imply temporal succession. It is also presumably why he contrasts this usage with the 'simultaneous' (*hama*) signification of *hepetai*, where *hama* even more exclusively picks out a temporal notion ('at the same time').

So even putting aside the 'potential' use of *hepetai*, we cannot assume that *hepetai* signifies 'at least concurrence' (and then ask what sort of concurrence Aristotle might have in mind); for we still have the 'subsequent' use to consider.

---

[6] Does learning entail having learned? Suppose I want to learn French and at my first class am taught the numbers one to ten. It is now true that I am learning French. Can we say that I *have learned* French? It depends on what we mean by this. It will now always be true that I have spent some time learning French (even if I never attend another class). In this sense learning entails having learned. But in no sense does my learning in such a case entail that I now understand French as such (I will not be able to order in a restaurant or ask for directions). So learning *X* does not entail having learned *X* if 'having learned *X*' is taken to mean 'understand *X* as such'. Aristotle explicitly rejects the idea that 'at the same time we are learning' we 'have learnt' in *Met.* Θ.6.1048b24–5.

On this notion, pleasure or pain (nominative) *hepetai* the emotions (dative) in the same way that understanding (nominative) *hepetai* learning (dative). If, as I have suggested, understanding *hepetai* learning in the sense that, all going well, understanding will *result from* learning, the implication for the emotions, on this signification, would be that pleasure or pain would *follow* or *result from* the emotion. Unlike the potential use, the connection could still be a necessary one (i.e. whenever we have an emotion we get a pleasure or pain), but it would be *sequential*. We would first have the emotion *and then* the pleasure or pain would ensue.[7]

As it happens, though, this view is no less implausible than that suggested by the potential use.[8] On this reading, emotions would be states that *bring about* a further state of pleasure or pain, but they would not be pleasures or pains themselves. And yet it is clear from a good number of Aristotle's specifications of emotions in both *Rhet.* and elsewhere (esp. *EE* III.7) that he views pleasure or pain as (at least) *part of* the emotional state. Many emotions are simply stated to be 'a kind of distress' (*lupē tis*)—fear (*Rhet.* II.5.1382a21), shame (II.6.1383b12–13), pity (II.8.1385b13), envy (II.10.1387b23), emulation (II.11.1388a32)—or, more simply, distresses—pity (II.9.1386b9, 26–7); indignation (II.9.1387a8–9, cf. *EE* III.7.1233b23–5); envy (*EE* III.7.1233b19–20)—or pleasures/joys—pride-in-another (*Rhet.* II.9.1386b30–1), schadenfreude (II.9.1386b33–1387a3).[9] If Aristotle thought that pleasure or pain was strictly speaking only something that resulted sequentially from the emotion, this would be incomprehensible.[10]

So, if we are to select from the three specifications of *hepetai* in *Rhet.* I.7, Aristotle must mean *hepetai* in the 'simultaneous' sense. On this view, pleasure or pain (nominative) *hepetai* the emotions (dative) in the same way that living (nominative) *hepetai* being healthy (dative). Living *hepetai* being healthy in the sense that those who are healthy are, by that very fact, *alive*, and their being healthy is simultaneously a manifestation of their being alive. If the cases were parallel, the implication for the emotions would be that those undergoing an emotion are, by that very fact, undergoing pleasure or pain, and their undergoing the emotion is simultaneously a manifestation of pleasure or pain. We end up with co-occurrence.

---

[7] Cf. Moss (2012a: 80–1n.26). [8] Cf. Viano (2021: 129n.9).
[9] I provide more detailed specifications of all these emotions in my Catalogue at the end of the book.
[10] Aristotle does appear to use *hepesthai* in the subsequent sense when characterizing the pleasure connected to anger. He claims that 'a certain pleasure' (nominative) must *hepesthai* 'all anger' (dative), namely, the pleasure that arises from the prospect of revenge (*Rhet.* II.2.1378b1–2). He explains that it is pleasant to think that one will get what one seeks (b2–3) and that a certain pleasure follows along (*akolouthein*) because of this (b8). The pleasure, in this case, is indeed subsequent *to anger*, which is itself most plausibly thought of as involving a representational *distress* (directed at an apparent slight). The pleasure is, though, plausibly thought of as an emotion in its own right. I discuss all these points further in Chapter 6 (see esp. **6.5** on the pleasure subsequent to anger; see also **4.3**).

It is worth stressing that this alone would not identify, or even in part identify, emotions with pleasures/pains. Two things could go along simultaneously like this and yet be distinct. Suppose all and only creatures with a heart also have a kidney, then having a heart (nominative) would *hepetai* having a kidney (dative) (and indeed vice versa), but having a heart is not to be identified, or in part identified, with having a kidney.[11] Indeed, in *NE* II.3 Aristotle claims:

> if the virtues are concerned with actions and emotions, and every emotion (dative) and every action (dative) *hepetai* pleasure and pain (nominative), for this reason also virtue will be concerned with pleasures and pains. (1104b13–16)

Here we are told not only that every emotion *hepetai* pleasure and pain, but also that every *action hepetai* pleasure and pain. The latter is pleasure and pain *in action*. Actions are clearly not *themselves* pleasures or pains, but pleasure or pain may non-accidentally accompany every (ethical) action (i.e. must supervene on such actions: II.3.1104b3–5).[12] The passage, however, leaves open the possibility that Aristotle intends something stronger with the emotions. If both actions and emotions *hepetai* pleasure and pain in the 'simultaneous' sense, such co-occurrence would be compatible with different sorts of relation. Pleasure and pain may supervene on all actions without actions themselves simply being types of pleasure or pain, whereas emotions could manifest the stronger relation.

In favour of the idea that Aristotle does indeed intend the stronger relation (identification or part identification) with emotions is the fact, already mentioned, that he defines many emotions (in *Rhet.* and elsewhere) *as* pleasures or pains (or as a *kind of* pain: *lupē tis*). In fact, it is possible that one of the supplementary qualifications provided in the *EE* II.2 specification seeks to *indicate* the way we should understand *hepetai* in that formulation. Aristotle claims that the emotions are accompanied by pleasure/pain *intrinsically* or *in their own right* (*kath' hauta*).[13] This would also accord with the fact that in *EE* II.4, when he refers back to the specification in *EE* II.2, Aristotle tells us that the emotions are defined or delimited (*diōristai*) by pleasure or pain (1221b36–7).[14]

The idea that the general specifications are intended to mark out emotions *as* pleasures or pains receives further support from the fact that in the ethical

---

[11] Cf. Quine (1961: 21). [12] See Price (2017: 200ff.) and the introduction to Chapter 5 below.
[13] In **10.8** I will propose that the 'for the most part' in the *EE* definition might qualify this, to account for some cases in which the states specified are not themselves representational pleasures or distresses (but link to such in looser, but still determinate, ways). The *kath' hauta* would thereby pick out a narrower class of *pathē* which just are such pleasures or distresses.
[14] 'Refers back': the II.2 passage is part of his distinction between emotions, capacities, and states (1220b10–19) and in II.4, just before the line mentioned in the text, Aristotle claims: 'base and excellent character must...consist in the pursuit or avoidance of certain pleasures and pains. This is clear from the distinctions we have made concerning emotions, capacities and states...' (1221b32–5). See also *EE* II.5: 'pleasures and pains arise from the aforementioned states and emotions' (1222b10–11).

formulations (though not in *Rhet.*) Aristotle claims that pleasure or pain 'in general' (*holōs*) accompany anger, fear, appetite, etc. When he provides lists which end in an 'in general' (*holōs*), what follows often specifies the general kind of which the items of the list are instances; that is, with '*a*, *b*, *c*, and in general *X*', *X* can often specify the general kind of which *a*, *b*, and *c* are specific instances (e.g. *Sens.* 1.436a9; *NE* I.4.1095b4–6; *Int.* 9.19a7–10; *Pr. an.* I.13.32b6–8, 11–13; *Top.* I.12.105a14–16; see also esp. *Phys.* IV.3.210a15–24).[15] And in the *NE* II.5 and *EE* II.2 specifications he lists various emotions and then adds 'and in general pleasure/pain'. Indeed, in *NE* II.6, the next chapter following the *NE* formulation, we do not even have the *hepetai* qualification to this. He claims that fear, confidence, appetite, anger, and pity 'and in general (*holōs*) pleasure and pain' may be felt either too much, too little, or just right (II.6.1106b16–23).[16] Once again Aristotle seems to be indicating that all emotions count as pleasures or pains.[17]

One might ask: if Aristotle intended to (in part) identify emotions and pleasures/pains, why express this with *hepetai* at all? Why not simply say, as the above passage may suggest, that emotions *are* pleasures or pains? It seems to me that his usage is most plausibly explained by the 'living *hepetai* being healthy' example he employed. Aristotle claimed that living *hepetai* being healthy '*but not vice versa*' (*toutō(i) de ekeino ou*) (1363b30–1). *Hepetai* indicates an *asymmetric* relation. While it is, in some particular case, possible *both* that *A* (nominative) *hepetai B* (dative) *and* that *B* (nominative) *hepetai A* (dative), these would be two distinct relations. In this respect, *hepetai* functions like 'implies' or 'entails' (i.e. '*A* (nominative) *hepetai B* (dative)' amounts to '*B* entails *A*').[18] This means that Aristotle can state that pleasure/pain (nominative) *hepetai* the emotions (dative) without that implying that the emotions *exhaust* all the possible types of pleasure or pain. The relation does not go the other way around: being an emotion (nominative) does not *hepetai* pleasure/pain (dative) because we can have pleasures or pains

---

[15] One can put this in terms of 'genus-species' so long as one is generous about how that is understood, since colours would clearly fit the remit and yet could be understood as a determinate-determinable relation *in contrast to* a genus-species relation (see the end of **2.4** below). It should be flagged, *pace* Nussbaum and Putnam (1992: 44), that *kai holōs* does not always indicate a kind/instance or genus/species relation (indeed, their own *De an.* I.1 (403a7) example most likely being a case in point). To see this, consider two of their supposed 'excellent examples' for *holōs* indicating a genus in *Met.* E.1. Aristotle writes: 'If then all natural things are analogous to the snub in their nature—e.g. nose, eye, face, flesh, and, in general (*holōs*), animal; leaf, root, bark, and, in general (*holōs*), plant…' (1025b34–1026b2). 'Animal' is not the genus of nose, eye, flesh, etc., it is the genus of e.g. dogs and cats. Instead, the genus of nose, eye, and flesh would be *parts of animals*. Similarly, with the plant example.

[16] Note, this list of emotions includes five of those from the *NE* II.5 specification of emotions (the previous chapter). There may be an issue with 'appetite' (*epithumia*), as we shall see in Chapter 8.

[17] The Stoics would later explicitly think of pleasure and pain as genera of the emotions (adding *epithumia* and *phobos*) (see esp. *SVF* III.394 and Graver 2007: 55–7). Aspasius seems to have thought that Aristotle counted pleasure and pain as genera of the emotions (Heylbut 1889: 42.27–47.2); on Aspasius' account, see Sorabji (1999). Cf. also Striker (1996: 292).

[18] Which makes the translations of Irwin (1985) and Reeve (2014, 2018) appropriate (see n.3 above).

that are not emotions; perhaps, for example, the pleasure of scratching an itch (cf. Plato, *Gorgias* 494c–e, *Philebus* 46a, 46c–47b) or the pain of stubbing a toe.[19]

A key obstacle for thinking that Aristotle holds that emotions just are kinds of pleasure or pain is a number of problematic cases. In particular, in *Rhet.* hating (*misein*) is explicitly said to be 'without pain' (II.4.1382a12–13). And, by implication, its contrary, friendly feeling (*philein*), would be without pleasure too. Again, it is unclear with a number of the 'contraries' of the emotions, e.g. mild-manneredness (*praotēs*) and shamefulness (*anaischuntia*)—which, according to the general specification in *Rhet.*, would seem to count as emotions—how to characterize the pleasure or pain dimension to the state. And we also have the qualification 'for the most part' in the *EE* specification to explain. What does this qualify?

These questions will prove more tractable later on, when we have more of Aristotle's account in place. I shall argue that hating and feeling-friendly-towards are not themselves emotional pleasures or distresses, but specify several such emotional states (7.4); and that the above 'contraries' of emotions indicate specific privations of emotional pleasures or distresses (Chapter 10). If this is right, it would be open for someone to maintain that Aristotle's use of *hepetai* in linking emotions to pleasure or pain is weaker than identification or part identification. It would still be stronger than the potential use of *hepetai*, insofar as we would still have an essential connection to pleasure or pain, but it would leave open the sort of relation the state might have to pleasure or pain. Emotions would *entail* pleasures or pains, but not in the same way in each case.[20]

Perhaps this may ultimately be the most cogent thing to say.[21] However, I would like to emphasize that we do have the large number of cases (indicated above) where the emotion seems to *be* a pleasure or pain, not merely imply one. And, as we shall also see, this is plausibly extended to some other problematic cases (e.g. confidence and feeling-grateful-for).[22] This should, I believe, encourage us to investigate how this broad set of cases is understood by Aristotle. Accordingly, I will (perhaps not uncontroversially) call the set of cases in which emotions are (at least in part) pleasures or pains 'the core set' and in the remainder of this part of the book will put to one side the cases in which pleasure or pain

---

[19] Cf. also the basic sensory/thought-based pleasures mentioned at the start of Chapter 5. On this picture, the *holōs* in the passage from *NE* II.6 just quoted might generalize to the broader genus of pleasure and pain (which would include not just emotions, but other kinds of pleasure/pain).

[20] So Rapp (2002: 550, 2013: 35–8).

[21] Note, on this view, Aristotle's phrase 'in general those things (dative) that *hepetai* pleasure and pain (nominative)' in *NE* II.5 would no more pick out emotions than it would actions (at least as the latter are characterized in the *NE* II.3 passage quoted above). Of course, on any account, Aristotle's specifications fall short of a definition of the emotions, seeing as he does not tell us the *differentia specifica* that marks out emotions from other types of pleasure or pain (see 6.5n.23). Nonetheless, one may well think that he would want to distinguish the way emotions *hepetai* pleasure or pain from the way actions do.

[22] These are discussed in 10.7 and 10.1, respectively.

are only implied in a looser way by the state that Aristotle refers to. But I shall eventually address the latter too (esp. Chapters 7 and 10) and, ultimately, admitting them may require us to extend the notion of 'emotion' beyond the conception implicit in the core set (or, as I shall suggest, allow broader and narrower notions of 'emotion'). But it is surely not implausible to envisage that the understanding of emotions implicit in what I am calling the core set of cases has a priority over the other cases, in the sense that the latter need to be understood in relation to them, rather than vice versa. And this is what I shall argue through the course of this book. At any rate, the understanding of emotions implicit in the core set surely warrants consideration in its own right.

2.2 The view that Aristotle holds that the pleasures and pains of emotions are non-representational

If it is clear, at least with a core set of cases, that Aristotle thinks that emotions are pleasures or pains, controversy sets in when we consider *what sort* of pleasures or pains he thinks emotions are, or whether he thinks emotions essentially involve *another component* besides the pleasure or pain, or (in part relatedly) what the relation is between the intentional state that apprehends the emotion's object and its pleasure or pain. My goal in the remainder of this chapter, and the two that follow, is to tackle these more controversial questions.

Let me first address what sort of pleasures or pains Aristotle has in mind. The controversy here concerns whether the pleasures or pains of emotions are *representational* or *non-representational*. W. W. Fortenbaugh advances the latter reading.[23] He tells us that he is 'not inclined' to accept that Aristotle 'views pain itself as an intentional state with cognitive content' (2002: 111n.1).[24] Instead, on his reading:

> [Aristotle] distinguishes between the cognition and the pain involved in emotions like fear, anger and pity. The former is intentional; the latter is so only in a derivative way, i.e., through the judgment that is its cause. (111)

On this reading, emotions occur when an intentional state that apprehends the object of the emotion (for Fortenbaugh, a judgement) causes a further non-intentional hedonic state. Such a reading would be compatible with the idea that the non-representational pleasures or pains in question are either bodily sensations or mental feelings, but in fact Fortenbaugh holds that Aristotle 'almost

---

[23] See also Leighton (1996: 219–20). For a contemporary account of emotions along these lines, see Goldstein (2002).

[24] He is here addressing Nussbaum's (2001: 64) view, which I consider in the next chapter.

certainly thinks of the pain and pleasure of emotion in terms of sensation' (111). However, I shall not take it to be an essential feature of this reading that the pleasure or pain has to be sensory. The key is that the pleasure or pain is non-representational.

One reading Fortenbaugh seeks to resist is that Aristotle *identifies* the pleasure or pain of the emotion with the intentional state that apprehends its object. On this view (which I consider in Chapter 3), the pleasure or pain of the emotion is just another way of referring to the intentional state that apprehends its object (with the two, as Aristotle would say, 'the same but different in being') and so the pleasure or pain must itself be representational. Against this, Fortenbaugh (2002: 111) appeals to a few cases in which Aristotle refers to the pleasure or pain as *resulting from* (*dia* + accusative) or *arising from* (*ek* + genitive) an apprehension of the emotion's object. Anger is, atypically for Aristotle's accounts of the emotions, characterized as a desire accompanied by a pain (*orexis meta lupēs*).[25] But the desire accompanied by pain is said to result from (*dia* + accusative) an apparent slight (*Rhet.* II.2.1378a30–1). Again, fear is said to arise from (*ek* + genitive) a *phantasia* of a future destructive or painful evil (*Rhet.* II.5.1382a21–2). We might also cite the pleasure that Aristotle associates with anger, namely, the pleasure that arises from (*apo* + genitive) the hope of being revenged (*Rhet.* II.2.1378b1–2). Fortenbaugh would suggest that these examples show that Aristotle thinks that emotions involve a judgement which causes a separate non-intentional state, a (sensory) feeling of pleasure or pain.[26]

I agree that insofar as these formulations separate the pleasure or pain of the emotion from the intentional state that apprehends its object they are problematic for the idea that Aristotle identifies the two (see also 3.2 below). But the characterizations do not show that he thinks the pleasures or pains in question are non-representational. The fact that he claims that the pains of anger and fear result or arise from an apparent slight or a future destructive evil is clearly compatible with him holding that the pains in question are *about* or *directed at* the slight or destructive evil. So too with the pleasure that arises from the hope of being revenged.[27] Characterizing these pains or pleasures as stemming from intentional states that apprehend their objects leaves it entirely open whether the pleasures or pains are representational or not.

In support of his view that we should think of the pleasure and pain as 'sensory', Fortenbaugh points out that in the *EE* specification of emotions (quoted in 2.1)

---

[25] I shall eventually argue in Chapter 6 that Aristotle in fact holds that the desiderative and emotional elements of anger can be separated out, and that anger counts as an emotion *qua* representational distress and a desire *qua* desire for revenge.
[26] He also (2002: 111) tries to extend this to other cases which are formulated with *epi* + dative. I resist this in the next section.
[27] Indeed, there is surely every reason to believe that this pleasure is representational: the subject of the anger is pleased *at the prospect of getting revenge*.

Aristotle refers to emotions as accompanied by 'perceptual (*aisthētikē*) pleasure or pain' (II.2.1220b14).[28] Now, of course, this qualification is dropped from the *NE* and *Rhet.* specifications (and *NE* is typically thought to be later than *EE*), so it may be that Aristotle himself ultimately decided it was inappropriate. But, in any event, even this qualification would not entail that the pleasures or pains of emotions are non-representational. This is because, first, perception itself, on Aristotle's view, can be a complex representational state. What he calls extrinsic (or 'incidental', *kata sumbebēkos*) perception is predicative in structure, i.e. involves taking something to be of a certain kind.[29] For example, one may perceive the white thing as the son of Diaires (*De an.* II.6.418a20–4, cf. III.1.425a24–7: 'the son of Cleon'). And, second, there is, in any event, no incompatibility between the idea that (occurrent) emotions essentially involve a perceptible element, in the sense that they have a felt phenomenological dimension (see 2.4n.54, 4.4, and 5.6), and their being directed at instantiations of the emotion's formal object (on which, see next section). They could be felt states that are so directed. Thus, while the qualifier 'perceptible' would imply the involvement of the perceptual capacity (the *aisthētikon*) and could indicate a phenomenologically felt dimension to emotions, it would not itself dictate that the pleasures or pains are non-representational.[30]

But if Fortenbaugh's points do not show that Aristotle holds that the pleasure or pains of emotions are non-representational, can we demonstrate the alternative?

2.3 Representational pleasures and pains

A central consideration supporting the idea that Aristotle holds that the pleasures or pains of emotions are representational is his use of (what I shall call) 'pain-at locutions' in specifying them.[31] The key marker for this is that in many of

---

[28] He also refers to *Phys.* VII.3.247a17–18. What I go on to say will apply to this too.

[29] An argument that this is a feature of all types of perception for Aristotle, can be found in Caston (unpublished). This also shows how such a reading can still preserve the requisite distinction between special and extrinsic perceptibles (as per e.g. *De an.* II.6). See also Sorabji (1993: 17–20). As noted in 1.2n.14, contra some commentators, there is no reason to think that extrinsic perception is not a genuine form of perception for Aristotle (see that note for references).

[30] Nor, relatedly, would the fact that Aristotle appears to think that emotions belong to the non-rational part of the soul (see e.g. *Pol.* I.5.1254b8). He may think this simply because they are pleasures or pains. But even if he holds it because they involve some felt element, that would not make the pleasures or pains non-representational. They can have a felt element and still be about apparent instantiations of their formal objects. It is also worth flagging that the idea that there is something perceptible about the pleasure or pain does not itself demand that the object of the emotion can only be apprehended by a perceptual state, at least not on any view that rejects the idea that the pleasure or pain of the emotion and the intentional state that apprehends its object are identical.

[31] This feature of Aristotle's has also been flagged by Sherman (1993: 17–18, 1997: 64–5) and Nussbaum (1994: 88, 2001: 64), and then elaborated on by Dow (2011: §2, 2015: §9.3).

Aristotle's definitions of emotions in *Rhet.* II he characterizes the pleasure or pain as *epi* (+ dative) the (apparent) object of the emotion. This suggests that he is construing the pleasure or pain as directed *at* that object. Aristotle writes:

> Let pity (*eleos*), then, be a sort of distress (*lupē tis*) at (*epi* + dative) an apparent destructive or painful bad thing happening to someone who does not deserve it, and one that a person might expect himself or one of his own to suffer, and this when it appears close at hand. (II.8.1385b13–16)
>
> ...indignation (*to nemesan*) is being distressed (*lupeisthai*) at (*epi* + dative) apparent undeserved doing-well. (II.9.1387a8–9)
>
> ...envy (*phthonos*) is a sort of distress (*lupē tis*) at (*epi* + dative) apparent doing-well in terms of the goods mentioned [wealth, power, etc. from II.9?], on the part of those like themselves, not in order that something accrue to the person himself, but because of those [possessing it]. (II.10.1387b23–5)
>
> ...emulation (*zēlos*) is a sort of distress (*lupē tis*) at (*epi* + dative) the apparent presence, in the case of others who are by nature like the person himself, of good things that are honoured and possible for someone to acquire, not owing to the fact that another has them but rather owing to the fact he himself does not. (II.11.1388a32–5)

We also see the same *epi* + dative formulation in three pleasure-based emotions specified in *Rhet.* II.9. What we might call 'pleasure-based indignation' (to distinguish it from the distress-based variant above) involves being pleased (*hēdesthai*) at (*epi* + dative) deserved doing-badly (1386b27–8).[32] What we might call 'pride-in-another' is joy (*chairein*) at (*epi* + dative) (someone else's) deserved doing-well (1386b30–1).[33] So, too, schadenfreude (*epichairekakia*) is joy (*chairein*) at (*epi* + dative) undeserved doing-badly (1386b33–1387a3; cf. *EE* III.7.1233b18–22, *NE* II.6.1107a9–11, II.7.1108a35–1108b6).[34] In each of these cases, I submit, the Greek is most naturally understood as indicating that Aristotle views the distress or pleasure (or joy, *chairein*) as *directed at* the object of the emotion.[35]

---

[32] Aristotle groups the pleasure- and pain-based variants as types of indignation (*nemesis*) in *EE* III.7 (1233b23–5). See **Cat.12** and **Cat.16** for more discussion. In the *Rhet.* II.9 passage he also allows that we can be *un-pained* (*alupos*) at deserved doing-badly (1386b27). On my view, though an interesting variant, this would not, strictly speaking, be an emotion at all (or would be so only in the sense of a privation; see **10.2–6**). (But it does show that Aristotle holds that one can apprehend the formal object of an emotion without experiencing a distress or pleasure-based emotion about that object.)

[33] Aristotle does not provide a name for the emotion. For a little more discussion, see **Cat.17**.

[34] For more discussion of Aristotle on this emotion, see **Cat.18**. See also the characterization of grief or longing in *Rhet.* I.11.1370b25–9 as 'distress at (*epi* + dative) [the loved one's] not being there' (1370b26); see **Cat.21**.

[35] Indeed, this is how e.g. Kennedy (1991) and Reeve (2018) translate; so too in related passages in e.g. Inwood and Woolf's (2013) translation of *EE* (III.7).

Fortenbaugh, though, disagrees. He wishes to read Aristotle's *epi* constructions as indicating a causal relation in line with his non-representational reading. He writes:

> Pity is defined as a certain pain that is based on (*epi*) apparent evil, destructive or painful, which befalls some underserving person (1385b13–14). Here, too, the relationship is one of cause and effect. When a man observes suffering and deems suffering unmerited, his judgment is cause of his emotion including feelings of pain. (2002: 111)[36]

But while 'based on' is a possible rendering of *epi*, there are indications that it is not what Aristotle had in mind in his formulations of the emotions. One point is that when Aristotle characterizes an emotion as 'pleasure/pain *epi* an apparent FO' (where 'FO' is the formal object of the emotion; see **1.3**), he is quite happy to drop the 'apparent' qualification on occasion. In *Rhet.* II.9 he refers to pity and indignation simply as (respectively) 'pain at (*epi* + dative) underserved doing-badly' (1386b9, b26–7, cf. b12) and 'being pained at undeserved doing-well' (*to lupeisthai epi tais anaxiais eupragiais*) (1386b10–11). And, in *EE* III.7, he refers to envy as 'distress at (*epi* + dative) deserved doing-well' (1233b19–20; see also *Top.* II.2.109b36–7, 110a1–2). Similarly, with the pleasure-based emotions I have just mentioned.[37] And yet, on Fortenbaugh's reading, it is only the intentional state that apprehends the object of the emotion (for him, a judgement) that has intentionality, strictly speaking. Hence, he would have to take these 'pain/pleasure at FO' formulations as in fact elliptical for

---

[36] In line with this 'on what grounds' was used as a translation of *epi poiois* at *Rhet.* II.1.1378a24 by W. Rhys Roberts in the *ROT*. Reeve (2018: *ad loc.*) translates 'for which sort of things'; Kennedy (1991: *ad loc.*) 'for what sort of reasons'. One could just as easily translate 'at what sort of things'. But I do not wish to press too hard on this. Aristotle has a variety of ways of referring to what was labelled *epi poiois* in *Rhet.* II.1 (*dia poia* at II.2.1380a1; *dia tinōn* at II.3.1380a8; *peri poia* at II.5.1383a15; *poia* at II.6.1383b11, II.8.1385b11; *epi tisi(n)* at II.7.1385a16, II.9.1387a7, II.10.1387b22; *dia ti* at II.9.1387b4; *ta poia* at II.11.1388a31) and it is not always clear that he has the same relation in mind. Most often, though, this section seems to pick out the object of the emotion (what the emotion is about), especially the formal object (note also *ha elousin*, 'those things they pity', at II.8.1386a4), as befits the idea that he intends the pleasures or distresses of emotions to be construed as directed at those objects. There is a sense, on my view, in which the pleasure or distress of the emotion is consequent on the intentional state that apprehends its object (see Chapter 4). It is just that, as I see it, the hedonic state is representational.

[37] On my view, the primary function of 'apparent' (*phainomenos*) in the definitions of the emotions highlighted previously is simply to indicate that the object may not be as it is represented as being, that is, to permit error. See Dow (2009: 153–5, 2015: 201) and **4.2** below. If this is right, nor is there any direct reference in any of those definitions to the intentional state that apprehends the emotion's object either. Such an intentional state will, of course, be indirectly presupposed—the fact that we have a non-factive intentional state doing the apprehending is why error is possible—but the 'apparent' *itself* will just register the fact that to experience, say, pity it need not be the case that someone has *actually* suffered some underserved misfortune, so long as one represents this. Nonetheless, in the cases just highlighted the interpretation of *phainomenos* is taken out of the equation, since Aristotle omits it entirely.

'non-representational pain/pleasure that is caused by the judgement that apprehends the FO', or some such. But while I agree that there must be an intentional state that apprehends the FO, Aristotle's shorthand is surely much more reasonable if he is construing the pleasures/pains as themselves representational. Note, he could easily, and less equivocally, have avoided using a preposition that suggests this. He could have said that the pain (in question) arises from (*ek* or *apo* + genitive) or results from (*dia* + accusative) the object in question. But he does not. Instead, he chooses a preposition that would quite naturally be construed as indicating that what follows the preposition is the object of the pleasure or pain. Note, too, when he does use the 'arise from' (*ek* + genitive) formulation, in the case of fear, he appears to refer directly to the intentional state that apprehends the object, viz. *phantasia* (see 2.2). Whereas in the cases cited above he does not. He individuates the emotions by pain/pleasure and formal object *alone*. The implication, I propose, is that he is taking the formal object to be the *object* of the pain/pleasure; that is, he is specifying what that emotion (as pleasure or pain) is about.[38]

Indeed, there are some cases where it seems clear that Aristotle has in mind pleasures or pains that are intentional states in their own right. In his discussion of feeling-friendly-towards, in *Rhet.* II.4, he writes:

> necessarily a friend is someone who shares in one's pleasure at good things and in one's pains at painful things,[39] not because of something else, but because of oneself. (1381a3–5)

Here we have a notion of a friend sharing in our pleasure or pain at good or painful things (happening to us: 1381a5–10). Fortenbaugh would have to say that our friends share in our pleasure or pain insofar as they have non-representational pleasures or pains that are based on (caused by) judgements about something good or painful (occurring to us). But this is not what Aristotle writes. He simply refers to the friend as taking pleasure or pain at good or painful things (happening to us). The pleasures and pains are themselves construed as representational.[40]

An even clearer, and more significant, example is Aristotle's specification of shame:

> Let shame be a sort of distress or disturbance about (*peri* + genitive) evils—whether present, past, or future—that appear to bring a person into disrepute. (*Rhet.* II.6.1383b12–14)

---

[38] His formulations here also fit well with the idea that he does not in fact view the intentional state that apprehends the object of the emotion as a component part of the emotion as such, as I shall eventually argue in Chapter 4.

[39] ἀνάγκη φίλον εἶναι τὸν συνηδόμενον τοῖς ἀγαθοῖς καὶ συναλγοῦντα τοῖς λυπηροῖς...

[40] I consider the emotions connected to feeling-friendly-towards (and its contrary, hating) in 7.4.

How can the 'about', here, be construed causally in the way Fortenbaugh needs? Surely, what follows it is intended to mark the object of the pain, what the pain is about or concerned with. But this fact is significant since, within his discussion of shame, Aristotle *also* characterizes the same relation with *epi* + dative. He writes:

> ...necessarily people feel shame (*aischunesthai*) at (*epi* + dative) such bad things as seem shameful (*aischra*) either for themselves or for those they care about. (1383b16–18)

If the first formulation with *peri* ('about') specifies the object of the pain, so does the second with *epi*. And if *epi* specifies the object of the pain here, this would be a good indicator that it is intended to signify that the pains (or pleasures) of emotions are directed at their objects (i.e. are representational) more generally.[41]

It is also worth emphasizing that the idea that the pleasures or pains of emotions are representational would not be a novel or strange thing for Aristotle to think. For, significantly, such a view seems to be *presupposed* by Plato and it is likely that Aristotle's understanding of the pleasure or pain involved in emotions starts off from an appreciation of Plato's views, especially as those are developed in the *Philebus*. In the latter, just as judging (*doxazein*) is about something, namely what is judged (*to doxazomenon*), so too pleasure (*hēdesthai*) is about something, namely something that pleases (*hō(i) to hēdomenon hēdetai*) (37a2–9). And just as if what one has judged is in error, one's judgement itself errs, so too if one's pain or pleasure is about something (*peri to*) in which one is erroneously pained or the opposite (*eph' hō(i) lupeitai ē tounantion hamartanousan*), it too errs (37e1–7). Of course, exactly what sorts of error Plato intends here, and the senses in which he thinks pleasures and pains can be 'false', is hotly debated.[42] But the basic idea that pleasures and pains are representational is taken as a given. Furthermore, in the emotional context, Plato will also use *epi* to characterize the directedness of pleasure or pain. For instance, Socrates refers to envy as a pain of the soul (48b8–9), but notes that the envious person will also manifest pleasure at (*epi* + dative) his neighbour's misfortunes (*epi kakois tois tōn pelas hēdomenos anaphanēsetai*) (48b11–12).[43]

---

[41] Note, too, Aristotle's definition of shame shows that his usage of 'disturbance' (*tarachē*) in this context is compatible with the pain of the emotion being representational. The disturbance, no less than the pain, it seems, is 'about' (*peri*) the object in question. Aristotle also characterizes fear as a 'pain or disturbance' (*Rhet.* II.5.1382a21–2, cf. also II.9.1386b16–20, on envy). I consider the significance of the addition in Chapter 7.

[42] See e.g. Penner (1970); Hackforth (1972: 72–3); Lovibond (1989–90); Frede (1993: xlv–liii); Harte (2004); Moss (2012b); Dimas (2019).

[43] This is what Aristotle will later call *epichairekakia*, i.e. schadenfreude. However, he links the envious person and the person who experiences schadenfreude in just this way in *Rhet.* II.9 (1386b33–1387a3), quoted in **Cat.18**.

2.4 Qualms about pleasure and pain being representational. Joy and distress

Perhaps what might prompt someone to attempt to read Aristotle as referring to non-representational pleasures or pains in this context is a general suspicion about the idea that pleasures or pains can be representational in the first place. It may be worth briefly addressing this. As we saw in 1.1, the hallmark of a state being intentional or representational is it being *about* or *of* something. And yet, as Tim Crane writes (of a view he rejects, see below):

> Consider a pain you may have in your ankle; what is it *of* or *about*? Silly question: it isn't *of* or *about* anything. And so, since intentionality is of-ness or about-ness, pain is not intentional. (1998: 232, his emphases)

And, as Crane notes (232), in line with this we find Colin McGinn, for example, arguing:

> bodily sensations do not have an intentional object in the way perceptual experiences do. We distinguish between a visual experience and what it is an experience of; but we do not make this distinction in respect of pains. (1982: 8)

If we think that pains are 'purely subjective qualities' whose 'existence consists in the existence of a subjective state that tells us nothing about the external world' (Crane 1998: 234–5), we will not find it plausible that they can be representational along the lines I have attributed to Aristotle. Hence, we could understand Fortenbaugh looking for alternatives, however much strain that places on the texts.

However, in response to those like McGinn, others, including Crane himself, have argued that even bodily pain is in fact representational. On this view, bodily sensation is a 'form of perceptual awareness of one's body' (1998: 237):[44]

> It is by experiencing bodily sensations that we come to be aware of the state of our body, and of events happening within it. The qualities of which we are aware in bodily sensation—the sensory qualities of hurting, feeling cold or warm and so on—are predicated in these experiences of parts of the body. When one feels a pain, one normally feels it to be in a part of one's body; and even when a pain is felt where there is no body-part in which to feel it—as in the case of phantom limb pains—what subjects feel is that their body extends further than it actually does. They do not feel as if their pain exists in mid-air, a few inches from where they have lost their limb. (237)[45]

---

[44] Crane is here characterizing the views of Armstrong (1968) and Martin (1993, 1995).
[45] As here, Crane thinks that a strong consideration in favour of this is that bodily sensations appear to have a felt location. He adds: 'An ache in my hand feels to be in my hand, not in my mind. Rather than being something which is contained within my body, it presents itself as something which

This makes such sensations manifest intentionality insofar as they, too, are about something: 'in the sensation, something is sensed: the body' (238).⁴⁶

But if even the idea that bodily pains can be representational is not as hopeless as it may have seemed, we should *a fortiori* have no qualms accepting that the sorts of pleasures and pains that Aristotle connects to the emotions are representational. For these are palpably *not* bodily sensations in the sense specified. Most of our emotions are not experienced about our bodies, but about evaluative properties that we ascribe to the world or our place in it (or to parallel imagined scenarios).⁴⁷ That is, they involve us representing some object as manifesting the formal object of the emotion. And insofar as they involve us experiencing pleasure or pain *about* an object that is represented as manifesting the formal object of the emotion, our emotions will palpably be representational. While we may, at least initially, have struggled to see how a pain in my foot is *about* anything, we can readily accept that we can be distressed *about* some impending event, real or imaginary, e.g. visiting the dentist or being confronted by some green slime in a movie. Similarly, if you have burnt yourself on the oven, while we may query (along the lines of McGinn) whether it sounds appropriate to say that *your* pain is about anything, it certainly sounds far less puzzling to say that if *I* am distressed by your pain, my distress is *about* your suffering insofar as it is directed at (pointed at, we might even say) your experiencing bodily pain from that source. Equally, if someone unscrupulous takes pleasure in the same event, we can see that their pleasure is representational: it is *about*, or *of*, or *directed at* your undergoing that suffering as such.

It seems to me that the unqualified word 'pain' is often taken to mean 'bodily pain' and to refer to bodily sensations such as might occur if one stubs one's toe or pulls a muscle (although it clearly can refer to 'mental' distresses too). Such is the

---

my mind can concentrate on, attend to and try to ignore...to concentrate on the ache, I must necessarily concentrate on the part of the body which aches...Attending to bodily sensations is achieved by attending to a part of the body where these sensations feel to be. This is because bodily sensation is a form of awareness, the awareness of things going on in one's body' (237).

⁴⁶ In his 2009 Crane considers Bain's (2003) problem of distinguishing between (i) 'seeing that one's body is disordered' and (ii) 'somatosensorily feeling the same thing' (2009: 480). He notes that while a number of philosophers have sought, in different ways, to account for this by appealing to a difference in intentional *content* (e.g. Tye 1995; Dretske 2000: 458; Bain 2003), there is a simpler explanation: 'the difference between feeling one's leg to be damaged and seeing it to be damaged is just the difference between *feeling* and *seeing*' (2009: 480; Crane's emphases). That is, it is a difference in intentional *attitude*, rather than intentional content (480). See **1.1**.

⁴⁷ 'Most', because, as we shall see (Chapter 8), in one case, appetite (*epithumia*), the emotion may well (often) concern bodily sensations. Nonetheless, even here the emotion will not itself be the bodily sensation, but a further distress directed at one's having, or at what causes one to have, the sensations in question. In effect, with regard to our forming emotions about it, our body becomes an object 'in the world'. (I put to one side Prinz's 2004 view, which appeals to a teleosemantic theory of representation to suggest that bodily feelings can themselves represent the formal objects of the emotions insofar as the former are reliably (functionally) connected up with the latter; although, note that even on this view the pleasures or pains of emotions turn out to be representational. For criticism of Prinz's view, see e.g. Deonna and Teroni 2012: 72–4.)

case, at least, in the contemporary philosophical literature we have just considered. The Greek word *lupē*, by contrast, can just as easily refer to 'pain of the body' or to 'pain of the mind' (as *LSJ* puts it; see *LSJ* s.v.).[48] But insofar as 'pain' may have a stronger connotation of bodily pain, and this is undesirable in the current context, I shall from now on use 'distress' instead of 'pain' in connection with Aristotle's account of the emotions. Let me flag, though, that I make this choice not because I am accepting that bodily pains are not themselves intentional states (I see the attractions of Crane et al.'s view), but because on the view I am ascribing to Aristotle emotions are not bodily sensations (sensations of the body), but hedonic states that typically extend outwards to the world and our place in it (or as that appears in our imagination).[49]

It is notable that 'pleasure' does not quite have the same connotation of being bodily as 'pain'. We can just as happily say that we experience a pleasurable sensation (e.g. when rubbing the stubbed toe or feeling the sun on one's face on a nice day) as we can say that we experience pleasure directed at our having completed some task or at someone we care about having achieved some success. In this respect, it is interesting that although Aristotle characterizes emotions in general (in the specifications quoted in 2.1) as accompanied by pleasure (*hēdonē*) or distress (*lupē*), and although he generally uses *lupē* for 'distress', he sometimes specifies pleasure-based emotions in terms of *chairein*, 'joy', rather than *hēdonē*. Greek, it seems, supplied him with another word that he felt was appropriate to use in this context.[50] While he writes of being pleased (*hēdesthai*) at someone's deserved doing-badly (*Rhet*. II.9.1386b27–8; 'deserved' indicated by *enantiōs*, by reference to 1386b26–7), he also refers to experiencing joy (*chairein*) at someone's deserved doing-well (II.9.1386b30–1, *EE* III.7.1233b25) and, indeed, to experiencing joy (*chairein*) at someone's undeserved *mis*fortune (*Rhet*. II.9.1386b33–1387a3; *EE* III.7.1233b22). The fact that with the first of these he a little later refers to experiencing joy (*chairein*) at the punishment of parricides and bloodthirsty murders (1386b28–30; so too *chairein* at *EE* III.7.1233b25) suggests that 'joy' and 'pleasure' are to some extent

---

[48] Relatedly, *The Cambridge Greek Lexicon* (Diggle 2021: s.v.) has 'annoyance, distress, anguish, pain'.

[49] For contemporary views with related ideas about the affective dimension of an emotion being essentially directed; see e.g. Greenspan (1988: e.g. 5–6, 31); Goldie (2000: esp. ch. 3); and Helm (2009). As noted at the end of 2.2, the pleasures or distresses of emotions may have some essential felt dimension insofar as they are occurrent states, but that would sit alongside (and be made determinate by: see end of this section) their being pleasures or distresses that are directed at objects of emotions in the sense specified. Emotions also essentially have a material or physical dimension for Aristotle, but again this does not undermine the current point. See Chapter 9.

[50] Greek has other words for 'pain', *lupē*, of course, some of which Aristotle uses in other contexts (see Cheng 2019). But, in his *Rhet*. I.11 discussion of pleasure/pain, it is notable that in his paraphrases or explanations of quotations of other authors, Aristotle refers to the different pain-words in the quotations (*anairon, ponoi, algos, goos*) with *lupē* or cognates (1370a10–11, 1370b4–5, 9, 1370b26–9), so he evidently thought it most appropriate in this context. See Cheng (2019: 54).

interchangeable.[51] But the use of 'joy' is notable. Indeed, we too use 'joy' in some of these contexts and it can seem particularly effective in indicating the representational nature of the emotion—we can say that those experiencing schadenfreude take joy *at* or *in* someone's misfortune.[52] In some contexts, though, 'joy' may suggest a certain kind of response that we do not think applies to all cases of a given emotion. In **10.7** I will argue that Aristotle holds that *confidence* (*to tharsos*) is a representational pleasure directed at the prospect of safety. But while one might be (over)joyed at such a prospect, one may, more simply, be pleased at the prospect of being-safe (quietly confident, or some such). Similarly, as we shall see in **10.1**, Aristotle recognizes an emotion of feeling-grateful-for (*charin echein*) some favour done. Again, while one might be (over)joyed at such a favour, one could, more simply, just experience pleasure at the favour. Consider the following passage from *Rhet.* I.11:

> there is a certain pleasure (*hēdonē*) that attaches to mourning and lamentation for a departed one, since there is pain at (*epi* + dative) his not being there and pleasure (*hēdonē*) in (*en* + dative) remembering and, in a way, seeing him, the actions he was doing, and what he was like. (1370b25–8)

While we clearly *can* be (over)joyed in such remembering, the hedonic response may, in some cases at least, seem more appropriately characterized as a representational pleasure (we take pleasure *in* remembering the lost loved one) than a joy as such. Indeed, Aristotle uses *hēdonē* here, not *chairein*.

For simplicity, I shall, from now on, generally stick to referring to representational 'pleasures or distresses'; but I shall also employ 'joy' for the former, on occasion, if it seems particularly appropriate.

Let me add one further note. The idea that emotions essentially involve pleasure or pain has been understood to mean that each pleasant emotion must manifest the same 'intrinsic property of experience' or 'feeling', and so too each painful emotion (cf. Deonna and Teroni 2012: 14–15). It is then objected that emotions are too diverse a bunch for this to be adequate: there is no one kind of

---

[51] So too, in *NE* II.7, he first refers to indignation, envy, and schadenfreude as concerned with distress (*lupē*) and pleasure (*hēdonē*) directed at (*epi* + dative) the fortunes of our neighbours (1108a35–1108b3) and then, a few lines later, refers to the person prone to schadenfreude (*ho epichairekakos*) as taking joy (*chairein*) (in another's misfortune) (1108b5–6). Cf. also Price (2017: 204–6). In *Top.* II.6 Aristotle notes that Prodicus used to divide pleasures (*hēdonai*) into joy (*chara*), delight (*terpsis*), and good cheer (*euphrosunē*), which are in fact names for the same thing, viz. pleasure (112b22–4). Cf. Plato's *Protagoras* (358a6–b3). However, in **Cat.20** I shall tentatively suggest that Aristotle may have placed *chara* (joy) on his lists of emotions in *NE* II.5 (1105b22) and *De an.* I.1 (403a18) to mark out various joys as a subgenus of the pleasure-based emotions.

[52] Which is not to say that 'pleasure' sounds inappropriate.

pain (or suffering) that runs through grief, jealously, envy, or shame, for instance.⁵³ But it is evident that there is little reason to understand Aristotle's view as open to such a charge. He thinks that emotions are forms of representational distress or pleasure, that is, *different kinds* of representational distress or pleasure. Hence, as we saw, in *Rhet.* he frequently refers to individual emotions as *lupē tis*, a *kind of distress* (fear: II.5.1382a21; shame: II.6.1383b12–13; pity: II.8.1385b13; envy: II.10.1387b23; emulation: II.11.1388a32). And the different kinds of pleasure or distress are specified in relation to their objects—i.e. what they involve the subject being distressed or pleased *about*—as distinguished by the emotion in question's formal object. Thus, although all emotions have to be classified as kinds of distress or pleasure, there need be no one identifiable felt state of distress that runs through all emotions that are representational distresses and no one felt state of pleasure that runs through all emotions that are representational pleasures. The distress of pity, for instance, concerns the undeserved suffering of another, the distress of fear the prospective pain or destruction of oneself. Insofar as these distresses have different objects, they are different distresses. Furthermore, each token emotion also has a determinate particular object, in addition to its evaluative object (see **1.3**). So there can be considerable specificity in the pleasure or distress of any particular token emotion.

Of course, it might still be asked: in virtue of what, then, do they *count* as distresses? But the answer to that need not attempt to point to some felt state that is common to both fear and pity (or particular tokens of these emotions). The distress of fear is specified in relation to its intentional object, as is the distress of pity, and the distress of envy, and so on. A better parallel for them might be colour. Different colours all count as colours, but red makes determinate some specific colour, as does blue, and yellow. They do not seem to share some isolatable common residue.⁵⁴ Similarly, the emotions can be distinct distresses or pleasures, without sharing some isolatable common residue of distress or pleasure in each case.⁵⁵

---

⁵³ See e.g. Solomon and Stone (2002: 423–5); Solomon (2003b: 167–9); Prinz (2010: 6–7).

⁵⁴ See also Harte (2014: 310–11). This would make the pleasures or distresses of emotions closer to a determinate-determinable relation, rather than one of genus-species. For an overview of the former distinction, see Wilson (2023). In her historical survey, she draws attention to Granger (1984) and Salmieri (2008), who suggest that Aristotle should be taken as anticipating the distinction.

⁵⁵ All this is of course compatible with occurrent emotions *having* a felt dimension (see end of **2.2**, **4.4**, and **5.6**). In line with the above, the felt dimension of an emotion would be made determinate by its pleasure or distress being directed at a particular instantiation of that emotion's formal object (see also n.49), where both the evaluative object of the emotion type and the emotion's particular object will play a role in determining the felt nature of any given token pleasure or distress. Note, also, if, as I hold (but am not assuming here; see **Intro.2**), emotions can form in response to a number of different intentional states (e.g. belief, *phantasia*, perception, perceptual imagination, uncommitted thought), this, too, could contribute to the different 'feel' of particular token emotions.

Conclusion

In this chapter I first argued that it is reasonable to think that Aristotle holds that at least a core set of emotions are pleasures or pains (**2.1**). I then turned to the question of what sort of pleasures or pains he thinks they are. I resisted Fortenbaugh's view that they are non-representational states (**2.2**) and instead argued that he holds that they are representational, i.e. are about or directed at the object of the emotion (**2.3**). In the final section, I tried to explain why there should be no general prejudice against such a view and why 'pleasure (or sometimes joy) or *distress*' is in fact better than 'pleasure or *pain*' (**2.4**).

3
Pleasure and Distress as Contributing to the Individuation of Emotion-Types

In the last chapter we saw that the pleasure or distress of an Aristotelian emotion is representational. Given, then, that the intentional state that apprehends the object of the emotion is itself representational, one may wonder whether they are not one and the same state. On this view, the pleasure or distress in question will not be a separate component of the emotion which, along with the intentional state that apprehends the object of the emotion, jointly composes it. Instead, the pleasure or distress and the intentional state that apprehends the emotion's object will just be two different ways of referring to the same state. They will be, as Aristotle would put it, *the same but different in being* (or *account*).[1] Such a view would explain my points in 2.3 about the formulations of the emotions: the object of the emotion, what comes after the 'at' (*epi*), will specify *both* the object of the pleasure or distress *and* the object of the intentional state that apprehends the object of the emotion. For the two will in fact be one and the same state. Let us call this reading of Aristotle's account of the emotions, 'the Identification view'. As we shall see (3.1), several commentators have advanced it.

We have, however, already seen one reason to be suspicious of such a reading (2.2). As Fortenbaugh noted, with some emotions Aristotle appears to view the pleasure or distress as *resulting from* or *arising from* the intentional state that apprehends its object. This does not seem compatible with him thinking that they are in fact one and the same state. I consider this a little further in 3.2. But in this chapter my main goal is to provide a very different argument against the Identification view, one which reveals something fundamental about Aristotle's view and, in turn, enables us to challenge many current accounts of emotions.

Any account of the emotions must explain how emotion-types can be differentiated from one another; how anger can be distinguished from indignation, for instance, or fear from thrill. I explain the problem this raises for accounts of the emotions in 3.3. I then show that the Identification view entails that Aristotle would differentiate emotion-types in a quite specific way (3.4). It, as it were,

---

[1] See e.g. *Phys.* III.3.202b14–16, where the road from Thebes to Athens is said to be the same as the road from Athens to Thebes, but different in being. The phrase can represent weaker relations than this example. See e.g. *NE* V.1.1129b26–7, where a subset, rather than co-extension, seems in play; see also *De an.* II.12.424a26–8, and for discussion my 2020 (56).

makes a prediction that can be assessed. Unfortunately, as I show in **3.5**, he clearly does not individuate emotions in the way the Identification view predicts, and hence cannot sensibly be construed as advancing that view. Significantly, the considerations I provide have ramifications not just for interpreting Aristotle, but for understanding how *any* account of emotions can differentiate emotion-types. In the last section (**3.6**) I employ this as part of an argument to show that emotions are not, even in part, perceptions or judgements. If this is on the right lines, contemporary perceptualists and judgementalists are in no less trouble than those advancing the Identification reading of Aristotle.

3.1 The Identification view

Several commentators appear to advance the Identification view as a reading of Aristotle. Martha Nussbaum (2001) writes:

> Aristotle's definitions of pain-linked emotions always speak of the 'pain at…', suggesting that he views pain itself as an intentional state with cognitive content. I believe this is correct in such cases…But [the pain] is not a noncognitive element, and we have already included it in our cognitive/evaluative account (64).[2]

Since Nussbaum is in the process of defending the view that emotions are judgements, and here tells us that the representational pain is 'already included' in that account, the pains in question must just be (aspects of) the judgements that, on Nussbaum's view, constitute emotions.

So too, albeit this time with perception in mind, Deborah Achtenberg (2002) claims:

> for Aristotle, emotion is both perception (of particulars as good or bad) and pleasure and pain since, according to him, pleasure and pain are themselves a type of perception (of particulars as good or bad). Perception of particulars as good is positive emotion, or pleasure, and perception of particulars as bad is negative emotion, or pain. (162)

---

[2] She goes on to suggest that we may also have non-intentional pains in connection with distressful emotions. Nussbaum's account in her 2001 drops reference to the intentional state *causing* the pleasure or pain (that is then so directed), which was in her 1994 (esp. 88). I consider *that* view in Chapter 4. (I am thus construing Nussbaum as advancing the Identification view in her 2001 and a dual-component view in her 1994, although it should be noted that her 2001 remarks are made in passing, while developing her own view.)

Once again, the intentional state that apprehends the object of the emotion (perception, for Achtenberg) is just another way of describing the pleasure or pain.

Finally, Jamie Dow proposes a similar view (2011, 2015: ch. 9). He argues at length that Aristotle thinks that emotions involve pleasures or pains that are directed at objects of emotion, and so are representational (2015: 155–61). He then suggests, admittedly somewhat tentatively (176–7), that Aristotle thinks that intentional states such as beliefs and perceptions might 'constitute' pleasures if 'their represented contents in some way include the effects of some pleasant object, and perhaps the pleasant object itself' (176). He gives the following example:

> Pitying Jessica, on this account, might be the painful judgement that she is suffering undeservedly (where what is painful about the judgement is its object: that she is suffering undeservedly). (179)

Although Achtenberg refers to perception and Dow and Nussbaum to judgement, this difference is not crucial for us here.[3] (In fact, in his 2015 it is clear that Dow would ultimately identify emotions with *phantasiai*, rather than judgements.[4]) On each of these interpretations, emotions are *both* pleasures or distresses *and* intentional states that apprehend their objects because the pleasures or distresses of emotions *just are* the perceptions/*phantasiai*/judgements that apprehend their objects.[5]

It is worth noting that although the Identification view insists that Aristotle holds that the pleasure or distress of an emotion is identical to the intentional state that apprehends its object, such a reading can still claim to be compatible with the idea that emotions have a distinctive phenomenological dimension, that is, are felt states. In fact, this is also something emphasized by contemporary philosophers who advance identification views of emotions, whether of a perceptualist or judgementalist stripe. Such views often reject 'add-on' theories,

---

[3] See **Intro.2**. As I noted there, I would reject all such mono-state readings of Aristotle (see my 2014a), but this does not matter for current purposes. We are just considering the relation between the intentional state that apprehends the object of the emotion, *whatever that may be*, and the emotion's pleasure or distress.

[4] He uses 'judgement' for illustrative purposes only (see 2015: 179n.73). In his 2015 he thinks Aristotle holds that objects of emotion are always apprehended by *phantasia*.

[5] In support of their Identification views, both Achtenberg (2002: 161–3) and Dow (2015: 177) (cf. also Sorabji 2000: 23–4) appeal to a tricky passage from *De an.* III.7.431a8–14, in particular: 'to feel pleasure or pain is to be active with the perceptive mean towards the good or bad as such' (431a10–11). There is much that could be said about this (and much that has) but, on the question at hand, it does not seem to entail the *identity* of the pleasure with the activity. The line would be compatible with the idea that wherever there is a pleasure or pain, there is an activity, without thereby *identifying* the two. Cf.: 'To sing a song is to be active with one's vocal cords'. Against identity, see also *NE* X.5.1175b30–5 (quoted in **5.1**). Dow also appeals (2015: 176) to Aristotle's account of pleasure in *NE* VII.12, albeit inconsistently (cp. 2015: 162). See **5.1**.

according to which the felt dimension of an emotion is subsequently 'bolted on' to the intentional component after the account of the latter has been provided.[6] But they nonetheless claim to embrace a phenomenological aspect to emotions. Perceptualists may stress that different sorts of perceptual states have different kinds of phenomenology and emotions are a distinctive kind of perceptual state, namely, *affective perceptions* with a 'felt' phenomenology. The phenomenological aspect of emotions, they might say, is an aspect or feature of such perceptions.[7] Similarly, a judgementalist might try to account for the 'heat and urgency' of emotions on the ground that 'they concern our most important goals and projects, the most urgent transactions we have with the world' (Nussbaum, 2001: 77).[8] Or else a judgementalist may say:

> Emotions are self-involved and relatively *intense* evaluative judgments...The judgments and objects that constitute our emotions are those which are especially important to us, meaningful to us, concerning matters in which we have invested our Selves. (Solomon 1993: 127; his emphasis)

So too with advocates of the Identification view as a reading of Aristotle. If Aristotle holds that the intentional state that apprehends the object of the emotion is just another way of describing the representational pleasure or pain, he could be indicating that emotions are not only intentional states, but *felt* intentional states, *distressing* or *pleasurable* intentional states. As Dow puts it: '[t]he fact that the judgement is painful accounts for its phenomenal character' (2015: 179).

Note, also, that those who identify emotions with perceptual states or judgements need not maintain that the phenomenological dimension of an emotion can in some sense be *reduced* to the state's representational content. Granted, since they identify emotions with the intentional state that apprehends the emotion's object, they must maintain that the phenomenological aspect of an emotion will at least supervene on such an intentional state (as a whole).[9] But this does not require that the phenomenological aspect of an emotion *reduces* to the intentional state (as a whole), let alone that it reduces to the representational content, which is only one part of the intentional state (alongside the state's intentional attitude;

---

[6] The terminology 'add-on theory' comes from Goldie (2000: 4, 40–1).

[7] 'Affective perception' is employed by Döring (2007: 375–6). See also Tappolet (2016: §1.4). Something similar is achieved by Roberts' (1988, 1996, 2003: e.g. 79–80) suggestion that emotions are *concern-based* construals. We should keep in mind that perceptualists typically only claim that emotions are analogous to literal sense-perceptions (see **12.2** below and e.g. de Sousa 1987: 149; Tappolet 2012: e.g. 212–13, 2016: §1.3–4; Döring 2007: 376, 2014: 130; although contrast Prinz 2004).

[8] Characterizing her own 'Neo-Stoic' view, not Aristotle's.

[9] Whether this will result in them denying the existence of 'qualia' will depend on what we mean by the latter. See Tye (2021).

see 1.1).¹⁰ Indeed, some perceptualists maintain that we can represent the same object non-emotionally, via a judgement, as well as emotionally, via a perception.¹¹

3.2 Cases in which Aristotle indicates that the emotion is distinct from the intentional state that apprehends its object

As mentioned, we have in fact already encountered (2.2) one objection to the Identification reading. In several cases Aristotle appears to indicate that the distress or pleasure of the emotion is distinct from the intentional state that apprehends its object. Anger (*orgē*) is characterized as a desire accompanied by a distress (*orexis meta lupēs*) that *results from* (*dia* + accusative) an apparent slight (*Rhet.* II.2.1378a30–1). Fear is said to *arise from* (*ek* + genitive) a *phantasia* of a future destructive or painful evil (*Rhet.* II.5.1382a21–2). And the pleasure associated with anger is said to *arise from* (*apo* + genitive) the hope of being revenged (*Rhet.* II.2.1378b1–2). If the pleasures or distresses or emotions arise or result from our apprehending the object of the emotion, the two would not appear to be one and the same state.¹²

Dow in fact addresses these cases, albeit in the context of arguing that the pleasures or distresses of emotions are representational (against Fortenbaugh's view that they are non-representational; as discussed in Chapter 2). But what Dow concedes at this point seems to be at odds with the Identification view he then goes on to advance. He agrees that Aristotle's accounts of the pleasure of anger, on the one hand, and fear, on the other, 'undoubtedly assert a causal connection between hope and pleasure in the one case and appearance of pain in the other' (2015: 160). But he maintains that 'the view that these pains and pleasures are representational has no difficulty with Aristotle's causal remarks about anger and fear' (160):

> After all, it is natural to suppose that causal relations would hold between thinking that something fearsome is the case and the state of feeling pain *at that same*

---

¹⁰ Insofar as reduction is taken to require property identity or entailment, supervenience does not entail reduction (see McLaughlin and Bennett 2018: §§3.2–3).

¹¹ Döring (2009a: 246), by implication from the fact that 'in the default mode' the emotion (= perception) generates a parallel belief, which can then be withdrawn while leaving the emotion (= perception) intact. In a note, Dow claims that we do not need to attribute to Aristotle the view that 'pleasure consists *solely* in the representational contents of experience having certain features'. Instead, 'the possibility is left open that Aristotle might have thought...that the representational contents of a motion of the soul could not alone properly account for the pleasurable "feel" of pleasure' (2015: 174n.69).

¹² See also *MA* 8.701b33–702a5, which refers to physical warming and cooling as 'following' (*akolouthein*: 701b34) *the thought* and *appearance of* an object (to be pursued or avoided), but as 'accompanied by' or 'with' (*meta*: 702a1, 4) the *pleasure* or *pain* of emotions (e.g. fear, confidence).

thing. Likewise, thoughts about getting vengeance are very likely to cause a state of pleasure *at getting vengeance*. (160; Dow's emphases)

I agree that Aristotle's specifications of these emotions do not preclude his thinking the pleasures or distresses in question are representational (see **2.2**). What is not so clear to me is how Dow can coherently combine such an understanding of fear and the pleasure of anger with his general Identification view. As we have seen, according to the latter, the judgement (say) that apprehends the object of the emotion is just another way of describing the distress or pleasure directed at that object. But if fear fits this model and, as per Dow's proposal above, thinking that something is fearsome *causes* the state of feeling pain at that same thing, then we would seem to have a representational distress *causing itself*. This is because the judgement that causes the distress would, given the Identification view, *itself* be just another way of referring to that distress. So too with the pleasure the stems from the hope of getting revenge or rectification. On the Identification view, thoughts about the prospect of getting revenge are just another way of describing taking pleasure at the prospect of getting revenge. But then in claiming above that thoughts about the prospect of getting vengeance *cause* the representational pleasure at the prospect of getting vengeance, Dow would be saying that a representational pleasure causes itself. For, according to his Identification view, thoughts about the prospect of getting revenge *are themselves* just another way of referring to a representational pleasure directed at the prospect of getting revenge. Hence, absent an explanation of how something can be a *causa sui*, Dow's overall view looks incoherent. And since at least something like a causal explanation of fear seems needed, it is the Identification view we should give up.[13]

In short, Aristotle's characterizations of these emotions suggests that he views the intentional state that apprehends the object of the emotion and its pleasure or distress *as distinct*. If this is right, the only remaining option for advocates of the Identification view would be to maintain that while he did not identify the pleasure or distress and the intentional state that apprehends the object of the emotion *in these cases*, he did with all other emotions. But besides this making his account uncomfortably hybrid, we would want some principled reason for his dividing up emotions in this way. I shall not pursue this further, however, for I will now go on (3.3–5) to develop a more general argument against thinking that Aristotle holds the Identification view.

---

[13] 'Something like' because in Chapter 4 I shall offer an alternative to a strict causal reading. But this will respect the gap between the intentional state and the pleasure or distress, and so will allow the latter to be *consequent upon* the former.

3.3 The Individuation problem

A requirement on any plausible theory of the emotions is that it explains how emotion-types can be individuated. Such individuation is typically thought to rely on specifying different evaluative (i.e. formal) objects for each emotion-type (see 1.3). In his classic treatment of the formal objects of emotions, Anthony Kenny noted (1963: 189) that there can be trivial and non-trivial specifications of formal objects. Trivial specifications are, for example, *fearful, shameful, pitiable,* or *angering*. Non-trivial specifications purport to provide substantial characterizations of the formal objects of the emotions that are both more informative and falsifiable. For instance, Aristotle links fear to the prospect of suffering some destructive or painful evil (*Rhet.* II.5.1382a21–2) and claims that *danger* is the 'sign' of such things (1382a27–32). Similarly, anger involves representing an *offence* (literally a belittling or slight: *oligōria*) directed at us by someone unfitted to offend us (*Rhet.* II.2.1378a30–2); shame involves representing *bad things that bring us into disrepute* (*adoxia*) (*Rhet.* II.6.1383b13–14); pity involves representing *undeserved destructive or painful bad things happening to another* (*Rhet.* II.8.1385b13–16); and so on.[14] Similarly, in contemporary philosophy, *danger* is often cited as the formal object of fear, *offence* as the formal object of anger.

Trivial specifications of the formal objects of emotions look like good candidates for individuating emotion-types. Relative to the class of emotions, fear is distinct from pity or shame, for instance, insofar as all and only cases of fear have the fearful as their object, whereas all and only cases of pity have the pitiable as their object and all and only cases of shame have the shameful as their object.[15] And note that if someone were to object to this by asking: cannot what is fearful also be the object of, say, *thrill*? We can answer that, in raising the objection, the questioner has failed to stick to trivial specifications. If we really have the latter in view, the formal object of thrill is not what is fearful, but what is *thrilling*. And so on with any emotion that plausibly has an object.[16]

---

[14] For both types of specification, see e.g. *EE* III.1.1229a33–5, quoted in 1.3n.25.

[15] Consider a perceptualist view that maintains that while fear is the perception of something fearful, we can still nonetheless judge something to be fearful as well (i.e. in a non-emotional way; see end of 3.1). On such a view, we will not be able to say, *relative to the general class of intentional states as such,* that *only* cases of fear have the fearful as their object (for some non-emotional judgements might too). But it would still be the case that *no other emotion* would have the fearful as its object. So, if we stick to trivial specifications of the formal objects, we could still say that *relative to the class of emotions* all and only cases of fear have the fearful as their object. And that is my claim. (I take 'the fearsome' (Tappolet 2016: §2.1; cf. D'Arms and Jacobson 2003: 133) to be an alternative expression of the trivial specification of the formal object of fear. 'The frightening' (de Sousa 1987: 122) would be the formal object of *fright* and will only be equivalent to the fearsome/fearful if fright and fear are the same emotion.)

[16] Contrast Teroni (2007: 401–2).

And yet we also of course want to know whether these trivial specifications of the formal objects of emotions align with substantive differences.[17] Does being thrilled by something involve representing an intentional object in a different way than fearing it? And it seems clear that to answer *this*, we shall need substantial specifications of the formal objects of fear and thrill.[18]

Suppose, then, it is proposed that *danger* is a substantive specification of the formal object of fear.[19] An objection to this proposal could be that we can be *excited* by (certain kinds of) danger.[20] But does this really threaten the idea that danger individuates fear? Perhaps not. For we might maintain that while all and only fearful things are dangerous, it is not the case that all and only exciting things are dangerous. We can be excited by things that are not dangerous. Thus, if a formal object individuates an emotion, danger cannot be the formal object of excitement. But it still could be the formal object of fear. At this point, however, we might ask: if danger can be the object of some kinds of excitement, how do we distinguish those forms of excitement from parallel fears? Why is danger not the formal object of both fear and the dangerous forms of excitement? Granted, the fearful and the excitable *as such* only partially overlap but, insofar as they do, they share the same formal object when specified substantively.[21] Furthermore, we might even say that there is an emotion-type which *is* this dangerous form of excitement, namely *thrill*. If so, thrill and fear will share the same substantive formal object. But then we will not be able to individuate fear and thrill by reference to their substantive formal objects. And yet fear and thrill seem to be different emotions.

Such cases thus pose a problem for the view that substantive specifications of the formal objects of emotions individuate them. Let us call this problem, 'the Individuation problem'. There seem to be only two possible options for dealing

---

[17] The trivial specifications can prompt us to look for more informative non-trivial ones. Cf. Kenny (1963: 192): 'If a man says that he is afraid of winning £10,000 in the pools, we want to ask him more: does he believe that money corrupts, or does he expect to lose his friends, or to be annoyed by begging letters, or what? If we can elicit from him only descriptions of the good aspects of the situation, then we cannot understand why he reports his emotion as fear and not as hope'.

[18] Also, obviously, views that hold that the formal object enters into the representational content of the emotion need not (implausibly) insist that *trivial* specifications of those formal objects do so (see e.g. de Sousa 1987: 122–3; Döring 2003: 222). The latter can simply be second-order properties implicitly ascribed owing to substantial specifications of the formal property being represented in the content.

[19] It might be worth flagging that the suggestion is *not* that what is *in fact* dangerous is the formal object of fear. We can of course generate a notion of y's being a danger-for-X independently of how X represents y (indeed, even if X doesn't represent y at all) (the CO_2 emissions in the house are dangerous, but not known about). But we are considering danger as a property that is represented by a subject, whether conceptually or non-conceptually, as applying to some object. On the other notion of danger, cf. Tappolet (2016: 51): 'As Prinz notes (2004: 63) being dangerous is a relational and response-independent property. Something that is dangerous for some being is something that is likely to cause damage to that being, by threatening its bodily integrity or more generally its well-being. This is a relational as well as a relative property…'.

[20] See e.g. Lyons (1980: 101) and Teroni (2007: 401–2).   [21] Cf. Lyons (1980: 101).

with the problem. Either (1) we stick with the idea that the formal objects of emotions *do* individuate them and try to resolve the problematic cases. Perhaps, for example, we could offer different specifications of the formal objects in question, or more fine-grained specifications, or perhaps we could argue that some apparently different emotions are in fact the same.[22] Alternatively (2) we give up on the idea that substantive specifications of the formal objects of the emotions individuate them. Here the challenge will be to explain *what does* individuate those emotions which are clearly not the same and yet not individuated by their formal objects. If fear and thrill share the same formal object, how do we account for the fact that they nonetheless appear to be different emotions?

While (1) and (2) seem live options, it is worth stressing that it is *not* an option to maintain, without further comment or explanation, *both* that (e.g.) danger is the formal object of fear *and* that the formal objects of emotions individuate them.[23] The combination of claims is not plausible: while an object's being represented as dangerous might be *necessary* for it to be an object of fear, its being so represented is not plausibly *sufficient* for the emotion to be fear rather than some other emotion. Hence an object's being represented as dangerous will not individuate fear.

---

[22] Roberts (2003: 193-5) thinks that fear is tied to negative ('aversive') prospects more generally—but that makes the problem I am highlighting even more pressing. We might also consider the 'threatening' as a substantive specification of fear (cf. Nussbaum 2001: 27, 126). But why cannot some people enjoy finding certain things threatening? Below (3.6) we will see Lyons provide a more fine-grained specification of fear.

[23] See e.g. de Sousa (1987: 122-3, cf. 2007: 328); Deonna and Teroni (2012: 76-8; although cp. Teroni 2007); Helm (2002: 15). Kenny himself seems to have been the source of the confusion here, although I doubt he was confused himself. He introduced the terminology into the modern discussion (taking it from medieval accounts) in a general way, not specifically tied to emotions. He writes: 'To assign a formal object to an action is to place restrictions on what may occur as the direct object of a verb describing the action' (1963: 189). He then provides a trivial application of this idea: 'Descriptions of formal objects can be formed trivially simply by modalising the relevant verbs: only what is edible can be eaten, only what is inflammable can be burnt, only what is tangible can be touched' (189). But the notion of 'placing a restriction' on what may occur as a direct object of a verb describing an action, and then modalizing this in the form '*only* what is F-able can be F-ed', only purports to provide *a necessary condition* for the object in question, not a jointly necessary and sufficient condition. (Note, Kenny only writes of assigning *a* formal object, not *the* formal object.) While it is more plausible (although still contestable, of course) that only what is represented as dangerous can be feared or only what is represented as an undeserved suffering (of another) can be pitied, this falls short of claiming that there cannot be *other emotional states* which could have those same objects, and maybe necessarily so. Perhaps only what is dangerous can be an object of *thrill* and only what is an undeserved suffering (of another) can be an object of *schadenfreude*. The fact (were it a fact) that all *fearful* things are represented as dangerous would be compatible with the fact (were it a fact) that all *thrilling* things are represented as dangerous, but the latter is not compatible with the claim that all *and only* fearful things are represented as dangerous. Yet it is the latter claim that must be substantiated if danger is to *individuate* fear.

3.4 How does the Identification view predict Aristotle would individuate emotions?

In light of the Individuation problem, the question I wish to raise for the Identification view (as a reading of Aristotle) is this: if he held this view, how would he respond to the Individuation problem? The Identification view, recall, claims that Aristotle thinks that the intentional state that apprehends the object of the emotion is just another way of referring to the representational pleasure or distress in question. Let us start with specifications of emotions as representational pleasures or distresses. We could try to distinguish fearing something from being thrilled by it as follows (where 'A' stands for 'intentional attitude' and 'C' for 'intentional content'; see 1.2):

(1) Distress (A): that p is dangerous (C).
(2) Pleasure (A): that p is dangerous (C).

For the sake of argument, let us agree that (1) characterizes the intentional state of fear and so involves representing an object as fearful, while (2) characterizes the intentional state of thrill and so involves representing an object as thrilling. According to the Identification view, (1) and (2) are just different ways of specifying the intentional states—the judgements, *phantasiai*, or perceptions—that apprehend the objects of these emotions. But *what* judgements/etc. can (1) and (2) be other ways of specifying? (1) cannot, it seems, simply be another way of characterizing:

(3) Judgement (*phantasia*, etc.) (A): that p is dangerous (C).

For (3) would look no more specific to (1), than to (2), and yet (1) and (2) are diametrically opposed emotions. Instead, it seems, the Identification view must distinguish the judgements (*phantasiai*, etc.) that it thinks are equivalent to (1) and (2) by reference to their intentional contents. Perhaps, respectively:

(4) Judgement (*phantasia*, etc.) (A): that p is distressingly dangerous (C),

and:

(5) Judgement (*phantasia*, etc.) (A): that p is enjoyably dangerous (C).

In this way, (4) would represent the object as distressingly dangerous, while (5) would represent it as enjoyably dangerous, and so (4) and (5) could be thought to correspond to (1) and (2) respectively.[24] The Identification view, then, would appear committed to the claim that when we come to specify the judgements (*phantasiai*, etc.) that emotions are to be identified with, Aristotle would solve the Individuation problem by *providing more fine-grained specifications of the formal objects in the representational contents* of a judgement (*phantasia*, etc.). That is, this reading would insist that he would advocate the first of the two strategies I mentioned at the end of the last section.

Before we conclude this, though, let us consider one other possibility. To account for the difference between (1) and (2), perhaps the Identification view could modify the intentional *attitude* of the judgement (*phantasia*, etc.), rather than the intentional *content*. Perhaps, that is, it could suggest that (1) and (2) are equivalent to:

(6) Distressful judgement (*phantasia*, etc.) (A): that *p* is dangerous (C),

and:

(7) Pleasurable judgement (*phantasia*, etc.) (A): that *p* is dangerous (C).

However, as I see it, the problem with this proposal is that either (a) the judgement (*phantasia*, etc.) aspect of (6) and (7) is equivalent to ordinary judging, in which case the distress or pleasure ceases to be representational in the right way; or (b) *distressful judging* and *pleasurable judging* now constitute two new *sui generis* attitudes, in which case we no longer have the Identification view, as originally conceived. Let me elaborate.

Suppose (a) we have the same common-or-garden notion of judging (*phantasia*, etc.) in play that we find everywhere. Then, it seems, the difference between (6) and (7) can only really amount to whether *we find* the very same judgement (*phantasia*, etc.) (that *p* is dangerous) either distressful or pleasurable. In both cases we, in effect, have the *same* attitude (judging, *phantasia*, etc.) + content combination. It is just that in one case that attitude + content combination is found distressful, in the other pleasurable. We might say, on this view, that *either* distress *or* pleasure can supervene on or emerge from that attitude + content combination and that which of the two emerges determines whether we feel fear or thrill. But the problem with this for advocates of the Identification view is that such a supervening distress or pleasure seems to have lost the requisite intentionality. Strictly speaking, only the judgement (*phantasia*, etc.) is actually representing the object of the emotion; the distress or pleasure simply emerges from such a

---

[24] Although in 3.6 I shall argue that this is in fact questionable.

judgement (*phantasia*, etc.) and does not represent that object itself.[25] But then (6) and (7), so construed, would not plausibly be identical to (1) and (2) in the way the Identification view seeks to establish. For the distress or pleasure in (1) and (2) *do* represent the object of the emotion, whereas the distress or pleasure in (6) and (7), on this reading, do not.

Suppose instead, (b), that (6) and (7) are taken to introduce two new *sui generis* intentional attitudes—*distressful judging* and *pleasurable judging*—which do not involve 'ordinary' or 'normal' judging. Recall (see **1.1**), intentional states represent objects in virtue of their attitude and content pairings. If we now distinguish between the intentional attitudes of *distressful judging* and *pleasurable judging*, these amount to two *new* kinds of judging, besides ordinary judging. The problem with this alternative, though, is that the Identification view was intended to provide a substantive identity between a judgement (*phantasia*, etc.) of value, on the one hand, and a representational pleasure or distress, on the other. Whereas, on the current proposal, we have actually identified the representational pleasures or distresses of emotions with two new *sui generis* intentional states (pleasurable judging and distressful judging). And, in fact, since, on the current proposal, distressful or pleasurable judging is not simply a matter (as it was with (a)) of finding normal judging pleasurable or distressful, it is unclear that these intentional states have really earned the right to be called *judgement* (*phantasia*, etc.) in the first place. If they truly are *sui generis* states, they are not really *judgements* (*phantasiai*, etc.) as such. But then we are effectively being told that *representational pleasures or distresses* (as per (1) and (2)) are to be identified with special types of *pleasurable or distressful representation*. So put, that appears to amount to little more than the idea that representational pleasures or distresses are *representational*. No substantive identification has been made.[26]

And yet the advocates of the Identification view *do* appear to be making a substantive identification between judgements/*phantasiai*/perceptions of value and representational pleasures or distresses. Nussbaum insisted that the pleasure or pain aspect of an emotion, on Aristotle's view, was not a distinct non-cognitive element, but was already included in the cognitive/evaluative account of emotions—by which she meant: judgements of value. Achtenberg identified pleasure and pain with evaluative perceptions (perception of particulars as good, perception of particulars as bad), not *pleasurable* or *painful* perceptions. And, finally, Dow proposed that emotions were normal beliefs or perceptions that

---

[25] The distress or pleasure can thus, on this view, only be said to be about the object of the emotion in a derivative sense, along the lines of Fortenbaugh's non-representational account (see **2.2**).

[26] We might also wonder whether distressful and pleasurable judging could feasibly be construed as distinct modes of apprehension alongside other modes. Judging is a mode of apprehension (see **1.4**). But what sort of mode of apprehension is *pleasurable/distressful* judging? While we can distinguish the intentional attitudes of judgement, *phantasia*, and perception themselves, and can understand how some acts of judging (etc.) might be pleasurable while others distressful, it is far from clear that the latter difference dictates that a distinct intentional attitude is in play.

might constitute pleasures if their 'represented *contents* in some way include the effects of some pleasant object or perhaps the pleasant object itself' (2015: 176; my emphasis). Look again at his example:

> Pitying Jessica, on this account, might be the painful judgement that she is suffering undeservedly (*where what is painful about the judgement is its object: that she is suffering undeservedly*). (179; my emphasis)

The pity equivalent of (6) (painful judgement that Jessica is suffering undeservedly) is glossed in terms of us having a judgement with an object that we find painful. What we find painful about the judgement is *what that judgement is about*. But then to distinguish between fear and thrill we will require a more fine-grained differentiation of their objects. For if the object is simply characterized as *danger*, it *alone* will not mark itself out as either painful or pleasurable. (Similarly, as we shall see in the next section, further differentiation will be needed to distinguish the notion of pity that Dow appeals to here from *schadenfreude*.)

The Identification view, then, does seem committed to specifying the judgements (*phantasiai*, etc.) that are putatively equivalent to (1) and (2) along the lines of (4) and (5). And so, when we come to specifying the judgements (*phantasiai*, etc.) that emotions are to be identified with, the Identification view is committed to claiming that Aristotle would solve the Individuation problem by providing more fine-grained specifications of the formal objects *in the representational contents* of the judgements (*phantasia*, etc.) in question.

3.5 How does Aristotle *actually* individuate emotions?

The problem, though, is that Aristotle does not seem to wish to individuate emotions in this way. It is true, let us acknowledge, that he *sometimes* distinguishes closely related emotion-types by reference to more fine-grained specifications of their intentional contents. Consider envy (*phthonos*) and emulation (*zēlos*). These are defined as follows:

> envy is a sort of distress at apparent doing-well in terms of the goods mentioned [wealth, power, etc. from II.9?],[27] on the part of those like themselves, not in order that something accrue to the person himself, but because of those [possessing it]. (*Rhet.* II.10.1387b23–5)
>
> emulation is a sort of distress at the apparent presence, in the case of others who are by nature like the person himself, of good things that are honoured and

---

[27] Reeve (2018: 271n.539) traces the goods back, via *Rhet.* II.9.1387a6–23, to *Rhet.* I.5–6.

possible for someone to acquire, not owing to the fact that another has them but rather owing to the fact he himself does not. (*Rhet.* II.11.1388a32–5)

Both of these emotions are about the doing-well of another, but the definitions reveal a key difference between them. Aristotelian envy involves distress directed at the other's doing-well *qua the other doing-well*. Aristotelian emulation involves distress directed at the other's doing-well *qua our not doing (as) well ourselves*.[28] These emotions, then, are demarcated by more fine-grained specifications of their intentional contents. However, we should note that to distinguish Aristotelian envy from Aristotelian emulation *any* account will need more fine-grained specifications of their intentional contents than 'doing-well of another'. For, with respect to formulations along the lines of (1) and (2), both emotions share *the same* intentional *attitude*—they are both forms of distress (*lupē*)—and so the intentional content is the only thing left to play with. So even views that do not equate (1) and (2) with judgements (*phantasiai*, etc.) will still have to distinguish envy and emulation with more fine-grained specifications of their intentional contents.

With other pairs or groups of emotions, however, Aristotle distinguishes them by reference to their intentional attitudes, not their intentional content. He thinks that both envy and emulation are to be contrasted with another emotion; namely, *taking pleasure* in the deserved doing-well of another—which, since he does not give it a name, we might call 'pride in-another' (see *Rhet.* II.9.1386b30–1 and **Cat.17**). If the evaluative object of this emotion is the deserved doing-well of another then in terms of its evaluative object alone some instances of pride-in-another would be indistinguishable from envy, others indistinguishable from emulation.[29] But, evidently, Aristotle thinks that it would be insofar as subjects *take pleasure in* someone's deserved doing-well *qua* the other doing-well ('Isn't it wonderful what she's achieved!', etc.) that their emotion would be distinguished from *envying* the other. And, equally, it would be insofar as subjects *take pleasure in* another's deserved doing-well *qua* their not doing as well ('I'm really pleased she's far outstripped me!', etc.) that their emotion would be distinguished from emulation. If he wanted to, Aristotle could thereby refer to these different pleasure-based emotions as 'non-self-referential pride-in-another' and 'self-referential pride-in-another', respectively, or some such, and maintain that envy and non-self-referential pride-in-another can share the same formal object, on the one hand, and emulation and self-referential pride-in-another can do so, on the other. But what he *does not do* is try to distinguish pride-in-another from

---

[28] Aristotle thinks that which of the two one is prone to experience is ethically significant: 'emulation is a decent thing characteristic of decent people, whereas envy is a base one characteristic of base people' (*Rhet.* II.11.1388a35–6). See 7.5.
[29] On the not unreasonable assumption that envy and emulation *can*, at least, concern *deserved* doing-well. For more on this, see **Cat.13** and **Cat.14**.

both envy and emulation by aligning the former with a judgement (*phantasia*, etc.) with the intentional content *pleasurable-for-me doing-well of another* (or some such), and the latter with a judgement (*phantasia*, etc.) with the intentional content *distressing-for-me doing-well of another*.

Here is another example. On Aristotle's view, the object of pity is the undeserved doing-badly (of another) (see *Rhet.* II.9.1386b9, b12, b26–7).[30] But, if we view this as the formal object of pity then another emotion Aristotle explicitly recognizes shares pity's formal object, namely *epichairekakia*, which can reasonably be translated by 'schadenfreude' (see **Cat.18**). What distinguishes these two emotions, on his view, is whether one *experiences distress* at the undeserved doing-badly of another (pity) or, conversely, *takes pleasure* (or *joy*: *chairein*) in it (schadenfreude). That is to say, Aristotle differentiates the two emotions not by reference to more fine-grained specifications of the intentional contents as they would appear in judgements (*phantasiai*, etc.)—say, the judgement that someone has suffered a pleasurable-for-me (or distressful-for-me) undeserved misfortune—but simply by reference to the intentional attitude of distress or pleasure itself.

Now I think that this goes hand in hand with (what I have called) Aristotle's 'pain-at locutions' (as specified in 2.3). For those locutions suggest that he is envisaging the distress or pleasure of an emotion to be *directed at* an object represented. Thus, if the objects that the distress or pleasure are directed at are *themselves* construed as manifesting the formal object of the emotion, the distress or pleasure of the emotion cannot be *built into* the specifications of the formal objects (for they are directed at it). But then Aristotle would have to hold that non-trivial specifications of the formal objects of the emotions will *never* individuate them. For they will be compatible with two different, and opposed, hedonic variations.[31]

The only alternative to this, it seems to me, is that the formal object of a given emotion is constructed out of its *attitude-content pairing* and so is not simply a function of the evaluative object as that is specified by the intentional content alone. Insofar as pity is a representational distress, it represents objects as distressful for the subject of the emotion (as well as, of course, the person pitied). So it could be said that the evaluative or formal object of pity is the evaluative

---

[30] In *Rhet.* II.8 Aristotle further specifies the object of pity as one that a person might expect to suffer herself (or at least one of her own) (1385b13–16). This does not affect the point I go on to make since the object of schadenfreude would at least include such cases even if it extended more broadly, and so we would still need a way of distinguishing pity (so specified) from equivalent cases of schadenfreude. In what follows, for simplicity, I shall operate with the pared down version of the formal object of pity.

[31] On this account, the trivial specifications of the formal objects of emotions will individuate them, but not non-trivial specifications. This is because the trivial specifications pick out the formal objects in a way that also guarantees the emotion's hedonic flavour (because they trivially specify all and only cases of the emotion-type), whereas non-trivial ones do not.

dimension of what pity represents *as a whole* (i.e. by its attitude-content pairing); namely, a distressful-for-me undeserved suffering of another (or some such). Let me spell this out further. If we characterize pity along the lines of fear in (1) (of **3.4**), it would be:

(8) Distress (A): that X has suffered some undeserved misfortune (C).

We could then say that the intentional object represented by such an intentional state is: a distressful-for-me undeserved suffering of another. Someone might then propose that it is *this* object that is the formal object of pity, not simply: suffering some undeserved misfortune. On this view, the formal object (FO) of pity would be:

(9) FO (pity): distressful-for-me undeserved misfortune of another.

How could this help the Identification view? An advocate of the Identification view could then suggest that (8) is equivalent to a judgement (*phantasia*, etc.) that possesses intentional content which specifies the formal object in (9) (along the lines of (4) for (1), with fear), namely:

(10) Judgement (*phantasia*, etc.) (A): that someone has suffered a distressing-for-me undeserved misfortune (C).

This would thereby enable the Identification view to distinguish between pity and schadenfreude, or fear and thrill, as required.

However, the problem with this strategy as an interpretation of Aristotle is the quite simple fact that we do not see him individuating emotions in this way. Instead, he sticks with formulations along the lines of (1), (2), and (8), which casts doubt on whether he would accept the putative identification of (8) with (10), or of (1) with (4) and (2) with (5). (And, as we shall see in the next section, I think he would be right to reject such identifications.) This is particularly clear from the opening of *Rhet.* II.9. Here, pity is first contrasted with indignation, with the former specified as distress at (*epi* + dative) undeserved doing-badly, the latter distress at (*epi* + dative) undeserved doing-well (1386b8–15). Indignation is then, in turn, contrasted with envy on the ground that while both involve distress directed at (*epi* + dative) doing-well, indignation's distress is directed at *undeserved* doing-well, whereas envy's is not (1386b16–20). And both indignation and envy are then, in turn, contrasted with fear, which we are told concerns distress pertaining to something bad happening to *oneself*, rather than another (1386b20–4). Furthermore, distress at (*epi* + dative) someone undeservedly doing-badly (= pity) is then contrasted with three pleasure-based emotions: (i) being pleased (*hēdesthai*) at (*epi* + dative) someone deservedly doing-badly (which we might call 'pleasure-based indignation'; see **Cat.16** and cp. **Cat.12**); (ii) being pleased at (*epi* + dative) someone deservedly doing-well (pride-in-another) and (iii) joy (*chairein*) at (*epi* + dative) someone undeservedly doing-badly (schadenfreude) (1386b25–1387a3). Emotions, that is, are distinguished by reference *both* to their formal objects *and* whether they are distresses or pleasures/joys. There is no hint that Aristotle would view each of these emotions as equivalent to judgements (*phantasiai*, etc.) that somehow attempt to incorporate the distress or pleasure of the emotions into their intentional contents. In fact, I maintain we *never* find him offering such an analysis.

Indeed—perhaps in light of such passages—it is notable that insofar as those advocating the Identification view do specify formal objects of the emotions, they do not attempt to build the distress or pleasure of the emotion into its intentional content in this way. As we saw, Dow proposed that pitying Jessica might *be* the painful judgement that she is suffering undeservedly, 'where what is painful about the judgement is its object: *that she is suffering undeservedly*' (2015: 179; my emphasis). On this view, the formal object of pity is undeserved suffering. But the problem with this account is that it would fail to distinguish the object of Dow's pity from the object of a parallel bout of schadenfreude that I might experience about Jessica in relation to the same situation. For both Dow's pity and my schadenfreude represent *the very same object* so specified—that Jessica is suffering undeservedly. This means that what is distressful about the judgement for Dow, and what is pleasurable about it for me, *cannot* simply be a matter of the judgement's object so specified. Dow's view thus fails to enable Aristotle to individuate the emotions. And yet Aristotle clearly does think that these two emotions are distinct *and* is quite able to differentiate them himself. They are differentiated along the lines of the formulations in (1) and (2) (*mutatis mutandis*), where (1) is clearly not equivalent to (3). That is, pity, as specified in (8), is distinguished from schadenfreude insofar as the latter is:

(11) Joy (A): that *X* has suffered some undeserved misfortune (C).

The upshot is that *Aristotle* appears to hold that non-trivial specifications of the formal objects of the emotions will not individuate them. Indeed, this falls out simply from the fact that he allows that we can experience joy or distress at *the very same object*. While the pitiable individuates pity, there is no non-trivial specification of the formal object of pity that individuates pity. For we can also experience *joy* at that *very same* object, whereupon our emotion will instead be schadenfreude.

3.6 Contrast with contemporary perceptualist and judgementalist views

My argument against the Identification view was possible because that reading required Aristotle to individuate emotions by reference to their intentional contents, and yet he clearly does not think that the correct way to go. But this invites us to ask: is Aristotle right? Perhaps he would have been better off advancing the Identification view? Let us address this in relation to accounts of emotions that identify them with perceptual states or judgements. Here are two different possible identifications:

(i) Identify the emotion with the intentional state that apprehends the object of the emotion.

And:

(ii) Identify the intentional state that apprehends the object of the emotion with a representational pleasure or distress.

Some contemporary perceptualists and judgementalists accept (i) without accepting (ii). By contrast, as we saw in **3.1**, Nussbaum (2001), Achtenberg (2002), and Dow (2011, 2015) appear to accept (i) and (ii) as an interpretation of Aristotle's account of emotions. I called the latter 'the Identification view', meaning by this an interpretation of what Aristotle intends in linking emotions to pleasure and distress. But now let us consider how contemporary views that advance (i) alone might attempt to deal with the Individuation problem.

We can follow the same steps of the argument we have provided against the Identification view, except that the contemporary philosophers *can* try to deal with the Individuation problem by enriching the intentional content of a judgement or perception. Since they are not trying to interpret Aristotle, it is no objection to them that *he* does not proceed this way. In line with this (and noting the issue about distinguishing fear from excitement we considered in **3.3**), William Lyons (1980) suggests:

> 'the dangerous' is at best only a very rough generalisation of the evaluative category peculiar to fear and to no other emotion. Fully to separate the evaluative aspects of fear and excitement one would have to go into more detail. At the least one would have to spell out the evaluation of the object as not merely 'dangerous' but 'disagreeably so' as well, for the person who is excited, even if by danger, cannot claim to find the danger disagreeable. (101)

Similarly, to deal with the Individuation problem perhaps a perceptualist or judgementalist could try to build 'disagreeable' or 'agreeable' (henceforth 'distressful' and 'pleasurable') into the intentional content of a judgement or perception.[32] Consider the following:

(1) Fear that *p*,
(2) Distress that *p* is dangerous,

and:

(3) judgement/perception that *p* is a distressful-for-me-now danger.[33]

Those who identify emotions with judgements or perceptual states must, it seems, commit to the identity of (1) and (3). But, if they bought into Aristotle's view that the distress of fear is directed at its object, they could throw in (2) as well and maintain (like the Identification view of Aristotle) that (1), (2), and (3) are each simply different ways of specifying the same thing.

It is certainly more plausible to suppose that (3) is equivalent to (1) than to the simple judgement/perception that *p* is dangerous. For, as we have seen, (3) looks to have a better chance of individuating fear from thrill. But is it really true that *judging* or *perceiving* that *p* is a distressful-for-me-now danger is the same as fearing that *p*? Many will insist that the answer depends on which of *judging* or *perceiving* we have in mind. Judgementalists will think that *judging* that *p* is a distressful-for-me-now danger is equivalent to fear, whereas perceptualists will think that *perceiving p* as a distressful-for-me-now danger is equivalent to fear. Accordingly, let us divide (3) into (3J) and (3P) depending on which of judgement or perception we have in mind.

There is an important difference between (1) and (3J) which can be appreciated by considering the distinction between (3J) and the judgement which, according to judgementalism, would be equivalent to thrill:

(4J) Judgement that *p* is a pleasurable-for-me-now danger

To distinguish fear from thrill it is crucial to account for their differing hedonic 'flavours': fear is a distressful emotion, thrill an exhilarating one. Do the differing judgements in (3J) and (4J) account for that difference? Do they account for the fact that fear *is itself* distressful and thrill *itself* pleasurable?

---

[32] To ensure the distress is attributed correctly, some disambiguation may be necessary. We could say, for instance, that envy concerns the distressing-for-*S* doing-well of *O*, or some such, where '*S*' refers to the subject having the emotion, and '*O*' the person apprehended as having done well. Similarly, with pity, we might say that the formal object of the emotion is a distressing-for-*S* *O*'s undeserved painful suffering of some destructive or painful bad thing. With fear, since the future anticipated pain might perhaps also be a distress, we may need a further attribution marker: a *distressing-for-S-now* future destructive or painful evil (of *S*), or some such.

[33] Perceptualists may prefer 'perceive *p* as a distressful-for-me-now danger', or other related locutions. This should be taken as read in what follows.

Reconsider (2). (2) *does* seem to guarantee that the agent is distressed by the danger. (2) specifies *distress that* p *is dangerous* as an intentional state. The state has an attitude (= distress) and a content (that *p* is dangerous). What a state represents is a function of the combination of both (1.1). But the intentional attitude of the state indicates the *mode* or *way* or *manner* the object specified in the intentional content is represented (see 1.1n.7). (2) thereby represents *p*'s being dangerous *as* distressful. And *that*, I suggest, entails being distressed by *p*'s danger. Similarly, a parallel version of (2) for thrill would entail a pleasure. Also reconsider (1). (1), too, seems to guarantee that the agent is distressed by the danger. It has the intentional attitude *fear* and the content *that* p. And the combination would seem to amount to: representing *p as* fearful. Now, if *danger* is the formal object of fear, representing *p* as fearful must involve representing *p* as dangerous. *But* representing *p* as fearful must *also* involve finding the dangerous *p distressful*, i.e. (1) must entail (2). Or, at least, if we are to distinguish fear *from thrill* via their different hedonic flavours, (1) must involve representing the dangerous *p* as *distressful*, rather than *pleasurable*. Similarly, a parallel version of (1) for thrill would entail representing the dangerous *p as* pleasurable.

But now consider (3J). What object does (3J) represent? This intentional state's attitude is judgement or belief and its content is: that *p* is a distressful-for-me-now danger. The attitude of judgement or belief represents something as *obtaining*: someone who judges that *p*, represents *p as* obtaining (belief that *p* is taking *p* to be true, but what the belief represents, its intentional object, is the state of affairs specified by *p as obtaining*). So what (3J) represents is that a distressful-for-me-now danger *obtains*. But then we can easily show that what (3J) represents is not identical to what (1) represents; nor, indeed, to what (2) represents. For (1) does not represent some object as obtaining, it represents some object as fearful. And (2) does not represent some object as obtaining, it represents some object as distressful. And this result, prompted by reflection on the difference between fear and thrill, is significant for more than one reason. First, the point in fact shows that fear cannot simply be equivalent to *any* judgement whatsoever, regardless as to how we specify that judgement's content. For judgements involve representing objects as obtaining, whereas fear does not. This seems important in explaining both recalcitrant emotions—emotions that conflict with our judgements—and our emotional responses to fiction, neither of which seem to involve us representing some object as obtaining.[34] For if fear itself does not entail a parallel judgement such as (3J), clearly such emotions seem far less problematic. Second, the

---

[34] Or, at least, with respect to the latter, not in an unqualified manner. 'I believe that Bertie and Haddock drank a lot of port' represents a state of affairs that fails to obtain if treated as meaning that I believe that there really was someone called Bertie (Wooster) who drank a lot of port with (Esmond) Haddock. But if taken as elliptical for: 'I believe that in *The Mating Season* Bertie and Haddock are portrayed as drinking a lot of port', it could represent a state of affairs that obtains. There is also a question about the respect in which we can have emotions about fictional events. I investigate this in relation to Aristotle in my MS. I examine recalcitrant emotions in Chapter 12 below.

consideration also calls into question whether (3J) could really account for the fact that fear is distressful. For does representing that a distressful-for-me-now danger *obtains* entail that I am distressed by the distressful-for-me-now danger that I represent as obtaining? Can I not represent a distressful-for-me-now danger as obtaining, but for some reason be detached from this and so *not* fear it? I am not now proposing to try to argue for this one way or the other. What I want to point out is that it at least makes sense to raise the question of whether even judgements that are as specific as (3J) could entail the hedonic flavour of (1) and (2).

Doubtless perceptualists will be buoyed by these results since they have long argued that emotions should not be identified with judgements. Indeed, problems with doing so (especially pertaining to recalcitrant emotions) were often part of the motivation for perceptualist views in the first place.[35] But they should be wary. For it is not clear their view fares any better. What does the attitude of 'perception' entail for how the object of (3P) is represented? There is clearly a difference between (3J) and (3P). The latter does not seem to imply, as seems to be the case with belief or judgement, that *the subject* takes things to be a certain way (we can perceive things are a certain way without endorsing that they are that way; cf. perceptual illusions). But perception of *p* would seem to imply that the intentional state *itself* presents the object specified by *p* as obtaining (under the relevant intentional description). Döring attempted to capture this by claiming that the subsystem of perception generates the *appearance of truth* (2007: 378–9, 2009a: 245). The subject may know full well that the object perceived is not, in fact, as it is perceived, but still perception *presents it* as obtaining, even if the subject is not for one second taken in. We can illustrate this by contrasting perception with perceptual imagination. Suppose that Pat fears Fido because she perceives Fido as dangerous.[36] But suppose this conflicts with Pat's judgement: she does not doubt for a minute that Fido is, in fact, a harmless old fluff-ball. Nonetheless, her perceiving Fido as dangerous still *presents* Fido-as-dangerous as obtaining—it provides the appearance of truth—even though she judges otherwise. To see this, contrast such a perception with Pat *perceptually imagining* Fido as dangerous. While Fido is lying curled up, placidly, in his basket, Pat might, for the fun of it, perceptually imagine Fido with gnashing teeth, chasing her up the garden. There is clearly a big difference between Pat having such a perceptual imagining and Pat *actually perceiving* Fido as dangerous.[37] And that difference seems to be captured by the idea that the subsystem of perception presents *appearances as truth*, whereas there is no such requirement with our perceptual imaginations.[38] But

---

[35] See esp. Roberts (1988, 2003: 89–93); see also Tappolet (2003: 109–10); Döring (2009a).
[36] For the original version of this example, see Greenspan (1980, 1981, 1988: 17–18).
[37] Even in the broad notion of 'perceiving' that perceptualists employ; see 12.2 below.
[38] A parallel difference is present in the contrast between belief and thought-based imaginations. That perception is an appearance of truth obviously makes it ripe for providing material for belief and knowledge, but note that (perceptual) imagination may also be able to do this in various ways; cf. Gendler and Liao (2019: §3.6).

then (3P) differs from (1) and (2) no less than (3J). For, even independently of whether the subject accepts that the object obtains, (1) and (2) do not themselves represent an object as obtaining, whereas (3P), it seems, does. Fear that *p* represents the object specified by *p* as fearful. A distress that *p* is dangerous represents a dangerous *p* as distressful. But neither the fear nor the distress, *as such*, represents a dangerous object as *obtaining*. And they are compatible with *the subject* not taking the object to be in fact dangerous (as perceptualists would agree), on the one hand, and with the subsystem of perception not presenting the object as dangerous (as perceptualists cannot agree), on the other. Recalcitrant fears are examples of the former and emotions we form about objects as presented by perceptual imaginings (if, e.g., Pat was amused by her perceptually imagining a rabid Fido chasing her round the garden) or in response to fiction may be examples of the latter.[39] But the bottom line is that (1) and (2) *as such* simply do not pronounce on the epistemological status of the object represented *at all*, whether from an agential perspective (judgement/belief) or from that of a subsystem (perception).[40]

It is also worth noting that this argument does not hinge on the plausibility or otherwise of our substantive specification of the formal object of fear in (3). Suppose we stick with the trivial specification of the formal object: *fearful*.[41] On this view, (1) is not equivalent to (3), but instead to:

(5) perception: *p* as fearful.

---

[39] Döring (2015) herself highlights the difference between perception and imagining: 'our occurrent perceptual state puts forward its content as *correct*. In contrast to, e.g. the content of imagination, the content of perception is subject to correctness conditions. In imagining myself winning the next Dressage World Championship, it does not seem to me to be, outright, that I could really succeed. By contrast, in perceiving the stick as bent, it does look bent to me' (395; her emphasis). But Döring fails to see how this imaginative possibility undermines perceptualism. Could one not *experience an emotion* about one's imagined winning of the next Dressage World Championship? Interestingly, in her 2007, Döring allows that one can experience emotions in response to perceptual imaginings, but only insofar as the latter has correctness conditions (see 1.5n.41). You might, e.g., 'lie awake at night, fearing that your boss will fire you, and your emotion may be an affective perception without this requiring that your boss is standing in front of you in your bedroom' (2007: 378). This allows the notion of 'perception' to include perceptual imaginations, but retains the idea that what one 'perceives' has the *appearance of truth*. But it is just the latter that I am suggesting is not necessary for emotion, as is evidenced by our emotional responses to purely imagined scenarios (such as Pat imagining Fido chasing her up the garden) and perhaps our emotional responses to fiction.

[40] Of course, the object that the fear or distress represents must come from *somewhere* and so there must be some intentional state that apprehends the object of the emotion (in the 'specifying' sense of 'apprehend' sketched in 1.4). Nonetheless, this does not *identify* the emotion with such an intentional state. The emotion itself does not intrinsically share the properties of the judgement, perception, perceptual imagination, thought, etc., which reveals its object. In Chapter 4 we shall see why (on Aristotle's view) this is so.

[41] Cf. Tappolet: 'there are good reasons to take fear to consist in the perceptual experience of something as fearsome' (2016: 53, cf. 2009: 328). Tappolet, I think, wants trivial specifications of formal objects, but seeks to deal with the triviality issue I raised about this (in 3.1) by appealing to a response-dependent view: a bit like defining red in terms of responding to red in normal conditions.

On the argument I have provided, fear cannot simply be equivalent to (5); for perception is a state that presents its object as obtaining (an appearance of truth), whereas fear simply presents it as fearful. Nor does the fact that the perception of something fearful represents an object as fearful entail that it is feared. For consider the following:

(6) Rejection: that a fearful *p* exists.

Here the intentional state represents a fearful object, but it represents the existence of that fearful *p* as not obtaining. And clearly no one would presume that (6) entails fear! Hence, it cannot simply be the case that an intentional state representing some object as fearful entails fear. (It is not that the characterization of *fear* needs further additions, it is that when you embed the fearful within other intentional states, we need not get the emotion.)

Also note that for all I have argued it could still be true that perceiving some object as fearful *does* entail fearing it (so too with judging it fearful). Even so, I maintain that fear *as such* cannot simply *be* such a perception (or judgement). For perceptions (or judgements) and fears essentially represent objects in different ways. It is no part of the intentional state of fear that its object is taken to obtain or is presented as obtaining. Yet this seems to be constitutive of belief and perception, respectively.

Finally, note that the argument I have developed applies no less to views that make perception and judgement *components* of emotions alongside other features.[42] For perceptions and judgements fail to represent objects in the way emotions do insofar as they make *an additional* representational contribution; namely, representing the object as obtaining (belief) or presenting it as obtaining (perception). And it is these *supplements* that entail that judgements and perceptions cannot be identified with emotions as such (see the end of 1.5). But the supplements will still be present if we add in other components alongside the perception or the judgement. Indeed, we may well be in a worse position if the additional proposed component itself introduces representational features that are not part of the emotion as such. But even if it does not, the extraneous contributions of the judgement or perception will remain, insofar as the account builds in one or the other as a component.

Conclusion

In this chapter I have considered the view that Aristotle holds that the pleasure or distress of an emotion is simply another way of referring to the intentional state

---

[42] See e.g. Marks (1982); Searle (1983: 29–36); and Green (1992: ch. 6).

that apprehends the object of the emotion (**3.1**). I argued against this reading by, first, pointing to some of his descriptions of emotions that resist such an analysis (**3.2**) and, second, showing that it entails that he would individuate emotions in a way that he palpably does not (**3.3–5**). I closed by arguing that Aristotle is right not to individuate emotions this way: emotions cannot simply be identified with judgements or perceptual states, even in part, since that would involve attributing to emotions representational commitments which emotions *as such* lack (**3.6**).

4
Emotions as Hedonic States That Are Formed *in Response to* Intentional States That Apprehend Their Objects

Thus far I have argued (1) that Aristotle thinks that (a core set of) emotions are, at least in part, pleasures or distresses, (2) that those pleasures or distresses are representational (both Chapter 2), and (3) that they are not identical with the intentional state that apprehends the object of the emotion (Chapter 3). But this picture invites two further questions. First, since the pleasure or distress of an Aristotelian emotion is not identical to the intentional state that apprehends its object, *what is the relation between the two*? Second, do the pleasure or distress of the emotion and the intentional state that apprehends its object form two *components* of the emotion, or is the emotion, strictly speaking, only to be identified with the former?[1]

In this chapter I tackle these further questions. I first (**4.1**) consider what relation Aristotle thinks holds between the intentional state that apprehends the object of the emotion, on the one hand, and the emotion's pleasure or distress, on the other. I consider three possible candidates: (mere) concurrence, a causal relation, and (what I shall call) an 'in light of' relation. I argue that the latter is most plausible. I then (**4.2**) turn to the question of whether Aristotle thinks that the intentional state that apprehends the object of the emotion should be considered a *component part* of the emotional state, or whether the emotion is best characterized as a representational pleasure or distress *alone*. On the basis of his specifications of a core set of emotions, I argue in favour of the latter. In 4.3 I address this reading in relation to a few cases where we find alternative formulations, but argue that they do not undermine the interpretation. The resulting view that emotions—as representational pleasures or distresses—are formed in light of the intentional state that apprehends their object contrasts sharply with many current accounts. According to them (as indeed previous interpretations of Aristotle), emotions are themselves *apprehensions of value*; whereas if the reading I have

---

[1] For the reason I pointed out in **2.1**, there is no third option that Aristotle thinks that the emotion is, strictly speaking, to be identified only with the intentional state that apprehends its object. He explicitly *defines* many of the emotions as 'a kind of distress' (*lupē tis*) (*Rhet*. II.5.1382a21, II.6.1383b12–13, II.8.1385b13, II.10.1387b23, II.11.1388a32) or simply as 'distresses' (*Rhet*. II.9.1386b9, 26–7, 1387a8–9; *EE* III.7.1233b23–5, 1233b19–20) or 'pleasures/joys' (*Rhet*. II.9.1386b30–1, 1386b33–1387a3).

developed is right, Aristotle rejects this. Instead, he thinks that emotions are hedonic *responses* to apprehensions of value. I consider this further, and some other implications, in 4.4.

4.1 What is the relation between the intentional state that apprehends the object of the emotion and the emotion's pleasure or distress?

If, as argued in Chapter 3, Aristotle does not identify (i) the intentional state that apprehends the object of the emotion and (ii) the emotion's pleasure or distress, we must now ask: how *are* (i) and (ii) two related? Return briefly (see 2.2) to Fortenbaugh's reading, according to which Aristotle holds that the pleasures or pains of emotions are non-representational sensations. How would such a view explain the relation in question? On the simplest understanding, we might interpret it as one of *mere concurrence* and nothing more. On this view, when we experience fear this is because of the simple concurrence of sensory pain and an intentional state of oneself as in imminent danger; when we feel pity this is owing to the mere conjunction of sensory pain and an intentional state of someone as having suffered some undeserved misfortune; and so on. Call such a reading 'the Mere-Concurrence view'.[2]

The Mere-Concurrence view has not been popular as a reading of Aristotle and it is not difficult to see why.[3] Such a view is highly implausible philosophically, and there is another non-representational view in the vicinity which is not implausible in the same way. Suppose I believe that David has suffered some undeserved misfortune, but I am not particularly upset by this. Then suppose that Malcolm walks along and stands on my foot and I feel pain. I now have both an intentional state that apprehends an object of an emotion (pity) and a pain. It seems, then, according to the Mere-Concurrence view, I am feeling pity for David. So too, as the Malcolm-induced pain in my foot gradually subsides, my pity for David diminishes no less. But this is clearly ludicrous. The Malcolm-induced pain in my foot has nothing to do with my construing David as having suffered some misfortune, and so should have no bearing at all on whether I am having an emotional reaction to that. The Mere-Concurrence view thus fails to connect the

---

[2] It might be thought that since this view insists that the emotion only occurs when both the pleasure or pain and the apprehending intentional state co-exist, it would entail an answer to our second question, viz. that the pleasure or pain and the apprehending intentional state must form two *components* of an emotion. But, strictly speaking, this is not so. For the view could maintain that although the emotion only occurs when the pleasure or pain and the apprehending intentional state co-exist, nonetheless the emotion as such is only to be identified with the pleasure or pain.

[3] Both Leighton (1996: 219) and Fortenbaugh (2002: 12) mention it only to dismiss it. Cf. Sherman (1993: 17–18). See also Nussbaum (1994: 88), discussed below.

intentional state that apprehends the object of the emotion and the pleasure or pain tightly enough.[4]

Fortenbaugh deals with this by linking the pleasure or pain and the apprehending intentional state *causally*.[5] On this view, Aristotle holds that emotions occur when the intentional state that apprehends the object of the emotion *causes* the subject to feel a separate, non-representational, pleasure or pain. Call this a 'Causal view'.[6] Fortenbaugh writes:

> Aristotle defines fear as a pain or disturbance resulting from (*ek*) the appearance of future evil (1382a21–2). The pain is different from the belief that danger threatens, but the two are intimately tied together as cause and effect. (2002: 111)

And Fortenbaugh thinks that this applies generally with Aristotle's account of the emotions. In each case, the subject's 'judgment is the cause of his emotion including feelings of [pleasure or] pain' (111). Just as fear occurs when one possesses an intentional state that apprehends one as in imminent danger and this *causes* pain, so too pity occurs when one possesses an intentional state that apprehends that someone has suffered some undeserved misfortune and this *causes* pain, and so on.

The Causal view clearly deals with the philosophical objection we levelled against the Mere-Concurrence view. Since, in my example, the pain I experience is not caused by my representing David as having suffered some undeserved misfortune, I will not count as feeling pity for him. Like the Mere-Concurrence view, the Causal view insists that if we experience pleasure or pain without the apprehending intentional state, we do not count as having the emotion. And, again like the Mere-Concurrence view, the Causal view insists that if we have the apprehending intentional state without the pleasure or pain, we do not count as having the emotion.[7] But, unlike the Mere-Concurrence view, the Causal view also insists

---

[4] The same would apply, *mutatis mutandis*, to a view that invoked non-representational mental feelings, instead of sensory pains.

[5] Fortenbaugh (1970: 57, 2002: 11–12) explicitly makes the move from the Mere-Concurrence view to a Causal view, although not explicitly in light of troubles with mere concurrence such as those mentioned above. See also Leighton (1996: 219), who *does* note the problem with the Mere-Concurrence view. Fortenbaugh instead highlights *Philebus* (37e10) and some passages from *Top.* as background to his making the shift. I discuss the passages in *Top.* in 6.1.

[6] Besides Fortenbaugh (1970: 57–60; 2002: 11–14, 111) and Leighton (1996: 219), causal views have also been advanced by e.g. Cooper (1996: 247), Striker (1996: 291–3), McCready-Flora (2014: 410). It is not always clear whether these authors wish to subscribe to the idea that the pleasures or pains are non-representational, however. Nussbaum (1994: ch. 3, 1996) also subscribes to a causal reading of Aristotle, but her view is *explicitly* representational. I consider it below. Causal views of emotions (where the emotion is caused by a cognition or evaluation) have also been advanced by some contemporary philosophers. See e.g. Wilson (1972: esp. 85ff.), Lyons (1980: 53ff.), Goldstein (2002), and Whiting (2011). Cf. also Scarantino (2010: §6.2), characterizing various theories in the psychological literature.

[7] The Causal view can permit this possibility if some defeater comes into play that blocks the causal connection from occurring.

that the emotion only occurs if the intentional state *causes* the pleasure or pain.[8] The fact that the Malcolm-induced pain in my foot happens at the same time as my believing that David has suffered some undeserved misfortune does not entail that I am experiencing *pity* for David because the Malcolm-induced pain is not caused by my believing that David has suffered some undeserved misfortune. Unless the pleasure or pain and the intentional state that apprehends the object of the emotion are *connected up* in the right way, we do not have emotions, but just two co-occurring states. And that sounds like the right result.

In support of his Causal view, Fortenbaugh appeals (2002: 12, 111, 2006: 72–3) to some cases in which Aristotle's language does sound more causal.[9] Anger is, atypically for Aristotle's accounts of the emotions, specified as a desire accompanied by a pain (*orexis meta lupēs*).[10] But the desire accompanied by pain is said to result from (*dia* + accusative) an apparent slight (*Rhet*. II.2.1378a30–1). Again, fear is said to arise from (*ek* + genitive) a *phantasia* of a future destructive or painful evil (*Rhet*. II.5.1382a21–2). And the pleasure of anger is said to arise from (*apo* + genitive) the hope of being revenged (*Rhet*. II.2.1378b1–2). Fortenbaugh would suggest that these examples show that Aristotle thinks that emotions involve an intentional state that apprehends the emotion's object *causing* a non-representational pleasure or pain.

Now, I have already argued (**2.2**) that these examples do not support Fortenbaugh's view that the pleasures and distresses that Aristotle connects to the emotions are non-representational. The fact that fear, for instance, arises from an appearance of a future destructive or painful evil does not show that the distress of fear is not *about* or *directed at* that evil. And, ultimately, in Chapter 2 I argued that we have good reason to believe that Aristotle does think that the pleasures or distresses of emotions are themselves representational. Nonetheless, one might think that the causal aspect of Fortenbaugh's view, as evidenced by the examples above, could survive intact if we instead combine it with representational pleasures or distresses. On this view, Aristotle would hold that emotions are representational pleasures or distresses when these are *caused by* intentional states that apprehend their objects.

In her 1994 (= 1996), Martha Nussbaum advances such a view.[11] Like Fortenbaugh, she claims that Aristotle holds that emotions require both a

---

[8] This will open the view up to deviant causal chains objections, i.e. cases in which the intentional state causes the pleasure or pain but in a deviant way. The standard response is to add that the causal connection must occur 'in the right way'. The difficulty is then to spell out what 'the right way' amounts to. Cf. Schlosser (2019: §3.2).
[9] Fear and anger are his prime examples. He also (2002: 111), as we saw, tried to extend his account to other cases which are formulated with *epi* + dative. I resisted this in **2.3**.
[10] 'Feeling-friendly-towards' (*to philein*), discussed in *Rhet*. II.4, is also characterized as a desire (wishing: *to boulesthai*) (1380b36–1381a1). I consider this in **7.4**.
[11] Cf. also her 1986 (383). This stands in tension with Nussbaum's Identification view, as specified in her 2001, considered in the last chapter. I return to this divergence in the next section.

characteristic or individuating belief and a pleasure or pain.[12] And, like Fortenbaugh, she rejects the idea that these come together as a matter of mere concurrence, with 'each available independently of the other' (88).[13] Instead, again like Fortenbaugh, she claims that they are related *causally*: pity's pain, for example, 'is produced by the thought of another's suffering' (88). Indeed, also like Fortenbaugh, Nussbaum supports her causal reading by appealing to Aristotle's characterization of fear as arising 'out of' (*ek*) a *phantasia* (88). But, crucially, unlike Fortenbaugh, Nussbaum holds that the pleasures or pains that are caused by the characteristic beliefs or judgements are *representational*. She appeals to (what I called in 2.3) Aristotle's 'pain-at locutions', in particular, to the fact that the distress of pity is described as directed at (*epi*) the appearance that someone is suffering. So, Nussbaum combines a causal view with *representational* pleasures or distresses and explicitly claims that *both* (i) the causal relation between the belief and the distress or pleasure—as highlighted by fear—*and* (ii) the intentional nature of the distress or pleasure—as highlighted by pity—*apply in each case*:

> both relationships are present in both cases, clearly: for it is equally true that pity's pain is produced by the thought of another's suffering—Aristotle's rhetorical analysis relies on this—and also that fear is pain *directed at* the imagined future evil. (88; her emphasis)

If this account is generalizable (on which, see 89–91), Aristotle would hold that emotions in general require both an intentional state that apprehends the formal object of the emotion and a representational pleasure or distress, and these two features would be linked together causally.[14]

One question we might raise about characterizing this relationship causally is whether such a reading is able to explain the way Aristotle individuates emotions, as discussed in Chapter 3. As we saw (3.5), he holds that possessing an intentional state that apprehends an object of an emotion is compatible with experiencing *either* pleasure *or* distress directed at that object, and so undergoing different emotions. Both Lottie and Monty might apprehend that someone has suffered some undeserved misfortune (tripped over, say), but Lottie experience distress at such a circumstance, while Monty be overjoyed by it. But then one might argue that it cannot simply be the case that the intentional state that apprehends the object of an emotion *causes* some specific emotion. How can Lottie's

---

[12] Like Fortenbaugh, Nussbaum advances a judgementalist reading of Aristotle, but this is not crucial for my current argument (see **Intro.2**).

[13] As with the shift from the Mere-Concurrence view to the Causal view, we want the intentional state that apprehends the object of the emotion to play some crucial part in the *explanation* of why the subject possesses the representational pleasure or distress, not merely to be something that just happens to coincide with it when we want to say the subject possesses the emotion.

[14] As we saw in **3.2**, Dow (2015: 160) also holds such a view for both fear and the pleasure arising from anger, even though that is inconsistent with his Identification view.

apprehending that someone has suffered some undeserved misfortune cause her to experience pity, if the very same intentional state causes Monty to experience schadenfreude?

But there is misconception here about what it would mean for an intentional state to cause a distress or pleasure. There is no general difficulty with the idea that the very same *A* can cause *B* in *X*, but *C* in *Y*. If I add red paint to some white paint, I will get a pink colour, whereas if I add the same red paint to some black paint, I will get a brown, or burgundy, or maroon colour. Nonetheless, we can still say that my adding the red paint *caused* the change in colour in both cases. Similarly, suppose I tell you a joke that could be construed by some as offensive. To someone of a certain disposition or persuasion, the joke could cause mirth and laughter, whereas to someone of an opposed persuasion, it could arouse disgust and consternation. But it still seems reasonable to say that *my telling the joke* caused these opposed reactions in the different people. Granted, we would have reason to doubt a causal view if there was no way to distinguish *X* and *Y* that could explain the differing causal effects of *A*. But we have no reason to assume this with Monty and Lottie. (Aristotle is clear that the dispositions to experience pity or schadenfreude (or emulation and envy) stem from different *characters*, good and bad, respectively; see *Rhet.* II.9.1386b25–1387a5, 1386b11–13, II.11.1388a35–8, 1388b24–6; cf. *NE* II.6.1107a9–11.) So a causal account of the link between the intentional state that apprehends the object of the emotion and the emotion's pleasure or distress can embrace the way Aristotle individuates emotions. It will have to say that if Lottie and Monty possess *the very same* intentional state there must be some difference between *them* that will explain their different emotions. But that seems a reasonable requirement.[15]

Nevertheless, I think that characterizing the relation between the intentional state that apprehends the object of the emotion and the emotion's representational pleasure or distress as a causal one is misleading. In fact, one reason for this stems from the agential variability just highlighted. I have suggested that Aristotle would claim that in response to apprehending someone as having suffered some undeserved misfortune, Lottie might experience distress directed at the misfortune, while Monty experience pleasure. Equally, Aristotle thinks that someone might experience no hedonic state at all. (Cf. his parallel claim that a good person may be either pleased *or unpained* at someone's *deservedly* suffering some misfortune; e.g. murderers getting their comeuppance (*Rhet.* II.9.1386b26–30).) But although such agential variability is *compatible* with a causal relation being in

---

[15] It might be worth flagging why the Identification reading cannot appeal to a parallel point. According to it, the pleasure or distress of an emotion and the intentional state that apprehends its object are just two ways of describing the same thing. But then, on that view, there *is simply no room* for the intentional state to cause pleasure in one person and distress in another. For possessing the intentional state that apprehends the object of the emotion entails possessing the pleasure or distress, since the latter is just another way of describing the former.

play, it is still potentially misleading to characterize the relation this way. If I say that *A*—the intentional state of apprehending someone as having suffered some undeserved misfortune—causes *B*—a *distress* directed at that misfortune—that implies, *ceteris paribus*, if *A* then *B*. But *A* no more causes *B* than it does *C*—a *pleasure* directed at that misfortune—or *D*—no representational hedonic state at all. Each of these are possible responses to *A* against the background of different character traits. So why single out the *A*→*B* relation as the causal one? That would be like saying that adding red paint to another paint causes it to turn pink, without specifying the colour of the other paint. Absent the background presuppositions about the subject (or paint), it does not seem reasonable to speak of a causal relation at this level of generality. Furthermore, since we need not have any hedonic reaction at all in response to the apprehending intentional state, we cannot even claim that *A* causes some representational hedonic state.

But there is another reason why causal talk seems inappropriate in this context. To see this, note that the relation between the apprehending intentional state and the pleasure or distress is not plausibly construed as causal in the way in which, say, having too much to drink on rugby day may cause Kevin to fall down the steps of the pub's loo, or the way in which seeing Salah score might cause an increased heart rate. We are in an intentional context and so the intentional state that apprehends the object of the emotion and the representational pleasure or distress are more intimately connected than mere cause and effect. The representational pleasure or distress must be *about* the object of the emotion as that is presented by the intentional state that apprehends the object. Of course, one might say in reply to this that we just need to specify the causal relation more determinately: the intentional state that apprehends the object of the emotion causes a representational pleasure or distress *about that object*. But, even here, characterizing the relation causally may seem to miss something. It is not simply that subjects form the apprehending intentional state and then *find themselves* with a pleasure or distress directed at the object of that state. Rather, the pleasure or distress seems to be formed about that object *as it is* presented by the apprehending intentional state and *in response to* that intentional state. This, I believe, makes it more appropriate to think of the pleasure or distress as formed 'in light of' the object as it is presented by the intentional state, rather than as *caused by* it. The pleasures and distresses seem to be *responses* to the intentional state that apprehends the object of the emotion, to be formed *in light of* the object as it is presented by that intentional state, not simply caused by it.[16] Note, as well, that this picture deals better with the variability in hedonic response previously mentioned. While, for the reason mentioned, it seems problematic to think of an intentional state of undeserved misfortune causing a representational distress, it

---

[16] See also Müller (2017: 290–1).

is not problematic to think of a representational distress forming *in light of* such an apprehending intentional state. For the 'in light of' relation points to the fact that the subject of the emotion may have a bearing on which hedonic response may ensue (or whether there will be one at all). Monty might form a representational pleasure in light of apprehending that someone has fallen over, Lottie a representational distress.[17]

It is perhaps worth stressing right away that in characterizing the pleasure or distress as forming *in light of* the object of the emotion (as that is apprehended by another intentional state), there is no implication that the hedonic response (when it occurs) is deliberate or planned, or even something that must be *experienced as* sequential to the intentional state that does the apprehending. It must *be* sequential, on this view, since the pleasures and distresses are said to result from or arise from the intentional state in question. But that does not mean that it is *experienced as* sequential.[18] The representational pleasure or distress can form so automatically and imperceptibly that one simply experiences it as directed at the object. There need be no perceivable or discernible gap between forming the apprehending intentional state and experiencing the pleasure or distress.

Finally, we should note that the 'in light of' understanding of the relation between the apprehending intentional state and the representational pleasure or distress is no less plausible than a strict causal view when we come to explaining Aristotle's characterizations of anger, fear, and the pleasure that arises from anger. In claiming that the desire-accompanied-by-distress of anger results from (*dia* + accusative) an apparent slight (*Rhet.* II.2.1378a30–1); that fear arises from (*ek* + genitive) a *phantasia* of a future destructive or painful evil (*Rhet.* II.5.1382a21–2); and that the pleasure stemming from anger arises from (*apo* + genitive) the hope of being revenged (*Rhet.* II.2.1378b1–2), Aristotle indicates that these hedonic states form *in consequence of* the apprehending intentional states in question. But the 'in light of' reading readily accommodates that. On this view, the desire-accompanied-by-distress of anger *results from* an apparent slight because it is formed *in light of* an apparent slight; the distress of fear *arises from* a *phantasia* of a future destructive or painful evil because it is formed *in light of* such a *phantasia*; and the pleasure associated with anger arises from the hope of being revenged because it is formed *in light of* such a hope. The language that Dow conceded (to Fortenbaugh) 'undoubtedly assert[s] a causal connection' (2015: 160) only really dictates that the hedonic aspect of the emotion is explanatorily downstream of

---

[17] The causal formulation would be equivalent to the claim that a representational pleasure *will* (absent some defeater) form in light of apprehending that someone has fallen over. But using 'in light of' does not require us to say this.

[18] Cf. *MA* 7.701a25–33. Indeed, so far as this view goes, it could be *experienced* as occurring *prior* to apprehending the object of the emotion, or it could be experienced about the object, even though the subject would deny having explicitly registered the object in the way in question. Cf. Scarantino (2010: §3); Majeed (2022).

the intentional state that apprehends its object. That is compatible with characterizing that relation as an 'in light of' one in the way specified, if this is to be distinguished from a causal one.[19]

4.2 What *are* emotions, for Aristotle?

If Aristotle holds that emotions involve a pleasure or distress that forms in response to ('in light of') an intentional state that apprehends the object of the emotion, we must now address what he wants to identify as the emotion itself. In particular, does he think that the apprehending intentional state and the pleasure or distress form *two component parts* of emotions, or does he think that, strictly speaking, the emotion is to be identified with the pleasure or distress *alone*?[20]

Concerning his non-representational causal view, Fortenbaugh sometimes appears to suggest the latter, viz. that the pleasure or pain alone is the emotion. He writes:

> When a man observes suffering and deems the suffering unmerited, this judgment is the cause of his emotion including feelings of pain. (2002: 111)

This implies that emotions would just be the pleasures or pains that are brought about by the intentional state (a judgement, for Fortenbaugh), not the complex of pleasure or pain *plus* the intentional state. But I suspect that the above was just a careless formulation on Fortenbaugh's part. For, in his more explicit statements, he seems committed to the view that the pleasure or pain and the apprehending intentional state form two components of an emotion. Concerning fear, he writes:

---

[19] If someone wants to grant all my substantial claims and maintain that the relation in question can still be construed as 'causal', I shall, ultimately, have no qualms with characterizing the relation that way. Nonetheless, for the reasons highlighted, I believe that 'in light of' is less misleading and so shall employ that formulation in what follows. Aristotle explicitly mentions 'cause' (*aitia*) in connection with the emotions in *Rhet.* II.9 (1386b8–1387a5). He claims that the various emotions he contrasts with pity (indignation, envy, fear, pleasure-based indignation, pride-in-another, and schadenfreude) differ 'owing to the causes mentioned' (*dia tas eirēmenas aitias*)' (1387a3–5). The only bit of causal language in what preceded occurred when he distinguished indignation and envy from fear: 'And what must be present alike in each and every instance [of envy and indignation] is that [the distressful disturbance] not be because something distinct will accrue to the person himself (*mē hoti auto(i) ti sumbēsetai heteron*), but because of (*dia*) his neighbour himself. For it will be neither envy nor indignation but rather fear if the distress and the disturbance are present because (*dia*) something bad will happen to the person himself because of the other's doing well' (1386b20–4). This is to treat facts as causing distresses in certain agents (note there is no direct mention of the intentional states that apprehend the objects). But, in any event, Aristotle need not be thinking here of an efficient cause rather than a teleological one; which, in an intentional context, would amount to a *reason* in light of which a response occurs along the lines I have specified. Cf. Hocutt (1974: 396–9).

[20] As noted, since Aristotle clearly defines many of his emotions in terms of pleasure or distress in *Rhet.* II, the reverse possibility—that the emotion is strictly speaking to be identified only with the intentional state that apprehends its object—is not a realistic option. Cf. Leighton (1996: 218–19).

> [Fear] is caused by the thought of imminent danger, so that the appearance of future evil, destructive or painful, is mentioned in the definition of [fear] (1382a21–2).[21] Fear is not some pain or bodily disturbance distinct from cognition. It is a complex phenomenon which necessarily involves not only painful disturbance but also the thought of danger. (2002: 12)[22]

Here fear is very clearly characterized as a complex of *both* pain *and* apprehending intentional state (judgement), with the latter causing the former.[23]

Now, clearly, Fortenbaugh's version of this view is not a serious candidate for me, since I have rejected his claim that the pleasures or distresses of Aristotelian emotions are non-representational. But, once again, the basic structure of his view may be salvageable if we replace his non-representational pleasures or pains with representational pleasures or distresses. And, once again, Nussbaum provides just such an interpretation. We saw in 3.1 that in her 2001 she appears to advance an Identification view, according to which Aristotle holds that the intentional state that apprehends the object of the emotion—which, on Nussbaum's reading, is a judgement—is just another way of referring to the representational pleasure or distress. On that view, Aristotle holds that emotions do not have separable components, but are one state that can be specified in two different ways: as judgements of value, on the one hand, or representational pleasures or distresses, on the other. But in her 1994 Nussbaum advances a different reading.[24] She still endorses a judgementalist reading, according to which emotions 'are individuated by reference to their characteristic beliefs' (88). But she here claims that this makes belief a 'component' of emotion, alongside 'the other constituent in the emotion, the feeling of pain or pleasure' (88):

> We cannot describe the pain that is peculiar to *fear*, or say how fear differs from grief or pity, without saying that it is pain *at the thought of* a certain sort of future event that is believed to be impending. But if the beliefs are an essential part of

---

[21] For the second bracketed 'fear' (the first is just a pronoun picking up 'fear' from the previous sentence), Fortenbaugh actually writes 'anger', but this must be a slip of the pen.

[22] See also his 1970 (58–61).

[23] The explanation of why Fortenbaugh appears to say otherwise in the first passage is that he seems to think that an efficient cause of X also counts as part of the essential specification of X: '[Aristotle] looks upon some sort of cognition as both essential to and also the efficient cause of emotional response... The thought of outrage is essential to anger... It is also the efficient cause of anger' (1970: 58–9, also 2002: 13). And, of course, if the emotion is the complex of pleasure or pain and judgement then, in one sense, in bringing about the pleasure or pain, the judgement *does* bring about the emotion, because the judgement brings about the pleasure or pain and the emotion only exists when we have *both* of these. But it certainly is not a general truth that efficient causes count as part of the essential specification of the thing caused: the house-builder is not part of the essential specification of a house (cf. *De an*. I.1.403a29–b7).

[24] I should again flag that Nussbaum's goal in her 2001 is not to characterize Aristotle, but develop her own view. Hence her discussions of Aristotle are very brief. Her 1994, though, is devoted to Aristotle. Her 1996 is, bar changes required for the extraction, the same as her 1994 (ch. 3).

the definition of the emotion, then we have to say that their role is not merely that of external necessary condition. They must be seen as *constituent parts* of the emotion itself. (88; Nussbaum's emphases)

If this analysis is generalizable (on which, see 89–91), Aristotle would hold that emotions essentially consist of two components: (1) a judgement that represents the formal object of the emotion and (2) a representational pleasure or distress.[25]

Now, Nussbaum's judgementalist reading of Aristotle is controversial.[26] Nonetheless, the general form of her account can be preserved while remaining neutral about her judgementalist interpretation if we simply replace 'judgement' with 'intentional state'. Let us call this reading 'the Dual-component view' and characterize it as follows:

[Dual-component view]: emotions have two distinct component parts; a representational pleasure or distress, on the one hand, and the intentional state that apprehends the object of the emotion, on the other.

Advanced as a reading of Aristotle, such a Dual-component view seems both able to account for his pain-at locutions (since, in line with my argument of Chapter 2, it employs representational pleasures or distresses) and to allow him to individuate emotion-types in the way he does (since, in line with my argument of Chapter 3, it does not identify the representational pleasures or distresses with the intentional state that apprehends their objects). It thus seems the most promising reading so far.

Nevertheless, I do not believe that this is Aristotle's view either. The reading may seem attractive when considering his specification of fear, since that does appear to make reference both to fear's hedonic dimension and to the intentional state that apprehends its object. Fear is said to be a sort of distress or disturbance arising from the *phantasia* of a future destructive or painful evil (*Rhet.* II.5.1382a21–2). But fear is atypical in being formulated this way (I consider other putative cases below). As we saw in **2.3**, in his definitions in *Rhet.* II Aristotle more commonly claims that individual emotions are directed at (*epi* + dative) an apparent (*phainomenos*) instantiation of the formal or evaluative object of the emotion. For instance, pity is 'a sort of distress (*lupē tis*) at (*epi* + dative) an apparent (*phainomenos*) destructive or painful bad thing happening to someone who does not deserve it' (II.8.1385b13–14); indignation (*to nemesan*) is 'being

---

[25] In my 2014a I also implied (in my title: 'Aristotle and the Cognitive Component of Emotions') that the intentional state that apprehends the object of the emotion is a component part of the emotion. Cf. also Price (2011: 119). I now reject this view. (But, to be fair to my previous self, that point played little part in the argument of my 2014a.)

[26] As discussed in **Intro.2**, although I reject a judgementalist reading (see my 2014a), I am remaining neutral on this matter for the purposes of this current book.

distressed (*lupeisthai*) at (*epi* + dative) apparent (*phainomenos*) undeserved doing-well' (II.9.1387a8–9); envy (*phthonos*) is 'a sort of distress (*lupē tis*) at (*epi* + dative) apparent (*phainomenos*) doing-well in terms of the goods mentioned [wealth, power, etc. from II.9?], on the part of those like themselves, not in order that something accrue to the person himself, but because of those [possessing it]' (II.10.1387b23–5); and so on.

How should 'apparent' be understood in these definitions? If the argument of Chapter 2 was correct in supposing that Aristotle is here specifying representational distresses—distresses that are about their objects—the 'apparent' would most plausibly indicate that the object need not in fact be as the emotion presents it as being. Aristotle would, in effect, be highlighting that the object of the emotion is an *intentional* object in the sense specified in **1.1**: the object need not in fact exist (or not under the relevant description). But that would give us no direct reference to the intentional state that apprehends the object of the emotion. Granted, there would have *to be* such an intentional state for the emotion to form. But Aristotle would be defining the emotion itself in terms of the representational distress alone.[27]

Of course, advocates of the Dual-component view will want to resist this. They may instead insist that the 'apparent' does provide a direct reference to the intentional state that apprehends the object of the emotion (most plausibly a *phantasia*, given the linguistic connection between *phainomenos* and *phantasia*).[28] But three considerations count against this suggestion.

First, as we saw in **2.3**, Aristotle is quite happy to revert to factive formulations of emotions, dropping the 'apparent' altogether. In *Rhet.* II.9 he refers to pity simply as 'distress at (epi + dative) undeserved doing-badly' (1386b9, b26–7, cf. b12) and indignation as 'being distressed at undeserved doing-well' (*to lupeisthai epi tais anaxiais eupragiais*) (1386b10–11); and, in *EE* III.7, he refers to envy as 'distress at (*epi* + dative) deserved doing-well' (1233b19–20; see also *Top.* II.2.109b36–7, 110a1–2). Indeed, some emotions are *only* specified by factive formulations. What I call 'pleasure-based indignation' (to distinguish it from the distress-based version) is characterized as 'being pleased at (*epi* + dative) deserved

---

[27] For the difference between a dual-component view and a view that identifies emotions with pleasures or distresses alone, consider the following analogy. A house only occurs when a builder puts the bricks and mortar in the right positions. But the house is the bricks and mortar put in the right position (as caused by a builder), not: the builder causing the bricks and mortar to be put in the right position. (*Building-a-house* might be the latter.)

[28] The latter presumption may perhaps explain why Nussbaum claims that Aristotle asserts that pity is defined as a painful feeling directed at 'the appearance' that someone is suffering (1994: 88), rather than at the person's *apparent suffering*. But, in fact, this would be problematic for her view, since, as noted, she advances a judgementalist reading. Many have appealed to the use of 'apparent' in the specifications of the emotions to support *phantasia*-based readings; see e.g. Cooper (1996: 247); Sihvola (1996); Striker (1996: 291); Achtenberg (2002: ch. 6); Nieuwenburg (2002); Price (2011: 116); Moss (2012a: 77–9). I resist this below; see also Dow (2009, 2015: 190, 201–3) and my 2014a.

doing-badly' (II.9.1386b27–8).²⁹ What I call 'pride-in-another' is specified as 'joy (*chairein*) at (*epi* + dative) (someone else's) deserved doing-well' (1386b30–1).³⁰ So too schadenfreude (*epichairekakia*) is joy (*chairein*) at (*epi* + dative) undeserved doing-badly (1386b33–1387a3; cf. *EE* III.7.1233b18–22, *NE* II.6.1107a9–11, II.7.1108a35–1108b6).³¹ As I see it, reverting to such factive formulations is a reasonable shorthand if one thinks that the emotion, strictly speaking, *just is* the representational pleasure or distress. It would be similar to me referring to emotions as 'about their objects', rather than always as 'about their *intentional* objects' (see 1.1). Granted, things might not always be as our emotions present them, but the factive case is paramount for the explanation and the error cases are understood by modification of that. The Dual-component view, by contrast, has to maintain that in these formulations Aristotle can only be gesturing or alluding to the emotions in question, not actually specifying them. For, in each case, he has left out any mention of an *essential component* of the emotion, namely, the intentional state that apprehends its object. And yet Aristotle appears to think that the characterizations are perfectly adequate.

Second, *phainomenos* ('apparent') is used in other contexts in the *Rhetoric*. And it quite clearly does not refer to an intentional state in its own right, but is instead employed to allow in error cases. Consider its use with regard to oratorical deductions, enthymemes.³² In *Rhet*. I.2 Aristotle writes:

> In cases of persuasion that operate through showing (*deiknunai*) or appearing to show (*phainesthai deiknunai*) something, just as in dialectical ones there is induction (*epagōgē*), deduction (*sullogismos*), and apparent deduction (*phainomenos sullogismos*), so it is like that here as well. For a paradigm (*paradeigma* ['example']) is an induction, and an enthymeme a deduction, and an apparent enthymeme (*to phainomenon enthumēma*) an apparent deduction (*phainomenos sullogismos*). For I call a rhetorical deduction an enthymeme, and a rhetorical induction a paradigm (*paradeigma*). (1356a35–b6)

---

²⁹ Aristotle groups these together as types of indignation (*nemesis*) in *EE* III.7 (1233b23–5). See **Cat.12** and **Cat.16** for more discussion.
³⁰ Aristotle does not provide a name for this emotion. For a little more discussion, see **Cat.17**.
³¹ For more on Aristotle on this emotion, see **Cat.18**.
³² On enthymemes, see: 'to show that if some things are so, something beyond them follows through them by their being so, whether universally or for the most part, is called in dialectic a deduction (*sullogismos*) and in rhetoric an enthymeme' (*Rhet*. I.2.1356b16–18; on which, see Reeve 2018: 175–6n.57). As Rapp notes (2022: §6.1): 'For Aristotle, an enthymeme is what has the function of a proof or demonstration in the domain of public speech. Since a demonstration is a kind of *sullogismos*, the enthymeme is said to be a *sullogismos* too...The word "*enthymeme*" (from "*enthumeisthai*—to consider") had already been coined by Aristotle's predecessors and originally designated clever sayings, bon mots, and short arguments involving a paradox or contradiction. The concepts "proof" (*apodeixis*) and "*sullogismos*" play a crucial role in Aristotle's logical-dialectical theory. In applying them to a term of conventional rhetoric, Aristotle appeals to a well-known rhetorical technique, but, at the same time, codifies and redefines the original meaning of "enthymeme": properly understood, what people call "enthymeme" *should* have the form of a *sullogismos*, i.e., a deductive argument'.

Just as we have deductions and apparent deductions, so too we have enthymemes and apparent enthymemes. But what makes an apparent enthymeme 'apparent'? Aristotle picks up enthymemes and apparent enthymemes in *Rhet.* II, first providing his discussion of the different *topoi* ('topics') of enthymemes in II.23 and then turning to apparent enthymemes in II.24. He opens the latter as follows:

> But since it is possible for a thing to be a deduction or for another thing not to be one, but to appear (*phainesthai*) to be one, necessarily it is also possible for a thing to be an enthymeme and for another thing not to be one, but to appear (*phainesthai*) to be one, since an enthymeme is a sort of deduction. (1400b34–1401a1)

He then goes on to provide a series of *topoi* for such 'apparent (*phainomenos*) enthymemes' (1401a1). We might, for instance, falsely deduce on the basis of a 'sign' (*ek sēmeiou*) of something:

> [for example] if someone were to say that Dionysius is a thief since he is wicked. For this of course is non-syllogistic. For not every wicked person is a thief, although every thief is wicked. (1401b12–14)

So too, we might falsely deduce by taking a non-cause as a cause:

> for example when the thing has happened at the same time as another or after it. For people take the coming-after-something as being because-of-something, and especially political policy makers—for example, as Demades took the policy of Demosthenes to be the cause of all evils since it is after it that the war came. (1401b30–4)

The implication is clearly that for a piece of reasoning to qualify as an enthymeme, it must *successfully* deduce and be a valid piece of reasoning.[33] Whereas when some reasoning only *looks* as though it deduces, but is in fact fallacious, it is called in dialectic 'an apparent deduction' (cf. *Top.* I.1.100b23–101a4) and in rhetoric 'an apparent enthymeme'.

Evidently, then, *phainomenos* ('apparent'), here, does not refer to an intentional state, a perceptual *phantasia*. It simply indicates that some pieces of reasoning only appear to be enthymemes (or deductions) when they in fact fail to be so. But since this is how Aristotle employs *phainomenos* in *Rhet.* here, we have defeasible expectation that this is how he is employing it elsewhere in the same text.

---

[33] This obviously does not automatically make enthymemes either sound or incontestable. As Aristotle notes, 'the deductions are based on reputable beliefs, and many things that seem to be so are contrary to one another' (*Rhet.* II.25.1402a33–4).

Accordingly, we have a defeasible expectation that in his use of *phainomenos* in his definitions of the emotions in *Rhet.* II Aristotle simply means to indicate that things may not be as the emotion presents them, and is not pointing to the intentional state that apprehends the object of the emotion.[34]

Third, the Dual-component view we are considering accepts that Aristotle's pain-at locutions (*lupē epi* + dative) indicate that the pleasures or distresses of emotions are representational. But, as I see it, this creates a problem for interpreting the *phainomenos* in those definitions as referring to the intentional state that apprehends the object of the emotion (as the Dual-component view has to maintain). For if what comes after the 'at' (*epi*) in the pain-at locutions is what the pleasure or distress of the emotion is *directed at* or *about*, and if *phainomenos* refers to the intentional state that apprehends the object of the emotion, then in the cases I mentioned at the start of this section, the distress would have to be directed *at the intentional state that apprehends the object of the emotion itself*. Pity, for example, would be distress directed at the *phantasia* that someone has suffered some undeserved misfortune. Indignation would be distress directed at the *phantasia* that someone has undeservedly done well. And so on. But this provides the wrong object for the emotion. Our emotions are not generally directed at our intentional states. Indeed, it is hard to see how it could be intelligible to *pity* or *envy* an intentional state (it is not clear we can cogently represent an intentional state as having suffered some undeserved misfortune or achieved some success). And even when the idea is at least intelligible, as, e.g., when an athlete may fear having negative thoughts, we certainly do not want to *define* the emotion to restrict it to such cases! Only in very specific circumstances are emotions about other intentional states, i.e. when those intentional states can themselves be construed as manifesting the formal object of the emotion in question. Thus, taking the 'apparent' to refer to the intentional state that apprehends the object of the emotion is not compatible with the idea that the pleasures or distresses of emotions are representational in the way that is revealed by Aristotle's pain-at locutions, i.e. as directed at the objects of the emotions themselves (as they are apprehended), rather than (implausibly) as directed at the intentional state that apprehends those objects.

In sum, Aristotle's (1) reverting to factive formulations that drop the *phainomenos*, his (2) use of *phainomenos* elsewhere in *Rhet.*, and (3) the *position* of *phainomenos* in relation to the representational pleasure or distress and the object of the emotion—as marked by the pleasure or distress being directed at (*epi*) the

---

[34] The usage cannot be quite the same since in the case of enthymemes we have 'enthymemes or apparent enthymemes', whereas in the case of the emotions we do not have, e.g., 'pity is distress at undeserved misfortune or apparent undeserved misfortune'. Nonetheless, the use of *phainomenos* elsewhere in *Rhet.* strongly suggests that it is error cases that he is trying to allow in. And, of course, he does at some points provide factive formulations, as I have mentioned. Dow (2009: 153–5, 2015: 201) also (rightly, in my view) draws attention to the broader use of *phainomenos* in *Rhet.*

phainomenos object of the emotion—suggest that the intentional state that apprehends the emotion's object is not specified in the definitions of these emotions. This indicates that the Dual-component view is not Aristotle's either. We should conclude that he does not define emotions as involving two separate components: (i) an intentional state that apprehends the object of the emotion and (ii) a representational pleasure or distress. He defines emotions as representational pleasures or distresses *alone*.[35]

4.3 Some other formulations

If my conclusion in the last section is suggested by Aristotle's definitions of the core set of emotions I have highlighted, we still need to address some cases which, though they link emotions to pleasure or distress, do not invoke the simple formulations just specified. (Other difficult cases besides these will be addressed in Part II and Chapter 10.)

Let me start with anger (*orgē*).[36] Aristotle defines this as follows:

> Let anger be desire accompanied by distress for apparent revenge (*timōrias phainomenēs*), because of an apparent slight (*dia phainomenēn oligōrian*) on the part of someone unfitted to slight the person himself, or those close to him. (*Rhet.* II.2.1378a30–2)

Given our analysis of *phainomenos* above, there is nothing especially puzzling here for my reading. Atypically with Aristotle's accounts of individual emotions, anger is specified as combining both a desire and a distress. But then if *phainomenos* is being employed to account for the error cases, Aristotle will need two of them; one to account for the possibility of error pertaining to the object of the distress (the apparent slight; see **6.2**) and another to account for the possibility of error with respect to the object of the desire. And this is just what we find. Just as the distress concerns what-presents-itself-as (= apparent) a slight (even if it was

---

[35] The account I am proposing fits well with the fact that in his general specifications of the emotions in *NE* and *EE* (quoted in **2.1**), Aristotle characterizes emotions *just* by reference to pleasure and distress: emotions are in general those things that are accompanied by or imply (*hepetai*—see **2.1**) pleasure or distress. At the start of *Rhet.* he claims that we need a 'theoretical grasp' (*theōrēsai*) of the emotions (as well as of character and virtue), 'that is, on which each of the emotions is and what sort of thing, and from what it arises and in what way (τί τε ἕκαστόν ἐστιν τῶν παθῶν καὶ ποῖόν τι καὶ ἐκ τίνων ἐγγίνεται καὶ πῶς)' (I.2.1356a22–5). On the interpretation I have offered, pleasure and distress mark out the 'what-it-is' (*ti esti*) of emotions and the specific evaluative properties that each emotion responds to (its formal object) mark out the particular kind of representational pleasure or distress in question (the 'what-sort': *poion ti*).

[36] I provide a fuller account of anger in Chapter 6.

not in fact a slight), so too the desire concerns what-presents-itself-as (= apparent) revenge or rectification (even if it will turn out not to be such).[37]

Next consider the pleasure that Aristotle associates with anger. He writes:

> A kind of pleasure follows all anger, namely, the one that arises from the hope of being revenged (*apo tēs elpidos tou timōrēsasthai*).[38] For it is pleasant to think (*oiesthai*) that he will get what he seeks... a kind of pleasure actually follows along (*akolouthein*) because of this... (II.2.1378b1–3, 8)

Here the pleasure does appear to be consequent on the hope and to arise from it. And I suspect that Aristotle has in mind a representational pleasure: the angry person is pleased *at the prospect of getting revenge*. In this sense, the pleasure will count as an emotion by my lights. But none of this supports the Dual-component view we specified. Aristotle is obviously not in the business of *defining* this emotion, he is simply indicating that it occurs in response to anger. On both my reading and the Dual-component view, emotions require an intentional state that apprehends the object of the emotion. It is just that on my view the emotion is, strictly speaking, the representational pleasure alone. But highlighting that the representational pleasure follows from the intentional state in question is obviously quite compatible with that.

Fear, by contrast, may appear more difficult for my reading. For, unlike his characterization of the pleasure arising from anger, Aristotle *does* appear to be defining fear when he claims:

> Let fear, then, be a sort of distress or disturbance arising from (*ek* + genitive) a *phantasia* of a future destructive or painful evil. (II.5.1382a21–2)[39]

---

[37] Some (e.g. Spengel 1867: *ad loc.*; Ross 1959: *ad loc.*) have excised the first *phainomenos* even though it is well attested in the manuscripts. As noted, in my view it is necessary since with anger we (atypically) have two different intentional objects (*qua* distress and desire, respectively). See also Cooper (1996: 255–6n.23). Cooper also corrects the mistaken tradition of translating *phainomenos*—in the case of anger alone—as 'conspicuous' (see e.g. Cope 1877: *ad loc.*; Roberts (*ROT: ad loc.*); Kennedy 1991: *ad loc.*; and Gastaldi 2015: 203–4): while the revenge has to be (taken to be) recognized as revenge by the person revenged upon (*Rhet.* II.3.1380b20–5), slights do not have to be 'conspicuous' to be deemed slights, and yet the same use of *phainomenos* is surely in play both times. Price (2009: 134, cf. 2017: 188n.23) appears to resist this by noting that one kind of slight, insult (*hubris*), involves doing and saying things that cause shame, and shame is public. But of course *hubris* is only one of the three kinds of slight and with the other two (contempt (*kataphronēsis*) and spite (*epēreasmos*)) there does not seem to be an essential *public* dimension, even if there must be a perceived injustice (*NE* V.8.1135b28–9). In any event, as Cooper notes (1996: 255–6n.23), and Price acknowledges (2009: 134, 142n.28), there is surely good reason to treat the occurrences of *phainomenos* here in the same way as the other emotions—and no one thinks 'conspicuousness' must be in play in each instance of those.

[38] Reeve (2018: 252n.427) cites *NE* IV.5.1126a21–2 as a parallel to this ('Taking revenge puts a stop to their anger by producing pleasure in place of pain'). But this conflates the pleasure that one will get from *exacting* revenge, with the pleasure of *anticipating* it.

[39] See also *Rhet.* II.9.1386b22–4 and *EE* III.1.1229a33–b1.

And yet here he appears to refer both to the emotion's distress and to the intentional state that gives rise to it (which apprehends its object). Does this not suggest that he is advancing a Dual-component view of this emotion?

In reply, one might propose that given (i) the use of *phainomenos* already highlighted and (ii) the linguistic connection between *phantasia* and *phainomenos* (*phainomenos* is a participle from the verb *phainesthai*, *phantasia* a noun deriving from the same ultimate route), Aristotle just intends *phantasia* in a way that corresponds to *phainomenos* in this context. On this view, *phantasia*, here, would not refer to an intentional state as such, but to the fact that the future destructive or painful evil need only be apparent, not real. This reading strikes me as possible, but in fact I do not need to appeal to it. For *even if* Aristotle means to refer directly to the intentional state that apprehends the object of the emotion (*phantasia* construed as an intentional state in its own right; see **1.2n.9**), this does not show that he intends to include that intentional state *as a component part* of the emotion as such.[40] For note, he claims that fear is a kind of distress or disturbance that *arises from* (*ek* + genitive) such a *phantasia*. This is quite compatible with him thinking that the emotion, strictly speaking, is the distress alone. It all depends on how we read the identification. Aristotle could, as the Dual-component view maintains, be intending to identify fear with two component parts, one of which forms in response to the other. Or he could, more simply, be identifying fear with the distress and then indicating how that distress comes about, namely, in response to an intentional state that apprehends such an object. The latter would, in effect, just be an alternative way of formulating an emotion. Aristotle would be highlighting the object of the distress by specifying the intentional state that apprehends that object. But, again, this is quite compatible with him thinking that, strictly speaking, the emotion is the distress *alone*.[41]

---

[40] Nor, I think, would it entail that fear can only be about its objects just insofar as they are represented by perceptual *phantasia*, rather than say, thought. The idea that fear arises from such a *phantasia* is clearly compatible with the idea that the object of fear may only be accessible via a thought *that operates on* such a *phantasia*, in line with Aristotle's notion of how thought operates on *phantasia* in *Mem*. 1.450a12–1, 22–5. (I discuss this in more detail in my MS.)

[41] It is also worth stressing that Aristotle's 'definitions' of the emotions in *Rhet*. II are not all of the same status. While with a core set of emotions—anger, shame, pity, indignation, envy, emulation (as well as what I have called 'pleasure-based indignation', 'pride-in-another', and schadenfreude)—Aristotle's definitions seem to provide a straightforward characterization of the emotion in terms of a distress or pleasure directed at the (apparent) manifestation of the evaluative object in question, a number of other specifications are more oblique. A good example is *feeling-grateful-for* (*charin echein*) where, as we will see (**10.1**), Aristotle does not define the emotion as such, but what we feel the emotion *for*, namely, a favour. Something similar also applies, I believe, with *feeling-friendly-towards* (*to philein*) and, by extension, its opposite, *hating* (*to misein*) in *Rhet*. II.4 (see **7.4**). Aristotle characterizes a closely related phenomenon as a helpful way of specifying the emotions he wants. So too, with confidence (*to tharsos*) in *Rhet*. II.5 (see **10.7**). Since Aristotle's specifications of individual emotions are not always of the same form (and can be looser or stricter), he need not hold that everything he mentions in his account of fear strictly speaking counts as part of what the emotion itself is. (In Chapter 10 I shall also address the various 'contraries' of emotions that Aristotle alludes to in his *Rhet*. specification of emotions (II.1.1378a21–2).)

Finally, consider shame (*aischunē*). In *Rhet.* II.6 Aristotle defines this as follows:

> Let shame be a sort of distress or disturbance about evils—whether present, past, or future—that appear to bring a person into disrepute (*peri ta eis adoxian phainomena pherein*). (1383b22–4)

We here get the idea that shame is a distress about bad things (*peri tōn kakōn*) with respect to their appearing to bring one into disrepute. It seems quite plausible that all Aristotle intends to indicate by *ta phainomena* in this definition is that the bad things in question are apparently disreputable to the subject, in the sense of 'apparent' we have specified for other emotions. Interestingly, though, later in his discussion, Aristotle refers to shame as 'a *phantasia* concerning disrepute' (1384a22). How should we understand this? I have a few observations. First, we should stress that Aristotle's gloss, here, lies outside his definition and presumably the formulation in the definition should take priority (he cannot intend to *identify* shame with an appearance of disrepute, since he has explicitly defined it as a distress or disturbance). Second, given that the gloss clearly refers back to the definition, we might well be expected to take the latter to inform the former. If so, the gloss could simply stand for: 'shame is [distress about] an appearance (*phantasia*) concerning disrepute (*peri adoxias*)', where *phantasia* is understood to be equivalent to *phainomenos* in the other definitions and simply intended to mark the possibility of error. Third, in line with this, we can explain why Aristotle might here employ this version. The shortened formular will, in effect, be picking out *the part of the definition* that Aristotle wishes to focus on at this point in his discussion, viz. the connection of shame to disrepute, which he then elaborates on via the notion of 'reputation' (*doxa*) and the opinions of those one takes account of (1384a21–5). Fourth, alternatively, in line with my comments about fear above, Aristotle may intend *phantasia* to indicate an intentional state in its own right, viz. the intentional state that apprehends the object of the emotion. But, if so, given that Aristotle does not appear to wish to identify such intentional states with the emotion's pleasure or distress (so Chapter 3), he must intend the gloss to allude to shame as *resulting from* or *arising from* such an intentional state. The gloss would, that is, be short for: 'shame is [what results from] a *phantasia* concerning disrepute', where *phantasia* marks an intentional state in its own right.[42] Either way, we have little reason to think that Aristotle's basic understanding of shame does not fall in line with the general account highlighted in the last section.

---

[42] As with fear (see n.40), I would resist the idea that such a reading would entail that shame could only be about is object just insofar as that object is represented by *phantasia*.

4.4 Response views versus apprehender views of emotions

In Chapter 3 I resisted (what I called) the Identification reading of Aristotle, according to which the pleasure or distress of an emotion is just another way of referring to the intentional state that apprehends its object. Against this, I argued that there is good reason to think Aristotle holds that the representational pleasure or distress of an emotion and the intentional state that apprehends its object are distinct states. In this chapter I have argued that the former forms in light of the latter, but that the two do not constitute separate components of an Aristotelian emotion (as the Dual-component view maintains). Emotions are representational pleasures or distresses that form in response to ('in light of') an intentional state that apprehends their object, but they are to be identified as representational pleasures or distresses *alone*.

The idea that emotions are responses to intentional states that apprehend their objects, rather than (even in part) such apprehending states themselves, contrasts sharply with many contemporary accounts of emotions. The latter typically consider emotions themselves to be intentional states that apprehend their objects.[43] Indeed, this is perhaps the dominant position now. The notion that emotions are intentional states that apprehend their objects falls out trivially with views that *identify* them (even in part) with evaluative judgements or evaluative perceptions. For if emotions *just are* (in part) evaluative judgements or perceptions then they themselves can be thought of as apprehending what the perceptions or judgements (they (in part) are) apprehend. If fear that Fido will bite me *simply is* (in part) judging that Fido will bite me is fearful then my fear will apprehend the object it represents. In coming to form the judgement (and so have the fear), I *form* an understanding of the world, and so apprehend it as I judge it (even if I am mistaken). Equally, if to fear that Fido will bite me *simply is* (in part) perceiving the prospect of Fido biting me as fearful then my fear will apprehend the object it represents—in coming to perceive Fido this way (and so have the fear) I apprehend the world as I perceive it (even if the world is not such).[44] On all such views, emotions will be special types of value apprehension. But even views that do not identify emotions with evaluative judgements or perceptions may still construe emotions as apprehending their objects or at least their formal objects. Indeed, this is so with Deonna and Teroni's 'attitudinal' account of emotions (2012: ch.7,

---

[43] Here and in what follows I have in mind 'apprehend' in the 'epistemic state' sense I specified in 1.4. Some of these views would also maintain that emotions are modes of apprehension in the 'epistemic access' sense. For the latter, see Müller (2017).

[44] This also holds of Prinz's (2004) 'indirect' perceptualist view, I think. On his view, emotions are bodily perceptions' (60) that represent formal objects insofar as they are 'reliably caused by' and 'set up by' (i.e. have 'the function of being caused by') 'relational properties that pertain to well-being' (66). Insofar as we come to have such a perceptual state, we come to represent the world in terms of the formal object of the particular emotion (62–3) and '[h]aving an emotion is literally perceiving our relationship to the world' (240; see also ch. 10 *passim*).

2014, 2015) considered in 1.5. On their view, emotions apprehend, via their own intentional attitudes, the evaluative property constitutive of the emotion in question (its formal object) to be applying to the particular object of the emotion (as that is apprehended by another intentional state, a 'cognitive base', e.g. judgement, perception, imagination, memory, etc.; see 2012: 5, 69; 2015: 300). Thus, on their view, no less than on those that (in part) identify emotions with evaluative judgements or perceptions, emotions play an important role in apprehending the world around us: they apprehend evaluative features of that world (whether or not it actually possesses them).[45] We might call all such views *apprehender* accounts of emotions.

Aristotle, by contrast, construes emotions as *responses* to intentional states that apprehend their objects, rather than such apprehending intentional states themselves. We might call such a view a *response* account of emotions.[46] On this view, the representational pleasures or distresses of emotions are about their objects *as those objects are apprehended by another intentional state*, and they form *in response to* such a state. We see a good example of the general kind of analysis I have in mind, here, in Aristotle's discussion of two types of *desire* in *NE* VII.6. He writes:

> reason or *phantasia* **informs us** that we have been insulted or slighted, and *thumos*, reasoning as it were that anything like this must be fought against, boils up straightaway; while *epithumia*, if reason or perception merely **says** that an object is pleasant, springs to the enjoyment of it. (1149a32–b1)

Thumos is here presented as a response to something that reason or *phantasia* has informed or *shown* us (*edēlōsen*; the third-person singular aorist of *dēloun*, to make visible, to manifest, show, exhibit, disclose). Similarly, *epithumia* is presented as forming in response to reason or perception telling us (*eipē(i)*, from *eipon*, 'said') something. The desires are not presented as *apprehending* either the particular or the evaluative object they pertain to, but as responses to intentional states that have apprehended such objects.[47] Similarly, as I understand him, Aristotle thinks that emotions are hedonic responses to objects as they are represented by another intentional state (reason, *phantasia*, perception, etc.). We might

---

[45] See also Teroni (2007).

[46] The idea that emotions are responses rather than apprehensions is not without its contemporary parallels. See e.g. Müller (2017, 2019) and Dietz (2018).

[47] See also *De an*. III.10.433b10–12. Although *thumos* and *epithumia* are desires for Aristotle, it is noteworthy that *epithumia* appears on both the *NE* and *EE* lists of emotions (quoted in 2.1) and *thumos* appears on the *EE* list (it seems to replace *orgē*, anger, in the *NE* list). I shall eventually argue (in Part II) that although Aristotle distinguishes desires from emotions, *epithumia* and *thumos* (at least insofar as the latter is synonymous with *orgē*) can count as both (Chapters 6 and 8, for *orgē* and *epithumia*, respectively). Here, I am using them as examples of states that are responses to other intentional states. But the fact that Aristotle views these states themselves as emotions obviously strengthens their importance for us; for the sense in which they are responses applies no less to their being emotions than to their being desires.

judge that someone has suffered some undeserved misfortune and, in response, experience distress (or pleasure) directed at that person's suffering. Or we might perceive that a bus is tearing down on us and, in response, experience urgent distress directed at the danger. In each case, the object of the emotion, what the representational pleasure or distress is about, is, in effect, *imported* from another source, viz. the apprehending intentional state. The representational pleasure or distress does not apprehend an object that we would otherwise not have apprehended. It instead involves us experiencing pleasure or distress at that object.

The view that emotions are representational hedonic responses to other intentional states that apprehend their objects, rather than such apprehending states themselves, has a number of advantages. First, in Chapter 12 I shall explain a significant philosophical advantage such a view has over apprehender views, viz. that it enables us to provide a coherent account of recalcitrant emotions, emotions that persist in light of a contrary judgement. Second, it explains the individuation of the emotions (3.3). The idea that there are different hedonic responses available to the very same object (as apprehended by another intentional state) allows us to distinguish fear from thrill, for example, and pity from schadenfreude. These pairs of emotions can be differentiated by the intentional attitude they possess towards specific manifestations of *the same* formal object as represented in the content.[48] We will have (with 'A' marking the intentional attitude and 'C' the intentional content):

[Fear]: distress (A) that *p* is dangerous (C);
[Thrill]: pleasure (A) that *p* is dangerous (C);

[Pity]: distress (A) that *X* has suffered some undeserved misfortune (C);
[Schadenfreude]: joy (A) that *X* has suffered some undeserved misfortune (C).

Third, the account may have an advantage in explaining the felt nature of occurrent emotions. As representational pleasures or distresses, emotions can be construed as intentional states that represent an intentional object. (This is the *analysis* of emotions that Aristotle is offering; see **1.5**.) In terms of the intentional objects of the above emotions, fear will represent *p*'s being dangerous *as* distressful, thrill will represent *p*'s being dangerous *as* pleasurable, and similarly, *mutatis mutandis*, with pity and schadenfreude. And, in characterizing the above emotions as representing such things *as* distressful (or pleasurable), the account refers to a subject's *feeling distress (or pleasure)* directed at those objects. Analysing emotions in this way thus purports to explain their experiential or felt dimension in a more intuitive way than views that identify them as, for example, judgements or

---

[48] Recall (**1.1**), on the model of intentional states that I am operating with in this book, an intentional state consists of both an intentional attitude and an intentional content and only together do they represent an intentional object.

perceptions (which instead present scenarios as obtaining or appearing to be the case, rather than as distressful or pleasurable as such; see 3.6). Many perceptions and judgements are not felt, so perceptualists and judgementalists have to say that there is something special about the perceptions and judgements that constitute emotions that means these perceptions and judgements *are* felt (see 3.1). Whereas, on Aristotle's view, the fact that *pleasure* or *distress* is the intentional attitude of the intentional state *itself* entails that the object is *found pleasurable* or *distressing*.

The interpretation I have provided also has important implications for understanding Aristotle's picture of the training of our emotional dispositions and, relatedly, the way emotions can impact on our decisions or verdicts (*kriseis*) (as developed in *Rhet.*).[49] These topics ultimately require detailed exploration and examination, which is beyond the scope of this book. But let me at least gesture in the general direction. Consider the contrast between apprehender accounts and the response view I have argued is Aristotle's. On an apprehender view, to change an emotional disposition will require changing the way one is disposed to apprehend an object of emotion. For, on such a view, emotions just are such apprehensions. On a judgementalist view, we would need to change the way we are disposed to judge a situation. If, for instance, one is prone to feel afraid of cats, this would be grounded in the view that cats are dangerous (if danger is the formal object of fear). One would therefore need to change one's tendency to judge that cats are dangerous—perhaps, e.g., one could be *persuaded* that cats are not dangerous and thereby lose the disposition to so judge them. On a perceptualist view, by contrast, going through such a process need have no tangible effect on our emotional state. For unless one ceases to *perceive* cats as dangerous, one's emotional disposition to fear them will remain. Instead, one will require some process that alters one's *perceptual* dispositions. And if (in some or many cases) a change in judgement will not itself achieve this, other forms of habituation may be needed; e.g. repeated exposure under controlled conditions, therapy, hypnosis, etc. Nonetheless, the process has the same *structure* as it does with judgementalism. We have to alter the way we apprehend the situation. And *if* we are successful, this alone will guarantee a change in emotional state.

Now, in **Intro.2** I stated that I am leaving it open in this book whether Aristotle thinks that objects of emotion must be apprehended by one state (judgement, *phantasia*) or whether (in line with the view I favour, but am not here assuming) they can be apprehended by a variety of intentional states. If objects of emotions have to be apprehended by judgements, then a judgement of danger (say) will be necessary for fear. If they have to be apprehended by perception, then an equivalent perceptual state will be requisite. But so too if different intentional states can

---

[49] As representational distresses or pleasures, emotions are also, of course, tied to motivation and to action, without themselves *being* motivational states. I explore this further in Part II and Chapter 11.

apprehend objects of emotion on different occasions (in line with the view I favour).⁵⁰ On this account, no less, there still has *to be* some such apprehending intentional state and, absent it, we will not be able to have the emotion. Crucially, though, on Aristotle's response account of emotions, such an apprehending intentional state is never *sufficient* for an emotion. The intentional state that apprehends the object of the emotion is only one part of the puzzle. Emotions are hedonic *responses* to such apprehensions. Apprehending cats as dangerous does not itself guarantee fear. One can be disposed to judge that cats are dangerous or disposed to perceive them as dangerous (or both) and yet still not be disposed to fear cats. Let us take 'apprehending cats as dangerous' to entail that the subject has the appropriate intentional state to underlie an emotion (whether judgement, perceptual state, or whatever). On Aristotle's response view, only if we are disposed to apprehend cats as dangerous *and* are also disposed to experience distress directed at cats so construed will we be disposed to experience fear of cats. Otherwise, we may experience thrill at cats so apprehended (if we are disposed to experience *pleasure* at (certain things) we apprehend as dangerous), or no emotion at all (cf. *Rhet.* II.9.1386b26–8). This means that *in addition* to a disposition to apprehend the emotion's object a certain way, we also have to have a *hedonic* disposition to experience a representational pleasure or distress directed at objects when they are apprehended that way. This further disposition—which, given the argument of this chapter, *is* the disposition to experience the emotion as such—will most plausibly be understood as an aspect of the subject's *character*.⁵¹ We can see the connection between our emotional dispositions and our character in *Rhet.* II.9:

> the one who is distressed at people undeservedly doing badly [= pity] will be pleased or not pained by their doing badly in the contrary way [= pleasure-based indignation or no hedonic state]—for example, no good person would be distressed at [= pity] parricides and blood-thirsty murderers when they are punished. For one should rejoice in such cases [= pleasure-based indignation], as in the case of those who deservedly do well [= pride-in-another], since both are just things that make a decent person rejoice... And all these belong to the same character, and the contrary ones to the contrary one. For the same person will be prone to schadenfreude (*epichairekakos*) and envy (*phthoneros*), since when

---

⁵⁰ Indeed, on my view the state need not even be perception (conceived of as 'appearance-as-truth') or judgement. It could be perceptual imagination or uncommitted thought (see 3.6). Hence, I ultimately want an even broader notion of 'apprehend' than the epistemic state sense. See 1.4.

⁵¹ Even if an emotion we undergo conflicts with our evaluative judgements, it still thereby points to something significant about us. We are not simply perceiving something a certain way, we are *affected* by that apprehension, whether we judge this reasonable or not. For broad and narrow notions of character, see my 2012 (249–51). For emotions that prompt actions which do not mark us out as a certain person ('character' in the narrow sense), see e.g. *NE* V.6.1134a17–23, V.8.1135b19–25; cf. *EE* II.8.1225a20–33 (and for discussion of these passages, see my 2006).

someone is distressed at the acquisition or possession of something [= envy], he necessarily rejoices at its lack or destruction [= schadenfreude]. (1386b26–32, 1386b33–1387a3; my glosses)

Aristotle here claims that the same underlying disposition could account for different emotions in different situations. Those who are prone to experience pity at undeserved doing-badly will experience pleasure-based indignation (or no hedonic state) at deserved doing-badly; those who are prone to experience envy at someone's deserved doing-well will be prone to schadenfreude at the same person's undeserved doing-badly. Insofar as emotional dispositions are dimensions of our characters, they will be products of our upbringing, education, and habituation. And, clearly, given that they are dispositions to hedonic states, and that these states form in response to certain kinds of apprehension, the development of such emotional dispositions will be a complex process which integrates habituating a disposition to apprehend things a certain way, as well as habituating a disposition to form certain hedonic responses in light of those apprehensions.

As mentioned, I am unable to explore this further here. But I would just like to close by mentioning an implication of this picture for the oratorical manipulation of decisions or verdicts (*kriseis*) via emotions (*Rhet.* II.1.1377b31–1378a5, 1378a19–21).[52] If our hedonic dispositions are bound to our character, an orator is not going to be able to alter our hedonic dispositions simply by argumentation (contra the judgementalist view; cf. *NE* X.9.1179b28–9: 'in general emotion listens not to argument (*logos*) but to force (*bia*)'). This implies, it seems to me, that to employ emotion-arousal as a means of persuasion, orators must first *know their audience*. An example will illustrate this. Suppose Susan, an orator, tries to make the adjudicators in her trial *pity* Kev, her client, by persuading them that Kev has just suffered some undeserved misfortune ('on the way here, he was bitten by a small dog... hasn't he suffered enough?'). If Susan succeeds in arousing pity, this might prompt the adjudicators to go easy on Kev. But suppose Susan has not done her homework and, in fact, is preaching to adjudicators who are prone to schadenfreude. Her persuasion, if successful, will not help Kev one jot. Instead, had she known that the adjudicators are also prone to all manner of fears (they are far from thrill-seekers), a better strategy for her might have been to attempt to persuade them that Kev is a *danger* to them ('Kev *sees* who you all are; others in similar situations have *disappeared* without trace... he has contacts everywhere to do his bidding', etc.).[53] The example illustrates how persuading someone to apprehend a situation a certain way is only going to be helpful against the background

---

[52] For 'decisions and verdicts' as a rendering of *kriseis*, see e.g. *Rhet.* I.3.1358b3–5, 9–10, I.13.1374b19–21.
[53] Cf. *Pol.* V.8.1308a27–30, where Aristotle suggests that those who are concerned about their constitution and seek to make the citizens 'like sentries on night-duty' who 'never relax their guard' should manufacture fears by making 'faraway dangers seem close at hand'.

of certain (assumed) hedonic dispositions. Hence, on this view, public oratory will be more than simply a matter of persuasion. One will need to know the probable underlying hedonic dispositions of the adjudicators or, if one does not, try to ascertain these quickly without cost to the verdict or decision (e.g. by testing the water on some more trivial matter first).

Conclusion

In this chapter I first argued (**4.1**) that the representational pleasure or distress of an Aristotelian emotion is best thought of as forming 'in light of' the intentional state that apprehends its object (rather than merely occurring along with it or being caused by it). I then showed that, strictly speaking, Aristotle thinks that only the pleasure or distress is to be identified with the emotion (**4.2–3**). This means that emotions, as representational pleasures or distresses, form *in response to* intentional states that apprehend their objects. I tried to unpack this idea and explain its significance in the final section (**4.4**). A major philosophical payoff of such an account of emotions will be developed in Chapter 12, in relation to recalcitrant emotions.

The argument of Chapters 2–4 has been worked out with respect to the core set of emotions that clearly involve a distress or pleasure (see **2.3**). But, as is well known, and as I flagged in **2.1**, there are several tricky cases to deal with. In particular, in *Rhet*. II.4 hating (*to misein*) is explicitly said to be 'without pain' (1382a12–13) and, by implication, its contrary, friendly-feeling-towards (*to philein*), would be without pleasure no less. So too, it is unclear with a number of the 'contraries' of the emotions—which, according to the general specification in *Rhet*. II.1 (quoted in **2.1**), would seem themselves to count as emotions—how to specify the pleasure or distress dimension of the state. I return to these states (and some other tricky cases) in Chapters 7 and 10. When I have considered them, I will also address some philosophical objections to the idea that emotions should be characterized as pleasures or distresses, viz. that there can be emotions that involve *both* pleasures *and* distresses and emotions that involve *neither* (**10.9**).

Aristotle on What Emotions Are. Giles Pearson, Oxford University Press. © Giles Pearson 2024.
DOI: 10.1093/9780191989292.003.0005

5
Emotions and the Account(s) of Pleasure in the *Ethics*

I have argued that Aristotle thinks that emotions are representational pleasures or distresses. But he explicitly discusses pleasure both in *Rhet.* (I.11) and in his ethical works (*NE* VII.11–14, X.1–5). Is my reading compatible with those accounts?

The *Rhetoric* presents an interesting interpretative puzzle, which I am not able to pursue in detail here. This stems from the fact that the account of pleasure Aristotle there provides—'a sort of movement of the soul, an intensive and perceptible settling down into its original natural state' (I.11.1369b33–5)—is strongly reminiscent of a Platonic notion of pleasure (found in esp. *Philebus* 31d–32b, also 42c9–d7, 43c4–6; see also *Timaeus* 64c7–d3). This is *prima facie* problematic for two reasons. First, Aristotle appears to reject such a view in his ethical works (esp. *NE* VII.12.1152b33–1153a17, X.3.1173a29–1173b20).[1] Second, he seems to associate the pleasures that do ('incidentally': *NE* VII.12.1152b34–5) connect up with processes of replenishment with bodily pleasures, especially those connected to nutrition (*NE* X.3.1173b7–20, cf. III.11.1118b8–21), and yet in *Rhet.* I.11 he includes a much wider range of pleasures (some examples below).

There have been a number of proposals to deal with the problem. Aristotle's discussion, here, is intended to provide material for enthymemes (rhetorical arguments). He is not, as he is in his *Rhet.* II discussion of emotions, seeking to enable the orator to engender pleasure or pain in an audience. Perhaps, then, the Platonic view could serve as a background theory for popular conceptions of pleasure that will be encountered in what follows (Rapp 2002: 463).[2] Or perhaps

---

[1] He also shows awareness of objections to the idea that pleasure could be any kind of movement (*kinēsis*) in his early *Topics* (IV.1.121a30–9), which undermines a developmentalist hypothesis to explain the problem. See Rapp (2002: 461–2); Price (2017: 185); cf. Frede (1996: 260). Reeve suggests that although the distinction between a movement and an activity is fundamental to Aristotle's philosophy (see esp. *Met.* Θ.6), the two are intimately connected (citing *Met.* Θ.3.1047a30–2, where Aristotle claims that the word 'actuality' (*energeia*) has been extended from movement to other things, for 'actuality in the strict sense is identified with movement'), and so we might 'accept the claim that "pleasure is *sort of* movement of the soul", as one Aristotle would himself accept—certainly for rhetorical purposes' (2018: 226, Reeve's emphasis). (Cf. also Dow (2015: 175–6) on the use of *tina* ('sort of') in the *Rhet.* I.11 definition.) But even if this is right, Aristotle would seem to view replenishment pleasures as limited (my second problematic reason).

[2] Rapp offers this as a modification of Gosling and Taylor's suggestion (1982: 196–9) that Aristotle employs a commonly accepted view which is close enough to the truth to suit the orator's needs. That view will not quite do as the definition looks more Platonic than popular (see Rapp 2002: 462–3; Price 2017: 185–6).

Aristotle may have considered the definition only a starting point and envisaged 'no unifying conception [of different kinds of pleasure] beyond a family resemblance whereby new types of pleasure relate, closely or loosely, to old ones' (Price 2017: 186).³ Or, again, it has been suggested that there are already representational elements inherent in the definition itself (Dow 2015: 163–76). On this view, the definition 'characterizes pleasure experiences as involving the representation of the subject as undergoing a restoration of their nature' (172).⁴ This is then extended to cases in which we take pleasure *at* an object we encounter (172–3).⁵

The point I would like to emphasize, though, is that however we resolve this it is tolerably clear that even in this chapter Aristotle intends to accommodate the representational pleasures or distresses of emotions we find in book II. Perhaps the clearest example of this is when, in connection with 'mourning and lamentation for a departed one' (*en penthesi kai thrēnois*), he refers to the subject as experiencing 'distress at (*epi* + dative) his not being there and pleasure in (*en* + dative) remembering him and, in a way, seeing him, the actions he was doing, and what he was like' (1370b26–8). But we also have angry people enjoying anticipating getting revenge (1370b31–2; more on this in **6.5**); people taking pleasure in the appearance of superiority that results from victory (some kind of pride) (1370b32–4); and finding honour and good reputation pleasant insofar as they result in the appearance that we have the qualities of an excellent person (taking pleasure in our (putative) excellent qualities) (1371a8–9). So whether we somehow try to view such cases as falling under the definition (difficult, but see Dow 2015: 163–76 for an attempt) or as extending (further, see n.5) the definition to other loosely related notions of pleasure or pain through a series of steps by family resemblance (as Price suggests), the chapter does explicitly recognize the representational pleasures and distresses that I have argued are integral to his account of the emotions.⁶ In this sense, at least, that discussion is unproblematic.

If we turn to Aristotle's official account(s) of pleasure in the ethical works, in one sense these too may appear unproblematic. This is because Aristotle is there clearly concerned with a different kind of pleasure, namely pleasure connected to 'activities'. I shall return to the 'connection' in question in **5.1**, but what sort of activities did he have in mind? Some think that they are to be identified with the

---

³ Price sees this as following the *Philebus* since, on his reading, the latter should be construed as 'offering a developing characterization of pleasure that branches and spreads, rather than a single identification of it with a process of restoration' (2017: 186).

⁴ Dow (2015: 168–70) appeals especially to *Timaeus* 61c–68d to support this.

⁵ Dow (2015: 166–8) notes that even to accommodate Aristotle's first examples we need to extend the strict process account. Aristotle claims, e.g., that habits are pleasant (1370a5–6) and justifies this by noting that habits are 'something like' (*homoion*) nature, since what happens often (= habit) is close to what happens always (= nature) (1370a6–9). This already extends the definition, which refers simply to a natural state, not things 'like' or 'similar to' a natural state. Dow takes the extension to suggest that the definition is intended more broadly. But one might just as well take it to support Price's idea.

⁶ This can be combined with Rapp's idea that the initial definition provides a background theory for popular conceptions, as I think Price intends his suggestion.

activities of thinking and perceiving (Bostock 2000: 160–3; Heinaman 2011: 8 and 8n.1; cf. Heinaman 1990: 92–8), others extend them to include exercising one's capacities (Taylor 2003: 14–15) which allows an enjoying of action. Anthony Price thinks that 'whenever one is enjoying anything, one is enjoying a thinking or perceiving' (2017: 200), but allows that one can also, in so doing, take pleasure in action (e.g. 'take pleasure in the thought of acting nobly' (202)).[7] Uncontroversially, though, 'activities' at least includes the activities of perceiving and thinking. But, with respect to our concerns, pleasures connected to, say, the activity of a sense organ in relation to a particularly fine sensory object (*NE* X.4.1174b18–23), or enjoying geometrical thinking (*NE* X.5.1175a32–3), seem different kinds of pleasure to the representational pleasures of emotions which, as we have seen, are not pleasures or pains flowing from such activities (of sense or thought), but pleasures or distresses *about* certain (evaluative) objects (as those are *represented* through some intentional state, such as perception or thought).[8] And, evidently, Aristotle may not have considered the latter sorts of pleasures or distresses to fall under his general account(s) in the ethical works or, indeed, even registered the idea of doing so.

Nonetheless, since these accounts, unlike the one in *Rhet*. I.11, are official ones that Aristotle explicitly endorses, and since pleasures in activities and the representational pleasures of emotions are each supposedly genuine cases of pleasure, it would be encouraging if the account(s) we find in the ethical works could, if extended, be seen as compatible with the representational pleasures of emotions. And, as we shall see, this is far from trivially so. This, then, is my topic in this chapter. I first consider and reject the idea that pleasures *just are* activities (5.1). I then outline and respond to two objections that might be levelled against the idea that Aristotle's view of emotions, as I have developed it, can be compatible with the account of pleasure we find in *NE* X (if we extend the latter to emotions). The first (discussed in 5.2–3) concerns the idea that even without *identifying* pleasures and activities in *NE* X, the connection he specifies between the two is still too tight for his account of the emotions. The second (addressed in 5.4–5) pertains to defective pleasures. I close by considering what Aristotle might mean in claiming that pleasure 'perfects' activity and how, on at least one plausible interpretation, this may enable him to give an account of the phenomenological or felt dimension of an occurrent emotion (5.6).

---

[7] Part of the issue here concerns accommodating Aristotle's claim that pleasure is not a process (*genesis*) (*NE* VII.12.1153a9–10, X.3.1173b4–20; and see e.g. Price 2017: 197–200). In *NE* X he gives the following examples of pleasures; enjoying geometrical thinking (5.1175a32–3), music (5.1175a34), building (5.1175a34), acting virtuously (3.1173a15, b29–31, 1174a6–8), or playing the flute (5.1175b3–6); and he refers to pains connected to writing and doing sums (5.1175b18–20). Price (2017: 200) also points to Aristotle's examples of playing dice and hunting in *NE* IX.12.1172a4.

[8] See also Dow (2015: 162–3).

5.1 Pleasures as activities

In *NE* VII.12 Aristotle may appear to specify pleasure as an 'unimpeded activity of a natural state' (1153a13–15). But if pleasures *are* activities (e.g. kinds of thinking or perceiving) then, extended to the account of the emotions, representational pleasures and pains would simply *be* perceptual states or thoughts. This is surely why Dow appeals to the *NE* VII.12 claim in support of his Identification reading of Aristotle (as sketched in 3.1). He claims that his interpretation more easily accommodates 'the insight that enjoying something is not something over and beyond that thing' (citing *NE* VII.12.1153a7–17). Instead, pleasure is 'an attribute of one's doing it, or some feature of the manner in which it is done' (2015: 176).[9]

However, if an implication of the view that pleasures or pains are themselves activities (and so types of perceiving or thinking) would be that emotions, as pleasures or pains, should be identified with the intentional state that apprehends the object of the emotion, then my argument in Chapter 3 suggests that Aristotle would have to reject the idea that pleasures or pains are themselves activities (or else he could reject the implication, and treat the two types of pleasure/pain as distinct). For, as we there saw, Aristotle appears to think that two agents can experience diametrically opposed emotions in response to the very same intentional state that apprehends the object of the emotion (e.g. pity or schadenfreude in response to perceiving that someone has suffered some undeserved misfortune).

Perhaps it might be proposed that we can accommodate this by identifying the pleasure with *another* thought or perceiving: not the one that apprehends the object of the emotion, but one that forms in response to that intentional state? But besides it being unclear what could confirm such a reading, or why Aristotle would be motivated to advance the view, such an interpretation faces the problem that in *NE* X.5 Aristotle *explicitly rejects* the idea that pleasures are to be identified with thoughts and perceptions.[10] He writes:

> [A] Pleasures involved in activities...are close to the activities, and so hard to distinguish from them that it admits of dispute whether the activity is not the same as the pleasure. Still, pleasure does not seem to *be* thought or perception— that would be strange; but because they are not found apart they appear to some people the same. (1175b30, 32–5)[11]

---

[9] It is still a little odd that Dow appeals to the *NE* VII account of pleasure at this point in support of his Identification view since he had earlier claimed: 'It does not seem to me that the accounts of pleasure and pain from the ethical treatises can be easily reinterpreted so as to accommodate the kinds of pain under discussion [viz. in Aristotle's account of the emotions]' (2015: 162).

[10] The reading would also lose the philosophical advantage that stemmed from *not* identifying pleasure with the intentional state that apprehends the object of the emotion, highlighted in 3.6.

[11] Owen (1971–2: 146) thought that this passage stands in tension with the book VII account, even though on his view the two treatments were answering different questions (see below). Gosling and Taylor (1982: 207) point out that if Owen is right on the latter, the passage cannot stand in tension. I think this is the right response. But Gosling and Taylor (207–8) also mention the idea that perhaps

Instead, in book X Aristotle characterizes pleasure as something that 'perfects' an activity (X.4.1174b23–33).[12] In light of the apparent discrepancy between books VII and X, many commentators have sought to clarify the aims of book VII. It is notable that it is only in book X that Aristotle explicitly formulates the question 'What *is* pleasure?' (4.1174b13); while book VII is compatible with him there instead seeking to characterize *pleasures*, that is, things we find pleasant.[13] The idea that we find unimpeded activities pleasant (book VII) is clearly compatible with the view that pleasure itself is not an activity itself, but something that perfects it (book X).

In any event, in line with [A], I shall from now on assume that Aristotle does not wish to identify pleasure as an activity and hence that my reading of his account of the emotions—which blocks the identification of emotions with thoughts and perceivings—is not *in this respect* incompatible with the account of pleasure in the *Ethics*.

5.2 The 'same activity, same pleasure' objection

One might still worry that Aristotle's account of pleasure in *NE* X connects the activity and the pleasure too closely for his account of the emotions, as I have developed the latter. For it might seem that he there holds that the very same perceptual or thought-based activity entails the very same hedonic result. In *NE* X.4 he claims:

> [B] in the case of each sense the best activity is that of the best-conditioned organ in relation to the finest of its objects. And this activity will be the most complete and pleasant. For, while there is pleasure in respect of any sense, and in respect of thought (*dianoia*) and contemplation (*theōria*) no less, the most

---

Aristotle only meant that it would be strange to say that perception or thinking *in general* is a pleasure (which would be compatible with book VII, since that insists they must also be impeded and of a natural state). This reading has been accepted by some subsequent commentators (e.g. Harte 2014: 312–3n.30). But it seems improbable. In the last clause of the passage Aristotle is surely referring to the thoughts and perceptions he had in mind in the previous clause, and yet he claims that *they* are not found apart (from pleasures). So, in the previous clause he cannot have meant 'thought and perception *in general*' (for perceptions and thoughts in general are not bound to pleasures; some are bound to pains, some are ahedonic). In any event, as noted, we do not need such a reading to avoid the tension Owen found—which, given his own account, is not there.

[12] On some readings of the bloom of youth parallel (quoted at the start of **5.6**), perfecting an activity might amount to little more than the activity itself; e.g. Gosling and Taylor (1982: 212) who take the parallel to refer to *the springtime of youth* supervening on *those in their prime*. However, as Price (2017: 191) notes: 'It could indeed be said that a springtime is added to *human beings* as they reach their prime. Yet to say that it supervenes upon *men in their prime* would be as odd to say…that the circle supervenes not only on *bronze*, but upon *bronze circle*. Hence we cannot identify the *hora* with the *akmē* of *hoi akmaioi*. Rather, it must be something extra that their *akmē* brings with it' (my emphases).

[13] See esp. Owen (1971–2); also e.g. Pakaluk (2005: ch. 10); Harte (2014: 309–14); Price (2017: 189–90).

complete is pleasant, and that of a well-conditioned organ in relation to the worthiest of its objects is the most complete. (1174b18–23)

Here we have a connection between 'subject' (sense, thinker, contemplator) and 'object' (something sensed, thought of, contemplated). And Aristotle holds that the best activity of the best subject in relation to the best objects will be most complete and pleasant. But a little later he claims that in such a scenario pleasure *must* ensue:

[C] when both sense-object and perceiver are of the best, there will always be pleasure, since the requisite agent and patient are both present. (1174b29–31)

Furthermore, while the conjunction of [B] and [C] only establishes a connection between the *best* subject/object combinations and the corresponding *best* pleasures, Aristotle seems happy to generalize a little further on:

[D] So long, then, as both the intelligible or sensible object and the discriminating or contemplative faculty are as they should be, the pleasure will be involved in the activity; for when both the passive and active factor are unchanged and related to each other in the same way, the same result naturally follows. (1174b33–1175a3)

The last part of this is particularly telling. Whereas in [B] and [C] Aristotle clearly had the best exemplifications of pleasure in mind, we now see that his point is intended to have very general application: whenever our perception/thought and their objects relate to each other in the same way, we naturally get the very same hedonic result (whether pleasure or pain).

But then this view would not seem extendable to Aristotle's account of the emotions. For, according to the latter, *both* pleasure *and* distress can (in different people) be bound to the *very same* perception or thought (e.g. pity *or* schadenfreude can be experienced in response to perceiving/judging that someone has suffered some undeserved misfortune). But here he appears to deny just this. When the same capacity is coupled with the same object, the same hedonic response seems to be entailed. Let us call this the 'same activity, same pleasure' objection to the idea that Aristotle's account of emotions is compatible with his view of pleasure in *NE* X.

5.3 Two responses to the same activity, same pleasure objection

Joachim Aufderheide (2016) suggests that the connection between 'subject' and 'object' in Aristotle's claim in [C] should be understood only *ceteris paribus*. On this view, the virtuous person will enjoy the perceptions and thoughts integral to virtuous actions *unless something interferes* (300; my emphasis). The *ceteris paribus* qualification needs to be assumed, Aufderheide insists, because:

> although a lover of *x* should enjoy *x*-ing, she may on occasion fail to do so because factors not related to the act may interfere with the agent's enjoyment. For instance, a virtuous person, a lover of the fine, may not enjoy her virtuous action because of severe bodily pain...pleasure is not conceptually guaranteed even if a lover engages in a beloved activity. The lover's character guarantees the pleasure (and other responses)—*as long as nothing psychologically interferes*. (300; my emphasis)

The idea is that if an agent is, e.g., in severe bodily pain then even perfectly operating perceptual/thought-based activity in light of the very best objects need not result in the pleasure in question (the most complete one). And, on this view, the interfering bodily pain can be independent of the perceiving/thinking even though it undermines the latter's ability to generate pleasure, such that the very same act of perceiving/thinking that would bring about pleasure if the pain were not present, will now fail to do so. If this is correct, Aristotle cannot be intending his claim in [C] as a conceptual truth.

If Aufderheide's interpretation of *NE* X is right, my reading of Aristotle's account of the emotions could potentially resist the same activity, same pleasure objection. The connection between an intentional state apprehending someone as having suffered some undeserved misfortune, on the one hand, and a corresponding distress, on the other, would only be *ceteris paribus*. We would be able to have the very same perception/belief of the suffering, without the distress, *if something 'interfered'*. Clearly, a further story would then have to be told about how, and why, say, a person's having a different character (see 4.4)—one which disposes her to take pleasure in such a circumstance—would sensibly count as 'interference'. But at least there would be a gap between the perceiving/thinking and the pleasure or distress that we could attempt to exploit. (Bear in mind we are considering the *extension* of the account in *NE* X to incorporate representational pleasures or distresses; the former is not specifically set up to accommodate them.)

However, Aufderheider's interpretation has been challenged (Price 2017: 194). In [C] Aristotle claims that when both object and perceiver are of the best, there will *always* be pleasure. He thus seems keen to stress precisely what, given Aufderheider's reading, he should not, viz. that pleasure will always ensue if the perceiving/thinking and the object perceived/thought are as they should be. And yet the sort of example Aufderheider mentions clearly needs dealing with. The obvious alternative is to maintain that the pain that Aufderheider envisages to be hindering the pleasure would only do so if (and to the extent that) it in some way hinders the subject from apprehending the object in question. In other words, one might suggest that in such a case the agent would not count as perceiving *the very same object*. This is Anthony Price's (2017) view. After noting that the word 'always', in [C], shows that Aristotle intends 'a stronger relation' than Aufderheide proposed, Price suggests:

> it seems better to suppose that the reference to the subject and object is now imprecise, and actually takes in an indefinite range of conditions that extends beyond what intuitively count as qualities of organ or object. A reluctant piece of perceiving can count as impeded if one has to *force* oneself to persevere; and a competing pleasure can have much the same effect as a proper pain (X.5.1175b16–17, 22–3). Thus the operation of a sense in good condition towards the best of its objects is naturally enjoyable—and *will* be enjoyed if there is no distraction or other impediment. (194)

On this view, the very same 'subject' and 'object' will not count as in play unless the same hedonic quality results, but an indefinite range of background conditions will have to be met for the same subject-object relation *to be* in play. On Price's reading, then, we do not say, with Aufderheide, that the same subject-object relation only *ceteris paribus* brings about pleasure. We instead say that lots of conditions have to be met for us to have the very same subject-object relation in play in the first place, but that when such conditions are met, the pleasure is guaranteed.

The latter reading seems preferable insofar as it accounts for the 'always' in [C]. But is *it* compatible with one person experiencing pleasure and another distress in response to the very same perceiving/thinking, as required by Aristotle's theory of emotions? On my view, it depends on how that reading is fleshed out. In particular, we need to see how Aristotle would apply the account to *defective* pleasures/pains.

5.4 The defective-pleasures objection

In *NE* X.5 Aristotle writes:

> [E] Now since activities differ in respect of goodness and badness, and some are worthy to be chosen, others to be avoided, and others neutral, so, too, are the pleasures; for to each activity there is a proper pleasure. The pleasure proper to a worthy activity is good and that proper to an unworthy activity bad…As activities are different, then, so too are the corresponding pleasures. Now sight is superior to touch in purity, and hearing and smell to taste; the pleasures, therefore, are similarly superior, and those of thought superior to these, and within each of these two kinds some are superior to others. (1175b24–8, 1175b36–1176a3)

As with the *NE* X.4 passages (5.2), it might seem that Aristotle is here claiming that for each activity there is a corresponding pleasure, and that the hedonic response only varies with a different activity. Applied to the emotions, this would entail that if two people perceive/think that another has suffered some undeserved misfortune (= same activity), the same hedonic response *must* result. And that would not make room for both pity (= distress) and schadenfreude (= pleasure) as possible responses.

However, Aristotle cannot mean that the same activity entails the same hedonic response in [E]. For, immediately after [E], he notes that while each animal 'is thought to have a proper pleasure, as it has a proper function—viz. that which corresponds to its activity' (1176a3–5)[14]—nonetheless 'in the case of men at least', pleasures 'vary to no small extent' (1176a10). For:

> [F] the same things delight some people and pain others, and are painful and odious to some, and pleasant to and liked by others. (1176a10–12)

On the surface, this would appear to say that the same activity might issue in a different hedonic response depending on what kind of person is in play. Applied to the emotions this would mean that in response to the very same perceiving/thinking (viz. that someone has suffered some undeserved misfortune) a virtuous person could experience pity, a vicious one schadenfreude. If so, [E] would have to be understood against the background of the relevant people involved. Aristotle would be referring to the pleasure proper to a worthy activity *as that would be experienced by a virtuous person*, and to the pleasure proper to an unworthy activity *as that would be experienced by a vicious person*. That way, he could allow that the very same worthy activity might be experienced as either painful or pleasant for opposed agents. Indeed, in line with these glosses, we might note that it is not as if virtuous agents would take pleasure in performing the actions vicious agents perform, nor vice versa (see esp. *NE* II.3.1104b3–13).

However, we might not be out of the woods yet. After [F], Aristotle writes:

> [G] This happens, too, in the case of sweet things; the same things do not seem sweet to a man in fever and a healthy man—nor hot to a weak man and one in good condition. The same happens in other cases. But in all such matters that which appears to the good man is thought to be really so. If this is correct, as it seems to be, and virtue and the good man as such are the measure of each thing, those also will be pleasures which appear so to him, and those things pleasant which he enjoys. If the things he finds tiresome seem pleasant to someone, that

---

[14] As can also be seen if we survey them species by species: 'horse, dog, and man have different pleasures, as Heraclitus says "asses would prefer sweepings to gold"; for food is pleasanter than gold to asses' (1176a5–9).

is nothing surprising; for men may be ruined and spoilt in many ways; but the things are not pleasant, but only pleasant to these people and to people in this condition. Those which are admittedly disgraceful plainly should not be said to be pleasures, except to a perverted taste. (1176a12–24)

This gives a gloss on 'same things' in [F] which could be problematic for us. On the account we have provided, Aristotle thinks that virtuous and vicious agents could form opposed emotions in response to the very same perceiving/thinking that someone has suffered some undeserved misfortune. [F] seemed compatible with this since it allowed the 'same things' to be pleasurable to some and distressful to others. But [G] might appear to restrict the sense in which the things in question are 'the same'. While they are clearly the same under *some* description, the question is whether they are *encountered as* the same by people who have different hedonic responses. And [G] may suggest otherwise. While the same food might *look* the same both to a person in a fever and to a healthy person, it will be perceived differently by them *when tasted*; as, say, sweet to someone healthy, sour to someone feverish. But, carried over to the emotions, this would suggest that while Aristotle could allow that both vicious and virtuous agents might see the same event occur (someone fall over and hurt herself, say), they might not see that event under the same evaluative description. And yet it is *just that latter sameness* that is required for virtuous and vicious agents to be able to form opposed emotions (pity, schadenfreude) in response to the *very same* perceiving/thinking. For the intentional state that apprehends the object of the emotion apprehends it evaluatively (as an *undeserved suffering*, or some such).

Concerning defective pleasures, Anthony Price (2017: 197) draws our attention both to the first half of [E] and also to the following passage:

[H] those things are both valuable and pleasant which are such to the good man; and to each man the activity in accordance with his own state is most desirable, and therefore to the good man that which is in accordance with virtue. (*NE* X.6.1176b25–7)

Price elaborates on both passages as follows:

To the short-sighted subject, fitting objects are close and medium-sized; to the subject who is hard of hearing, they are loud, while to the sufferer from hyperacusis they are soft. What is required is a correspondence between subject and object...such that his sense-organs can function in a way that best approximates to that of the normal subject. (Nowadays we have spectacles, hearing aids, and earplugs all carefully calibrated to bring this about artificially.) In the case of action, virtuous or vicious, we can say something that is loosely analogous: vicious action is pleasant to the vicious agent to the extent that he stands to it as the virtuous agent stands to virtuous action—which, in Aristotle's view, will be imperfectly. (197)[15]

On this model, the subject-object relations that generate pleasure are established by well-functioning organs and if a defective organ is to experience something approximating to the pleasure that a well-functioning organ experiences, the object will have to be altered accordingly, so that an equivalent subject-object relation emerges. Those who are short-sighted, for instance, will have to move the object closer to them (or themselves closer to the object). In the very same conditions, then, a well-functioning organ and a defective organ will not be assured the same hedonic result. For although the object is the same in both cases, the *intentional* object is not: the intentional object that the defective organ encounters will be one that a well-functioning organ would encounter in different conditions (if the object were considerably further away, for example), under which it may not be pleasant at all. Indeed, what a well-functioning organ finds pleasant may well be found *unpleasant* by a defective organ. If that happened, the intentional object generated by the subject-object relation would be equivalent to the intentional object a well-functioning organ would encounter when it experiences something painful. Similarly, in the 'loosely analogous' case of virtuous and vicious actions. Here, too, the subject-object relation that generates pleasure in objects of a certain quality in the virtuous person will have to be replicated (by adjustments in the object) if the vicious agent is to experience something approximating to that very same pleasure. Again, then, in the very same conditions a virtuous and a vicious agent will clearly not be guaranteed the same hedonic result. For, as with the sensory case, their intentional objects will differ and the intentional object that the vicious agent would encounter will approximate to one that the virtuous agent would encounter in a different situation. To the self-indulgent agent, for example, the amount of food and drink that the temperate agent finds *excessive* may appear *just right*. And when faced with what the temperate agent counts as *just the right* amount of food and drink, the self-indulgent agent may deem that *meagre*.[16] And, as is clear from this example, what a virtuous agent finds pleasant may well be found *unpleasant* by the vicious agent. If that happened, the inten-

---

[15] Price (197) goes on to explain: 'He may engage in it keenly, and he may have the satisfaction of achieving things he intends to achieve. Yet he will fail, as we may put it, to *identify* fully with what he does. His pleasures will come into conflict since they are unnatural (I.8.1099a11–13), and he will be full of regrets (IX.4.1166b5–25). Aristotle ascribes this to his being "thoroughly bad and impious" (1166b5). It equally comes of his being human, and so (if he is not brutish, cf. VII.6.1149b27–1150a8) partly good'.

[16] Cf. *NE* II.8: 'the courageous man appears rash relatively to the coward, and cowardly relatively to the rash man; and similarly the temperate man appears self-indulgent relatively to the insensible man, insensible relatively to the self-indulgent, and the generous man wasteful relatively to the stingy man, stingy relatively to the wasteful. Hence also the people at the extremes push the intermediate man each over to the other, and the courageous man is called rash by the coward, cowardly by the rash man, and correspondingly in the other cases' (1108b19–26).

tional object generated by the subject-object relation in vicious agents would be equivalent to the intentional object virtuous agents encounter when they experience something as painful.

But then, once again, Aristotle's account of the emotions would seem incompatible with the view of pleasure so fleshed out. For, according to the model just sketched, virtuous and vicious agents always take pleasure in (something approximating to) the very same intentional objects. They differ only in that such intentional objects are generated in them by their encountering different things. Both those who are temperate and those who are self-indulgent will take pleasure in what they view as the right amount of food, but the amount in question will vary considerably. But if virtuous and vicious agents always take pleasure in (something approximating to) the same intentional objects, there would seem to be no room for two agents to experience diametrically opposed emotions in response to the *very same* intentional state; no room, that is, for two different agents both to perceive someone as suffering some undeserved misfortune (same intentional object), but one to experience pity, the other schadenfreude (different hedonic responses).

It is worth stressing why this result cannot be taken as indirect support for an Identification reading of Aristotle (3.1). Advocates of that view might suggest that we should embrace the above implications and say that Aristotle would insist that there must be some difference in the apprehending intentional state if there is to be a different hedonic result (for, on their view, these are two ways of referring to the very same state). Unfortunately, though, with regard to the emotions, restricting ourselves to this model of defective pleasures implies something that Aristotle would view as absurd. Suppose two people—one virtuous, one vicious—encounter the same situation. Perhaps David comes off his bike rather nastily and looks to be in considerable discomfort. If the virtuous person experiences distress at that situation and the vicious person pleasure, the above model implies that they must in fact have different intentional objects in view. Well, so be it, you might say. But the model also implies that the vicious person must apprehend an intentional object that, were the virtuous person to encounter it, would generate pleasure. And yet given that David has clearly fallen heavily off his bike and is writhing in pain, what pleasure-based emotion might a *virtuous* agent experience directed at *that*? In fact, there is one possibility. In *Rhet.* II.9 Aristotle claims that good or decent people will experience pleasure at *deserved* misfortune (1386b27–30), an emotion he elsewhere characterizes as a kind of indignation (*EE* III.7.1233b23–5).[17] But then, applying the model above, we would be forced to say that rather than experiencing schadenfreude (joy at David's undeserved

---

[17] 'For the one who is pained at people undeservedly doing-badly will be pleased or not pained by their doing-badly in the contrary way—for example, no good person would be distressed at parricides and blood-thirsty murderers when they are punished. For one should rejoice in such cases, as in the case of those who deservedly do well, since both are just things that make a decent person rejoice' (*Rhet.* II.9.1386b26–32).

misfortune), our vicious agent actually experiences mistaken pleasure-based indignation (joy at David's deserved misfortune). This seems bizarre enough, but there is worse to come. For the model under review would also be committed to claiming that *vicious* people can *never* experience schadenfreude. For Aristotle is very clear that this is not an emotion a *virtuous* agent would ever feel:

> not...every emotion admits of a mean; for some have names that already imply badness; e.g. schadenfreude, shamelessness, and envy...for all of these and suchlike things imply by their names that they are themselves bad, and not the excesses of deficiencies of them. It is not possible, then, ever to be right with regard to them; one must always be wrong. (*NE* II.6.1107a8–15)

If, then, schadenfreude necessarily involves experiencing pleasure at someone having suffered some underserved misfortune (and see **Cat.18** for evidence Aristotle thinks so), a vicious person could never experience it. For, on the model we are considering, whenever vicious people experience pleasure, they encounter (something approximating to) the intentional object that virtuous people would experience were they confronted by something that warrants pleasure. But there are *no* cases in which a virtuous agent would experience the pleasure of schadenfreude. And yet it would clearly be ludicrous to suggest that no one can experience schadenfreude or, indeed, envy—for the same would apply, *mutatis mutandis*, to it too—and clearly ludicrous (given that he explicitly specifies both emotions and, indeed, devotes a whole chapter to envy) to suggest Aristotle thinks this. So, contra the Identification view, it needs to be possible for virtuous and vicious agents to experience contrary hedonic emotional responses to the very same apprehension of the situation.

5.5 A reply to the defective-pleasures objection

Are we, then, forced to admit that Aristotle's understanding of defective pleasures in *NE* X.5 shows that his account of pleasure in *NE* X cannot be applied to his view of the emotions? In fact, I think that seeing the problem emerge in this way should prompt us to reconsider whether Aristotle is really committed to the picture of defective pleasures we have sketched. Or, rather, it is not that there *cannot* be defective pleasures as spelt out by Price, along the lines of [E] or [H] (and suggested, too, by the example in [G] of sweet things appearing different to healthy people and those in a fever). It is instead the idea that such a model constitutes *the only way* an agent can experience a defective pleasure or pain that should be questioned.[18]

---

[18] It is unclear that Price is committed to this, but he offers no other model for defective pleasures.

All Aristotle actually claims in [D] is that the same subject-object relation entails the same hedonic result. In modern parlance we can refer to this as an instance of supervenience. *A* supervenes on *B* just in case the same *B* entails the same *A* (though not vice versa) or, equivalently, that there can be no change in *A* without a change in *B* (though not vice versa). If some particular pleasure supervenes on some particular subject-object relation, this means that every time we get that particular subject-object relation we must have that particular pleasure or, equivalently, that we cannot cease to have that particular pleasure without there being some change in the subject-object relation. *However*, given that the pleasure is said to supervene on the subject-object relation *as a whole*, a change in *either* the subject *or* the object could be sufficient for a different hedonic output. In line with this, then, [G] need not be taken *to restrict* the way in which [F] can apply, but just to provide one sort of case. *Sometimes* a different hedonic output will ensue because we encounter the same thing under a different description (as with the sweet case in [G]). But this is compatible with the idea that *at other times* a different hedonic output ensues *even though* the object is encountered under *the very same* description. For, so long as *the subject* is sufficiently altered, we will still have a different subject-object relation.

Thus, we do not have to assume that in order to experience a defective pleasure, vicious agents must in some way replicate the subject-object relation of virtuous agents, so that they, in effect, possess the same intentional state as the latter. Their different constitution can *itself* account for why they might not have the same hedonic response as virtuous agents. Granted, *virtuous agents* cannot ever experience schadenfreude. If they encounter someone they perceive as having suffered some underserved misfortune then, given their constitution, they could only experience distress at that situation, viz. *pity* for the person in question. But there is nothing ruling out *vicious agents* from experiencing schadenfreude. They can perceive the situation in the very same way as virtuous agents, i.e. see the same person as having suffered some underserved misfortune, but, because they have a different character, experience pleasure directed at that situation.[19] Nothing in Aristotle's discussion of pleasure in *NE* X, so far as I can see, rules out this option.

On this reading, we can say that pleasures (or distresses) supervene on a subject-object combination, where the 'object' is an 'intentional object'. And if two people encounter the same situation, but have different hedonic responses, there could be two different reasons for this:

---

[19] Relatedly, in *NE* III.2 Aristotle notes that we cannot simply identify those who make the best choices with those who have the best opinions (1112a9) since 'some people form better opinions but, owing to vice, choose what they should not' (1112a10–11). If vicious agents can form the right opinion about a situation, but still choose acts that they should not, they can also view a situation in the same way as virtuous agents but, owing to vice, experience a different emotion about it.

(1) The fact that they are different subjects may mean that they encounter different intentional objects when they enter into this subject-object relation. This is the model suggested by Price's analysis of [E] and [H]. The fact that the amount of food that a temperate agent would find *ample* would be found *meagre* by the self-indulgent agent will account for their different hedonic responses upon eating the very same amount of food.

Alternatively:

(2) The fact that they are different subjects may mean they have different hedonic responses directed at the very same intentional object. This is the case that I have highlighted with the virtuous experiencing pity, the vicious schadenfreude, in response to the very same intentional object.[20]

Both sorts of case are compatible with the supervenience relation stated in [D] and, if Aristotle's account of pleasure in *NE* X is to be compatible with his account of the emotions, *NE* X should be taken to allow both.[21]

Thus, to answer the question posed at the end of 5.3, I think we can endorse Price's response to the 'same activity, same pleasure' objection so long as we flesh it out in a way that permits both (1) *and* (2) above and does not restrict us to (1) alone.

5.6 Pleasures as 'perfecting' activities

If Aristotle's account of pleasure in *NE* X can be viewed as consistent with his account of the emotions, let us now briefly consider what he means there by claiming that pleasure 'perfects' the activity.[22] For, applied to emotions as representational pleasures or distresses, this may be able to give us a sense in which occurrent emotions are phenomenologically 'felt' states. The key lines, of course, are in *NE* X.4:

---

[20] There will be *a sense* in which virtuous and vicious agents represent the same situation (the undeserved misfortune) differently. They will either represent the intentional object so apprehended as pleasurable (vicious) or distressful (virtuous). (And it is in this that their distress or joy *consists*: to be distressed or joyful about some situation is to represent that situation as distressful or joyful.) But this is compatible with virtuous and vicious agents apprehending the object in question *in the very same way*. For their pleasure or distress is a *response* to that apprehending (the perceiving/thinking) and involves a further representation.

[21] Cases of the second kind are required by his understanding of pity and schadenfreude (and the other cases discussed in **3.5**), as well as the *NE* III.2 passage in n.19. Cases of the first kind are required by his claim that actions of the courageous appear rash to the cowardly (see n.16) and suggested by [G]. Allowing the second kind will permit Aristotle to say that adulterers can take pleasure in their adulterous acts *as such*, without somehow taking themselves to be acting virtuously.

[22] I use 'perfects' (*teleioi*) rather than 'completes' following Strohl (2011) and Price (2017).

pleasure perfects the activity. But pleasure does not perfect it [sc. the activity] in the same way as the object perceived and the faculty of perception do, if they are good...Pleasure perfects the activity not as the corresponding permanent state does, by its immanence, but as an end which supervenes as the bloom of youth does on those in the flower of their age. (1174b23–5, 31–3)

The analogy is a matter of considerable dispute, the detail of which I cannot enter into here.[23] But let me just briefly sketch two interpretations of what Aristotle intends in claiming that pleasure perfects an activity.[24]

On one interpretation pleasure is simply the perfection—the perfection itself—that occurs when the best objects are encountered by the best senses. This is Matthew Strohl's (2011) reading:

A perfect activity of awareness is one where a capacity in a good condition is active in relation to a fine object...pleasure is a certain aspect of perfect activity of awareness, namely, *its very perfection*. That is, pleasure is the character that such an activity has in virtue of the good condition of the capacity being activated and the fineness of the object it is in relation to. (259; Strohl's emphasis)

Strohl provides the example of the activity of listening to music:

In the most perfect case, the listener will be someone with flawless hearing who has had a great deal of practice listening to complicated pieces and whose capacities for listening have been perfected thereby. The piece of music that serves as the object of her activity of listening will be among the finest things to hear, and therefore will be such as to make full use of her perfectly developed capacities for listening when they are active in relation to it. (262)

As Strohl notes, Aristotle focuses on the most perfect cases, but he clearly thinks that we can have pleasures that are less than perfect. Those who are perfect at listening may still experience a lesser pleasure in a less than perfect piece; those with a less than perfect capacity for listening may still experience something approximating to a perfect pleasure with a less than perfect piece, and so on. Nonetheless, on this view, the subject and the sense-object give rise to a perceptual activity and, if that activity is good, its goodness itself will be pleasure. Hence, as the goodness of the activity tends towards perfection, so does the pleasure. On this view, pleasure is brought about when subject and object contribute to

---

[23] See Warren (2015) for discussion of the background to the analogy. For one interpretative option we should rule out, see n.12 above.
[24] For a recent alternative, see Machek (2022). Three traditional readings in the literature (summarized by Gosling and Taylor 1982: 241–2) are rebutted by Strohl (2011: 272–7).

bringing about perceptual activity. But the activity itself, when good, is not itself pleasure. Pleasure is the good*ness* of the activity, the *goodness itself*.²⁵

On Anthony Price's (2017) reading, by contrast, pleasure is not the perfection of the activity of the best sense in relation to the best object—call this 'perfection$_1$'—but a further perfection that occurs when perfection$_1$ occurs—call this 'perfection$_2$'. This further perfection is a necessary feature of the first perfection, but not part of its essence as good (a necessary, but non-essential, feature; an *idion*; Price cites *Top.* I.5.102a18–30).²⁶ A motivation for this view is Aristotle's recognition that when virtuous agents find an action *noble*, this is distinct from their finding that same act *pleasant in so far as it is noble*. With the latter, they take pleasure *in* the act's being noble. Since it is their acting nobly (perfection$_1$) that they are finding pleasant, the perfection$_2$ that is pleasure, on this view, is a necessary feature of their acting nobly (= perfection$_1$). But pleasure is not this perfection$_1$ itself:

> If the pleasure that he takes in a virtuous action were identical to its perfection$_1$, it could not be this *in which* he takes pleasure. Thus pleasure indeed constitutes an *extra* perfection (i.e. perfection$_2$), though it is one that is sequential and not accidental... This new perfection is experiential but not accidental: it enhances the activity, already conscious, of which it is an inseparable companion. (193; Price's emphases)

On this view, while the best pleasure will only occur when subject and object are at their best, pleasure is neither to be identified as the activity that occurs when subject and object are such (see 5.1), nor to be identified with that activity's perfection (= perfection$_1$). Rather, it is an extra perfection (= perfection$_2$) that necessarily occurs when perfection$_1$ occurs. It is an experiential perfection of that perfect activity, which is sequential to it, but which enhances it still further.²⁷

Let us see how these different accounts would apply to the emotions. Suppose virtuous and vicious subjects both apprehend (through perception or thought) that someone has suffered some underserved misfortune. Virtuous people will form a distress directed at that object (= pity). The fact that they are virtuous entails that when they apprehend this object, they experience distress in response. But, on Strohl's reading, the distress itself just is the badness (imperfection, flawedness) that virtuous subjects experience in response to the activity. Whereas,

---

²⁵ For how this reading meshes with the bloom of youth analogy, see Strohl (2011: 278–83).
²⁶ In permitting such properties, Aristotle distances himself from a modal characterization of essential properties (as advanced by e.g. Kripke 1980): only a subset of necessary properties will be essential ones. For contemporary resistance to modal characterizations, see e.g. Fine (1994). For more discussion, see Atkins and Robertson Ishii (2020).
²⁷ Cf. Shields (2011: 208–9). For how Price's reading can mesh with the bloom of youth analogy, see his 2017 (193).

on Price's account, the badness (imperfection, flawedness) is distinct from the distress. The badness involves experiencing the event as bad or hurtful for the person concerned, or some such, and while the distress necessarily goes along with this (in the virtuous), it is sequential to the badness, experiential, and diminishes or mars the perceiving (or thinking) beyond its badness. Vicious people, by contrast, while apprehending (through perception or thought) the very same suffering, form a pleasure directed at that object (= schadenfreude). And their pleasure cannot be found apart from their perceiving (or thinking) that the person has suffered some undeserved misfortune. But, on Strohl's reading, the pleasure itself just is the perfection/goodness that vicious agents experience in response to the activity. Whereas, on Price's account, the perfection/goodness is distinct from the pleasure. The perfection$_1$/goodness will amount to these agents finding the event good, or some such, whereas the pleasure is a second perfection, a perfection$_2$, that necessarily goes along with this (in the vicious), but something that is sequential to it, experiential, and which enhances the perceiving (or thinking) of the suffering beyond its initial perfection$_1$.

Now, given that the distress or pleasure, here, are themselves representational, i.e. about the person who has suffered the undeserved misfortune, this means that these two accounts are different ways of fleshing out the respect in which the representational distress or pleasure is distress*ful* or pleas*urable*. On the first view, the distressfulness or pleasurableness of the representational distress or pleasure (directed at the suffering) *just is* representing its badness or goodness. On the second view, the distressfulness or pleasurableness of the representational distress or pleasure is a further experiential feature of the encountered badness or goodness in the event: representing the person's suffering the undeserved misfortune *as* distressful or pleasurable.

As I see it, insofar as the second reading more readily accounts for the difference between agents finding something noble, on the one hand, and their finding that noble thing pleasant, on the other, and insofar as it also provides a more immediate explanation of the *phenomenological* aspect of the emotions—their felt status—it seems the preferable reading (see end **2.2**, **2.4n.55**, **4.4**).

Conclusion to Part I

In this part of the book I have argued for an interpretation of what Aristotle thinks emotions are. Any plausible reading must accept that he holds that emotions are, at least in part, pleasures or pains/distresses (**2.1**). But this left many possibilities on the table. I first argued that he holds that those pleasures or distresses are representational, rather than, as has been claimed, non-representational sensations or feelings (**2.2–3**). I next argued that he does not simply identify such representational pleasures or distresses with the intentional state that apprehends the emotion's object (Chapter 3). And, finally, I resisted the view that he incorporates the intentional state that apprehends the emotion's object into the emotion as a separate component alongside the representational pleasure or distress. Instead, I argued that he thinks the emotions *just are* representational pleasures or distresses (4.2–3). They essentially link to the intentional state that apprehends the object of emotion insofar as they are formed *in light of* (rather than, e.g., caused by) the latter (4.1), but they are not, even in part, such intentional states themselves. Finally, in this current chapter, I considered Aristotle's understanding of the emotions, so construed, in relation to the account of pleasure we find in *NE* X. Although in the latter Aristotle is addressing taking pleasure *in* a (sensory or thought-based) activity, rather than representational pleasures or distresses as such, I argued that the two accounts can be viewed as compatible. Indeed, in his idea that pleasures 'perfect' activities, we may have some indication as to how his construing occurrent emotions as pleasures or distresses could help explain their experiential or felt nature.

In the book thus far, I have also commented on some aspects of Aristotle's view from a philosophical perspective. I defended the integrity of offering an analysis of emotions in terms of other intentional states against a recent objection to such a project (1.5). I showed that viewing the pleasures or distresses of emotions as representational is relatively unproblematic, and that taking emotions to be hedonic states of this kind does not commit us to thinking of different emotion-types as involving the very same *feelings* (2.4). I argued that Aristotle's analysis of emotions seems preferable to judgementalist and perceptualist accounts, since the latter seem to involve extraneous representational additions to the basic emotional response as such, which precludes them from explaining the full range of emotions (3.6). And I contrasted Aristotle's view of emotions as *responses* to intentional states that apprehend their objects with the more common current view that they are such apprehending intentional states themselves (4.4). In this respect, a further significant philosophical payoff of Aristotle's view will be developed in Chapter 12, viz. that it provides a plausible account of recalcitrant emotions.

In what follows I will also address the bodily or material dimension of emotions (Chapter 9) and some other problematic cases for the analysis of emotions as representational pleasures or distresses (Chapter 10). But, before I turn to these matters, I must first consider Aristotle's view on the relation between emotions, as representational pleasures or distresses, and *desires*. For my claim that he thinks that emotions are representational pleasures or distresses *alone* may appear to have a very obvious counter-example, viz. *anger*, which he in part defines as a desire. And, in line with anger, some think that he holds that emotions involve desires more generally. Addressing this is the goal of Part II of this book and anger is first up.

PART II
EMOTIONS AND DESIRES

6
Anger (*Orgē*)

In the first part of this book I argued that Aristotle holds that emotions *just are* representational pleasures or distresses. But, in fact, at several points we have already encountered an emotion that may seem to resist this basic picture. The first state that Aristotle discusses in his catalogue of emotions in *Rhet*. II, anger (*orgē*), is actually defined as a 'desire accompanied by a distress' (*orexis meta lupēs*), not simply a distress (II.2.1378a30–2). Even if the distress, here, is representational, anger is very clearly not *just* a representational distress, but also essentially involves a desire. Might this suggest, more generally, that Aristotle thinks that emotions themselves involve desires? Some commentators think so. Here is John Cooper:

> as we saw especially clearly in the case of anger, Aristotle seems to recognize three central elements as constituting the emotions—they are agitated, *affected* states of mind, arising from the ways events or conditions *strike* the one affected, which are at the same time *desires* for a specific range of reactive behaviours or other changes in the situation as it appears to him or her. (1996: 250; Cooper's emphases)[1]

In the second part of the book I resist this by addressing not just anger, but also a number of other considerations that might appear to link emotions to desires.

In this chapter I tackle anger itself. Contra Cooper, I argue that the correct conclusion to draw from Aristotle's analysis of anger is not that emotions involve desires, but that anger is more than just an emotion. In Chapter 7 I address several other considerations that might be invoked to support the idea that Aristotle holds that emotions involve desires (e.g. his characterization of some emotions in terms of a disturbance (*tarachē*); and his accounts of feeling-friendly-towards (*to philein*) and hating (*to misein*) in *Rhet*. II.4). I argue that none of these threatens the view that he has a clearly defined notion of emotions as representational pleasures or distresses *alone*. Finally, in Chapter 8 I consider *appetite* (*epithumia*). This appears on the lists of emotions in the ethical works (see 2.1) and yet in

---

[1] Cooper admits that Aristotle 'does not draw special attention to this common structure' and 'does not accord equal attention to each of the three elements in the case of every emotion he discusses' (251). He concludes that 'one cannot say more than that there seems to underlie Aristotle's discussions of the emotions in *Rhetoric* Book II an emerging general theory along these lines' (251).

those works Aristotle appears to view appetite as one species of *desire*. I propose that he can coherently think that it is *both* if he models appetite (or at least a class of appetites) along the lines of anger, i.e. as involving both a desire and a representational distress.

On my view, although Aristotle thinks that emotions can *prompt* desires (against the background of certain desiderative dispositions) and although he thinks they can form components of states that include desires, he does not think that they are, even in part, desires themselves. I reserve discussion of whether Aristotle is *right* to distinguish emotions from desires in this way for Part IV (Chapter 11), when I contrast his view with a contemporary motivational account of emotions and examine, more generally, the various representational roles that emotions are said to play (e.g. descriptive, imperative) according to different theories.

My concern in this chapter, though, is anger itself. I first consider some passages in the *Topics* in relation to anger's genus (**6.1**). I then turn to Aristotle's definition in the *Rhetoric* and characterize anger's distress (**6.2**). I next examine the relation between anger's distress and its desire (**6.3**) and specify the sense in which anger is an emotion (**6.4**). I then consider another emotion that Aristotle connects to anger, namely, the pleasure that stems from the hope of revenge (**6.5**). I close by examining why he thinks of anger as essentially involving both an emotion (a representational distress) and a desire (for revenge or retaliation or rectification: *timōria*) (**6.6**).

6.1 *Topics* on the genus of anger

A number of scholars have highlighted that the *Topics* may indicate that there had been some debate concerning the genus of anger in the Academy.[2] Here, the candidates appear to be not merely distress and desire, but also the intentional state that apprehends the object of the emotion, namely, a supposition (*hupolēpsis*) of a slight (*oligōria*). There are four principal references to anger that are relevant for us:

(1) In *Top*. IV.6 the question is raised whether pain (*lupē*) or supposition of a slight (*hupolēpsis oligōrias*) is the genus of anger, and it is claimed that both are predicated of anger in *what it is* (*ti esti*) (127b30–2).

---

[2] See e.g. Striker (1996: 288 with 300n.6); Dow (2015: 151); cf. Fortenbaugh (2002: 94–5); Viano (2014: 13–17). *Top*. is generally thought to be an early work, a product of Aristotle's time in the Academy. And since he is there concerned with dialectical reasoning—its methods and mistakes—the examples he employs need not manifest his own views (even at an earlier stage in his thought) (they only need to illustrate the point about reasoning methods or argument type he is seeking to illuminate). Nonetheless, the examples we find here do at least indicate the sort of views that he explicitly considered, and so one or more of them clearly could represent his actual view.

TOPICS ON THE GENUS OF ANGER   139

(2) In *Top*. VI.13 Aristotle refers to a putative definition of anger as 'pain accompanied with (*meta*) a supposition (*hupolēpsis*) of being slighted' (151a15–16), and he notes:

> For what this means to say is that it is because of (*dia* + accusative) a supposition (*hupolēpsis*) of this sort that the pain occurs; but to occur because of (*dia* + accusative) a thing is not the same as to occur together with (*meta* + genitive) it in any of the aforesaid ways [specified at 150b32–151a1; e.g. when something else contains both of them, or being in the same place or time; see **6.3**]. (151a16–19)

(3) In *Top*. IV.5 Aristotle addresses a view that distinguishes the distress of anger from anger itself. He writes:

> Sometimes…people state any kind of attendant feature (*to parakolouthoun*) as the genus, e.g. pain as the genus of anger and belief as that of conviction. For both of the aforementioned things follow (*parakolouthein*) in a certain way upon the given species, but neither of them is genus to it. For when the angry man feels pain, the pain has appeared in him earlier (*proteras*) than the anger; for his anger is not the cause (*aitia*) of his pain, but his pain of his anger, so that anger is not pain unqualifiedly (*haplōs*). (125b28–34)

Here, it seems, the distress of anger occurs *before* the anger itself and is the cause of the anger.

(4) Finally, in *Top*. VIII.1 we seem to have the view expressed that anger is a desire. Aristotle characterizes anger as 'a desire for revenge owing to an apparent slight' (*orexis timōrias dia phainomenēn oligōrian*) (156a32–3).

Perhaps there is no way to extract an entirely consistent position that respects all aspects of these remarks, but they nonetheless remain instructive. The basic understanding of anger as involving or requiring a series of elements is manifest. In (1) we get the idea that both the intentional state that apprehends the slight (here said to be a 'supposition' (*hupolēpsis*); cf. *De an*. III.3.427b24–6) and the distress of anger are essential to it. In (2) we get the notion that the supposition (*hupolēpsis*) in question leads to the distress or, as we might put it, that the distress is formed in light of the intentional state that apprehends the slight (so **4.1**).[3] In (3) we get the idea that the distress itself does not count as anger, but rather anger is formed in light of the distress. This would make sense if Aristotle is here identifying anger *as such* with the desire for revenge alone. For while distress at

---

[3] This specification dovetails nicely with the idea that emotions (as representational pleasures or distresses) are formed *in response to* the intentional state that apprehends the object of the emotion, as argued in Chapter 4.

the slight is formed in light of the supposition that one has been slighted (= (2)), the desire for revenge is in turn formed in light of the distress. Hence if, in (3), Aristotle is envisaging anger to be the desire for revenge, it would indeed come after the distress (even though, as he says, the distress may continue with the anger). This understanding of (3) would, of course, in turn mesh with (4), which characterizes anger simply as a desire for revenge owing to an apparent slight.

If we take (3) seriously, the distress of anger would not, strictly speaking, seem to be a part of what anger itself is (contra (1)): anger would instead, presumably, be identified with a desire (for revenge) alone (as per (4)). The distress would instead be what brings about or prompts such a desire. Why might someone—whether Aristotle or not—have been tempted by such a view? One point to note is that there is an asymmetry between the distress and the desire. While we have to desire revenge *for* something (whether or not it actually occurred)—this being built into the notion of *revenge* or *retaliation* (*timōria*)—there is clearly scope for someone to experience distress in response to a slight and yet fail to desire revenge. Indeed, in **6.6** we will see evidence that Aristotle thinks this a very real possibility. And yet it is also clear from his definition of anger in *Rhet.* II.2 that he holds that the desire for revenge is *necessary* for anger: one will not count as angry *unless* one desires revenge. (One may be despondent or resentful, perhaps, but not angry.) I also pick this up in **6.6**. But if it is only when one desires revenge or rectification for a slight that one *counts* as angry, one might well think that anger, strictly speaking, is to be identified with the desire alone: anger only occurs just insofar as, and to the extent that, such a desire arises.

Nonetheless, even on the view that anger is, strictly speaking, to be identified with the desire for revenge alone, the *Top.* passages do not eliminate the distress from the analysis. It, too, is essential to anger. This is explicit in (1) and (2) and why the distress is called an 'attendant feature' (*to parakolouthoun*) in (3). And, presumably, it is what the desire specified in (4) forms in response to. There has to be, it seems, something painful or distressing that we desire revenge *for*. This understood, there might seem to be a rather fine line to draw between maintaining that anger should be identified with the desire for revenge alone, on the one hand, and holding that it should be identified as a distress-*cum*-desire, on the other. For, on either alternative, *both* a desire for revenge *and* the distress that led to it are necessary for anger. The difference would seem to amount to maintaining that anger essentially *indicates* a distress (but is not itself, even in part, such a distress, since it is the desire alone), on the one hand, and holding that anger essentially *involves* a distress (i.e. is, in part, the emotion), on the other. Passages (3) and (4) in *Top.* point in the direction of the former reading, passage (1) the latter.

6.2 The distress as part of anger

The definition of anger in *Rhet.* II.2 indicates that the latter is Aristotle's own (considered) view. He writes:

> Let anger be desire accompanied by distress (*orexis meta lupēs*) for apparent revenge, because of (*dia* + accusative) an apparent slight on the part of someone unfitted to slight the person himself, or one of those close to him. (*Rhet.* II.2.1378a30–2)[4]

If the *position* of the desire and the distress in the definition indicates anything, it would seem that *desire* is the genus of anger. For, as Aristotle claims in *Top.* VI.5, 'the genus is intended to signify the what-it-is, and is placed first of the things said in the definition' (142b27–9).[5] Even so, Aristotle does not here define anger simply as a desire (for revenge), but as a desire *accompanied by a distress* (*orexis meta lupēs*). This specifies the distress as an *essential part* of anger, not something that is merely necessary as a prompt for it.[6]

The object of the desire of anger is explicitly specified as revenge or rectification (*timōria*). It also seems clear that Aristotle is claiming that this desire is brought about by an apparent slight from someone. But, in fact, although the distress is mentioned in the definition in *Rhet.* II.2, its object is not explicitly specified. Given that being slighted by someone is distressful, one may not unreasonably presume that the distress of anger, no less than the desire, is brought about by the apparent slight. It would involve, that is, being distressed *at* (*epi* + dative) or *about* (*peri* + genitive) the slight (see 2.3).[7]

Before we conclude this, however, we should consider an alternative. For, within the chapter on anger, we get a discussion of a pain that Aristotle connects to the emotion, but it is not the one I have just specified. He writes:

> [People] are angry when they are pained; for the one who is pained seeks something. If, then, anyone in any way directly obstructs, for example, a thirsty man

---

[4] For the double use of 'apparent' (*phainomenos*) in this definition, see 4.3n.37.

[5] Note, with respect to the desire and the distress we *can* talk in terms of a genus-species relation, where this is distinguished from a determinate-determinable relation (see the end of 2.4 and 2.4n.54 for references); for the desire and the distress are independent features which, added together, compose the state as a whole.

[6] 'Desire accompanied by pain' (*orexis meta lupēs*) would contrast anger with rational desire (*boulēsis*), which Aristotle elsewhere characterizes as *painless desire* (*Top.* VI.8.146b2). But it would not distinguish anger from appetite (*epithumia*), which is also said to be *meta lupēs* (see e.g. *NE* III.11.1119a4). But, of course, with both anger and appetite, the desire and the 'pain' have further specifications. Anger's desire is for revenge (*timōria*), appetite's for pleasure (*boulēsis*, by contrast, is desire of the good). Anger's 'pain' is specified below; appetite's in Chapter 8.

[7] Cf. also Nussbaum (2016: 18).

from drinking, or if he does not do so directly, appears to be doing the same thing, or if he acts against him or does not assist him in acting, or annoys him in some other respect when he is so disposed [sc., seeking something because he is pained], at all such people is he angry. That is why those who are ill, poor, at war, in love, thirsty—in general, those with an appetite and not successful in satisfying it—are irascible, that is, easily provoked to anger, especially towards those who slight their present condition. For example, the one who is ill is easily provoked because of things related to his illness, the poor one because of things related to his poverty, the one at war because of things related to the war, the one in love because of things related to his love, and likewise too in the other cases. For each is prepared by his present affection to follow the path toward his particular anger. (1379a11–24)

What we have here is a specification of a general background condition which disposes people to anger. If people are pained, they seek something: presumably, their distress indicates that something is not right which they would prefer to be rectified.[8] For example, those who are ill (painful state) want to be healthy, those who are poor (painful state) want to be rich, those who are thirsty (painful state) want a drink, those at war (painful state) want to be victorious, and so on. But then suppose another person interacts with such subjects and either appears to thwart the satisfaction of their desire or not show the correct support, or otherwise belittle their condition. The subjects will then be prone to get angry with that person. They may construe themselves as having been slighted and form a new desire, namely, for retaliation against the slighter.[9]

Given that this 'pain' (pain as a background condition) *is* explicitly discussed in *Rhet.* II.2, we should briefly address why it nonetheless cannot be the distress mentioned in the definition. The most obvious point against this is that it would provide Aristotle with an account that is both far too restrictive for his purposes and far too restrictive to be plausible. Clearly, I do not *already* need to be in a distressing condition in order to take offence at something you do or say. One species of offence or slight (*oligōria*) is manifesting wanton aggression (*hubris*). This, we are told, 'consists in doing or saying things that involve shame for the one who suffers them, not in order that something or other [beneficial] may come for the agent himself, or because something [bad] has happened to him, but in order to take pleasure in it' (1378b23–5). But it is clearly not a condition on you doing or saying such things to me that I am *already* in some painful state: the doing or saying can itself bring about a distress, without having to 'tap into' an existing

---

[8] Reeve glosses the 'seeks something' as '[n]amely, relief from pain' (2018: 253). But this is not quite right. It is not relief from the pain, as such, that we seek. Rather, we seek what is causing the pain to stop doing so. We do not, e.g., want to take a knockout pill to cure our distressful fear that a lion might eat us; we want the lion to go away (which will then mean we cease to be distressed).

[9] Cp. Harris (2001: 59).

one. Instead, the pain that Aristotle highlights in the passage quoted is simply one of the conditions under which someone may be more irascible. This could clearly be useful for orators since if they know of some pre-existing malaise in their audience they can, if it is expedient, use that as a way of generating anger. But this is clearly not necessary.[10] This explanation fits the location of the passage above in Aristotle's chapter on anger. He divides his discussions of individual emotions under three heads: the 'at what', the 'conditions under which', and the 'at whom' (II.1.1378a22–6). The 'at what' section typically considers the evaluative or formal object of the emotion, while the 'at whom' part generally specifies the target of the emotion (see 1.3).[11] But the passage quoted above occurs in anger's 'conditions under which' section. This section often simply highlights those who are particularly prone to the emotion (rather than, say, offering strict conditions for the occurrence of the emotion). For example, in his discussion of pity Aristotle lists a number of kinds of people who are prone to pity: those who have already suffered and escaped, older people (because of their wisdom and experience), weak people, those who are more cowardly, and so on (II.8.1385b23–6). Clearly, he is just providing us with a list of people who might be prone to pity, not specifying conditions that would apply in every case. Similarly, in his chapter on indignation (*nemesis*), when he claims that those who think they are worthy of great goods, or those who are ambitious or desirous of things, are prone to indignation at the apparent undeserved doing-well of another (II.9.1387b5–8, 9–11), these are just types of people who are particularly prone to the emotion. So too, I suggest, with the background pain in anger: such a pain will make people irascible, but it is far from necessary. Indeed, in line with this, Aristotle's other case in the 'conditions under which' section of anger provides another way in which a pain can be contingently related to anger: '[f]urther, [a person is disposed to anger] if he happened to be expecting the contrary, since what is to a high degree contrary to belief pains more, just as what is to a high degree contrary to belief delights more, if what is wished for comes about' (1379a24–6).

By contrast, the 'pain' mentioned in the *definition*, since it contributes to specifying the state (anger is a 'desire accompanied by distress'), seems essential to anger. Hence, the pain in question is surely, as initially suggested, the distress formed in response to the apparent slight, not a background pain that would, if present, make us irascible.[12] The upshot of this section, then, is that in contrast to

---

[10] Note, in such cases we have two different states prompting two different desires: a painful state (illness, poverty, thirst) prompting a desire to alleviate it (get healthy, get some money, get something to drink), and an apparent slight prompting a desire to get revenge on the slighter.

[11] The exception is shame, given the self-reflective nature of this emotion. See 1.3n.29.

[12] It is perhaps worth noting that there is nothing odd in Aristotle *not* providing an explanation of the former distress in his subsequent discussion. We do not generally get such a discussion with the other emotions either.

passages (3) and (4) from *Top.*, but in line with passage (1), Aristotle's considered view is that distress at an apparent slight is an essential part of what anger itself is.

6.3 The desire of anger as both brought about by (*dia*) and accompanied by (*meta*) the distress

If Aristotle holds that anger incorporates *both* a desire *and* a distress, we still need to establish more precisely the relation between the two. In the *Rhet.* II.2 definition the desire (for revenge) accompanied by distress (*orexis meta lupēs timōrias*) is said to be brought about by (*dia* + accusative) an apparent offence or slight (*dia phainomenēn oligōrian*). In fact, what seems to be going on is that the subject experiences distress in response to (*dia*) an apparent slight and then *in turn* forms a desire in response to (*dia*) the distress.[13] There are, that is, two transitions in the formation of anger and, as we shall see in **6.6**, a subject could in principle fail to complete either, and thereby fail to be angry. To be angry the subject must, first, move from apprehending an apparent slight to experiencing distress directed at that slight and then, second, move from experiencing distress at the apparent slight to desiring revenge for the slight. We have already considered the first transition in the last section. Its result is the representational distress (*lupē*) that the definition refers to (hence the *dia phainomenēn oligōrian*, 'because of an apparent slight', applies to the distress, no less than the *orexis*, the desire). The second transition is required insofar as a desire for revenge is *a response to* something (this is built into the notion of *revenge* or *retaliation* (*timōria*)); and what it is a response to is not simply a slight, but a slight that has brought about distress. A slight that seemed warranted, for instance, might not bring about such a desire (hence the 'on the part of someone unfitted to slight the person' in the *Rhet.* II.2 definition).[14]

However, Aristotle appears to think that anger requires *more* than merely these two transitions. In passage (2) from *Top.* in **6.1**, Aristotle *criticized* a definition of anger as *distress accompanied by* (*meta* + genitive) *the supposition of being slighted* on the ground that what was *really* meant was that the distress is 'due to' or 'on account of' (*dia* + accusative) the supposition, and so (given this) the relation does not count as a genuine case of 'being accompanied by' (*meta* + genitive) (151a14–15). Examples of genuine 'being accompanied by' (*meta* + genitive) relations, by contrast, are (i) *A* and *B* occurring together within something else (Aristotle's example is justice and courage being found within the soul), (ii) *A* and *B*

---

[13] Or 'in light of' (**4.1**). There need be no perceived temporal gaps here; see towards the end of **4.1**.
[14] The latter transition is also suggested by the formulation of the desire of anger in *De an.* I.1, the desire to *return* pain (*antilupēseōs*) (403a30–1), which implies there was an initial pain that one seeks to rectify (see also **6.6** below). But see **9.4** for some limitations of such a formulation. The two transitions at least preserve the *structure* we gathered from the *Top.* passages: an offence or slight prompts a distress which, in turn, prompts a desire.

being in the same place, and (iii) *A* and *B* taking place at the same time (150b32–151a1). But, of course, *Rhet.* specifies anger as a 'desire accompanied by distress' (*orexis meta lupēs*). This suggests that while the desire of anger is formed in response to (*dia* + accusative) a distress at the slight (hence it is a desire to *retaliate*), nonetheless, for the overall state to count as *anger*, the distress in question *must remain present while the agent desires revenge*. That is, for the subject to count as angry, the desire for revenge must not merely be formed in response to (*dia* + accusative) a distress (at a slight), it must also be *accompanied by* (*meta* + genitive) that distress. The two must be *co-present* in anger.[15] Such co-presence is alluded to in passage (3) from *Top.* ('when the angry man feels pain, the pain has appeared in him earlier than the anger': the prior pain is clearly still present when the angry man feels pain), but it is more explicit still in other passages. In *Rhet.* II.4 Aristotle claims, quite generally, that anger, in contrast to hating, is *with pain* (*meta lupēs*) (1382a12–13), where it seems clear that it is occurrent instances of anger and hating that he has in mind—hence he reiterates: 'for the angry person is pained (*ho orgizomenos lupeitai*), whereas the one who hates is not' (1382a13).[16] He makes the same claim in *Rhet.* II.3—'anger involves pain' (1380b1)—and even more directly in *Pol.* V.10: 'anger is present with distress' (*hē orgē meta lupēs parestin*) (1312b31–2) (cf. also *NE* IV.5.1126a21–2, VII.6.1149b20–1; *EE* III.1.1229b31–2; *MM* II.6.1202b26–7).

Aristotle thus appears to hold not merely that anger essentially *involves* both a desire and a distress (with the former formed in light of the latter: **6.2**), but that the distress must *remain present* alongside the desire if the subject is to count as angry.

6.4 Anger as an emotion

With this in place, let us now turn to consider the sense in which anger is an emotion. If anger essentially incorporates both a desire and a distress in the way I have specified, is it not a clear counter-example to my claim that he thinks that emotions are representational distresses or pleasures *alone*? Here we come to the nub of the issue with anger. It has simply been assumed by commentators that Aristotle thinks that anger counts as an emotion with respect to *both* aspects of it: the desire and the distress.[17] On this assumption, Aristotle cannot think that emotions, as such, just are representational distresses or pleasures. But this is an assumption we simply do not have to make. Anger, for Aristotle, can still legitimately

---

[15] This shall be important later on. See **9.4**.
[16] I consider this passage with respect to hating in **7.4**.
[17] So Cooper (1996: 249–51). As we noted in the introduction to this chapter, Cooper then seeks to generalize on the basis of anger for emotions as a whole (251). See also Striker (1996: 293); Rapp (2013: 35; cf. 2002: 568); and Dow (2015: 148–9n.13, cf. 179 for the general applicability).

count as an emotion, and be listed and discussed as such, even if it does so *only with respect to one of its essential components*, namely, its representational distress. To preserve his general view of emotions as representational distresses or pleasures, as developed in Part I, all we need to accept is that anger essentially incorporates two different states; a desire and an emotion. One will not count as being angry without both a distress at a slight and a desire for revenge (formed in response to the distress). But the requirement that anger incorporate both these states does not collapse the distinction between the desire of anger and the emotion of anger. Insofar as anger incorporates a desire (an *orexis*), it specifies an object of desire (an *orekton*) which (under the right conditions) will motivate pursuit. And the object of the desire of anger is revenge (*timōria*). And insofar as anger incorporates an emotion (a *pathos*), it involves a representational pleasure or distress. And the object of the distress of anger, what the distress is directed at, is an apparent slight (*oligōria*).[18] Both the emotion and the desire remain distinct in anger, even though anger essentially requires both.[19] The desire (for revenge) must be formed in light of the distress (at the slight) and, as we have seen, both the desire and the distress must co-exist for anger to occur. But all this is compatible with *the emotion of* anger fitting Aristotle's general model of emotions as representational pleasures or distresses *alone*. *Qua* emotion, anger is simply a representational distress. Granted, anger is *not just* an emotion, but insofar as it is, it fits the rubric.[20]

6.5 Another emotion connected with anger and the implications of this

As we have already seen (4.3), Aristotle thinks that anger is also connected to a representational pleasure. Let us consider this a little further. In *Rhet.* II.2 he writes:

> A kind of pleasure follows all anger (*kai pasē(i) orgē(i) hepesthai tina hēdonēn*), namely, the one that arises from the hope of being revenged (*apo tēs elpidos tou*

---

[18] Both the emotion and the desire can be said to provide formal objects of anger. *Qua* emotion anger's formal object is *slighting* (or offence), *qua* desire it is *revenge*.

[19] Compare preferential choice (*prohairesis*), which we are told can be characterized as either 'desiderative thought' (*orektikos nous*) or 'intellectual desire' (*orexis dianoētikē*) (*NE* VI.2.1139b4–5, cf. also III.3.1113a11 and VI.2.1139a23, which specify preferential choice as 'deliberate desire' (*bouleutikê orexis*), and *EE* II.10.1226b16–20, 1227a3–5). These formulations may be intended to indicate a more intimate relation than we get with the distress and desire of anger; whereby the deliberation and desire do not ultimately end up as numerically distinct states within the choice.

[20] Note that even if Aristotle stuck to the view expressed in passage (3) from the *Topics*—that the distress is, strictly speaking, to be distinguished from anger itself—anger would still essentially *indicate* a distinct and unique emotion. It would just be that, strictly speaking, anger would not itself be (in part) identified with the emotion, but with the desire that results from it (when it does). But, as his definition of anger in *Rhet.* II.2 shows, this is not Aristotle's own view.

timōrēsasthai). For it is pleasant to think that he will get what he seeks... a kind of pleasure actually follows along (*akolouthein*) because of this. (1378b1–3, 8)

Note that here we appear to find the 'subsequent' use of *hepetai* (glossed by *akolouthein* in b8) (see **2.1**). Pleasure follows (*hepesthai*) anger (dative) (or, equivalently, anger (dative) is followed by (*hepesthai*) pleasure) *subsequently*. It is worth stressing that this does not undermine our argument in **2.1** concerning the use of *hepetai* in Aristotle's general specifications of the emotions—in fact, the exception almost proves the rule. Anger *itself* is to be identified as a desire-*cum*-emotion, that is, as a desire for revenge accompanied by distress at an apparent slight. But anger also *leads to* a (subsequent) pleasure; a pleasure which is itself most plausibly construed as representational and so would count as an emotion in its own right. The pleasure that arises from the hope of getting revenge is presumably directed at just that: the prospect of getting revenge. In fact, since Aristotle claims that this pleasure follows 'all' anger, he seems to think that anger *essentially* leads to this second emotion. This point notwithstanding, the representational pleasure is clearly envisaged to be subsequent to anger itself (construed as the desire for revenge owing to distress at a slight) insofar as it pertains to the prospect of satisfying the desire of anger.[21] Hence, although it essentially follows from anger, this representational pleasure is not specified in anger's definition.

The fact that we have both a pleasure and a distress connected with anger has been thought to have implications for whether Aristotle could think that pleasure and distress are genera of the emotions. Jamie Dow (2015) writes:

> [Aristotle] seems to have seen anger as essentially involving *both* pleasure *and* pain (1378a31–b2): since each thing can only have one genus, he would be forced to say that at least one of pleasure and pain was not anger's genus. But if in the case of anger it is possible for a passion to be *essentially* (say) a pleasure without that's [sic.] being its *genus*, it is unclear why there is any motivation for making the strong claim about pain's [sic.] being its *genus*. The same seems to apply to the passions in general. (149n.13; his emphases)

However, there are several things wrong with this. First, pleasure or pain *could* be genera *of the emotions*, without one or the other being the genus of anger.[22] As we have seen, *anger* is essentially *both* a desire *and* an emotion. Second, the pleasure connected to anger seems to be something that essentially *follows* anger, not a part of what anger itself is. Third, even if (counterfactually) Aristotle had included the pleasure alongside the distress and held that both form part of what anger

---

[21] Aristotle notes that the angry person must view revenge as a real possibility: *Rhet.* II.2.1378b1–4, I.11.1370b13; and see **6.6** below.

[22] I am taking the genus/species relation in a broad sense which includes determinate/determinable relations (see the end of **2.4** and **2.4n.54**).

itself is, why should we assume that each state can only have one genus? Dow's conclusion is the wrong one to draw. Gisela Striker (1996) draws the correct one:

> If pleasure and pain are to serve as the genera, then their species can hardly be treated as mixtures of both. This does not rule out mixed feelings, of course; but instead of describing each emotion as itself a mixture of pleasure and pain, one would now speak—quite plausibly—of mixtures of emotions: hope and fear, for example. (292)[23]

The claim is that emotions are species of pleasure or pain. Clearly, this implies that no individual emotion can be both a pleasure and a pain. That is the truth in Dow's claim. But the idea that emotions are species of pleasure or pain does not imply that no state can involve both a pleasure and a distress. It could clearly do so if it itself included two emotions. On this view, anger could be one emotion *qua* representational distress and another emotion *qua* representational pleasure. So too, indeed, anger could be one emotion *qua* representational distress, another emotion *qua* representational pleasure, *and also* incorporate a desire for some desired end. But, in fact, we have reason to believe that anger's representational pleasure, strictly speaking, *follows* it, rather than forms part of what it itself is. So, as it happens, anger is just to be identified with a desire (for revenge) plus one emotion (distress at an apparent slight). The second emotion it is connected to (pleasure at the prospect of getting revenge) is only something it essentially leads to. Nonetheless, it remains quite a busy state!

6.6 Why does Aristotle think that anger essentially involves a desire?

On my view, then, contra Cooper, Aristotle's account of anger does not show that he thinks there are emotions that *are*, in part, desires (or, generalizing, that all emotions are such). Instead, it shows that there can be states that essentially involve both emotions and desires. In line with this, the representational distress of anger and its desire are specified as distinct elements in the definition (anger is an *orexis meta lupēs*, a desire accompanied by a distress). But this invites us to ask: why does Aristotle insist that anger essentially (i.e. as part of its definition)

---

[23] Striker is alluding to the reading of Aristotle's account of the emotions by Dorothea Frede (1996) as 'mixed feelings'. Striker thinks that a *phantasia* with a specific content serves as the *differentia specifica* for the different emotions. If characterizing the account in terms of genus-species, I would instead treat *the (apparent) instantiation of the formal object* as the *differentia specifica*. This is because on my view Aristotle does not think (i) that objects of emotions can only be apprehended by *phantasia* (see my 2014a), nor (ii) that the intentional state that apprehends the object of the emotion is a component part of the emotion (4.2).

includes a desire in the first place? In this last section of the chapter I consider this further.

To begin with it is worth stressing that he does not think that subjects *must* desire revenge simply because they have apprehended an apparent slight directed at them. This is clear from part of his definition:

> Let anger be desire accompanied by distress for apparent revenge, because of an apparent slight *on the part of someone unfitted to slight the person himself*, or one of those close to him. (*Rhet.* II.2.1378a30–2; my emphasis)

The part of the definition I have italicized suggests that if a slight appears to come from someone who is (as you see things) *fitted* to slight you, you may not desire revenge in response and so may fail to count as angry.[24]

Indeed, there is additional evidence that apprehending a slight need not even trigger the *distress* of anger, let alone its desire.[25] One of the (three) species of slight that someone may direct at us is 'spite' (*epēreasmos*). Aristotle specifies this as:

> an impediment to the wishes (*boulēseis*) [of the other], not in order to get something for himself, but in order that the other not get it. (1378b18–20)

But Aristotle also explicitly lists spite (alongside anger itself and accusation (*diabolē*)) as productive of enmity (*echthra*) in his discussion of hating in *Rhet.* II.4 (1382a2–3). And yet not only is hating sharply distinguished from anger there (1382a3–15), it is explicitly said to be 'without pain' (1382a12–13). So, it seems, subjects could apprehend an apparent slight (*qua* spite) without experiencing distress at that slight. They could experience painless hate instead.[26]

Aristotle's account of hating also suggests that we can even form a desire to harm someone in response to an apparent slight (*qua* spite) without such a desire counting as the desire for revenge that is constitutive of anger. In *Rhet.* II.4 he claims that angry people seek pain (*lupēs ephesis*) for the person they are angry with (cf. *De an.* I.1.403a30–1: 'desire to return pain'), whereas those who hate 'seek evil' (*[ephesis] kakou*) for the person they hate (1382a8), and he explains this as follows:

---

[24] See Konstan (2006: 55–6), referencing slaves (cf. *Rhet.* II.3.1380a15–18). Slaves aside, it would seem that someone could reasonably think that a slight is fitting: suppose I have akratically wronged you, I may judge that I deserve the slight (see *Rhet.* II.3.1380b16–18). Aristotle links anger to perceived injustice in *NE* V.8.1135b28–9.

[25] I suppose we might have expected that at least some of those who viewed the slight at fitting would not have been distressed by the slight. But I shall now cite further evidence.

[26] Or they might have just expended their anger on someone else; see II.3.1380b10–13 and Rapp (2002: 565).

for the angry person wishes [his revenge] to be perceived, whereas to the latter [sc. the hating person] it makes no difference, and painful things are all perceptible, whereas the greatest evils are the least perceptible ones, [for example], injustice, lack of practical wisdom. For the presence of evil does not at all cause pain. (1382a9–12)

In *Rhet.* II.3 Aristotle links this idea to the notion that angry people wish for the revenge to be recognized and acknowledged as revenge by the one they are angry with (1380b20–30), whereas this is clearly not required with hating.[27] Thus, while people who hate desire evil for that person, their desire is to be distinguished from the desire for revenge that is constitutive of anger. It is neither distress-fuelled, nor recognition-seeking.[28] (Hating will, though, as we shall see in 7.4, entail some other representational pleasures and distresses about the hated person.)

What if the slight appeared to you to be by someone *unfitted* to slight you *and* you experience distress at it as such? Would *this* now entail a desire for revenge? Aristotle would certainly think that one *should* form a desire for revenge in such a scenario.[29] But he may still think that it is *possible* that such a desire would not ensue. In *NE* IV.5 he writes:

> those who are not angry at the things they should be angry at are thought to be fools, and so are those who are not angry in the right way, at the right time, or with the right persons; for such a man is thought not to grasp (*aisthanesthai*) things nor to be pained (*lupeisthai*) by them, and, since he does not get angry, he is thought unlikely to defend himself; and to endure being insulted (*propēlakizomenon anechesthai*) and put up with insult to one's friends is slavish. (1126a4–8)

Although such a person *is thought* or *seems* (*dokein*) not to grasp or be distressed by the slight, the text is compatible with Aristotle envisaging that the subject has nonetheless done these things (rather than, e.g., failed to notice what should be noticed). On this reading he would be emphasizing that unless distress at the slight results in a desire for revenge (and the behaviour that would follow;

---

[27] I shall try to make the desiderative structure of hating more perspicuous in 7.4, after deriving my specification of it from the definition of feeling-friendly-towards (*Rhet.* II.4.1380b37–1381a1) (given that Aristotle tells us to grasp what hating is 'from its contrary' (II.4.1382a1–2)).

[28] Therefore, hating and anger would doubtless involve a different physical dimension. Cf. *De an.* I.1 which suggests that a material definition of anger might be 'boiling of the blood and hot stuff around the heart' (403a31–b1). This must connect to the fact that anger is a quite specific desire for revenge formed in response to distress at a slight, rather than just a desire to bring about bad for another. I come to the material/physical dimensions of emotions in Chapter 9.

[29] He thinks that there is a *virtue* pertaining to experiencing anger (to the right degree, at the right time) (see e.g. *NE* IV.5; *EE* III.3). Cp. Nussbaum (2016).

although see n.32), the subject will fail to be angry. And since anger is normatively required in the envisaged scenario, the subject will thereby appear 'slavish' (*andrapodōdes*).

If, then, Aristotle may perhaps even allow that distress at an (apparently) inappropriate slight might not lead to a desire for revenge, why does he include both the distress and the desire in his definition of anger? The answer, I think, must simply be a consequence of the *applicability of the concept* of *orgē* (anger), as Aristotle understands it: in order *to count* as angry, on his view, one must feel some impulse to action. In this respect it is worth emphasizing that the desire of anger, as he sees it, is not merely an idle wish, but provides a goal that is deemed at least feasible.[30] In *Rhet.* I.11 he writes:

> no one is angry at someone on whom it appears impossible to take revenge, nor at those who are greater than themselves in capacity, [that is,] either they feel no anger or less anger. (1370b13–14)

In *Rhet.* II.2 he connects this with the pleasure of anger:

> all anger must entail some sort of pleasure, namely, the one from the hope of being revenged. For it is pleasant to think that he will get what he seeks, and no one seeks things that appear impossible for him to attain, and the angry person seeks what is possible for him. (1378b1–4)

Even if one judges that one should not take revenge (now)—because, say, to do so would be significantly contra one's best interests—one must, on Aristotle's view, at least view revenge as *possible* (revenge must be *feasible*, we might say, even if not *advisable*).[31] So although other responses *can* occur in light of an apparent slight,

---

[30] Konstan (2006: 56) gives an example of this from the *Iliad*: 'the priest Chryses and his patron god Apollo react very differently to Agamemnon's refusal to free Chryses' daughter...Chryses pleads and offers a ransom; when he is threatened and harshly dismissed, he obeys his fear, although he suffers inwardly (*Iliad* I.33–4). He appeals to Apollo to take revenge in his behalf (42), but is not said to experience anger in his own right. Apollo, however, is "angry in his heart" (*khōomenos kēr*, 44) and immediately punishes the Greeks for this slight to his divinity; he is, of course, entirely capable of doing so'.

[31] One could, of course, be mistaken in thinking that revenge is a real possibility. Those who 'spend their time in taking revenge through thinking' (II.2.1378b8–9) are not satisfying an idle wish with thoughts, then, but anticipating getting the revenge they view possible. Note, it is not that idle wishes cannot count as desires (*orexeis*) for Aristotle. We can have *boulēseis* for things that are impossible, e.g., to rule all humankind or to be immortal (*NE* III.2.1111b22–3; *EE* II.10.1225b32–4). Rather, it is that the *orexis* of anger cannot be idle but must instead be deemed feasible (if not advisable) to act on. Also, note there is no implication that one must attempt to act in order to count as angry. One may judge it inappropriate to pursue retaliation in this context and so resist one's desire for it (the famous Greek example is Odysseus and the suitors; see the opening of Homer's *Odyssey* book XX; and Plato's *Republic* IV.441b, III.390d). Aristotle often treats *orgē* and *thumos* (one of his three species of desire) as equivalent (see my 2012 (ch. 5) and 7.1n.5 and 7.5n.56 below). But he explicitly allows that we may be akratic with respect to *thumos* (see esp. *NE* VII.6 *passim*) and where there is the possibility of *akrasia*,

Aristotle seems to view it as a condition on the *applicability* of anger that one not only (i) experience distress at the apparent slight, but (ii) desire to *rectify* the slight and (iii) view doing so as *feasible*. (Without (iii), one may instead be reduced to resentment or despondency.) Such a proactive and emotional response to the slight seems to be constitutive of what it means *to become angry* (*orgizesthai*) by the slight, on his view. One will not *count* as being angry without it.[32] This feature of anger, as he construes it, may simply be a consequence of the connotations of the Greek term. While Aristotle can certainly offer corrective accounts of phenomena, especially if pretheoretic (or, indeed, theoretic) conceptions are conflicting, he tends not to employ terms in a way that completely contradicts their current usage. To that extent he respects the linguistic practices and conceptual schemes of his time. Apprehending that one has been insulted and yet not in any way 'boiling up' in reply, will mean that one cannot feasibly be said to be experiencing anger (*orgē*).[33]

Conclusion

In this chapter I have argued that Aristotle's account of anger as a-desire-accompanied-by-distress does not stand in tension with his general account of emotions—as developed in Part I—as representational pleasures or distresses *alone*. Anger essentially involves both a desire and a representational distress. *It*, therefore, is more than simply an emotion. But, *qua* emotion, it just is a representational distress (although it also leads to a representational pleasure). It therefore

---

there is the possibility of *enkrateia*, of resisting one's desire for revenge because it conflicts with what one judges to be in one's best interests (cf. *NE* VII.4.1148b10–14). It is not, strictly speaking, *acting on* the desire, then, that is required for anger, but *possessing it* (cp. Harris 2001: 57–8).

[32] Cf. Frede: 'The rage of Achilles is Aristotle's prime example, just as it was Plato's. Achilles does not feel only pain at being humiliated by Agamemnon. If he did, that state would not be called anger, at least not according to Aristotle. To be called "anger", it must at the same time contain the desire for retaliation and the hope of achieving it. And that is what the *Iliad* is all about. It is the song about Achilles' wrath *and* his revenge' (1996: 269; Frede's emphasis). Achilles' anger with Agamemnon was of course a paradigmatic case for the Greeks. (His emotion directed at Hector at the end of the *Iliad*, though, seems importantly different, at least from Aristotelian *orgē*; see Konstan 2006: 48–55.) Aristotle refers to Achilles (and quotes lines from the *Iliad*) in his discussion of anger in *Rhet.* II.2 (1378b31–5). Clearly, it is inconceivable to imagine *Achilles* calmly taking a slight from Agamemnon—he would always make the transition from slight to desire for revenge. But not many of us are Achilles. Nonetheless, to count as angry, for Aristotle, we must make the transition.

[33] Cf. Harris (2001: ch. 5); Allen (2002: esp. 50–9); Konstan (2006: ch.2). In *NE* IV.5 Aristotle claims that the mild-mannered person (*praos*) 'is not revengeful but, rather, considerate to others' (1126a2–3). And yet he also claims that the mild-mannered person does get *sore* or angry (*chalepainein*: 1126a1). Does this imply that we can experience anger without desiring revenge after all? No. Mild-manneredness (*praotēs*) in this sense (cp. the sense in *Rhet.* II.3 discussed in **10.3**) is a trait of character. All Aristotle means is that in general a person with such a character trait will not be prone to get angry (and so will not be a revengeful sort of person). This is why he characterizes the trait as straying too close to the vice of deficiency (1125b27–8, 1126a1–2, a36–b1). The true mean, he tells us, has no name (1125b27–9).

fits the general account. In the final section I explored why Aristotle characterizes anger as essentially combining both an emotion and a desire. He appears to hold that neither apprehending a slight as such, nor even being distressed at it (= the emotion) *entail* the desire of anger (for revenge). Rather, the reason anger (*orgē*) essentially involves a desire seems to stem from the conditions of applicability of the concept of the state, as Aristotle understands it.

7
Some Other (Putative) Links between Emotions and Desires

The fact that anger incorporates a desire in its definition was surely a major factor in prompting a number of commentators to think that Aristotle holds that emotions essentially incorporate a desire.[1] If one thinks of anger as a whole as an emotion, it clearly involves a desire as a component. I have argued that we can deny the antecedent, here, and preserve the idea that emotions are representational pleasures or distresses alone. Anger can essentially *involve* an emotion without that implying that emotions themselves involve desires. But if there were other considerations in favour of the general thesis, we may still have reason to affirm the antecedent. Perhaps Aristotle held more generally that all emotions have representational pleasures or distresses *and* desires as components?

The chief consideration *against* this thesis is that the vast majority of emotions in *Rhet.* are not defined in terms of a desire. Bar anger and feeling-friendly-towards (I shall come to the latter) there are no direct references to desires in the specifications of the states listed in *Rhet.* II at all.[2] In particular, with fear, shame, and all the emotions concerning (un)deserved doing-well/badly (envy, pity, other-directed pride, schadenfreude, and pleasure- and distress-based indignation), there is no explicit mention of a desire in their definitions. (I sketch all these emotions in my Catalogue at the end of the book.) If Aristotle thought that

---

[1] For some who make the general claim (besides Cooper discussed in Chapter 6), see e.g. Engberg-Pedersen (1983: 136); Sherman (1993: 19); Nussbaum (1994: 83); Cates (2003: 331–2); Taylor (2006: 98); and Centrone (2015: 154); cf. also Frede (1996).

[2] Where a 'direct' reference would either be to Aristotle's general term for all types of desire, *orexis*, or one of its three species; *boulēsis* ('wish', 'rational desire'), *thumos* ('anger', 'spirit'), or *epithumia* ('appetite') (*EE* II.7.1223a26–7, II.10.1225b24–6; *De an.* II.3.414b2; *MA* 6.700b2 (also *MM* I.12.1187b36–7); cf. *De an.* III.9.432b5–6; *EE* asserts these are the only *orexeis* at II.10.1225b24–6). Anger refers to an *orexis* (*meta lupēs*), feeling-friendly-towards to wishing (*boulesthai*) which, most plausibly, indicates a *boulēsis* (see 7.4). Note, the *orexis* of *orgē* (anger) should not itself be considered a *thumos*. Otherwise, as I noted in my 2012 (117), we would get a reduplication problem of the kind Aristotle identifies elsewhere (e.g. *Met.* Z.5.1030b28–1031a1). *Thumos* (in this guise) would amount to an *orexis* for revenge, but in *Rhet.* II.2 *orgē* itself is characterized as an *orexis* for revenge. Hence, if the *orexis* in that definition were *itself* a desire for revenge, *orgē* would be *a desire for revenge for revenge*, which is clearly nonsense. (Aristotle makes just this point with *epithumia*—as both itself 'of the pleasant' and also '*orexis* of the pleasant'—at *SE* 13.173a39–40.) Rather, with anger, the overall state, *orexis meta lupēs* (+ their complements: (apparent) revenge and (apparent) slight, respectively) can be said to be *orgē* or *thumos* (at least insofar as *thumos* manifests *orgē*; see 7.1n.5 and 7.5n.56).

pity, for instance, essentially involved a desire, he could quite easily have characterized it, like anger, as an *orexis meta lupēs*, a desire accompanied by distress. As anger shows, and as we shall also see with feeling-friendly-towards, he is happy to include a desire in a definition if he thinks the state in question involves one. But, with pity and the emotions just mentioned, he shows no interest in doing so. This provides strong support for the view that he does not think that emotions in general essentially incorporate desires.

But more needs to be said, for there are other considerations to address. First, some have claimed that in his discussion of motives for action in *Rhet.* I.10 he treats emotions generally as types of desire. Second, it might be argued that while Aristotle does not *directly* refer to a desire in the definitions of other emotions, he sometimes *indirectly* refers to one insofar as he characterizes some emotions as kinds of 'disturbance' (*tarachē*). Third, one may argue on the basis of his discussion of fear's role in courage and its coordinate vices (in the ethical works) that Aristotle has a motivational understanding of this emotion in particular. And, finally, in *Rhet.* II.4 Aristotle defines feeling-friendly-towards simply in terms of a desire and, by implication, its contrary, hating, which is explicitly said to be 'without pain' (1382a12–13), would also be such. In this chapter I tackle these considerations in turn. I first argue that *Rhet.* I.10 need not be read as equating emotions and desires, but instead as referring to desires that are prompted by emotions, or to emotions that are component parts of states that include a desire (as with anger) (7.1). I next argue that whatever Aristotle means by 'disturbance' in this context, its inclusion does not undermine the general picture of his account of emotions as representational pleasures or distresses alone (7.2). I then propose that while the notion that Aristotle has a motivational understanding of fear in the ethical works does have some plausibility, such a usage must sit alongside his understanding of fear as a representational distress alone, not replace it (7.3). And with regard to feeling-friendly-towards (and by implication hating) I argue that there is evidence to suggest that Aristotle here defines a state (a desire) which indicates the presence of *two* distinct emotions. But the emotions themselves are simply representational pleasures/distresses alone. Defining the desire is, in effect, a convenient shorthand for specifying the emotions in question (7.4)

If I am right, Aristotle observes a distinction between emotions and desires. Clearly, though, he thinks that emotions, as representational pleasures or distresses, often link to and interact with desires in interesting ways. I explore this further in 7.5 by examining how emotions, without themselves being (in part) desires, may nonetheless (contingently) prompt desires against the background of other desiderative dispositions of the subject. The upshot is that emotions may form part of states that incorporate desires (as with anger) or prompt desires against the background of other states, but are not themselves, even in part, desires.

7.1 Motives for action in *Rhet.* I.10

It has been claimed that emotions come up in two different 'theoretical frameworks' in *Rhet.*: as motives for action in I.10 and as 'instruments of persuasion' in book II (see Striker 1996: 289–91 and Viano 2010). On this view, Aristotle separates 'the desiderative from the cognitive aspect of the emotions' (Striker 1996: 289) and, at least in book I, may be treating emotions *as* desires. One commentator even tries to see the I.10 framework (so construed) as the general model for his account of emotions in *Rhet.* as a whole (Frede 1996: 266–9). But even the more modest claim that I.10 shows he had a recognizable notion of emotions *as* desires—as motives for action—would appear to undermine my view that he thinks the two distinct. So let us investigate further. In I.10 he is providing argumentative material for forensic speech ('accusation and defence'), in particular with respect to the motives for injustice. There are two different sections where emotions are feasibly in play.

1. In the opening part of I.10 he points out that it is owing to vice and *akrasia* that people deliberately choose to do harm and evil (1368b12–14). And he provides a series of examples where people act unjustly owing to different vices; for instance, 'the ungenerous person does injustice where money is concerned; the self-indulgent where the pleasures of the body are concerned; the soft (*ho malakos*) where comfort is concerned' (1368b16–18), and so on. After his examples (which run on until 1368b23), he generalizes: 'and likewise each of the others with respect to its underlying sort of [depravity] (*mochthēria*)' (1368b23–4; *mochthēria* implied from 1368b14–15). But he then notes: 'this will be clear partly from what we said about the virtues and partly from what we will say about the emotions (*pathē*)' (1368b25–6). The back reference is to his discussion of virtue in I.9, while the forward reference is most plausibly to his discussion of the emotions in book II. And since this gloss immediately follows the generalization, it appears to invite us to extend the kind of analysis just given to other cases.[3] But how do emotions fit in here? Within the examples themselves there were several references to emotions. Most clearly, we were told (i) that the cowardly person does injustice 'where dangers are concerned', 'for they abandon their comrades because of fear' (1368b18–20); and (ii) that the quick-spirited person (*ho oxuthumos*) does injustice because of anger (*orgē*) (1368b20).[4] It is clear here that emotions are cited as prompting certain kinds of action (in certain kinds of

---

[3] It could (in addition) refer to further clarifying or further elaborating on the existing examples.
[4] We also have the bitter person (*ho pikros*) doing injustice because of revenge (1368b21), where the bitter person is a kind of person disposed to anger (see *NE* IV.5.1126a19–22) and revenge is treated as the co-relative of (the desire of) anger (*Rhet.* I.10.1369b11–12); and the shameless person (*ho anaischuntos*) doing injustice because of contempt for reputation (*di' oligōrian doxēs*) (1368b22–3), where shamelessness is treated as an emotion in *Rhet.* II (see **10.5** and **Cat.8**).

people). However, what is *not* stated is that emotions are (in part) *themselves* desires. Fear could be envisaged as *prompting* a desire to flee *in a cowardly person* (more on this in 7.3). And anger, as we saw in Chapter 6, can be taken to motivate actions insofar as it incorporates both a desire (for revenge) and an emotion. So too, the invited extension to other cases permits that emotions could prompt desires in certain kinds of agent or form parts of states that include desires, without themselves (even in part) *being* desires. This reference to emotions in I.10, then, does not entail that Aristotle thinks that emotions *are* themselves (in part) desires.

2. Aristotle's discussion then broadens into providing an account of why people do anything whatsoever (1368b32ff.). The relevant part for us is about actions that are due to ourselves and of which we are ourselves the cause (1368b37–1369a1). Aristotle claims that these stem either from habit (*ethos*) or from desire (*orexis*) and, if the latter, either from rational desire (*dia logistikēn orexin*) or from non-rational desire (*di' alogon [orexin]*) (1369a1–2). Rational desire is then identified as 'wish' (*boulēsis*), i.e. desire of the good (*orexis agathou*); while anger (*orgē*) and appetite (*epithumia*) are identified as non-rational desires (*alogoi orexeis*) (1369a2–4). Interestingly, 'anger', *orgē*, in this chapter seems to be treated as synonymous with 'spirit', *thumos*, since in the summary list of all the causes of action, which immediately follows the division just noted, the latter replaces *orgē* (1369a7).[5] Thus far, then, Aristotle is clearly thinking of anger (*qua thumos*, 'spirit') as a *desire*. Again, this is unproblematic for me since I maintain that anger consists of both a desire (for revenge) *and* an emotion (distress at an apparent slight), with the desire and emotion numerically distinct states. Referring to anger as a desire, on this view, does not identify desires with emotions, it just picks out anger by reference to one of its components. Anger *is* a desire (an *orexis*), but it is an emotion (a *pathos*) no less.

---

[5] As I discussed in my 2012 (ch. 5), there is evidence elsewhere that Aristotle often treats *orgē* and *thumos* as synonyms. Note, contra Scheiter (2013) and Saenz (2018), my claim there was *not* that there is never any scope for a broader use of *thumos* in Aristotle (see e.g. 2012: 129–31), just that most often he appears to have his account of *orgē* in mind. Saenz claims that this is 'false' and that Aristotle has a broader notion of *thumos* in play in which it is 'the faculty that cognizes social value' (85). But besides any concerns we might have about this in its own terms, his chief support for the broader notion, it turns out, is an interpretation of the components of *orgē* in *Rhet.* II.2-3 (80–2, 85). Saenz claims that *anger* requires cognition of social value. Evidently, appealing to features of Aristotle's account of *orgē*—and how it (allegedly) involves cognition of social value—is not going to show that there is notion of *thumos* which is broader than *orgē* insofar as it (*thumos*) involves cognition of social value! That said, as noted, I am (and *was*) happy to accept that in some passages Aristotle may have a broader notion in mind. My claim was (and is) that *frequently* he appears to treat *orgē* and *thumos* as synonyms, and I see nothing in Saenz or Scheiter to suggest otherwise (I refer the reader to the passages I discussed in my 2012 (111–17) in support; see also 7.5n.56 below).

In the next section of the text (1369a7–31) Aristotle argues that we do not need further to divide his causes of action according to stages of life, states of character, or other related things. This is because in each case the action is still ultimately due to either anger, appetite, or rational desire. Within this chunk, however, there may appear to be a generalization to other emotions. Aristotle writes:

> For if the young happen to be prone to anger (*orgiloi*) or appetite, they do not do actions of this sort owing to youth, but owing to anger (*orgē*) and appetite. Nor is it owing to wealth or poverty—rather the poor happen to have an appetite for money owing to their lack of it, while the rich happen to have an appetite for unnecessary pleasures owing to their abundant resources. But these people too will do the actions they do, not owing to wealth or poverty but owing to appetite. Similarly, both the just and the unjust, and the others said to do the actions they do in accord with their states [of character], do them owing to the same causes, since they do them either owing to rational calculation (*dia logismon*) or owing to *pathos* (*dia pathos*). (1369a9–18)

Noting that the *dia alogon orexin* ('owing to non-rational desire') of 1369a2–3, in the original division, is now picked up by '*dia pathos*', Gisela Striker (1996) suggests:

> one might conclude that all the passions are supposed to be covered by 'spirit and appetite' and that they are all to be seen as irrational desires. (289)

But although one 'might' conclude this (and Frede 1996: 268 appears to), it would, I think, be an unjustified stretch to do so. We should first note that it cannot be taken as a given that anytime we read '*pathos*' Aristotle simply means 'emotion'; for he uses the term in a number of different ways.[6] Instead, I suspect he could just be employing *dia pathos* as a shorthand for *dia alogon orexin* ('owing to non-rational desire'), similar to the way he uses *dia logismon* ('owing to reasoning') in the same phrase as a shorthand for *dia logistikēn orexin* ('owing to rational desire') (from 1369a2). In the passage (quoted above) running up to the mention of *dia logismon* and *dia pathos*, Aristotle only explicitly tracks each of the stages of life or states of character back to either anger (*orgē*) or appetite. And it is notable that as the chapter progresses, and he goes on to chart what is enacted in line with each of the causes of action, when we come to desire there is no generalization from *thumos* and *epithumia* to cover other emotions. Once again, we only have *dia logismon* ('owing to rational calculation')—through which is performed what appears advantageous (*sumpherein*) (1369b7–11)—'spirit or anger'

---

[6] See Bonitz (1870: s.v.); Rorty (1984); and Rapp (2002: 543–5).

(*thumos kai orgē*)—through which acts of revenge are taken (1369b11–12)—and appetite—through which is done what appears pleasant (1369b15–16). The three-fold division of desire, that is, remains in play and there is no suggestion that 'anger and appetite' is intended to cover all emotions and mark them all out as desires, as Striker proposed. Admittedly, Aristotle then takes his division as a cue (1369b28–31) to consider pleasure in more detail in *Rhet.* I.11 ('the advantageous' is taken to be covered by his previous discussion in I.6) and the range of things that count as pleasant and painful in I.11 is very broad (see the introduction to Chapter 5). But while this implies that he has a broad notion of *epithumia* in play, it clearly does not imply that every other emotion besides anger (which remains narrowly connected to the desire for revenge) is now somehow conceived *as a species of epithumia* (I come to *epithumia* in Chapter 8). All that is required, once again, is that insofar as desires are bound up with emotions—when, e.g., a desire is prompted by an emotion or an emotion forms in response to a desire being satisfied or thwarted—the desires will ultimately have to fall under one of Aristotle's three species. That may ultimately prove problematic for his account *of desire*, but it is not a flaw in his theory *of emotions* (as representational hedonic states).[7] And it certainly does not show that he here envisages emotions in general to be (in part) desires.[8]

There is a further point, though. Recall, on my reading, Aristotle thinks that anger is a state that combines *both* a desire (for revenge) *and* an emotion (distress at an apparent slight). Anger, then, *is* an emotion (*qua* representational distress). In addition, in Chapter 8 I will argue that there may be a sense in which at least a good subset of *epithumiai* also have the same overall structure as anger. Such *epithumiai* will, that is, involve a numerically distinct emotion (a representational distress) *and* a desire (for pleasure). If this is right, it is even less problematic for Aristotle to use *dia pathos* to pick up 'anger and appetite'. For both of these (or at least a decent subset of *epithumiai*) would themselves count as emotions (*qua* incorporating a numerically distinct representational distress). And so even if *dia pathos* at 1369a18 refers to 'emotion', it need not refer to *all* emotions. It could just pick up anger and *epithumia*—the states he has been specifying and discussing—by reference to *their* emotions. This would not *equate* desires and emotions. It would just be a handy shorthand to the extent that the two non-rational desires that he wishes to refer to *themselves incorporate* (distinct) emotions (representational distresses).[9]

---

[7] I discuss how it may be a problem for Aristotle's account of desire in my 2012 (ch. 8).
[8] I should stress that Striker thinks the theoretical framework of *Rhet.* II moves Aristotle in the direction of distinguishing desires and emotions (1996: 291–3), but she does here entertain the possibility that in I.10, at least, he might view emotions as desires. Viano (2010: 14) also claims Aristotle equates the two in *Rhet.* I.
[9] Aristotle also uses *dia pathos* to pick up *thumos* and *epithumia* in *NE* III.1.1111b1–2 but, again, there is no indication that he means anything other than his two species of desire. (And, once again, to the extent that these *are*, in part, emotions, *dia pathos* is reasonable in any event.)

On my view, then, *Rhet.* I.10 is consistent with the account of anger I developed in Chapter 6: emotions are not themselves desires but can (a) form part of states that also incorporate a desire or (b) prompt desires against the background of other desiderative dispositions. In the relevant parts of I.10 Aristotle's focus is on desires (*orexeis*), not emotions as such, even though (as I see it) two of these states (anger and appetite) include (or, with appetite, can include) emotions.

7.2 Emotions as involving a 'disturbance' (*tarachē*)

With some emotions Aristotle refers to a 'disturbance' (*tarachē*) alongside the distress. So fear (*phobos*):

> Let fear be a sort of distress or disturbance (*lupē tis ē tarachē*) arising from the appearance of a future destructive or painful evil. (*Rhet.* II.5.1382a21–2)

And shame (*aischunē*):

> Let shame be a sort of distress or disturbance (*lupē tis ē tarachē*)[10] about evils—whether present, past, or future—that appear to bring a person into disrepute. (*Rhet.* II.6.1383b22–4)

Again, we also find envy (*phthonos*) characterized in terms of a disturbance and, by implication, pity (*eleos*) and indignation (*nemesan*) too—albeit not in their definitions. In *Rhet.* II.9 Aristotle claims:

> It might seem, though, that envy is also opposed to feeling pity in the same way, as being of the same kind (*genos*)—even the same thing—as indignation; but it is a distinct thing. For though envy too is a disturbing pain (*lupē men gar tarachōdēs kai ho phthonos estin*) and is directed at doing-well (*epi eupragia(i)*), it is not about someone underserving of it, but about an equal and similar. (1386b16–20)

Thus, even though Aristotle did not specify envy, pity, and indignation in terms of a disturbance in their definitions, the above passage suggests that he nonetheless views them as disturbing distresses. Could this connection between emotions and disturbances at least *indirectly* indicate that he thinks that they too involve desires?

How would this work? It might be proposed that the 'disturbance' here is a vestige of the process account of pleasure we find in Plato (see esp. *Philebus*

---

[10] Reading *ē* rather than *kai* in 1383b13, with the OCT and MS A.

31d4–9 and following; also *Timaeus* 64c7–65b3), which is also echoed in Aristotle's account of pleasure (and pain) in *Rhet.* I.11 (1369b33–5) (see the introduction to Chapter 5). Roughly, on this account, pain is experienced when there is a disturbance or disruption of a natural state of the subject, pleasure when the disruption is restored. If pain is connected to a disturbance in some such way, one might take it to imply a *desire* for the restoration.[11] Now, clearly, for this suggestion to have any plausibility it will have to be adjusted in line with the sorts of representational distresses we are concerned with. But perhaps Aristotle's use of 'disturbance' in the above specifications could be thought to indicate that he thinks that such distresses disrupt our balance or harmony (or some such) and so are intrinsically states we want to get out of? On this view, since we do not like being disturbed or troubled, we will seek to be free of whatever it is that is making us such. As Aristotle writes in his discussion of anger: 'the one who is pained seeks something' (*Rhet.* II.2.1379a12).[12]

I believe we should resist this idea. First, note its limited applicability. Some emotions are representational pleasures, not representational distresses, and these could not sensibly be characterized by reference to a disturbance. Perhaps it might instead be suggested (in line with the Platonic account) that such emotions should be construed as the *restoration* of such a disturbance? This would require us to take each pleasure-based emotion (schadenfreude, feeling-grateful-for, pleasure-based indignation, etc.) as a response to our satisfying a pre-existing desire, however unexpected the event in question was.[13] But even if that could be substantiated (perhaps by appealing to very general desiderative dispositions of the agent that lie in the background; see **7.5**), it would not support the idea that such emotions *are* (in part) desires: satisfying a desire is not itself a desire. So appealing to the use of *tarachē* that occurs with some of the emotions is not going to help show that *all* emotions are (in part) desires.[14]

---

[11] So Frede (1996: 271). On the status of the *Rhet.* I.11 definition, see e.g. Gosling and Taylor (1982: 196–9); Rapp (2002: ii: 461–5); Dow (2015: 163–77); Price (2017: 185–8); and the introduction to Chapter 5 above. On the view I am considering, we say that if a state involves a disturbance or disruption then one experiences a painful disturbance that one seeks to rectify (i.e. for what would rectify it). Aristotle appears to criticize the process account in *NE* (VII.12.1152b33–1153a17, X.3.1173b4–20), instead viewing pleasure as supervening on an activity (see **5.1**).

[12] Cf. Frede (1996: 276), who wants to construe emotions, for Aristotle, as 'mixed feelings', that is, as essentially involving *both* pleasure *and* pain. Faced with thereby having to find pleasures connected to, e.g., fear, longing, and mourning, she suggests that the pleasure they contain is 'usually remedial', namely, 'the pleasure of getting rid of what bothers us'. Cf. also Fortenbaugh (2006: 79–81). For criticism of Frede's view, see Striker (1996: 290–3).

[13] Cf. Rapp (2002: 568–9).

[14] If a pleasure-based emotion is itself the satisfying of a desire, it cannot itself coherently involve a desire for that desire to be satisfied. If, e.g., pride-in-another (see *Rhet.* II.9.1386b30–1 and **Cat.17**) is the satisfying of a desire that X deservedly do well, it cannot itself coherently involve a desire that X deservedly do well (X has *done* well, that is why one is having the emotion). In what way, then, *could* a pleasure-based emotion involve a desire? Perhaps: a desire for the events (which the representational pleasure is about) *to continue*, so that the emotion may continue? But the event may be a one off and pleasurable as such (e.g. a chance meeting, or someone unexpectedly doing-well), in which case a

In fact, though, the use of 'disturbance' in the specifications above does not show that Aristotle thinks those emotions *are*, even in part, desires. The Platonic background suggests that pain is a disrupted state. But a disrupted or disturbing state is not *itself* a desire, even if we (typically) want to get out of disrupted or disturbing states.[15] And yet the emotions in question are *themselves* characterized as 'distresses or disturbances' (shame, fear) or 'distressful disturbances' (envy, pity, and indignation). Thus, even if such emotions entailed desires, those desires would be distinct from the emotions in question *as such* and would only occur *as a result of* them. Hence the most one could hope to get out of 'disturbance' is that such emotions *entail* a desire, insofar as they involve a psychic imbalance that we seek to restore, not that they *are themselves* (in part) desires (although I shall soon question whether there really is 'entailment' here anyway).

What else might the 'disturbance' be intended to signify? I suggest that we might, rather, think that its appearance in the specifications of shame and fear is simply intended to indicate that the distress can (but need not) be of a certain kind. The definition of shame suggests that the disturbance, no less than the distress, must be representational and about the same object as the distress: one is distressed or disturbed *about* (*peri*) evils that appear to bring one into disrepute. This may indicate that the 'disturbance', here, is just intended to flag that the distress can be highly troubling or traumatic (so Aristotle means: 'a distress or a highly disturbing distress', or some such). This reading receives support from the use of 'disturbing' (*tarachōdēs*) in the *Rhet*. II.9 passage quoted above. As noted, 'disturbance' (*tarachē*) is not employed in the definitions of those emotions, but in *Rhet*. II.9 is simply added as an adjectival qualification of the distress itself. And, once again, the disturbing distress of envy is explicitly said to have the object that the distress was directed at in the official definition. Aristotle seems to

---

desire for it to continue may not make sense. Indeed, some pleasures may be perfect in their novelty or transience, or in the first-time completion of something, and lose their lustre if repeated. As Aristotle notes: 'Some things delight us when they are new, but later do so less...for at first the mind is in a state of stimulation and intensely active about them, as people are with respect to their vision when they look hard at a thing, but afterwards our activity is not of this kind, but has grown relaxed; for which reason the pleasure also is dulled' (*NE* X.4.1175a6–10). (I would instead suggest that while it may be the case that experiencing pride-in-another is dependent on our background dispositions—one has to be prone to take pleasure in another's success—the emotion itself is simply a hedonic *response* to someone deservedly doing-well; where the latter may or may not have been desired in advance and may or may not make sense to wish to continue; see Chapter 11.)

[15] The *Philebus* refers to a disruption (*lusis*) or destruction (*phthora*) of the nature of the animal (31d5, 32b2–3) and specifies hunger, thirst, and being too hot or cold as such disruptions (31e–32a). While such disruptions will standardly lead to desires which, when satisfied, will bring the restoring pleasure, the pain or disruption *as such* is not *itself* a desire—it is just a painful state. The *Philebus* also characterizes the hope of being restored as a pleasure and the expectation of a painful bodily disruption as a pain (32b9–c5). These seem to be emotions, rather than desires (even if they typically prompt desires), insofar as they seem to be hedonic responses to how one construes the situation. Contrast the notion of 'hope' in the next section, which may be a *boulēsis* (one of Aristotle's three species of desire). See also Dimas (2019: 127). (Note, a state can be both a desire and a distress without that implying the desire *is* the distress, as we saw with anger in Chapter 6.)

be emphasizing that emotions can be particularly poignant distresses, ones that disturb or rock us.[16]

7.3 Fear and desire (and more on 'disturbance')

Let us consider fear further. Insofar as we associate fear with a desire, we may think that it would be a desire to escape or flee the feared object.[17] Aristotle writes:

> [a] [For people] to be afraid there must be some hope (*tina elpida*) of being saved from what they are anxious about. [b] A sign (*semeion*) of this is that fear makes people inclined to deliberate, whereas no one deliberates about hopeless things. (*Rhet.* II.5.1383a5–8)

It could well be that [a] alludes to a general wish (*boulēsis*) to be saved. Indeed, such a desire would even be compatible with one recognizing that one will not be able to bring about the desired end oneself. Some of Aristotle's examples of wishes (*boulēseis*) in *NE* III.2 concern things that 'could in no way be brought about one's own efforts', e.g. that an actor or sportsperson win a competition (1111b23–4). Relatedly, in order to feel fear, we may need to have at least some, however faint, hope of being saved from the feared object, even if that would involve someone else coming to the rescue. On this view, the Spartans at Thermopylae—recognizing they had no hope of escape or being saved—could not have felt fear (although see n.22 below). But how, precisely, does fear relate to such a hope? Note, first, fear is not plausibly construed as *prompting* such a hope. The hope to be saved from the fearful object was a condition of one experiencing fear in the first place. The claim is that to be able to experience fear, one must think that it is *possible* to escape the feared thing, and hope for such an escape. We cannot, on this view, fear the *inevitable* (although we could clearly have other negative emotions, e.g. sadness, despondency, etc.). Similarly, with [b] we are told that a sign of this (viz. that a necessary condition for fear is a hope of safety) is that fear inclines one to deliberate. The deliberation in question clearly pertains to how to get out of the predicament one faces. Aristotle holds that deliberation pertains to things that are in our power and can be done (*NE* III.3.1112a30–1), and is directed at an

---

[16] Rapp (2002: 549) suggests that *tarachē* could indicate a certain kind of pain, namely, pain felt at the prospect of a future pain. He then proposes (631) that with shame this might pick out the cases in which the emotion is future-directed (i.e. distressful anticipation of the discovery of a shameful action one has already committed but which has not yet been revealed, or of a shameful deed not yet done). But the use of *tarachōdēs* in the *Rhet.* II.9 passage counts against this suggestion since pity, envy, and indignation are not future-directed in the way fear or such cases of shame are.

[17] Indeed, on one view, attributed to the Stoics, fear simply *is* 'a non-rational shrinking or aversion of an expected danger' (*SVF* III.391).

end supplied by *boulēsis* (*NE* III.5.1113b3, cf. III.2.1111b26–9). So the fact that fear makes us inclined to deliberate is an indicator that it requires a hope to be saved from the fearful thing. (This allows that in some cases we may recognize that we cannot do anything and so deliberation is pointless. So long as there is still a hope that *someone* might save us, the necessary condition for fear can be satisfied.) But, once again, fear does not prompt this hope. The hope is a condition for the fear. Nor, second, can the hope in question be sensibly construed as a *part of* fear. Fear does not involve being distressed at the hope of being saved. Equally, fear is not a distress at the danger accompanied by (*meta*) hope of being saved, in the way that anger is a desire for revenge accompanied by distress at a slight (*orexis meta lupēs*). The definition of fear explicitly specifies it as distress at the danger alone—it is a distress that arises from the appearance of a future destructive or painful evil (*Rhet.* II.5.1382a21–2). The hope of being saved, then, it seems, is *a background condition* for fear to occur, not part of what fear itself is.[18]

It is of course true that fear *can* prompt a desire to flee the feared object. Aristotle tells us that a coward 'fears the things he ought not, in the way he ought not' (*NE* III.7.1115b34–5) and is 'in a way a despairing sort of person, since he fears everything' (III.7.1116a2–3). And he notes that the coward flees from the things he fears (see e.g. *NE* II.2.1104a20–1, III.8.1116b15–22, V.2.1130a18, 30; *Rhet.* II.6.1383b19; cf. *NE* III.7.1116a12–15). It is surely plausible that it is the coward's fear that prompts his desire to flee: his *distress* at the danger motivates him to run away (*Rhet.* I.10.1368b18–20).[19] And yet it is clear that Aristotle thinks that fear only operates this way *in the coward*, and hence that the subject's *character* plays a crucial role in linking fear to motivation. For he also holds that those who are courageous feel fear and yet lack the motivation. In *NE* III.7 he claims that with some things it is beyond a human being's power not to fear them (unless insane), whereas with others it is possible to fear or not fear them (1115b7–10). And yet Aristotle explicitly claims that courageous people will not only fear the things that it is beyond human capability not to fear, but also the things that are *not* beyond human capability not to fear (1115b10–12). These are, though, things it is possible to fear more or less (1115b13–14), and the courageous are distinctive in that they fear them in the way they should and when they should (1115b18) (and, unlike the cowardly, do not fear to any extent things that are not frightening

---

[18] The 'hope' (*elpis*) that is mentioned in the specification of *confidence* (*to tharsos*) (*Rhet.* II.5.1383a17–18)—'[confidence's] hope of things providing safety involves a *phantasia* of them as being close at hand'—should, I believe, be understood more along the lines of *expectation*, not a wish (*boulēsis*) for something that may or may not transpire. For it is an expectation or anticipation of safety that will prompt confidence, not the (perhaps faint) wish for it. For hope as *expectation*, see *Mem.* (1.449b10–11, 27–8), where it is simply the contrary of memory and could be translated 'what is expected or anticipated'. For more on confidence, see **10.7**.

[19] Similarly, optimistic people (*hoi euelpides*) are confident (*tharrein*) in danger but, unlike those who are courageous, 'only because they have conquered often and against many foes' (III.8.1117a9–11). This is why when their adventures do not succeed, they run away (1117a15–16). It seems plausible that as their confidence turns to fear, so too their fear prompts a desire to flee.

at all (1115b14–15, 17)). But in a situation demanding courage, the courageous, though feeling fear, are not motivated to run away:

> the courageous person is as dauntless (*anekplēktos*) as humanly possible. Therefore, while he will fear even things that are not beyond human capability, *he will face them* as he ought and as reason directs, for the sake of the noble; for this is the end of virtue. (1115b10–13; my emphasis)[20]

So while fear will prompt a desire to flee in the coward (*Rhet.* I.10.1368b18–20), it will do no such thing in the courageous person, at least not in a situation demanding courage.[21] Hence, the motivational 'output' of an emotion can be contingent on the character of the person who experiences the emotion.[22] So although fear will prompt a desire to flee in the coward, it is not part of the definition of fear that it prompts such a desire, since we can be afraid without the desire. The connection between emotions and desires, it seems, operates against a background of desiderative dispositions supplied by the subject's character. I shall return to this in 7.5.[23]

---

[20] See also *EE* III.1.1228b26–7. Vigani (2017) claims that Aristotle 'never portrays the courageous person as experiencing fear when standing firm' (326). On her view, while there may be room for a fear of missing the target (325–6), and while Aristotle does allow that courageous agents would feel fear outside the context of courage (e.g. confronting an earthquake), he thinks that *in the exercise of their courage* courageous people are fearless (326). The passage quoted counts against Vigani's reading. For it is *the very things* that courageous people here *face* and *stand up to*—qua courageous—that they fear. Indeed, Aristotle's goes on: 'But it is possible to fear *these things* (*tauta*) more, or less, and again to fear things that are not fearful as if they were' (1115b13–15); and he then proceeds to sketch the various vices. It is, that is, the same things that the various vicious characters fail to respond appropriately to that the courageous agent both stands up to (in accordance with right reason and for the sake of the noble) *and*, we are told in 1115b10–13, *also fears*. This is why, as we will see, we need two notions of fear to explain Aristotle's view: fear as a distress and fear as a motivation. The courageous can be motivationally fearless, and hence stand up to fearful things, while simultaneously experiencing fear (as a distress) of them. The repeated claim that the courageous are fearless in *NE* III.6 needs to be understood as tacitly referring to 'motivational fear', given what is then claimed in III.7. See also Brady (2005) and my 2014b.

[21] A passage in *EE* III.1 suggests that Aristotle may allow someone to have a *slight* desire to flee and still count as courageous, but he still leaves open the possibility that there may be no desire at all (1228b17–29); see my 2012 (243–4). Note, even the 'or slightly' possibility would still generate a disparity between the magnitude of the fear cognized and the desiderative/motivational response.

[22] Note, it can still be a condition on the fear of courageous agents that they hope to be saved. They may think that it is *through fighting* that they can be saved. But even if they see death as likely, by standing firm they may be saved from something they fear more than even death, namely disrepute (see *NE* III.6.1115a12–14, III.8.1116a27–9, 1116b22–3; and see Plato's *Apology* 28c3–9, in turn alluding to Homer's *Iliad* XVIII 91ff.; see also my 2009 (131–2); contrast Curzer 2012: 22 and Vigani 2017: 324–5). Aristotle claims that to fear disrepute is 'right' (*dei*), 'noble' (*kalon*), 'good' (*epieikēs*), and 'modest' (*aidēmōn*), and not to fear it is 'shamelessness' (*anaischuntos*) (1115a12–14) (although cp. *NE* IV.9 and Jimenez 2020: 137; and, for a resolution, Raymond 2017: 139–41).

In this sense the Spartans at Thermopylae could feel fear, but not of death. They could fear acting disreputably by running away. And they could hope to be saved from *that*, so far as it is possible for them to stand firm.

[23] In *NE* III.12 Aristotle claims that cowardice comes about 'because of pain' (1119a21–2). The 'pain', here, is presumably the pain of fear (cf. III.7.1116a1–2). But III.12 continues: 'but pain upsets and destroys (*hē lupē existēsi kai phtheirei*) the nature of the person who feels it, whereas pleasure [which the self-indulgent person pursues] does nothing of the sort' (1119a23–4). Might this be the 'disturbance' which leads to a desire? Perhaps. But only in the coward. The remark about pain appears

Aristotle may yet have a notion of fear as motivational, but in my view this does not threaten his understanding of fear, *qua* emotion, as a representational distress, nor the idea that 'disturbance' (*tarachē*) in the definition of fear does not entail a desire. As we have seen, in *Rhet.* II.5 he in part defines fear by reference to a disturbance (*tarachē*). But, in his discussion of courage in the *NE*, he makes it clear not only (i) that the courageous agent experiences fear (in the passages we have highlighted) but also (ii) that the courageous person is *un*disturbed (*atarachos*) (III.8.1117a19, III.9.1117a31). One way of dealing with the apparent tension (fear/disturbed in *Rhet.*, fear/undisturbed in *NE*) is to note that Aristotle also recognizes a sense in which courageous people are *fearless* (e.g. *NE* III.6.1115a16, 32–4), and it is most plausibly in precisely *this* sense that they count as *atarachos*, undisturbed. The sense in question is that in the appropriate situation they will *face up to* the feared object or *stand firm* (see the *facing* of the fearful things in 1115b10–13, quoted above). Being fearless, in this sense, amounts to a disposition to act. Indeed, on this notion, those who succeed in *standing up to* things that we view as fearful will count as fearless, whether they (a) experience fear as a representational distress and yet *are not moved by it* (as with the courageous), or (b) do not experience fear as a representational distress at all, as would seem likely with the excessively fearless people that Aristotle mentions in *NE* II.7 (1107b1) and III.7 (1115b24–8).[24] And it is in this motivational sense that the courageous person counts not only as fearless, but as 'undisturbed' (*atarachos*). Aristotle claims that it is the mark of the braver person 'to be fearless and undisturbed (*atarachos*) in sudden alarms' than in those that are foreseen (III.8.1117a18–19) and he claims that the person who is 'undisturbed in the face of' things that inspire fear and 'bears himself as he should towards these' is more truly brave (III.9.1117a30–2).

It seems, then, that Aristotle operates with *two* notions of fear, *both* of which *could* be said to entail a disturbance (*tarachē*). First, there is a representational distress about some prospective danger. This requires a hope of safety as a background condition and may, in certain kinds of character, prompt a desire to flee. With this I have suggested that the disturbance (*tarachē*) is no less representational than the distress and amounts to little more than a gloss on the

---

to be a quite general one, but we know that the courageous agent, though experiencing appropriate fear, either does not desire to flee at all or does so only 'very slightly' (see n.21).

[24] For the motivational notion of fear, cf. also *De an.* III.9: 'even when the [intellect] contemplates something to be avoided or pursued, it does not straightaway command avoidance or pursuit, e.g. it often thinks of something fearful or pleasant, but it does not command being afraid (*ou keleuei phobeisthai*), although the heart is moved, or, if the object is pleasant, some other part' (432b29–433a1). This seems to envisage a scenario in which the intellect thinks of something that one would expect to command motivational fear (avoidance), but (for some reason) this does not happen. (NB: this passage also shows that Aristotle holds that one can think of something dangerous without feeling fear, contra cognitivist readings.) Insofar as courageous people are motivationally fearless, there is no issue with distinguishing them from enkratic agents (with respect to fear). Courageous people do not have any substantial clash of desires. Cf. Vigani (2017).

distress, perhaps along the lines that it can be significant or potent. Second, there is a motivational tendency to flee from something dangerous. In this sense of fear, 'disturbance' (*tarachē*), like the motivational tendency itself, indicates that one is in a position one seeks to escape from. And, in this sense, 'disturbance' *will* indicate a motivational tendency—it will amount to agents being averse to the situation they are in.[25] In *Rhet.* II Aristotle is concerned with fear in the first sense, and that is, on my reading, the sense in which it qualifies as an emotion *as such*.[26]

As confirmation that Aristotle employs 'undisturbed' (*atarachos*) in different ways, we might also compare *NE* IV.5, in the discussion of the virtue concerned with anger:

> The mild-mannered person (*ho praos*) tends to be undisturbed (*atarachos*) and not led (*agesthai*) by his passion (*pathos*), but to be angry in the manner, at the things, and for the length of time, that reason dictates. (1125b33–1126a1)

If we think that Aristotle means here that the mild-mannered person is not led (to act) by his emotion *because* such a person is undisturbed (rather than, say, simply alluding to such a person as manifesting the conjunction of two independent features), this may indicate a notion of 'disturbance' that would at least entail a desire to act (cf. Price 1995: 125). However, 'undisturbed', here, *cannot* entail that the person has 'no desire' (for revenge) since, as we saw in Chapter 6, anger *itself* entails one, and the mild-mannered person *will* be angry and seek revenge when it is appropriate to do so, as the passage itself suggests.[27] Instead, 'undisturbed' must here amount to *not being led astray* or *not being led to overact*, or some such. But clearly the notion of 'disturbed' that corresponds to *this* will not work in the accounts of fear or shame. For, I take it, no one wants to claim that it is *part of the definition* of fear or shame that in order to experience either emotion, one must be *led astray* by such states. That would seem absurdly strong (and the courageous

---

[25] Hence, that notion will not be well explained by the process account of pleasure we considered in 7.2, since the latter did not itself appear to be motivational.

[26] I suppose it might be suggested that Aristotle's definition of fear in *Rhet.* II.5 itself permits both variants. Insofar as he claims that fear is a distress or (*ē*) disturbance, one could propose that it *need not* include both. In this way, the courageous person could experience fear *qua* distress, but be fearless *qua atarachos*. But reading the 'or' (*ē*) this way might be pressing the definition too hard given, as we saw, Aristotle is happy to gloss his definition of envy (which was in terms of a distress alone) by reference to a disturbing distress. That suggests, if anything, that *tarachē* in *Rhet.* is just an innocent gloss on the distress, amounting to the possibility that the distress may be especially potent or disturbing. Price (1995: 125) seems to think that in the *NE* Aristotle wants a notion of fear-without-disturbance. For this to be compatible with *Rhet.* II.5, Price would *have to* read the latter in the disjunctive way I have just proposed. On the view developed above, by contrast, while courageous agents may well be disturbed in the sense in which they experience fear as a representational distress—that is, insofar as their distress concerns something that deeply upsets them (since they are facing death)—they will be undisturbed in the sense which corresponds to their being fearless—they will be unruffled behaviourally and be motivated to stand firm regardless. Not much, I think, hinges on which way we go.

[27] Although Aristotle does concede that mild-manneredness (*praotēs*) is not quite the right term for the mean, since mild-mannered people err of the side of the deficiency (1125b26–9, 1126a1–3).

agent a clear counter-example). So, since Aristotle uses 'undisturbed' in different ways, we are at liberty to resolve the apparent tension between the *Rhet.* II.5 definition and the *NE* passages along the lines proposed; that is, by appealing to different senses of 'disturbance' corresponding to the different senses of fear we have already sketched.[28]

7.4 Feeling-friendly-towards (*to philein*) and hating (*to misein*)

If Aristotle's accounts of anger, fear, and his use of 'disturbance' in characterizing some emotions does not show that he thinks that emotions themselves essentially incorporate a desire, and so does not threaten the reading I have offered, I may nonetheless seem to be on thinner ice when it comes to his accounts of feeling-friendly-towards (*to philein*) and hating (*to misein*) in *Rhet.* II.4. His discussion of the former has frequently been a source of concern for commentators.[29] The problem is twofold. First, Aristotle defines feeling-friendly-towards in terms of a desire, not a pleasure (or distress), and there is no mention whatsoever of pleasure (or distress) in the definition. Second, the desire that Aristotle specifies is *boulēsis* (he uses the verb, *boulesthai*, in the definition itself, and the noun *boulēsis* later on: 1381a7). But *boulēsis* is a rational desire (*De an.* III.9.432b5; *Rhet.* I.10.1369a1–4; *Top.* IV.5.126a13; cf. *De an.* III.10.433a23–5) and is never found on his lists of emotions, which seem to be classified as non-rational.[30] But if feeling-friendly-towards has been found problematic, it is fair to say that hating (*to misein*) has caused even more puzzlement.[31] For if hating was going to be either a distress or a pleasure, it would surely be the former.[32] And yet, as noted, Aristotle explicitly states that while anger is accompanied by distress

---

[28] When Aristotle claims in *Pol.* that certain types of pre-emptive action can occur because of fear (e.g. V.3.1302b21–4, V.10.1311b36–40), he could feasibly have in mind either notion of fear.

[29] See e.g. Cooper (1996: 244, 247); Striker (1996: 301n.13); Fortenbaugh (2002: 104–7); Konstan (2006: ch. 8); Price (2011: 120); Moss (2012a: 75n.15); Rapp (2013); Dow (2015: 153–4).

[30] In *Pol.* Aristotle refers to an emotional part of the soul (as distinct from the rational part) (I.5.1254b8) and, in both ethical works, the emotions, as listed at *NE* II.5.1105b21–3 and *EE* II.2.1220b12–14, are plausibly thought of as belonging to the non-rational part of the soul (*NE* I.13.1102b28–1103a3; *EE* II.1.1219a26–32). (In accordance with his division of the soul into a strictly rational part and a non-rational part that can obey it, Aristotle divides virtues into two kinds, intellectual and ethical (*NE* I.13.1103a3–7; *EE* II.1.1220a4–12), and it is ethical virtue that he is investigating when he insists that virtues, while not themselves emotions, are states (*hexeis*) in virtue of which we stand well or badly with regard to them (*NE* II.5.1105b25–8; *EE* II.2.1220b9–10, 18–20).) Exactly why he thinks emotions are non-rational is debatable but, on my view, it is compatible with him holding that a variety of intentional states can apprehend objects of emotions (see **Intro.2**). I address this in my 2014a and, more fully, in my MS. See also **2.2n.30**

[31] See e.g. Leighton (1984: 138, 1996: 218, 232–3n.14); Cooper (1996: 247–9); Striker (1996: 301n.13); Fortenbaugh (2002: 104–7); Konstan (2006: ch. 9); Price (2011: 120) Moss (2012a: 75n.15); Dow (2015: 153–4).

[32] So Cooper (1996: 248): 'it does not seem plausible to identify it as essentially a feeling of pleasurable excitement of any kind (however much, like anger, it might involve pleasurable thoughts about what you will do to the one you feel that way toward if you get the chance'.

(*meta lupēs*), hating is *ou meta lupēs*, 'without pain' (*Rhet.* II.4.1382a12–13). Hence, it has seemed that here, in his catalogue of emotions, he explicitly admits a state that contravenes his own general specification in *Rhet.* II.1—according to which emotions are accompanied by pleasure or distress (see **2.1**).

The problem with both feeling-friendly-towards and hating is compounded by the fact that it seems clear, both here and elsewhere, that Aristotle wants to include them. Besides having their own chapter in *Rhet.* II (II.4), they are also employed (in verbal forms) as examples of how emotions may bear on the decisions or verdicts (*kriseis*) of listeners in *Rhet.* II.1 (1377b31–1378a3; so too *Rhet.* I.2.1356a15–16) and appear on lists of the emotions in *De an.* I.1 (403a16–18) and *NE* II.5 (as *philia* and *misos*: 1105b21–3), with the latter also claiming that emotions are accompanied by (*hepetai*) pleasure or pain (see **2.1**).

The resolution to the difficulty that I prefer is as follows. As I see it, Aristotle does not intend to characterize either feeling-friendly-towards or hating as emotions *themselves*. Instead, he views specifying them as an economical way of pointing to a *pair* of emotions which are implied and explained by them (so we have four emotion-types in total). His discussion thereby indicates the emotions that he wants by defining states that are *themselves* unemotional rational desires (*boulēseis*).[33] On my view, this is not the only occasion in *Rhet.* II where Aristotle defines a state that is not itself an emotion in order to indicate one (or more) that is. He also does precisely this with gratitude (*charin echein*) in *Rhet.* II.7, as we shall see in **10.1**.

Here is the definition of feeling-friendly-towards in context:

[A] Let us say whom people love (*philein*) and hate (*misein*), and because of what, after having defined friendliness (*philia*) and feeling-friendly-towards (*to philein*). [B] Let feeling-friendly-towards, then, be wishing (*boulesthai*) for someone what one thinks to be good things, for his own sake not for one's own, and to be productive in action of such things so far as one can.[34] And a friend is

---

[33] By contrast, Rapp (2013: 35–8) allows feeling-friendly-towards to count as an emotion, but takes it to indicate that *hepetai* permits emotions to have a looser connection to pleasure or pain than I have specified. He writes: 'pleasure and pain are among the components of fully fledged emotions, but it is nowhere determined what functional role they are supposed to play. I take the formula "are followed by pleasure and pain (*hepetai*)" not as temporal succession, but as something like an implication: if there is an emotion, there are also occurrences of pleasure and pain—no matter how they are related to the other components of the emotion' (36). On this view, even though feeling-friendly-towards is a desire, it *itself* counts as an emotion simply because it entails pleasure and pain. Of course, 'entailing pleasure or pain' cannot itself be sufficient for an emotion (for one thing, ethical *actions* also entail pleasure or pain (cf. *NE* II.3.1104b13–18), but are not themselves emotions). So Rapp will have to find other 'components' of emotions to prevent his understanding of the pleasure/pain 'component' allowing just anything that implies pleasure or pain to count. The argument of this book so far has been that there are no other components. But see **10.8** (on 'for the most part' in the *EE* II.2 specification) and Chapter 9 on the material dimension.

[34] This connects feeling-friendly-towards with what Aristotle calls *eunoia* ('good will') in the *Ethics* (see e.g. *NE* VIII.2.1155b31–4). Aristotle also links *philia* and *eunoia* at *Rhet.* II.1.1378a18.

one who loves and is loved in return; and people think they are friends when they think they are both this way. [C] These things being presupposed, a friend is necessarily (*anankē*) someone who shares in one's pleasure at good things and in one's pains at painful ones (*philon einai ton sunēdomenon tois agathois kai sunalgounta tois lupērois*), not because of something else, but because of oneself. For all enjoy it when the things they wish for come about, and are pained when the contrary ones do, so that the pains and the pleasures are signs of wish (*boulēsis*). (II.4.1380b35–1381a7)[35]

In [A] Aristotle announces that his aim is to characterize whom people love and hate and because of what. He will do this in the remainder of the chapter (1381a7ff.). But in [B] he first provides a definition of feeling-friendly-towards in terms of wishing (*boulesthai*) for someone what one thinks to be good things. This, I believe, refers to rational desire, *boulēsis*, which is distinct from the non-rational desires of appetite (*epithumia*) and spirit (*thumos*).[36] *Boulēsis* does not count as an emotion itself by Aristotle's own criteria: it is not a representational pleasure or distress (see *Top.* VI.8.146b2), but rational desire for the good.[37] But Aristotle then goes on to show, in [C], how feeling-friendly-towards, so construed, implies two kinds of emotion. A friend shares in one's pleasure at good things and in one's distress at painful things, and not because of something else, but because of oneself. Such pleasures and distresses are therefore a 'sign' or 'marker' (*sēmeion*) of the wish (*boulēsis*) itself.[38] We thereby find two emotions associated with feeling-friendly-towards:

(1) Pleasure at (the prospect of)[39] someone getting good things—*qua* the person getting them, not insofar as it benefits you.

And:

---

[35] Aristotle continues: 'And friends are the ones, then, to whom the same things are good and bad and who are friends and enemies with the same people, since it is necessary for them to wish for the same things. So the one who also wishes for another the very things he wishes for himself is evidently a friend to him' (1381a7–10). I think this already begins the 'to whom' section.

[36] Cooper (1996: 254n.9) suggests that Aristotle might be using a broader notion of *boulesthai* 'that permits it to cover at least some nonrational desirings' (citing *Rhet.* II.12.1389a8 as a possible parallel). But the connection between *boulesthai* and thinking good (*oietai agatha*: 1380b37) in the definition shows that Aristotle has the narrow notion of *boulēsis* in mind. Cf. '*boulēsis* is *orexis* of the good, for no one wishes (*boulesthai*) for something except when he thinks it is good (*hotan oiēthē(i) einai agathon*)' (*Rhet.* I.10.1369a2–4). This also counts against Scheiter's (2013) suggestion that feeling-friendly-towards lies in the *thumoeides*, as a way of accounting for *Pol.* VII.7.1327b40–1238a1.

[37] References for the rational side of this were given at the start of this section. For the connection between *boulēsis* and the good, see *NE* III.4.1113a23–4, V.9.1136b7–8; *EE* VII.2.1235b23; *Rhet.* I.10.1369a2–4; *Top.* VI.8.146b5–6, 146b37–147a1; cf. *EE* II.7.1223b6–7, 32–3, II.10.1227a18–31. For some discussion, see my 2012 (ch.6).

[38] This would, I take it, be what Aristotle would call a 'necessary' sign in *Rhet.* I.2.1357b1–21 (hence 'all' in 1381a6 and 'necessarily' (*anankē*) in 1381a3).

[39] The 'sharing' in pleasure and distress would presumably cover not just cases in which the other is actually perceived to get good or bad things, but also the *prospect* of the other getting such.

(2) Distress at (the prospect of) someone getting painful things—*qua* the person getting them, not insofar as it harms you.

These emotions might be characterized as *taking pleasure in someone's (prospectively) doing-well* and *feeling distress in someone's (prospectively) doing-badly*. The suggestion, then, is that Aristotle specifies the desire of feeling-friendly-towards in order to indicate these two emotions, which are explained by it.

Similarly with hatred. We are told that enmity (*echthra*) and hating (*to misein*) are to be grasped theoretically (*theōrein*) from their contraries (II.4.1382a1-2), but Aristotle does not actually provide a definition of either. If hating is the contrary of feeling-friendly-towards, we might define it as follows:

Hating is wishing for someone[40] what you think to be bad things, for the person's own sake not insofar as it benefits you as such, and to be productive in action of such things so far as you can.[41]

Hating can thus reasonably be contrasted with anger in the way we find in *Rhet.* II.4: 'anger involves pain, whereas hate does not involve pain (for the angry person is pained, whereas the one who hates is not)' (1382a12-13). Hating itself, like feeling-friendly-towards, is a *rational desire* (*boulēsis*) and, as such, is painless.[42] We can also understand *Pol.* V.10's contrast between anger and hatred:

But hatred (*to misos*) [employs rational calculation (*logismos*)] more [than anger does]. For anger involves pain (*meta lupēs*), so that it is not easy to calculate rationally (*logizesthai*), whereas hatred (*echthra*) does not involve pain (*aneu lupēs*). (1312b32-4)

If, like feeling-friendly-towards, hating is a kind of rational desire, it will not only be painless, but may itself involve reasoning and thinking.[43]

---

[40] Aristotle will extend this to kinds of people in II.4; we can hate *thieves* or *sychophants* (1382a6-7).

[41] Cf. '[anger] seeks (*ephesis*) pain for its object, whereas [hatred] seeks evil (*kakon*) (for the angry person wishes [his revenge] to be perceived, whereas to the latter it makes no difference; and painful things are all perceptible, whereas the greatest evils (*ta malista kaka*) are the least perceptible ones, [for example], injustice, lack of practical wisdom). For the presence of evil (*parousia tēs kakias*) does not at all cause pain' (*Rhet.* II.4.1382a8-12).

[42] As noted in 6.6, it seems that anger and hating can have the same cause, namely spite (*epēreasmos*) (II.4.1382a2). Indeed, Aristotle claims that anger itself can produce hatred (1382a2).

[43] Hence, as we saw in 7.1, on his list of causes for action in *Rhet.* I.10, Aristotle can replace *boulēsis* with what is done 'owing to reasoning' (*dia logismon*) (1369a6-7, picking up *boulēsis* in 1369a3-4; which in turn picks up 'rational desire' (*logistikē orexis*) in 1369a2) (there is obviously a clear Platonic background to this: *Republic* IV.439c-441c). Although desires which occur as a result of *deliberation* for the good are *boulēseis*, I argue in my 2012 that Aristotle does not think that this is required for *boulēsis*, nor what makes this desire rational (178-89).

Similarly, however, like feeling-friendly-towards, we can easily see that hating will imply parallel (contrary) emotions to those we found with feeling-friendly-towards:

(3) pleasure at (the prospect of) someone getting bad things—*qua* the person getting them, not insofar as it benefits you.

(4) distress at (the prospect of) someone getting good things—*qua* the person getting them, not insofar as it harms you.

And, as with the emotions implied by feeling-friendly-towards, these emotions might be characterized as *pleasure in someone's (prospectively) doing-badly* and *distress in someone's (prospectively) doing-well*.[44]

It is also, I think, easy to see how all four emotions connected to feeling-friendly-towards and hating could be relevant for the orator. As Aristotle notes in *Rhet*. II.1:

things do not appear the same to those who love (*philein*) and those who hate (*misein*)...To the one who loves (*philein*), the person about whom he makes his judgement seems not to do injustice or to do little injustice, but to the one who hates (*misein*), it is the contrary. (1377b31, 1378a1–3)

Of course, this would apply no less to *feeling-friendly-towards* and *hating* themselves, than to the emotions these desires produce, but nonetheless the emotions will also do the job: if I experience pleasure directed at (the prospect of) an accused *doing-well* (where my pleasure is for the accused's own sake, not for some benefit of mine) and a parallel distress at (the prospect of) that person *doing-badly*, this will incline me to see that person as doing no justice or little injustice.

My account of feeling-friendly-towards and hating is similar to Dow's (2015: 153–4). He claims that these states are not emotions themselves but 'dispositions' to emotions. And he too points to the passage immediately following the definition of feeling-friendly-towards as showing that this state 'involves a disposition to feel pleasure along with a friend at good things, and pain at distressing or painful things' (153). However, Dow thinks that there is a problem with integrating hating in a parallel way. He says that doing so 'is awkward as an interpretation of 1382a12–13', quoted above, 'because hostility is contrasted with anger—and it is clearly *episodes* of anger that are in view' (154; his emphasis). Consequently, Dow asserts that Aristotle '*should have said*' (154; his emphasis) that hating is a disposition to emotions, even if he did not in fact. On my view, Dow has been misled by

---

[44] These emotions could be distinguished from schadenfreude and envy, respectively, to the extent that the latter invoke the notion of *desert* (*axia*). See **Cat.13** and **Cat.18**.

the notion that hating is a disposition. Hating and feeling-friendly-towards are not dispositions *as such*. They are desires (*boulēseis*). But they are desires that dispose one to certain emotions. In the passage that Dow cites, Aristotle is contrasting an episode of anger with an episode of hating, where the latter is a desire. And they are distinguished *precisely* in the way he claims: since hating is a rational desire, it is not accompanied by pain. But, still, hating disposes an agent to emotions, viz. the representational pleasures and distresses highlighted. And it is, on my view, these emotions that Aristotle is trying to specify by his discussion of the desire.[45]

So construed, it is worth emphasizing the different ways emotions are involved in anger, on the one hand, and feeling-friendly-towards and hating, on the other. While anger *is*, in part, an emotion (distress at an apparent slight), feeling-friendly-towards and hating are not emotions themselves. They are desires. But these desires are convenient ways of specifying a pair of emotions that are entailed by them (entailed: *anankē*: *Rhet.* II.4.1381a3). Someone with these desires will have certain emotional responses when those desires are satisfied or thwarted (or at the prospect of such). For example, with the desire of feeling-friendly-towards, one will be disposed to experience pleasure at (the prospect of) the person getting good things and distress at (the prospect of) the person getting bad things. *Mutatis mutandis*, with hating.[46]

7.5 Emotions and background desiderative dispositions

If the argument of this chapter is on the right lines, we have no reason to reject the idea that Aristotle thinks emotions are representational pleasures or distresses alone (as is suggested by the fact that the majority of his definitions of emotions do not mention a desire).[47] Nonetheless, as we have already seen with anger, fear,

---

[45] Thus, when Aristotle places feeling-friendly-towards and hating on his lists of emotions, he could mean: 'the friendly emotions' and 'the hating emotions', or some such. Since each specifies a pair of emotions, this could be his best way of referring to them. But for an alternative to this, see 10.8.

[46] By contrast, the account of *epithumia* I provide in Chapter 8 *is* directly parallel to anger. The emotion will be part of what *epithumia* is, not simply entailed by (the prospect of) its satisfaction or thwarting. This befits the fact that *epithumia* is cross-posted as both a desire and an emotion (see n.2 above and n.56 below; also Chapter 8 nn.1, 12). Also, given the parallel with feeling-friendly-towards and hating, we might further distinguish certain *reactive* emotions that may result from (the prospect of) the desire of anger being satisfied or thwarted. As we have seen (**6.5**), Aristotle draws attention to one of these himself: a representational pleasure concerning the prospect of getting revenge. But equally, insofar as one takes oneself to have achieved it, anger would presumably also be associated with a representational pleasure concerning *having got* revenge (and so having rectified the slight) (cf. *NE* IV.5.1126a21-2)—unless, of course, one misjudged the reward getting revenge would bring.

[47] There are two other ways (I can think of) that one might attempt to argue that emotions essentially involve desires, neither of which is compelling. (1) In *De an.* I.1 Aristotle provides a schematic definition of affections of the soul that involve the body, as follows: 'Being angry is [A] a particular movement (*kinēsis tis*) of a body of such and such a kind, or a part or potentiality of it, [B] as a result of this (*hupo toude*) [C] for the sake of that (*heneka toude*)' (403a25-7). With anger, [C] might be

and feeling-friendly-towards/hating, emotions can link up with desires in interesting and important ways. I close this chapter by offering some further thoughts about this.

With respect to the link between our background desiderative dispositions and the motivational impact of our emotions (as we saw with fear), it is interesting to consider a passage where Aristotle links emotions to specific desiderative responses:

> Emulation (*zēlos*) is a decent thing (*epieikes*) characteristic of decent people (*epieikoi*), whereas envy (*phthonos*) is a base one (*phaulon*) characteristic of base people (*phauloi*)—for the decent person, because of emulation (*dia ton zēlon*), is ready to attain the good things (*paraskeuazei tunchanein tōn agathōn*), whereas the base person, because of envy (*dia ton phthonon*), is ready for his neighbour not to have them. (*Rhet.* II.11.1388a35–b1)

It seems plausible that Aristotle is here characterizing emulation as prompting a desire to attain the good things we experience the emotion about (honoured goods, e.g. virtues and what is beneficial: 1388b11–12), and envy as prompting a desire (or wish) that the neighbour one is envious of does not have the goods in question (e.g. wealth, power, and the like).[48] To work as both the stated verb for the emulation clause and the implied verb in the envy clause, 'being ready for' (*paraskeuazein*) must, in this context, amount to something like 'be eager for', or some such.[49]

---

taken to refer to the desired end of anger (*De an.* I.1 characterizes a 'formal' account of anger as 'desire to return pain or something of sort' (403a30–1)). Now, given that prior to the schematic definition, we have just had two lists of states that include emotions (403a7, 17–18), it might be suggested that Aristotle is indicating that each emotional state should be defined along the lines of the schematic definition and so involves a desired end. But note that *perception* was on the first list and does not seem to have an end as an intentional object (and if Aristotle had some broader notion of 'end' in mind, such as contributing to the functioning of the animal, or some such, [C] need not pick out desires anyway). In any event, even if he had a narrower notion of an end as an intentional object in mind, his schematic definition need not imply that every state *has all the specified features*. An inclusive schema could include features that not every state has as such. (2) Another route some might be tempted by (see Tuozzo 1994; Charles 2006) would commit Aristotle to the following: (i) emotions are (in part) cognitions of value; (ii) cognitions of value are (in part) desires; hence (iii) emotions are (in part) desires. I have argued that Aristotle rejects (i) in Part I of this book (emotions are *responses* to such cognitions). I argue he rejects (ii) in my 2020; see also *NE* III.2.1112a9–11, discussed in 5.5n.19).

[48] Emulation is 'a sort of distress at the apparent presence, in the case of others who are by nature like the person himself, of good things that are honoured and possible for someone to acquire, not owing to the fact that another has them but rather owing to the fact he himself does not' (*Rhet.* II.11.1388a32–5). Envy is 'a sort of distress at apparent doing-well in terms of the goods mentioned [wealth, power, etc., from II.9?], on the part of those like themselves, not in order that something accrue to the person himself, but because of those [possessing it]' (*Rhet.* II.10.1387b23–5). Reeve (2018: 271n.539) traces the goods in question back, via II.9.1387a6–23 on indignation, to *Rhet.* I.5–6.

[49] Reeve (2018: *ad loc.*) renders 'setting himself up to'. The *ROT*'s (*ad loc.*) 'take steps to secure' / 'take steps to stop' and Sherman's (1993: 19) 'take steps to secure' / 'take steps to thwart' seem to me to go beyond the Greek.

But insofar as emulation is *itself* a decent thing, characteristic of decent people, and prompts a desire to achieve the goods in question, and insofar as envy is *itself* a base thing, characteristic of base people, and prompts a desire that the envied person does not have the goods in question, there would seem to be a contrast between these emotions, on the one hand, and fear, on the other. For although fear *can* prompt a desire to flee or escape the feared object, it need not do so—it does not in the courageous—whereas the desires associated with emulation and envy seem to follow simply from the emotions themselves. But, equally clearly, the connection between the desiderative response to the emotion and the subject's character is not broken here. It is not that emulation and envy prompt their respective desires *regardless* of the subject's character. Rather, having a certain character is (for the most part) a background condition for having these emotions.[50] One is disposed to experience them *if* one possesses a character of a certain kind (decent or base), and the desires in question follow from this, given the emotion. Emulation prompts a desire for good things (viz. those possessed by the person one feels emulation about) because emulation is experienced by decent people. Envy prompts a desire that one's neighbour does not possess the good things in question because envy is experienced by bad people. Indeed, in *NE* II.6 Aristotle cites envy (alongside schadenfreude and shamelessness) as an emotion that does not admit of a mean but which implies by its very name that it is wrong (1107a8–11).[51] So just as the motivational effect of fear varies depending on whether we are courageous or cowardly, so too the desires stemming from

---

[50] I should flag that here and in what follows the regularities are only 'for the most part'. Just as an akratic person can perform an unjust act without being unjust (*NE* VII.8.1151a10; also e.g. V.6.1134a17–23, and for discussion my 2006) and we sometimes act out of character (perhaps, e.g., owing to tiredness or undue stress; cf. Stocker 1979 and Svavarsdottir 1999), it may be possible to experience envy without being bad. (Nonetheless, there will be a broader notion of 'character' according to which the akratic agent's character is different from the virtuous agent's *insofar as the former is prone to akrasia*; see my 2012: 249–51.)

[51] The fact that emulation is itself praiseworthy (so too pity and indignation: see *Rhet.* II.9.1386b8–15) and envy, schadenfreude, and shamelessness are themselves blameworthy appears to qualify Aristotle's claim in *NE* II.5 that emotions should be distinguished from virtues on the ground that 'we are neither praised nor blamed for our emotions (for the man who fears or is angry is not praised, nor is the man who simply feels anger blamed, but the man who feels it in a certain way), but for our virtues and our vices we *are* praised or blamed' (1105b31–1106a2). Some see Aristotle contradicting himself here (Cairns 1993: 412–13), others seek to find an 'in-between' or 'mixed' category of states that has some features of emotions, some of virtues (Jimenez 2020: 154–8). I would instead suggest that he need not intend his distinction to be exhaustive. He has several ways to distinguish emotions from virtues in *NE* II.5 and this one does at least serve to show the two are not co-extensive. Experiencing fear or anger (his examples above) is not *as such* praiseworthy or blameworthy, since both virtuous and vicious agents will experience these emotions. Rather, we must experience fear or anger *in a certain way* (*pōs*: 1106a1). Hence emotions *as such* are not virtues or vices. But this is compatible with *some* emotions being themselves praiseworthy or blameworthy. (Aristotle often demonstrates that two things are not identical by showing that they are not co-extensive. See e.g. *De an.* III.3, where we are told that (i) perceiving is not thinking since all animals have the former, but very few the latter (427b7–8, 12–14); (ii) *phantasia* is not reason, since some animals have the former, but not the latter (428a24); and (iii) *phantasia* cannot be knowledge, since the former can be correct or incorrect, the latter only correct (428a16–18).)

emulation and envy emerge against a background of different desiderative dispositions, in line with the subject's character. The difference is that with emulation and envy the desires are correlated with the emotions since the latter are themselves correlated with the possession of a certain character, whereas fear is experienced by different kinds of character (courageous, cowardly) with correspondingly differing motivational effects. With each emotion, though, desires and motivations are correlated with a given emotion relative to a given character.[52] And note that here, too, Aristotle does not say that emulation and envy *are*, in part, desires. We have the desires in question because of (*dia*) the emotions. The latter *prompt* the desires (in such people). They are not (even in part) the desires themselves.[53]

Something similar can be said if we return (see **6.2**) to Aristotle's claim in his discussion of anger that the person who is pained seeks something (*Rhet.* II.2.1379a12). Note, this permits the pain and the desire to be distinct, with the latter forming in light of the former. Aristotle is here referring to 'those with an appetite' who 'are unsuccessful in satisfying it' (1379a17–18). The 'pain' in question could refer to the painful or distressful state (hunger, illness, poverty, being at war: 1379a16–17) that prompts the appetite, or to the pain of not being able to satisfy the desire (or both). Aristotle claims that such people are 'irascible, that is, easily provoked to anger, especially toward those who belittle their present condition' (1379a18–19). They have this disposition because they cannot satisfy their appetite. But insofar as Aristotle would want to say that those who are pained seek something because the pain prompts them to try to alleviate what causes the pain, this should be understood to hold only against the background of a set of desiderative dispositions. Some people in certain situations may be disposed to *tolerate* the distress (as we might tolerate a distressful slight if we deem it a 'fitting' response to our own unjust action; see *Rhet.* II.2.1378a32 and II.3.1380b16–18; and **6.6**). Others may view the distress as something they must *face up to* and *confront* (as with Aristotle's courageous agent), which may not alleviate it at all. Any desiderative response to quell the pain requires, as a background, that no such blocking feature is in play. Perhaps we might say that *ceteris paribus* one who is pained will seek to be rid of what it is that brings about the pain?[54] But, of course, other things will only be equal if there is no reason for the person not to seek to be rid of the pain at hand that trumps forming the desire in question. Indeed, consider Aristotle's example of illness. If there is something we can do, the pain may well prompt a desire to do it (call a doctor; get some medicine). But if we recognize that there is nothing we can do, our desire may slide into more of

---

[52] So too with the actions that are prompted by disdain or contempt (*kataphronēsis*) referred to in *Pol.* (e.g. V.10.1311b40–1312a20). On disdain, see **Cat.15**.

[53] Envy is also associated with desires for the good things the envied person has (*Rhet.* II.10.1388a1–5). But in that instance the desire is (like the hope connected to fear; see **7.3**) a background condition for the emotion: envious people desire the goods and so feel distress at their neighbour getting them. It is only the latter distress that is the occurrent emotion, strictly speaking.

[54] We have to formulate this carefully. See **6.2n.8**.

a desiderative hope, a wish to get better. Which desires, if any, form in response to pains we possess will evidently depend on our understanding of the situation and our basic background dispositions.[55]

On my account, then, Aristotle thinks that emotions can prompt desires against the background of other desiderative dispositions or character traits. But emotions are not, even in part, desires themselves. They are representational pleasures or distresses alone. This reading fits well with the idea that while desires sometimes appear on Aristotle's lists of emotions, emotions do not, more generally, appear on his lists of desires.[56] Desires can appear on lists of emotions insofar as they involve representational distresses or pleasures, but representational pleasures or distresses are not, as such, desires. The reading also fits with the basic root meaning of the general terms. *Pathos*, which is here used by Aristotle for 'emotion', is derived from *paschein*, 'to suffer', and clearly indicates something *undergone* (see *EE* II.2.1220b5–6).[57] Hence Aristotle claims that in respect of the emotions (*ta pathē*) we are said to be moved (*kineisthai*), rather than disposed (*diakeisthai*) (*NE* II.5.1106a4–6). Whereas *orexis*, which is Aristotle's general word for desire, a term he may even have coined for its usage, derives from the verb *oregesthai*, which means 'to reach out for', 'strive towards'.[58] But, most simply, this reading aligns with the fact that the majority of the states discussed in *Rhet.* II are not defined in terms of desires and we see so few references to desires in the longer discussions. If Aristotle thought that emotions were essentially in part desires, this would be downright mysterious.

Conclusion

In this chapter I have argued that Aristotle distinguishes between emotions and desires. On my view he holds that emotions are representational pleasures or

---

[55] Which is of course not to say that we cannot have irrational desires that fly in the face of our beliefs.
[56] *Epithumia* or *thumos* (or both) are frequently included in his lists of emotions: *NE* II.5.1105b21–3, II.6.1106b18–20; *EE* II.2.1220b12–14. Interestingly, in the *NE* lists just mentioned we find *orgē* and *epithumia*, but not *thumos*, whereas in the *EE* list we find *thumos* and *epithumia*, but not *orgē* (see also *NE* IV.5 and *EE* III.3). Again, in *De an.* I.1 we find two lists, the first including *epithumia* (*epithumein*: 403a7), the second *thumos* (403a17) (*thumos* here seems to replace *orgē* which was on the first list (as *orgizesthai*), but not the second). (In my 2012:115–16 I chart the interplay of *thumos* and *orgē* in *De an.* I.1, which goes beyond this simple replacement of one by the other on the lists.) But although *epithumia* and *thumos* appear on lists of emotions, we do not find any other emotions (fear, shame, pity, envy, etc.) appearing on his lists of desires. (As noted in 7.1, in *Rhet.* I.10 Aristotle does name *orgē* and *epithumia* as the two non-rational desires (alongside rational desire, *boulēsis*) (1369a1–4). But, moments later, *orgē* is picked up by *thumos* (1369a7) and so Aristotle is evidently using *orgē* and *thumos* interchangeably.) It will doubtless be difficult to view some of the desires prompted by other emotions as one of Aristotle's three species of desire, given the latter's objects (on which, see my 2012: chs. 4–6). But the account of those, which surely stems from Aristotle's appropriating Plato's tripartite division of motivations for action (esp. *Republic* IV.436aff.), looks like it needs expansion and revision anyway (see my 2012: ch. 8).
[57] See also Bonitz (1870: s.v.); Rorty (1984); and Rapp (2002: 543–5).
[58] See Nussbaum (1986: 273–6) and my 2012 (19–21).

distresses *alone*. So construed, they can, for sure, prompt desires (as with fear, envy, and emulation). And they can also be the results of desires (as with feeling-friendly-towards and hating). Again, they can even form parts of states that essentially also incorporate desires (as with anger). More generally still, as hedonic responses to intentional states that apprehend evaluative objects, they have the capacity to tap into and engage our desiderative dispositions. Indeed, having some such disposition (in the form of a state of character) can even align with experiencing a certain emotion (as with envy and emulation). All this notwithstanding, as I understand him, Aristotle holds that emotions are not *themselves*, even in part, desires.

8
Appetite (*Epithumia*)

Before we leave Aristotle on the relation between emotions and desires, I would like to consider one further state which, despite appearing on the lists of emotions (*NE* II.5.1105b21–3, II.6.1106b18–20; *EE* II.2.1220b12–14; *De an.* I.1.403a7), is conspicuous in not receiving separate treatment in the *Rhet.* II catalogue; namely, *epithumia* (pl. *epithumiai*), standardly translated by 'appetite'. I first consider whether he considers *epithumia* to be an emotion in *Rhet.* (**8.1**). I next address whether he thinks that all *epithumiai* are painful and the implications of this (**8.2**). I close by examining whether we can specify a coherent notion of *epithumia* as an emotion (**8.3**).

8.1 Does Aristotle consider *epithumia* an emotion in the *Rhetoric*?

Epithumia paradigmatically picks out pleasure-based bodily desires connected to, e.g., hunger, thirst, and sex.[1] The fact that it does not receive separate treatment in the *Rhet.* II catalogue of emotions might be taken to indicate that here, at least, Aristotle does not count it as an emotion, strictly speaking. But why might he want to distinguish between bodily appetites and emotions? Martha Nussbaum (not discussing Aristotle, as such) suggests the following distinction. A bodily appetite, such as hunger, is a '*push*' insofar as it 'arises relatively independently of the world, as a result of the animal's own bodily condition, and it is this condition that causes the appetite to represent an object that it then seeks' (2001: 131). Emotions, by contrast 'are *pulled* into being by their object, and by the seeming importance of the object', hence 'intentionality is at their very core' (131). This means that 'bodily appetites do not go away if there is no object of the right sort around':

> Hunger, to say the least, persists in the absence of food. Indeed, since they are value independent drives, [bodily appetites] do not go away even if the person is convinced that an object of the appropriate sort is actually harmful: if I am

---

[1] See e.g. *NE* III.11.1118b8–27, VII.12.1153a32–3; *De an.* II.3.414b11–16; *Sens.* 5.443b20–31; *Hist an.* VI.18.571b8–10, VII.1.581b20–1; *PA* II.17.661a7–9, III.14.675b25–7; *MA* 7.701a32; *Gen an.* I.4.717a24, VII.1.774a3–6. For more discussion, see my 2012 (92–100).

thirsty at sea, my knowledge of the danger of drinking salt water does not stop me from wanting to drink it. (131)[2]

Emotions, by contrast, on Nussbaum's view, 'do go away when the relevant beliefs about the object and about value alter' (131):

I do not get angry when I am not aware of a wrong to which I ascribe significance; and if I am convinced that the wrong did not really take place, or was not really a wrong, my anger will go away. (131)[3]

In fact, as we shall see in Chapter 12, Nussbaum is overly optimistic about emotions' responsiveness to reason (although cp. her remarks at 233–4). And yet we sense there is something to her contrast.[4]

However, we have to account for the fact, as noted, that *epithumia* appears on Aristotle's lists of the emotions elsewhere. Stephen Leighton (1996) proposes that Aristotle has broader and narrower notions of *pathē* in mind. In the general specifications in the ethical works (*NE* II.5.1105b21–3, II.6.1106b18–20; *EE* II.2.1220b12–14) he just characterizes emotions in terms of pleasure and distress. But in *Rhet.* II.1 (1378a19–21) he adds that it is owing to emotions that people differ in respect of their judgements (*kriseis*). According to Leighton, this provides an additional criterion for a narrower class of *pathē*. *Epithumia* is a desire for the pleasant and is itself characterized as painful (see **8.2**). Hence, it satisfies 'the pleasure/pain test' (1996: 224) and so can reasonably appear on broader lists of *pathē* when Aristotle only has that criterion in mind. However, it fails the other criterion required for the narrower class of emotions proper. Emotions 'require judgments, judgments subtle and complex in structure' and 'because of this, emotions are themselves alterations of judgments' (225). *Epithumia*, by contrast, is 'devoid of reason' (quoting *EE* II.8.1224b2) and is instead 'suited to a causal analysis'; as when in hunger or thirst or sexual desire, one responds to a physical yearning (224). In line with this, Leighton quotes (226) a nice passage from *NE* III.5:

It is assumed that there is no gain in being persuaded not to be hot or in pain or hungry or the like, since we shall experience these feelings nonetheless. (1113b27–30)

---

[2] This relates to Nussbaum's further claim that appetites are 'object-fixated' and 'value-indifferent' (appealing to Plato's *Republic* IV: thirst is for drink, hunger for food: 437d–e), whereas emotions are object-flexible (for different kinds of object) and value-suffused (130). This seems questionable to me—appetites are for bodily *pleasure* and pleasure is a 'value'. Indeed, it is clear that *in some sense Republic* IV views appetites as pleasure-based (see e.g. 436a10–b1, 439d6–8).

[3] She does go on to qualify the force of the contrast this presents with appetites, by allowing that the latter 'can be modified by teaching and habit, and can thus have at least some of the focused intentionality and value selectivity characteristic of emotions' (132).

[4] Cf. also Fortenbaugh (1970: 64–70) and Price (1995: 120–1).

If, then, unlike *epithumia*, emotions *are* subject to persuasion and are elicited by 'grounds' rather than 'causes', we would have a principled reason for Aristotle's omitting *epithumia* from his *Rhet.* II catalogue.

This is an interesting suggestion. The extra clause of the *Rhet.* specification is certainly dictated by its context, since the 'judgements' it concerns are *kriseis* which, in the oratorical domain, amount to verdicts (in a judicial sphere) or decisions (in a deliberative sphere) (see esp. *Rhet.* I.3.1358b3-5, 9-10, I.13.1374b19-21). And no doubt this context had a bearing on the emotions Aristotle selected to discuss. Furthermore, although one might (as I would; see **Intro.2**) resist the idea that Aristotle holds that belief or judgement is necessary for emotion (even human emotion)—let alone the notion that emotions *are themselves* 'alterations of judgments'—nonetheless, given his goal of enabling the orator to arouse or abate emotions in an audience (insofar as that bears on their *kriseis*) (*Rhet.* II.1.1378a26, II.11.1388b29), emotions which form in response to beliefs, or which at least track them, would seem more germane.[5]

However, Leighton's view is ultimately untenable. Aristotle allows that *epithumia* can be formed in response to 'reason' (*logos*) (*NE* VII.6.1149a34–b1; see also the *Rhet.* I.11 passage discussed in **8.2**) and so the contrast that Leighton presents is not unequivocal in the first place. But, more tellingly still, there are clear indications that *even in Rhet.* Aristotle thinks *epithumia* counts as a full-fledged emotion. Immediately after discussing the individual emotions in *Rhet.* II, he turns, in II.12, to consider people's 'characters' (*ēthē*), 'that is, of what sorts people are with regard to their emotions (*pathē*) and states (*hexeis*), as well as with regard to their stages of life and fortunes' (1388b31–2). But, in line with his general policy of not repeating himself in *Rhet.*, he notes that he has already discussed emotions and states (of character) earlier, and of the former he writes: 'by emotions (*pathē*), I mean anger (*orgē*), *epithumia*, and the like, about which we spoke earlier' (1388b32–4). That is to say, *immediately after* his discussion of the individual emotions, *epithumia* is *explicitly* listed as an emotion and, indeed, one Aristotle *has already discussed*.

Leighton sees the problem this passage poses and suggests it is 'an uncareful moment' on Aristotle's part (1996: 237n.37). But this seems a little desperate and, in any event, will not do. For the passage is matched by another that occurs *just before* the individual discussions of the emotions, where Aristotle is in fact *explicating* the idea that *emotions bear on judgements*, the very thing Leighton insisted *epithumia* could not do. For, in *Rhet.* II.1, *epithumia* is one of his examples of this:

to a person with *epithumia* and of good hope (*kai tō(i) men epithumounti kai euelpidi onti*), if something in the future is a source of pleasure (*ean e(i) to*

---

[5] See my 2014a for some discussion of these points, which are addressed in greater detail in my MS.

esomenon hēdu), it appears (*phainetai*) that it will both come about and be good; but to someone who is unemotional (*apathei*) and discontented (*duscherainonti*), the contrary. (1378a3–5)[6]

I suppose it might be suggested that Aristotle here slides to a broader use of *epithumia*, where it indicates desire (*orexis*) or hope more generally. But given that the defining feature of *epithumia* is that it is for pleasure (see **8.2**), the connection to pleasure in the passage suggests otherwise. We appear to have:

If someone (i) has an *epithumia* and (ii) is of good hope, then if something in the future is a source of pleasure, it appears both that it will happen [consequence of (ii)] and that it will be a good thing [consequence of (i)]. Whereas if someone (iii) lacks the *epithumia* (and so is unemotional) and (iv) is pessimistic ('discontented'), it appears that it will not happen [consequence of (iv)] or that, if it does, it will not be a good thing [consequence of (iii)].

Thus, we have a clear correlation between possessing *epithumiai* and the way things appear to us—correlations which Aristotle evidently thinks would be helpful for orators in affecting the judgements of an audience. In particular, the fact that instilling an *epithumia* for something will make that thing appear good (*qua* pleasant) may be useful in a deliberative context, when, e.g., trying to influence assemblymen (see *Rhet*. I.2.1356a14–16, I.3.1358b4–7, II.1.1377b20–8) or, more generally, advising on a private decision (*Rhet*. I.3.1358b9–10).[7]

The *conjunction* of this passage *immediately before* the individual accounts of the emotions in book II and the reference to *epithumia* as an emotion *immediately after* them dictates that we must reject Leighton's proposal. Aristotle treats *epithumia* as a full-fledged emotion in *Rhet*. But, if so, why does he not provide a separate discussion in book II? Here Gisela Striker (1996) has a suggestion. As discussed in **7.1**, she emphasizes that we find discussion of *pathē* not merely in book II's catalogue, but also (and here she follows Frede 1996) in the discussion of motives of action in book I's treatment of forensic speeches. As we noted, in *Rhet*. I.10 Aristotle sets out his threefold division of desire (*orexis*) into *boulēsis* ('wish'), *epithumia*, and *orgē/thumos* ('anger'/'spirit') (1368b37–1369a4).[8] And yet when he comes to elaborate on these desires more fully (1369b7ff.), something interesting happens. The reader is flagged *forwards* to the book II discussion for more on

---

[6] Reeve (2018: *ad loc.*) translates *duscherainonti* in a5 as 'disgusted', but it is clearly intended to be the opposite of *euelpidi* in a3, so 'discontented' seems better. *Apathei* looks to be Aristotle's way of trying to specify an 'opposite' for *epithumia* (presumably a 'privation' opposite; see Chapter 10).

[7] At the same time, this usage of *epithumia* does not seem especially likely to be bound to bodily urges of the assemblymen or those making decisions, even though it retains the connection to pleasure. For broader notions of *epithumia*, see below.

[8] As I noted in **7.1**, *orgē*, at 1369a4, is picked up by *thumos*, at a7; we also have *dia thumon kai orgēn* at 1369b11 (where the *kai* is presumably epexegetic).

anger (1369b14–15). But, with *epithumia*, Aristotle claims that through it is done whatever seems to be pleasurable (1369b15–16) and then goes on to discuss pleasure at length in *Rhet.* I.11, with many references to *epithumia* in that discussion. Striker suggests:

> As is his custom in the *Rhetoric*, Aristotle avoids repetition by dealing with a subject only once, even if it should be considered from different perspectives. So he does not pick up *epithumia* again in Book II, and he does not emphasize the role of the passions as motives for action in the longer section, leaving it to the reader to figure out how passionate desire may influence judgment (II.1.1378a4) or how envy or fear, for example, would lead to action. (289)[9]

In fact, as we have seen, Aristotle does at least provide *epithumia* as an example of how emotions may influence judgement.[10] But the idea that, come book II, he may have taken his discussion of *epithumia* to have *already been provided* would account for his including it as an emotion both immediately before and after the book II catalogue and, indeed, for why he refers to it as already spoken of in *Rhet.* II.12.[11]

8.2 Are all *epithumiai* painful?

If Aristotle considers *epithumia* to be a full-fledged emotion in *Rhet.*, we need to understand how he can sensibly do this. In Chapter 6 I suggested that it is insofar as anger involves a representational distress (directed at an apparent slight (*oligōria*)) that it counts as an emotion (*pathos*), whereas it is insofar as it aims at revenge or rectification (*timōria*) that it counts as a desire (*orexis*) (with revenge its object of desire (*orekton*)) (see **6.4**). Relatedly, it is interesting to note that Aristotle not only repeatedly characterizes *epithumia* as a desire for pleasure—indeed, this seems to be definitional of it—he also frequently characterizes it as 'involving pain' (*meta lupēs*).[12]

---

[9] I resisted the notion that *Rhet.* I.10 provides a notion of emotions *as* motives for action in **7.1**.

[10] Something Striker herself alludes to in another note (301n.10), quoted below.

[11] Striker illustrates Aristotle's avoidance of repetition with another case: 'The most striking example of this kind of economy is character as a "means of persuasion": instead of explaining how speakers may convince an audience of their moral wisdom and reliable character, Aristotle simply refers the reader back to his collection of common views about the virtues of speeches of praise or blame in I.9, saying that "one would use the same things to establish one's own good character as one would for another person" (II.1.1378a16–19). He can hardly mean that the best way to present oneself as a morally good person consists in extolling one's own virtues, and so the reader is left with the task of adapting the materials given in I.9 to a different purpose for which some further advice might well have been helpful' (300n.9).

[12] *Epithumia* is desire (*orexis*) for the pleasant: *Top.* VI.3.140b27–8, *SE* 173a39, *De an.* II.3.414b5–6, *Rh.* I.11.1370a17–18, cf. *NE* III.12.1119b5–7; or, more simply, 'of' or 'for' the pleasant: (*tou*) *hêdeos*; e.g., *Top.* VI.3.140b28, *SE* 13.173a39, *NE* III.2.1111b17, *EE* II.7.1223a34, II.8.1224a37, VII.2.1235b22, *PA* II.17.661a8; or that what is in accordance with *epithumia* is pleasant (*ta kat' epithumian hēdea*: *NE* III.1.1111a32–3); or that through *epithumia* is done whatever appears pleasant (*Rh.* I.10.1369b23;

At first sight, this might seem helpful with regard to construing *epithumia* as an emotion. For it suggests that, like anger (*orgē*), it too can count as an *orexis meta lupēs*, a desire accompanied by pain.[13] In fact, though, the 'pains' in question seem importantly different. As we have seen (**6.2**), the 'pain' in anger has an intentional object and is directed at a slight (*oligōria*) (hence 'distress' seems more appropriate). Whereas the pain in *epithumia* seems to be bodily. As noted, prime examples are hunger, thirst, and sexual desire—which suggests that a typical *epithumia* would involve a bodily discomfort, e.g. feeling an unpleasant lack of food or a dry throat, and a pleasure-based desire to alleviate that unpleasant state.[14]

Concerning Leighton's view that Aristotle intends to exclude *epithumia* from the emotions, Striker claims:

> [Leighton] overlooks the crucial passage in I.11 in which Aristotle distinguishes between emotional *epithumiai* and bodily cravings, as well as the mention of *epithumia* as influencing judgment in II.1. (1996: 301n.10)

We have already flagged the latter, but by the former Striker appears to mean:

> everything for which we have an *epithumia* within us is pleasant. For *epithumia* is desire (*orexis*) for the pleasant. Of *epithumiai*, though, some are non-rational (*alogon*), whereas others involve reason (*meta logou*). By non-rational ones I mean those where people do not have an *epithumia* (*epithumein*) on the basis of some supposition (*ek tou hupolambanein*). Those that are by nature are said to be of this sort,[15] like those that are present in us through the body; for example, for nourishment, namely, thirst and hunger, and for a particular kind (*eidos*) of nourishment, a particular kind (*eidos*) of *epithumia*; those connected with taste, sexual pleasures, and, in general, with objects of touch; and those of smell, hearing, and sight. Those that involve reason (*meta logou*), on the other hand, are those where people have an *epithumia* (*epithumein*) on the basis of being persuaded (*ek tou peisthênai*). For there are many things that people have an *epithumia* (*epithumein*) to look at (*theasasthai*) or acquire (*ktēsasthai*) after hearing about them and being persuaded. (1370a16–27)[16]

---

cf. *Top.* VI.8.146b36–147a5). *Epithumiai* involve pain: see, e.g., *EE* II.10.1225b30–1 ('*epithumiai* always involve pain'), *NE* III.2.1111b16–17, III.11.1119a4, VII.12.1152b36, 1153a32–3; *Top.* IV.5.126a9–10; cf. also *NE* VII.4.1148a21–2, *De an.* II.2.413b23–4.

[13] Striker suggests: 'A definition of *epithumia* parallel to that of *orgē* can perhaps be inferred from I.10.1369b15–16 together with I.11.1370a17–18: *orexis meta lupēs phanimonenou hēdeos*' (1996: 301n.14), 'a desire accompanied by pain for an apparent pleasure'.

[14] I discuss this further in my 2012 (ch. 4.1) and provide many examples. There is a broader notion of *epithumia* in Aristotle, but it seems equally likely that it is 'without pain'. See below (this section) and also my 2012 (ch. 4.2).

[15] On 'natural', here, see *NE* III.11.1118b9, 15, 19.

[16] Kassel (1976: *ad loc.*) marks this passage as a later addition by Aristotle himself. However, if that were right, it could hardly be part of the reason for the initial exclusion of *epithumia* from book II.

The second category may seem to provide us with a notion of *epithumia* that goes beyond bodily appetites (although note that we are not actually provided with any specific examples of this category).[17] But is Striker's suggestion that *epithumia* only counts as an emotion insofar as, and just to the extent that, it has this broader use?[18] That seems to be the implication of her contrast between 'emotional *epithumiai*' and 'bodily cravings' in the passage above.

One problem with this is that when *epithumia* is included as a *pathos* in the *NE* or *EE* lists, no such restriction seems to be in play. Indeed, one would more naturally assume that the notion of *epithumia* Aristotle has in mind is the one prevalent in those works, viz. bodily appetites of the kind relevant to temperance and self-indulgence (*NE* III.10–12; *EE* III.2).[19] A second problem is that if we extend the notion of *epithumia* to include anything we might find pleasurable on the basis of persuasion, or to non-bodily pleasures more generally, it is unclear whether the connection to pain is preserved, since the pain we had in view pertained to a painful disruptive bodily state. Indeed, Striker herself resisted (rightly, on my view) Frede's (1996) proposal that Aristotle is developing an analysis of emotions as 'mixed feelings'—in line with Plato's account in the *Philebus*—on just this ground. She notes:

> When [Aristotle] speaks of the pleasure that comes from victory or from the impression that one is superior to others (*phantasia huperochēs*, 1370b33–4)—I suppose we might call this a kind of pride?—it is difficult to regard the desire to excel as a perceived lack or disturbance of the natural state, unless, of course, one takes it that being superior to others is everybody's natural condition. And while feeling inferior might count as distressing, leading to a desire to surpass or at least be even with one's peers or competitors, such feelings need not inevitably precede or accompany the pleasure of feeling superior: some people clearly enjoy competition and feel quite confident that they will succeed. Obviously, we might declare passionate desire to be always painful by definition, but these examples would seem to throw doubt upon such an assumption. (1996: 291; I quote 1370b33–4 in the next section)

---

[17] *What* are desiring to 'look' or 'gaze' at as a result of being persuaded? A beautiful person, a statue, a building, a city? And what are motivated to 'acquire'? Wealth, a new book, some precious gem, a piece of fruit?

[18] Reeve claims: 'In Aristotle's own somewhat technical use of the term, an *epithumia* is one sort of *orexis* (desire)...Here, however, and throughout this chapter, the term seems to be used in its loose and popular sense to refer to any sort of desire' (2018: 227). This must be wrong. The passage begins by reminding us that *epithumia* is *orexis* of the pleasant. '*Epithumia*' is used in a broad way, but it retains its specific connection to pleasure and does not simply collapse into *orexis*.

[19] Notwithstanding that *NE* III.1 speaks of *epithumiai* for health and learning (1111a31). In *NE* II.3 temperance and self-indulgence are connected to bodily pleasures (1104b5–7), in II.5 his list of emotions begins with *epithumia* (1105b21; so too II.6.1106b18–19), and then in III.10–12 the bodily pleasures of temperance and self-indulgence are explained in terms of *epithumiai*.

186 APPETITE (EPITHUMIA)

I agree. But since Aristotle explicitly claims that a desire for feeling superior is an *epithumia* (I.11.1370b33–4), it seems that such a desire need not involve pain. And yet if such *epithumiai* do not involve pain, how can they count *as emotions*? Note, their connection to pleasure cannot help. That holds only insofar as they are *desires*: pleasure is the *orekton*, the object of desire, of an *epithumia*. And, as with anger, it is not insofar as *epithumia* counts as a desire that it counts as an emotion as such.

8.3 Emotional *epithumiai*?

What we really needed was a sense in which *epithumia* was tied to a distress that was *representational*, i.e. has an intentional object.[20] In pointing to non-appetitive *epithumiai*, Striker presumably sought to direct us to such, even though she actually went on to illustrate cases in which no pain was required at all. In fact, though, we do get a case in *Rhet.* I.11 that may provide an example of the requisite kind:

> there is a certain pleasure that attaches to mourning and lamentation for a departed one; since there is pain (*lupē*) at (*epi* + dative) his not being there and pleasure in remembering and, in a way, seeing him, the actions he was doing, and what he was like. That is why it made perfect sense to say, 'Thus he spoke, and stirred in all of them the longing for weeping.' (1370b25–9; the quote is from Homer: *Iliad* XXIII.108, *Odyssey* IV.183)

Aristotle seems to be referring to grief: *distress at* (specified with *epi* + dative) *the loss of someone close to us*, or some such. He does not here specifically refer to a *desire* for the pleasure he mentions and it may seem odd to think that such a pleasure must have been preceded by an occurrent *epithumia* for the pleasure of remembering the loved one. More likely, one just naturally shifts from feeling grief to then remembering the loved one, and finds such imaginative encounters pleasurable. But the example is one of a series to illustrate how 'a sort of pleasure follows along with most *epithumiai*, since people enjoy a certain pleasure when they remember that they got something or anticipate that they will get it' (1370b15–16). So Aristotle must be envisaging the pleasure to be connected to an *epithumia* in some way. Presumably, some more general *epithumia* is thought to lie in the background. We see a related tracing of pleasure to *epithumia* in the passage in I.11 that Striker alluded to about victory:

---

[20] As we saw in **2.4**, there may be a sense in which bodily pleasures and pains *are* intentional, but not one that corresponds to emotions (which are directed at their evaluative objects). Cf. also Goldie (2000: 51–7) on a way that bodily states in emotions might be directed at objects through a kind of 'borrowed intentionality'. It is, though, non-borrowed intentionality we seek.

And victory is pleasant, not only for those who love victory, but for all. For an appearance of superiority results, which all have an *epithumia* for, whether mild or more intense. (1370b32–4)[21]

Those who love victory presumably have an *epithumia* for it. But even if we do not have an *epithumia* for victory, on Aristotle's view, we still find it pleasant. Why? Because we all have an *epithumia* (whether mild or more intense) for appearing superior to others, and victory is one of the things that make us feel superior. Similarly, while we may not have a specific *epithumia* for remembering our lost loved one (although we *could*), our pleasure in doing so might still reflect an *epithumia*, namely, an *epithumia to be with* our lost loved one once more. And, clearly, such an *epithumia* would explain why we find remembering our loved one pleasant.[22] But, equally, such an *epithumia* seems essentially connected to the representational distress that Aristotle specified: distress at the loss of the loved one. Perhaps, then, we might characterize an *epithumia* of such a kind as involving an intentional distress—*distress at the absence of a lost loved one*—alongside the desire for the presence of the loved one? We would then finally have an *epithumia* of the right *kind* to be 'emotional', viz. one that has a distress that is intentional.

Relatedly, we saw in 6.2 (also 7.5) that in *Rhet.* II.2—in connection with a pain that can serve as a background condition for anger—Aristotle refers to poverty, illness, and war as painful or distressful and, in turn, prompting *epithumiai* to relieve them (1379a11–12, 16–17). It is quite plausible that (at least some manifestations of) these *epithumiai* involve representational distresses. We could, for instance, have an *epithumia* for money accompanied by distress at our poverty. Indeed, in *Rhet.* I.10 Aristotle refers to a poor man who has an *epithumia* for wealth (1369a12–13; also *NE* VII.4.1148a25) and, in *NE* III.10, to a distress directed at (*epi* + dative) money matters (1118a1). Or we might experience distress at being ill (not just the bodily pain of the illness) accompanied by a desire for health (cf. *NE* III.1.1111a31), or distress at the possibility of being vanquished accompanied by a desire for victory (cf. *NE* VII.4.1148a26). Or, again, we might feel distress at our ignorance or poor education accompanied by a desire for learning (*NE* III.1.1111a31), or distress at being dishonoured accompanied by a desire for honour (*NE* VII.4.1148a26). And so on.[23]

---

[21] Following Kassel (1976: *ad loc.*) in reading *mallon* with the MSS in b34, rather than the OCT's *mala*.
[22] This might be construed as a kind of *longing* or *pothos* for the loved one still to be living—see my discussion of *pothos* in **Cat.21**.
[23] In each case the 'accompanied' is intended to be understood in the sense in which anger is a desire accompanied by distress (see **6.3**), i.e. the distress is *both* that in light of which the desire forms *and also* must persist alongside the desire if the state is to count as an emotion. (In my 2012: 103, I resisted Bostock's 2000: 34n.8 claim that in such passages Aristotle 'slips' to a wider usage of *epithumia*, in which there is no clear distinction between *epithumia* and *boulēsis*. In each case Aristotle retains *epithumia*'s definitive connection to pleasure which distinguishes it from *boulēsis*.)

Note, I am not proposing that every appetite for a non-bodily pleasure *must* be accompanied by a representational distress. I do not, for instance, see why this should be the case with the example of superiority that Striker drew our attention to. Nor does it seem plausible that distress at the possibility of being vanquished must accompany every appetite for victory. But if at least a good set of *epithumiai* could be construed as such, this might account for Aristotle's allowing *epithumia* to count as an emotion in *Rhet*. As Striker put it, some *epithumiai* would be 'emotional'.

But what about *epithumiai* connected to bodily appetites? And what about the appearance of *epithumia* on the lists of emotions in the ethical works, where the most obvious notion would be appetitive (although note the references above to a broader notion of *epithumia* in the ethical works)? In fact, once we have opened up the idea that *epithumiai* may incorporate a representational distress, there seems little reason in principle to think that Aristotle could not connect such distresses to bodily appetites too. Suppose, owing to not having eaten for most of the day, you feel famished and experience a very unpleasant bodily discomfort. Quite commonly, I propose, you might also experience a *distress* directed at the bodily discomfort, i.e. become *distressed at* or *by* your physical discomfort: it *upsets* you. Furthermore, sometimes the situation may not be easily resolved. Suppose the hunger results from a punitive diet, or think of the longing a recovering alcoholic or drug addict may have for a drink or hit, or the yearning of someone deeply sexually frustrated. Such people may experience not merely the physical pang of the lack in question, and a pleasure-based desire to satisfy it, but also an enduring representational distress directed either at the physical pain (at the fact that they have the pain), or at the lack of what would relieve it. Bodily pains can be significantly upsetting in a number of ways.

We find a notion of *epithumia* which plausibly involves a representational distress, and which cuts across bodily and non-bodily cases, in *Rhet*. II.7. Aristotle writes:

> Needs are desires (*orexeis*) and, among desires, especially the ones that involve distress at what is not attained (*hai meta lupēs tou mē gignomenou*). *Epithumiai* are such things, for example, love (*erōs*), and those desires felt in sufferings of the body and in times of danger (for the one who is in danger has an appetite (*epithumein*) for something and so does the one who is in pain (*ho lupoumenos*)). (1385a21–5)

In the opening sentence we have a clear notion of a desire that involves a representational distress. The distress that accompanies such desires is *about what is not attained*, that is, is *directed at* the perceived absence of something. In the second sentence we are told that *epithumiai* are such desires and are given examples *both* of cases where the desire involves a bodily pain *and* of cases where it does not ('in times of danger...'—note that in the bracketed clause this case is *explicitly* distinguished from the case where the person is *in pain*, hence the latter must pick up the bodily sufferings mentioned prior to the bracket). But both sorts of case—*epithumia* with or without bodily pains—fall under the general category of desires that are accompanied by a representational distress, as specified in the first sentence. In cases with bodily pains, then, we are presumably to envisage situations in which the subject experiences a bodily pain and, in response, forms a desire (to rectify that) accompanied by a distress at the lack of what would rectify it ('what is not attained'). Whereas in the danger case, we are presumably to imagine the subject having an *epithumia* to be *safe* (from some danger) accompanied by a distress at the lack of safety ('what is not attained'). The 'love' example could perhaps be construed along either lines, depending on whether we have a desire for sexual pleasure in response to physical discomfort, or some kind of non-bodily yearning for (say) the presence or company of the loved one. In each case the desire (or desire-*cum*-pain, with the former) would be accompanied by a representational distress at the perceived lack in question.[24]

The formal object (*qua* emotion) of such *epithumiai*, whether bodily appetites or not, might then be characterized as *(bodily) pain, or a lack of something, or something's absence*; where lacks and absences would not be restricted to what would rectify a bodily pain or discomfort, but could include the loss or absence of a loved one, or the lack or absence of health, wealth, honour, etc. This notion of *epithumia* would run:

> *Epithumia*: a desire for a (rectifying) pleasure accompanied by distress at a bodily pain, or discomfort, or bodily lack, or other lack or absence.[25]

Note how the definition encompasses appetites in which one's distress pertains to a bodily state (at the fact that one feels a bodily pain, or at the lack of what would rectify such a pain), no less than desires in which one's distress pertains to a non-bodily state, such as poverty, honour, and lack of friendship. When one is hungry and craving food, one experiences bodily pain, but if one is distressed about one's bodily pain (the fact one has the bodily pain), or about the lack of what would rectify it, one's appetite will be emotional insofar as it involves a representational

---

[24] In *NE* III.11 Aristotle writes: 'the self-indulgent man is so called because he is pained more than he ought to at not getting pleasant things (even his pain being caused by pleasure)...he is pained both when he fails to get them and when he has *epithumiai* (*epithumein*) for them (for *epithumia* involves pain)' (1118b30–2, 1119a3–4). This seems to mark the pain of *epithumia* as bodily and to distinguish it from the representational distress of not having the things in question. But our *Rhet.* II.7 passage suggests that bodily pain, representational distress, and pleasure-based desire can all come together in *epithumia*.

[25] Or (parallel to anger): desire accompanied by distress (*orexis meta lupēs*) for an apparent pleasure because of (*dia*) an apparent bodily pain, or other lack, or absence.

distress. Similarly, when one longs for the presence of a loved one owing to distress directed at their absence, this will fit the account no less.

With emotional *epithumiai* pertaining to bodily pains, it is worth noting that there are two possible relations the distress may have to the desire of the *epithumia*. The desire could (i) form in response to the representational distress (in a way parallel to anger; see Chapter 6) or (ii) form (primarily or predominantly) in light of the bodily pain or lack itself. To admit both options, we might say that each of the following count as the desire being 'accompanied by' a distress: (i) cases where the desire is formed in light of the distress (and the distress persists alongside the desire) and (ii) cases where the desire is formed (predominantly) in light of the bodily pain or lack, but a representational distress accompanies the desire (and perhaps contributes to it).

The upshot is that while, as Striker emphasized, it seems unlikely that every desire for pleasure must be preceded by a pain, let alone a bodily pain, it could be that in listing *epithumia* as an emotion, Aristotle is trying to characterize *epithumiai* that involve some kind of distressful lack, whether those *epithumiai* involve bodily pains or not.

Conclusion to Part II

In Part II we have considered the relation that Aristotle thinks holds between emotions and desires. On my view, he thinks that emotions can prompt desires (as fear may prompt a desire to flee), or be the results of desires or aversions being satisfied (as pride may result from a success or shame from an unwanted public exposure), or be implied by our possessing certain desires (as with feeling-friendly-towards and hating; see 7.4). Again, emotions can form part of states that incorporate desires (as with anger (Chapter 6) and the emotional *epithumiai* of this chapter). More generally, Aristotle thinks that an emotion's connection to motivational states is dependent on our desiderative dispositions (as, e.g., fear will motivate flight in the cowardly, but not in the brave). Indeed, some emotions may themselves align with certain sorts of character and thereby (to that extent) imply certain desiderative dispositions (as with envy and emulation; see 7.5). Nonetheless, these connections notwithstanding, I have argued that Aristotle holds that emotions are not *themselves*, even in part, desires. Desires and emotions form two distinct categories of intentional state.

If this is Aristotle's view, it invites the further question: is he *right*? After all, some current philosophers and psychologists hold that emotions are types of desire or action tendency (see Chapter 11 n.1 for references). I take this up in Chapter 11 and suggest there are reasons for thinking that Aristotle's account is preferable to such views. I also consider there the sorts of representational role emotions play according to various theories. Aristotle's picture, I shall suggest, is distinctive. On his view, emotions themselves play neither a descriptive role (which may instead be played by the intentional state that apprehends the emotion's object), nor a prescriptive role (as may be played by the desires that emotions connect up with). Instead, emotions play a *reactive* or *responsive* role: they are representational pleasures or distresses that are formed in response to intentional states that apprehend their objects (so Part I).

PART III
THE MATERIAL DIMENSION OF EMOTIONS AND SOME PROBLEMATIC CASES

9
The Material or Bodily Dimension of Emotions

In this part of the book, I consider two further challenges to my reading of Aristotle's account of emotions as representational pleasures or distresses. First, pertaining to the material or bodily dimension of emotions (this chapter). Second, concerning some problematic cases that Aristotle appears to count as emotions but which (at first sight, at least) do not seem to be representational pleasures or distresses in their own right (Chapter 10).

I have claimed that Aristotle thinks that emotions *just are* representational pleasures or distresses. My aim in so characterizing his view was twofold. First, as we saw in Part I, to emphasize that the intentional state that apprehends the object of the emotion does not itself form a component part of the emotion. Instead, emotions are *responses* to such states (are formed 'in light of' them). Second, as we saw in Part II, to indicate that emotions are not themselves desires or motivational states, even if they interact with the latter in important ways (and some states, such as anger, can incorporate an emotion alongside a desire). But, of course, in another respect it is abundantly clear that Aristotle does not think that emotions are *just* representational hedonic states. For he very obviously thinks that emotions are also in some way material states (see esp. *De an.* I.1.403a25–7, quoted and discussed below; and *PA* II.4). Any account must accept this. However, when Aristotle comes to discuss the material dimension of emotions, some of his claims have been thought to imply something more problematic for my reading, viz. that any definition or specification of an emotion that does not explicitly incorporate its material dimension must be essentially 'inadequate', prone to 'errors' and 'mistakes', and even 'empty' (Charles 2009: 5, 10, 11, 14; cf. Corcilius 2008: 156–8). On such views, emotions cannot sensibly be understood at all, or at least not without significant misrepresentation and misunderstanding, unless we integrate their material element in precisely the correct way in their specifications. If this were true, what I shall call '*Rhet.*-style definitions'—definitions of the form 'pleasure/distress directed at an apparent instantiation of the formal object of the emotion' (for 'formal object', see **1.3**)—would be inadequate specifications of emotions.

In this chapter I explore these views and defend the integrity and validity of *Rhet.*-style definitions. On my view, Aristotle thinks that understanding emotions simply in terms of representational pleasures or distresses does not mislead or misrepresent. Such specifications are alternative ways of specifying the enmattered states, ones which are more germane in many contexts. I begin, in **9.1**, by introducing two (rival) versions of the problematic reading, both of which commit Aristotle to the idea that any adequate definition of states such as the emotions must make explicit reference to their material dimension. I discuss these readings in relation to a key text (part of *De an.* I.1) and sketch two reasons Aristotle's claims have been thought to undermine *Rhet.*-style definitions; namely, that the latter (i) fail to be co-extensive with definitions that make direct reference to their material dimension and (ii) are explanatorily impotent. However, in **9.2** I show that it is clear that Aristotle holds that *Rhet.*-style specifications of emotions—ones which do not make direct reference to their material dimension— are perfectly adequate in a number of other contexts (not just *Rhet.*, but in his ethical works, and in *Pol.* and *Poet.* too). Furthermore, in some of these it is also clear that he nonetheless holds that emotions are essentially enmattered—but that this is only worth drawing attention to at certain points. This gives us reason to see if *De an.* I.1 can be read as compatible with those texts and, if it can be, whether we can answer the concerns mentioned above ((i) and (ii)). In **9.3** I argue that *De an.* I.1 can be read as maintaining that we only need to make explicit reference to the material dimension of an emotion *in a natural science context*, not every context. And in **9.4** I show that *Rhet.*-style definitions, when correctly understood, do not fall foul to (i) or (ii). The upshot is that we should accept that Aristotle thinks that *Rhet.*-style definitions are perfectly legitimate specifications of emotions, adequate for many investigatory frameworks. I close the main part of the chapter, in **9.5**, by providing revised *un*problematic versions of the problematic readings that restricts them to a natural science context and so leaves *Rhet.*-style definitions intact in many other kinds of investigation. While, ultimately, I can leave it open which of these revised readings is more plausible—since both are unproblematic for the argument of this book—in **Appendix 1** I do address whether *De an.* I.1, at least, gives us reason to prefer one or the other. In **Appendix 2** I consider a passage from *De an.* I.1 where Aristotle provides some examples that purport to show that emotions involve the body (403a19–24) and establish that this, too, is compatible with my reading.

9.1 Two problematic readings

Here are two interpretations of how Aristotle understands the material dimension of the emotions that would be problematic for the account developed in this book:

> [Material component requirement (MCR)]: Aristotle holds that states such as the emotions cannot be adequately defined or specified without direct reference to their specific material components (e.g. boiling of the blood).[1]

---

[1] Note, I formulate MCR in such a way that it does not make direct reference to a 'formal' dimension to the state. See n.12 below.

[Enmattered form requirement (EFR)]: Aristotle holds that states such as the emotions cannot be adequately defined or specified except by reference to forms that are themselves directly specified as essentially enmattered (e.g. a desire-for-revenge-boiling-of-the-blood).

David Charles (2009, 2011: 77–83, 2021) commits to EFR and I shall draw extensively from his views in what follows.[2] But either MCR or EFR would be damaging for Aristotle's account of the emotions, as that has been developed in this book.[3] Specifications of emotions as hedonic responses to an apparent instantiation of the emotion's formal object do not make direct reference to either a material component or an enmattered form.[4] Hence, if either MCR or EFR were true, Aristotle would hold that *Rhet.*-style definitions are inadequate ways of defining emotions.

What is the basis for either MCR or EFR in Aristotle? A key text for the emotions is *De an.* I.1.[5] In this introductory chapter Aristotle raises the question of whether any properties of the soul are specific (*idion*) to it alone or whether they are all common (*koina*) to the body as well (403a3–5). His answer is that it is at least clear that states such as anger (*thumos*), mild-manneredness (*praotēs*), fear, pity, confidence (*tharsos*), joy (*chara*), feeling-friendly-towards (*to philein*), and hating (*to misein*) involve the body and so are common to the body as well, since 'at the same time as these [occur] the body is affected in a certain way' (403a16–19).[6] He then offers some further considerations in support of the claim that the affections of the soul involve the body (403a19–24)—which I address in **Appendix 2**—and concludes that it is therefore clear that they are 'principles in matter' (*logoi en hulē(i)*) (or 'enmattered accounts': *logoi enhuloi*) (403a25)[7]

---

[2] See also esp. Peramatzis (2011).

[3] Caston (2009) explicitly resists Charles view (in the latter's 2009) and advances what Charles would call a 'pure' form reading (see below). See also e.g. Nussbaum and Putnam (1992); Wedin (1996); Johansen (2012: 157, 168); Shields (2016: 101–2). It is not clear to me, though, that these commentators commit to MCR, rather than the weaker version of this thesis that I go on to specify in **9.5**. At any rate, MCR needs dealing with no less than EFR.

[4] This leaves open the possibility that they could *indirectly* entail how the material dimension of the state should be specified, against the background of other material facts and assumptions, as we shall see. But that idea is weaker than MCR or EFR, as specified.

[5] To defend his general picture of Aristotle's specification of natural objects, Charles (2021) appeals to a number of other texts across the corpus (e.g. *Met.* Z.10–11 in his long ch. 2). I am unable to address all his considerations here but, as we shall see, doing so will not end up crucial for my argument.

[6] In a prior list (403a7) he included perception, which has caused some debate. See e.g. Nussbaum and Putnam (1992: 42–50); Burnyeat (1995: 433 and n.38, 2001: 129–30, 2002: 82n.143); Sorabji (2001: 56–9); Caston (2005: 281–5); Charles (2021: 30–2).

[7] Both variants are attested in the manuscripts, although Shields (2016: 98) claims that the latter, though preferred by many contemporary editors and translators, 'derives from inferior manuscripts and commentaries from late antiquity'. He suggests: '[t]he difference is more than mere nuance, if the latter (*logoi enhuloi*) is understood to carry the suggestion that psychic states are themselves *essentially* material, while the former (*logoi en hulē(i)*) stops short of that claim, asserting only that psychic states are merely *realized* in matter' (98, his emphases). It seems to me, though, that either textual variant could be understood in either way and so there will not be much mileage gained from the variation alone. Cf. Wedin (1995: 218n.41).

and for this reason study of them is 'at once the province of the *phusikos*', the investigator into nature (403a27–8). Now, clearly, the fact that Aristotle thinks emotions *involve* bodily processes does not itself imply MCR, let alone EFR. He could think that elaborating on or referring to the material dimension of such states is not needed in all contexts. However, in what follows, he distinguishes (403a29–b9):

(1) Someone who only specifies the formal aspect—the form (*eidos*) and principle (*logos*)—of a state such as anger. Such a person Aristotle calls the *dialektikos*, the dialectician (403a29). 'A desire to return pain (*orexis antilupēseōs*)' is given as such a specification for anger (403a30–1).
(2) Someone who only specifies the material aspect of such a state. Such a person Aristotle initially calls the *phusikos*, the investigator into nature (403a29). 'Boiling of the blood and the hot stuff around the heart' is given as such a specification for anger (403a31–b1).
(3) Someone who specifies the-form-'in'-the-matter (for the sake of some end) (403b3, 6–7).

Aristotle then re-asks which of (1)–(3) the *phusikos* really is (403b7) and subsequently proposes that the *phusikos* is 'concerned with everything which is a function or affection (*erga kai pathē*) of such and such a body and such and such a matter' (403b11–12). And he appears to treat this characterization as equivalent to viewing the *phusikos* as (3)—the person who investigates the-form-in-the-matter—not (2)—the person who only investigates the material aspect.[8] Relatedly, just after he had stated that emotions are enmattered accounts, he provided what we might call his 'schematic definition' of states such as anger:

> Hence their definitions are such as: 'Being angry is [A] a particular movement (*kinēsis tis*) of a body of such and such a kind, or a part or potentiality of it, [B] as a result of this (*hupo toude*) [C] for the sake of that (*heneka toude*)'. (403a25–7)

Those who advance MCR will understand [A], here, to refer to the material component of the state, of which 'boiling of the blood and hot stuff around the heart' (403a31–403b1) was Aristotle's specification for anger.[9] They will say that this

---

[8] There are a number of thorny details about the text which I am skirting here, but I am aiming to provide a broad-brush characterization that would be acceptable to most, since this is all I require for my purposes.
[9] Code and Moravcsik (1992: 130–1; cf. also Wedin 1995: 189) instead hold that 'movement' (*kinēsis*) in the schematic definition does not form part of the material specification, but instead refers to anger as a whole. The matter, on their view, is specified solely by the clause 'a body of such and such a kind, or a part or potentiality of it' (i.e. they would place [A] after *kinēsis tis*). They write: 'the boiling of the blood is not matter for the anger; rather, the boiling is *kinēsis* of blood, the blood being a part of the body, and hence matter' (1992: 131). Although the point is not crucial for me, I instead suspect that Aristotle is trying to characterize *a material process—boiling of* the blood—as the 'matter' of

shows that Aristotle thinks that adequate definitions of states such as anger must make direct reference to their material component, but that (contra EFR) this can be specified independently of the form of the state. Hence, however we ultimately understand [B] and [C] and their relation to the formal aspect of the state, the advocate of MCR will say that Aristotle holds that an adequate definition of such a state must make direct reference to its matter.[10] If so, *Rhet.*-style definitions would be inadequate.

Advocates of EFR will see things differently. Charles writes:

> The definition, the defining formula, of anger, the composite, is to be given in terms of the form alone...the definition of the composite, anger, will not include anything beyond the form. It will not contain (*pace* the purist reading) reference to material parts of the composite in addition to the form...the relevant type of account (*logos*) refers to a distinctive type of essentially enmattered form...an impure form. (2021: 24)

On this view, the schematic definition does not refer directly (in [A]) to a distinct material *component* of anger. Rather, the whole specification picks out a form, but one that is itself essentially enmattered. Relatedly, on this view, when Aristotle refers to 'enmattered accounts' (403a25), he is referring to the form itself as enmattered.[11] And, as above, Charles calls such forms 'impure', in contrast to 'pure' forms which are not specified as enmattered (as may be the case, e.g., with the forms of mathematical objects).

Let us employ the phrase 'the material dimension' of a specification (of states such as anger) in a way that is neutral between whether that is specified as a distinct material component, along the lines of those advancing MCR, or as embedded in an impure form, as with those who advocate EFR. Both MCR and EFR agree that states such as anger cannot be adequately defined without direct reference to their 'material dimension', so construed.[12]

---

anger. Two considerations favour this reading. First, it is what he actually claims. When he provides the specification—*boiling of the blood and hot stuff around the heart* (403a31–b1)—he states that someone defining anger with this would give the matter (403b1). Code and Moravcsik will have to say he misleads, here, and provides a specification of the matter, but not only the matter. Yet absent a prior preference for their view, there seems little reason to assume this. Second, if there is a worry about the material aspect of anger being a process—boiling—it should be appeased by the fact that it fits with Aristotle's earlier remark that 'at the same time as the [affections of the soul] occur the body is affected in a certain way' (403a18–19). When anger or other emotions occur, the body is affected (*paschein*), i.e. *changed*, in a certain way. This suggests that states such as emotions involve material processes. See also **9.2**.

[10] [C] presumably refers to 'revenge' in the case of anger. [B] presumably refers to 'an apparent slight' or 'distress at an apparent slight'. See **6.2** and **7.5**n.47.

[11] See also Peramatzis (2011: 106).

[12] Note that, as I have formulated it, MCR does not make direct reference to the formal dimension of the state. This is helpful since, among other things, it allows advocates of MCR to leave it open whether there is something between what Charles calls a 'pure' formal specification (which he believes suffers from the defects I address in **9.4**) and an 'impure' one in line with EFR. As I see it, *Rhet.*-style

Why, according to MCR or EFR, would Aristotle think that reference to the material dimension of states such as anger is essential to an adequate definition of them? Charles provides two principal considerations.[13] First, definitions which fail to refer to a material dimension will fail to pick out the correct *extension* of the state. This is illustrated by the possibility that someone could have a cold (non-blood-boiling), calculating desire for revenge without being angry (2021: 19–20, 2009: 9–10). Second, earlier in *De an.* I.1, when discussing the relation between having an account of what a thing is (*to ti estin*) and the attributes (*ta sumbebēkota*) which follow from the essence, Aristotle claimed that 'definitions which do not enable us to ascertain the attributes nor even make it easy to guess about this' have been stated 'dialectically' (*dialektikōs*) and 'to no purpose' (or 'emptily': *kenōs*) (402b25–403a2). Charles (2021: 23–4) links this to the 'dialectical' definition of anger we found in *De an.* I.1, the desire to return pain (*orexis antilupēseōs*), and suggests that it would succumb to such a charge. Since *Rhet.*-style definitions at least look along the same lines as such a definition, the worry is that they would too.

I shall later argue (**9.4**) that neither of these concerns applies to *Rhet.*-style definitions, when correctly understood. But let me first provide an independent argument that should make us doubt both MCR and EFR.

9.2 A reason to be suspicious of both MCR and EFR

One problem with both MCR and EFR is that it seems abundantly clear in a number of other works that Aristotle treats *Rhet.*-style specifications of emotions as perfectly adequate in their own terms. Furthermore, it is also apparent in some of these that he nonetheless still thinks that emotions *are* essentially enmattered, but that referring to this dimension of such states is not relevant in all situations.

In his *Rhet.* II catalogue Aristotle certainly *thinks* that he is providing adequate accounts of the emotions, fit for his purposes. He explicitly states that his goal is to enable orators to engender (*empoiein*: II.1.1378a26; *engignetai*: II.11.1388b29) or abate (*dialuetai*: II.11.1388b29) emotions in their audience, so as to bear on the latter's decisions or verdicts (*kriseis*). But, crucially, for his accounts of the emotions to achieve this, they have to be adequate for such a purpose. And that seems

---

definitions are not impure forms in Charles' sense (see **9.5**), but nor are they susceptible to the issues he finds with pure forms. Of course, though, it is open for those who advance MCR to specify a formal dimension for emotions that would be pure forms in Charles' sense. And I shall sometimes refer to an advocate of MCR who advances views about the formal aspect of the state as well. (Leaving out reference to the 'form' of the state in MCR also allows its advocates to take a view on the material aspect of the schematic definition, without having to say precisely how the form of the state relates to that definition.)

[13] He, of course, takes these to favour EFR but, as I see it, they could also be advanced in some form by those who advance MCR. In any event, they need dealing with.

to require that they are both sufficiently well specified and *true*, or at least that Aristotle thinks they are. So advocates of MCR or EFR are going to have to say that the Aristotle of *De an.* I.1 would (now) reject this (so Charles 2009: 10n.19).[14]

But in a number of other works, too, *Rhet.*-style definitions or specifications of emotions, whether explicitly stated or implicitly invoked, seem to be treated as perfectly adequate in their own right. In his ethical works, with respect to mean states 'in the emotions (*en tois pathēmata*) and concerned with the emotions (*peri ta pathē*)' (*NE* II.7.1108a31),[15] Aristotle characterizes envy, indignation, and schadenfreude only in terms of representational distresses or pleasures, not by reference to specific heatings or chillings that must accompany them.[16] Envy, we are told, is distress at someone's deserved doing-well (*EE* III.7.1233b19–20; cf. *NE* II.7.1108b4–5, *EE* II.3.1221a38–40). Indignation (*nemesis*) is distress at someone's undeserved doing-well (*NE* II.7.1108b3–4; *EE* III.7.1233b23–5). And schadenfreude (*epichairekakia*) is joy at someone's undeserved doing-badly (*EE* III.7.1233b21–2; *NE* II.7.1108b5–6).[17]

In other cases, Aristotle's working understanding of particular emotions is more implicit, but even so it is clear that it is *Rhet.*-style specifications that lie in the background, not ones that make explicit reference to their material dimension. Courage, he tells us, concerns fear and confidence. With respect to fear, he writes:

> plainly the things we fear are terrible things (*phoboumetha de dēlon hoti ta phobera*), and these are, to speak without qualification, evils (*kaka*); for which reason people even define fear as expectation of evil (*prosdokia kakou*). Now we

---

[14] As noted in **Intro.1n.11**, I take the older reading, according to which the accounts of emotions found in *Rhet.* are merely a matter of commonplace opinions (which Aristotle employs without any commitment to their truth), to be long refuted (see **Intro.1n.11** for references). Aristotle's aim in providing accounts of the emotions in *Rhet.* II is not to provide orators with colourful examples which can be employed in speeches (even if they can double as such) but to enable them to affect the decisions or verdicts (*kriseis*) of their listeners. To achieve this, he must think the accounts are true. He typically introduces his definitions of individual emotions in *Rhet.* II with *estō*, 'let E be...' (II.2.1378a30, II.3.1380a8, II.4.1380b36, II.5.1382a21, II.6.1383b12, II.7.1385a17, II.8.1385b13) or something equally concessive; e.g. *ei gar esti to nemesan*...'for if indignation is...' (II.9.1387a9–10); *eiper estin ho phthonos*...'if envy is...' (II.10.1387b23); *ei gar estin zēlos*...'for if emulation is...' (II.11.1388a32). The reason for this, I believe, is because the definitions are not *argued for*. A treatise on rhetoric is not the place to conduct investigations into the best definitions of emotions. But Aristotle needs the definitions to be adequate and true if they are to achieve their stated purpose, and so must be giving us the best accounts he has. See also Rapp (2002: 542).

[15] On what Aristotle might mean by these, see Raymond (2017: 118ff.).

[16] *NE* mentions these states in its initial survey of virtues and vices in II.7 (II.7.1108a30–b6), but tells us: 'about these states there will be an opportunity of describing elsewhere' (1108b6–7). However, Aristotle does not pick them up in his more detailed characterizations of virtues and vices that follow (where one would have expected them after the discussion of shame (*aidōs*) in *NE* IV.9). Thankfully, we have the *EE* III.7 version to supplement.

[17] For more on these emotions, and some complications in their specifications, see **Cat.12, Cat.13, Cat.18**. Cf. also regret (*metameleia*) (*NE* III.1.1110b18–24, 1111a20–1, IX.4.1166b22–5; *Rhet.* II.3.1380a14–16).

fear all evils, e.g. disrepute, poverty, disease, friendlessness, death, but the courageous man is not thought to be concerned with all... (*NE* III.6.1115a7–12)

This picks out the key feature of Aristotle's definition of fear in *Rhet.* that it is concerned with evils ('Let fear be a sort of distress or disturbance arising from (*ek*) the appearance of a future destructive or painful evil' (II.5.1382a21–2)).[18] What you will not find, though, is any reference to chilling of the blood which, according to advocates of MCR or EFR, the Aristotle of *De an.* I.1 thinks required for an adequate specification. So too in *EE* III.1, where Aristotle refers to fear as concerned with 'whatever appears capable of producing pain that is destructive' (1229a33–5) and 'to the kind of pain that appears to be imminent and whose nature is capable of extinguishing life' (1229a39–b1).[19]

Similarly, in *NE* IV.5's discussion of the virtue and vices concerned with anger (*orgē*).[20] While there are vestiges of the *Rhet.* account of anger in play—we have the notion of being abused foully (*propēlakizomenon*: 1126a7), which seems equivalent to being slighted, and to retaliating (*antapodidonai*: 1126a17, 21) and revenge (*timōria*: 1126a2, 22, 28, 30), we do not have any reference to boiling of the blood.[21]

Again, in *Pol.* and *Poet.* it is *Rhet.*-style characterizations of the emotions that lie in the background. In *Pol.* V.8 he claims that those who are concerned about their constitution and want to make the citizens defend it (so that 'like sentries on night-duty' they 'never relax their guard') should manufacture fears 'and make faraway dangers seem close at hand' (1308a27–30). This directly echoes *Rhet.* II.5's insistence that fear requires the dangers to be near, rather than far off (1382a24–7). But there is no reference to the fact that the material dimension of fear is chilling of the blood. See also *Pol.* V.10, where anger is said to involve distress and to be for revenge (1311a34–5, 1312b32–3; cf. also V.11.1315a24–31).

---

[18] Note, Aristotle does not commit to the 'expectation of evil' definition (which is Platonic; see *Protagoras* (358d6) and *Laches* (198b9); see also *Rhet.* II.5.1382b29–30). Instead, it is, I think, taken for granted by him here that fear is a distress. He later refers to the courageous agent, who feels fear, as 'distressed at [the prospect of] death' (III.9.1117b11) (this follows because the person is virtuous and life is best worth living for such a person). His understanding fear as a distress will also contribute to its explaining the motivational impulses of the coward and what is so exceptional about the courageous person (see **7.3**). See also *NE* II.3.1104b7–8.

[19] Note, the specifications in *Rhet.* and *EE* are narrower than that in *NE* insofar as they restrict fear to 'destructive or painful evils', which would be distinguished from, e.g., fear of friendlessness (see *Rhet.* II.8.1386a5–11). See also *Cat.*7.

[20] Aristotle claims that there is no word for the mean state. The closest is *praotēs*, 'mild-manneredness', but he thinks that this strays too close to the deficiency because 'the mild-mannered person is not revengeful but, rather, considerate to others' (1126a1–3). On Aristotle's view, 'to put up with insulting treatment (*propēlakizomenon*: be foully abused) and to stand by watching while this happens to one's kin is slavish' (1126a7–8). Cp. Nussbaum (2016).

[21] The closest we get to a reference to anything physical is his calling people who manifest one of the (several) vices of excess 'hypercholic' (*akrocholoi*). But *cholos* most likely has its metaphorical meaning in this context (see *LSJ* s.v.). In any event, there is no mention of boiling blood.

Similarly, in *Poet.* 13 pity is specified by reference to its formal object, viz. that it is about (another's) undeserved misfortune (*peri ton anaxion dustuchounta*) (1453a4).

And yet while Aristotle clearly thinks that *Rhet.*-style specifications of emotions are adequate in a number of works, it is nonetheless notable that he still appears to think that occurrent emotions do essentially *possess* a material dimension in some of these. Just as in *De an.* I.1 he suggests that the material dimension of anger could be something like 'boiling of the blood around the heart', so too we know from elsewhere that he thinks that fear is a kind of chilling of the blood.[22] But after he has discussed the individual emotions in *Rhet.* II.2–11, Aristotle turns to stages of life (youth, prime, old age) in II.12–14. And in II.13 he contrasts the old with the young in a respect that draws on their physical make-up. He claims that the old are 'cowardly and fearful about everything ahead of time' (1389b29–30):

> for their disposition is the contrary of that of the young—for they are chilly, whereas the latter are warm, and so old age has paved the way for cowardice, since in fact fear is a sort of chilling (*ho phobos katapsuxis tis estin*). (1389b30–2)[23]

In claiming that fear *is* a sort of 'chilling' (*katapsuxis*), Aristotle is surely alluding to the idea that fear involves chilling of the blood. Similarly, the young are 'warm' and in II.12 he tells us that, like those drinking wine, they 'are warmed through and through due to their nature' and that this, in conjunction with the fact that they have not experienced much failure, accounts for their being hopeful (1389a18–20). They are also noted to be spirited, which is said to 'prevent fear' (1389a25–7).[24] It seems, then, that the 'warmth' of the young goes hand in hand with them being prone to anger or spirit, which is a boiling of the blood, and the 'coldness' of the old goes hand in hand with their being prone to fear, which is itself a kind of chilling (consider the parallel: the young have neural plasticity and so are more able to learn new skills).

In *Rhet.*, then, Aristotle appears to think *both* that *Rhet.*-style definitions of emotions are adequate in their own terms *and* that emotions are essentially enmattered. It is also clear that he thinks that the latter is only worth mentioning in a certain context, but *not* when defining the states for the purposes of his *Rhet.* II catalogue.[25]

---

[22] See *PA* II.4.650b27–30, IV.11.692a23; *De resp.* 20.479b20–6; *Probl.* II.31.869b7, X.60.898a6, XI.36.903b12, XXVII.1, XXX.1.954b13.

[23] Cf. also *Pol.* VII.17.1336a20–1; *Probl.* XXX.1.954b39–955a18.

[24] For the occurrent incompatibility of anger and fear, see also *Rhet.* II.3.1380a33–4, II.5.1383b6.

[25] Note how *Rhet.* II.13 refers to fear *only* by reference to its material dimension, i.e. *without* explicit reference to its being a representational distress. See also *PA* II.4, where Aristotle connects types of blood to types of character. He tells us both that fear 'chills' and that *thumos* is 'productive of heat', and he links the natural cowardly or aggressive dispositions of different types of animals to whether their blood is 'excessively watery' (650b27–30) or 'excessively fibrous and thick' (650b33–651a4). But we do

Similarly, in *NE* Aristotle seems to understand occurrent emotions as essentially possessing a material dimension. This is presumably why, in *NE* X.8, he refers to emotions as stemming from our composite nature (1178a20–1).[26] But the point is clearest in his discussion of shame (*aidōs*) in *NE* IV.9:

> *Aidōs* should not be described as a virtue; for it is more like an emotion than a state of character. It is defined, at any rate, as a kind of fear of disrepute (*phobos tis adoxias*), and produces an effect similar to that produced by fear of terrible things (*kai apoteleitai tō(i) peri ta deina phobō(i) paraplēsion*). For people who are ashamed (*hoi aischunomenoi*) of themselves blush, and those who fear death turn pale. Both shame and fear, therefore, seem to be in a sense bodily conditions, which is thought to be more characteristic of an emotion than of a state [of character] (*hexis*). (1128b11–15)[27]

Aristotle defines *aidōs* as fear of disrepute and then notes that fear and shame have similar effects—fear turns us pale, shame makes us blush.[28] Note that these are bodily *effects* of fear and shame, not the material dimension of those states themselves (which would be specified by processes of the blood). The conclusion that fear and shame are somehow bodily (or 'bodily in a way', *sōmatika pōs*: 1128b14) seems to be inferred from the fact that they (can) have bodily effects

---

not have the notion that fear and *thumos* involve representational distresses (or desires). Cf. also *De an.* I.4, where Aristotle refers to being angry and being afraid simply in terms of their consisting in the heart's being moved in a certain way (408b7–8). This could actually prove problematic for Charles' thesis that Aristotle holds that adequate specifications of emotions must make reference to an enmattered form. For, in the above, no 'formal' dimension is specified. Of course, Charles is not claiming that Aristotle holds there are no ways of referring to emotions that do not explicitly invoke enmattered forms. Trivially we can *refer* to 'anger' and, if Charles is right, we must be referring to something which could not be adequately defined except in terms of an enmattered form. However, in the passages mentioned we have material specifications without any corresponding 'formal' ones. And yet Charles claims: '[t]he relevant type of material process (in the case of anger) is one which is essentially directed towards revenge. *It is the presence of this goal that makes the relevant material process the one it is*' (2021: 32; my emphasis). But no such goal is stated, or deemed necessary to state, in the above contexts. The view I am proposing, by contrast, allows that different specifications can be relevant and adequate in different contexts.

[26] Note also the connection between emotions and the body a little earlier in X.8 (1178a14–16). Cf. also *NE* VII.3.1147a14–17.

[27] For more on the relation between *aidōs*, as characterized here, and *aischunē* (= 'shame' in *Rhet.* II.6), and the relation between shame and fear, see **Cat.7**.

[28] These (presumably contingent) effects of fear and shame are somewhat 'similar' (*paraplēsion*) in that they are both bodily, not in that they are the same bodily effect (blushing is not the same as turning pale). Given that Aristotle is here viewing shame as a species of fear, the contrast is between the physiological effects of (i) 'fear of terrifying things', on the one hand, and (ii) 'fear of disrepute', on the other. Cf. also *Probl.* XI.53.905a5–16, which, after mentioning the notion that *aidōs* is a kind of fear (*phobos tis*), claims that in those feeling afraid the heat *fails* in the upper part of the body (ἐκλείπει ἄνωθεν τὸ θερμόν), whereas in those feeling *aidōs*, the heat in the region of the breast *travels upwards* (ἄνω ἔρχεται τὸ θερμὸν περὶ τὰ στήθη), as is shown by the fact that they blush. For the link between shame and blushing and fear and pallor, see also *Cat.* 8.9b11–33. For more on how Aristotle understands the physiological process in fear, see *De resp.* 20.479b20–6.

(the latter is *evidence* that shame and fear are themselves bodily conditions).²⁹ Because those states themselves involve material changes, they can produce physiological effects. And the pallor of those who feel fear is doubtless to be explained, on Aristotle's view, by the notion that fear involves chilling of the blood. We find a similar divide between the material dimension of a state and its effects in *MA* 7:

> whenever there is an alteration on the basis of heating or cooling or some other such affection around the heart and in some imperceptible part of within it, it makes a considerable difference to the body, causing blushings and palings and shiverings and shudderings and their opposites. (701b28–32)

Blushing, turning pale, and shuddering are physiological effects of the underlying material processes.

It seems, then, in *NE* no less than in *Rhet.*, Aristotle holds *both* that *Rhet.*-style specifications of emotions are adequate in their own terms *and* that emotions are material states. Indeed, *NE* IV.9 is particularly telling for his taking the two to be compatible. For the *definition* (*horizetai*: 1128b11) of *aidōs* as 'fear of disrepute' looks like a *Rhet.*-style specification. Certainly, it does not mention the

---

²⁹ Sometimes Charles refers to the material dimension *of anger* in physical terms (he claims Aristotle wants 'the best account of the relevant type of specific physical process, whatever that turns out to be' (2021: 22n.8)), whereas at other times in more phenomenological terms ('[m]any think that there is a distinctive form of tense or stressful desire for revenge which can be distinguished phenomenologically (as a type of desire) from the cold calculating desire to get one's own back' (2021: 20; also 'getting hot and bothered', 'hot under the collar' in his 2009: 11). Since Charles thinks that with states such as the emotions the physical cannot be defined in abstraction of the psychological, nor vice versa, perhaps he wants both? (Although, note, there is surely *some* level of physical description which we would not experience phenomenologically *as such*: just as we cannot feel our neurons firing nor, I take it, would Aristotle think that we can feel the fibres in our blood; see *PA* II.4). But it is at least crucial to distinguish features of a state *itself* from its *effects*. Boiling of the blood around the heart seems intended to supply a feature of anger *itself*, whereas blushing seems to be an *effect* of shame. Of course, it may not always be easy to divide these up. And while emotions clearly can have (contingent) physiological *effects*, it is also plausible that insofar as Aristotle thinks that occurrent emotions *are* pleasures or distresses, he holds that they *themselves* essentially have some phenomenological or felt aspect (see end 2.2, 2.4n.55, 4.4, and 5.6). Cp. de Sousa and Scarantino (2018: §2): 'A widely shared insight is that emotions have components, and that such components are jointly instantiated in prototypical episodes of emotions. Consider an episode of intense fear due to the sudden appearance of a grizzly bear on your path while hiking. At first blush, we can distinguish in the complex event that is fear an evaluative component (e.g., appraising the bear as dangerous), a physiological component (e.g., increased heart rate and blood pressure), a phenomenological component (e.g., an unpleasant feeling), an expressive component (e.g., upper eyelids raised, jaw dropped open, lips stretched horizontally), a behavioral component (e.g., a tendency to flee), and a mental component (e.g., focusing attention)'. Aristotle would hold that some of these are effects of emotions, rather than parts of them, e.g. the expressive and the behavioural (e.g. anger might make us 'shake our fist'; cf. *Rhet.* III.16.1417b1–2). He would also insist that the evaluative is not a 'component' of the emotion, but what the emotion is formed in light of (so Part I). But the physiological and the phenomenological can still be parts of what emotions are. (The facial expressions associated with emotions of course generated a whole research programme: basic emotion theory; see de Sousa and Scarantino 2018: §8.1 for a summary.)

material dimension of *aidōs*.[30] But we are then told that *aidōs*, so construed, produces physiological effects, as befits the fact that it itself is in some sense bodily.[31] Aristotle thus sticks to the idea that *Rhet.*-style definitions of emotions are appropriate *even at the very point* he is drawing attention to their material dimension. It is hard not to draw the conclusion that here, no less than in *Rhet.*, he held that the material dimension of emotions is only worth drawing attention to in certain contexts and does not need to be referred to in any adequate specification of them.[32] Just as the notion that fear involves chilling of the blood is not deemed necessary to include in its definition in the *Rhet.* II catalogue (when Aristotle is trying to provide accounts of emotions that will enable orators to alter their listeners' decisions or verdicts), so too his view that, e.g., anger essentially involves boiling of the blood around the heart seems to be deemed unimportant for the purposes of charting the virtue that pertains to this very emotion, and the variations among the vices coordinate to that virtue.

This, it seems to me, leaves us having to choose between one of two alternatives. Either (1) we take Aristotle to think that definitions along the lines of the schema in *De an.* I.1 (which do make explicit reference to the state's material dimension) are not required in all contexts. On this reading, he would hold that lower-level descriptions of the processes of the blood involved in the emotions are simply irrelevant for most purposes; e.g. when instructing an orator how to engender or abate emotions, or when thinking about the role emotions play in ethics, politics, or tragic drama (or, we may add, philosophical psychology). Instead, *Rhet.*-style definitions, as true specifications that pick out the same states, will be adequate in such contexts. This will require us to reject MCR and EFR as stated, for they are not restricted to a certain kind of investigatory framework (although we shall see in **9.5** it will still permit revised versions of those claims). Alternatively (2) we take *De an.* I.1 to conflict with the accounts we find elsewhere and insist that Aristotle would, by its lights, view those accounts as

---

[30] Aristotle claims that *aidōs* is defined 'at any rate' (*goun*) as fear of disrepute. The 'at any rate' could be intended to distance him from the definition, suggesting that this is how *aidōs* has been defined, whether correctly or not. The definition is Platonic (see *Euthyphro* 12b–c; cf. also the Pseudo-Platonic *Definitions* (416a9)). It differs from the definition of *aischunē* in *Rhet.*, which does not seem to view shame as a species of fear. See **Cat.7**. But it is still clearly a *Rhet.*-style definition, rather than one which explicitly invokes the material dimension of the state.

[31] With regard to the *argument* in this stretch of *NE* IV.9, while Aristotle does establish that the occurrent emotion of shame is not a virtue as such, one wonders why he did not address whether the *disposition* to feel *aidōs*—as manifested by someone who is *aidēmōn*—could be a virtue. See esp. Raymond (2017: §2); see also Broadie and Rowe (2002: 334). The disposition to feel *aidōs* is addressed in the remainder of the chapter. I think states of character must be bodily states too, for Aristotle. See e.g. *NE* X.8.1178a20–1, where he ascribes them, no less than emotions, to our composite nature; see also the *Rhet.* II.12–13 passages above and *PA* II.4. Aristotle's contrast in *NE* IV.9 is presumably to the effect that shame and other emotions involve an *occurrent* material dimension or process (boiling or chilling of the blood, etc.), whereas states of character do not (they are material states that are dispositions to undergo such a material feature).

[32] Cf. also Rapp (2002: 552) and Gottlieb (2021: 29).

inadequate. Given the quantity of *Rhet.*-style specifications (whether explicit or implicit) across a range of works, this would presumably have to be supplemented with a strong developmental hypothesis to explain the change in view (since it was clearly not just a one-off slip), according to which the Aristotle of *De an.* I.1 has now ceased to view *Rhet.*-style definitions as adequate (so *NE* will now have to come out as an early work).

Insofar as Charles accepts EFR, he is committed to (2). Indeed, in his 2009 he explicitly claims that the Aristotle of *De an.* I.1 would reject *Rhet.*-style definitions (10n.19). Those who advocate MCR would also have to accept (2), since MCR commits Aristotle to the view that *any* adequate specification of an emotion must make reference to its material component. But since (1) holds out the possibility that Aristotle does not contradict himself, or need a developmental hypothesis to avoid this, it is *prima facie* more attractive than (2). It will become compelling, I believe, if we can do two further things. First, show that in fact *De an.* I.1 is compatible with the idea that the material dimension of emotions need not be specified in every investigatory framework. Second, establish that it is reasonable to think that *Rhet.*-style definitions *are* adequate in their own terms; in particular in response to the concerns raised at the end of **9.1**. I tackle the first of these in the next section, the second in **9.4**.[33]

9.3 Different requirements of different investigations

We have seen that if Aristotle held either MCR or EFR, the accounts of emotions we find in a number of key works would be undermined. Given this, we should reconsider whether he really commits to either MCR or EFR in *De an.* I.1. If there was a way of respecting his claims there that did not entail either of them, it would clearly be preferable. I believe there is such a reading. It is very clear in *De an.* I.1 that Aristotle is concerned with characterizing what the natural scientist, the *phusikos*, investigates in particular. When listing the three options—investigating the form, the matter, or the form-in-the-matter—he asked: which of these *is the job of the phusikos* to investigate (403b7)? Equally, at the end of the chapter he explicitly contrasts his account of what the *phusikos* investigates with the tasks of practitioners of other investigations, e.g. (i) craftspeople, such as carpenters and doctors (403b13–14), (ii) mathematicians (403b14–15), and (iii) those who investigate 'first philosophy' (403b15–16).[34] The investigation into the affections of the

---

[33] In fact, if we can do these things, the principle of charity might *demand* that we adopt my reading; cf. Davidson (1973–4: 19).

[34] Aristotle claims that 'the *phusikos* is concerned with everything which is a function or affection of such and such a body and such and such a matter' and notes that 'anything not of this kind is the concern of someone else, and in some cases of a craftsman perhaps, e.g. a carpenter or doctor' (403b11–14). This might initially surprise us. It is not as if the craftsperson or doctor *are not*

soul, insofar as they are properties common to body and soul (403a3–10), falls within natural science. Hence Aristotle is concerned with how the *natural science investigation* of states such as the emotions should go. And this is what the schematic definition (quoted in **9.1**) is intended to specify. But that clearly leaves entirely open whether there can be true accounts of the emotions that are entirely adequate for other investigatory frameworks. We can agree, then, that the *phusikos—the natural scientist—*needs to provide accounts of states such as the emotions that make direct reference to their material dimension (form-in-matter accounts, however that is understood; see **9.1**) and that from that investigatory framework, *Rhet.*-style definitions will be insufficient. However, it clearly does not follow that *Rhet.*-style definitions are inadequate *tout court*. Aristotle could quite consistently hold that the account required for an investigation into *psuchē* (soul) as a branch of the study into *phusis* (nature) is not required for other investigations, which can themselves be equally legitimate ways of approaching the same phenomena.[35]

In *Met.* E.1 Aristotle writes:

And since natural science (*phusikē*), like other sciences, confines itself to one class of beings, i.e. to that sort of substance which has the principle of its movement and rest present in itself, evidently it is neither practical nor productive. For the principle of production is in the producer—it is either reason or art or some capacity, while the principle of action is in the doer—viz. choice, for that which is done and that which is chosen are the same. Therefore, if all thought is either practical or productive or theoretical, natural science must be theoretical,

---

concerned with forms-in-perceptible-matter. But Aristotle's point is presumably that the *phusikos* is concerned with things that are functions or affections of natural bodies *simply as such*, i.e. in terms of developing a theoretical understanding of the phenomena in question. Whereas craftspeople have other ends in sight and this will dictate the relevant analysis. House-builders cannot build a house without having an understanding of the materials involved and how they interact. But they do not need to know the chemical or atomic properties of the materials they are employing. Surgeons will not be able to perform surgery successfully without an understanding of the physical properties of the flesh/organs/etc. they are to operate on. But they do not need to know the precise chemistry of what is going on at a molecular level. Cf. also Johansen (2012: 156) and Charles (2021: 33n.28). I will argue that something similar applies to the emotions. For the investigations of the mathematician, see **Appendix 1(d)**.

[35] See also Fortenbaugh (1970: 50) and Nehamas (1992: 295). Cf. also *Met.* E.1: 'we must not fail to notice the nature of the essence and its formula, for, without this, inquiry is but idle. Among things defined, i.e. essences, some are like snub, others like concave, and these differ because snub is bound up with matter (for what is snub is a concave *nose*), while concavity is independent of perceptible matter. If then all natural things are analogous to the snub in their nature—e.g. nose, eye, face, flesh, bone and in general animal; leaf, root, bark, and in general plant (for none of these can be defined without reference to movement—they always have matter), it is clear how we must seek and define the essence in the case of natural objects, and also why it belongs to the *phusikos* to study soul to some extent, i.e. so much of it as is not independent of matter' (1025b28–1026a6). Natural phenomena, *qua* natural, cannot be defined without reference to their matter. Hence, the *phusikos*'s investigations must refer to the matter. But, again, this does not entail that there cannot be investigations into the same phenomena from perspectives other than natural science as such.

but it will theorize about such being as admits of being moved, and only about that kind of substance which in respect of its formula is for the most part not separable from matter. (1025b18–28)

Investigations differ relative to their subject matter. Natural science, for Aristotle, is a theoretical discipline, concerned with knowledge as such. The study of the soul (*psuchē*)—or that in virtue of which living things are alive—falls under this (*Met*. E.1.1026a5–6).[36] Hence a theoretical account of emotions (as among the 'affections of the soul' (*ta pathē tēs psuchēs* or *ta tēs psuchēs pathē*: *De an*. I.1.403a3, 16))[37] would be the province of natural science, and would make reference to their perceptible matter (as specified by Aristotle's biology and chemistry). But we also need accounts of emotions that we can employ in rhetoric (a productive discipline), ethics and politics (practical disciplines), and, indeed, *poetics*, which concerns the literary arts.[38]

The general idea that Aristotle thinks that different investigations can legitimately employ different specifications of the same phenomenon is well illustrated in his ethical works. In *NE* I.13, after noting that he has established (i.e. in *NE* I.7) that 'happiness is activity of soul in accordance with perfect virtue' (1102a5–6), Aristotle emphasizes that the virtue he is referring to is 'of the soul' (1102a16–17) and tells us that this means that the investigator into politics—the *politikos*—must study the soul too (1102a18–19, 23). However, the *politikos* must do so, he insists, 'with these objects in view' and 'just to the extent which is sufficient for the questions we are discussing'—for 'further precision would perhaps involve more labour than our purposes require' (1102a23–6). We do not, it appears, need the same kind of analysis for each of our investigations.[39] His point becomes clearer in what follows. He offers some working notions that are sufficient for his current

---

[36] That is, 'at least to the extent that it is not independent of natural matter' (1026a6). This makes room for some types of thought to be different, on Aristotle's view, but not necessarily *human* thought (see *De an*. I.1.403a8–10 and *Met*. Λ.7). Cf. Shields (2016: 100–1).

[37] Charles (2021: 30–1) proposes that the first formulation picks out a broader set of states (i.e. including perception: 403a7) than the second, which concerns the emotions specifically.

[38] Rhetoric is characterized as 'craft-like' (*technikon*) in *Rhet*. I.2.1355b31–4 and in a sense it is clear what the end is, viz. helping the orator persuade. There is some debate about the purpose of the *Poetics*. See e.g. Ford (2015); Destrée (2016).

[39] I suppose it might be suggested that this indicates that Aristotle is accepting that his analysis may only be roughly right. Near the beginning of the *NE* he notes that given the variable nature of the subject matter of ethics (i.e. just and fine actions 'which exhibit much variety and fluctuation' (I.3.1094b14–16)), we must be content with reasoning that 'indicates the truth roughly and in outline' (1094b20–1). Similarly, when we speak about things 'which are only for the most part true' we must expect only 'premises of the same kind to reach conclusions that are no better' (1094b21–2). The principle that is being invoked in these passages is that we must 'look for precision in each class of things just so far as the nature of the subject admits: it is evidently equally foolish to accept probable reasoning from a mathematician and to demand demonstrative proofs from a rhetorician' (1094b23–7). But this cannot be his point in *NE* I.13. For it is not the *subject matter* that in this case dictates the nature of our analysis. On the contrary, we know full well that a more detailed analysis of the soul *can* be completed (and, indeed, is completed by Aristotle himself in *De an*.). Rather, it is the nature of the current investigation.

purposes, namely, that one part of the soul is non-rational and another rational (1102a26–8). And he even gives us an indication of the sort of detail that would be unnecessary:

> Whether these parts are separated as the parts of the body or of anything divisible are, or are distinct by definition but by nature inseparable, like convex and concave in the circumference of a circle, does not affect the present question. (1102a28–32)

These further questions about the elements so distinguished—whether they are separable, like the parts of the body or other divisible things, or inseparable by nature but nonetheless distinct in definition (as with mathematical properties; see **Appendix 1(d)**)—*simply do not affect the present question*. The *excessive labour* (1102a25) that Aristotle has in mind, then, pertains to attempting to provide details that are simply *inconsequential for the investigation at hand*. While one of the options about the soul that Aristotle mentions will nonetheless *be* true—or at least some resolution between them obtain—and in an investigation into the soul this will be important[40]—*which* is true is *irrelevant* for current purposes. At the same time, though, the ethical division itself counts as a *true* one. As Aristotle writes in the parallel *EE* passage:

> It makes no difference if the soul is or is not divisible into parts (*diapherei d'ouden out' ei meristē hē psuchē out' ei amerēs*); it *still has* different capacities (*dunameis*), including those we have mentioned [viz. a rational one and a non-rational capacity that can obey reason]. (1219b32–3; my emphasis and gloss)

The issue concerns *what kind of* detail is pertinent for a given discipline. Similarly, I wish to propose, with the accounts of emotions that Aristotle provides in different investigatory frameworks.

Relatedly, in the ethical works we also find Aristotle *directing* the reader to a natural science investigation which he does not there provide because it is not germane to his current ethical inquiries. In his discussion of *akrasia* in *NE* VII.3, having just sketched his account of akratic ignorance (1146b31–1147a24), he writes:

> The explanation of how the ignorance is dissolved, and the akratic person regains his knowledge, is the same as in the case of the man drunk or asleep and is not peculiar to this condition; we must hear it from the natural scientists (*para tōn phusiologōn akouein*). (1147b6–9)

---

[40] See e.g. *De an.* II.2.413b13–32, III.9.432a15–b7, III.10 433a31–b13; and cp. Plato's *Timaeus* 69b–70e.

And he says no more. It is, then, not simply that some details need not be addressed because their resolution does not make a difference for a certain investigation. It is also that some details that are, strictly speaking, the job of the natural scientist can be pushed to one side.[41] So too, I propose, the lack of reference to the boiling or chilling of the blood in *Rhet.*-style definitions does not undermine their appropriateness when we are not doing natural science, as Aristotle conceives of it.

In fact, Aristotle may think that such details are not just unnecessary, but actually unhelpful or hindering. In *Top.* VI.1 he writes:

> Incorrectness falls into two branches: first, the use of obscure language (*to asaphei tē(i) hermēneia(i) kechrēsthai*) (for the language of a definition ought to be the very clearest possible, seeing that the purpose of rendering it is to make something known); secondly, if the account is in a more extended form than is necessary (*ei epi pleion eirēke ton logon tou deontos*) (for all additional matter in a definition is superfluous). (139b12–17)

This, in turn, is echoed in *Rhet.* I.10:

> we should consider our definitions as adequate in each case if they neither lack perspicuousness nor are [too] exact (*mēte asapheis mēte akribeis*). (1369b31–2)[42]

Why might Aristotle think that references to the boiling or chilling of blood would be 'too exact' in his *Rhet.* II catalogue or his ethical works? Consider Aristotle's analogy of the house-builder (*De an.* I.1.403a3–7). The house-builder does not need to understand the molecular properties of stone and wood in order to fashion and fit a joist. Indeed, it is not merely that such details are unnecessary, it could also potentially *mislead* and *confuse* house-builders to fill their minds with such details. Or consider surgeons. Surgeons do not need to know what is going on at the atomic level in cells when they are making the cut, and filling their heads with such detail might not be a shrewd move when they have scalpel in hand. So too if orators fill their heads with thoughts about the boiling or chilling of blood (or fibres in the blood, or, for us, neurological synapses firing), this might make them lose sight of their aim, which is simply to *engender* or *abate* emotions

---

[41] It seems likely that the explanation that Aristotle has in mind is one for the *phusikos* because it involves a material explanation tied to the body. In *Phys.* VII.3 he claims that even though we are unable to use our knowledge when we are drunk, asleep, or ill, we do not say, when we know once more, that we have now *acquired* knowledge again (247b13–17). Rather, it seems, a bodily condition has *blocked* our access to knowledge that we nonetheless in some sense retain (247b17–248a6). Explaining this will quickly embroil us in detailed accounts of the physical processes by which this occurs (cf. *Somn.* 3.456b17–28 for the physical changes in sleep), accounts which Aristotle does not want to get bogged down with in his ethical works.

[42] Cf. Striker (1996: 287–8) and Dow (2015: 163–4); and cp. Gosling and Taylor (1982: 197–8).

in their audience insofar as that might bear on the latter's decisions or verdicts (*kriseis*), not to understand the emotion's physical make-up as such. Indeed, an analogy Nietzsche employed in a different context seems apt: a full-blown scientific account of the material aspect of anger (which, on Aristotle's view would refer, e.g., to fibres in the blood and the processes through which the blood is heated, etc.) might well be about as much use to the practicing orator as the chemical analysis of water would be to a boatman facing a storm.[43] There is, of course, such an analysis of water to be had, but knowledge of it is not really going to help a boatman encountering adverse weather conditions.

Note, finally, there is no implication, here, of a kind of relativism to the effect that there is no underlying truth of the matter, with the different conclusions of various disciplines neither more nor less true, or only true relative to the assumptions of the discipline. The suggestion is that the accounts provided in *Rhet.* and *De an.* are different specifications of the same underlying truths about emotions, ones that are more or less germane for different kinds of investigatory framework.[44]

9.4 Addressing concerns about the extension of *Rhet.*-style definitions and their explanatory power

In **9.2** I showed that Aristotle clearly thinks that *Rhet.*-style specifications of emotions are adequate in a number of works (and in some of these he also explicitly takes them to possess a material dimension). This suggested that a reading of *De an.* I.1 that did not commit us to MCR or EFR would be preferable. In **9.3** I provided such a reading, viz. that the requirement to define states such as anger according to the schematic definition (whether that is understood to invoke an impure form or a material component; see **9.1**) only applies if we are concerned with full natural science specifications of such states. But at the end of **9.1** I noted two considerations that have been provided for thinking that definitions which leave out direct reference to the material dimension of these states would be inadequate. It is alleged that such specifications (i) fail to capture the correct extension of these states and (ii) are explanatorily 'empty' in that they do not allow us to derive other properties of the states. If these concerns were legitimate, we may still feel the pull to embrace the otherwise non-preferable reading and insist that Aristotle's most considered view is either EFR or MCR. So let us now address these concerns, taking each in turn.

---

[43] Nietzsche has in mind the usefulness of knowledge of a metaphysical world (*Human All Too Human*, §9).
[44] Indeed, even an account that invoked a notion of anger that did not pick out all and only instances of anger (as with the bare desire for revenge; see **9.4**) would still be attempting to characterize this underlying truth. It would just be a poorer one.

(1) The extensionality worry

In his 2009 Charles writes:[45]

> If one does not think of fear and anger as enmattered in certain types of perceptual matter, one will, in [Aristotle's] view, make mistakes in one's reasoning about those affections. One will fail, for example, to know when and why they occur. (5)

To illustrate, he points to Aristotle's house analogy (*De an.* I.1.403b3–7):

> if one does not think of a house as enmattered in certain types of perceptual matter, one will, as a builder or architect, make mistakes in one's reasoning about house construction. One will not know how or where to build successfully. What you build may fail to keep out wind or weather. It may not even stand up. (6)

Charles expounds more on anger as follows:

> One has to introduce reference to the bodily state (material cause) to distinguish the specific type of desire for revenge which defines anger ... desire for revenge has to be enmattered in this kind of matter [i.e. boiling of the blood] if it is to be the type of desire which defines anger, and not be, for example, the cold calculating desire of the aged. Any dialectician who might be tempted to define anger simply as the desire for revenge would not succeed in giving a fully adequate definition of the phenomenon. (10; my gloss)[46]

On this view, definitions of anger such as *the desire for revenge* are inadequate because they fail to specify the *particular type* of desire for revenge required for anger, and so fail to pick out the correct extension of the state.

---

[45] I draw from Charles' 2009 here because he develops these points more explicitly there than in his 2021. But the claim that definitions that fail to mention the material dimension are prone to error is still present in the latter (see e.g. 21, 28, 44).

[46] Charles claims (2009: 9, 2021: 29) to find reference to a cold desire for revenge in the old in *Rhet.* itself—somewhat ironically, given that he thinks we should reject *Rhet.*-style definitions on this basis; although the passage in question, II.13.1390a15ff., falls outside the *Rhet.* II catalogue. In fact, I do not see an explicit reference to cold desires for revenge here. All we are told of the old is that their *thumoi* are 'sharp but weak' (1390a11), that they live more in accordance with rational calculation (*logismos*) than character (*ēthos*) (1390a15–16), and that 'the unjust actions they commit are due to *kakourgia* ('malice', 'wickedness'), not *hubris* ('insult', 'wanton aggression')' (*Rhet.* II.13.1390a17–18; see also *Pol.* IV.11 which distinguishes the very poor and the very rich on the same basis: 1295b1–11). (*Hubris* is, of course, one of the three species of 'slight' (*oligōria*) Aristotle specifies in *Rhet.* II.2 (see 1378b23–35). But, in *Rhet.* II.13, *hubris*—which the old do not act on—is cited as a *motivator* of (unjust) action, something one may get angry and seek revenge *in response to*, not a revenge-seeking motivation itself. So too (by implication) *kakourgia*—which they do act on—is cited only as a cause of unjust action without any indication that it is itself a revenge-seeking motivation.) Nonetheless, I am happy to accept that Aristotle would want to distinguish cold desires for revenge from anger.

From the perspective of *Rhet.* it is natural to object that Aristotle did not there define anger simply as the desire for revenge, but as a desire for revenge *accompanied by distress at an apparent slight* (II.2.1378a30–1; and see **6.2–3**). In fact, even in *De an.* I.1 he does not characterize the formal account of anger as a desire for revenge (*orexis timōrias*), but as a desire to return pain (*orexis antilupēseōs*: 403a30–1).[47] And while a bare desire for revenge only implies that one desires revenge *for something*, this formulation seems more directly to imply that the person is seeking to *return* pain or distress to the other. But then what is wrong with the following reply to the extensionality worry: while a bare desire for revenge may not pick out all and only cases of anger, the specifications in *Rhet.* II.2 and *De an.* I.1 do achieve this insofar as they require that the subjects experience a distress that they seek to rectify? Indeed, it may seem quite plausible that it is the lack of the distress that explains why a cold desire for revenge is *cold*. The old-timers that Charles refers to can plausibly be construed as emotionally unaffected by the perceived wrong done to them. They just coldly reason that the wrong will have to be rectified and some suitable punishment meted out in return. Those who are angry, by contrast, differ from such cold-hearted old codgers. They experience distress *at*—are *hurt by*—the wrong done to them. In this way, it seems, we can rule out a cold desire for revenge as counting as anger without having to make direct reference to anger's perceptual matter.

Charles disagrees. On his view, parallel concerns apply with the *Rhet.* II.2 account:

> Similar remarks will apply if one uses the fuller account of anger offered in the *Rhetoric*: the desire for revenge brought on by pain attendant on the appearance of an unjustified slight (1378a30ff). For the old can have a desire for revenge of this type without being angry. [i] The desire for revenge may outlive their past pain. Or [ii] even if their pain endures for as long as they desire revenge they may succeed in detaching themselves sufficiently from it so as not to be angry. (2009: 10n.19, numerals added)

On this view, since such a definition 'does not refer to any type of material process' or 'specify the relevant desire in a matter-involving way' (14), it can be satisfied even though we only have a cold desire for revenge, not one enmattered in boiling blood.

However, as I see it, while Charles' examples may have bite with respect to the bare 'desire to return pain' formulation of *De an.* I.1, they do not undermine the

---

[47] A fact obscured by some translations (e.g. Hamlyn 1993: *ad loc*; Shields 2016: *ad loc.*) which translate 'desire for retaliation'. The *ROT* (for example) translates more literally, as does Charles himself in his 2021 (24). Aristotle appears to wish to indicate that such a definition is somewhat loose; he adds: 'or something of the sort' (403a31).

account of anger we find in *Rhet.* II.2, when that is correctly understood. A desire to return pain is clearly compatible either with the original pain no longer being current (= [i]), or with detaching oneself from the pain in question (= [ii]).[48] Hence, if the pain must link more directly to the desire than in either of these scenarios (to rule out cold desires for revenge), merely possessing a desire to return pain would be compatible with the subject not being angry. But the account of anger we find in *Rhet.* II.2 can be seen to block both [i] and [ii]. With [i], we saw in **6.3** that in characterizing anger as a desire *accompanied by* (*meta*) distress in *Rhet.* II.2, Aristotle is most likely indicating that the desire and the distress must *co-exist* if the subject is to count as angry.[49] Indeed, he emphasizes this point in a number of other texts as well (e.g. *Rhet.* II.3.1380b1, II.4.1382a12–13; *EE* III.1.1229b31–2), most explicitly in *Pol.* V.10: 'anger is present with distress' (*hē orgē meta lupēs parestin*) (1312b31–2). Thus, while the desire must form in light of the distress, Aristotle holds that the distress itself must *remain present* if the subject is to count as angry.[50] Someone who is not *currently* distressed by the slight, then—even if they once were—will not count as angry, on Aristotle's view. [i] is blocked.

With [ii], we need to note, first, that it is not the *mere* conjunction of *distress at a slight* and *desire for revenge* that makes one angry (such that Aristotle's definition of anger would be satisfied by those who get distressed at a slight and then, *independently* of the distress, form a desire for revenge (owing to the slight)). It is surely more plausible that Aristotle is envisaging that the desire of anger is formed *in light of* the distress of anger. (Indeed, this fits the formal definition of anger in *De an.* I.1: a desire *to return* pain.) But then, second, it is, I suggest, plausible that Aristotle holds that the desire for revenge gets its heat—that is, is specifically one of anger—just insofar as and to the extent that it is 'fuelled' by the distress it is formed in light of. One will count as angry, on this view, just insofar as one's desire for revenge directly reflects the distress which the apparent slight gives one. ('You slighted me; that *hurts*—just you wait!') So construed, while the distress is directed at the slight, the desire for revenge would itself make essential reference not just to the slight, but to the *distress* one experiences at it. If so, in contrast to the simple *desire for revenge* or even the *desire to return pain* formulation, the desire of anger as envisaged in *Rhet.* II.2 would not be able to become 'detached' from the distress in the way Charles envisages. [ii] is also blocked.

---

[48] Note, Aristotle holds that we could want to harm another in response to an apparent slight (*sub specie* 'spite': *epēreasmos*) without being angry (see **6.6**). However, in that case spite is said to produce hating (*Rhet.* II.4.1382a2–3) which, unlike anger, is 'without pain' (*Rhet.* II.4.1382a12–13). So such a desire *to get even* would not straightforwardly count as a desire *to return pain*. See **7.4**.

[49] This is supported by his contrasting the implications of *meta* + genitive and *dia* + accusative in definitions of anger in *Top.* VI.13. See **6.3** and, for the passage, **6.1**.

[50] This befits the fact that it is occurrent outbursts of anger he is after in *Rhet.* II.2; see **Intro.1**.

The upshot is that unlike the 'dialectical' 'desire to return pain' of *De an.* I.1, the *Rhet.* II.2 definition can plausibly be understood to secure the correct extension of anger, even though it does not make direct reference to boiling of the blood, or the like.

Note, too, the sorts of example that Charles invokes can only even appear *prima facie* troubling with Aristotle's account *of anger*, not emotions as such. As we have seen, he thinks that emotions just are representational pleasures or distresses; that is, pleasures or distresses about an apparent manifestation of the formal object of the emotion. With such states there is no gap of the kind Charles tries to exploit. To generate cases in which the desire for revenge came apart from the emotion of anger, Charles appealed to situations in which the distress of anger was either not concurrent with the desire or was not connected up correctly with it. But since Aristotle thinks that emotions themselves just are representational pleasures or distresses (or so I have argued), they clearly cannot be separated in such a way. The pleasure or distress must be present *if the emotion is*. And the pleasure or distress must be directed at a particular instantiation of the emotion's formal object if we are to have that specific emotion-type instantiated.[51]

Finally, note that if *Rhet.*-style definitions do, after all, secure the correct extension of emotions (or, at least, it is plausible Aristotle thinks so), and if emotions, on Aristotle's view, essentially possess a material dimension, then he must think that *Rhet.*-style definitions are just *alternative ways* of specifying the enmattered states. They pick out such states without making direct reference to the state's material dimension. I shall return to this shortly, in the process of addressing the second concern.

(2) The explanatory worry

Aristotle claims that 'definitions which do not enable us to ascertain the attributes nor even make it easy to guess about this' have been stated 'dialectically' and 'to

---

[51] By contrast, characterizing, e.g., pity as a response to apprehending someone as having undergone some undeserved misfortune will not demarcate it. For, as we have seen (**3.5**), Aristotle thinks that another diametrically opposed emotion can form in response to the same apprehension, namely, schadenfreude (*pleasure*, rather than distress, at such misfortune). Indeed, he even thinks that in response to apprehending the object of an emotion, it is possible to experience *neither* pleasure *nor* distress (see *Rhet.* II.9.1386b27–8). In this sense, characterizing emotions by reference to the intentional state that apprehends its object will fail to specify them sufficiently, since it will not isolate a particular emotional response. Such specifications will still provide helpful *necessary* conditions for different emotions (via the formal object), but the sorts of error Charles alludes to could emerge in one's reasoning if one relied on them alone. The suggestion is that the same cannot be said for Aristotle's specifications of emotions as representational pleasures or distresses. And this is crucial if such accounts are to fulfil their stated purpose in *Rhet.* and elsewhere (see **9.2**).

no purpose' (or 'emptily': *kenōs*) (402b25–403a2).⁵² Charles (2021: 23–4) thinks that definitions that do not make explicit reference to the material dimension are such. On his view:

> one would not be able to derive the other, bodily, features of anger...from a dialectical definition (403a20ff). It does not provide the resources to explain why people are angry in certain bodily conditions and not in others...Even if the dialectical definition were to succeed in marking out the correct extension of 'anger', it would not provide the resources to explain why anger has the bodily causes, concomitants, and consequences it does. It will be, in Aristotle's terms 'empty and vain' (403a2). (23–4)

Since *Rhet.*-style definitions do not make explicit reference to the material dimension of emotions (whether as a distinct component or in an impure form), they may appear susceptible to such a charge. If this means they have no explanatory power at all, they will indeed be 'empty'.

There are two things to say in reply here. First, let us accept that *we* cannot derive the idea that the material dimension of anger should be specified as boiling of the blood around the heart from the *Rhet.* definition. I suppose one might wonder whether this may not in fact be a strength of such a definition since, I take it, *we* would not want to specify the material dimension of anger by reference to calorific blood. The definition may therefore have a chance of being *true*, whereas one that explicitly invokes boiling blood (whether as a separate component or as part of an impure form) presumably will not. But, as Charles notes (2021: 22n.8, cf. 29), we may be able to take Aristotle's specific account of the material dimension of the state as a 'placeholder' for whatever the correct account is. Let us grant this, for the sake of argument.⁵³ However, if what I have argued in (1) of this section is right, Aristotle would think that the correct natural science

---

⁵² 'Dialectical' or 'logical' (*logikōs*) can, as here, have a pejorative sense in Aristotle (see esp. *Gen. cor.* I.2.316a5–14). In *this* sense, I believe Aristotle would not view *Rhet.*-style definitions as such.

⁵³ One might wonder how Charles can propose this, given he thinks that Aristotle holds that we cannot define anger without *explicit* reference to its material dimension. But crucial for him is not boiling of the blood, but that the desire is specified as a 'hot' one (which rules out cold desires for revenge). In line with this, Charles translates Aristotle's material specification of anger (403a31–b1) as 'seething of the blood around the heart and the hot' (2021: 22) and suggests that 'and the hot' may indicate 'a possible clarification of the phrase "the blood around the heart"' (22n.8). On this view, Aristotle is alluding 'to the best account of the relevant type of specific physical process, whatever that turns out to be' and his theory does 'not require commitment to...calorific fluid!' (22n.8). (Charles also later suggests that 'and the hot' may 'indicate a physical genus of which blood boiling is a species' and that while anger is 'essentially a hot desire for revenge', it may be 'variably realized in different types of heat' (29).) The Greek for the phrase specifying the material dimension is: *ho de zesin tou peri kardian aimatos kai thermou*. *Thermou* (of the hot) and *aimatos* (of the blood) are genitives and are both specified as boiling. So *boiling hot (stuff)* would have to be the generic specification if Charles is right. Hamlyn translates: 'boiling of the blood and hot stuff around the heart' (cf. Shields 2016: 'boiling of the blood and heat around the heart'). He thereby takes *tou* to govern both *thermou* and *aimatos*. On this reading, the boiling hot (stuff) is specified to be around the heart, no less than the relevant blood.

account of anger (which includes reference to the material dimension) and the *Rhet.* II.2 specification (which does not) are extensionally equivalent. But then the latter definition will at least have indirect implications for the material dimension of the state. In fact, given enough other physical/material assumptions, it may well directly entail a specific material description of the state, or at least enable us to 'guess at' (*eikasai*: 403a1) it. Indeed, Aristotle appears to think that the pleasures or distresses of emotions themselves entail the relevant material dimension of such states, as he understands them. In *MA* 8 he writes:

> roughly speaking, painful and pleasant things[54] are all accompanied by (*meta*) some cooling and warming.[55] This is clear from the affections (*pathēmata*). For occurrences of confidence and fear and sexual arousal (*tharrē gar kai phoboi kai aphrodisiasmoi*) and other painful and pleasant bodily things (*ta alla ta sōmatika lupēra kai hēdea*) occur sometimes in some particular part accompanied by (*meta*) warming and chilling, and sometimes in the whole body. (701b37–702a5)

The reference to sexual arousal and other pleasant and painful bodily things seems to indicate that by 'affections', here, Aristotle has in mind a broader category than just emotions.[56] But since fear and confidence are specifically mentioned we know the category at least *includes* emotions. The claim is that we cannot have the pleasures or distresses of emotions *without* the relevant heatings and chillings in the body. Hence, if we refer to emotions *as* representational pleasures or distresses, Aristotle would say that we are, in so doing, picking out states that essentially involve the relevant material processes. But, in any event, if (i) the *Rhet.*-style specification of anger picks out all-and-only-instances of it, and (ii)

---

[54] Nussbaum (1978: *ad loc.*) adds 'the thought and *phantasia* of' as an explanatory gloss before 'painful and pleasant things' (*ta lupēra kai hēdea*; which she translates 'the painful and the pleasant'). But this has no basis in the text itself and should be rejected. She no doubt added the gloss because Aristotle had just claimed: 'But warming and cooling necessarily follow the thought and *phantasia* of those things [sc. the object of pursuit and avoidance: 701b34], for the painful is to be avoided and the pleasant to be pursued' (701b34–6). However, Nussbaum misses the structure of the passage. Having stated (in the lines quoted in the main text) that pleasure and pain are *themselves* accompanied by heating and chilling, Aristotle then picks up on the thought and *phantasia* of the objects of pursuit and avoidance, at 702a5, via the notions of memory and anticipation which, 'using such things as images, are causes of them, sometimes to a lesser extent and sometimes to a greater' (702a5–7). (The distresses or pleasures *themselves* entail the heating or cooling in a way a judgement or *phantasia* of the object of the emotion does not (see n.51) and the emotion is to be identified with the former, not the latter—so Part I.)

[55] Nussbaum (1978: *ad loc.*, 1976: 153–4), after Moraux (1959: 366), transposes 701b36-7 to here (which she translates: 'although we do not notice this when it happens in a small part'). I follow the new edition in Rapp and Primavesi (2020: *ad loc*) in not transposing the line.

[56] I take the 'or other pleasant and painful bodily things' to generalize from 'sexual arousal', but it would be possible to take it to generalize from all three of 'fear, confidence, and sexual arousal', in which case the first two would count as bodily pleasures and distresses, no less than the last. Even if Aristotle had this in mind, it would not make emotions bodily sensations in the way discussed in Chapter 2. Emotions are about apparent instantiations of their formal objects, but as pleasures or distresses they would be bodily in the way emotions are in general, i.e. as specified in *De an.* I.1.

anger essentially involves the body being affected in a certain way (*De an.* I.1.403a3–5), we know (iii) that the material dimension of the state (whatever it in fact is) must be occurring when the *Rhet.*-style account is instantiated. This, I suggest, will at least give us a sound basis for *investigating* that dimension. And *if*, as Aristotle appears to have thought, such an investigation reveals that the material dimension of anger is boiling of the blood around the heart, that would in turn allow us to investigate *that* material feature and look for further correlations (such as, in *PA* II.4.650b27ff. (see **9.2**n.25), he asserts holds between creatures with lots of fibres in their blood and dispositions to spirit or anger, on the one hand, and creatures with watery blood and fear/cowardice, on the other). In short, while *Rhet.*-style definitions do not themselves make direct reference to material processes such as boiling of the blood, if we accept that they are extensionally equivalent to definitions that do make such reference, they will appear to provide a basis for investigating what those material processes are. If so, contra Charles, they *will* 'provide the resources to explain why people are angry in certain bodily conditions and not in others', and *will* enable us at least to investigate 'the bodily consequences of anger' (2021: 23–4).[57]

Second, I also think we need to take on board the implications of the argument I provided in **9.2–3**. When Aristotle claims in 402b25f. that 'definitions which do not enable us to ascertain the attributes nor even make it easy to guess about this' have been stated 'dialectically' and 'to no purpose' (or 'emptily'), he did not, as Charles presumed, explicitly state that it was the *bodily* causes, concomitants, and consequences that he was getting at. His point, rather, appears to be a general one about definitions. Definitions have to be able to do some *explanatory work* in order to avoid being 'empty'. Now, in **9.3** we saw that Aristotle not unreasonably thinks that different investigations have different requirements and that the kind of questions addressed, and the information or detail provided, may differ relative to the investigation. And while *Rhet.*-style definitions may, as just suggested, at least indirectly facilitate an investigation into the material dimension of the state, they may be more *directly* relevant to grasping other properties and consequences of the state. While definitions have to be able to do some explanatory work to avoid being 'empty', they can do so *relative to the investigatory frameworks they pertain to*.

In line with this, we can see that Aristotle clearly thinks that *Rhet.*-style definitions allow us to derive other significant properties of these states, ones that are more germane for the oratorical or ethical context these specifications of emotions are invoked in. In *Rhet.* itself he explicitly derives further properties from

---

[57] With *Rhet.*-style specifications we have: distress/pleasure *at* an apparent instantiation of the formal object of the emotion (see **1.3**). As I see it, the different combinations of distress/pleasure and apparent instantiations of the distinct formal objects will fix the relevant material specifications of the individual emotions, *whatever those turn out to be* (subject to our background physical theories and assumptions).

his definitions on a number of occasions.[58] And his definitions explicitly constrain other features of his analysis of the emotions pertaining to his threefold structure.[59] His specifications also allow him to distinguish emotion-types from each other[60] and enable him to infer the account of the 'contraries' of his primary emotion-types.[61] Equally, and most crucially (given his aims in *Rhet.* II), his specifications (and subsequent discussions) of individual emotions allow him to explain how engendering or abating the emotions will affect an audience's decisions or verdicts.[62]

Again, in the ethical context, Aristotle's specifications of emotions allow him to chart the virtues and vices, or dispositional states more generally, that correspond to the emotion in question (see esp. *EE* III.7 and *NE* IV.9). And they allow him to specify their motivational influence (against the background of various desiderative dispositions) in the way examined in Chapter 7. So too, in the *Pol.* V.8 passage discussed in **9.2** (1308a27–30), the feature of fear drawn from a *Rhet.*-style definition—that fear requires dangers to be close at hand—is cited as something that those concerned about their constitution could use to help manufacture fear (they can try to make faraway dangers seem close at hand) insofar as this might make people take a firmer grip on their constitution. Again, in the *Poet.* text cited in **9.2**, the feature of pity drawn from a *Rhet.*-style account, viz. that its formal object can be specified as (another's) undeserved misfortune (13.1453a4), enables us to see that tragedy, which should elicit our pity in the tragic character, should not concern wicked people passing from bad fortune into good fortune (for then there is no misfortune at all), nor thoroughly depraved people falling from good fortune into bad fortune (for they *deserve* their misfortune) (13.1452b36–1453a4). Evidently, then, Aristotle does not view *Rhet.*-style definitions as 'empty' in the way the *De an.* I.1 text suggests a purely 'dialectical' one

---

[58] E.g. 'If, then, this is what anger is, the angry person must always be angry at some particular person...because the individual has done or is going to do something to him or one of those close to him, and all anger must entail some sort of pleasure, namely the one from the hope of being revenged...' (II.2.1378a32f); 'If, then, this is what fear is, necessarily the sorts of things that are fearsome are whichever ones appear to have a great capacity for destroying or causing harms that lead to great pain. This is why even the signs of such things are fearsome...In fact, this is what danger is...' (II.5.1382a27f); 'If, then, what has been defined is shame, necessarily people are ashamed of such evils as seem shameful either for themselves or for those they care about. And works due to vice are like this...' (II.6.1383b15f). See also *Rhet.* II.4.1381a3f.

[59] E.g. 'since shame is an appearance of disrepute...necessarily a person feels shame in front of those he takes account of...' (II.6.1384a21f); 'and the things they pity are clear from the definition. For whichever painful or distressing things are destructive are all pitiable, and whichever are ruinous, and whichever evils having magnitude of which luck is the cause' (II.8.1386a4–5); 'it is also clear why people envy, whom they do, and by being disposed in which way, if indeed envy is a sort of distress at...' (II.10.1387b22–5). See also II.7.1385a16–17, II.11.1388a31f.

[60] See esp. *Rhet.* II.9.1386b8–1387a5, where Aristotle distinguishes a series of emotions in terms of representational pleasures and distresses: pity, distress-based indignation, envy, fear, pleasure-based indignation, pride-in-another, and schadenfreude. (= **Cat.11–13, Cat.5, Cat.16–18**.)

[61] E.g. 'Since it is now evident what fear is...it is also evident on the basis of this what being confident is...' (II.5.1383a13–15); see **10.7**. See also II.4.1382a1–2, II.6.1385a14–15.

[62] See e.g. II.2.1380a2–5, II.3.1380b31–4, II.4.1382a16–19, II.5.1383a8–12, II.7.1385a29–33.

would be. On the contrary, they do all the work required of them in the contexts they are invoked.

In short, the argument of this section strongly suggests that Aristotle thinks that *Rhet.*-style definitions are neither subject to 'errors'/'mistakes', nor 'empty' in the way a bare dialectical definition (e.g. the desire to return pain) might be. Instead, they are extensionally equivalent to (correct) specifications that make explicit reference to their material dimension, and they allow us to derive or postulate all manner of other properties that are crucial for the investigations Aristotle is conducting.

9.5 Restricted versions of MCR and EFR

Charles directs much of his argument against the idea that natural states such as the emotions (and natural entities more generally) can be adequately specified in terms of a combination of a 'pure' form and an independently specifiable material component. But Charles' specification of a 'pure form' *is* one which is compatible with different material dimensions even at a broad level, a bit like *sphericity* could be realized in numerous different materials. With the emotions, this leaves us with 'dialectical' definitions, such as the desire for revenge, which seem compatible with cold (non-emotional) or warm (emotional) manifestations (e.g. 2021: 23), and Aristotle may well think that such definitions are limited.

If the argument of the last section is along the right lines, though, *Rhet.*-style definitions are not 'pure forms' in this sense. Would this mean that Charles may, after all, wish to view *Rhet.*-style definitions as 'impure' formal specifications of the emotions? I doubt this. On his reading, a specification that does not make '*explicit* reference to any physical feature' is one of a 'pure form' (2021: 19; my emphasis) and Aristotle thinks that an 'adequate' definition of anger 'must specify the relevant desire in a matter-involving way' (37). The material dimension, on his view, plays a role 'in determining the identity of the psychological states themselves' (37n.34) and one cannot 'define anger as a given type of desire which is fully determinate without *explicit reference to specific types of matter* internal to the organism' (37; my emphasis).[63] Whereas, in direct opposition to this, *Rhet.*-style definitions do not make explicit reference to the state's material dimension.

My central claim in this chapter is that we should reject the idea that Aristotle thinks that any definition that does not make explicit reference to the material dimension of an emotion (whether as a distinct component or in an impure form) is inadequate. *Rhet.*-style definitions, when correctly specified, secure the right extension of such states (with anger, for example, the definition ensures we have a 'hot', rather than 'cold', desire) and enable us to derive other properties pertaining to

---

[63] Although, as we noted (9.4(2)n.53), Charles does not think that this has to refer to calorific fluid, but can just be some more generic material feature.

the state. Indeed, against the background of his other physical theories and assumptions, Aristotle clearly holds that his hedonic specifications of emotions entail the relevant material dimension of such states (**9.4(2)**). He therefore thinks that *Rhet.*-style definitions are both adequate in their own terms and explanatorily potent.

In **9.1** we saw two ways of understanding the material dimension of the schematic definition in *De an.* I.1; as referring to (1) a material component of the state (MCR) or (2) an enmattered form (EFR). But however we read the schematic definition, it seems clear that it *does* demand direct reference to the material dimension of such states.[64] I have suggested (**9.3**) that this does not jeopardize *Rhet.*-style definitions once we see that *De an.* I.1 is telling us how a *natural science* specification must go and not demanding the same from *any* adequate definition. Since states such as the emotions are essentially enmattered (are common to body and soul), and since the natural science investigation concerns providing accounts of natural phenomena as such, natural science definitions must make reference to their material dimension. The key point, though, is that if *Rhet.*-style definitions reliably pick out such states, they must (as Aristotle sees it), pick out *the very same states* as those specified by (true) natural science accounts. They must just be alternative ways of specifying those states. And if, as I have argued, *Rhet.*-style definitions are explanatorily potent in their own terms (**9.4**), and are more germane to employ in many contexts (see end **9.3**), we can, in many other investigations, *operate simply with them*.

What is wrong with MCR and EFR, then, is that they fail to *restrict* Aristotle's claims in *De an.* I.1 *to the relevant investigatory framework*. But, so restricted, either could still be plausible (and, in any event, natural science definitions of such states, as per the schematic definition, must make reference to their material dimension). That is, we might have:

[Restricted material component requirement (RMCR)]: Aristotle holds that natural science definitions of states such as the emotions cannot be adequately specified without direct reference to their specific material component (e.g. boiling of the blood)

Or:

[Restricted enmattered form requirement (REFR)]: Aristotle holds that natural science definitions of states such as the emotions cannot be adequately specified except by reference to forms that are themselves directly specified as enmattered (e.g. a-desire-for-revenge-boiling-of-the-blood).

Since RMCR and REFR are restricted to the natural science context, they both permit that *Rhet.*-style definitions may be perfectly adequate in other contexts.

---

[64] For one complication with the schema (besides whether we should accept MCR or EFR; or, rather, the more restricted versions of these I will now go on to formulate), see **9.1n.9**.

Advocates of RMCR might then argue that in the correct natural science definitions of emotions (along the lines of the schematic definition) there is a distinguishable material *component* of the state. Advocates of REFR will insist that the schematic definition specifies an impure form, and that the business of natural science is to specify such impure forms, to reflect the fact that these states are essentially psycho-physical. So recast, I do not need to resolve this debate here (although I will provide some reflections on *De an.* I.1 itself in **Appendix 1**). For, whoever is right, the resolution does not bear on the fact that Aristotle evidently thinks that *Rhet.*-style definitions (as alternative ways of specifying the very same states as those defined by natural science) are entirely adequate outside of the natural science investigation. In effect, my argument is simply that so long as the above debate is restricted to the correct *natural science* specification of the emotions, it leaves Aristotle's accounts of emotions, as developed in this book, intact.[65]

Conclusion

In this chapter I have argued that Aristotle's claim in *De an.* I.1 that states such as the emotions need to be specified with a material dimension (**9.1**) does not undermine his accounts of emotions as representational pleasures or distresses as developed in this book. Lower level material descriptions, in terms of processes in the blood and heating or chilling, for instance, will only be required for certain kinds of investigation (natural science ones), or worth flagging in certain contexts (as with *Rhet.* II.13 and *NE* IV.9) (**9.3**). But Aristotle holds that *Rhet.*-style definitions are extensionally equivalent to ones that specify their material dimension and are explanatorily significant (**9.4**). And treating emotions as representational pleasures or distresses will typically be adequate not merely with respect to instructing the orator, but also for investigations into, for example, ethics, political philosophy, aesthetics, and (from our perspective) philosophical psychology more generally (**9.2**). Indeed, outside the natural science context, detailing the processes of the blood involved in emotions may not only be unnecessary, but actually hinder the investigation at stake. Just as surgeons do not want to be filling their heads with details about what is going on at the atomic level when they are making the cut, so too if orators were to fill their minds with details about boiling or chilling blood, this may hinder their ability to engender or abate emotions in their listeners (**9.3**).

---

[65] I leave to those advancing such views to explain how their reading intersects with the efficacy of *Rhet.*-style definitions. Perhaps an advocate of RMCR might propose that *Rhet.*-style definitions are more detailed formal specifications that 'hypothetically necessitate' the correct material dimension, whatever that is (cf. Johansen (2012: 157, 168) and *Phys.* II.9)? Perhaps an advocate of REFR could (after all; cp. the beginning of this section) say that they are another way of specifying the impure form that specifies the compound? And there may be other ways. All I will insist on is that there must *be* some such reconciliation, given that Aristotle clearly thinks that *Rhet.*-style definitions are true, acceptable to employ, and explanatory significant in a host of other investigatory frameworks.

Appendix 1: Does Aristotle advance RMCR or REFR in *De an.* I.1?

A full discussion of whether we should accept RMCR or REFR (see **9.5**) is beyond the scope of this book.[66] However, I would briefly like to consider this in relation to *De an.* I.1. I address four points: (a) '*touton*' in 403b3; (b) 'from both' at 403b8–9; (c) the putative inadequacy of 'pure' forms; and (d) the parallel with mathematics. As I see it, *De an.* I.1 is compatible with RMCR, and may even favour that reading.

(a) '*Touton*' in 403b3

A key passage for Charles is the following:

> [1] But the student of nature and the dialectician would define each of these differently, e.g. what anger is. For the latter would define it as a desire to return pain or something of the sort, the former as the boiling of the blood and hot stuff round the heart. [2] Of these, the one gives the matter, the other the form (*eidos*) and principle (*logos*). [3] For this (*hode*; viz. the *logos*) is the principle of the thing (*logos tou pragmatos*), [4] but this (*touton*) must be in a matter of such and such a kind if it is to be. (403a29–b3)

Charles points out that 'this' (*touton*) in [4] is masculine and that the nearest masculine noun is *logos* (*eidos*, 'form', is feminine). On his view, this implies that the *logos* itself must be enmattered if it is to be a definition (of the thing). He writes:

> Aristotle explicitly identifies the form with the definition or defining formular [Charles' glosses on *logos*] (403b2). The latter formula itself, he says, has to be enmattered to be the defining formula of this thing: it must refer to the matter. If so, the form must itself be enmattered: a matter-involving form. The definition, the defining formular, of anger, the composite, is to be given in terms of the form alone. If definition and form are identified in this way, the definition of the composite, anger, will not include anything beyond the form. It will not add (*pace* the purist reading) reference to material parts of the composite in addition to the form. (2021: 23–4)

We thereby very quickly arrive at (R)EFR. But perhaps *too* quickly. Let us grant that [2] identifies the form (*eidos*) and the *logos*. Does [4] entail that the *logos* itself (and therefore the form) must be enmattered if it is the principle (*logos*) of the

---

[66] Charles advances many considerations in favour of his view (which is, in fact, EFR, not REFR), drawing from a number of different texts. See also esp. Peramatzis (2011).

thing? Not for me. In [3] Aristotle claims that the *logos* is the *logos of the thing* (*tou pragmatos*). 'The thing', here, is the composite state. Then, in [4], he tells us that the *logos* must be enmattered 'if it is to be'. But what does Hamlyn's 'it', here, refer to? The Greek is just *ei estai*, 'if [it] is to be', no subject is specified. Charles takes the implied subject to be, once again, the *logos* and, on his view, 'Aristotle is focusing on what is required for an adequate definitional account' (22n.9) (rather than, say, the *existence* of the form). He translates: '...and must be enmattered if it is to be the definition [of this thing]'. (Strictly, 'the definition' should also be in square brackets, since the subject is not explicitly stated.) However, advocates of RMCR could instead suggest that the implied subject is simply 'the thing' (the *pragma*) from [3], not 'the definition of the thing'. They could then claim that it is the existence of the thing, the composite, that Aristotle is concerned with. We would have: 'For the *logos* is the *logos* of the thing, but the *logos* must be in a matter of such and such a kind if the thing is to exist'. On this reading, since we are concerned with physical things, not abstract ones, the *logos* must be realized in suitable matter if the thing in question is to exist.

(b) 'From both' (403b8–9) and the example of the house (403b3–7)

Aristotle asks which of the following is the *phusikos*; (i) 'the one concerned with the matter, but ignorant of the *logos*'; (ii) 'the one concerned with the *logos* alone'; or (iii) 'the one concerned with what results from both' (*ex amphoin*) (403b7–10). Charles claims that the account that results 'from both' the matter and the *logos* is an 'impure form'. But Aristotle *distinguishes* the *logos* from the matter and then claims that the *phusikos* is the one who is concerned with what results *from both* the *logos* and the matter. It seems, then, that the matter is not *part of the specification* of the *logos* in the way Charles requires.[67] So too, with Aristotle's house example:

> One [will define a house as] the *logos* of some such kind, viz., a covering to prevent destruction by winds, rain, and heat, but someone else will say [that a house is] stones, bricks, and timber, and another again that it is the form in them for the sake of these other things. (403b3–7)

Charles claims (2021: 23) that the *logos* specification is a pure form, the material specification is a purely material one, and that their conjunction is an impure form. But Aristotle is concerned with the correct *definition* of a house. And the *logos* is not identified with the form-in-matter account. The dialectician's definition,

---

[67] Clearly (i) would be concerned with just the matter and (ii) with what Charles would call a 'pure' form. But if natural scientists are concerned with what results from both *of these*, they put together a pure form with a specification of the matter, contra Charles' reading.

'a covering to prevent...', is said *to be* the *logos*. And it only forms *part of* the third proposal, which seems to be a combination of the purely formal and purely material specifications. If we had a pure form for the first proposed definition, it would seem that the third proposal would also invoke a pure form. And Aristotle's preferred definition would refer to the form realized in suitable materials (for some end).[68]

(c) The putative inadequacy of 'pure' forms

On Charles' view, Aristotle thinks that we need 'to define the form [of anger] explicitly in an impure way as a hot-boiling-of-blood type of desire for revenge'; for we 'could not explain the presence of the relevant bodily features on the basis of a pure form alone' (2021: 23). Similarly, with the house example. Charles claims:

> A pure form could not be used as the basis of the explanation of why houses are made from stones and wood or how they resist wind and heat in the way they do... The relevant type of covering is defined as one made from stones, logs, and the rest: it is a made-from-these-materials type of covering. This is why it successfully keeps out rain and heat in the way it does. (23)

Clearly, advocates of RMCR also think that Aristotle holds that in the natural science context we cannot define anger simply by reference to a (pure) form. Such investigations require reference to the material dimension of the state. But they would insist that this does not commit us to (R)EFR, just RMCR. Charles believes he can refute such a view no less. He claims (41) that if we say that anger—'defined as the combination of desire for revenge *and* boiling of the blood'—requires the presence of boiling blood, this would 'trivialize Aristotle's demand that one derives from the essence of the phenomenon its other necessary features' (citing *De an.* I.1.402b21–5). He also raises a philosophical objection against such a view. He asks us to imagine those who desire revenge in a cool calculating way while at the same time suffering from boiling blood. Perhaps, e.g., they have been rigged up by a skilled neuroscientist 'so that the very same antecedent event triggers both a cold desire for revenge and a boiling of their blood (which the patients regard as an unwelcome distraction from the calculated and dispassionate desire for revenge)' (20). On Charles' view, such people are not angry because 'even if all the components for anger are present, they are not unified in the right way to yield the required type of desire' (20).

It seems to me that advocates of RMCR should reply that as they read the schematic definition the natural science account of anger requires that the material feature occurs 'as a result of this' (*hupo toude*) and 'for the sake of that' (*heneka toude*)

---

[68] Which seems to be *precisely* how Aristotle describes such a definition of a house in *Met.* H.2.1043a12ff.

(403a25–7). They are thus not claiming that anger is simply the *conjunction* of a desire for revenge and boiling of the blood;[69] even if, on their view, the various elements of anger do remain distinguishable in its definition. So too with the house example. The definition was not simply the *conjunction* of bricks, stones, etc., *plus* the specification of the covering. Those elements were combined *for the sake of* something else, which constrains the way the matter and form can be combined. This suggests, contra Charles, that other relevant properties about, e.g., anger (or a house) can be derived from such definitions.[70] Equally, if the matter of anger does not occur as a result of a specific cause and for the sake of a certain end, we will not have anger. So if a trigger causes both a desire for revenge *and* independent boiling of blood, this would not count as anger, since the material dimension would not be occurring for the sake of the end of anger, but independently (owing to the trigger). As Charles writes:

> there is one specific type of boiling blood found in angry people, which is made the one it is by its being a desire-for-revenge-type of boiling blood. This one (non-accidentally) unified type of process exemplifies a distinctive type of boiling of the blood: a for-revenge-type of blood-boiling. (2021: 35)

Advocates of RMCR should say the same thing.[71]

(d) The parallel with mathematics

Charles thinks he can prove his reading of *De an.* I.1 (= EFR) by reference to Aristotle's contrast between natural properties (such as the emotions) and mathematical properties (403a11–16, b14–15, 16–19) (lines, points, the straight, and the curved are given as examples in the chapter: 402b18–21, 403a12–16). Concerning mathematical properties, Aristotle writes:

> The properties which are not separable, but which are not treated as properties of such and such a body, but in abstraction, are the concern of the mathematician. (403b14–15)

Charles claims that this provides a basis to distinguish mathematical properties from states such as the emotions as follows:

---

[69] This would be parallel to the Mere-Concurrence view we considered in **4.1**, which suffered from a related deviant causal chains objection.
[70] Note, too, these are the only elements that Charles' account can itself appeal to. It is just that, on his view, these elements combine to provide a specification of an 'impure' form.
[71] He adds: 'A psycho-physical form determines the specific type of boiling involved. It makes the matter be the matter it is. This is why in talking of anger there is reference to the (one) process, "a certain type of process" (403a26), not to several' (35). Advocates of RMCR should say that the same applies given their understanding of the schematic definition, absent reference to impure forms.

anger and fear: their form is existentially inseparable and inseparable in thought from perceptual matter

geometrical objects: their form is existentially inseparable from but separable in thought (and definition) from perceptual matter. (2021: 26)

And he claims that since 'the form of anger (desire for revenge) cannot be thought of or defined in abstraction from matter, it must be defined in ways which essentially are matter-involving' (26).

Once more, we quickly arrive at (R)EFR. But, again, perhaps too quickly. The natural thing for advocates of RMCR to say is that Aristotle is not comparing the *forms* of such properties, but the form-matter compounds of them. He is, that is, comparing the compound state, anger, with mathematical properties. On this reading, Aristotle is saying that anger, the compound, only exists in perceptual matter and so (in the natural science investigation) needs to be defined by reference to both its form and its perceptual matter. But the situation is different with mathematical properties. Like natural states or objects, they can in fact only be *found* in perceptual matter (they are existentially inseparable), but, unlike natural states or objects, they are not treated as properties of such and such a material body, but instead in abstraction of such bodies (they are definitionally separable).[72]

However, Charles objects that 'so interpreted, Aristotle fails to compare like with like' (27). For he 'should surely have compared his accounts of the two compounds...not his account of the abstracted geometrical line and that of the whole compound, anger'. But, Charles claims, had he proceeded this way 'he would not have discerned any significant difference between the two cases' and so since he is clearly seeking 'to contrast and not to assimilate' the two cases, 'this purist reply undermines the point he is trying to establish' (27).[73]

But Charles' reply is specious. On the reading we are considering, Aristotle is contrasting mathematical properties (and the mathematician) with natural properties (and the natural scientist) and his contrast works by pointing out what these properties have in common, on the one hand, and how they differ, on the other. They have *in common* that such properties are, in fact, only ever found in perceptual matter. Just as states such as the emotions essentially involve the body

---

[72] See also Caston (2009: 35–7). Similarly, with Aristotle's example of 'the snub' (see e.g. *Phys.* II.2; *SE* 31.181b37–182a3), which he uses to illustrate the way natural entities are not independent of natural matter. Snub is essentially enmattered since snub is a concave *nose*, whereas concavity itself is independent of perceptible matter (*Met.* E.1.1025b30–4). Charles (2021: esp. ch. 2, 2009: 7–8; cf. Peramatzis 2011: esp. 111–15, 122–32) sees this as an example of something that can only be defined by an impure form; his opponent as something that can only be adequately specified as a composite (cf. the way *sphericity* is the form, in the sense of shape (*morphē*), of a bronze sphere (e.g. *Met.* Z.8 *passim*) and how, in *Met.* Z.5, Aristotle refers to snubness as 'compounded out of the two [concavity and nose] by the presence of the one in the other' (1030b17–18); see also Caston (2009: 44–7). I am obviously unable to attempt to resolve this dispute here.

[73] See also Peramatzis (2011: 105–6).

(and so are existentially inseparable from their perceptible matter), so too, on Aristotle's view, mathematical properties are not in fact separable from the bodies in which they exist (and so are also existentially inseparable from perceptible matter). They *differ* in that mathematical properties are not treated by the mathematician *as* inseparable—and so as properties of such and such a body—but in abstraction (403b14–15) from the bodies in which they in fact exist. When investigating how many right angles the angles of a triangle are equal to (402b20–1), for example, mathematicians need not consider the material dimension of the properties in question. Natural properties, by contrast, cannot be treated by the natural scientist in abstraction from the bodies in which they exist. Natural scientists must, therefore, treat/investigate the natural objects/states *as* enmattered. Hence the schematic definition, as understood according to RMCR.[74]

Charles also points out (2021: 28) that earlier in *De an.* I.1 (403a11–16), when considering the relation between the separability of the soul and whether there are properties that are specific to it alone, Aristotle notes that if there is nothing specific to the soul alone, the situation would be like the straight insofar as it is straight. Aristotle claims that a straight thing (a compound object), insofar as it is straight, would touch a bronze sphere at a point, but if we separate the straight from a body it would touch nothing (a geometric line cannot touch anything). The straight *qua* straight (as part of a compound), by contrast, is itself inseparable since it is always found in some body (403a11–16). The idea is that straight objects have causal and physical properties that geometrical objects do not, given that geometry involves treating objects that are not in fact separable *as if* they were separable. And when treated as separable, objects do not have causal or physical properties. But Charles concludes from the passage:

> This is an instance of a more general claim: geometrical forms cannot interact with physical objects. (2021: 28; see also 2009: 8–9)

If Aristotle is claiming that geometrical *forms* cannot interact with physical objects, and so can be defined without reference to their matter, one might think that this is the crucial difference between such forms and the enmattered forms that, according to REFR, Aristotle thinks are used to define states such as anger and fear.

Advocates of RMCR should reply that in taking the passage to refer to geometrical *forms* Charles begs the question. Why not, instead, take it refer to geometrical *entities* (form-matter compounds)? Such entities cannot interact with physical objects and in this respect they differ from states such as anger. That is why the mathematician can define such entities without reference to perceptual matter, whereas the natural scientist cannot define states such as anger and fear

---

[74] Note how, in line with **9.3** and **9.5**, this formulation is relativized to *the natural science investigation*, i.e. it entails RMCR, not MCR.

without reference to their perceptual matter (in line with RMCR). But this does not generate impure forms. Perhaps Charles is assuming that geometrical entities *are* pure forms, such that the straight abstracted from perceptible matter could only be a form? If so, there is evidence that Aristotle would reject this view. He appears to think that mathematical objects are not matter*less*, but have their own special kind of matter—intelligible matter (see *Met*. Z.10.1036a9–12, 11.1037a2–5, cf. K.1.1059a14–16). The mathematician abstracts away from perceptible matter, but not from matter as such (see esp. Mueller 1970: e.g. 163–4; also Menn 2010: 200–1).

Finally, note that 403a11–16 treats *un*separated mathematical objects as *directly parallel* to natural states that are common to body and soul ('if there is nothing peculiar to the soul, it will not be separable, *but will be like* (*kathaper*: exactly like) that which is straight, to which, *qua* straight, many properties belong, e.g. it will touch a bronze sphere at a point' (403a11–14)). States such as anger are *exactly like* the straight, when the straight is treated as inseparable. But, on Charles' view, if Aristotle thought this he would hold that we could define anger by reference to distinct material and formal components (2021: 26). Charles rejects this reading because Aristotle later claims that states such as the emotions are inseparable from the natural matter in which they occur, 'and not in the same way as a line or a surface' (403b16–19). But, given the parallel the earlier passage emphasizes, we might rather infer that Aristotle is referring to *abstracted* mathematical objects in the later passage, as specified in the lines in between the two passages (403b14–15). While both natural states and mathematical properties are not in fact separable, the mathematician can (by abstraction) treat mathematical properties as if they were separable. In *this* sense anger is not inseparable in the same way as a mathematical object: the natural scientist cannot treat states such as anger as if they were separable, whereas the mathematician can so treat mathematical properties.

Appendix 2: Aristotle's examples to show that the emotions are in part bodily

After claiming in *De an*. I.1 that at the same time as the 'affections of the soul' (*ta pathē tēs psuchēs*) occur, the body is affected in a certain way (403a16–19), Aristotle provides some further support for that claim. He writes:

> This is shown by the fact that [i] sometimes when severe and manifest misfortunes (*pathēmata*) befall us we are not provoked [to anger] (*parozunesthai*) or feel fear. While [ii] at other times we are moved by small and hardly seen things (*hupo mikrōn kai amaurōn*) when the body is aroused and is as it is in anger. This is even further evident; for [iii] men may come to have the affections (*en tois pathesi*) of the frightened although nothing frightening is taking place. (403a19–24)

How should these examples be understood and do they bear on the argument of this chapter?

We must keep in mind that the considerations are intended to provide *evidence* or *support* for the claim that emotions involve the body. So we need to see how the body or material dimension of emotions is necessary to explain such phenomena, or at least how that is highly probable. One general point to note about the examples as a group is the way they involve a decreasing shift in the intensity or significance of the object that the emotion is felt (or not felt) about. In the first example we have *severe and manifest misfortunes*, in the second we have *small and hardly seen things*, and in the third we have *nothing whatsoever*. Severe—small—none. The emotional response (or lack of it) must, then, dovetail with these events to generate a discrepancy that in each case is to be explained by reference to the body. In the first case the severe and manifest misfortunes are coupled with no emotion, when presumably we would expect one. In the second, the small and hardly seen things are coupled with an emotion, when presumably we would have expected only a very minor emotional response (or none at all). And, in the final example nothing whatsoever taking place is coupled with an emotion, when we would not have expected one. As I understand it, the final case is intended to be a more evident (*mallon phaneron*) case *than the second* of how emotions must involve the body. It is *of the same kind* as the second case because it involves the subject experiencing an unwarranted emotion. It is *more evident* because whereas in the second some very minor emotion might have been warranted (but not an emotion of that intensity), in the third the emotion occurs in response to no misfortune whatsoever.[75]

The key to understanding the first example is to note that although in this case we are not provoked to anger or fear, we must nonetheless apprehend ourselves as undergoing some 'severe and manifest misfortune'. For if we were simply *unaware* of the misfortune, the body would not be needed to explain why we were not emotionally affected. So the idea must be that *given* that we apprehend ourselves as undergoing some severe and manifest misfortune, the bodily or material dimension of fear or anger is required to explain why we nonetheless do not feel an emotion.[76]

This example is clearly compatible with the idea that, given his other background physical assumptions, Aristotle holds that the representational pleasures or distresses of emotions entail their material dimension (see **9.4(2)**). We have a case in which, for some reason, people are in a condition whereby in spite of apprehending themselves as, e.g., facing some severe danger or malicious offence, they fail to *get distressed* about this. What might Aristotle have in mind? In *Rhet.* II.3 he writes:

---

[75] Charles (2009: 6n.18, 2021: 20–1n.6) fails to see the structure here and so takes *touto* ('this') in 403a23 to refer back to the general claim at 403a18–19 that at the same time as one undergoes an affection, the body is affected in a certain way. Oddly, in his 2021 (20) he fails to translate the 'this is still further evident' (*eti de mallon touto phaneron*) (403a22–3) at all.

[76] See also Rapp (2002: 551).

people become mild-mannered when they have spent their anger on someone else. This happened in the case of Ergophilus. For though the people were more embittered against him than against Callisthenes, they let him go because they had condemned Callisthenes to death on the previous day. (1380b10–13)

As we shall see in **10.3**, Aristotle thinks that mild-manneredness (*praotēs*) is the opposite of anger. Although the people in question surely still viewed Ergophilus as worthy of their ire, their anger towards him dissipated (they became mild-mannered) because, after venting on Callisthenes, they had (for the time being) run out of energy for further anger. It seems that by the time they got to Ergophilus, the physical state underpinning their anger towards him (boiling of the blood) had been discharged (their blood had cooled through the retaliation on Callisthenes) and so they could not remain angry with him. Again, such a picture is clearly compatible with my reading: just as the material dimension of the state disappears in them, *so too will their distress at the slight*, and they will just be left with the notion that although Ergophilus *warrants* their retaliation, they no longer feel inclined to exact it.

Here is another possible case. In *NE* III.7, when Aristotle turns to the vices connected to courage, first up is:

he who exceeds in fearlessness has no name...but he would seem to be a sort of madman or insensitive to pain if he feared nothing, neither an earthquake nor the waves, as they say the Celts do not. (1115b24–8)[77]

Such a person might, one may presume, perceive the danger, and be able to apprehend it as such, but fail to experience distress at it, and so fail to experience fear.[78] In line with Chapter 7, to account for this we would have to appeal to the agent's *character*. Hence, if a state of character (pertaining to, e.g., fear, anger, or appetite) is realized in one's bodily condition, this would explain how the fact that emotions involve the body would be required to accommodate such cases.[79] The acquired character state (as realized in something physical) will have to block experiencing distress at a situation that one apprehends as horrific. And that would only make sense if emotions are themselves physical.[80]

---

[77] On 'neither earthquake nor the waves' see **1.3n.30**.

[78] Aristotle's *example*, here, may not actually be an instance of the vice he is specifying, but one of brutishness (see my 2018: 135). But the general point applies and, indeed, cases of brutish fears stemming from disease may well provide good examples of the general kind (i.e. where the body has a key role to play in accounting for the fear).

[79] On states of character being realized in one's bodily condition, see **9.2n.31**.

[80] See also the *NE* IV.5 passage quoted in **6.6** (1126a4–8). If Aristotle there intends to allow the possibility that someone could apprehend a slight, but not experience distress at it, and so not be angry (see **6.6**) then, once again, we would have an example of the requisite kind. And, once again, we would explain the absence of the emotion by reference to the character dispositions of the agent in question, which are themselves material states.

The key to understanding the second and third examples is to note that even though we are told that sometimes people are moved by small or hardly seen things (second example) or something that is not frightening at all (third example), in both cases the people in question must still apprehend themselves as encountering the object of the emotion. This is because in both cases it is clear that the people experience an emotion and, *on any account of the matter*, a necessary condition for experiencing an emotion is possessing an intentional state that apprehends the emotion's object. Indeed, the subjects must also experience *distress* directed at the apparent instantiation of the emotion's object. For, again on any account, fear and anger, for Aristotle, entail a distress (**Cat.1** and **Cat.5**). The body, then, is being invoked to explain why the agent experiences an emotion *even though* only something small and hardly seen is present (hence only a minor emotion could, at best, be warranted) (second example) or, indeed, *nothing at all* (hence no emotion whatsoever is warranted) (third example).[81]

In the second example Aristotle claims that this can occur when the body is aroused and is as it is in anger. He seems to have in mind cases where the body is already *primed* so that a trigger that otherwise might be overlooked or discounted is in fact treated as a full-blown manifestation of the formal object of the emotion.[82] Again, this is clearly compatible with the idea that the distress alone can indicate a material dimension to the emotion. The background physical condition will help explain why the subject is prone to experience distress at the apparent instantiation of emotion's object. We are half way there already, so to speak. As with the young in *Rhet.* II.12 (or the bulls in *PA* II.4; see **9.2n.25**), some subjects are in a physical state that makes them more prone to anger or spirited responses (cf. also Dow 2015: 221). Perhaps we can find an example (or something close) of the sort of thing Aristotle has in mind in a passage we scrutinized in **6.2** (also **7.5**) from *Rhet.* II.2 (1379a11–24). He there points to how people can be in a background condition that makes them prone to anger. When people are pained, he suggests, they seek something. For example, those who are 'ill, poor, in love, thirsty—in general those with an appetite' (1379a16–17) seek what would relieve their illness, poverty, lust, or thirst. Aristotle claims that each such person

---

[81] Charles claims that these examples show that if we omit reference to the body, we 'fail to state the conditions under which someone is (or comes to be) in these emotional states' (2021: 21, cf. also 28). But while they are clearly intended to show that emotions are bodily states, they do not entail that there cannot be accounts of emotions that explain the conditions under which one has them, but which do not make explicit reference to bodily or material features. They do not, that is, entail EFR (or even MCR). Aristotle is arguing that emotions involve the body and that in the natural science context, which addresses this dimension of such states directly, we therefore need reference to their material dimension (= RMCR). But we do not have anything stronger than this.

[82] Contra Heinaman (1990: 101) and Burnyeat (1992: 23) (cf. Rapp 2002: 551), Aristotle does not say that the subject is *not* angry (as Wedin notes too: 1995: 194; 1996: 20). But equally the body being in a state 'as it is when it is in anger' could be taken more or less loosely. See the example I go on to provide, where we have a bodily condition found in some of those who are angry, which is not itself boiling of the blood, but can be co-present with boiling of the blood and explanatory of it.

'is prepared by his present feeling to follow the path toward his particular anger' (1379a23–4). Such people are, that is, easily prompted to take offence with respect to their particular condition and so some minor quibble or question, or some such, may then be pounced on and taken as a full-blown slight. Here, then, the fact that subjects are in a prior condition which is itself in part bodily—i.e. distress or pain (hence illness, thirst)—and which is at least consonant with the material condition of anger, helps explain their anger at such a minor quibble.

In the third example Aristotle once again has in mind cases where, given the circumstance, a bodily condition is required to explain why someone would apprehend the object of the emotion and experience pleasure or distress directed at it. But, in contrast to the second example, in this case there is not even any actual event, however small or hard to see, that can be construed as prompting the emotion. Why would such a case require emotions to be in part bodily? The idea may simply be that since there is nothing external that could explain the emotion, the explanation for it must stem from internal causes alone and that such internal causes will plausibly be bodily in nature (cf. Charles 2009: 6).[83] Alternatively, Aristotle may have in mind cases in which the subject experiences fear in spite of believing that there is nothing fearful present at all. In order for this to be possible, subjects would have to respond emotionally to something that merely (perceptually) appears dangerous, even though they believe otherwise (hence the 'nothing at all fearful' will pertain to the subject's beliefs about the situation). In such a scenario, the state's being bodily would presumably be manifest through its bodily effects (shuddering, pallor, heart rate, sweating, etc.), which occur in spite of the subject believing there is nothing fearful going on at all (cf. *NE* IV.9.1128b11–15 (quoted in **9.2**); *De an.* III.9.432b29–433a1; *MA* 11.703b6–8). Again, neither of these readings suggests that the representational pleasures or distresses of emotions do not themselves (at least indirectly) entail the relevant material dimension of the state (cf. Wedin 1995: 196, 1996: 20). Both thereby accord with the argument of this chapter.

Aristotle on What Emotions Are. Giles Pearson, Oxford University Press. © Giles Pearson 2024.
DOI: 10.1093/9780191989292.003.0010

---

[83] Perhaps an example could be the irrational fears of children (a monster in the kitchen), which have no ground in the content of their perceptual appearances-as-truth (see **3.6**). Again, perhaps delusional/hallucinatory states associated with illness might fit. Cf. *Insomn.* 2: 'persons in delirium of fever sometimes think they see animals on their chamber walls, an illusion arising from the faint resemblance to animals of the markings thereon when put together in pattens; and this sometimes corresponds with the emotional states of the sufferers, in such a way that, if the latter be not very ill, they know well enough that it is an illusion; but if the illness is more severe they may actually move according to the appearances' (460b11–16). Clearly, there is some external trigger (the pattern on the wall), here, but it provides *no reason at all* for the subject to envisage danger and be distressed by it ('nothing frightening taking place': 403a23–4). The illness, it seems, can push sensory appearances (*phantasmata*) before one and, for Aristotle, the latter have a physical dimension (see Caston 1998: 259–60), so the body would be needed to explain the appearance in the first place, via the illness. (There would then be a further material dimension, via the disposition to experience an emotion in light of the appearance (see first example), since emotions are not, on Aristotle's view, apprehensions of objects of emotions, but hedonic responses to such apprehensions—so Part I.)

10
Some Problematic Cases and the Supplements in the *EE* Specification of the Emotions

In this chapter I consider some states that Aristotle mentions in his *Rhet.* II catalogue of emotions that may seem problematic for the interpretation of his account of emotions as representational pleasures or distresses. I first (**10.1**) consider *Rhet.* II.7, where Aristotle defines 'favour' (*charis*). This has been considered problematic by some commentators but, in line with some others, I argue that by defining 'favour' Aristotle is actually trying to specify feeling-grateful-for (*charin echein*), which can be seen as a representational pleasure and so to fall in line with his general analysis. I then turn to consider a set of problematic cases stemming from the fact that Aristotle's account of the individual emotions in *Rhet.* is developed as a series of 'opposites' (anger/mild-manneredness; fear/confidence; and so on). This feature of his account is intelligible insofar as it purports to provide orators with the flexibility to affect the decisions and verdicts (*kriseis*) of their audience in whichever direction is necessary. But some of Aristotle's 'opposites' are problematic for his understanding of emotions as representational pleasures or distresses. I first introduce the problem (**10.2**). I then consider, in turn, mild-manneredness (*praotēs*) (op. anger) (**10.3**), not-being-grateful-for or being-put-out (op. feeling-grateful-for) (**10.4**), and shamelessness (op. shame) (**10.5**). In light of the problematic cases, I consider (**10.6**) one recent suggestion that Aristotle did not even intend to count them as emotions. However, attractive as this proposal may seem, I argue that it is ultimately untenable. Instead, I suggest that he appears to view these opposites as extending the category of emotions to include 'privations' (*stereseis*) of specific representational pleasures or distresses. I next (**10.7**) address whether confidence (*to tharsos*), as specified in *Rhet.* II.5, should be considered a representational pleasure in its own right or some such privation-emotion (of fear). I argue in favour of the former. To close my discussion, I examine (**10.8**) the supplements we find in the *EE* II.2 general specification of the emotions (1220b12–14), which distinguish it from those in *Rhet.* and *NE* (all quoted in **2.1**). I round off the chapter by addressing some more general philosophical objections to Aristotle's contention that emotions are pleasures or distresses (**10.9**).

10.1 Feeling-grateful-for (*charin echein*)

It is not even universally agreed what emotion Aristotle is trying to characterize in *Rhet.* II.7.[1] At the beginning of the chapter he writes:

> Those toward whom people feel grateful (*charin echein*), and why, and how—by being disposed in the relevant way [they feel it], will be clear after having defined favour (*charis*). Let a favour, then, in the sense in which the person who has received it is said to feel grateful (*charin echein*), be a service provided to one in need, not in return for anything, nor in order that the provider get something, but in order that the recipient get something. (1385a16–19)

Traditionally, it has been thought that insofar as Aristotle characterizes an emotion at all here, it must be connected to kindliness or benevolence. And yet this seemed problematic. John Cooper sums up the difficulties well:

> Awkwardly, Aristotle defines *charis* (what I am translating as 'kindly feelings') in II.7 in terms of action, not feeling: it is 'helping someone in need, not in return for anything nor for the good of the one helping, but for that of the one helped'. Formally, then, the person who 'has *charis*' is the one who acts in this helping way; the definition apparently makes no reference to the emotion that might lead to such action. Or does it? Perhaps one should take Aristotle's reference to helping actions as indicating, elliptically, the emotion that leads to them (akin to friendly feelings, I suppose: a warm feeling of attachment to someone, with a desire to do that person good for her or his own sake). But of course what Aristotle should primarily be telling aspiring orators about is a feeling that they need either to engender in or remove from their audience's mind. And in what follows in II.7…he seems to limit himself to discussing the means of showing an audience that someone has shown *them charis* or failed to do so. (1996: 242–3; Cooper's emphasis)

The way out of the problem, though, is to notice that Aristotle is not in fact trying to characterize kindly feeling or benevolence (or some such) at all, but instead *feeling-grateful-for* something. As Gisela Striker notes:

> The Greek phrase *charin echein* normally means 'to be grateful', and once we realize that this is the topic of the chapter, it is also clear that Aristotle is

---

[1] See e.g. Cope (1877: 87, 89); Grimaldi (1988: 127–8); Kennedy (1991: 149); Cooper (1996: 242–3); Striker (1996: 301n.15); Fortenbaugh (2002: 107–9); Rapp (2002: 645–6); Konstan (2006: ch. 7); Price (2011: 120); Moss (2012a: 75n.15); Dow (2015: 152–3); Gottlieb (2021: 26).

following his usual schema, dealing with people 'toward whom', 'on account of what', and 'in what state of mind' gratitude is felt. (1996: 301n.15)²

If we look back at the opening passage of II.7, it is clear, I think, that the state Aristotle seeks to specify is *charin echein*, not *charis*. He claims that we can see how the threefold schema applies to *charin echein* after we have first defined *charis*. And, as Striker notes, *charin echein* normally means 'to be grateful'.³ Why, then, does Aristotle define *charis*? Striker proposes:

> Aristotle presumably resorts to a definition of favour (*charis*) because no formal definition of gratitude (*charin echein*) was available. (1996: 301n.15)

I am not sure about this. Aristotle is more than capable of coming up with a definition of his own even if he has not been handed one. Indeed, a formal definition is not hard to come by:

> Feeling-grateful-for is a kind of pleasure at an apparent favour received.

However, clearly such a definition is not particularly informative until you have an account of 'favour'. Hence I suggest that Aristotle defined *charis* because he thought doing so would be the most helpful way of unpacking the emotion he seeks to specify—since what we feel grateful for is *receiving a favour*. This is why, on my view, he writes that what *charin echein* is 'will be made *clear*' once we have defined *charis*.⁴ In any event, so characterized, the emotion evidently falls unproblematically in line with the general account: it is a kind of representational pleasure. It is also clear why this emotion would be relevant to orators: if they can make it so that the judges feel grateful towards their client, those judges may be less inclined to convict or more inclined to overlook certain misdemeanours.

---

² See also Rapp (2002: 645–6) and Konstan (2006: ch. 7).
³ Note, though, that in his final lines about *charin echein* and its opposite (at the very end of II.7 in Kassel's 1976 edition of the Greek text; at the very beginning of II.8 in Ross's 1959 OCT), Aristotle writes: 'about *charizesthai* and *acharistein*, let this much be said' (1385b11). This is somewhat problematic, for *charizesthai*, unlike *charin echein*, typically refers to *doing a favour*, not being grateful for receiving one (*charis* can mean both *kindness* on the part of the doer (doing a favour) and also, frequently with the infinitive, *charin echein*, gratitude on the part of the receiver). So too *acharistein* typically refers to *being thankless* or *showing ingratitude*, not feeling ungrateful for having been treated a certain way. (For all, see *LSJ* s.v.) However, perhaps Aristotle may just be using *charizesthai* and *acharistein* as loose ways to refer to the feelings that we have in response to such actions, in the way he did with *charis* in the first place? (Alternatively, it could be that the linking line was added by a later editor of the text who shared the traditional misreading.)
⁴ This way former interpreters come out as deficient in failing to pick up his strategy, not Aristotle for being unable to provide the definition that is, indeed, entailed by his remarks.

10.2 Introducing the tricky 'opposites'

Several other problematic cases for the thesis that emotions are representational pleasures or distresses are generated by Aristotle seeking to provide 'opposites' or 'contraries' (*enantia*: 1378a22) for his core emotions. Of course, one can immediately see why it would be helpful for orators to be able to engender not just, e.g., emotions connected to feeling-friendly-towards but also emotions linked to hating (see 7.4): they will then have the flexibility to affect the judges in whichever way they require. But it may seem that rather than providing pleasure-based emotions that are correlates of the distresses of, e.g., anger, fear, shame, and pity, Aristotle does something else. Here is Striker once more:

> most of the alleged 'opposites' of the emotions treated in these chapters are not the emotional states that might correspond to the impression that some good thing has happened or will happen, but rather the state of mind corresponding to the absence of the specific distress. So calmness is opposed to anger, confidence (rather than relief) to fear, shamelessness (rather than, say, pride) to shame, while pity, rather than being opposed to something like taking pleasure in other people's good fortune, is opposed to two different forms of distress: righteous indignation (*nemesis*) and envy or jealousy (*phthonos*). The system of 'opposites', as these examples already show, does not work very well. (1996: 292)

In fact, I think Striker is too quick with pity. Although Aristotle's discussion is compressed (*Rhet*. II.9.1386b8–1387a5), pity is contrasted not just with righteous indignation and envy, but with a whole series of emotions, some of which are indeed representational pleasures (see **Cat.11–15** and the Appendix to my Catalogue at the end of this book). But the worry Striker expresses for the other 'opposites' is legitimate. In the general specification of emotions in *Rhet*. II.1, Aristotle's examples were 'anger, pity, fear and other such things, *and their opposites*' (1378a21–2, my emphasis). Even if we overlook the fact that the opposites are not necessarily the ones we would expect, the worry is that they are not really emotions at all, but *the absence of* the emotion they are supposedly opposite to. Let us consider this further by looking in more detail at some of them.

10.3 Mild-manneredness (*praotēs*)

Aristotle's most substantial discussion of an 'opposite' is mild-manneredness (*praotēs*), which even gets its own chapter (II.3). He begins:

> [1] Since becoming angry (*to orgizesthai*) is the contrary of becoming-mild-mannered (*to praünesthai*) and anger (*orgē*) to mild-manneredness (*praotēs*), we

must [2] grasp by being disposed in which way people are mild-mannered (*praoi*), to whom they are mild-mannered (*praōs*), and because of what sort of things they become mild-mannered (*praünontai*). [3] Let, then, becoming-mild-mannered (*praünsis*) be a settling down and coming to rest (*katastasis kai ēremēsis*) of anger. [4] If, then, people are angry at those who have slighted them, and slighting is voluntary, it is evident that they are mild-mannered (*praoi*) towards those who do none of these things, or do them involuntarily, or are only apparently of this sort. (1380a6–12)

The problem, here, is twofold. First, the state that Aristotle actually defines in [3], becoming-mild-mannered (*praünsis*), seems to be a *process*, a 'settling down and coming to rest', rather than some (even briefly) stable affection or intentional state. Second, the process is specified simply in terms of the *ceasing-to-be* of its contrary emotion—anger—not as something positive in its own right.

In my view, there is something significantly different going on with being-mild-mannered (*praotēs*), but we should not be thrown by the fact that Aristotle defines a process. We just need to observe precisely what he claims and recall—as we saw clearly in **10.1**—that he does not always *define* the state that he wants to include as a *pathos* at the start of his discussion.[5] In the passage, Aristotle seems to be operating with a distinction between *becoming*-mild-mannered (*to praünesthai, praünsis*), on the one hand, and *being*-mild-mannered (*praotēs*), on the other.[6] Only being-mild-mannered (*praotēs*) is explicitly said to be the contrary of anger (*orgē*) (= [1]). Hence, we should assume that just as Aristotle found it helpful to define *charis* (favour), rather than the emotion he was after (being-grateful-for: *charin echein*), so too he here finds it helpful to define *becoming*-mild-mannered (*praünsis*) instead of *being*-mild-mannered (*praotēs*). But the state that Aristotle wishes to specify for his catalogue of emotions—the state that is the actual contrary of anger—is the state *that results from* the process he defines, not that process itself.[7]

---

[5] This holds, in my view, not just with feeling-grateful-for (**10.1**), but feeling-friendly-towards (**7.4**).

[6] In this respect I follow Reeve (2018) who, of *praünsis*, notes: 'This rare noun, which occurs only here in Aristotle, seems to denote some sort of process, and so to be close in meaning to the middle-passive *praünesthai* used at II.3.1380a6' (255n.449). In fact, *praünsis* clearly does denote a process since that is how it is defined in [3]. The key, as Reeve also notes (2018: 255n.449), is not to equate this process with *praotēs* (see above). (For some reason Reeve fails to translate *praünontai* in 1380a8 (I added it above)—it is not redundant, in my view, given the distinction Aristotle appears to be operating with between *becoming*- and *being*-mild-mannered.)

[7] Aristotle may reasonably want to specify the process for practical reasons: we will be able to make someone who is angry cease to be so. Cp. Cooper (1996: 242) who, in noting that the definition 'explicitly makes it [*praünsis*] simply a settling down and quieting of anger', insists that this is a 'lapse' and that Aristotle *does* 'mean to treat feeling mildly as a separate emotion'. This, on my view, is doubly wrong. There is no lapse and yet (as we shall see) *praotēs* is not a positive 'feeling' in its own right—it is simply the absence or privation of anger.

However, since that state is, in effect, the *absence* of anger, we can arrive at it in two ways. We can *either* go through the process (the settling down and coming to rest of a pre-existing angry condition), in which case *becoming*-mild-mannered (*praünsis*) would lead to one *being*-mild-mannered (*praotēs*), i.e. when one's anger has abated. *Or* we can simply not be angry in the first place. That Aristotle has the latter in mind too can be seen in [4]—which begins the 'at whom' section of the discussion (see 1.3n.29)—when, having reminded us who we are angry at (those who voluntarily slight us), his first category of people we *are* (rather than become) mild-mannered (i.e. are *praoi*) towards is specified as people who have not slighted us at all ('those who do none of these things'). This suggests that he cannot merely be intending to characterize the process of becoming-mild-mannered in this chapter: we count as in the state he specifies to be the opposite of anger, being-mild-mannered (*praotēs*), insofar as we have not been slighted *at all*.[8]

This suggests that what Aristotle is seeking to provide in his ensuing discussion—as he flags in [2]—is (a) how we can make someone mild-mannered if they already happen to be angry ('because of what sort of things they become mild-mannered (*praünontai*)'), (b) the general conditions under which someone will not be angry or disposed to anger in the first place ('by being disposed in which way people are mild-mannered (*praoi*)'), as well as (c) the sort of people towards whom we are mild-mannered (*praōs*), whether we have a prior state of anger or not.[9] This would obviously give the orator maximum flexibility either to calm the judges' existing anger or to put them in a state in which they are not naturally disposed to anger.

And, indeed, this is *precisely* what we see in what follows. As noted, [4] begins the at-whom section. Let us now consider it as the start of that section and continue:

> If, then, people are angry at those who slight them, and slighting is something voluntary, it is evident that they are mild-mannered towards those who [i] do none of these things, or [ii] do them involuntarily, or [iii] are only apparently of this sort. And [iv] toward those wishing to do the contrary of what they have [in fact] done. And [v] toward all who are such toward themselves (for no one

---

[8] Interestingly, according to *Rhet.* I.11, becoming-mild-mannered (*praünsis*) would seem to count as a pleasure. Aristotle there specifies pleasure as 'a sort of movement of the soul, an intensive and perceptible settling down (*katastasis*) into its original natural state' (1369b33–5). For the limitations of this definition, see Chapter 5 (intro.) and e.g. Gosling and Taylor (1982: 196–9); Rapp (2002: ii: 461–5); Dow (2015: 163–77); Price (2017: 185–8). Nonetheless, the notion that becoming-mild-mannered is a 'settling down' (*katastasis*) clearly echoes that definition. But even if *becoming*-mild-mannered is (sometimes) experienced as pleasant, the *pathos* that Aristotle wishes to characterize by defining *praünsis* seems to be *being*-mild-mannered, i.e. *praotēs*: as emphasized, it is the latter that is explicitly stated to be the contrary of anger in [1].

[9] This applies his threefold structure: conditions-under-what, at-whom, and because-of-what (*Rhet.* II.1.1378a22–4).

seems to slight himself). Also, [vi] toward those who admit and regret (for taking as just recompense their being distressed at (*lupeisthai epi*) what they have done, they cease to be angry). (1380a9–16)

Here Aristotle is envisaging cases where the person has either *not done* anything anger-inducing (= [i]), or *only appears to* have done some such, but did not in fact do so (= [iii]), or who did in fact slight us, but there are *mitigating circumstances* (= [ii], [iv], [v], [vi]). And the state of mild-manneredness itself is most plausibly construed as the state that we are either in *by default* (with [i]) or which *we arrive at* after learning that the slight was only apparent or is otherwise mitigated (with [ii]–[vi]).

The examples that follow (still within the at-whom section) accord with this analysis as well: we have those who humble themselves before us and do not dispute with us; those who are serious towards the serious; those who have shown us great favour; those who are begging a favour and entreating us; and those not being wantonly aggressive (*hubristai*) or satirizing (*chleuastai*) or slighting us (1380a22–30). These all appear to be people that we will not feel angry towards as such.[10] Indeed, Aristotle then *explicitly* goes on to specify some people we 'do not get angry at' (*ouk orgizontai*: 1380a33), e.g. those whom we fear ('for it is impossible to be afraid and angry at the same time') or those we feel shame in front of (1380a32–4); as well as people we are 'not angry at or less angry at', namely, those who did things because of their own anger (1380a34–b1). Once again, we count as mild-mannered in these cases, it seems, simply because we are not angry.

When we come to the 'under what conditions' section of the discussion, Aristotle explicitly emphasizes: 'people whose condition goes contrary to being angry are mild-mannered' (1380b2–3). Again, we count as mild-mannered, it seems, simply insofar as we are not angry. Hence Aristotle goes on to list a series of conditions under which we are not prone to feel anger:

for example, in a condition of amusement, of laughter, in a holiday mood, in a condition of prosperity, of success, of satisfaction—in general in a condition of painlessness,[11] of pleasure that does not result from wanton aggression, and of decent hope. (1380b3–5)

---

[10] With the first of these ('those who humble themselves before us and do not dispute with us'), Aristotle explains 'for they appear to agree that they are inferior, inferior people are afraid, and no one who is afraid slights—indeed the fact that anger ceases towards those who humble themselves is something that even dogs make clear by not biting those who are sitting' (1380b23–6). This example can clearly work whether there is an existing condition of anger or not: we will cease to be angry with those who humble themselves before us and we will not be prone to be angry with those who are generally such.

[11] This directly contrasts with the pained background condition which made us disposed to anger that we discussed in 6.2.

Or again, when we have spent time with our anger (1380b5–6), or have spent our anger on someone else (1380b6–13), or if we pity the offenders (1380a13–15), or, most explicitly, if we think that we ourselves have done an injustice and so are suffering justly, for 'anger does not arise at what is just' (1380b16–20)—that is, it seems, we count as being-mild-mannered simply insofar as we are *not angry*. And he provides further examples in what follows (1380b20–30).[12]

When he closes his chapter by highlighting guidance for the orator, Aristotle alludes both to cases in which there is a prior state of anger and ones where there is not:

> It is clear, then, that those who wish to make their listeners become mild-mannered (*katapraünein*) should speak from these topics, making, on the one hand (*men*), the listeners be of that sort and, on the other (*de*), rendering those with whom they are angry as either fearsome, or worthy of being ashamed in front of, or as having shown them favour, or as involuntary agents, or as deeply pained at what they have done. (1380b31–4)

The 'on the one hand', here, refers to disposing the listeners (= judges) to being mild-mannered without a pre-existing condition of anger as a background, whereas the 'on the other hand' refers to making listeners who are currently angry (with their client) cease to be so, and thereby bringing about a condition of mild-manneredness.

If the above analysis is right, the state that Aristotle wants to characterize as the opposite of anger, mild-manneredness (*praotēs*), would seem to amount to:

> *the absence* or *privation* of anger, whether that occurs after a process of becoming-mild-mannered, or because of a pre-existing condition one possesses, or simply because of the absence of any cause of anger.

If so, mild-manneredness is not a positive emotion in its own right. For it is not a specific representational distress or pleasure.[13] Whether this means it should not

---

[12] What about the 'because of what sort of things we become mild-mannered' specified in [2] of the opening passage? Aristotle seems, reasonably enough, to take this to be manifest from the rest of his discussion. After providing a series of examples of those to whom we are mild-mannered, he writes: 'and, in general, the things that make us become mild-mannered (*ta praünonta*) should be looked for from their contraries' (1380a31–2) (i.e. the things that make us angry). See also below.

[13] Or is there an alternative interpretation? Konstan (2006: ch. 3) thinks so. While conceding that Aristotle initially addresses cases 'to counter anger by redescribing the nature of the offence that has aroused it' (83), he points out that when Aristotle claims that we are *praoi* with those who are serious towards the serious ('for it seems to them that they are being taken seriously, rather than being disdained (*kataphronein*)'), and towards those who have shown us greater favour, or towards those who are begging a favour and entreating us, or those who are not arrogant or insulting towards people like us (1380a26–31), he is not 'obviously' referring 'to a case in which an offender exhibits some form of contrition' but perhaps instead 'to some respectful comportment in and of

be classified as a *pathos* at all, as was already doubted by Cope (1877: 42), is a question we shall return to (**10.6**). But let us first examine two more of Aristotle's 'opposites': the contraries to feeling-grateful-for and shame, respectively.[14]

10.4 Not-being-grateful-for or being-put-out (*ou charein echein*)

We find a related situation with the opposite of feeling-grateful-for (*charin echein*), which is also sketched in *Rhet.* II.7. Aristotle here describes how people could be shown not, in fact, to have provided one with a favour (even though they had been presumed to). It might be shown, for example, that they were providing the service *for their own sake*, or that they had provided the service *by luck*, or *through compulsion*, and so on (1385b1–5). In such a circumstance, we would no longer feel grateful for the service under consideration. This would clearly be relevant for orators since, when germane, they could try to show that we should not in fact be feeling grateful to the person in question because, e.g., the service was not actually a favour. But, just like becoming-mild-mannered (*praünsis*), the process of ceasing to be grateful would seem simply to result in the privation or absence of the feeling of gratitude. In this sense, not-being-grateful-for (*ou charein echein*; cf. *to acharistein*: 1385b11) would not be a representational distress in its own right, but simply the state of not feeling grateful.[15]

However, Aristotle goes on to note:

---

itself' (84). But Konstan infers from this: '[i]n these instances, we are *praoi* just because of the consideration, or rather the deference, of others, and not necessarily because of some appeasement. *Praotēs*, it would appear, is elicited by reverence or other admiring or self-abasing signals on the part of the others that elevate our standing or esteem' (84). Konstan thereby suggests that *praotēs* might be defined as: 'a desire, accompanied by pleasure, to treat someone kindly, on account of a perceived gesture of respect' (85). But the textual basis for this reading is slender. Although we do not need a prior state of anger in such cases, nor did we with [i] in 1380a9–16, quoted above. And it is surely more plausible that Aristotle is here providing further instances of that case, i.e. the sort of people we are not angry at, rather than indirectly and obliquely trying to specify some positive desire-cum-emotion which is integral to his understanding of the state. Indeed, Konstan ends up conceding that his own reading might not be Aristotle's, but only Aristotelian (2006: 89). Furthermore, as we shall see, mild-manneredness is not an isolated case.

[14] In *NE* IV.5 Aristotle uses *praotēs* to characterize the virtue connected to anger. It is clear that there *praotēs* is being treated as a state (of character), a *hexis*, rather than a *pathos*. As a *hexis*, *praotēs* does involve experiencing anger: the *praos* is 'undisturbed and not led by emotion, but becomes angry (*chalepainein*) in the way, at the things, and for the length of time, that reason specifies' (1125b34–1126a1). However, even in this context the connection to the privation of anger is apparent: he notes that, strictly speaking, the virtue connected to anger does not have a name, and that *praotēs* tends towards the deficiency (1125b27–9) because the *praos* is not revengeful (*timōrētikos*) but inclines towards forgiveness (*sungnōmonikos*) (1126a1–3). (Note, there is *no* association with Konstan's positive desire-cum-emotion here either (see last note): the *only* emotion that is germane to *praotēs*, as a state of character, is anger.)

[15] So Striker: 'His advice about the 'opposite' [of *charin echein*] is clearly meant to show how one can persuade people that they have no reason to be grateful' (1996: 301n.15).

> It is a sign of disfavour if a small service is not provided or if the same, equal, or greater services are provided to enemies (for it is clear that in neither case are these for our sake). Or if someone has provided a worthless service and knows it (for no one agrees to having a need for worthless things). (1385b7–10)

Here, it seems, the subject has apprehended that a service that could reasonably have been bestowed on one is *lacking*. That could well generate a parallel emotion to the representational pleasure we saw with *charin echein* (feeling-grateful-for), which we might characterize as 'being-put-out', or some such:

> Being-put-out is a kind of distress at the lack of a favour being bestowed that was hoped for.[16]

So perhaps we can find a representational distress in Aristotle's discussion of this opposite. Nonetheless, he seems to have no concern for restricting the opposite to this emotion rather than to an absence or privation of feeling-grateful-for.

10.5 Shamelessness (*anaischuntia*)

An even clearer privation is shamelessness. The account of this is provided along with shame at the start of *Rhet.* II.6 (and borrows from it):

> [and let] shamelessness (*anaischuntia*) [be] a sort of belittling (*oligōria*) and lack of feeling (*apatheia*) about these same things [viz. evils—whether present, past, or future—that appear to bring a person into disrepute]. (II.6.1383b14–15)

No more is said about shamelessness until the final lines of II.6, which run:

> These, then, are the things that concern shame; it is clear that we shall be well-equipped with things concerning shamefulness from their contraries. (1385a14–15)

The feeling (*pathos*) that shamelessness involves lacking and owing to which it can be characterized as a lack of feeling (or 'unemotional'), *apatheia*, is obviously shame itself. Shamelessness is *apatheia* 'about these same things', i.e. the things that shame concerns. That is, shamelessness involves *failing* to feel shame about

---

[16] This again fits the fact that *Rhet.* II.7 concerns gratitude, not benevolence or kindness (**10.1**). The distress is directed at some ingratitude shown towards you, not to you yourself being unkind or malevolent (which would be the opposite of kindly feeling or benevolence). Konstan (2006: 82, 161–3) misses the positive emotion connected to being-ungrateful-to.

those things. When shameless people commit shameful acts they will not feel shame. Again, then, shamelessness seems to be a *privation*, an *absence* of an emotion, rather than a genuine emotion in its own right. Of course, people who do not feel shame when they perform shameful acts will have no qualms about performing such acts. If this amounts to a disposition of such subjects, they may be said to possess shamelessness as a state of character ('they are shameless people').[17] But Aristotle seems to want to characterize an occurrent lack of shame, the privation of the emotion of shame (which is itself a distress) as such, as a state in its own right.

Aristotle also mentions shamelessness in *Rhet.* II.3. He writes:

> we punish more severely those who dispute and deny...the cause of this is that to deny evident facts is shamelessness, and shamelessness manifests belittling (*oligōria*) and [in particular] disdain (*kataphronēsis*)—at any rate, we feel no shame before those we deeply disdain. (1380b17–18, 19–21)

Once again, he is here linking shamelessness to a belittling (*oligōria*), and this is further specified in the II.3 passage above as a disdaining (*kataphronēsis*)—one of the three species of slight (*oligōria*) in *Rhet.* II.2 (1378b14–15). But, here, the disdain is specifically linked to a person. We feel no shame (i.e. are shameless) before someone we disdain, hence disputing and denying some evident fact (such as that it was you who broke the vase) is a manifestation of our disdaining the person and hence shamelessness, since we would not do this if we respected the person and so felt shame. Again, shamelessness seems to amount to little more than the privation or lack of the emotion of shame.

With shamelessness, then, we have as clear a case as we could want of an 'opposite' which is not a representational distress or pleasure in its own right.[18] Doubtless, those who are shameless may experience pleasure-based emotions in relation to their shameless acts, but Aristotle seems just to be aiming to specify the opposite of shame in terms of not being distressed when acting disreputably.[19]

---

[17] So *NE* II.7: 'he who falls short or is not ashamed of anything at all is shameless (*anaischuntos*)' (1108a34–5).

[18] Cf. also Konstan (2006: 82–3, 99–100).

[19] Similar to the way *praotēs* is used to refer to a character trait in *NE* IV.5 (10.3n.14), so too shamelessness is used to refer to a dispositional trait in *NE* II.7 and *EE* III.7 (where the shameless person is one of the bad characters corresponding to the person who is *aidēmōn* or 'modest'). In *NE* II.7 the shameless person is characterized as 'not ashamed of anything at all' (1108a34–5), in *EE* III.7 'as one who cares about no one's opinions' (*mēdemias phrontizōn doxēs*) (1233b27–8). Shamelessness is also specified as a trait of character in *Rhet.* I.10, where once again the connection to belittling reputation is explicit: 'a shameless person [commits unjust acts] because of belittling reputation' (*ho d' anaischuntos di' oligōrian doxēs*) (1368b22–3). See also Aristotle on old people in *Rhet.* II.13: 'And they are more shameless than prone to shame (for since they do not care equally about what is noble and what is advantageous they are belittling (*oligōrein*) of their reputation)' (1390a1–3).

10.6 Were these opposites even intended to count as *pathē*?

The three opposites we have looked at in 10.3–5, then, seem (at least primarily, given the *being-put-out* notion of not-being-grateful-for) to be privations of representational pleasures or distresses, rather than hedonic states themselves. This may prompt one to wonder whether Aristotle intended them to count as emotions (*pathē*) in their own right in the first place. Jamie Dow suggests:

> it seems plausible that Aristotle's accounts of the 'opposite' passions do not stand on their own, but should be taken as part of a pair in which they are presented. Thus, these 'opposites' are not themselves passions but are privations of their opposite, which in each case *is* a passion. (2015: 154; Dow's emphasis)

In support of this, he flags Aristotle's characterization of shamelessness as an *apatheia*, which he translates 'emotionlessness'. More generally, he notes:

> To the extent that each of these states involves no pleasure or pain (as merely the privation of another kind of state), strictly speaking, it does not belong in a list of the *pathē*. But there is clearly an important sense in which these states do belong exactly where we find them. The aspiring orator needs to know both how to arouse and to dispel each type of emotion, and—insofar as Aristotle has things to say about what we might call the 'privations'—this is exactly the kind of thing he says about them, and the kind of explanation he offers of why it is useful to understand how to bring someone into such a state. (154–5)

This is obviously an attractive idea and I agree about the usefulness of specifying the opposites for the orator. But, unfortunately, the notion that Aristotle does not count these opposites as *pathē* flies in the face of the evidence, both here and elsewhere.

First, he seems explicitly to count the opposites as emotions in his general specification of emotions in *Rhet*. II.1. He claims that emotions are 'those things owing to which people, by undergoing change, differ in their judgements, and which are accompanied by pain and pleasure—for example, anger, pity, fear and other such things, *and their contraries* (kai ta toutois enantia)' (1378a19–22; my emphasis). Second, in *De an*. I.1 being mild-mannered (*praotēs*) is placed on a list of the emotions of the soul (*pathē tēs psuchēs*: 403a16)—alongside spirit (*thumos*), fear, pity, confidence (*tharsos*), joy (*chara*), feeling-friendly-towards (*to philein*), and hating (*misein*). Indeed, each of these *pathē* is explicitly said to involve the body (*meta somatos*: 403a16–17), 'for at the same time as these the body is affected in a certain way' (403a18–19) (for more on this, see Chapter 9). Third, even our paradigm privation, shamelessness, seems to count as a *pathos* at *NE* II.6. Having provided his definition of virtue (at 1106b36–1107a2), Aristotle claims:

But not every action nor every *pathos* admits of a mean; for some have names that already imply badness, e.g. schadenfreude, shamelessness, envy, and in the case of actions, adultery, theft, murder; for all of these and suchlike things imply by their names that they are themselves bad. (1107a8–13)

Here shamelessness, too, is treated as a *pathos* in its own right.[20]

It seems, then, that rather than exclude the opposites as *pathē*, Aristotle wishes to *extend* the category of *pathē* of the soul *to include* privations of representational pleasures or distresses.[21] In this respect, we need to note that he appears to think that in some sense privations are positive states in their own right, not simply nothing at all. In *Met*. Z.7 he writes:

even contraries have in a sense the same form; for the substance of a privation is the opposite substance, e.g. health is the substance of disease; for it is by its absence that disease exists. (1032b2–5)[22]

Disease is the privation of health (see also *Met*. Z.7.1033a7–13), but it is not nothing. It is a specific lack: disease exists by the very specific lack of health (hence Aristotle refers to the 'substance of a privation' (*hē ousia tēs sterēseōs*)). Applied to our cases, while the opposites in question do not count as representational pleasures or distresses in their own right, Aristotle may still nonetheless want to characterize them as *pathē* insofar as they involve *quite specific lacks*, which indicate an absence of a particular contrary. Only insofar as we are *not angry* do we count as being-mild-mannered, only insofar as we are *not feeling grateful for* something do we count as *lacking-gratefulness*, and only insofar as we do not feel shame do we count as manifesting *shamelessness*. Shamelessness is not nothing at all, but the quite specific lack of the emotion of shame. Just as blindness is a privation (*Met*. Δ.22.1022b28) insofar as it is the absence of sight, but being blind will count as a quality of a person, so too, on this view, the opposites of the emotions are privations and indicate the absence of particular emotions, and yet can count as properties of people no less. (For example, shamelessness, it seems, is the *pathos* of lacking the *pathos* of shame.)

This said, we can clearly draw a distinction between what we might call 'positive emotions' or 'emotions proper'—specific representational pleasures or distresses—on the one hand, and lacks or privations of such emotions, on the other. And while I think that we will sometimes quite happily refer to someone who is

---

[20] Note, Aristotle had just provided his general specification of the emotions in *NE* II.5 (1105b21–3, quoted in 2.1), which explicitly mentioned envy (cf. II.6.1106b16–20; also quoted in 2.1). Hence, by *pathos* he most likely means 'emotion'.

[21] Note also that Aristotle uses *apatheia* ('lack of feeling') to characterize the opposite of appetite (*epithumia*) in *Rhet*. II.1.1378a3–5; quoted in **8.1**.

[22] See also e.g. *Met* Δ.22 and *Phys*. II.1.193b19–20.

disposed to fail to experience an emotion as someone who has a positive state (a shameless person, for example, as someone who just does not feel shame), we will not (I think) characterize the specific lacks that Aristotle has in mind as emotions as such. To have an emotion, we must actually undergo some occurrent pleasure or distress, not merely fail to undergo it. And while some of Aristotle's 'opposites' count as positive emotions in their own right, e.g. indignation (*nemesis*), which, as a representational distress, we are told is 'most opposed' to pity (*Rhet.* II.9.1386b8) (in spite of the fact that Aristotle will actually list a series of 'opposites' here, as can be seen in my Catalogue at the end of this book), the three opposites we considered in 10.3–5—though defined by reference to such pleasures and distresses—do not.[23]

10.7 Confidence (*tharsos*)

In **10.3** we saw Striker claim that 'confidence', for Aristotle, is also just the absence of a specific distress, namely, the distress of fear. Let us now consider this further.

Interestingly, Aristotle may appear to specify confidence (*to tharsos*) just by reference to the intentional state that apprehends its object. The *Revised Oxford Translation* makes it sound as though in *Rhet.* II.5 he attempts to provide a strict definition of confidence, translating the relevant lines as follows: 'it [sc. confidence] is, therefore, the imaginative expectation (*meta phantasias hē elpis*) of the nearness of which keeps us safe and the absence or remoteness of what is terrible' (1383a17–19). Confidence, on such a view, would be some kind of 'imaginative expectation'. But let us look at the specification in context. Here is Reeve's (2018) translation:

> Since it is now evident what fear is, what the fearsome things are, and by being disposed in which way each is afraid, it is also evident on the basis of this what being confident is, what sorts of things people feel confident about, and by being disposed in which way people feel confident, since confidence is the contrary of fear, and what inspires confidence, of what is fearsome. So [confidence's] hope [or 'expectation': *elpis*] of things providing safety involves [or 'is accompanied by': *meta*] a *phantasia* of them as being close at hand and of fearsome things as either non-existent or as being far away. (1383a13–19)

This account of confidence is clearly intended to be informed by the discussion of fear just given. And the key to it, I think, is to grasp that in the lines the *ROT* translation implies are attempting to define confidence, Aristotle is in fact only

---

[23] Note, Aristotle's including the privations of representational pleasures or distresses as emotions does not fit Rapp's (2013) view discussed in 7.4n.33: here there is only *the lack of* pleasure/distress.

intending to characterize the intentional state that gives rise to it (in light of which it forms). This of course relates to a novel feature of Aristotle's formulation of fear that we considered in **4.3**, viz. that, in contrast to his specifications of other emotions, Aristotle's definition explicitly mentions not merely the distress of fear (and what it is directed at) but the intentional state that it arises from (fear is a 'distress or disturbance arising from a *phantasia* of a future destructive or painful evil': II.5.1382a21–2). His specification of confidence seems to be indicating the parallel intentional state that gives rise *to it*. His reference to a '*hope*' (or *expectation*: *elpis*) of safety may be intended to indicate not merely that we are concerned with the *prospect* of safety, but a prospect that is apprehended as *likely* or *probable*. Aristotle seems, in effect, to be claiming that confidence arises from apprehending oneself as safe from possible harm or as having access to things that can keep one safe from harm. But such a specification of course leaves entirely open whether confidence should be considered a representational pleasure in its own right. Indeed, it would be *compatible* with him *taking it for granted* that confidence is a representational pleasure. On the other hand, the specification would seem no less compatible with him viewing confidence as the privation of fear, as Striker suggests, and along the lines we saw with mild-manneredness, not-being-grateful-for, and shamelessness.[24]

Are there any indications elsewhere that might resolve this?[25] In the *NE* specification of emotions confidence is listed next to fear as 'accompanied' by pleasure or distress (II.5.1105b21–3) (see **2.1**); but then, as we have seen, mild-manneredness is also placed on a list of emotions in *De an.* I.1 (403a16–18), and it seems to be a privation. However, a strong indication that Aristotle would view confidence as a representational pleasure in its own right is provided by the *MA* 8 passage we considered in **9.4**. Aristotle writes:

---

[24] Note, either way confidence does not threaten the idea (argued for in Chapter 4) that Aristotle holds that emotions are *responses* to intentional states that apprehend their objects, not those apprehending intentional states themselves.

[25] Given the privation-emotions, we clearly cannot establish confidence is a pleasure simply from its being fear's opposite (contra Moss 2012a: 80 and my 2009: 124). Nor can we infer it simply from the fact that confidence arises from apprehending the prospect of safety (contra Cooper 1996: 245), since I see no reason one could not judge that one will be safe, but be hedonically ambivalent about that (or, if, e.g., suicidal, distressed by it). Cooper (1996: 253n.4) claims that Aristotle 'carelessly' 'equates those experiencing confidence simply with those who are *apatheis* under certain circumstances', citing *Rhet.* II.5.1383a28. Dow follows suit and claims that Aristotle here describes confidence 'as being "without emotion" (*apatheis*)' (2015: 154n.32). But this is a mistake stemming from failing to observe that Aristotle is here characterizing what conditions, if present, will dispose one to confidence (in line with his threefold structure). As Cooper notes, the feeling that Aristotle is referring to people being free from in 1383a28–9 is fear. Reeve (2018: *ad loc.*) translates: 'people become free from the feeling [of fear] in two ways: either by not having been put to the test or by having the means to help'. The fact that people are *disposed to* feel confident when they are in such a condition does not *identify* confidence with such a disposition. Similarly, as we saw in **6.2**, Aristotle claims that those who are in pain are disposed to anger, especially if one belittles their condition. But he does not mean they *are* angry insofar as they are in such a condition. (Nobody might in fact trigger an angry response.) Indeed, the pain is not even a necessary condition for anger. But while the absence of the relevant fear is a necessary condition for confidence, this certainly does not imply that such an absence *is itself* confidence.

roughly speaking, painful and pleasant things are all accompanied by (*meta*) some cooling and warming. This is clear from the emotions. For occurrences of confidence and fear and sexual arousal (*tharrē gar kai phoboi kai aphrodisiasmoi*) and other painful and pleasant bodily things (*ta alla ta sōmatika lupēra kai hēdea*) occur sometimes in some particular part accompanied by (*meta*) warming and chilling, and sometimes in the whole body. (701b37–702a5)[26]

The emotions of fear and confidence are here given as *examples* of how painful and pleasant things are accompanied by chilling and warming. It seems that just as fear is taken by Aristotle to be a distress, so too confidence is construed by him as a pleasure in its own right, not simply the absence of the distress of fear.[27] As a representational pleasure, a definition might run:

Confidence is: pleasure at the (apparent) prospect of safety.

Or some such.[28]

10.8 The supplements in the *EE* specification of emotions

I would now like to consider Aristotle's general specification of the emotions in *EE* II.2 which includes a number of additions to those in *NE* II.5 and *Rhet*. II.1 (all quoted in **2.1**). Aristotle writes:

By emotions (*pathē*) I mean things like spirit, fear, shame, appetite, in general things that for the most part (*epi to polu*) are accompanied by (*hepetai*) perceptible pleasure or pain in their own right (*kath' hauta*).[29] (1220b12–14)

The idea that emotions are accompanied by (*hepetai*) pleasure or pain is common to the *NE* II.5 and *Rhet*. II.1 specifications and was examined in **2.1**; as was the 'in general' (*kai holōs*), which also occurs in *NE* II.5 (but not *Rhet*. II.1). And I have

---

[26] See **9.4** for some notes on this passage (nn.54–6).
[27] Cf. also *NE* III.9, where the fact that the pleasant end which courage sets before itself (1117b3, viz. acting nobly: 1117b9) may be a source of confidence perhaps suggests that it too is a pleasurable state. Certainly, Aristotle's discussion of confidence in *NE* III.6–9 seems to treat confidence as a positive state in its own right, not simply the absence of fear (see e.g. III.7.1115b15–19, 1115b33–1116a2, III.9.1117a29–30; and my 2009). Aspasius also takes Aristotle to hold that confidence is a pleasure (Heylbut 1889: 43, 22–4; 46, 18–19). For the notion that confidence, in contrast to fear, involves 'warming', cf. also *Rhet*. II.12, where being hopeful is said to be a source of confidence (1389a25–8) and is referred to as being 'warmed through' (1389a19), while fear is said (in *Rhet*. II.13) to be a 'sort of chilling' (1389b32).
[28] Cp. Cooper (1996: 254n.12), who offers a definition with reference to *phantasia* that attempts to mirror the definition of fear.
[29] λέγω δὲ πάθη μὲν τὰ τοιαῦτα, θυμὸν φόβον αἰδῶ ἐπιθυμίαν, ὅλως οἷς ἕπεται ὡς ἐπὶ τὸ πολὺ ἡ αἰσθητικὴ ἡδονὴ ἢ λύπη καθ' αὑτά.

already provided a brief comment on the 'perceptible' at end of 2.2 (see, in addition, n.35 below). But what about the 'for the most part' (*epi to polu*) and the 'in their own right' (*kath' hauta*)?

Clearly since these further supplements are dropped from *NE*, which is the direct parallel for the *EE* specification in terms of its function in the text, and the former is usually thought the later text, we should not be *overly* concerned by these supplements, which are not further explained.[30] But let us nonetheless consider what Aristotle might have meant. Michael Woods (1982, 1992) and Stephen Leighton (1984) take the 'for the most part' to qualify pleasure or pain.[31] They thus have to allow that some (token) emotions, according to this specification, *are not* connected to pleasure or pain. As Woods sees it, 'Aristotle must mean that it is true of each of these affections that it is mostly accompanied by pleasure and pain' (1992: 101); that is, that each of the emotions for the most part involves pleasure or pain, but there can be instances of them that do not. Leighton (1984: 136) rightly objects to this idea (as first presented in Woods' 1982) that the distress in question is typically mentioned *as part of the definition* of the individual emotions (see 2.3), which suggests that it cannot be a contingent feature. Instead, he proposes that the 'for the most part' should be taken to indicate that 'certain *pathē* are without pleasure and pain' (1984: 136). And he then points to hating (*to misein*) as being just such a case, since it is treated as an emotion (appears on the lists, etc.) but is explicitly said to be 'not accompanied by pain' (1984: 138).[32] Against this, it might seem odd for Aristotle to define a state by reference to a feature that only holds of its instances for the most part (cf. Woods 1992: 101). But, also, the proposal invites the question: in virtue of what would hating then count as an emotion if it lacks any connection to pleasure or pain? Indeed, when Aristotle refers back to the *EE* II.2 specification in *EE* II.4, he tells us that the emotions are defined or delimited (*diōristai*) by pleasure or pain (1221b36-7).[33] Furthermore, if this were what he intended to accommodate by the 'for the most part', it is odd that in the parallel *NE* specification (II.5.1105b21-3) he explicitly lists hatred *and yet omits* the qualification (see also Price 1995: 119).

Anthony Price instead proposes that 'for the most part' qualifies 'perceptible', not 'pleasure or pain', which leaves Aristotle able to link all emotions to pleasure or pain. On Price's view, 'Aristotle must think that a special kind of pleasure or pain attaches to most affections, though not all' (2011: 115, see also his 1995: 119-20). But the

---

[30] The function in both cases is to distinguish states (of character) (*hexeis*) from other related states; viz. emotions (*pathē*), on the one hand, and capacites (*dunameis*), on the other.
[31] Cf. also Fortenbaugh (2002: 110).
[32] Cf. also Achtenberg (2002: 176) and Moss (2012a: 81n.27).
[33] 'Referring back': the II.2 passage is part of his distinction between emotions, capacities, and states (1220b10-19) and in II.4, just before the line mentioned, Aristotle claims: 'necessarily the character must be bad or good by its pursuit or avoidance of certain pleasures and pains. This is clear from our classification of the emotions, capacities and states...' (1221b32-5). Cf. *EE* II.5: 'pleasures and pains arise from the aforementioned states and emotions' (1222b10-11).

exceptions Price has in mind are, once again, hating and feeling-friendly-towards.[34] With these, he claims 'there is no mention of a *phantasia* that connects with a pain or pleasure that is in part somatic': 'loving [= feeling-friendly-towards] is defined in terms of "wishing" (*boulesthai*), which is rational desire, and acting' (2011: 120). However, this is to focus on these states *qua* desires, not *qua* the emotions those desires entail (see 7.4). Price is alive to the latter too (120) and, indeed, appears to think that that connection brings them 'within' Aristotle's 'bare formulations' (citing the general specifications of emotions in *Rhet.* II.1 and *NE* II.5). But if it is the connection of feeling-friendly-towards and hating to representational pleasures or distresses that makes it appropriate for Aristotle to include these states on his lists of emotions, it is unclear why including them would demand the 'for the most part' qualification. In any event, we have not been given any reason for thinking that *the pleasures or distresses* connected to feeling-friendly-towards and hating would be any less 'perceptible' than with other emotions, yet it was the 'perceptible' that the 'for the most part' was meant to qualify, on Price's view.[35]

What else could the 'for the most part' indicate? My preference would be to take it to be required given the 'in their own right' (*kath' hauta*: intrinsically) supplement. Emotions are *for the most part* things that are accompanied by perceptible (i.e. occurrent) pleasure and distress *in their own right*. Then Aristotle would be flagging that we include as emotions some states that are not accompanied by perceptible pleasure or distress *in their own right*. This would fit with the fact that *both* these qualifications are subsequently dropped from the *NE* and *Rhet.* specifications: without the 'in their own right' we do not need the 'for the most part'. In the context of our discussion in this chapter, the obvious candidates for states that Aristotle would wish to count as emotions but which do not involve pleasure or distress *in their own right* would be the privation-emotions. As we have seen, these only indicate the privation or lack of a representational pleasure or distress. But equally, Aristotle might be referring (as well) to feel-friendly-towards and hating. As we have seen (7.4), these are not representational pleasures or distresses in their own right—they are desires—but they do essentially entail such pleasures and

---

[34] Price also mentions (2011: 120) 'kindness' (*charis*), but he has the mistaken interpretation of *charin echein* discussed in **10.1**.

[35] At the end of **2.2** I suggested that the 'perceptible' may simply indicate that there is some felt phenomenological aspect to emotions insofar as they involve the perceptual capacities being engaged (see also **2.4**n.55, **4.4**, and **5.6**). I suppose it may instead be suggested that the 'perceptible' indicates that emotions are directed at objects the representation of which essentially requires perception or perceptual *phantasia* (cf. Price 2011: 114–15). As I see it, this would not preclude the idea that emotions can be about their objects just insofar as those objects are represented by thought (see **Intro.2**), since Aristotle holds that thoughts operate on perceptible *phantasmata* and yet is happy to claim that memory is an exercise of perceptual *phantasia* even while explicitly acknowledging that we can have thought-based memories. In fact, Aristotle claims that it is *phantasmata* that are remembered in their own right (*kath' hauta*), whereas thoughts are remembered by being extrinsically connected (they are connected *kata sumbebēkos*) to such a *phantasma* (*Mem.* 1.450a12–14, 22–5). This opens up the possibility that the 'in their own right' (or 'intrinsic') in the *EE* specification could mark that emotions are in their own right directed at objects that are apprehended by perception or perceptual *phantasia*, but extrinsically directed at objects that are apprehended by thought.

distresses. Aristotle could be flagging that feeling-friendly-towards and hating can count as 'emotions' insofar as we extend the term to states that essentially indicate the presence of such pleasures or distresses by entailment (*anankē*: *Rhet.* II.4.1381a3).[36] In this way, he would be broadening the class of emotions to include not just states which are in themselves (*kath' hauta*) representational pleasures or distresses, but also states which indicate, specify, or are otherwise essentially bound to such representational pleasures or distresses, even if they are not such themselves (as with privation-emotions or certain desires). This would, of course, account for the fact that 'and their contraries' is included in the *Rhet.* II.1 specification of the emotions in the way we saw, and for why mild-manneredness appears on the list of emotions in *De an.* I.1 (403a16–18), and why shamelessness seems to count as an emotion in *NE* II.6 (1107a8–13) (see **10.6**). And it would explain why feeling-friendly-towards and hating also appear on lists of the emotions in *De an.* I.1 (403a16–18) and *NE* II.5 (in the latter case as *philia* and *misos*: 1105b21–3). Most interestingly, though, it would also indicate that Aristotle has a notion of what we might call 'emotions proper' (*pathē kuriōs*), one which *excludes* the privation-emotions and the desires of feeling-friendly-towards and hating *as such*. 'Emotions proper' would be those states that are representational pleasures and distresses *in their own right* (*kath' hauta*). It is just such a notion of emotions that I have been trying to characterize in relation to Aristotle's views in this book.[37]

10.9 Some potentially problematic cases for Aristotle's view and replies

Is the notion of 'emotions proper' that I have just specified a good one? I shall provide some more general philosophical reflections in the final part of this book. But let me close this part by considering some potentially problematic cases.

One might object to the notion that emotions are representational pleasures *or* representational distresses by insisting that some emotions essentially involve *both* pleasures and distresses. Addressing hedonic views more generally, Deonna and Teroni (2012: 15) propose that *nostalgia* and *scorn* might be such. If they are

---

[36] We might say that the representational pleasures or distresses are *per se* accidents of feeling-friendly-towards and hating. This reading would not affect the understanding of 'perceptible' outlined in the previous note since that interpretation does not *require* the 'in their own right' to be making the point I proposed: Aristotle could still have that understanding in mind even if not drawing attention to it with the 'in their own right' (just as he can say that memory belongs to the *phantastikon* or primary perceptible part without intending to rule out thought-based memories).

[37] On this reading, when Aristotle drops the qualifications in the *NE* II.5 specification, he is simply employing the broader notion of *pathē*, and does not, as he did via the qualifications in the *EE* version, indicate the narrower class. Note how my reading still leaves a tight notion of *hepetai* (as specified in 2.1). (Contrast the view of Rapp 2013, discussed in 7.4n.33.) The idea is that in the *NE* II.5 specification Aristotle has a broader notion of *pathē* in mind, not a looser notion of *hepetai*. A state qualifies as a *pathos*, in this broad sense, if it essentially specifies a representational pleasure or distress (or, as with feeling-friendly-towards and hating, one of each), where privations can also be said to do this.

right, emotion-types *as such* could not simply be identified with (representational) pleasures or distresses. Some could be both.

In fact, we have already seen how Aristotle could reply to this objection. In our discussion of his account of anger, I noted (**6.5**) that his view is perfectly compatible with the idea that some states might incorporate *both* a representational pleasure *and* a representational distress, and so be hedonically ambivalent.[38] The notion that emotions are representational pleasures or distresses does not itself rule this out. What Aristotle would insist, though, is that such a state would essentially incorporate *two* emotions (cf. Striker 1996: 292). We would not have a hedonically ambivalent emotion, but a state incorporating two emotions, each with just one hedonic flavour.

Suppose we focus on emotions themselves, not states that are composed of them. Might it not be the case that some emotion-types cannot be classified as either pleasures or distresses because they can come in different forms? Deonna and Teroni raise the problem of *surprise* in this regard, pointing out that there can be both 'positive' and 'negative' surprises (2012: 15). This sounds right. In general terms, surprise seems to concern *unexpected or unanticipated outcomes, events, or circumstances*. But, clearly, some surprises can be positive (e.g. being unexpectedly given some money) and others negative (e.g. a shock death). Hence, we cannot identify surprise *as such* with a representational pleasure or distress.

How might Aristotle reply? It seems to me that he would claim that positive surprises are representational pleasures and negative surprises representational distresses. He could then either claim that the blanket term 'surprise' actually covers *two* distinct emotion-types positive surprises and negative surprises[39]— or maintain that while surprise *as such* might not indicate a specific representational pleasure or distress, each token surprise would nonetheless do so.

But is it even plausible to suggest that each individual surprise must be a pleasure or distress? Deonna and Teroni resist this no less. Concerning the view that 'every particular emotional *episode* essentially has a certain hedonic quality', they object:

> Once again, surprise looks like an exception: some episodes of surprise are hedonically neutral. And hedonic neutrality is not a hedonic quality as such, it is just the absence of any hedonic quality. (2012: 15)

Here I think Aristotle would say that insofar as you are neither pleased nor distressed about the unanticipated outcome or event, you do not have an emotion proper about it (though you might have a privation-emotion). If we still nonetheless want to say that

---

[38] Although, as I flagged, this does not, as a matter of fact, occur in anger itself, on Aristotle's view: while it essentially involves a representational distress (at an apparent slight), the pleasure of anger is something that (necessarily) occurs *as a result of it*, not *as part of it*. Anger does, though, essentially involve both a distress and a *desire*. See Chapter 6.

[39] Cf. the fact that he appears to hold that we can have pleasure- and distressed-based versions of indignation (*nemesis*) (although they also have different formal objects: deserved misfortune and undeserved fortune, respectively). See **Cat.12** and **Cat.16**.

you can be surprised by the outcome, he will say that some manifestations of surprise will not count as emotions (proper). On this view, surprise *as such* would not specify a particular emotion (proper), although we can have emotions (proper) about events we are surprised by and just insofar as those events are surprising. The latter would occur to the extent that we experience *distress* or *pleasure* at an apparent manifestation of an object of surprise (an unexpected event or outcome). But does this not sound right? Suppose you learn of something that you were not expecting, but you are neither distressed nor pleased by that outcome *one jot*. Would we not—to the extent that this description of the situation sounds plausible—think that you were not emotionally affected by the surprising event?[40] (To this extent, our notion of 'emotion' matches what I have called 'emotions proper', not Aristotle's broader notion which includes privations.) In fact, we might think that there is reason to reject the idea that surprise *as such* is an emotion-type. For, on the standard view, emotions have evaluative (or formal) objects (see 1.3), but while all surprises seem to concern unexpected events, what is the *evaluative* object of a surprise? It is unclear there is one for surprise *simpliciter*. We might say that *positive* surprises concern *good unexpected events* and *negative* surprises concern *bad unexpected events*, but if surprise *simpliciter* does not have a formal object, surprise *simpliciter* would not be an emotion (proper) (on the assumption that having a formal object is *necessary* for an emotion (proper)). Similarly, with surprises that are hedonically neutral: we could not say, with such events, that they were either good or bad.

Any account of emotions, if it is to be informative, must exclude some states and include others. Aristotle's account at least enables us to say clearly *why* (and, as with surprise, to what extent) any given state counts or fails to count as an emotion proper. The formal object of the emotion must be apprehended, and the subject must form a representational pleasure or distress about that object as it is apprehended. An interesting feature of this account is that it facilitates locating emotions bound up with states that are not, or need not be, emotions proper themselves. Anxiety, depression, and ecstasy are sometimes offered as cases of emotions which need not have a specifiable target or formal object.[41] One can be anxious or depressed without being anxious or depressed *about* some specifiable thing under the guise of some determinate evaluative object. Insofar as this seems a reasonable description of (at least some) cases of anxiety or depression, Aristotle would say that they are not themselves emotional states. But, clearly, they could still, quite easily, *link to* specifiable emotional states. Someone who is

---

[40] Similarly, merely perceiving or judging that someone has suffered some undeserved misfortune is not to undergo an emotion proper, on Aristotle's account: only when one experiences pleasure or distress directed at that scenario does one experience an emotion proper. Indeed, Aristotle explicitly recognizes that we can have a hedonic response *or fail to do so to the very same event*. Just as he contrasts pity (distress at undeserved doing-badly) with indignation (distress at undeserved doing-well), so too he claims that one who is distressed at undeserved doing-badly, will take pleasure (*hēsthēsetai*) or be un-pained (*alupos*) at *deserved* doing-badly (*Rhet*. II.9.1386b27–8). Only the first of these will count as a representational pleasure, and so an emotion proper (although perhaps the latter could count as a privation-emotion).

[41] See e.g. Kupperman (1995: 345–7) and, for a reply, Dalgliesh (1997: 88–9).

anxious or depressed may be prone to manifest specifiable representational distresses, e.g. at the prospect of leaving the house, or going to work, or facing people. And the connection between the objectless states and specific emotions could contribute, in part, to explaining why we feel uneasy excluding such states from the realm of emotions full stop. Such states would also, of course, share with emotions that they are distressful states to be in. Another example is romantic love. This has a particular object, a *target* in the sense specified in 1.3, but it is unclear that there is a specific evaluative object that one represents as applying to one's object of love.[42] In this sense, love may not itself qualify as an emotion, for there may not be a specific representational pleasure that it involves. But love could certainly *prompt* representational pleasures and distresses, which do have such evaluative objects. This may help to explain why love is clearly bound up with emotions, but is itself in some sense ineffable.

Conclusion to Part III

In this part of the book I have addressed some further potential difficulties for my interpretation of Aristotle's account of emotions as representational pleasures and distresses. In Chapter 9 I explored the material aspect of emotions and showed that while Aristotle thinks emotions essentially involve a material dimension, this does not threaten the integrity of his account of emotions as representational pleasures or distresses *alone*. And in this chapter I considered some other states that he characterizes in his *Rhet.* II catalogue that may seem problematic for the notion that he thinks emotions are representational pleasures or distresses. Some of these, on closer inspection, did not in fact provide counter-examples (feeling-grateful-for; confidence) (10.1, 10.7). But our discussion did reveal that Aristotle recognizes a category of emotion-privations (10.2–6), states which specify the absence of a determinate representational pleasure or distress. Taking my cue from the supplements in the *EE* specification of the emotions, however, I suggested that we can still find in Aristotle a notion of 'emotions proper' (*pathē kuriōs*), which picks out representational pleasures or distresses *in their own right* (*kath' hauta*) (10.8). In the final section I suggested that Aristotle's notion of emotions (proper) as representational pleasures or distresses can deal with some (putative) knock-down objections that have been raised against hedonic views. I also pointed out that it has interesting implications for what we should say about some objectless intentional states that seem close to emotions (e.g. some kinds of anxiety) or about states that seem bound up with emotions and to possess an intentional target but do not specify a determinate formal object (as with love).

Aristotle on What Emotions Are. Giles Pearson, Oxford University Press. © Giles Pearson 2024.
DOI: 10.1093/9780191989292.003.0011

---

[42] See e.g. Kraut (1986) and Rorty (1986).

PART IV
FURTHER PHILOSOPHICAL CONSIDERATIONS AND A SIGNIFICANT PHILOSOPHICAL ADVANTAGE

11
Contrast with a Contemporary Motivational Theory. Which Representational Role(s) Do Emotions Play?

In this book I have sought not only to argue for a particular reading of Aristotle's account of what emotions are but also, at various points, to relate his account to matters in contemporary philosophy and, where appropriate, to highlight the philosophical interest and putative merits of his views (see, e.g., Chapter 1 *passim* (but esp. 1.5), 2.4, 3.3, 3.6, 4.4, and 10.9). Having now completed my core interpretation of Aristotle's account (bar my Catalogue of his emotions at the end of the book), in the two chapters that constitute this final part of the book, I provide some further philosophical reflections and point to a major philosophical advantage, one which adds weight to the plausibility of his account. In this chapter I contrast his account of emotions with a contemporary view according to which emotions are motivational states in their own right, and I examine more generally the different representational roles emotions play according to different theories. In the following chapter I develop a significant philosophical advantage of Aristotle's account, namely, how it can contribute towards providing a plausible explanation of recalcitrant emotions.

In Part II of the book I argued that Aristotle distinguishes emotions from desires. As I understand him, he holds that emotions are not, even in part, desires or motivations. They are representational pleasures or distresses *alone*. If this is correct as an interpretation, it invites the question: is Aristotle right? After all, the view that emotions either are or at least essentially involve desires or motivations (or action tendencies or states of action readiness) has pedigree in modern discussions of the emotions—in both philosophy and psychology.[1] In this chapter I consider the merits of Aristotle's view, as I have developed it, by critically appraising a recent account of emotions as motivations. According to Andrea Scarantino's 'Motivational theory of emotions', emotions are 'action control systems designed to prioritize the pursuit of some goals over others' (2014: 156). On this view, we

---

[1] At least going back to Dewey (1894, 1895). In psychology, see esp. Frijda (1986, 2006). A number of philosophers have developed accounts of emotions in terms of belief-desire pairs; see e.g. Marks (1982); Searle (1983: 29–36); and Green (1992: ch. 6). I examine Scarantino's (2014) recent attempt to defend a motivational account of emotions in what follows. See also Maiese (2011).

need to find 'action tendencies' pertaining to 'relational goals' for each emotional state. I first consider some difficult cases for such an account (11.1). I then examine Scarantino's explanation of *acting emotionally* and argue that Aristotle's view has an advantage (11.2). I close by addressing the different representational roles (e.g. descriptive, prescriptive) emotions may be thought to play, according to different theories (11.3).

11.1 Problematic cases for a motivational theory of emotions

An attractive feature of Aristotle's view that desires and emotions are distinct is that we have no trouble explaining cases where we possess an emotion and yet appear to lack any coordinate motivation or action tendency. Such cases are obviously more problematic for views that maintain that emotions are themselves motivations. How, for example, could a motivational view of emotions explain cases of *sadness, grief*, or *depression*, in which the subject appears to experience no particular motivation or action tendency? Here, Scarantino has an interesting proposal. He suggests that the goal of sadness, grief, and depression is simply: *not to relate as such*.[2] On this view, *not to engage with the world* is itself the aim or goal of such states. He writes:

> The sad/grieving/depressed person is disengaged from the world in an undifferentiated fashion, in the sense that there is not much of anything that they wish to do. (2014: 171)

It may be worth stressing that Scarantino is *not* claiming that *those undergoing* these emotions aim at such a goal. Rather, he is saying is that this is the goal embodied in the emotions *themselves*—they manifest such a goal. He might also have proposed that these emotions should be identified with an *aversion* to doing anything.[3]

Scarantino's proposal invites two further questions. First, if, on the one hand, these emotions share *the same* action tendency and if, on the other, emotions *just are* such action tendencies, then sadness, grief, and depression would have to be the same emotion. If this is unacceptable, the theory cannot simply say that emotions *just are* action (here *in*action) tendencies, even if they essentially involve them. Scarantino will in fact ultimately accept this. He builds in a 'descriptive side' to the emotion as well—an appraisal aspect, which specifies the emotion's formal object or 'core relational theme'.[4] This dimension of an emotion may then potentially be invoked to individuate emotions with the same action tendencies.

---

[2] Cf. Frijda (1986: 71).
[3] Cf. Sinhababu (2009), who counts both 'positive desire' and 'aversion' as kinds of desire.
[4] In this respect he contrasts his theory with Frijda's (1986, 2006), which he otherwise draws heavily on. On Scarantino's view, Frijda's theory 'only accounted for the imperative side' of emotions (2014: 177).

Nonetheless, Scarantino claims that this descriptive aspect of an emotion should not be construed as a distinct 'component' alongside the 'imperative' aspect (the action tendency).[5] Instead, on his view, emotions have a 'mind-to-world-to-mind (or dual) direction of fit: they represent how things are (mind-to-world) and how things are to be (world-to-mind) at the same time' (2014: 177). I shall return to this in 11.3 below.

Second, we might ask whether the (in)action tendency cited really is necessary for the emotions in question. In particular, reactions to grief seem varied. Some may well want to disengage. But others might want to 'keep busy', insofar as doing so helps them avoid facing the horror of the situation. Aristotle's account of emotions readily accounts for the variation. Grief, on his view, will be (something like) distress at the loss of someone close or significant to one (cf. *Rhet.* I.11.1370b25–6). But how this interacts with our action tendencies will vary according to the desiderative dispositions of the subject in question. In some, such a distress may well result in a desire to withdraw, or a desire to wallow in the grief. But in those with different desiderative dispositions, it may instead result in a desire to keep busy, or a desire for company (as ways of coping with the loss). Given that emotions, on Aristotle's view—as representational pleasures or distresses—only prompt motivational tendencies against a background of relevant desiderative dispositions (see 7.5), such variability can be readily accommodated. But a view which seeks to isolate specific action tendencies for each emotion type will clearly struggle with such variation.[6]

Indeed, some emotions seem inherently compatible with a wide range of goals. This may be the case with *joy*, for instance. Interestingly, Scarantino has a parallel proposal for joy to the one he invokes for sadness/grief/depression. On his view, the goal of joy is simply: *to relate as such*. He writes:

> The joyful person is ready to engage in an open range of actions, and actively prepares for this open engagement with the world with a generalized state of arousal. (2014: 171)[7]

---

[5] Such a view is what Scarantino calls 'Belief and Desire Cognitivism'. More on this view in 11.2.

[6] An account appealing to a broader notion of desire, rather than simply motivational action tendencies, might appear more promising with grief (cf. Gaut 2007: 212–13). Grievers could perhaps be said, say, to desire the lost loved one be still around, even if this cannot (reasonably) motivate action. But even here we might want to distinguish (i) cases where grievers yearn for the lost one to be present again and (ii) cases where they accept that the lost one is gone and that nothing can reverse this, but are just sad about the loss. One might instead try to model grief as a response to an aversion being realized (cf. the discussion of shame and pride below; and 11.3). In *NE* III.2.1111b19–26 Aristotle recognizes desires (*bouléseis*) that do not directly entail (attempted) pursuit or avoidance (see my 2012: 24–32 for discussion). For resistance to the view that such desires really constitute counterexamples to the claim that having a desire that *p* entails being disposed to act in ways that you believe will bring about *p*, see Wall (2009).

[7] Cf. Frijda (1986: 38). On Scarantino's theory, then, we have three possibilities: 'we distinguish between *focused action tendencies* such as fear and disgust, which have specific relational goals, *unfocused action tendencies* such as joy, which has the generic relational goal of relating as such, and *inaction tendencies*, which have the generic relational goal of not relating as such' (2014: 171).

I suppose one might object that someone who experiences joy may simply just want to bask in it and do nothing. If Scarantino replied that this, too, could be a manifestation of the goal of relating as such, we might worry that the thesis is edging towards trivialization and unfalsifiability. More generally, though, we might ask what makes a person who is ready to engage in an open range of actions count as experiencing *joy*, rather than simply open to engage in lots of different actions (*willing*). Once again, Aristotle's account of emotions appears to have an advantage. Since, on his view, emotions are pleasures or distresses, he can obviously distinguish between someone who is merely open to engaging in lots of different actions and someone who is open in such a way *owing to their experiencing the pleasure of joy*.[8]

It is important to acknowledge that a theory of emotions as action tendencies can accommodate some variability in such tendencies. As Scarantino notes:

> Flexibility is related to the fact that the same emotion can lead to a number of different actions depending on the circumstances. In fear, we may run, but we may also freeze, shut a door, make a phone call, brandish a gun, keep as quiet as possible, and so on. (2014: 158-9)[9]

Such flexibility is permitted by the theory because the relational goal that is posited as the end of the emotion is an 'abstract goal' that needs to be 'situated in a *concrete context* in order to guide bodily changes' (169; Scarantino's emphasis). Following Frijda (1986: 88), Scarantino claims:

> Fear is associated with the action tendency of 'avoidance', associated with the relational goal of achieving one's 'own inaccessibility' (henceforth, one's own safety) with respect to a certain stimulus. (169)

Clearly, the variety of responses cited above could be concrete ways of realizing the abstract goal of achieving one's safety. Freezing may prevent us from being seen, shutting a door may prevent us from being accessible, and so on.

---

[8] And, once again, he would suggest that being so motivated would be a *response* to the emotion—against the background of a certain desiderative disposition—not (part of) the emotion itself as such. He may still have an issue in isolating a formal object that the pleasure of joy is directed at, though. Aristotle includes *chara* (joy) on two of his lists of emotions (*NE* II.5.1105b22; *De an.* I.1.403a18), but it is unclear how he understands it or whether he thinks it has some determinate formal object, and therefore unclear how he would deal with the difficulty it poses. See **Cat.20**. One possibility I mention there is that he may view *chara* as a subgenus (under pleasure) of various different joyful emotions, which could then be further differentiated.

[9] As Scarantino notes, though, 'flexibility is constrained': '[a]lthough there are many different things we can do when we are in the grip of an emotion, not everything goes. For example, people who are in the grip of fear of a tiger coming their way do not generally take a nap, nor do they approach the tiger to pet it. Similarly, people who are in the grip of anger towards their lover do not generally start juggling balls in the air, nor do they invite their lover out for a nice dinner' (159).

Nonetheless, in order for emotions to be (or essentially incorporate) action tendencies, individual emotions must be tied to a specific relational goal. If there were instances of fear which did not involve the relational goal of achieving safety, fear could not simply be (or essentially incorporate) an action tendency specified by that relational goal. In which case either Scarantino's theory would be false or it would have mistakenly identified safety as the action tendency of fear. But in fact, as we saw in 7.3, Aristotle's account of courage purports to provide just such an example. On his view, courageous agents feel fear but are very definitely not motivated to achieve safety. Rather, they attempt to face the danger *even if* they know full well that fleeing would bring about safety and standing firm is more likely to result in their death. Now, of course, even when people feel motivated to achieve safety this does not entail that they must *attempt to act* on that motivation. They could resist the motivation. But, on Aristotle's view, those who are courageous are distinct from enkratic agents in that they are not riddled with conflict. And yet, as we saw, he is insistent that courageous people nonetheless feel fear.

By contrast, Aristotle's own account of emotions permits people to feel fear (distress at the prospect of pain or death) without being motivated to achieve safety. Although, as we have seen (7.3), in order to feel fear they must possess some *hope* of safety, and so safety must be seen as a possibility, their fear need not actively *prompt*, let alone in part involve, an active motivation to seek safety.[10] In support of this consider Tim, who is genuinely afraid of a sponsored parachute jump he inadvertently agreed to take part in, but who, once he has nailed his colours to the mast, so to speak, has no serious desire or motivation to call the thing off or get out of it. Indeed, the notion that courageous agents experience fear would be compatible with them being motivated to pursue a course that makes safety *less likely*. On the motivational theory of emotions this seems unintelligible.

Now, clearly, different theorists can propose that we carve up the emotional landscape as they see fit. If someone wants to insist that we will only count as feeling fear insofar as we possess an accompanying relational goal of achieving safety, so be it.[11] Aristotle would then say that fear, so described, is not simply an emotion but, like anger, an emotion-*cum*-desire, a desire (*orexis*) for safety accompanied by distress (*meta lupēs*) at an apparent danger. But he would, I think, point out that you would then have to say that the courageous agent's distress at the prospect of pain and death is not fear.[12] Similarly, he could point out that you would

---

[10] So too Goldie (2000: 36): 'I can recognize something as dangerous and not be motivated at all to act as I ought...and that could be so even if I had feelings of fear towards that thing'. Note, Aristotle's claim that emotions *need not* prompt desires is compatible with him thinking that in some cases, with certain people, a very strong emotion can effectively impel action (see *EE* II.8.1225a20–33; and my 2006: 230–1).

[11] Cf. Scarantino (2010): 'representing the snake as dangerous by fearing it is *sufficient* for being motivated in a specific way, namely to avoid it' (761; Scarantino's emphasis).

[12] Just as he maintains that unless you form a desire for revenge, you will not count as angry (6.6).

have to maintain that in spite of his telling you that he is terrified of the parachute jump, Tim will only count as genuinely afraid if he has to wrestle with a desire to bail (out of the jump, not the plane). Well, if you insist, let us grant that as well. Nonetheless, Aristotle would point out that such distressful states *themselves* seem to be negative emotions directed at danger. And, if this is right, and they do not entail any particular relational goal, they remain problematic for the motivational theorist.[13]

Similar problems, it seems to me, attach to retrospective *shame* (shame about an action one has performed).[14] This seems more appropriately described as a *reaction* to something one *has been* motivated to do, rather than an action tendency itself. So what could its relational goal be? Scarantino suggests: *disappearing* (2014: 181). But while some people may seek to disappear as a result of feeling shame, this does not seem constitutive of the emotion. Some might seek to do public penance and thereby face up to their failing. Others might react by trying to do something noble or honourable, as if hoping the shameful act will be forgotten about or at least mitigated. Indeed, all manner of relational goals seem possible for someone experiencing shame and yet it quite clearly is not, as per Scarantino's understanding of joy above, simply a desire to relate as such! This fact about retrospective shame fits part and parcel with it not itself being an action tendency, but instead, as just mentioned, a *response* to some action one has already performed.

This is still more manifest with *pride*. One kind of pride concerns something one has achieved.[15] But while one will have been motivated to perform the act that one is proud of (e.g. win a competition; calculate 47^2 in one's head) or motivated to bring about the state of which one is proud (e.g. giving up smoking; losing weight), the emotion itself concerns *what one has achieved*, not some further motivational tendency. Such pride may, of course, contingently relate to further action tendencies. But further action tendencies are not necessary for it. One may have achieved something that one has no further intention of trying to do again;

---

[13] Whereas the fact that anger incorporates an emotion that need not be accompanied by the desire (so **6.6**) is clearly unproblematic for Aristotle. Such an emotion is not, *on its own*, anger, even though anger essentially involves that emotion and Aristotle can refer to anger as an emotion by reference to it.

[14] Aristotle also allows that we can experience shame about an action that we are performing or will perform (see *NE* IV.9.1128b18, 31–2; cf. the temporal neutrality in the definition of shame in *Rhet.* II.6.1383b12–14). For more on shame (*aidōs*, *aischunē*), see **Cat.7**.

[15] Although pride is not included in *Rhet.* II's catalogue of the emotions (shamelessness is said to be shame's opposite, not pride), in *Rhet.* I.11 Aristotle writes: 'And victory is pleasant, not only for those who love victory, but for all. For an impression (*phantasia*) of superiority results, which all have an *epithumia* for, whether mild or more intense' (1370b32–4; following Kassel in reading *mallon* with the MSS as opposed to the OCT's *mala*). This looks to be some kind of *pride* (or perhaps it could become some kind of *arrogant feeling* if unjustified or taken too far?). But, equally clearly, Aristotle seems to think of the emotion as arising from *satisfying* a desire (a pleasure-based *epithumia*) rather than prompting one (see also **8.3**). The emotion might be characterized as: 'joy at an apparent victory—insofar as that makes one appear superior to others', or some such.

indeed, one may view the act as *undesirable* to attempt again.[16] Nor need pride relate to the goal of *placing oneself into the open*, if we sought a parallel to Scarantino's *disappearance* for shame (*exposing oneself* could be misconstrued!). Some who are proud of some achievement want public acknowledgement, but others shy away from it and feel extremely awkward at the prospect of it.[17]

Similarly, *relief* would seem more aptly characterized in terms of something that one anticipates occurring (but is averse to) being *unrealized* or *averted*, rather than as an action tendency itself. Relief at learning that your loved one was not caught up in the terrorist attack in spite of being in the vicinity, for example, will no doubt co-exist with a desire for the loved one's continued well-being. But the emotional response of relief is more plausibly characterized as a reaction to a desire being satisfied, or to something one feared not being realized, than an action tendency in its own right.[18]

11.2 Acting emotionally

Scarantino contrasts his account of emotions with prior theories that have attempted to build desires into emotions as one *component* alongside a belief (as the other component).[19] He argues that such a view—which he calls *Belief and Desire Cognitivism*—is not sufficient for explaining 'being motivated to act *emotionally*' (2014: 163; my emphasis). Let us consider his counter-example. He writes:

> Consider Regular Matt and Twin Matt. By hypothesis, these two Matts are similar in all relevant respects—e.g. IQ, moral values, age, physical ability, eyesight, etc.—except for the fact that Regular Matt is an ordinary guy who works in a bank whereas Twin Matt is a Delta Force marine trained not to become afraid in dangerous circumstances.[20] Twin Matt and Regular Matt are visiting a circus after hours and realize that a tiger has escaped her enclosure. Let us assume that

---

[16] Think of someone who has accomplished some feat that was extremely dangerous. E.g. in 2012 Felix Baumgartner plummeted for about 24 miles towards earth (then a record), but then promptly gave up skydiving. Or think of sportspeople who, having succeeded in something exceptional, then retire (e.g. Nico Rosberg in F1). Indeed, someone may have attempted something always viewed as a one off, whether or not it was successful, and still feel pride at the success if it occurred.

[17] Cf. also Goldie (2000: 78–9) on the possibility of there being no desires involved when we experience pride-in-another; on which, see **Cat.17**.

[18] Again, emotions formed in response to something trivial or transient may be problematic for the Motivational theory, e.g. pleasure directed at seeing someone you pass in the street with an affable face or at someone's witty turn of phrase. Our emotions may simply be responses to such encounters and not involve any desire (even for the state to continue—one may like its transience).

[19] See n.1 for some references to those who have advanced such a view.

[20] So specified, it is highly improbable that Regular Matt and Twin Matt would have the same 'physical ability', but I do not think that this matters in what follows.

they both form a desire to get away from the tiger and believe that they will achieve such objective by running away from the tiger, so they both run away. Furthermore, suppose that these action-explaining beliefs and desires are caused in both Matts by the belief that the tiger is dangerous and by the desire to avoid dangerous things. (162–3)

Scarantino then points to the different reactions of the two Matts. First up:

Delta Force-trained Twin Matt coldly assesses the situation, remembering where the exit he just passed through is located. Without breaking sweat or trembling, he quickly moves towards the exit, while picking up a small child he finds on his way out. Once Twin Matt realizes that the exit door is closed from the outside, he recalls having seen a documentary indicating that standing still without looking at the tiger is the best way to neutralize it, and so he proceeds to remain entirely motionless while holding the child as the tiger approaches. (163)

By contrast, here is how things pan out for the other Matt:

Regular Matt, on the other hand, starts to tremble and sweat profusely, forgets where the closest exit is located even though he just passed through it, mistakes a shadow for a second approaching tiger, and starts running in a random direction while trampling upon a small child and leaving him face down on the ground. After he reaches a faraway exit, he realizes the exit door is closed from the outside. Although he also remembers watching a documentary on the advantages of standing still when a tiger is around, he cannot bring himself to do it, and so he frantically climbs a small tree well within the reach of the tiger while the tiger approaches. (163)

The example is a problem for Belief-Desire Cognitivism because while both Matts are, by hypothesis, motivated by the very same belief-desire pair, only Regular Matt's actions 'display the urgency, partial informational access, constrained flexibility, and bodily underpinnings of prototypical emotional actions' (163). Only Regular Matt, that is, feels fear. But then emotions cannot simply be belief-desire pairs.

I shall accept this as an objection to Belief-Desire Cognitivism, so construed. But how does Scarantino's Motivational theory of emotions explain the difference between the two Matts? He writes:

the difference between Regular Matt and Twin Matt is that only the former is seized by a prioritized avoidance tendency that 'clamours for attention and execution', constraining Regular Matt's ability to perform compatibility and executive controls. Twin Matt, on the other hand, is relying on standard practical reasoning, without having to deal with a state of action readiness that monopolizes attention, pre-empts access to relevant information, prepares the body for action, etc. (173)

Having such a state of action readiness, on Scarantino's view, is constitutive of fear. This does not imply that to experience fear we must all behave in a similar way to Regular Matt. The effects of such an action readiness come in degrees and, indeed, can be subject to rational control (which may either extinguish the emotion or channel it into emotionally planned action (174)). Nonetheless, an emotion, on this view, is essentially 'a prioritizing action control system' (178) and action control systems become prioritized by virtue of the 'functional components of *Precedence* and *Preparation*'—that is, owing to the fact that the 'action-tendency *takes precedence* over other actions and states of action readiness' and that we 'are not simply ready for action, but *actively preparing for it*' (170; my emphases). (Remember, prioritization comes in degrees.) So, while we will not all have to act like Regular Matt in order to be in the grip of fear, Regular Matt does at least provide an example of *impulsive emotional action*. Such action, on Scarantino's view, manifests:

> *urgency*, namely a preference for early versus late action, *partial informational access*, because the investment in information gathering and its quality are constrained by the pre-existence of a prioritized action tendency, and *bodily underpinnings*, because one of the elements of control precedence is bodily preparation. (173; Scarantino's emphases)[21]

Let us grant that Regular Matt has such a motivational tendency. The contrast between the two Matts nicely illustrates a difficulty with theories that identify emotions with beliefs or perceptions. It seems that both Matts can have the very same beliefs about the danger, or perceive the danger in the same way, but only Regular Matt experience fear. Scarantino will explain this difference by reference to the idea that only Regular Matt forms the prioritized action tendency of fear. But the question we must press is: does this difference really determine the specific emotional response of Regular Matt, viz. the fact that he is *afraid* of the tiger?

I would resist this. At the risk of the circus becoming overcrowded, let us introduce a third Matt, 'Inverse Matt'. Inverse Matt is the same as the other two Matts, except that he has become a serial thrill-seeker. He loves danger and thrives on it. He spends all his free time bungee jumping, skydiving, base jumping, diving off

---

[21] This distinguishes the case from emotionally planned action; e.g. 'taking legal action against one's landlord out of anger one month after a heated confrontation, buying a gift for a friend out of gratitude one week after having received his visit at the hospital, writing a letter of complaint to the IRS out of anger every April 15 for years after having been audited' (174).

cliffs, climbing mountains without ropes, and so on. Faced with the tiger loose in the circus, Inverse Matt also forms the desire to get away from it (he is a thrill-seeker, not suicidal—he does not want to die) and believes that he will achieve this objective by running away. So he runs away. Nonetheless, since Inverse Matt has become so accustomed to *enjoying* danger, let us imagine that he cannot help but experience *thrill* at the danger he is facing. At the same time, since he is not accustomed to experiencing just this type of danger, let us suppose that his thrill does not help him in the situation at hand (give him a cliff to dive off to escape the tiger, it would be another matter). In fact, as it happens, his somewhat delirious pleasure directed at the danger results in precisely the same sort of chaotic behaviour we saw with poor old Regular Matt, with the result that the tiger is spoilt for choice. The point is that on the face of it there seems little reason to think that the emotion of *thrill* might not result in the same impulsive emotional action tendencies as *fear*, i.e. manifest a similar degree of urgency, partial informational access, and bodily underpinnings. And, insofar as it does, those who are greatly thrilled might, owing to their thrill, make equivalently bad decisions as Regular Matt does (owing to his fear). They might, that is, manifest *thrilled panic*. Of course, at the end of the escapade, stuck up the hopeless little tree, as it dawns on him that he has come a cropper, Inverse Matt's thrill may finally revert to fear. Nonetheless, until then it seems possible that his thrill could prompt the very same action tendencies as Regular Matt's fear.

But thrill is clearly not fear. In fact, they are diametrically opposed. On the Aristotelian view we have developed, fear involves experiencing *distress at* an (apparent) danger, whereas thrill involves experiencing *pleasure at* an (apparent) danger.[22] This suggests that Regular Matt's fear is not well captured by his action tendency. Rather, what distinguishes his emotion from Inverse Matt's is that he experiences distress at the danger whereas Inverse Matt experiences pleasure at it. Both emotions can then go on to *interact* with other desiderative dispositions of those who possess them and, in so doing, prompt action tendencies. In Regular Matt, his fear prompts the self-defeating action tendency Scarantino specified. In Inverse Matt, his thrill plays the same role. This is possible, on Aristotle's view, against the background of the two Matts' differing dispositional make-ups. As Aristotle would see it, then, the action tendencies that Scanantino highlights with Regular Matt are *products* of the emotionality of his fear, not that emotionality itself. And they are such products only against the background of his particular desiderative/dispositional make-up.

There is a further point to make here as well. As noted, the fact that Twin Matt *recognizes (i.e. judges) or perceives the very same danger* as the other Matts, but does not experience fear, seems hard to square with views which identify

---

[22] Contrast, e.g., Morreall (1985: 96–7), who conflates the two. What prompts such conflation, it seems to me, is the fact that fear and thrill share the same formal object (danger, or some such).

emotions with judgements or perceptual states. So too, though, the fact that Inverse Matt *experiences the same action tendencies* as Regular Matt, but does not experience fear, seems no less problematic for the Motivational theory. But, if Aristotle is right, someone could experience fear without experiencing the relational goal that Scarantino thinks essential for fear. Suppose we add a fourth Matt into the mix, Courageous Matt. Courageous Matt may, unlike Twin Matt (throughout) and Inverse Matt (until the end), experience distress directed at the danger of the tiger (given the prospect of injury or death). But, since he is courageous, Courageous Matt will be so disposed that in a situation such as this his fear will not motivate him to make all the foolish moves of the Regular and Inverse Matts. Indeed, if faced with no other alternative, Courageous Matt may grab a nearby chair and courageously attempt to drive back the tiger and thereby save others (perhaps the child that both Regular Matt and Inverse Matt trod on). Scarantino would say that Courageous Matt, like Twin Matt, does not feel fear (his distress does not incorporate the relational goal of fear). Aristotle would disagree. On his view, Courageous Matt could experience just as much distress at the danger posed by the tiger as Regular Matt—and so count as afraid—even though, given *his* dispositional background, he is not motivated to run away or flee (his fear would only prompt the latter if doing so would be consonant with what he judges he ought to do). And he is certainly not disposed to panic.

11.3 Which representational role(s) do emotions play?

In Part I of this book I examined Aristotle's account of the relation between emotions, on the one hand, and the intentional state that apprehends the object of the emotion, on the other, and argued that he thinks that the former is formed *in response to* the latter (and *in light of* it, rather than *caused by* it). In Part II I clarified the relation that he thinks holds between emotions and desires/motivations. This places us in a position to attempt to specify the representational role(s) that emotions *themselves* play, according to Aristotle's account, and to contrast his view with those of others. Again, Scarantino is helpful in addressing this question. He distinguishes between two such roles emotions could play (2014: 77):

(A) A *descriptive* role: Emotions represent what obtains.
(B) An *imperative* role: Emotions represent what needs to obtain.[23]

[23] The distinction between such representations is often couched in terms of different 'directions of fit' (see e.g. Platts 1979: 256–7; Searle 1983: 7–8; Humberstone 1992; Smith 1994: 115). Since I agree with Frost (2014) that this is ultimately a bogus notion, I have avoided using the terminology. Unlike directions of fit, distinguishing roles (A) and (B) does not posit a symmetry between the two roles; nor does it entail that there cannot be states that play both roles; nor that there cannot be other roles to play (as, indeed, I shall suggest below). (For an attempt to revive something sensible out of the notion of directions of fit, see Archer 2015.)

Which role(s) do emotions play according to various theories of emotions?

If emotions *just are* judgements or perceptual states, they would seem *themselves* only to play the first of these roles. A judgement or perception that one is in distressful imminent danger (cf. **3.4**, **3.6**) does not *itself* represent what *needs to* obtain. Nor does a judgement or perception that one has been slighted or that someone has suffered an undeserved misfortune. Emotions may well *prompt* the subject to form a state which plays such an imperative role, but they would not themselves be such states on these views.

By contrast, a theory that characterizes emotions *just* as action tendencies, without correlating those tendencies with the different emotions' formal objects, would claim that emotions only play the imperative role.

Scarantino thinks that both kinds of theory are inadequate. While the former accounts for the descriptive side, but fails with regard to the imperative side, the latter accounts for the imperative side, but needs 'to be supplemented' with a descriptive side (2014: 177):

> Suppose that fear is a prioritized avoidance tendency with the relational goal of achieving safety… This fact *per se* does not explain why fear is about dangers. (177)[24]

In this respect, as already flagged (**11.1**), although he calls his own theory 'The Motivational Theory of Emotions', his account is to be distinguished from views that simply identify emotions with desires or action tendencies (and so as *only* playing the prescriptive role). As Scarantino sees it, emotions 'do not merely represent relational goals', they 'also represent facts' (177). They play both roles.

Belief-desire cognitivists agree. On their view, emotions have a descriptive role insofar as they involve beliefs and a prescriptive role insofar as they involve desires. Emotions play these two roles, on this account, by virtue of having two different *components*: beliefs and desires.

As we have seen (**11.2**), Scarantino also rejects this view since it fails to explain how two people with the same beliefs and desires may differ emotionally. Instead, on his theory, emotions involve both the descriptive and prescriptive roles, but as a 'unified whole', rather than as distinct components. To achieve this dual role for them, he adopts a teleosemantic theory of representation and maintains that emotions both (i) represent facts 'by having the function of being elicited by them' and (ii) '*at the same time*' possess 'the function of achieving a certain relational goal' (2014: 178; Scarantino's emphasis).[25] On this view:

---

[24] This is Scarantino's (2014: 177) objection to Frijda's (1986, 2006) view.

[25] A teleosemantic notion of representation was also employed by Prinz to account for how emotions, construed as 'bodily perceptions' (2004: 60), nonetheless represent formal objects insofar as they are 'reliably caused by' and 'set up by' ('have the function of being caused by') 'relational properties that pertain to well-being' (66). Scarantino claims (2014: 178) that he accepts Prinz's

> fear is about dangers because it is a prioritized avoidance tendency/reflex with the informational-cum-motivational function of achieving the relational goal of one's own safety while correlating with dangers. Anger is about offenses because it is a prioritized attack tendency/reflex with the informational-cum-motivational function of achieving the relational goal of removing an obstacle while correlating with offences. (178)

My arguments against Scarantino's view in the last two sections have just focused on the idea that emotions essentially involve a prioritized action tendency. But clearly his account, as specified above, is going to have to defend the coherence of the idea that there can be intentional states that are at once both descriptive and prescriptive, and yet not further decomposable.[26]

Let me consider one further view before coming to Aristotle's. Like Scarantino, Deonna and Teroni (2012, 2014, 2015) link emotions to actions. But, as they see it, emotions themselves only play the descriptive role.[27] Emotions are 'states of felt action readiness' (2012: 81), where the bodily stances are 'felt bodily attitudes directed towards the world' (80). However:

> There is no sense in which feeling one's body poised to act towards a perceived object, i.e. the emotional attitude, aims at being fulfilled. (83)

Rather, emotions are 'evaluative stances or attitudes we take towards the world' (83). (On their view, emotions have cognitive 'bases' which supply the particular object of the emotion.) Furthermore, they think that emotions are 'correct' if the object they concern does in fact have the evaluative property they represent it as having (see 1.5n.41). For instance:

> Fear of the dog is an experience of the dog as dangerous, precisely because it consists in feeling the body's readiness to act so as to diminish the dog's likely impact on it (flight, preemptive attack, etc.), and this felt attitude is correct if and only if the dog is dangerous. Similarly, anger at someone is an experience of her as offensive, precisely because it consists in feeling the body's readiness to act so

---

'teleosemantic framework' for explaining how emotions represent facts, 'namely that they do so by having the function of being elicited by them', but that he 'supplements' it 'with the idea that emotions have *at the same time* the function of achieving a certain relational goal' (his emphasis). Prinz himself draws on the teleosemantic theory developed by Dretske (1981, 1986); see Prinz (2004: 52–5). For more on the general approach, see Schulte and Neander (2022).

[26] These would look like what Jimmy Altham (1986: 284) termed 'besires' or, in the perceptual variant, what we might call 'persires' (see my 2020: 40). Altham was characterizing McDowell (1978; see also e.g. McNaughton 1988: at e.g. 109; Little 1997; and Swartzer 2013). Some have suggested that Aristotle advances such states (without using the terminology); see e.g. Tuozzo (1994); Charles (2006, 2015); cf. also Moss (2012a: 45). I reject this in my 2020 (40–3 and appendix).

[27] Still using the language of direction of fit (see n.23 above), they claim emotions possess 'mind-to-world direction of fit' (Deonna and Teroni 2012: 83).

as to retaliate one way or another, and this felt attitude is correct if and only if the person is or has been offensive. (81)

Deonna and Teroni thereby identify emotions as *felt* states of action readiness, not action tendencies themselves. And because, on this view, the felt state of action readiness is correct only insofar as the object in the world it pertains to manifests the formal property constitutive of the emotion in question, they hold that emotions can be said to describe the world as manifesting that formal property. Thus, even though Deonna and Teroni's account essentially links emotions to action tendencies, emotions themselves, on their view, only play the descriptive role. In this respect, their theory is like the versions of Perceptualism and Judgementalism just mentioned, and unlike the others we have sketched.[28]

As I understand Aristotle, he thinks that, strictly speaking, emotions play *neither* of the two roles Scarantino identifies. They instead play what we might call a *reactive role*. They are *reactions* or *responses* to an intentional state that apprehends an object of emotion. If there is a state connected to emotions that plays the descriptive role, it will be the latter: the intentional state that apprehends the object of the emotion. However, even here I would resist Scarantino's claim that such a state must be purporting to provide a description of *what obtains*. That would seem to fail to make room for recalcitrant emotions (see Chapter 12) or our emotional responses to fiction (or our emotional responses to perceptual or thought-based *imaginations* more generally; see 3.5). Nonetheless, the intentional state that apprehends the object of the emotion will frequently be purporting to provide a description of what obtains. But emotions themselves, on Aristotle's view, are not such intentional states. Nor are they, as Deonna and Teroni claim, states that play a descriptive role by being attitudes of felt action readiness that map on to the apparent formal properties of emotions. On Aristotle's view, although emotions bear important relations to states that play a descriptive role (they are often, though not always, formed in light of them), they are not such states themselves. Instead, as we have seen, they are *responses* to such states; that is, are formed *in light of* them.

Equally, on Aristotle's view, emotions are not themselves states that play a prescriptive role. As we have also seen, they do bear interesting relations to states that play such a role. They may, for instance, be consequent upon a state that plays a prescriptive role being *satisfied* (relief, pride) or *thwarted* (regret). And, against the background of other desiderative dispositions of the subject, they may *prompt*

---

[28] Of course, the plausibility of their view will hinge on both the idea that emotions essentially involve a felt state of action readiness, and also on the notion that, insofar as they do, those felt states can be said to describe the world as manifesting the emotion in question's formal object. (With respect to the former, note how they have to deal with shame and admiration (2012: 81), and cp. my remarks on shame in **11.1**, and note also the other examples they themselves bring up, viz. pride (also considered in **11.1**) and regret. How does sadness manifest a felt action readiness?)

a state that plays a prescriptive role (e.g. fear may prompt a desire to flee). And they can form part of a complex state that has a prescriptive role (as with anger, for Aristotle). But they are not *themselves* states that play such a prescriptive role.

It is also worth noting that Aristotle's view that emotions are representational pleasures or distresses can more readily explain their prompting states with a prescriptive role than judgements or perceptions alone can (cf. Nussbaum 2001: 135–7). For the fact that we experience *distress* at an apparent danger more readily explains why we would want to avoid it than our simply registering a danger does (although, even on Aristotle's view, the desire does not necessarily follow, as we have seen with his analysis of courage). Someone who is not distressed by the danger, but still recognizes it (e.g. the tiger's handler), or someone who is thrilled by it, may be motivated differently (although, with the latter, once again, this need not be so; as our example of *thrilled panic* showed in 11.2). So too, we can more readily account for people being motivated to help another whom they judge has suffered some undeserved misfortune, if they experience *distress* directed at the other's misfortune (pity), rather than merely register that person's suffering (through belief or perception) or, indeed, experience *pleasure* directed at it (schadenfreude).

Given, then, that Aristotle holds that emotions themselves play neither a descriptive nor a prescriptive role, clearly they do not play both such roles together, whether by incorporating two different states as distinct components (as Belief-Desire Cognitivism maintains) or themselves being one incomposite but hybrid state (as Scarantino holds). They can, of course, be bound up with desires and, in cases such as anger, we may say that they are a component of a state that essentially includes a desire. But the emotion itself is not, even in part, the desire. Anger is an emotion insofar as it is a representational distress alone.

Thus, while they bear interesting relations to states that play descriptive and prescriptive roles, on Aristotle's view, emotions themselves play only (what we might call) a *reactive* role:

(C) A *reactive* role: Emotions are responses to (are formed in light of) intentional states that apprehend their objects.[29]

In playing such a role, emotions are distinct from states that apprehend their objects, on the one hand, and states that prompt actions in response to their existence, on the other. Instead, as hedonic responses, emotions will typically be

---

[29] Although I cannot argue the point here, I think it is plausible that *desire* also plays a reactive role. It, too, can be considered to be a response to an intentional state that has apprehended an intentional object—in its case, an object of desire (*orekton*) rather than an object of emotion (see esp. *NE* VII.6.1149a32–b1). Desire also, of course, plays a prescriptive role.

products of our formed characters (in the broad sense) (see **4.4**). In this way, and to this extent, emotions are indicative of *who we are*.[30]

Conclusion

In this chapter I have contrasted Aristotle's account of emotions—as representational pleasures or distresses alone—with a motivational account, according to which emotions essentially involve motivations or action tendencies. I first argued that Aristotle's view gives a better explanation of why many emotions do not seem to connect to desires or motivations in the way the Motivational theory of emotions proposes (**11.1**). I then showed that his view also gives a superior account of *acting emotionally* than the Motivational theory, which itself appeared to improve in just this respect on Belief-Desire Cognitivism (**11.2**). Finally, I addressed which representational role or roles emotions play according to various theories. In contrast to other accounts, Aristotle's view implies that emotions play neither a descriptive nor a prescriptive role (nor both), although they do bear interesting relations to intentional states that play these roles. Instead, emotions themselves play only what I termed a 'reactive' or 'responsive' role (**11.3**).

Aristotle on What Emotions Are. Giles Pearson, Oxford University Press. © Giles Pearson 2024.
DOI: 10.1093/9780191989292.003.0012

---

[30] Of course, character can already be involved in helping us to see certain things in a certain way. The extremely rich cake may not appear pleasurable to one possessing the virtue of temperance. But not all cases are like this. Two people can experience diametrically opposed emotions (pity, schadenfreude) in light of the same informational input—or so Aristotle holds (see Chapter 3 and **5.4–5**). My parenthetical 'broad sense' alludes to the fact that we can experience emotions that conflict with our character in some narrower sense (one which aligns with our preferential choices), as with akratic/enkratic agents. But here, too, there is a sense in which akratic agents' emotions are indicative of who they are: they are people who can form emotions that fly against their considered choices (see my 2012: 249–51). One might suggest that there are other states that can have a bearing on the occurrence of emotions without even forming part of our characters in this broad sense, e.g. tiredness or illness. But one might instead view these as trying circumstances which provide a more fine-grained discrimination of the character of the agent in question (contrast e.g. Doris 2002). I should also flag that in *EE* III.7 (1234a23–33) Aristotle allows that emotions, as 'natural', 'tend to natural virtues' (with 'each virtue found both naturally and also otherwise, viz. as including *phronesis*' (see also *NE* VI.13 *passim*)): 'envy contributes to injustice (for the acts arising from envy are aimed at others); righteous indignation contributes to justice; while shame (*aidōs*) contributes to temperance—which is why some even defined temperance under that heading'. This may give us a sense in which some of our basic emotional dispositions are innate (since natural virtues are states we are born with: *NE* VI.13.1144b1–8).

12
Explaining Recalcitrant Emotions with Aristotle

In this chapter I examine a significant philosophical advantage of Aristotle's view, namely, its ability to provide a plausible explanation of recalcitrant emotions. As a first approximation, these are emotions that persist in the light of a conflicting judgement. The challenge posed by such emotions is, first, to explain their existence and, second, to explain their irrationality (to the extent that such emotions are irrational). As noted in **Intro.2**, in the contemporary literature there has been a debate concerning whether emotions are best thought of as (in part) identical to a certain kind of belief or judgement, or instead as (in part) identical to, or essentially involving, perceptual states (or perceptual construals), or, as a third option, as (in part) identical to a certain kind of quasi-judgement, such as, passive assent or inclination to assent.[1] And a key bone of contention (a touchstone, if you like) for all such views has been their implications for our understanding of recalcitrant emotions. I begin this chapter (**12.1–3**) by showing that each of these views fails to account for either the existence of recalcitrant emotions or their irrationality (or both). I next (**12.4**) highlight an alternative view, according to which objects of emotions can be apprehended by a variety of intentional states and do not demand agential assent.[2] I argue that while such a view has a significant advantage over other accounts with respect to accounting for the *existence* of recalcitrant emotions, it too, on its own, cannot account for their irrationality. I next (**12.5**) address the idea that the irrationality of recalcitrant emotions (when they are irrational) should be characterized as a kind of *practical* or *motivational* irrationality. I show how Aristotle's account of the relation between desires and emotions (as developed in Part II) helps reveal the limitations of such an approach. I then (**12.6**) argue that the further features of Aristotle's account of emotions developed in this book—viz. that they are hedonic states that are formed *in response to* intentional states that apprehend their objects—can explain the irrationality of recalcitrant emotions (when they are irrational).[3] I close (**12.7**)

---

[1] For (i) references to some who advance such views, (ii) the 'in part' here, and (iii) different uses of the terminology, see **Intro.2nn.19–20**.

[2] I ascribed this view to Aristotle in my 2014a and have a significantly revised and expanded development of the idea in my MS.

[3] *Taken together*, then, the two dimensions of my reading of Aristotle's account of emotions (in my 2014a/MS—as per last note—and in this book) provide him with the ability to explain not just the existence of recalcitrant emotions, but also their irrationality (when they are irrationality). The

by considering emotions that are irrational *by warrant* and show that recalcitrant emotions, when they are irrational, are just one kind of emotion that fall into this more general class. This last section will also reveal why, and when, recalcitrant emotions *need not* be irrational.

Here are two examples of recalcitrant emotions, with different emotion-types.[4] First, take a well-discussed case in the literature, originally by Patricia Greenspan:

> After a violent attack by a rabid dog...I find myself with a persistent fear of *all* dogs, even toothless old Fido, the loveable pet of a friend of mine, whose harmlessness I am sure of. When Fido approaches, my heart beats wildly, I feel an urge to flee, and perhaps I even find myself thinking: 'Fido is going to bite me!' I would deny, though, that I really believe this. (1980: 162)[5]

For ease of reference, let us refer to this as 'Pat's fear'. Second, take a case of recalcitrant anger. Suppose Jimmy gets angry with Chris—a work colleague—because he believes Chris has slighted him. Jimmy thinks that Chris has cracked some joke implying that Jimmy's performance on some important administrative task was poor. But then imagine that Jimmy finds out that Chris was not slighting him at all—the joke was not directed at his putative poor performance, but at the impossibility of the task set by the administrators. Nonetheless, suppose that Jimmy cannot stop himself imagining Chris' inanely grinning face as indicative of Chris slighting him, and Jimmy's anger does not abate, or not entirely, even though he now readily accepts that Chris did not in fact slight him. Let us refer to this as 'Jimmy's anger'.[6]

---

flexibility in the intentional state that apprehends the object of emotion will allow him to explain the existence of the different kinds of recalcitrant emotion that seem possible. And the idea that they are hedonic responses to such intentional state, not simply those intentional states themselves, will enable him to explain their irrationality (when they are irrational). If this is correct, it is no small indication that his account, so understood, is worthy of our attention. My discussion should be construed as considering what Aristotle's account of emotions, as developed, implies for our understanding of the emotions. He did not himself explicitly address the problem such emotions pose. Did he even acknowledge the phenomenon? That might depend on how we interpret certain examples. See esp. *De an.* I.1.403a22–4, discussed in Chapter 9 Appendix 2, and e.g. *MA* 11.703b6–8; *NE* IV.5.1126a9–11; *EE* VII.2.1235b26–9; *Pol.* VII.1.1323a29–30; *Rhet.* II.3.1380b10–14. See also, Rapp (2002: 565); Moss (2012a: 106–7); Dow (2015: 219–22).

[4] Keeping two different examples in mind, with different emotions, will help us avoid any bias pertaining to the fact that the emotion that is most frequently discussed in the literature is fear.

[5] See also her 1981 and 1988 (17–18).

[6] I have tried to give an example of anger that would fit Aristotle's account of *orgē* (see Chapter 6). For a simpler case, consider the following. Suppose I am in a rush to get to work and need a shirt from the dryer I had set going before heading to bed. I run to the dryer and discover that shortly after I had left it to get on with what it does best, the blankety-blank appliance had put up a firm *nolle prosequi* and switched itself off. Much-needed shirt is still soaking wet. I become filled with rage, level some of the fruitier expletives I know in its direction, shake my fist, and even contemplate laying a hefty boot on the blighter. At the same time, I know full well, of course, that it does not have intentional states, and did not fail deliberately. I do not *really*, that is, believe it tried to thwart me. Cf. Chrysippus (*SVF* III.478). For another emotion, consider Rawls' (1972: 482) case of a person raised in a strict religious

12.1 Judgementalism and recalcitrant emotions

The judgements that judgementalists hold are involved in emotions will typically be to the effect that the evaluative (formal) object of the emotion is instantiated in some particular circumstance; e.g. that the dog is dangerous or that one has been offended. It has often been argued that judgementalism faces significant difficulties explaining the *existence* of recalcitrant emotions.[7] Although I think this is correct, it is important to specify precisely what the problem is. Judgementalism is committed to the view that Pat's fear necessarily incorporates the judgement that Fido is dangerous and Jimmy's anger the judgement that Chris offended him. But, as we have seen, Pat and Jimmy also consciously judge that the opposite is the case. It seems, then, that judgementalism is committed to claiming that recalcitrant emotions involve agents holding contradictory beliefs (that Fido is and is not dangerous; that Chris did and did not intend offence). Now, judgementalists might insist that this is in fact a *merit* of their view insofar as it enables us to account for the *irrationality* of recalcitrant emotions. Holding contradictory beliefs would look to be irrational and so if recalcitrant emotions are themselves irrational, they could be such insofar as they are an instance of the former.[8] Let us formulate not holding contradictory beliefs as a principle of rationality. Believing *p* and not-*p* looks to be a case of *inconsistency*. Accordingly, we might try to postulate a consistency principle for beliefs as a requirement of rationality:

Consistency principle: Rationality requires of you (whichever person you are) that you do not, at the same time, both judge that *p* and judge that not-*p*.[9]

---

sect who has been taught that going to the theatre is wrong, and still feels guilty attending the theatre even though he no longer believes this (although, as it happens, Rawls denies, on motivational grounds, that such a subject has 'proper feelings of guilt').

[7] See e.g. Greenspan (1980, 1981, 1988: e.g. 17–19); Helm (2001: 41-6); D'Arms and Jacobson (2003: 129); Brady (2007: 274, 2009: 414–15); Deonna and Teroni (2012: 54–5); Benbaji (2013: 579).

[8] See Grzankowski (2017). See also Naar (2020); Majeed (2022); and cf. Benbaji (2013: 579). The falsity of judgementalism sometimes seems to be inferred from the mere fact that it is committed to claiming that recalcitrant emotions involve contradictory beliefs (e.g. Goldie 2009: 236–7; Deonna and Teroni 2012: 54–5). Others note that in ascribing incoherence to the subject, the judgementalist imputes 'too much irrationality' (Helm 2001: 45; Brady 2007: 274, 2009: 414; Grzankowski 2017). But we need to be more precise still, I think. (Grzankowski (2017: 644) goes on to propose that it must instead be an underlying assumption of the objection to judgementalism that recalcitrant emotions *do not* make the agent irrational. This seems to me to be a mistake. It is that the agent is not *that* irrational, or that the irrationality is not accounted for in terms of contradiction. Agents are irrational *insofar* as they have recalcitrant emotions (at least insofar as those conflict with a rationally held judgement; see 12.7.)

[9] We might want something stronger than this for a general account of rationality (see, e.g., the waverer example in n.11 below). But for the cases we are interested in, it will do. Döring's (2015: 387) formulation—'Rationality requires of you (whatever person you are) that you do not both judge that *p* and judge that not-*p'*—is *too* strong. Suppose a long time ago I believed *p* but then gradually came to realize that *p* is false and now believe not-*p*. I would flout Döring's principle, but surely need not be irrational. We minimally need to build in some kind of temporal restriction. Döring is drawing from Broome, but the latter does include such a restriction (e.g. 2013a: 154–6).

Since, according to judgementalism, Pat and James flout this principle, they will count as irrational.

It is worth emphasizing, though, that the judgementalist cannot straightforwardly infer from the fact that Pat and Jimmy flout the Consistency principle that they possess irrational *emotions*. For simply violating that principle does not as such prioritize or impute one of the pair of judgements (which only together generate the violation) over the other. As far as the principle goes, it could be the belief that conflicts with the emotion that is the source of the inconsistency and irrationality. So if the recalcitrant emotion is itself to be shown to be the source of the agent's irrationality, and so irrational itself, the judgementalist will have to tell a story about why, in the cases in question, we think that it is the judgement required by the emotion (e.g. that the dog is dangerous) that makes the subject flout the Consistency principle.[10]

Be that as it may, the charge against judgementalism is not that in ascribing contradictory beliefs to the subject, it cannot give an account of the irrationality of recalcitrant emotions. The charge is that it cannot explain the *existence* of such emotions in the first place. In effect, the objection is that it does not seem plausible in the sorts of case we have in mind that those possessing the emotion *judge* that things are the way their emotion represents them. This is because such agents are both *conscious* of their emotion and the way it represents things—and so must therefore be conscious of the judgement the emotion (putatively) is or involves—and yet *at no point do they accept* that things are as their emotion represents them. On the contrary, they *flatly reject* that they take things to be the way their emotion represents them. Thus, since the emotion and the judgement that conflicts with it occur *at the very same time*, and since we cannot in this case attribute to the subject a subconscious or unconscious belief to explain the situation (for the subject is all too aware of the emotion and the way it represents things), it becomes hard to see how the emotion could itself be or involve a belief or judgement.[11]

Of course, we may grant that *sometimes* we misrepresent our own take on the world (perhaps, e.g., we might think that we believe something that we are

---

[10] Note, we are trying to explain *recalcitrant* emotions, not just any irrational emotion. The judgementalist could allow that some emotions are irrational simply because they involve a subject forming a judgement that the subject does not have good evidence for (even if it seems perfectly reasonable to the subject). But, in the cases we are interested in (i.e. recalcitrant emotions), the agent must see the emotion as causing the problem and in some sense *reject* it. See **12.7**.

[11] The fact that the emotion and the conflicting judgement take place at the same time blocks the idea that the subject is *wavering* between p and not-p (see Nussbaum 2001: 86; cf. Benbaji 2013: 579 on a 'vacillator' who alternates between beliefs 'but at no time holds both'). And the fact that the agent is conscious of the emotion blocks the idea that the belief is sub- or unconscious (some judgementalists have appealed to such beliefs to explain emotions that would otherwise be problematic—typically supplemented with explanations for why the agent holds the belief, e.g. habit/upbringing (Nussbaum 1999: 814, 2001: 35–6, 233–4), wishful-thinking (cf. Helm 2015: 426), or trauma. As Benbaji notes (2013: 579): 'we may uphold contradictory judgments, provided they are kept distinct in our mind'. But in the cases at hand they are not. (On the possibility of unconscious emotions, see Deonna and Teroni 2012: 16–17, and for further references, 2012: 27).

actually more sceptical of). But to make the above charge stick against judgementalism, we need not commit to the view that all our beliefs are transparent to us. The problem is that judgementalism seems committed to claiming that *in spite of* the way things appear to them, such subjects must in fact either (i) believe that things are as the emotion represents them, or (ii) not really experience the emotion after all, or else (iii) have an emotion that does not actually contradict their other judgement.[12] But while we can accept that in *some* cases one or the other of these might be in play, it is not clear what could justify the claim that *every* putative case must be such, other than, that is, a prior assumption that judgementalism is true.[13] Note, too, as Greenspan points out (1988: 19), attributing a judgement in line with the emotion does not seem consonant with the subject's other behaviour: Pat is not prone to warn others that Fido might kill *even at the very point* she is supposedly in the grip of the belief.[14] And she can be firm in the belief that contradicts the emotion, use it in reasoning, appeal to it at other times, and so on. Subjects of such recalcitrant emotions do not typically experience themselves as believing *p* and not-*p*. They experience themselves as having emotions that they repudiate. And while they may, on occasion, be mistaken in such self-attributions, it is the universality of the judgementalist's claim that makes their view implausible: according to judgementalism, insofar as such subjects would categorically reject that they believe the situation is as their emotion represents it, they must *always* be mistaken.[15]

12.2 Perceptualism and recalcitrant emotions

Perceptualist theories insist that the object of an emotion is apprehended by something analogous to sense-perception. We need the 'analogous', here, because on the view under consideration emotions are not *literally* sense-perceptions.

---

[12] For (i): perhaps, in some variants, Jimmy may not quite be able to shake off the belief that Chris slighted him. Or he may temporarily lose sight of the fact that Chris did not really slight him (cf. Price 2011: 119n.16; Moss 2012a: 132). For (ii): perhaps Jimmy only *imagines* he is angry with Chris, but is not really angry. For (iii): perhaps one of the beliefs may have a displaced object. Jimmy might think that he is angry with Chris about the insult, but really his negative emotion is about Chris' views on a subject they fundamentally disagree about (cf. de Sousa 1987: 177; Helm 2015: 425–6). Or perhaps one of the beliefs is conditional on certain evidence, whereas the other is an all-out unconditional judgement (cf. Davidson 1980: 37–41; Benbaji 2013: 587ff.).

[13] Cf. Grzankowski (2017: 647ff.). Also note that the judgementalist cannot appeal to the idea that recalcitrant emotions must involve hasty or dogmatic judgements. Pat can fear even the thought of going next door when she is calmly sat down at home telling herself that her fear is ridiculous. (Cf. Benbaji's response (2013: 579) to Nussbaum's appeal to *habit* to explain recalcitrant emotions.)

[14] Perhaps it might be said that her belief is non-universalizable: the neighbours *own* the dog and she knows they are treated differently by it. But suppose she went to the house with someone else unknown to the dog, again there seems little reason to think that she would warn the other. She repudiates the emotion.

[15] See also Grzankowski (2017: 650).

Sense-perceptions have corresponding sense-organs (transducers), but the suggestion is not that there is a dedicated emotion organ. It is that emotions are analogous to sense-perceptions.[16] We might say, on this view, that objects of emotions are apprehended by *perceptual* states. And, as with judgementalist views, perceptualist theories typically claim that the perceptual states in question apprehend the particular object of the emotion under the guise of its evaluative (or formal) object.

It is widely thought that perceptualism fares rather better than judgementalism in explaining the *existence* of recalcitrant emotions (although see below).[17] For perceptual states *can* persist in the light of conflicting judgements. As perceptualists note, this is one respect in which we *are* able to press the analogy with sense-perception.[18] In the Müller-Lyer illusion, perceiving the lines as of different lengths can happily persist in light of one's judging that they are the same length.[19] So too, perceptualists argue, insofar as emotions are, or essentially involve, perceptual states, they can persist in light of a conflicting judgement. With our examples, they might propose that Fido perceptually *appears* dangerous to Pat, even though she believes he is actually a harmless old softy, and Jimmy perceptually construes Chris as having slighted him, even though he believes Chris did no such thing.[20]

---

[16] See e.g. de Sousa (1987: 149); Döring (2007: 376; 2014: 130); Tappolet (2012: e.g. 214–15); cf. Brady (2009: 415). See also e.g. Brady (2013: 46–52) and Helm (2015: 418–20) on the parallels between emotions and sense-perceptions. I am here concerned with what Deonna and Teroni (2012: ch. 6) call 'direct' perceptualist theories (e.g. Roberts 1988, 1996, 2003; Tappolet 2000, 2016; Döring 2007, 2009a, 2009b, 2014), rather than the 'indirect' perceptualist theory of esp. Prinz (2004), which links perceptions of bodily states to an emotion's formal object via a teleosemantic theory of representation (see 11.3n.25). For resistance to direct perceptualist theories, see e.g. Salmela (2011); Brady (2013: ch. 3); and Helm (2015).

[17] Indeed, in this respect contemporary perceptualists have appealed to recalcitrant emotions to support their view; see e.g. Roberts (1988, 2003: 89–91); Tappolet (2003: 109–10, 2012: esp. 210); Döring (2014, 2015). As indicative, see Tappolet (2003: 109–10) where that 'the evaluative content of an emotion is of the same kind as the content of perceptual experiences' (i.e. non-conceptual) is 'suggested by the fact that emotions are to a large extent isolated from our higher-order cognitive processes and thus from our deliberative faculty. *As we all know, it is possible to experience fear while judging that what one is afraid of is not dangerous*' (my emphasis). Recalcitrance is taken to justify isolation from higher-order cognitive processes, which is taken to justify the perceptual analogy. So too Tappolet (2012: 210): 'Emotional recalcitrance actually directly militates in favor of the perceptualist account…'. Cf. also her 2009: 328–9.

[18] See e.g. Döring (2007: 379–80, 2009a: 243–4, 2014: 132); Tappolet (2012: 210).

[19] Aristotle appeals to a similar case to distinguish *phantasia* from belief. The sun appears about a foot across, even though we believe it to be bigger than the known world (*De an.* III.3.428b2–4; cf. *Insomn.* 2.460b18–22). Plato gives another example: something appears crooked when seen passing through water even though we know it is really straight (*Republic* X.602c10-11).

[20] Depending on how we describe him, one might wonder whether one could sensibly perceptually construe Fido as dangerous. Greenspan called him 'toothless' (1980: 162). In reply, the perceptualist may point out, first, that a minimal condition for fear is viewing something under the guise of its formal object. Hence if danger is the formal object of fear, and Pat fears Fido, she must view Fido as dangerous in some respect. Perceptualists might also stress, second, that they are only committed to the perceptual *analogy*. Perceptual states are not restrained in the way sense-perceptions are. Pat's perceptual construals can run out of kilter with her actual sense-perceptions. Perhaps she could even fear a Fido stuffed by an amateur taxidermist? (But if one is struggling to understand Pat's fear, simply

This (putative) advantage concerning the existence of recalcitrant emotions notwithstanding, there is nonetheless a well-rehearsed objection to perceptualism pertaining to these self-same emotions. This concerns its ability to account for their *irrationality*.[21] The parallel with sense-perception is again instructive. No one is inclined, I take it, to claim that it is *irrational* to see the lines in the Müller-Lyer illusion as having unequal lengths even though we believe they are the same length. It is not as if we think that were we to count as fully rational, we should train ourselves to *stop* seeing the lines as of unequal length—the sensory experience is just how things perceptually appear to us.[22] Analogously, then, why, according to perceptualism, should it be *irrational* for Fido to appear perceptually dangerous to Pat, even though she rationally believes otherwise? That is just the way Fido appears to her and is perfectly compatible with her contrary belief.

Of course, with both perceptual illusions and recalcitrant emotions, subjects may experience internal conflict to the extent that their perceptual reports provide information that contradicts their beliefs (lines as (un)equal; Fido as (not) dangerous). But, in fact, given perceptualism, in *neither* case do subjects contradict themselves; for perceiving that *p* does not contradict believing that not-*p*. To see this, consider converting the perceptual appearance into a belief. 'I believe that Fido *appears* dangerous' does not contradict 'I believe that Fido is not dangerous'. One can simultaneously hold both beliefs without flouting the Consistency principle. Things *can* in fact appear dangerous without being dangerous, and so one can simultaneously believe they appear dangerous while also believing they are not.[23] Similarly, something can perceptually appear dangerous to you, without that contradicting your belief that it is not dangerous.[24] Now, doubtless perceptualists will view this as a merit of their theory. Positing a

---

replace it with a different case. A snake may appear dangerous—its writhing reptilian skin slithers across the floor, its tongue flashes in and out, its orange eyes are fixed on you—but you at the same time believe it harmless—the handler is present and stresses it is non-venomous and can only digest things about the size of a small mouse or vole.)

[21] At least going back to Helm (2001: 41–6). See also Brady (2007, 2009); Dow (2009: 147); cf. Döring (2007, 2009a, 2009b, 2014, 2015). As noted, I do not think that recalcitrant emotions must be irrational, but the point would apply to those cases in which they are. In particular, such emotions are irrational so long as the belief they conflict with is itself rationally formed. See 12.7.

[22] Not to *see*, but if we acted in accordance with a perceptual illusion, the act would be. See Döring's (2015: 391) example, replying to Helm (2015: 422), of acting on a mirage. This is relevant for the practical irrationality idea we consider in 12.5. As Döring points out (2009a: 246), we are sometimes able to recalibrate our sense-perceptions with our beliefs, as with seeing one's train move at a station when in fact it is a close-by train moving.

[23] I am not suggesting that the belief that something appears a certain way and it perceptually appearing a certain way are the same or equivalent. Perhaps one could believe that something does not appear dangerous but still perceptually construe it as dangerous. But the manoeuvre does show that the perception of *p* and the belief that not-*p* do not contradict each other.

[24] Another parallel is with Moore's paradox. While something seems wrong with 'I believe that *p*, but not-*p*' ('I believe the lines are the same length, but they are not the same length'), the perceptual variant, 'I perceive that *p*, but not-*p*', seems fine ('I perceive the lines as different lengths, but in fact they are the same length'). The underlying point is that we have different intentional attitudes directed at the contradictory content in question, and this means that the attitude + content combinations do

contradiction in such cases was, after all, what caused trouble for judgementalism. But if, according to perceptualism, subjects do not violate the Consistency principle in having a recalcitrant emotion, we are owed an explanation of why they are *irrational* in having such an emotion (when it conflicts with their rationally held beliefs). And if the *subject* is not irrational in having a recalcitrant emotion, how can that emotion *itself* be irrational? We can hardly claim that the emotion is irrational insofar as it makes the agent irrational, if the subject is not irrational in the first place.

And yet—so the objection runs—we *do think* that recalcitrant emotions are irrational (when they conflict with our rationally held beliefs).[25] Pat firmly believes that Fido is a toothless old fluff ball, and yet nonetheless fears him. That seems irrational. So too, Jimmy believes—quite rationally—that Chris did not insult him and so his anger seems unwarranted or irrational. There thus seems to be an important *disanalogy* between sensory illusions and recalcitrant emotions at just this juncture. While seeing the lines in the Müller-Lyer illusion look different lengths does not seem irrational even in light of one's contrary judgement, fearing Fido *does* seem irrational insofar as it conflicts with one's rationally held judgement that he is harmless.[26] Although there is 'conflict' (so construed) in both sensory illusions and recalcitrant emotions, the conflict involved in the latter seems to be of a different kind. Recalcitrant emotions seem to be states for which the subject can rightly be criticized (see Helm 2015: 420-1). And yet if perceptualism were true, why should this be so? Why should it be any more *irrational* for Pat to fear Fido than to see the lines in the illusion look different lengths? While perceptualism might seem able to account for the *existence* of recalcitrant emotions, it seems unable to account for their *irrationality*.[27]

We can generally see two sorts of reply by perceptualists in the literature. Some (e.g. Roberts 2003: 92) point to putative *practical* differences between emotions and sense-perceptions and claim that it is these that explain the irrationality of the former in contrast to the latter. Others (Döring 2014, 2015) have argued that perceptualism cannot account for the irrationality of recalcitrant emotions, but

---

not represent contradictory states of affairs. Hence Döring talks of 'conflict without contradiction' (2007: 380, 2009a: *passim*, 2009b: 292-4, 2014: 132-4).

[25] As noted, I shall later argue (12.7) that recalcitrant emotions *need not* be irrational, but even when they are, there is a further question: are *subjects* necessarily irrational in having such an emotion? Clearly, if they *act on* the emotion, their *action* would be irrational, but what if they resist it? Is *Pat* irrational simply for having an irrational recalcitrant fear? I think we *do* want to say this. *She* should not have the emotion. If recalcitrant emotions are not necessarily irrational, a subject's possessing a recalcitrant emotion does not entail that she is irrational. But possessing *an irrational* recalcitrant emotion does.

[26] Some things might naturally be thought of as having a dangerous *appearance*, e.g. a hissing snake (see n.20 above). We may then say they *warrant* being seen as dangerous. Perhaps. But this would not make it rational to fear the snake if one knows full well that it is harmless.

[27] Of course, perceptualists who maintain that emotions are perceptual states + something else could try to account for the irrationality of such emotions by appealing to the 'something else'.

that that is no defect of perceptualism. For, on this view, in spite of the way it may appear, recalcitrant emotions are *never* in fact irrational in the first place.[28]

I shall tackle both these responses in 12.5. But, for now, let us return briefly to whether perceptualism really can account for the *existence* of all cases of recalcitrant emotions. In fact, this too may be questionable. For, like judgementalism, it also places a restriction on the sorts of recalcitrant emotions that are possible which we may find implausible. First, since according to perceptualism objects of emotions are *only ever* apprehended by perceptual states, the view rules out cases in which the object of the emotion is apprehended by *thought*. But could not Pat's fear sometimes pertain to Fido as represented by thought, rather than a perceptual state? Uncommitted thoughts, no less than perceptual states, can clearly co-exist with beliefs or judgements to the contrary. So, could not a recalcitrant fear of flying, for example, just centre on thoughts connected to the prospect of being a mile above the ground in a machine that could potentially fail, rather than anything especially *perceptual* about the scenario (e.g. visualizing a plane crash). Of course, there may frequently be perceptual dimensions to envisaged scenarios, but why *must* there be if the subject is to have an emotion? Why *cannot* the emotion be about its object *just insofar as* it is represented by thought, rather than perception?

Second, the intentional attitude of 'perception' may itself implausibly rule out some cases. As we have seen, unlike judgementalists, perceptualists do not hold that possessing an emotion implies that *the subject* must assent that things are as the emotion represents them. Nonetheless, on their view, a perception of *p* does imply that *perception itself* presents the object specified by *p* as obtaining (under the relevant intentional description). Roberts (1988: 191) originally emphasized this by claiming that emotions are '*verisimilar*' perceptual construals, in the sense that 'in the emotion the situation looks to the subject as if it is actually as he is construing it' (2003: 92).[29] Döring attempted to capture the point by noting that the 'subsystem' of perception generates the *appearance of truth* (2007: 378–9, 2009a: 245). So although the subject may know full well that the object perceived

---

[28] Tappolet (2012) seems to want a third option (as well as the practical option). On her view, the irrationality accusation indicates two things. (i) '[T]hat something *ought* to be done to improve the reliability of that emotional system' (219; her emphasis). This is a practical claim (and a questionable one to infer on the basis of recalcitrant emotions—see 12.5; also Döring (2014: 126–30). (ii) '[T]hat something is wrong with the system that is responsible for the emotional reaction' (219). She suggests that emotions are more 'plastic' than sense-perceptions and so there is 'good reason to subject emotions to rational requirements and to consider inaccurate emotions not just inaccurate but also irrational' (219). In reply, we might ask why their plasticity (the fact that it may be possible for us to do more about them (cognitive therapy, drugs, etc.) makes recalcitrant emotions, as such, irrational? What requirement of rationality is the emotion as such flouting? (Further, as Helm (2015: 421–2) notes, we can also shape or reshape some sense-perceptions: 'my mishearing the trumpet as a violin involves perceptual capacities that can be refined, such that I can be criticized for the lack of refinement in my hearing'. Cf. Döring 2009a: 246.)

[29] He later (2003: 92) dropped the term, but not the idea: he takes the very same point to be included in his notion of 'construal'.

is not, in fact, as it is perceived (as with recalcitrant emotions), it is still nonetheless the case, on this view, that perception *presents it* as obtaining. However, is such a perceptual appearance always required for emotions? Contrast Fido with *Snarler*, a dog who snarls and froths at the mouth whenever he sees strangers, but who is ultimately harmless (having a condition a bit like a doggy version of Tourette's syndrome).[30] We can readily make sense of Pat's perception of Snarler as dangerous as having the appearance of truth, even though she judges that, like Fido, he is in fact a harmless old fluff ball. But *what about Fido*? Fido does not, it seems, even perceptually appear dangerous (Greenspan described him as 'toothless' (1980: 162)). So how can perceptualists explain this case? They do not, I think, have to deny that such cases are possible (cf. **12.2n.20**). For, as we noted, their view is that objects of emotions must be apprehended by percept*ual* states, not literal sense-perceptions. Pat can have a perceptual appearance or construal of Fido as dangerous (chasing her up the garden and trying to bite her, or some such) even if he can only ever actually be *seen*, toothless, curled up in his basket.[31] Nonetheless, the perceptualist maintains that if such a perceptual state is to underlie Pat's recalcitrant emotion, it must remain an appearance-as-truth. On this view, even in cases of recalcitrance, i.e. where she judges otherwise, if she is to fear Fido, Pat must in some sense be unable to prevent herself from perceptually construing the toothless old mutt as a serious threat. But the problem is that on the surface this still rules out cases of recalcitrant emotions that seem possible. Why *cannot* Pat fear Fido (the dog as she takes him to be) on the basis of her perceptual (or, indeed, thought-based) *imaginations* about him, without her in any sense experiencing those as appearances-as-true? Suppose Pat sees toothless, flea-bitten old Fido placidly curled up in his basket, looking more like he is on his last legs than a hound of the Baskervilles. But suppose, in spite of this, Pat finds herself *imagining* Fido with gnashing teeth, chasing her round the garden. This may not affect her perceptual construal of Fido as she encounters him. Her imagining him this way is quite compatible with her continuing to have an appearance-as-truth of Fido as harmless (toothless, placid, etc.)—it need not, that is, involve her suffering from some kind of perceptual delusion. But could she not, on the basis of her perceptual imagination, nonetheless fear Fido? If so, in such a case, it would be Fido *as imagined*, not Fido *as perceptually construed* (appearance-as-truth), that serves as the basis for her recalcitrant fear. On what ground could perceptualists rule out this possibility? After all, on their view, we can fear Fido on the basis of a perceptual construal of him (appearance-as-truth)

---

[30] It does not matter if this example is remotely plausible—we could replace it with one in which we have a *person* who *does have* Tourette's.
[31] Relatedly, as Döring notes, you may 'lie awake at night, fearing that your boss will fire you, and your emotion may be an affective perception without this requiring that your boss is standing in front of you in your bedroom' (2007: 378).

in spite of the fact that we do not assent that he is that way. So why cannot a perceptual imagination serve just as well? In both cases, Pat's fear will be irrational insofar as it conflicts with her rationally held judgement that Fido is harmless. So how can the perceptualist reasonably restrict the ways in which subjects can be irrational? There are a lot of ways to go wrong! In effect, the issue here is that in committing to the idea that emotions essentially involve appearances-as-truth, perceptualists make assent of at least the *subsystem* of perception a requirement for emotion. But given that we are considering emotions that conflict with our rational judgements, why should even assent of this subsystem be required? Indeed, in line with this, we may well think that the strongest indicator that it is not is provided by our emotional responses to fiction. If we can form genuine (or 'literal') emotions in response to fictional scenarios while knowing they are fictional, emotions cannot require an appearance-as-truth.[32]

12.3 Quasi-judgementalism and recalcitrant emotions

In light of the fact that judgementalists seem unable to account for the existence of (at least some) recalcitrant emotions, while perceptualists seem unable to account for their irrationality, some philosophers have sought a middle route that does both. Bennet Helm, for instance, argued against judgementalism on the ground that 'conflicts between emotions and judgments do not verge on incoherence, for they are readily intelligible and happen all the time' (2001: 42).[33] But he also resisted what he called 'anti-judgmentalism', namely, views which deny that emotions as such involve 'assents'.[34] Although anti-judgementalists escape assimilating conflicts between emotions and judgements to incoherence, it is nonetheless unclear, Helm suggests, that 'they are thereby able to provide a proper understanding of the resulting irrationality' (42). For if emotions do not involve assent, 'in what sense are they in rational conflict with judgment?' (43). Thus, while judgementalists falsely conclude that emotions are judgements of a certain kind, anti-judgementalists stray too far in the opposite direction and falsely conclude that emotions do not require assent at all. On Helm's view, in each case 'the conclusion presupposes the implicit premise that all assent is judgmental' (43) and '[t]he way out is to deny this premise':

---

[32] Of course, some will deny the antecedent here; e.g. Walton (1978, 1990: 195–204, 1997). A parallel difference between perceptual states and perceptual imaginations is present between belief and thought-based imaginations. That perception is an appearance-as-truth obviously makes it ripe for providing material for belief and knowledge, but note that perceptual (imagination) may also be able to do this in various ways; cf. Gendler and Liao (2019: §3.6).

[33] Here he is consciously following Greenspan (1980, 1981, 1988).

[34] He intends 'anti-judgmentalism' to pick out a broader category than 'perceptualism', including, e.g., Greenspan's view that the cognitive attitude involved in emotions is propositional *thought*.

emotions must be understood as a kind of assent if we are to make sense of rational conflict with judgment at all, but not a kind that can be reduced to judgment if we are to make sense of that conflict as something other than incoherence. (43)

We thus have a clearly articulated attempt to find a middle route between judgementalism and perceptualism. Helm himself went on to argue that emotions are 'passive assents' (2001, 2002, 2009, 2015), while another quasi-judgementalist, Michael Brady, instead claims they are 'inclinations to assent' (2009).[35]

The question we must raise is whether such quasi-judgementalist views really can steer a course between the Scylla of judgementalism and the Charybdis of perceptualism.[36] In characterizing emotions as 'passive assents' Helm means that they are 'states of consciousness that for the most part come over us in a way very much like that of perception, without our having to do anything more than (passively) be receptive to them' (2001: 66).[37] But I believe that for our purposes we can bypass assessing the plausibility of this idea or considering whether it generates a sharp enough contrast with judgement (cf. Roberts 2003: 92). This is because passive assents are still *assents*. Helm thus still holds that emotions involve assenting that things are a certain way. And by 'assent', here, he means *agential assent*, not merely the assent of what Döring calls a 'subsystem' (Döring 2009a: 245, 2009b: 293), e.g. perception. He means, that is—as is required for him to distinguish his view from perceptualism—assent of the subject 'as a whole', rather than merely 'a part' of her (as Dow 2015: 199 puts it).[38] Indeed, Helm is

---

[35] Brady (2007, 2009) also appeals to practical differences. See **12.5n.56** below.
[36] Grzankowski (2020: 509) refers to this as a search for a 'Goldilocks' attitude.
[37] Helm also thinks that emotions are 'disclosive' (rather than 'cognitive') assents (2001: 143–4). Basically, the idea is that whether a vase, say, has value to me is not independent of me in the way that whether a cat is sat on the mat is. If the vase has value (or disvalue) for me, any emotional response I have to it will rationally commit me to other emotional responses and, in this way, emotions are 'disclosive of import': 'the import of the object is both made intelligible by the pattern of assents to import and itself acting as a standard of warrant for these assents' (144). If, e.g., I *fear* that my vase is about to be destroyed, I should, rationally, feel *relief* if it somehow escapes this, or *sadness* (or *horror*) if the worst happens. Again, if we experience a positive emotion to something good that has happened, we rationally ought to experience a corresponding negative emotion if what had happened was instead something bad (68). Emotions thereby involve a kind of commitment and 'are not isolated mental states', but possess 'rational connections to other mental states, including other emotions' (67). (See also his 2002: 17 on commitment.) Now, clearly, even ordinary judgements rationally commit me to other responses. If I believe that the cat is on the mat, I ought rationally to suppose that she is not on the bed. Helm might reply that such a belief will my not disclose my values in the way an emotion does. But that is just because it is not an *evaluative* judgement. Indeed, Helm himself goes on to argue (2001: ch. 5) that evaluative judgements also have disclosive assent, no less than emotions, and he is surely right. If I judge that my vase is amazing, I ought also to judge that its needless destruction is horrendous. So this feature of Helm's view does not distinguish it from the idea that emotions are evaluative judgements.
[38] Cf. Döring: 'we treat our emotions and perceptions as cognitive mental subsystems whose function is to register stimuli so as to provide us with information about our environment' (2009a: 245; after Jones 2003). While perceptual experience has 'the appearance of truth' (2009a: 245), the 'crucial difference to judgement and belief is that, in regarding our emotions and perceptions as generally

explicit on this front when he criticizes Roberts' view (see the latter's 2003: 92–3) that emotions (as construals) involve assent only of 'part of the person' but not the 'whole person' (so too Döring maintains that in recalcitrant emotions '*the subject* does not contradict himself' (2009b: 292; my emphasis)). Helm complains that such a view 'does not make sense of the idea that it is *the agent—the whole person*—who is irrational when the repudiated emotion persists, and not merely the emotion itself' (2001: 45n.17; my emphasis).[39] But then whether the 'assents' in question are passive or active, recalcitrant emotions involve subjects—as a whole—both assenting to *p* and not-*p*. They do not, let us grant, flout the Consistency principle, as that was stated in 12.1, since that principle was formulated in terms of judgements. But they do flout a closely related principle, formulated in terms of assent:

Consistency principle2: Rationality requires of you (whichever person you are) that you do not, at the same time, both assent that *p* and assent that not-*p*.

Now I suspect Helm will not be unhappy with this result. It is, of course, for this reason that he believes his account avoids the pitfalls of perceptualism. For it entails that with recalcitrant emotions we have genuine rational conflict with a judgement.

But the problem is that in insisting that the subject of a recalcitrant emotion flouts Consistency principle2, Helm faces the same problem the judgementalist faced, viz. explaining the existence of all putative cases of recalcitrant emotions. On this view, Pat both assents, as a whole, that Fido is a dangerous killing machine (via the passive assent that underlies her emotion) and assents, as a whole, that Fido is a non-dangerous old fluff ball (with her judgement). So too, Jimmy both assents, as a whole, that Chris slighted him (via a passive assent) and assents, as a whole, that Chris did not slight him (via belief or judgement). But when spelt out this way, it is easy to see that assigning one part of the source of the contradiction to passive assent (rather than, as with Judgementalism, both parts to judgements) does not alter the fact that the account views subjects (as a whole) contradicting themselves. And the problem is that this is not how subjects experience the matter in the cases under review. On Helm's reading, Pat must assent as a whole (not

---

reliable cognitive *systems*, we do not regard the content of each particular *element* of the system as true. This privilege is reserved for the elements of the system of judgment and belief' (2009a: 246; her emphases). See also Roberts: 'what the emotion "says" is not always agreed to by the subject of the emotion, and it is *that* agreement that would be required for the emotion to be a judgment *by the subject*' (1999: 795; his emphases). Cp. Helm (2001: 45n.17).

[39] Cf. also his analysis of the motivational consequences of emotions against the perceptualist view: 'That my fear...persists in motivating me, despite the repudiation, indicates that it not merely presents me with the appearance of danger but that I in some sense continue to assent to the presence of that danger; otherwise, I can have no reason, not even a bad one (as the repudiation would suggest), to be motivated in this way' (2001: 44).

merely with a subsystem or part of her) that Fido is a dangerous killing machine, and Jimmy must assent as a whole that Chris slighted him. But this is not so. Pat knows full well that Fido is a harmless old fluff ball and Jimmy knows full well that Chris did not really slight him. It is just that Pat still fears Fido and Jimmy still experiences anger at Chris regardless. Granted, Helm claims that the emotional affirmation is a form of passive assent, not the active assent of belief or judgement. But what sort of assent is in play seems irrelevant: Pat simply *does not* experience herself *assenting*, as a whole, that Fido is a canine version of Harold Shipman—full stop. She *does not accept that she—as a whole—assents to the view that Fido is dangerous*. She wholeheartedly rejects this. Helm's account thus strays too close to judgementalism.[40]

Brady's account suffers from a related defect. On his view, emotions are 'inclinations to assent' (the agent 'leans towards', 'is subject to some kind of pressure to accept', 'is tempted by', 'is moved to endorse' the evaluative judgement or construal (2009: 420–1)). And recalcitrant emotions come out as irrational because 'it is epistemically irrational to be inclined to assent to something that one has determined to be false' (428).[41] But, as I see it, Pat is quite at liberty to maintain that she feels *no* inclination to assent to the judgement that Fido is dangerous. So too, Jimmy need not be 'tempted' to think that Chris really did slight him. And I see no reason to insist that their protestations *must* be mistaken.[42]

Granted, we can imagine cases where it does seem as though the agent may be inclined to assent to the way the emotion presents matters. Reconsider *Snarler* (12.2), who snarls and froths at the mouth when he sees strangers, but is ultimately harmless. Here we might both accept that the dog is not dangerous and yet nonetheless feel an inclination to accept that he is. However, as the examples of Pat and Jimmy show, not all cases of recalcitrant emotions involve this feature. In fact, the example of Snarler points to a further problem with Brady's view.

---

[40] Cf. Benbaji (2013: 585–6). Note too, as Brady pointed out (2009: 420), it is far from clear that Pat's fear retains the commitment to other emotional states that Helm thinks important in such evaluative feelings. Given that she does not believe that Fido is dangerous, is Pat rationally required to feel relief when he fails to bite her? (But see Benbaji 2013: 586–7 on this objection.) Note, there may well be cases where the conflict is not as severe as it is with Pat's fear and Jimmy's anger (cf. Helm 2015: 430; his example of Joe may be such). But the issue is what Helm's account is committed to saying in *our* cases. For further objections to Helm from the perceptualist viewpoint, see e.g. Döring (2007: 381n.16, 2009a: 245, 2014: 394f.).

[41] Brady also notes (2009: 428) that such agents are emotionally inclined to accept the situation they judge to be false even though they are aware there are *no good reasons* to accept this construal. This concerns *how* a recalcitrant emotion inclines us to believe (i.e. on the basis of no good reason), not merely *what* it inclines us to believe (i.e. something false). This difference is irrelevant for what I go on to say. Brady's third way in which recalcitrant emotions are irrational—viz. that they 'incline' one to invent reasons in support of the emotional construal—is clearly a highly contingent matter. Brady (427) also points to aspects of practical irrationality with recalcitrant emotions. I consider those in 12.5.

[42] Indeed, even by Brady's own lights (see last note), Pat and Jimmy may accept that there are 'no good reasons' to endorse the way the emotion presents things. But then in what sense does the emotion *incline* them to accept things are otherwise? On the basis of a reason they themselves view as *bad*?

Suppose we have a recalcitrant fear when encountering Snarler. The *irrationality* of this fear could not stem from it inclining one to assent to the view that Snarler is dangerous. For, surely, on the basis of Snarler's frothing at the mouth, growling, barking, and grinding his teeth, *it would be rational* to be *inclined* to assent that Snarler is dangerous, even if one knows otherwise. Those features of Snarler look like pretty good reasons—to me at any rate—to be at least *inclined* to assent that Snarler is dangerous.[43] Rather, the irrationality of a recalcitrant fear of Snarler would have to pertain to the fact that such a fear conflicts with one's rationally held judgement to the effect that, appearances to the contrary, Snarler is really just a big softy.

In short, with some examples, such as those of Pat and Jimmy, Brady's proposal fails to admit the full range of cases we seek to explain. In this respect, it has a parallel fault to judgementalism. With other examples, such as Snarler, it fails to account for the irrationality of the emotion that the subject experiences. In this respect, it suffers from a parallel flaw to perceptualism. Once again, it seems, safe passage through the Scylla and Charybdis has eluded us.[44]

12.4 A view that allows that objects of emotions can be apprehended by a variety of intentional states

In my 2014a I argued, against many interpretations of his view, and in contrast to all the views just discussed, that Aristotle holds that objects of emotions can be apprehended by a variety of intentional states (belief, perception, *phantasia*, uncommitted thought, perceptual imaginations) and hence that neither agential assent, nor even the assent of a subsystem, is necessary for emotions.[45] The details of that argument are not relevant here, but the resulting position is. For such a view clearly has the capacity to explain the *existence* of the recalcitrant emotions that the accounts we have considered cannot.

---

[43] Interestingly, this suggests that if Pat felt inclined to accept that Fido was dangerous, such an inclination would be irrational: there are no parallel perceptual cues that suggest that Fido is dangerous. But that does not mean that her emotion involves such an inclination. As far as she is concerned, she feels no such inclination. This just goes to show that being inclined to accept, in such cases, is independent of the irrationality of the emotion.

[44] For further considerations about the 'inclination to accept' aspect of Brady's view, see e.g. Tappolet (2012: 218–19); Döring (2014: 128); and Helm (2015: 423–4).

[45] I develop these views more extensively and systematically in my MS. Parallel to the contemporary accounts of emotions, some have held judgementalist readings of Aristotle (e.g. Nussbaum 1994; Frede 1996; Leighton 1996; Knuuttila 2004; and Dow 2009) others perceptualist accounts (e.g. Cooper 1996; Sihvola 1996; Striker 1996; Achtenberg 2002: ch. 6; Nieuwenburg 2002), and still others what I call 'quasi-perceptualist' accounts (Price 2009, 2011; Moss 2012a; Dow 2014, 2015). ('Quasi-perceptualist' insofar as they hold (in slightly different ways) that Aristotle thinks that the capacity with which we apprehend objects of emotions is a perceptual state (as with perceptualist readings), but that agential assent is also required (as with judgementalist readings).

If objects of emotions can be apprehended by intentional states that do not require agential assent, we can admit the cases of recalcitrance that judgementalists and quasi-judgementalists could not account for. For, on such a view, neither the Consistency principle nor Consistency principle2 must be violated with recalcitrant emotions. Pat may reasonably avow that in no sense does she assent 'as a whole' that Fido is dangerous. Equally, if emotions can be about their objects just insofar as those objects are represented by (uncommitted) thoughts or perceptual imaginations, we can admit the cases perceptualists could not. Pat may experience fear but still sincerely avow that in no sense does it even *appear-as-truth* to her that Fido is dangerous (as when her emotion is a response to perceptually imagining Fido as dangerous, without this appearing-as-truth to her).

But while such a view seems to fare better with accounting for the existence of the various kinds of recalcitrant emotion that seem possible, it may seem no better than perceptualism with explaining their irrationality. Indeed, it may appear worse still. For, in order to account for the existence of the above cases of recalcitrance, the view in question embraces not only the idea that *agential* assent is not required for undergoing an emotion (which allows it to admit the cases judgementalists and Helm's quasi-judgementalist view cannot), but also the notion that assent *of a subsystem* is not requisite (which allows it to admit the cases perceptualists cannot). But, as we saw when considering perceptualism, if agential assent is not required with recalcitrant emotions, it is hard to see why there is rational conflict between the emotion and the judgement. Subjects can, quite rationally, believe that something is a certain way and it appear (through, e.g., perception) to them that it is another. And the same issue applies *a fortiori* if assent *of a subsystem* is not even required in recalcitrant emotions (if, that is, we can form emotions in response to perceptual imaginations or uncommitted thoughts). How can there be rational conflict between recalcitrant emotions and judgements in cases in which the object of the emotion does not even *appear-as-truth* to the subject?

It seems, then, that in avoiding the Scylla—accounting for the existence of the cases of recalcitrant emotions that other views could not—the approach in question nonetheless ends up lost to the Charybdis—failing to account for their irrationality.

12.5 Practical irrationality and recalcitrant emotions

At the end of **12.2** I noted that faced with the difficulty of accounting for the irrationality of recalcitrant emotions, some perceptualists point to practical differences between emotions and sense-perceptions, and insist that it is these that explain the irrationality of the former, in contrast to the latter. On this approach, we should accept that there is no theoretical irrationality with recalcitrant emotions—and so agree that seeing Fido as dangerous is *itself* no more irrational than seeing the stick bend as it enters the water—but nonetheless maintain that recalcitrant emotions count as irrational insofar as they involve us in *practical irrationality*. One key idea here is that recalcitrant emotions have a connection to motivation and action that is lacking in sensory illusions. Robert Roberts writes:

> The [phobic's] fear has a personal depth and life-disrupting motivational power that the illusion lacks. The bent stick is, at most, puzzling; the fear is personally compelling. (2003: 92)[46]

Similarly, Döring (2014) suggests that the intuition that recalcitrant emotions are irrational, whereas sensory illusions are not, is due to the fact that:

> recalcitrant emotions interfere to a much greater extent with the reasoned pursuit of our goals than recalcitrant perceptions because, by contrast with perceptions, emotions have *motivational force*...Emotions continue to move us to act even after we have rejected their content. I may reject my fear of falling as unwarranted, and yet be moved to give in to it...Because of their motivational force, recalcitrant emotions cannot easily be kept from interfering with the reasoned pursuit of our goals. (128, her emphasis; see also 135)

She does point out that perceptual illusions can also interfere with our goals:

> Perceptual illusion due to refraction need not be an obstacle to achieving your goals in the bent-stick-in-water-illusion, but in trying to catch a fish with your bare hands it will certainly be. (128)

'Nonetheless', she maintains, 'the crucial difference between emotions and perceptions is that only the former motivate action' (129). The thought seems to be that we must first possess the goal of trying to catch the fish before the refraction of the water will prove problematic, whereas emotions themselves motivate action and so provide us with goals on their own. Thus, when those goals conflict with our reasoned aims, the emotion can itself be thought of as interfering.[47]

---

[46] Roberts goes on: 'This means that when the subject dissociates from his fear by denying its propositional content, it is like denying a part of himself, whereas denying his visual impression [as in optical illusions] is not' (92). But, as others have noted, it is not obvious why recalcitrant emotions must be considered a part of oneself or, insofar as they do, that there need be anything irrational in denying such a part (cf. a drug addict) (see Benbaji 2013: 584; Brady 2009: 418). Roberts adds another idea which I think may have more merit—I quote this below (**12.6n.66**).

[47] Cf. de Sousa and Scarantino (2018: §7.1): 'there clearly is some measure of irrationality involved in recalcitrant emotions: unlike perceptual illusions, they motivate us to act'. Contrast Helm (2001: 43-4). As we shall see, Döring will go on to argue that we should not think of the emotion itself as irrational in such cases, but only the actions we perform owing to them.

Now in Part II I argued that Aristotle thinks that emotions themselves—as representational pleasures or distresses—only motivate us against a background of other desiderative dispositions we possess (although they can also be embedded in states that also contain a desire, as with anger). But let us bracket that for now and just work with the idea that emotions link to desires/motivations in some important way. Given this, perhaps we could say that insofar as recalcitrant emotions motivate us in ways that conflict with our rational aims, they are practically irrational?

Akratic action—where we are motivated to pursue a goal we judge we should not—is typically taken to be practically irrational (although see 12.7). So perhaps we could view recalcitrant emotions as irrational along the lines of *akrasia*? Let us follow Döring (2015: 389)[48] and try to state what goes wrong in akratic action as a principle of rationality:

Enkratic[49] **principle**: Rationality requires of you (whichever person you are) that if you rationally believe at *t* that you yourself ought to φ at *t*, then you intend to φ at *t*.[50]

Susan flouts this principle if, for example, in spite of rationally believing that she should go for a gruelling 5-mile jog in the rain after work, she fails to intend to do this.[51] Applied to recalcitrant emotions, the idea would be that they motivate actions that are contrary to our reasoned aims and so prompt us to flout this principle.

Döring (2014: 129, 2015) raises a problem with this idea. She claims that, strictly speaking, 'it is the *actions* caused by recalcitrant emotions which are irrational insofar as they interfere with the reasoned pursuit of our goals...not the *emotions themselves*' (2014: 129, her emphases; see also 135). And we can see what she might have in mind. Insofar as emotions involve or lead to desires or motivations, they can be said to prompt us to intend to act, but it is the intending to act itself that flouts the Enkratic principle, not what prompts such intending.

---

[48] Döring is herself following Broome (2010: 290, see also 2013a: e.g. 22–5 and esp. §9.5, and 2013b).

[49] *Pace* Döring and Broome, I will not refer to 'the principle of *enkrasia*' as an equivalent. There is no such Greek word—it should be *enkrateia*. Broome has been made aware of this (2013a: 30n.25) but claims he wishes to invent his own term to avoid the connotation which *enkrateia* has of mastery over temptation. But insofar as 'the principle of *enkrateia*' would have that connotation, so too would 'the Enkratic Condition' (which Broome is happy to use; 2013a: 88). And using '*enkrasia*' will, for Classical scholars at least, jar more than the original misleading connotation.

[50] Döring and Broome do not have the 'rationally' before 'believe'. I address this in 12.7. The principle I cite is elliptical for a longer version in Broome which is intended to rule out a series of other loopholes (see 2010: 290, 2013a: 170–2, 2013b).

[51] The purpose of linking the principle to intending rather than simply to action is that if Susan did form the intention to go on the gruelling 5-mile jog, but was then somehow prevented from doing so—she became trapped in a lift, perhaps—she would not count as flouting the principle.

Susan flouts the principle insofar as despite rationally believing that she should go for the gruelling 5-mile jog, she fails to intend to do that. Similarly, Alan flouts the principle insofar as despite rationally believing that he ought not smoke, he intentionally does so.[52] Perhaps emotions prompt such intendings or failures of intending. But, strictly speaking, it is not the emotion that prompts the intending that flouts the principle, and so is irrational, but the (intending) to act, or failing to, itself.

In conjunction with the idea, discussed in 12.1, that (some) recalcitrant emotions do not flout the Consistency principle, Döring takes this to imply that there is *no* sense in which (such) recalcitrant emotions themselves count as irrational. But this seems too quick. A version of Pat who has to fight against a desire or motivation to run away from Fido seems irrational, not just the Pat who gives into the desire and forms the intention to run away. Similarly, a version of Jimmy who has to fight against his desire to poke Chris on the snout seems irrational, no less than the Jimmy who actually does so poke Chris (or forms the intention to). While emotions themselves do not flout the Enkratic principle, there still seems to be something wrong with those who *strongly desire* or *are motivated to* run away from Fido, even if they resist the desire or motivation stemming from their emotion and do not intend accordingly, and so do not flout the principle. Fido is entirely harmless and they know it. This suggests we need another principle of rationality to capture that. Consider:

Motivation principle: Rationality requires of you (whichever person you are) that if you rationally believe at t that you yourself ought not to φ at t, then you should not be motivated to φ at t.

Consider Mr Tempted, who is tempted to start smoking, even though he judges he should not smoke. Suppose Mr Tempted forms some quite strong desire/motivation to give smoking a go, but nonetheless resists it because he judges he should not smoke. Mr Tempted is rational according to the Enkratic principle because he has resisted his desire/motivation to act against what he judges he ought to do. But he comes out as irrational by the lights of the Motivation principle, since he is motivated to do something that he judges he should not. This seems the right result.

---

[52] It matters how we understand 'motivation' here. If we take it to amount to 'intending to act' and emotions (can) involve motivations, then emotions can flout the Enkratic principle. So, to capture 'Alan can be motivated to smoke but not intend to (insofar as he resists his motivation)', we need a weaker notion of 'motivation'. But, equally, if 'motivation' can extend to any trivial desire or whim, the principle becomes absurdly strong. A passing whim to try a cigarette will make me irrational if I judge I should never smoke. We need something in between. Perhaps: a motivation is something that would lead to intending to act in the absence of a restraining belief, or some such? At any rate, in the examples I provide, I give motivations with the right degree of strength.

But now consider Ms Quitter, who is trying to give up smoking. Ms Quitter is doing very well. She experiences many desires to smoke, but so far has resisted the lot. She therefore does not flout the Enkratic principle (having not formed the intention to smoke). But she seems to flout the Motivation principle, for she rationally judges that she ought not to smoke and yet nonetheless finds herself motivated to smoke. But do we want to say that Ms Quitter's motivation to smoke is practically *irrational*? This would seem rather harsh, for the motivation seems to occur as a *consequence* of her *sticking to* what she rationally judges she ought to do. But perhaps we can accommodate this intuition if we revise the Motivation principle slightly:

Pointless Motivation principle: Rationality requires of you (whichever person you are) that if you rationally believe at t that you yourself ought not to φ at t, then you should not be motivated to φ at t, unless your being so motivated is rationally acceptable to you as a side-effect of your not φ-ing.

Mr Tempted still comes out as practically irrational by this principle, since (we may presume) he does not see any further purpose served by his being motivated to try smoking.[53] The motivation is, then, an unacceptable side-effect of sticking to his belief.[54] Ms Quitter, by contrast, now comes out as practically rational, since her being motivated to smoke is rationally acceptable to her as a side-effect of her sticking to her goal of quitting. The Pointless Motivation principle also seems to give the right answer with the variants of Pat and Jimmy mentioned above. For we can assume that Pat does not see her being motivated to flee Fido as an acceptable side-effect of her rationally believing that he is not dangerous (and so nothing to flee from) and that Jimmy does not see his being motivated to poke Chris on the snout as a rationally acceptable side-effect of his rationally judging that Chris has not in fact slighted him (and so does not warrant having his snout poked).

So can the Pointless Motivation principle account for the intuition that recalcitrant emotions—at least of this kind, not as in Ms Quitter—are irrational? Not for Aristotle, on my reading, and for a similar reason that Döring gave for thinking that recalcitrant emotions are not shown irrational by reference to the Enkratic principle. For, as we saw in Part II, he separates emotions from any desires or motivations they might lead to. Emotions *just are* representational pleasures or distress. Hence, it would not be the *emotions* themselves that would be irrational

---

[53] If he did, it *may* perhaps be rational for him to smoke. Suppose he rationally believes that it is only by trying smoking that he will be able to stop himself having the desire to smoke. Or suppose his curiosity starts to overwhelm him to such an extent that unless he tries smoking, even if only once, it could consume his whole life.

[54] Which of course does not mean that he should revise his belief to escape the charge of irrationality. See **12.7**.

insofar as they prompted motivations that led someone to flout the Pointless Motivation principle. It would just be the motivations themselves. On Aristotle's view, the irrationality of Pat's *fear* cannot be accounted for by its motivational properties, since fear *itself* does not have motivational properties (at least, not in the sense in which, as in *Rhet.* II.5, it is just a representational distress, i.e. qualifies as an emotion; see 7.3). It might *lead to* a motivation, given some background conditions, but it itself is not a motivation. With anger, of course, the situation is different, since on his view anger does essentially involve a desire/motivation. However, on my reading, Aristotle does not think that it does so *qua* emotion. Qua emotion, anger is a distress at an apparent slight and so is not itself a motivation either. Thus, it could only be *being motivated in light of* a recalcitrant *emotion* that is irrational, not the emotion itself. Hence, if emotions are not themselves, even in part, desires or motivations then since the Pointless Motivation principle only speaks for motivations, it cannot account for the irrationality of recalcitrant emotions.

However, the Pointless Motivation principle *does* look like it could account for the irrationality of recalcitrant instances of states such as anger, i.e. states that do essentially involve a desire or motivation, *at least with respect to their desire/motivation*. For insofar as possessing such a state would involve the agent flouting the Pointless Motivation principle, it would look to be irrational. Since, on Aristotle's view, Jimmy will not count as being angry with Chris unless he desires revenge, the Pointless Motivation principle could account for why Jimmy's recalcitrant anger, at least *qua* desire/motivation, is irrational. Even though Jimmy does not believe that Chris has slighted him, and so does not see poking Chris on the snout as warranted, and even though he does not see any further end to be served by so poking, Jimmy's recalcitrant anger, insofar as it itself includes the desire/motivation to poke, will come out as irrational.[55]

But, on my view, this just serves to highlight how, if we are seeking to account for the intuition that recalcitrant emotions are irrational insofar as they conflict with a rationally held judgement, appealing to practical irrationality is somewhat of a red herring (cp. my 2014a: 202–3). That thought could plausibly only account for the irrationality of all cases of recalcitrant emotions if (a) all recalcitrant emotions essentially involve desires/motivations and (b) recalcitrant emotions are only irrational just insofar as, and to the extent that, they themselves involve such motivations. Concerning (a), in the last chapter I gave grounds for resisting the idea that emotions themselves involve desires/motivations. However, and more crucially, even if (some) emotions could involve motivations, why think that (b) would be true in any event? Do we not still think that there is something wrong with a version of Pat who, though not motivated to run away from Fido, still nonetheless experiences

---

[55] Cf. Gaut's proposal that an emotion will count as irrational 'if it motivates action, though its subject lacks motivation-relevant beliefs' (2007: 223).

distress directed at the prospect of Fido harming her (while knowing full well that he cannot)? Similarly, although anger essentially involves a desire for Aristotle, it also involves an emotion, a representational distress. And, regardless as to the desire/motivation, do we not think that there is something wrong with Jimmy insofar as he experiences *distress directed at* Chris' having slighted him (while knowing full well that Chris has done no such thing)? Insofar as fear and anger involve such representational distresses, they would seem to be subject to rational criticism, independently of any motivational aspect they may (or may not) possess. The challenge to explain recalcitrant emotions remains.[56]

12.6 Hedonic irrationality and the response view of emotions

Aristotle, I have argued, would, strictly speaking, deny that *emotions* can flout the Pointless Motivation principle and be irrational insofar as they do. For, on his view, emotions themselves are not, even in part, motivations. And, indeed, I think we do want to say that Pat's emotional response to Fido would be irrational even if she was not motivated to flee him. The fact that she finds herself distressed at the danger that Fido poses, even though she knows full well that he is completely harmless, seems enough. Focusing on possible links between recalcitrant emotions and practical irrationality has, I think, actually made us lose sight of the sort of cases we were originally trying to account for. They were not ones where we had an emotion that conflicted with a judgement *that we should not do something*. They were ones where we had an emotion that conflicted with a judgement *that the evaluative property of the emotion did not obtain*. Pat was afraid of Fido in spite of rationally believing him to be harmless. Jimmy was angry with Chris in spite of rationally believing that Chris had not slighted him. Can we explain how Pat's recalcitrant fear and Jimmy's recalcitrant distress at Chris' slight are

---

[56] Even those who hold that emotions can themselves involve motivations might claim that not all emotions are such and that some of the latter can be recalcitrant (e.g. a recalcitrant sadness or pride). Equally, with motivation-involving emotions, they may claim that a recalcitrant emotion need not (only) be irrational *qua* its motivation, but (may also) be so (say) *qua* the agent being upset. My objection to invoking practical differences to account for the irrationality of recalcitrant emotions might not apply to Brady's (2007, 2009) appeal to the idea that emotions involve 'persistence of attention' which 'functions to enhance the subject's perception of emotional stimuli' (2007: 281) to explain how recalcitrant emotions are irrational insofar as they are a 'waste of limited resources' (2009: 427). But that view has other problems, not least that it cannot be sufficient to make a recalcitrant emotion irrational since we can waste limited resources without being irrational. Cf. Helm (2015: 423): 'Sometimes we have excess attentional resources and we may then seek out opportunities to use them up rather than be bored, as when I watch a rerun of a banal TV show I have already seen. It seems Brady must say either that such "wastes" are just as irrational as in the case of recalcitrant emotions or that it would be rationally permissible to experience recalcitrant emotions when I'm otherwise bored. Surely neither of these is right'. For further objections to the practical side of Brady's view, see Tappolet (2012: 216–18) and Benbaji (2013: 584).

irrational, even without reference to any motivations these emotions may or may not prompt (or, on some views, involve)?

Let us take a step back. Consider the following:

[A] The rationality of fear of X, where X is rationally believed to exist, requires one to believe, rationally, that X is dangerous.[57]

[A] itself seems unobjectionable. If one's fear of X (where X is something that one rationally believes to exist) is to be rational, one must rationally believe that X is dangerous. But let us consider how different accounts of the emotions would gloss 'fear of X' in [A]? Judgementalism would gloss 'fear of X' (or at least 'fear of X *qua* judgement'—to allow in Dual-component views) in [A] as:

[B] The rationality of believing X is dangerous [= fear of X], where X is rationally believed to exist, requires one to believe, rationally, that X is dangerous.

[B] looks like a trivial truth. Recalcitrant emotions will come out as irrational, according to [B], when the subject experiences the fear, but does not (rationally) believe that X is dangerous. Pat simply does not believe that Fido is dangerous, hence her fear of him cannot be rational. However, as we saw in **12.1**, the problem with judgementalism is that it cannot explain the *existence* of Pat's fear. For, on this view, Pat's fear itself involves her believing that Fido is dangerous. And yet Pat would adamantly deny that she believes that Fido is dangerous and, in at least some cases, we have little reason to doubt her. She can know full well that the old sausage is harmless, but still fear him.

Helm's quasi-judgementalist view, as discussed in **12.3**, fails for a similar reason. On his view, 'fear of X', in [A], would be glossed with 'passive assent that X is dangerous':

[C] The rationality of passive assent that X is dangerous [= fear of X], where X is rationally believed to exist, requires one to believe, rationally, that X is dangerous.

While not a trivial truth, [C] is nonetheless plausible. As we saw, on Helm's view, 'passive assent' involves the subject assenting, as a whole, that something is so and so. Accordingly, it would seem reasonable to suggest that for such assent to be rational, the subject must rationally believe that X is dangerous. If Pat rationally believes that Fido is not in any way dangerous, it is hard to see how it could

---

[57] I adapt this formulation, with changes, from the first half of Gaut's 2007 criterion (220). It is important that the belief itself is rationally held (whether or not it is correct). If you irrationally believe, e.g., that someone is following you, fearing on that basis would also be irrational. See **12.7**.

nonetheless be rational for her to assent passively, as a whole, that he is in fact dangerous. But then this view fails for the same reason as judgementalism: it cannot explain the *existence* of Pat's fear. For, on this view, Pat's fear itself involves her passively assenting, as a whole, that Fido is dangerous. And yet Pat would adamantly deny that she, as a whole, assents, passively or otherwise, that Fido is dangerous. And, in at least some cases, we have little reason to doubt her.

Brady's quasi-judgementalist suffers from a parallel defect. As we saw (**12.3**), he thinks that emotions are 'inclinations to assent'. But Pat need not even be *inclined* to assent that Fido is dangerous either. She can know full well that he is harmless, and feel no such inclination, but fear him regardless. Brady's account is thus also unable to account for the existence of the full range of recalcitrant emotions. But his view may suffer from a further defect. According to it, [A] should be glossed as:

[D] The rationality of being inclined to assent that X is dangerous [= fear of X], where X is rationally believed to exist, requires one to believe, rationally, that X is dangerous.

But this version of [A] looks as though it could be false. Recall Snarler (**12.3**), who barks, growls, grinds his teeth, froths at the mouth, and snarls at strangers, but is in fact completely harmless. It would seem highly demanding to insist that if one is to be rationally *inclined* to assent that Snarler is dangerous, one must rationally believe that he is in fact dangerous. His appearance of being dangerous, one might think, could make it rational to be *inclined* to assent that he is dangerous, even if one rationally believes he is not.

As we saw (**12.2**), perceptualist views have more success in accounting for the existence of some of the recalcitrant emotions the above views struggled with. We can perceive something as dangerous without believing it to be dangerous. Furthermore, perceptualists can point out that in order for fear to be attributable to Pat at all, she must apprehend Fido under the guise of fear's formal object. And since Pat does not believe that Fido is dangerous, her *perceiving him as dangerous* is a possible option. However, as we also saw (**12.2**), perceptualism's problem is that it cannot explain the *irrationality* of Pat's fear. According to it, [A] should be glossed as:

[E] The rationality of perceiving X as dangerous [= fear of X], where X is rationally believed to exist, requires one to believe, rationally, that X is dangerous.

But even more clearly than [D], [E] looks false. For why should it be a condition on the rationality of *perceiving* something as dangerous that one rationally *believes* it dangerous? Whether or not one is inclined to assent that Snarler is dangerous, it is hard to deny that *he appears* dangerous. And surely many would *perceive* Snarler as dangerous even after knowing full well that he is just as harmless as toothless old Fido. But equally, if we do not let such a perceptual state affect our beliefs, it would seem very harsh to charge us with irrationality simply because we continue to perceive him this way despite rationally believing him harmless. Indeed, in some sense, the perceptual cues *warrant* perceiving Snarler as dangerous even though we believe otherwise. He *looks* dangerous.[58] Similarly, the perceptual cues in the Müller-Lyer illusion seem to warrant *seeing* the lines as of unequal length even when one believes they are not—that is how the lines *look* to well-functioning eyes. Of course, there may be a difference between these two kinds of case. The Müller-Lyer illusion only concerns our sensory apparatus, whereas with perceptualist theories of emotions 'perception' is treated as only analogous to sense-perception (see 12.2). And perhaps this difference means that in light of the rationally held belief that Snarler is not dangerous, it may be *possible* to construe him perceptually as harmless.[59] Let us grant this, for the sake of argument. Nonetheless, just as we do not demand that once we believe that the lines in the Müller-Lyer illusion are of equal lengths, we must, on pain of irrationality, *see* them as having the same length, so too, I suggest, we would not demand that once we rationally believe that Snarler is harmless, we must, on pain of irrationality, cease to perceive him as dangerous—*even if* such a perception were possible. That would surely set the bar of rationality too high. At some level, after all, Snarler *does* look dangerous. Indeed, it is not even clear to me that it would be epistemically *desirable* in such cases to cease to perceive the dog as dangerous since, as we shall see in the next section, the perceptual cues could be necessary for one to overturn a belief whose warrant is beginning to be called into question. At any rate, if it is not rationally required to stop perceiving Snarler as dangerous even though one rationally believes that he is harmless, the rationality of perceiving that X is dangerous cannot require that one rationally believe that X is dangerous. So [E] is false and cannot be a correct gloss of [A].

With Fido, of course, the perceptual cues do not point in the direction of his being dangerous. But if [E] is false, perceiving him as dangerous cannot be irrational *owing to the fact* that one also rationally believes that he is not dangerous. So why think of perceiving him as dangerous as irrational at all? As we saw in 12.2, such a perception does not *contradict* the belief. Granted, we may be surprised that Pat perceives Fido as dangerous despite believing him harmless. And, given his manifest perceptible features, we might even marvel at how she can do this.

---

[58] So too, it may seem perceptually warranted (or at least not unwarranted) to perceive Fido as harmless, even if one were to believe, contrary to his appearance, that he is actually *lethal*. 'He does not *look* lethal', we might say in justifying our perception.

[59] Similarly, as Döring points out (2009: 246), we may sometimes be able to 'recalibrate' our sense-perceptions with our beliefs, as with seeing one's train move at a station, when in fact it is a close-by train moving.

We may even want to say that her perception of Fido as dangerous is unwarranted insofar as it fails to match Fido's perceptible features. But we still cannot say that Pat's perceiving Fido as dangerous is irrational *insofar as it clashes with her rationally held belief that Fido is harmless*, that is, insofar as her perception is recalcitrant. For perceptions do not become irrational simply by clashing with a rationally held belief. (Hence perceiving Snarler as dangerous is not irrational simply because it clashes with the rational belief that he is harmless.) But, then, if Pat's perceiving Fido as dangerous is not irrational insofar as it clashes with her rationally held belief and if, further, perceptualists cannot appeal to motivational features to support the charge of irrationality either (given our starting assumption in this section), they may seem forced to withdraw the claim that recalcitrant emotions are irrational at all.[60]

However, if another account of recalcitrant emotions was available that could explain their irrationality (when they are such), we might prefer to draw the conclusion that it is the perceptualist theory that is flawed rather than withdraw the claim that recalcitrant emotions are (or at least can be) irrational. (As the old saying goes: one person's *modus ponens* is another's *modus tollens*.) But what alternative is available? As we have seen, in Pat's case we need an intentional state at least as uncommitted as a perception just to explain the *existence* of the emotion. Anything stronger than that—a judgement, a passive assent, or even an inclination to assent—and we lose that ability. And, as noted (12.2), we may on some occasions want something weaker than perception (appearance-as-truth), viz. something that does not even entail the assent of a subsystem (e.g. perceptual or

---

[60] As mentioned, one perceptualist has bitten this bullet. Döring argues that appearances notwithstanding recalcitrant emotions are not in fact irrational. On her view, irrationality consists in flouting either the Consistency principle or the Enkratic principle, but recalcitrant emotions do not flout the former (they only provide 'conflict without contradiction') and, if they prompt us to act akratically, it is only the *action* that is irrational, strictly speaking, not the emotion itself. As we saw, this left out the Pointless Motivation principle. But, in fact, even the Pointless Motivation principle will not help perceptualists explain the irrationality in question, unless they maintain that, in addition to being perceptual states, emotions are also essentially motivational (and, note, it is not sufficient simply for them to *prompt* motivations—for then we could still say that it is the motivation, not the emotion as such, that is irrational). I provided reasons for doubting that emotions essentially involve motivations in Chapter 11 but, in any event, states that look very much like emotions still seem to be subject to rational criticism even if they do not involve a motivation. Pat's being upset by the prospective danger of Fido looks irrational (given she believes him harmless) even if she is not motivated to flee. Jimmy's distress at Chris' slight seems irrational (given he believes no slight occurred) even if he does not form a desire to exact revenge in light of it (and so does not count as angry by Aristotle's lights). And we still have the *difference* to account for between such states and sensory illusions. Even when they are separated from motivations to act, recalcitrant emotions still seem irrational in a way that sensory illusions do not. Döring's account collapses this distinction. She appeals to motivational differences to account for the intuition that there is a line to draw between sense-perceptions and emotions, but then insists that this difference does not make the emotions themselves irrational (only the actions they prompt). Whereas I have argued that even though motivational differences *can* make a recalcitrant state irrational (to the extent that the state flouts the Pointless Motivation principle), appealing to motivations does not help explain the irrationality of recalcitrant emotions. At least, not given my reading of Aristotle. For, on that view, emotions do not involve motivations at all. They are representational pleasures or distresses *alone*.

thought-based imaginations). But if we have anything weaker than a judgement or assent in play, how can we explain the irrationality of the emotion? We are back to the Scylla and Charybdis.

Here is where the other features of Aristotle's account, as developed in this book, come to the fore; namely, (i) the fact that (on his view) emotions are hedonic states (representational pleasures or distresses) and (ii) that they are *responses* to intentional states that apprehend their objects (rather than such apprehending intentional states themselves). The latter idea, in particular, permits us to say that Pat's fear can on some occasion involve her perceiving Fido as dangerous without identifying that fear with the perceptual state. With respect to our concerns here, the first key advantage of this view is that it allows us to distinguish between sensory illusions and recalcitrant emotions in the way perceptualism cannot. Aristotle can say that *evaluative perceptions* are just like sensory illusions in that neither is irrational simply insofar as they persist in the presence of a contrary judgement (i.e. are recalcitrant). Just as it is not irrational to see the Müller-Lyer lines as of different lengths (even though one judges otherwise), nor is it irrational to perceive Snarler (or indeed Fido) as dangerous (when one judges otherwise). But since, on his view, emotions are not simply perceptions of value, this still leaves him able to say that *fearing* Snarler or Fido, given the contrary judgement, *is* (or at least can be) irrational. On his view, we should gloss 'fear of X' in [A] as follows:

[F] The rationality of distress at X's (apparent) danger [= fear of X], where X is rationally believed to exist, requires one to believe, rationally, that X is dangerous.

According to [F], Pat's fear comes out as irrational because she is distressed at the danger of Fido while rationally believing him harmless. Note that since this account does not directly specify the intentional state that apprehends the object of the emotion, it can allow that any number of different intentional states may, in different circumstances, play that role (that there must be one at all is revealed by the 'apparent'). But, in the case at hand, since Pat does not *believe* that Fido is dangerous, her emotion cannot be formed in response to her rationally believing that he is. So her emotion must be formed in response to some other intentional state; a perceptual state, or a perceptual imagining, or perhaps an uncommitted *thought*. In this way, the view can account for the *existence* of the recalcitrant fear.[61] But, equally, since Aristotle's view does not *identify* the emotion with the, e.g., perception, but instead takes it to be *a response to* it, his view can still distinguish fear

---

[61] Indeed, as noted (see 12.2, 12.4), it has more resources to explain this than perceptualism since (a) it need not insist that the object of the emotion is perceptual in character (even though it can permit that it is), and (b) it does not have to insist that the apprehension is an appearance-as-truth.

from sensory illusions. On his account, it is Pat's *being distressed at* the prospective danger of Fido, as this is formed *in response to* her, e.g., perception of him as dangerous, that is irrational (given that she rationally believes that Fido is harmless), not her, e.g., perception itself. Similarly, although it is not irrational to perceive Snarler as dangerous even when one rationally believes that he is harmless, it *is* irrational, on Aristotle's picture, to be *distressed at* the prospective danger of Snarler, in response to, e.g., perceiving him as such, when one rationally believes that he is in fact harmless.

Why does our becoming *distressed at*, and in response to, the (perceived) danger make the recalcitrant fear irrational in a way that the mere perception of danger did not? In the background, here, there is another principle of rationality:

> **Hedonic principle**: Rationality requires of you (whichever person you are) that if you rationally believe at *t* that *A* (which you rationally believe to exist) does not manifest the *FO* of emotion type *E*, then you should not experience distress or pleasure directed at *A* (insofar as you nonetheless represent *A* as manifesting the *FO*).

Here '*A*' is the particular object and '*FO*' the formal object of the emotion (see **1.3**). Note that the Hedonic principle gives the right answer with Fido and Snarler, and also with Jimmy's experiencing distress at Chris' (in fact inexistent) slight. Although Fido and Snarler are rationally believed to exist, neither are believed to manifest danger, and so to experience distress directed at them, *qua* manifesting that danger, is irrational. Whatever the basis of the distress (a thought or some perceptual appearance), it does not warrant fearing *Fido* or *Snarler themselves*, since they are rationally believed to be harmless. While it may not be irrational to *perceive* Fido or Snarler as dangerous even though one rationally believes they are not, it is irrational to be *distressed at the danger posed by* Fido or Snarler when one rationally believes that neither of the dogs is dangerous.[62] So too, although Jimmy will not count as irrational just insofar as he perceptually construes or has a thought of Chris as slighting him, his being distressed at Chris slighting him, in response to such a perception or thought, will come out as irrational since he resolutely does not believe that Chris in fact slighted him (and is rational in so believing).

To see this more clearly still, and to see precisely what is being claimed to be irrational, consider another example. Suppose Lottie sees a snake at a safari park and, reassured by the expert handlers, rationally forms the belief that it is not

---

[62] This leaves intact the difference between Fido and Snarler, viz. that perceiving Snarler as dangerous seems to have more perceptual warrant than perceiving Fido as dangerous. For, as we have seen, in neither case is the irrationality of recalcitrantly fearing Fido or Snarler to be accounted for in terms of perceiving them as dangerous.

dangerous. I will not here want to say that Lottie is irrational for nonetheless perceiving the snake as dangerous. As with Snarler, some things might warrant perceiving them as dangerous, and the snake might be one of them. Nor will I insist that Lottie must be irrational if she experiences distress at a snake she *imagines* to be dangerous—a snake, perhaps, like the one she encounters, that she imagines to be highly dangerous. If you experience emotions about imagined objects, that is, as I see it, up to you.[63] What I do want to insist on, though, is that if, on the basis of the snake perceptually appearing dangerous, Lottie experiences distress directed at the prospective danger *of the snake that she rationally believes to be harmless*, then she is irrational. What one justifiably believes to be harmless cannot warrant distress at its prospective danger. The fact that in this scenario Lottie perceives the snake as dangerous, then, provides her with no ground whatsoever for experiencing distress directed at the snake she sees in front her. She can experience distress at an imagined snake if she likes, but it cannot be rational for her to experience distress at the danger of the *actual* snake, as she believes it to be, when she justifiably believes it to be entirely harmless.[64]

The same can be said of representational pleasures. Suppose Monty rationally forms the belief that his mother has suffered some undeserved misfortune (she appears to fall over, bang her leg, and be in pain) and suppose Monty experiences pleasure directed at that turn of events (schadenfreude). But then suppose, much to his *chagrin*, he grasps that his mother has not in fact suffered the underserved

---

[63] Although I will say that irrationality *can* reappear here if the subject's emotion fails to match her imagined scenario. We also might on some occasions want to say that Lottie's choosing to experience such an emotion (so far as she can choose this) could be irrational, as I discuss in n.65.

[64] Contrast Greenspan's (1988) view. She views emotions as 'compounds' of two elements: 'affective states of comfort or discomfort and evaluative propositions spelling out their intentional content' (where the evaluative proposition is then glossed as a 'thought') (1988: 4). And she maintains that the affective component of emotions 'gives them a special role to play in rational motivation, as "extra-judgmental" reasons for action' (4, see also 6, 8). The motivation stemming from the (dis)comfort is later (31) said to be 'intended to capture a first-person motivational assessment of affect, corresponding to whether an agent would naturally seek or avoid *a given affective state*' (31; my emphasis). However, Greenspan is clear that the discomfort of an emotion is not itself a motivation or desire: '[d]iscomfort is here construed as a state that an agent would naturally want to escape from—not itself a desire, but a source of desires, under appropriate circumstances' (31). This account would suggest that a recalcitrant fear is irrational insofar as it motivates us to escape our discomforting fear when we judge that we have no such reason to be so motivated. One problem with this view is that fear is not a state that motivates the subject to get rid of *it* as such. We are motivated to get away from (or deal with, or some such) *the thing we are afraid of*. We would not, for example, be motivated to take a knock-out pill to deal with our fear of a lion on the loose. We want to get away from the lion (which will result in our no longer feeling fear). More crucially for our current concerns, though, this account does not show that the recalcitrant emotion is *itself* irrational since although the emotion *prompts* a motivation which conflicts with one's judgement, it is not itself that motivation (see also Helm 2001: 45; Benbaji 2013: 583–4). The account I have offered, by contrast, does purport to show that the emotion is itself irrational. It involves experiencing distress at the danger of *X*—an *X* you rationally believe to exist—when you rationally believe that *X* is harmless. (We need the 'an *X* you believe to exist' in this formulation to account for our emotional responses to fictional scenarios. This is why, in the paragraph above, I allow that Lottie *may* be rational in experiencing distress directed at an *imagined* snake—what is irrational is her experiencing distress at the *actual* snake, as she believes it to be.)

misfortune he presumed she had (she was putting it on, very convincingly, to tease him—you can see what sort of family we have before us). He is now under rational pressure to drop the belief. Well, let us suppose he does just this. But suppose that he nonetheless finds himself perceptually *imagining* that his mother has suffered the undeserved misfortune he had originally seen her as suffering. Perhaps, just as Jimmy knows that Chris has not slighted him, but might not be able to stop himself perceiving Chris as having done so, so too Monty might not be able to (or want to) stop conjuring up the image of his mother as having really suffered the misfortune. So be it. We cannot stop Monty perceptually construing his mother that way and Monty may not be able to do so himself (for a little while at least). While the perceptible features of the situation can no longer provide evidence for the belief that his mother suffered the misfortune, they can still remain perceptually vivid to him. But then suppose that Monty also finds himself *experiencing pleasure* directed at the perceptually imagined scenario. He enjoys perceptually imagining his mother as having suffered the underserved misfortune. I will not, off-hand, insist that such an emotion is irrational (you might want to claim that it is immoral or shows that Monty is a product of his family, but establishing any link between those claims and a charge of irrationality would require notoriously hard work). But what I *will* insist on is the following. If, on the basis of perceptually imagining his mother to have suffered some undeserved misfortune, Monty takes pleasure *at his mother actually having suffered some undeserved misfortune*, his representational pleasure would be irrational. For he believes, quite rationally, that his mother has not in fact suffered any such misfortune. This is directly parallel to Lottie experiencing distress at the danger of the actual snake, on the basis of a perceptual state that she repudiates. Monty believes, quite rationally, that his mother has not suffered the misfortune, so while he might enjoy *imagining* her suffering the undeserved misfortune, he cannot rationally enjoy her *actually* suffering the undeserved misfortune (as believed). Hence, if he nonetheless finds himself continuing to experience pleasure at his mother's actually having suffered some misfortune, his schadenfreude will be recalcitrant and irrational (it will persist in light of a rationally held conflicting belief).

Note that this account of the irrationality of a recalcitrant emotion is compatible with the idea that one could *rationally* seek to bring about such an irrational emotion in oneself. Suppose that Pat is undergoing a course of cognitive therapy and part of the process requires her to try to make herself experience the irrational fear. Then it will be rational for Pat to put herself in the position where she may be prone to experience her irrational fear of Fido (e.g. go to her neighbours' house). Similarly, with Lottie's fear of the snake. Suppose Lottie discovers that someone she is attracted to finds it adorable if people display irrational fears when those fears are not discernibly faked. It may be rational for Lottie to arrange it so that she experiences her irrational fear. So too if Monty enjoys his schadenfreude most of all when he irrationally experiences the joy directed at his mother herself, even though he knows she has not experienced the misfortune, it may be rational for him to experience such a joy (unless you have proved on moral or other grounds that this must be irrational). Nonetheless, we will not say that Pat's or Lottie's fears, or Monty's schadenfreude, in such situations, are *themselves* rational. We will say that it might be rational for them to try to bring about those irrational emotions, but not that those emotions thereby somehow themselves become rational. Suppose I know that my irrationally always looking on the bright side of life makes me feel good about myself and has other health benefits for me. That might make it rational for me to continue irrationally always looking on the bright side of life. But it would not make irrationally always looking of the bright side of life itself rational.[65]

In short, while it is not irrational to perceive some X (an X one rationally takes to exist) as having property Y, even though one rationally believes that X does not in fact have property Y, it *is* irrational to experience distress or pleasure at X (an X one rationally takes to exist) insofar as one perceives X to have property Y, when one rationally believes that X does not have property Y. We can also put this as follows: it is irrational to experience distress or pleasure at X (as one rationally believes X to exist) insofar as one perceives X to have property Y, when one

---

[65] For this reason, with the Hedonic principle we do not need anything equivalent to the exception clause that we included with the Pointless Motivation principle (**12.5**). Hence I reject Gaut's claim that '[a]n occurrence of an emotion is irrational if experiencing it involves suffering to no point' (2007: 225), which he thinks applies to both 'actual' as well as 'imagined' scenarios. Experiencing an emotion that involves one suffering to no point is not *itself* irrational. One might be rationally justified in thinking that things are the way one's emotion presupposes they are, but one's emotion in fact involves one suffering for no purpose (e.g. one might be rationally justified in believing that one's team has lost, and be distressed at that, when in fact the result will be overturned for reasons one could not rationally have foreseen). What is irrational is *choosing* to experience an emotion that involves one suffering to no point. In fact, even this is not quite right: what is irrational is choosing to put oneself in a situation in which one can rationally expect to suffer to no point (as might be the case, e.g., if we chose to watch a fictional tragedy in the expectation that we would experience great distress, but rationally expect to gain *nothing whatsoever* from doing so).

Note, I can irrationally choose to experience an emotion that I then rationally experience. Given that I should realize that I would experience terror, not thrill, by letting someone smear me in a jelly that will prompt some cockroaches to crawl all over me and bite me, it would doubtless be irrational for me to choose to let this happen (assuming I see no other purpose in this). But when I am jellied up and see the insects marching towards me, my fear of them will doubtless be rational.

Of course, if one persists in imagining a scenario one is distressed by, while at the same time rationally believing that there is no point to the distress, one's emotion (the distress) will be irrational. But it will be irrational because irrationality travels upwards. Persisting in imagining the scenario, knowing full well that it brings the pointless distress, is itself irrational (even if one cannot stop oneself doing so). Hence one's emotion, as a response to such an irrational imagining, will inherit the irrationality. But, contra Gaut, experiencing distress at an imagined scenario is not intrinsically irrational if it involves one suffering for no purpose. Indeed, such a distress is not even irrational if, upon experiencing it, one rationally judges that one is suffering for no purpose. For one may have no rational ground, before imagining the scenario, for believing that imagining it will generate the distress and the latter may be an appropriate response to the imagined object.

rationally believes that X does not have property Y. In experiencing fear directed at poor old toothless Fido, Pat was doing just this.⁶⁶

12.7 Rationality as warrant: Dexter, Huckleberry Finn, and poisonous frogs

In the last section I argued for an interpretation of the irrationality of Pat's recalcitrant fear of Fido that highlighted how the fear was a response to a perception or thought of danger that she did not believe obtained. But with some recalcitrant emotions, it may seem that it is the emotion that is rational, not the belief. Consider:

Dexter. Suppose Susan has some new neighbours and they have a dog, Dexter, whom they assure her is perfectly safe. Susan has no reason to doubt their testimony: they seem nice, honest, people. However, as Susan sees more of Dexter, she finds herself perceiving him as dangerous. It is not just that, like Snarler, he froths at the mouth, grinds his teeth, and snarls, it is also that he seems to lose control and not always obey his owners. Suppose, in addition, the neighbours' testimony begins to look a little shaky. Perhaps they let slip that Dexter attacked someone in the past but insist he is safe 'now'. Suppose, too, the perceptual counter-evidence begins to look stronger still. Perhaps Dexter lunges towards Susan at one point, fangs at the ready, but is pulled back just in time by one of the neighbours. Imagine this continues—testimony looking increasingly flimsy, perceptual evidence looking increasingly compelling. And suppose Susan eventually becomes

---

[66] After providing his motivational explanation of recalcitrance (as discussed in 12.5), Roberts adds: '[t]his explanation does not reduce the difference between the two cases to pure motivation (a mere behavioral tendency to recoil from the phobic object). The power and trouble resides also and necessarily in its perceptual or affective character: that the phobic object is personally upsetting because it *appears threatening*' (2003: 92; his emphasis). Stripped of his claims about motivation, I agree that the source of the fear is the object's appearing threatening—although I deny both that this must be perceptual (it could be a non-perceptual thought) and that it requires an appearance-as-truth. But obviously more needs to be said. Helm (2001: 44, 2015: 422) objects that at the point at which the emotion is recalcitrant, the appearance is *repudiated*; it is a *mere* appearance. He goes on to note that since my recalcitrant fear does motivate me (I would say, *can*), I must in some sense accept the appearance (2015: 423). But there is a confusion here. In these cases, we are distressed at X (which we take to exist) on the basis of its appearance, even though we do not believe (or accept) that X is as it appears. Our emotion is irrational insofar as the distress effectively presupposes that the thing is as one rationally believes it is not. But in such a case we are not distressed at the mere appearance of a dangerous X. We are distressed at X (which we take to exist) being dangerous (on the basis of its appearance). Given this, we can also be motivated by the recalcitrant emotion, subject to our background dispositions. Granted, we do not believe the thing has the property it appears to have. But that is why our fear is irrational. We fear it on the basis of its appearance, even though we do not believe it has the property it appears to have. But, *given* that we fear the thing, we can be motivated accordingly. We are not motivated by our distress at the mere appearance of X as F (like a mirage: 422); we are motivated by our distress at X—given that X appears F—even though we do not believe that X is F.

afraid of Dexter on the basis of the perceptual evidence. Nonetheless, since she is a trusting soul, let us assume that she continues to believe the testimony (which has not been retracted) that Dexter is safe.

Susan now has a recalcitrant fear, but it may seem that it is her fear that is rational and her belief irrational. Her belief should give more weight to the perceptual evidence in light of the flimsy testimony, but it does not.

In my view, this example brings out an important point: recalcitrant emotions are not irrational simply insofar as they are recalcitrant. If the belief that the recalcitrant emotion conflicts with is itself *irrationally* held, and if the emotional response pertains to what one does in fact have reason to believe, then the emotion, not the belief, will be rational. Since, given the evidence available to her, Susan's belief should be revised, it is irrational. But insofar as her fear forms in response to the evidence available to her (the perceptual information, what happened in the past, etc.), and not in response to her belief, Susan's emotion looks rational. While Pat's fear of Fido is irrational insofar as it involves her being distressed about the danger of harmless docile Fido on the basis of a perceptual or thought-based construal that Pat has no warrant to think matches reality, Susan's fear of Dexter, by contrast, seems rational insofar as it involves her being distressed about the dangerous Dexter on the basis of perceptual or thought-based construals that Susan *does have* warrant to think match reality. The fact that she does not *believe* in line with those perceptions and thoughts is a failing of her belief, not her emotion. Recalcitrant emotions, then, are not irrational *because* they are recalcitrant. They are irrational just to the extent that they themselves lack *warrant*.[67] In our examples in the previous section, this was guaranteed since we stipulated that the beliefs that the recalcitrant emotions conflicted with were rationally formed. Given this assumption, the recalcitrant emotions, which conflicted with such beliefs, had to be irrational. But that is simply because such an assumption *entailed* that the recalcitrant emotions lacked warrant. And the Hedonic principle diagnosed what was wrong with them (given that assumption). But if we retract that assumption, recalcitrant emotions need not be irrational.[68]

---

[67] Rationality has to pertain to what we can respond to, but it does not have to pertain to what we *are in fact* aware of. Instead, it pertains to: what *we should* be aware of. If I am not aware of some feature of a situation through negligence, wishful thinking, or carelessness, but could reasonably be expected to grasp it, I may be charged with irrationality. We may be able to find some such normative notion in Aristotle via his notion of ignorance 'of the universal' (*NE* III.1.1110b32–1111a2). On his view, it is not ignorance of the universal, but ignorance of the particular circumstances of an action that make it involuntary. But he does not claim that ignorance of the universal is not *possible*. He claims we are *blamed* for it; that is, *we ought* to know such universals.

[68] 'Need not' because there would seem to be scope for both the belief *and* the conflicting emotion to be irrational. Suppose the belief is irrationally formed, as in my example. That does not *itself* entail that any emotion that conflicts with that belief is rational. If the conflicting emotion was based on something which does not support believing that Dexter is dangerous, e.g. his name alone, which

With Dexter, the assumption is withdrawn and the position reversed: the belief is irrational, the recalcitrant emotion rational.

Parallel cases to Dexter (concerned with motivation and intention) have been considered in the literature as instances of 'inverse' or 'rational' *akrasia*.[69] Suppose, in line with her belief that Dexter is not dangerous (backed by her neighbours' flimsy testimony), Susan forms the normative belief that she ought not to flee from Dexter even when he seems 'frisky' (as the neighbours put it). But then suppose that Susan acts on the basis on her recalcitrant emotion and does indeed flee. In that scenario, she has acted against her normative judgement about what she ought to do, and so her action is akratic. And yet Susan's action seems *rational* insofar as it was grounded on her emotion, which, I have argued, is itself rational. So, in such a scenario, Susan would seem to manifest inverse or rational *akrasia*.

However, the idea that there can be rational *akrasia* has been resisted. Let me consider this further by examining Döring's (2015) rejection of the idea.[70] The much-discussed example in the literature is that of Huckleberry Finn.[71] Döring provides a neat summary of the essentials of the example:

> Huckleberry Finn...after having helped his friend Jim to escape from slavery, decides to turn him in but finds himself doing just the contrary when he is given the opportunity to do so. Instead of turning Jim over to the slave hunters, Huck lies out of growing friendship and sympathy in order to protect the fugitive slave, thereby doing what he believes is wrong according to every moral principle he ever held to be true. (386)

Döring grants that 'Huck does respond correctly to reasons' and she notes that if rationality were understood along the lines of such responsiveness, this 'would mean that Huck, even though he is akratic, is rational' (386). But she resists this. She writes:

> we have an intuitive sense that, given his belief that he ought to turn Jim in, Huck *is* irrational in not forming the intention to turn Jim in. His irrationality

---

reminds you of someone dangerous, it too would be irrational. By contrast, note that there does not seem to be scope for both the belief and a conflicting emotion to be *rationally* formed. If there is overriding evidence available (whether perceptual or whatever) that points one way or the other, the subject should believe in line with the evidence, and it would be irrational to have a conflicting emotion. Whereas if the available evidence does not firmly support one hypothesis over the other, the rational response will be to remain uncertain. (This might still make it rational to stay clear of Dexter, since being uncertain about whether a dog might bite may provide sufficient reason to stay clear.)

[69] Aristotle himself recognizes these cases and calls them 'good *akrasia*'; see *NE* VII.2.1146a16–21, VII.9.1151b17–22. See also Audi (1990); McIntyre (1990, 2006); Arpaly and Schroeder (1999); Arpaly (2003: ch. 2); Jones (2003); Tappolet (2003).

[70] See also Hinchman (2013).   [71] After Bennett (1974).

consists in the fact that his attitudes—specifically his believing he ought to turn Jim in and his not intending to—fail to fit together in the way that they should: they are incoherent. (386)

So Döring wants to say that it would have been rational for Huck to turn Jim in, given his belief. This is so because (following Broome) she thinks rationality consists in:

satisfying certain requirements of coherence between one's mental attitudes—such as the enkratic principle that, if you believe that you ought to φ then you intend to φ, or the consistency principle that you not judge both that p and then judge that not-p. (387)[72]

And, crucially, to view 'coherence' as the key, here, is to understand 'the logical scope of "requires"' as ranging 'over the entire conditional' of the requirement (389):

that is, it is a rational requirement on you that (if you believe at t that yourself ought to φ, then you intend at t to φ). Hence, [the Enkratic principle] does not require of you that you make some specific change in your attitudes. Rather, what is required of you is that you either intend to φ, or not believe that you ought to φ. Proceeding in any of these ways would allow you to escape from the state of having an incoherent combination of attitudes. (389)[73]

According to such a formulation of the Enkratic principle, one is irrational only to the extent that one's belief and intending conflict. Now, in line with the view I have developed in this section, I too accept that one's intending *need not* be rationally at fault. If Susan forms an intention to flee Dexter in light of her recalcitrant fear, her intention will be rational even though it conflicts with her belief (since her fear is a rational response to what she has reason to believe), while her belief is irrational. Hence, to accommodate such cases, I need another principle. Something like:

Inverse Enkratic principle: Rationality requires of you (whichever person you are) that if you rationally intend to φ at t, then you believe at t that you yourself ought to φ at t.

---

[72] In fact, as noted, Döring thinks that these are the only principles we need. On that basis she argues that recalcitrant emotions are not irrational. See **12.6n.60**.
[73] I omit reference to 'enkrasia' in line with my comment in **12.5n.49**.

Just as you will flout my version of the Enkratic principle (i.e. with 'rationally believes'; see 12.5) if you have a rationally held belief, e.g., that you should reply to some work emails at *t*, but fail to intend to do so, so too you will flout the Inverse Enkratic principle if you have a rationally formed intention (formed, e.g., in light of perceptual or other evidence) to avoid Dexter, but (on the strength of flimsy testimony) fail to believe this. Since, on my view, rationality is a matter of *warrant*, it is not open for us, in any given case, which of either the belief or the intention to revise.

Döring, by contrast (after Broome), holds that rationality is solely a matter of *coherence*:

> following Broome, I start from the assumption that rationality (and hence the rationality of emotion) is to be understood in terms of coherence, and not in terms of responsiveness. On the conception of 'rationality as coherence (between mental attitudes)', being rational is most fundamentally a matter of internal coherence between a subject's attitudes. Accordingly, the norms of rationality are codified as structural requirements on the relations between a subject's attitudes that must hold insofar as she is not irrational. (2015: 385)[74]

Given the notion of rationality as coherence, Döring will only charge you with irrationality *just to the extent* that your belief and intention conflict. So far as the Enkratic principle goes, then, you will *cease* to be irrational, on her view, just so long as your belief and intention concur, and from the perspective of rationality it does not matter *one jot* which you change. It can *never*, that is, so far as this principle of rationality goes, be any more rational to revise one's belief in line with one's intending rather than one's intending in line with one's belief. Hence, on Döring's view, even though we might say that Huck has most reason (is warranted) to not turn Jim in, nonetheless '*given* his belief that he ought to turn Jim in, Huck *is* irrational in not forming the intention to turn Jim in' (386; first emphasis mine, second Döring's). This is simply because his attitudes (belief/intending) 'fail to fit together in the way that they should: they are incoherent' (386).

On my view, by contrast, it could be rational to revise *either* your belief *or* your intention, but *which* it is rational to revise depends entirely upon the available evidence you should be taking into account. If your belief is irrationally formed and flies in the face of the available evidence and if, in contrast, your intention

---

[74] She goes on: 'This is in contrast to "rationality as responsiveness (to reasons)": on this conception, being rational is most fundamentally a matter of being informed by what really are reasons' (385). In fact, my notion of rationality is not well characterized as responsiveness *to what really are reasons*. This is because, as I see it, if all the evidence that you could reasonably be expected to take account of points in favour of believing that *p*, it would be rational for you to believe that *p*, even if in fact not-*p* (so too, *mutatis mutandis*, with intending to φ). My notion of rationality, then, is best characterized as responsiveness *as warrant*.

responds appropriately to said evidence then, from the standpoint of rationality, you ought to revise your belief in line with your intention. Whereas if your belief is rationally formed and your intention is an irrational response then, from the standpoint of rationality, you ought to revise your intention.

A first reason to be suspicious of Döring's view is that we normally think that irrationality 'travels upwards', so to speak. If, for instance, Monty forms the irrational belief that there are killer monsters under his bed and fears accordingly, we do not—I take it—want to say that Monty's fear is rational *given his belief.* Rather, we want to say that Monty's fear is irrational *because* it is grounded in an irrational belief. But Döring's account points in the opposite direction: rationality is, on this view, simply a matter of coherence. Thus, if it is ever appropriate to say that an emotion could be rationally formed on the basis of a belief,[75] Monty's fear would be a rational response to an irrational belief. But do we really want to say that Monty's fear in such a scenario would be *rational*?

I think not. To see just how counter-intuitive Döring's view is, consider the following example. Before it closed, Bristol Zoo possessed some little (6-centimetre) bright yellow frogs behind glass cases. At first glance, these looked quite pleasant and one might easily imagine enjoying letting one hop around on the palm of one's hand. But, as one noticed the accompanying sign, one learned they were in fact poison golden frogs, some of the most poisonous amphibians on earth, each with enough toxin to kill ten adult humans. Now, let us suppose, after reading the notice, one rationally forms the belief that the creatures are deadly. But also suppose that one nonetheless cannot help but *perceive* them as harmless—they do not *look* deadly, but rather like little rubber toys a baby would play with. Then imagine that one forms an emotion about the frogs—the killing machines themselves—in response to this perception. Perhaps one experiences pleasure directed at the prospect of having some of the frogs hop up and down on one's hand, or some such. And suppose that one's emotion persists despite one knowing full well that this would not be harmless fun, but instant death. We will all agree, I presume, that since one's emotion persists in light of one's conflicting belief, it is recalcitrant. I will further say that the emotion is irrational since it presupposes that one believes that the frogs are harmless (it is about the frogs as one believes them to be), in spite of the fact that one rationally believes they are murderous. Now, in this case, Döring would allow that if one possessed the normative judgement not to pick up the frogs and then sought to act on one's emotion to do so, one would be irrational (for one would then flout the Enkratic principle). But, on her view, that irrationality would stem simply from the fact that one has incoherent attitudes. There is nothing irrational *as such* with

---

[75] Which, for Döring, would be doubly wrong since, on her view, emotions (i) cannot be rational or irrational and (ii) are, in any event, perceptual states.

intending to act in accordance with one's emotion. One is irrational only insofar as and just to the extent that this intention clashes with one's normative judgement. And yet note what this implies. Suppose that, somehow, one were gradually able to get oneself to *change* one's normative belief so that it aligns with one's intention to pick up the frogs (self-hypnosis or some such). When one's normative belief and emotion finally align, one's intention to act on the emotion *will no longer be irrational*, by Döring's lights, because one will no longer possess the clash of attitudes. There is no longer any 'incoherence'. But note, further, that *the very act of making oneself believe in line with one's emotion* must, given Döring's account, be a process *through which* one makes oneself rational. For, on this view, it is owing to this process that one rids oneself of irrationality. Hence, in making oneself believe—in spite of the overwhelming evidence to the contrary—that the frogs are harmless, one would be making oneself *rational*. If this sounds bizarre enough, we can quickly make the scenario more so. Suppose one has just witnessed the frogs kill five people. Nonetheless, if one can somehow get oneself to believe (by hypnosis, drugs, or whatever) that the frogs are harmless, one will, thereby, through that very process, have eradicated one's irrationality and achieved the sanctity of rationality.

In fact, Döring's position is even more counter-intuitive than this. For even though she holds this view about rationality, she also holds that we can respond correctly or incorrectly to reasons. On her view, in acting akratically, Huck, though irrational, 'responds correctly to reasons' (2015: 386). Indeed, on her view, recalcitrant emotions 'can point us to reasons that we would not have gained without them' (399). The recalcitrance of Huck's sympathy 'leads him to reason his way out of the conflict, and it does so by pointing to possible reasons that Huck could not have gained without his emotion' (399). Furthermore:

> It is not that Huck earlier *overlooked* those reasons; rather they were not *accessible* to him. Prior to experiencing sympathy for the runaway slave Jim, Huck would not have thought of slavery as wrong, for the wrongness of slavery does not follow from the moral principles he had hitherto accepted. In Huck's case, the onset of his sympathy has led him to the explicit formulation of new, better, more comprehensive moral principles. (399; Döring's emphases)

As should be clear, I agree that emotions can be indicators of reasons. Susan's fear responds to evidence which undermines the flimsy considerations in favour of her belief that Dexter is harmless. But I want to say that insofar as the reasons are both available and compelling, it would be *irrational* for us not to respond appropriately to them. And there are compelling reasons, freely available, in favour of not picking up the sinister frogs. It would, therefore, I say, be irrational to intend to pick one up.[76] Whereas Döring is committed to saying that *even though* there are compelling *reasons*, freely available, dictating that one ought not to believe that one should pick up the frogs, nonetheless, given that one intends to pick one up, it would be *rational* for one to *alter* one's belief in favour of believing that one should pick up a frog. For, in so doing, one would bring one's belief in line with one's intending (to pick up a frog) and the Enkratic principle, as Döring understands it, does not require 'that you make some specific change in your attitudes' (389). On this view, it can be rational for one to do what one has compelling and overriding reason not to do, even when that reason is freely available to one. Indeed, it can be so even when one *acknowledges* the fact that one has the compelling and overriding reason. For one may acknowledge that one has compelling reason not to change one's belief so that it aligns with one's intention but, for all that, on Döring's account, were one to do so, that would make one rational and eradicate one's irrationality. This, I propose, is close to a *reductio* of Döring's view: to allow rationality and reasons to become so dissociated is surely unpalatable.

Since this is *so* counter-intuitive, it is worth considering what went wrong. Döring appeals to the following intuition: even though Huck responds correctly to reasons, we have 'an intuitive sense that, given his belief that he ought to turn Jim in, Huck *is* irrational in not forming the intention to turn Jim in' (386). The intuition hinges on the idea that *once he has formed* this judgement, the judgement dictates what sort of intentions he should form. I suggest that the reason we might have this intuition, insofar as we do, is *on the prior assumption* that the normative judgement is more likely to have been weighed in deliberation and so is more likely to be rational. But if, in spite of this, it is not rational, I do not think that we would be inclined to assume that *getting* one's intentions to align with such a judgement would *make one* rational, as my examples, and indeed the example of Huck himself, show.

There is a further factor, I think, in the example employed. Of course, things are more complicated with Huck. This is obviously not because *we* do not all know that slavery is wrong and that it would, therefore, be wrong for Huck to hand Jim (or anyone else, for that matter) over to the slave hunters. Rather, it is because we are unsure whether, given the evidence that *Huck* has to go on (and the evidence that he ought to be aware of), it would be rational *for him* to hand Jim over. Note that the reasons that *Huck* responds to do seem more connected to his relationship with Jim, his sympathy and friendship, than to the wrongness of slavery. On this basis, had he hated Jim, he might well have turned him in. We

---

[76] Note, I am assuming that I do not have reason to kill myself. Take away that assumption and I may have reason to pick up a frog. I speak of 'evidence' favouring not just a belief, but also an intending. I do not need to take a stand on what makes one have good practical reasons for the purposes of this argument. So far as the argument goes, they could be constructed entirely in terms of the agent's desires or there could be a practical reality which demands a certain response.

appreciate that it can be incredibly hard to address, rationally, evidence that runs counter to one's deeply ingrained moral principles, principles that have been inculcated through one's education and upbringing and, in addition, are the societal norm. In making this observation I am not, of course, suggesting that slavery was ever remotely justified—it palpably was not. Nor am I, unlike Döring, claiming that it would in fact have been rational for Huck to hand Jim over. But I am claiming that it can be rational for us to believe things that are false or intend to do things that we in fact have no reason to do. If all the available evidence points in favour of believing that p or φ-ing then, rationally, I should believe that p or intend to φ. But p might still be false for all that and the evidence in favour of φ-ing might mislead. We do not always have access to, nor normatively ought to be able to access, the relevant facts. Furthermore, even when we do have some sort of access to the features of the situation that would dictate a response one way or the other, sometimes accessing those features and giving them due weight can be extremely difficult. And, when this is the case, we may not want to call those who fail to make the correct call 'irrational'. As Berys Gaut writes:

> When we call someone irrational...the accusation cannot be of failing to be maximally rational, for this would be an extremely demanding standard, given all the reasons that are potentially relevant in any particular domain, and most people on most occasions might well be judged to be irrational by this standard. Rather, we must be adopting a lower standard in making this accusation: the irrational person is a person who fails to achieve some *minimal* standard of rationality. The reasons that he or she fail to recognise or to respond to appropriately would be those that are readily available, graspable, being clear and evident. How to specify this notion more exactly is a moot issue. (2007: 217)

Note that the reasons that Huck responds to *are* available to him. They are what his intention not to hand Jim in reflects and what underlies his sympathy. But they are presumably not 'clear and evident' to him, since otherwise he most likely would not have formed a belief contrary to that intention in the first place. There are many cases in which reasons are strictly speaking available, but where it is quite understandable for us to fail to respond to them because it would be very demanding on us to grasp them and respond to them adequately. In such cases, we do not, I take it, want to charge the person with irrationality for failing to respond to those reasons. As Gaut notes, that would make being rational far too demanding and succumbing to irrationality far too easy. So cases such as Huck's, where our intuitions are perhaps not as clear as we would like them, are not going to be good ones for working out our account of rationality. For, *given* the evidence *he* can readily access, it is perhaps less clear what Huck should do. Of course, other evidence that slavery was wrong was available, but given Huck's circumstances and background, it may be very hard for him to access that, or appreciate it properly, if he does. And yet, as the frog case shows, when it is 'clear and obvious' that believing or acting in a certain way would flout what we have reason to believe or do, we cannot achieve rationality *simply* by making ourselves have a coherent set of attitudes. If those attitudes are hopelessly lacking in evidential support, and we are readily aware of this, it would clearly be irrational to make ourselves coherent by coming to have them.[77]

Conclusion to Part IV

In this final part of the book I have considered some additional philosophical merits of Aristotle's account of the emotions. In Chapter 11 I argued that insofar as his account views emotions as distinct from desires and motivations, it is preferable to a recent motivational theory. I also explored the different representational roles emotions play according to different theories of emotions. In this chapter I have highlighted a major philosophical advantage of Aristotle's account, viz. that it enables us to explain both the existence and the irrationality of recalcitrant emotions, when, that is, the latter *are* irrational. For such emotions need not be irrational. They will be so if the judgement they conflict with is itself rationally formed. In such cases, besides any motivations or actions they may prompt, we can understand their irrationality as pertaining to the fact that we experience distress or pleasure directed at something in a way that would only make sense if we believed it possessed a property that we rationally believe it does not in fact possess. Contra judgementalism, such irrational emotions are not themselves beliefs, nor, contra quasi-judgementalist views, are they passive assents or inclinations to assent. Pat does not believe that Fido is dangerous, nor does she passively assent that he is, nor need she even be inclined to assent to this. Rather, they seem to be *responses to* perceptions, perceptual imaginations, or uncommitted thoughts. Such perceptions (etc.) need not *themselves* be irrational, however. It seems rather harsh, for instance, to insist that it must be irrational *to perceive* Snarler as dangerous. Rather, what is irrational is *to experience an emotion about Fido or Snarler* on the basis of one's perception (etc.) when one rationally believes that Fido and Snarler are harmless. Granted, too, one may be mistaken. Snarler may have taken a turn for the worse and become dangerous (as Dexter is). But if one's belief that Snarler is harmless is *rationally* held, then being distressed at Snarler's being dangerous—the dog himself, as he is believed to be—is irrational. Nonetheless, such recalcitrant emotions are not irrational in virtue of being recalcitrant. They

---

[77] Note, in line with this, the stronger the testimony and the weaker the perceptual evidence with Dexter, the less inclined we will be to think that responding in line with the perceptual evidence would be rational, *even if it turns out to be true* that Dexter is dangerous. Rationality must pertain to what the agent can respond to, not to what is in fact true. Contrast de Sousa and Scarantino (2018: §10.1).

are irrational because, without being beliefs themselves, they presuppose the truth of a belief that one rationally rejects. This means that recalcitrant emotions can also be rational if they persist in light of an *irrational* judgement. For, in such a scenario, they could be highlighting evidence one has reason to observe.

On my view, the fact that Aristotle's hedonic response account of emotions enables him to explain recalcitrant emotions, whereas contemporary views seem to struggle in just this respect, is a key indicator that he is on the right lines. It could be that as one of the first philosophers to develop a theoretical account of the emotions and to apply it systematically to a good number of cases, Aristotle managed to develop a theory that is superior to many recent attempts. At the very least, it surely deserves our attention and scrutiny.

Catalogue of Aristotle's Emotions as Representational Pleasures or Distresses

I close this book by providing a Catalogue of Aristotle's emotions as representational pleasures or distresses. The goal is specifically to chart the representational pleasures and distresses that Aristotle links to the various states he discusses or mentions in this context. Thus, with some states bound up with emotions, the emotion may only form a part of the state (as with anger) or the emotion may only be implied by the state (as with the emotions connected to feeling-friendly-towards and hating). In such cases, I shall provide the original specification of the state in question and then indicate the emotions I take Aristotle to be characterizing. To avoid repetition, I shall, where appropriate, refer the reader to other parts of the book for more detailed discussion.

To keep the Catalogue within sensible bounds, I have had to invoke some criteria for inclusion. Mine are as follows. I include the states that are discussed in the *Rhet.* II catalogue of individual emotions, including their 'opposites', and also the emotions discussed at the start of II.9.[1] In addition, I also include any other states which are referred to on the lists of the emotions in *NE* II.5 (1105b21–3), *EE* II.2 (1220b12–14), and *De an* I.1 (403a16–18).[2] But that is where I draw the line. Adopting these criteria for inclusion may well be both too inclusive—we shall struggle to characterize some of those on the latter lists—and not inclusive enough—it will doubtless leave out many representational pleasures and

---

[1] Right at the end of *Rhet.* Aristotle provides another list of emotions (III.19.1419b25–6). Some of these are unsurprising—pity (*eleos*), anger (*orgē*), hatred (*misos*), envy (*phthonos*), and emulation (*zēlos*)—but we also have *deinōsis* and *eris*. *Deinōsis* is only used by Aristotle in *Rhet.* (see also II.21.1395a9, II.24.1401b3). Reeve (2018: 289n.660) suggests that it doubles for indignation (*nemesis*), discussed in **Cat.12**. Concerning *eris*, 'strife', Reeve (2018) notes that it is has not been previously mentioned and 'is not obviously a feeling, and in this respect resembles *diabolē* ("accusation"), for which it may be serving as proxy (this would explain its unheralded introduction at this late stage)' (374–5n.1211). *Diabolē* itself occurs on a list—alongside pity and anger—at *Rhet.* I.1.1354a16–17. But *diabolē* is not an emotion, it is an activity. For more discussion, see Dow (2015: 111–16) and Reeve (2018: lvi–lvii, 160). Dow rejects the idea that 1354a16–17 is providing a list of emotions. Either way, *eris* in III.19 remains puzzling.

[2] *Aidōs* appears on the *EE* II.2 list. I address it under shame below (see **Cat.7**). *Thumos* appears on both the *EE* II.2 and *De an.* I.1 lists. Insofar as *thumos* counts as an emotion, I take it to be covered by my discussion of *orgē* below (distress at an offence) (see Chapter 7 nn. 5, 56). There is also a list in the *MM* (I.7.1186a11–14) with anger (*orgē*), fear (*phobos*), hatred (*misos*), longing (*pothos*), emulation (*zēlos*), and pity (*eleos*). Although I do not believe this work is by Aristotle, all these will be discussed below, since they are already covered by my existing criteria.

distresses, some of which will be important for Aristotle.[3] But any catalogue needs workable criteria for what it includes and if readers feel aggrieved that a personal favourite has missed out, they are at liberty to add to the catalogue at their leisure! As it is, we already have twenty-one entries in the pantheon and some of these will end up covering more than one emotion.

In my characterizations of the emotions as representational pleasures or distresses, I shall simply refer to the pleasures or distresses as directed at their (evaluative, formal) objects. But it must be understood that the objects are intentional objects. As we saw in 4.2, in many of his definitions Aristotle indicates this by his use of 'apparent' (*phainomenos*). To avoid potentially misleading constructions, though, I will leave out the 'apparent' in my own specifications (although not in quotations, of course), but it should be assumed. For instance, when I refer to the emotion of anger as distress at an offence or slight (*oligōria*), it should be understood that I mean: distress at an apparent offence or slight, where the 'apparent' indicates that the offence may not be as presumed.

In an **Appendix** to this Catalogue I provide a tree diagram charting the emotions which pertain to (un)deserved doing-well or -badly.

1. Anger (*orgē*) (*Rhet.* II.2)

In *Rhet.* II.2 Aristotle defines anger as follows:

> Let anger be desire accompanied by distress (*orexis meta lupēs*) for apparent revenge, because of an apparent offence (*oligōria*, lit. belittling or slight)[4] on the part of someone unfitted to treat the person himself, or one of those close to him, with offence. (1378a30–2)

I have argued (Chapter 6) that there are two states that compose anger, a desire and an emotion. The desire is for revenge or retaliation or rectification (*timōria*). The emotion, which the desire is formed in light of, can be characterized as:

> Distress at an offence (slight, belittling = *oligōria*) [on the part of someone unfitted to treat you, or one close to you, with offence].

In his subsequent discussion of the formal object of the emotion (II.2.1378b11–1379a9), Aristotle provides three species of offence or *oligōria*:

---

[3] E.g. regret (*metameleia*), which is clearly a representational distress; see *NE* III.1.1110b18–24, 1111a20–1, IX.4.1166b22–5; *Rhet.* II.3.1380a14–16. Cf. also distress at telling a lie (regret, guilt, shame?) in *NE* VII.2.1146a16–21. For more discussion of regret in Aristotle (and ancient philosophy more generally), see Warren (2021).

[4] On the limitations of construing anger in terms of 'slighting', see e.g. Nussbaum (2016: 19–21).

disdain (*kataphronēsis*), spite (*epēreasmos*),⁵ and insult or wanton aggression (*hubris*).⁶ These appear to be properties we ascribe to actions or behaviour. But for disdain as a kind of emotion, see **Cat.15** below.

As we saw in **6.5** anger also leads to another emotion. Aristotle writes:

> A kind of pleasure follows (*hepesthai*) all anger, namely, the one that arises from the hope of being revenged (*apo tēs elpidos tou timōrēsasthai*). For it is pleasant to think that he will get what he seeks...a sort of pleasure actually follows along (*akolouthein*) because of this. (1378b1–3, 8)

This emotion is not a component of anger itself. It follows (*hepesthai, akolouthein*) anger, in the 'subsequent' sense of *hepetai* (see **2.1**). But the emotion results from anger and is brought about by it. It can be specified as follows:

> Pleasure at the prospect of (or hope of) getting revenge.

For more discussion on anger and its emotions, see esp. Chapter 6.

2. Mild-manneredness (*praotēs*) (*Rhet.* II.3)

Concerning anger's 'opposite', Aristotle writes:

> Since becoming angry (*to orgizesthai*) is the contrary of becoming-mild-mannered (*to praünesthai*) and anger (*orgē*) to mild-manneredness (*praotēs*), we must grasp by being disposed in which way people are mild-mannered (*praoi*), to whom they are mild-mannered (*praōs*), and because of what sort of things they become mild-mannered (*praünontai*). Let, then, becoming-mild-mannered (*praünsis*) be a settling down and coming to rest (*katastasis kai eremēsis*) of anger. (II.3.1380a6–9)

---

⁵ With spite (*epēreasmos*), we thwart another's wishes not in order to get something ourselves, but to prevent the other from getting it (1378b18–20). The offence arises because we are not trying to get something ourselves (b20). If we thought the other could harm us, we would fear rather than slight the person (b20-1). Similarly, if we thought the other could do us good, we would try to make friends (b21–3). Spite is also said to be productive of enmity and hatred (II.4.1382a1–2).

⁶ After discussing his three species of *oligōria* (1378b20–1379a9), Aristotle then turns to discuss (i) the conditions-under-which we experience anger (1379a10–30) and (ii) at-whom we feel anger (the target of the state) (1379a30–b37) (this is in accordance with his tripartite schema for addressing the emotions: *Rhet.* II.1.1378a22–9). At the point he turns to (i), Reeve (2018) notes: 'Having discussed contempt [Reeve's translation of *oligōria*] in a preliminary way, Aristotle now returns to his tripartite schema introduced at II.1.1378a24–6. However, there is no focused discussion of the sorts of things because of which one gets angry, because here the people we are angry at also represent the things because of which we are angry' (253n.436). This seems a mistake. In other cases, we still have a discussion of the because-of-what, even when the target is also because-of-what we experience the emotion (e.g. pity: II.8.1386a4–16; envy: II.10.1387b35–1388a5). Rather, I suggest the discussion of *oligōria* and its three species *is* the discussion of the because-of-what of anger.

In **10.3** I argued that the state that Aristotle wishes to characterize here is being-mild-mannered (*praotēs*) (which is said to be the opposite of anger at the beginning of this passage).[7] But we arrive at being-mild-mannered either by being in a condition which blocks anger, or by having a *prior* state of anger which is then calmed (hence, given the latter, we also need the specification of *becoming* mild-mannered, *praünsis*, at the end of the passage), or, most simply, by simply not having our anger aroused. In this way, I proposed, we could specify it as:

> The *absence* or *privation* of anger, whether that occurs after a process of becoming-mild-mannered, or because of a pre-existing condition one possesses, or simply the absence of any cause of anger.

Mild-manneredness, therefore, does not appear to be a representational pleasure or distress in its own right. Instead, it seems to be a specific privation of a representational distress, viz. of anger. Nonetheless, as we saw in Chapter 10, Aristotle seems to treat such determinate privations as 'emotions' in one broad use of that term. For more discussion, see **10.3** and **10.6**. See also **10.8**.

3. Feeling-friendly-towards (*to philein*) (*Rhet.* II.4)

In *Rhet.* II.4 Aristotle defines feeling-friendly-towards as follows:

> Let feeling-friendly-towards (*to philein*) be wishing (*to boulesthai*) for someone what one thinks to be good things, not for one's own sake but for his, and to be productive in action of such things so far as one can. (1380b36–1381a1)

Feeling-friendly-towards is here defined as a type of desire (*orexis*), namely, a wish (*boulēsis*). On my view, this indicates that Aristotle does not think that the state is itself an emotion. However, in **7.4** I suggested that he includes it in his *Rhet.* II catalogue as an economical way of specifying two emotions.[8] For, in the passage that immediately follows the definition above (1381a1–7, quoted in **7.4**), Aristotle links feeling-friendly-towards to a pair of emotions that can be specified as follows:

> Pleasure at (the prospect of) someone getting good things—*qua* the person getting them, not insofar as it benefits you.

---

[7] *Praotēs* is also on the *De an.* I.1 list (403a17).

[8] *To philein* also appears on the *De an.* I.1 list (403a18) and is used as an example in *Rhet.* II.1 to illustrate how emotions can change one's judgements (*kriseis*) (1377b31–1378a3). *Philia* appears on the *NE* list (II.5.1105b22).

And:

> Distress at (the prospect of) someone getting painful things—*qua* the person getting them, not insofar as it harms you.

For more discussion, see 7.4. See also **10.8**.

4. Hating (*to misein*) (*Rhet.* II.4)

No specific definition of hating is provided in *Rhet.* II.4. It is said to be the contrary of feeling-friendly-towards.[9] At the start of the discussion, Aristotle writes:

> Where enmity (*echthra*) and hating (*to misein*) are concerned, it is evident that they are to be grasped from their contraries. And the things productive of enmity are anger (*orgē*), spite (*epēreasmos*), and accusation (*diabolē*). (1382a1–3)

The subsequent discussion is short and focuses on contrasting hating with anger. In 7.4 I argued that if we follow Aristotle's directive of understanding hating from its contrary, we arrive at:

> Hating is wishing for someone[10] what you think to be bad things, for the person's own sake not in so far as it benefits you as such, and to be productive in action of such things so far as you can.

Again, this is a desire, not an emotion. But, as with feeling-friendly-towards, it relates to a pair of emotions as follows:

> Pleasure at (the prospect of) someone getting bad things—*qua* the person getting them, not insofar as it benefits you.

And:

> Distress at (the prospect of) someone getting good things—*qua* the person getting them, not insofar as it harms you.

For more discussion, see 7.4 (also **6.6, 10.8**).

---

[9] *To misein* also appears on the *De an.* I.1 list (403a18) and is used as an example in *Rhet.* II.1 to illustrate how emotions can change one's judgements (*kriseis*) (1377b31–1378a3). *Misos* appears on the *NE* list (II.5.1105b22).

[10] Aristotle will extend this to *kinds of* people in II.4; we can hate *thieves* or *sychophants* (1382a6–7).

5. Fear (*phobos*) (*Rhet.* II.5)

In *Rhet.* II.5 Aristotle defines fear as follows:

> Let fear be a sort of distress or disturbance arising from the appearance of a future destructive or painful evil. (1382a21–2)

As I understand him, Aristotle here intends to identify fear as a representational distress concerning future destructive or painful evils. The formulation above specifies that it arises in response to an intentional state that apprehends its object (see **3.2** and **4.3**). After further clarifying that the evils he has in mind must be of significant magnitude, and near rather than far off (1382a22–7), Aristotle writes:

> If this is what fear is, necessarily the sort of things that are fearful (*ta toiauta phobera einai*) are those that seem to have great potentiality for destruction or for causing harms that lead to great pain. Therefore, even the signs (*ta semeia*) of such things are fearful things (*phobera*). For [the sign of such things makes] the fearful thing (*to phoberon*) appear near at hand. This is *danger*—the approach of something fearful. (1382a27–32)

This suggests that we can characterize fear as:

> Distress at the prospect of a destructive or painful evil or the signs of such (= *danger*).[11]

For further discussion of fear, see **3.2**, **4.3**, **7.2–3**, and **9.2**. For a broader notion of fear in *NE*, see **Cat.7**.

6. Confidence (*to tharsos*) (*Rhet.* II.5)

Aristotle treats confidence as fear's contrary. After discussing fear, he writes:

> Since it is now evident what fear is, what the fearsome things are and by being disposed in which way each is afraid, it is also evident on the basis of this what being confident is, what sorts of things people feel confident about, and by being

---

[11] Cf. *EE* III.1: 'Generally speaking the fearful is what is productive of fear, and that in turn is whatever appears capable of producing pain that is destructive. Those who anticipate some other type of pain might perhaps get a different type of distressful emotion, but it will not be fear. Examples would be what one feels on foreseeing that one will experience the distress of envy, or the sort of distress associated with emulation or shame. Fear, on the other hand, is restricted to the kind of pain that appears to be imminent and whose nature is capable of extinguishing life' (1229a33–b1). Cp. *NE* III.6.1115a7–12 and **Cat.7** below. See also *Rhet.* II.9.1386b20–4.

disposed in which way people feel confident, since confidence is the contrary of fear, and what inspires confidence, of what is fearsome. So [confidence's] hope of things providing safety involves a *phantasia* of them as being close at hand and of fearsome things as either non-existent or as being far away. (II.5.1383a13–19)

I suggested in **10.7** that it is most plausible to think that Aristotle is not here defining confidence, but simply characterizing the intentional state that gives rise to it. But I pointed out that there is evidence elsewhere (esp. *MA* 8.701b37–702a5) that he holds that confidence is a pleasure (rather than simply the privation of fear). As the representational pleasure that is the contrary to fear, confidence would be:

Pleasure at the prospect of safety.

At the end of *Rhet.* II.5 Aristotle claims that anger inspires confidence (1383b6; cf. *Rhet.* II.3.1380a33–4, II.12.1389a18–20). Presumably the thought is that anger makes us less concerned about danger (as the aggressor we, perhaps unjustifiably, feel safe) (see also *NE* III.8.1116b24–30). In *Rhet.* II.12 he also associates being hopeful with confidence: 'to hope (*elpizein*) for something good is a source of confidence (*tharraleon*)' (1389a27–8; also *euelpides* at 26) (cf. also *NE* III.8.1117a9–15).

For more on confidence, see **10.7**.

7. Shame (*aischunē*) (*Rhet.* II.6) and *aidōs* (on *EE* II.2 list and discussed in *NE* IV.9)

In *Rhet.* II.6 Aristotle defines shame (*aischunē*) as follows:

Let shame be a sort of distress or disturbance about evils—whether present, past, or future—that appear to bring a person into disrepute. (1383b12–14)

Paradigmatic examples of things that bring us into disrepute are, he claims, actions owing to vice (cowardice, injustice, self-indulgence, meanness, dishonour, etc.).[12] It is also worth noting that the evils or bad things (*kaka*) need not be ones that *we* have, are, or are about to commit *ourselves*, but can also be about those of others closely

---

[12] According to *Rhet.* II.6, besides acts (performed from vice), we can also be ashamed of: omissions stemming from vice (see e.g. 1383b19–20); acts (or omissions) that are *signs* or *indicators* (*sēmeia*) of vice (e.g. 1383b25, 29–30; 1383b33–1384a2); objects that implicate one with vice (1384b17–20); being deficient (either voluntarily or involuntarily) in some honourable quality shared by all, or most, of a group of which we are a member (1384a8–15); having something done to us (either voluntarily or involuntarily) that involves us in dishonour or censure (1384a15–20). See also Fussi (2015: 124–6).

related to us in some way (1383b17–18, 1385a1–3). The emotion of shame, then, on Aristotle's view, should be understood as the following representational distress:

Distress at evils—whether present, past, or future—that bring one into disrepute.

In *NE* IV.9 Aristotle defines *aidōs*, also often translated by 'shame', as 'a kind of fear of disrepute' (*phobos tis adoxias*) (1128b11–12). This would mark *aidōs* out as a species of fear (cf. *NE* III.6.1115a10).[13] It might be thought that this ties *aidōs* to prospective shame (since fear concerns prospects), whereas *aischunē*, as defined in *Rhet.* II.6, was explicitly temporally neutral (see the definition above). But in fact the situation is more complex. First, Aristotle also uses *aischunē* in *NE* IV.9 and it is unclear whether he thinks there is a sharp distinction between the two in that chapter.[14] Second, *NE* IV.9 also explicitly recognizes *both* retrospective *and* prospective shame.[15] The key, on my view, is to note two different ways shame can be bound to prospects; first, pertaining to the act one is ashamed of; second, with respect to the disrepute itself. *NE* IV.9 restricts *aidōs* to prospects in the second sense (it is *fear of* disrepute), but is temporally neutral with regard to what one is ashamed of (so one could be afraid of the disrepute caused by an action one has performed or is tempted to perform). The *Rhet.* II.6 definition specifies that what one is ashamed of is temporally neutral, but does not comment on the temporal status of the disrepute. This opens up the possibility that the two specifications are consistent and both ultimately view shame as 'fear of disrepute'.[16] But, in fact, this is not so—the two accounts do diverge. First, *Rhet.* II.6 does not restrict *aischunē* to prospective disrepute, but explicitly allows it to range over *both* prospective disrepute *and* present disrepute (1384b27–1385a3; present case beginning at 1384b31, prospective case beginning at 1384b35–6). Second, in *Rhet.* Aristotle appears to view fear more narrowly than in the *NE*, so even cases of shame concerning prospective disrepute may not count as a species of fear. While in *NE* III.6 we are told that we 'fear all bad things, e.g. disrepute, poverty, disease, friendlessness, and death' (1115a10–11),[17] in *Rhet.* II.5 we are told we do not fear

---

[13] Cp. Plato's *Laws* 646e4–647a6. In *NE* II.7 Aristotle refers to a disposition to feel *aidōs*: '*aidōs* is not a virtue, but praise is extended to the *aidēmōn* person…the bashful person (*ho kataplēx*) is ashamed of everything, while he who falls short or is not ashamed of anything is shameless (*anaischuntos*), and the intermediate person is *aidēmōn*' (1108a32, 34–5). So too *EE* III.7: '*aidōs* is a mean state (*mesotēs*) between shamelessness (*anaischuntia*) and bashfulness (*kataplēxis*). The one who cares about no one's opinions is shameless. The one who cares about everyone's opinions alike is bashful. The one who cares about the opinion of those who appear decent is *aidēmōn*' (1233b26–9). In *EE* Aristotle would call such a disposition a *dunamis* ('capacity', 'potentiality', or perhaps 'disposition'), rather than a *hexis* ('state (of character)') (II.2.1220b14–20; cp. *NE* II.5.1105b23–5). See also Cairns (1993: 401–11) and Raymond (2017: 112–17).

[14] For those who think he uses them interchangeably in *NE* IV.9, see e.g. Cope (1877: II.71); Burnet (1900: 200); Gautier and Jolif (1970: 322); Guthrie (1981: 368); Irwin (1985: 330); Grimaldi (1988: 105); Taylor (2006: 235); and Inglis (2014: 279n.28). For those who see a distinction, see e.g. Cairns (1993: 415, 417) and Konstan (2006: 95).

[15] Prospective: 1128b18, 31–2; retrospective: e.g. 1128b19–21, 29–30.

[16] As e.g. Fussi (2015: 117) and Higgins (2015: 3) hold.

[17] Cf. also e.g. *Pol.* VI.5.1320a24–6, which refers to fears (of the rich) about expense.

all things 'but only those capable of [causing] great pains and great destructions' (1382a23–4). And in *Rhet.* II.8 Aristotle specifies the latter as 'the various sorts of death, assaults on the body, ill-treatment, old age, diseases, and lack of food' (1386a7–9)—which all seem to be *physical* in nature—and he *contrasts* these with other bad things, such as friendlessness or scarcity of friends (1386a9–11).[18] The upshot is that *Rhet.* II.6's account of shame is broader than *NE* IV.9's. But this is not because it is temporally neutral with regard to what we are ashamed of (e.g. acts)—*both* accounts are neutral in this way—but because it is temporally neutral with regard to the disrepute (shame can pertain to a disrepute we are presently encountering, not just to one we envisage in the future). And, unlike *NE* IV.9, *Rhet.* II.6 would not appear to view any kind of shame as a species of fear.[19]

For more discussion of shame, see **4.3** and **7.2**.

8. Shamelessness (*anaischuntia*) (*Rhet.* II.6)

The account of shamelessness is provided along with shame at the start of II.6 and borrows from it:

> [and let] shamelessness (*anaischuntia*) [be] a sort of belittling (*oligōria*) and lack of feeling (*apatheia*) about these same things [viz. evils—whether present, past, or future—that appear to bring a person into disrepute]. (1383b14–15)

As I noted in **10.5** there does not seem to be a determinate representational pleasure or distress specified here. Aristotle appears to be including shamelessness as the specific privation of shame. But, as we saw in **10.6**, there is nonetheless evidence that he treats it as an emotion (e.g. in *NE* II.6 he lists it alongside schadenfreude and envy as an emotion that it would always be wrong to experience: 1107a8–11). In these respects, it falls into the same category as being-mild-mannered (*praotēs*) (**Cat.2**). For further discussion, see **10.5–6**.[20]

9. Feeling-grateful-for (*charin echein*) (*Rhet.* II.7)

At the beginning of *Rhet.* II.7 Aristotle writes:

> Those toward whom people feel grateful (*charin echein*), and why, and how—by being disposed in the relevant way [they feel it]—will be clear after having defined favour (*charis*). Let a favour, then, in the sense in which the person who

---

[18] See also *EE* III.1.1229a33–b1, quoted in n.11 above, for a notion of fear closer to *Rhet.* than *NE*.
[19] For a bit more on the opening of *NE* IV.9, see **9.2**. For a systematic analysis of the chapter as a whole, see Raymond (2017). For another important discussion, see Jimenez (2020: chs. 5–6).
[20] For a dispositional notion of shamelessness in *NE* II.7 and *EE* III.7, see n.13 above.

has received it is said to feel grateful (*charin echein*), be a service provided to one in need, not in return for anything, nor in order that the provider get something, but in order that the recipient get something. (1385a16–19)

As we saw in **10.1** Aristotle should here be understood to be defining favour (*charis*) in order to help with the specification of the emotion of *feeling-grateful-for* (*charin echein*). One feels grateful for having been done a favour. The emotion itself is a representational pleasure, presumably along the following lines:

Feeling-grateful-for is a kind of pleasure at a favour received.

For further discussion, see **10.1**.

10. Not-being-grateful-for or being-put-out (*ou charin echein*) (*Rhet.* II.7)

This is the contrary of feeling-grateful-for. As we saw in **10.4** Aristotle does not provide a definition of this opposite, but instead explains how people can be shown to have not, in fact, provided one with a favour (even though they had been presumed to). For example, it could be shown that the people were actually providing the service *for their own sake*, or had provided it *by luck*, or *through compulsion*, and so on. But while such things would give one reason to cease to feel grateful (and so would be useful to the orator), we do not thereby have a specific representational distress demarcated. Instead, all we appear to have is simply the privation of feeling-grateful-for. In this sense, not-being-grateful-for would be like being-mild-mannered (**Cat.2**) and shamelessness (**Cat.8**): it would be classified as an emotion (in a broad sense) insofar as it is the determinate privation of feeling-grateful-for (see **10.6**).

However, Aristotle goes on to note:

It is a sign of disfavour if a small service is not provided or if the same, equal, or greater services are provided to enemies (for it is clear that in neither case are these for our sake). Or if someone has provided a worthless service and knows it (for no one agrees to having a need for worthless things). (II.7.1385b7–10)

Here, one has grasped that a service that could reasonably have been bestowed on one is *lacking*. That could well generate a parallel emotion to the positive emotion of feeling-grateful-for (**Cat.9**), viz:

Distress at the lack of a favour bestowed (that was hoped for).

This is a matter of feeling distress at some ingratitude shown to one. We could characterize it as *being-put-out*.

11. Pity (*eleos*) (*Rhet.* II.8)

In *Rhet.* II.8 Aristotle defines pity as follows:

> Let pity, then, be a sort of distress at an apparent destructive or painful bad thing happening to someone who does not deserve it, and one that a person might expect himself or one of his own to suffer, and this when it appears close at hand. (1385b13–16)

Later in II.8 he claims:

> the things they pity (or: pitiable things: *ha eleousin*) are clear from the definition. For whichever painful or distressing things are destructive are all pitiable, and whichever are ruinous, and whichever evils having magnitude of which luck is the cause. (1386a4–7)

As examples of things that are painful and destructive, Aristotle mentions: death, bodily injury and afflictions, old age, diseases, lack of food. As examples of evils that come through chance, he mentions friendlessness, scarcity of friends, ugliness, weakness, disablement, and evil coming from a source from which good ought to have come (1386a7–13). According to *Rhet.* II.8, then, pity is:

> Distress at a destructive or painful bad thing happening to someone who does not deserve it, and one that we might expect ourselves or one of our own to suffer, and this when it is close at hand.

Interestingly, though, when distinguishing pity from other emotions in *Rhet.* II.9, Aristotle provides a shorter formulation. Pity is: distress at undeserved doing-badly (*lupeisthai epi tais anaxiais kakopragiais*: 1386b9; *ho lupoumenos epi tois anaxiōs kakopragousin*: 1386b26–7; *epi tois anaxiōs prattousi kakōs*: 1386b12).[21] Similarly, in *Poet.* he claims that pity concerns undeserved misfortune (*peri ton anaxion dustuchounta*) (13.1453a4). More generally, then, we might characterize pity as

> Distress at the undeserved doing-badly or misfortune of another.[22]

---

[21] 'Sympathy' (*sunachthesthai*) is also said to have this object (1386b12–13). Cf. *NE* IX.10.1171a6–8.

[22] In *Rhet.* II.13 Aristotle writes: 'The old too are inclined to pity, but not because of the same thing as the young (for the latter are so because of a love of human beings, whereas the former are so because of weakness, since they think that all sorts of [bad] things are close at hand for themselves to suffer, and this, as we saw, tends to arouse pity)' (1390a18–21). The back reference is clearly to II.8 (the definition and 1386a29–b7). But, in fact, in *Rhet.* II.8 Aristotle treats the self-referential aspect of pity as *definitional* of the emotion: it is stated in the definition and stressed in a subsequent explanatory passage (1385b16–23; and note *anankē* at 16). Nonetheless, *Rhet.* II.13's notion of the young experiencing pity because of a love of human beings shows that Aristotle does at least recognize a non-self-referential version of pity.

For a little more discussion, see **3.5** and **4.4**.[23]

12. Distress-based indignation (*to nemesan*) (*Rhet.* II.9)

At the start of his formal discussion of indignation, in *Rhet.* II.9, Aristotle defines the emotion as follows:

> indignation (*to nemesan*)[24] is being distressed (*lupeisthai*) at (*epi* + dative) apparent undeserved doing-well (*anaxiōs eupragein*) (1387a8–9).[25]

In the more detailed account that ensues, we find further indications of the kinds of good fortune that Aristotle has in mind, e.g. *wealth* and *power*. (We are said to experience indignation *at* (*epi* + dative) these things: 1387a13.)

Interestingly, in *NE* and *EE* Aristotle classifies the person prone to indignation (*ho nemesētikos*) as a virtuous mean between someone prone to envy and someone prone to schadenfreude (see **Cat.13** and **Cat.18** below). And he offers specifications of the emotions that correspond to the various states of character. In *NE* II.7, as in *Rhet.*, *nemesis* is said to be distress at (*epi* + dative) undeserved doing-well (1108b3–4). In *EE* III.7 he tells us that what the ancients (*hoi archaioi*) called *nemesis* is:

> being distressed at (*epi* + dative) undeserved doing-badly or doing-well and joy (*chairein*) at (*epi* + dative) deserved doing-badly and doing-well.[26] (1233b23–5)

This is fascinating since it seems to group more than one emotion (in terms of pleasure/distress + object) under the same term. On this account, *nemesis* includes:

(i) Distress at undeserved doing-badly [of another];
(ii) Distress at undeserved doing-well [of another];
(iii) Joy at deserved doing-badly [of another];
(iv) Joy at deserved doing-well [of another].

---

[23] See also e.g. Nussbaum (1994: 87).
[24] In *Rhet.* II.9 Aristotle uses *nemesan* rather than *nemesis*, except once (1386b22). Kennedy (1991: 155) suggests that this may be because *nemesis* had come to take on the meaning of 'divine retribution'. But (a) Aristotle makes the link to the gods himself in *Rhet.* II.9 whilst still using *nemesan* (1386b13–15) and (b) he is happy to use *nemesis* for the emotion in his ethical works (*NE* II.7 1108a35–1108b1, *EE* III.7.1233b24).
[25] The same specification, less the 'apparent', had in fact already been provided earlier in II.9, when Aristotle had contrasted various emotions with pity (1386b10–11). See also *Top.* II.2.110a3.
[26] τὸ λυπεῖσθαι μὲν ἐπὶ ταῖς παρὰ τὴν ἀξίαν κακοπραγίαις καὶ εὐπραγίαις, χαίρειν δ' ἐπὶ ταῖς ἀξίαις.

But there really seem to be *four* emotions here. And elsewhere Aristotle would certainly not characterize at least one of them as indignation. In the terms of *Rhet.*, (i) is *pity* (**Cat. 11**), not (any kind of) indignation; (ii) is (distress-based) indignation, as just sketched, which we find in *Rhet.* and *NE*; while (iii) and (iv) are mentioned in *Rhet.* II.9 but not given a name. I shall come to them shortly. At any rate, *nemesis* in the sense of (ii)—the *nemesis* of *Rhet.* and *NE*—I shall call 'distress-based indignation' to mark it as a distress. This is:

Distress at undeserved doing-well [of another].

13. Envy (*phthonos*) (*Rhet.* II.10)

In *Rhet.* II.10 Aristotle defines envy as follows:

envy is a sort of distress at apparent doing-well in terms of the goods mentioned [wealth, power, etc. from II.9?],[27] on the part of those like themselves, not in order that something accrue to the person himself, but because of those [possessing it].[28] (1387b23–5)

This specification of envy does not state that the doing-well of the other is deserved and a number of scholars think that Aristotle takes envy to allow that the apparent doing well of the other can be either deserved or undeserved.[29] This is supported by a passage in *NE* II.7, where Aristotle claims:

the indignant person is distressed at (*epi* + dative) undeserved doing-well, the envious person, going beyond him, is distressed at (*epi* + dative) all doing-well. (1108b3–5)

So specified, distressed-based indignation (**Cat. 12**) and envy overlap, with the undeserved cases being both. However, in contrast to this characterization, in *EE* III.7 Aristotle claims:

Envy is distress at (*epi* + dative) deserved doing-well. (III.7.1233b19–20)[30]

---

[27] Reeve (2018: 271n.539) traces the goods back, via *Rhet.* II.9.1387a6–23, to *Rhet.* I.5–6.
[28] In the opening line of *Rhet.* II.10, just before the definition, the *epi poiois* ('because of what') feature is referred to as *epi tisi* ('because of whom') (and distinguished from both *tisi* ('at whom') and *pōs echontes* ('under what conditions')) (1387b22). The formal object of this emotion does, of course, essentially make reference to a person. It is *someone's* doing-well.
[29] See Mills (1985: 10); Ben-Ze'ev (2003: 106, 109–11); Sanders (2008, 2014: e.g. 67); Castelli (2015).
[30] ὁ μὲν φθόνος τὸ λυπεῖσθαι ἐπὶ τοῖς κατ' ἀξίαν εὖ πράττουσιν ἐστίν. Cf. also *EE* II.3.1221a38–40 and *Top.* II.2.109b36–7, 110a1–2.

On this view, envy concerns the *deserved* doing-well of the other and so is distinct from distressed-based indignation.

It might be thought that since the *Rhet*. II.10 definition leaves out the notion of desert Aristotle has the broader notion of envy in mind in *Rhet*. But the matter is not so straightforward. On the one hand, in *Rhet*. II.9 he writes:

> It might seem...that envy is also opposed to feeling pity in the same way, as being of the same kind (*genos*)—even the same thing—as indignation; but it is a distinct thing. For though envy too is a disturbing distress and is directed at doing-well, it is not at someone undeserving of it, but at an equal and a similar. (1386b16–20)

Here it is explicitly stated that envy is *distinct from* indignation insofar as it is *not* directed at doing-well that is *undeserved*. This may suggest that in the subsequent *Rhet*. II.10 definition, the idea that envy concerns the deserved doing-well of another was simply taken for granted. Admittedly, the II.9 passage does not *explicitly* state that envy concerns the *deserved* doing-well of the other. It only asserts that envy is directed at 'an equal and a similar' (a point echoed in the II.10 definition: 'on the part of those like themselves'). Some take this to imply that envy simply does not address the desert dimension of the other's doing-well at all (see e.g. Ben-Ze'ev 2003: 106, 109–10; Sanders 2014: 61; Castelli 2015: 224). But one might instead think that the 'equal and similar' of II.9 could itself be intended to signify the desert in question. If Aristotle assumes that envious people think that *they themselves* deserve such goods (see also below) then, in line with the *EE* specification above, he could also be assuming that they construe *those they envy* as deserving the goods too. That is, envious people could deem the envied person to deserve the goods *because* or *insofar as* they deem the envied person to be 'an equal and a similar'. (Where envy is then aroused because the envied person actually possesses the goods, whereas those who are envious do not.) In line with this, in *Rhet*. II.9 Aristotle also claims that a person who is prone to experience distress at people undeservedly doing-badly (= pity) is also pleased (or at least not pained) by someone deservedly doing-badly, since these belong to the same character, and then adds that 'the contrary [emotions] belong to the contrary [character] (*ta enantia tou enantiou*)', before going on to refer to a person who is prone to both envy and schadenfreude (1386b25–1387a3).[31] Envy and schadenfreude are considered the contraries of emotions that are explicitly stated to invoke the notion of desert. In any event, as noted, the II.9 passage *does* explicitly claim that envy 'is a distinct thing' (*esti d'heteron*) from indignation in that it, unlike indignation, does

---

[31] Aristotle also recognizes a dispositional state corresponding to envy at *EE* II.3.1221a38–b2 and *NE* II.7.1108b4–5.

not concern a doing-well that is *undeserved*. That would seem to suggest that if the doing-well is construed as undeserved, the emotion would not count as envy.

On the other hand, as examples of good things that people envy in *Rhet*. II.10, Aristotle mentions deeds or possessions that are achieved through fame and honour (and so cause us to love fame or honour), *and also gifts of fortune* (*eutuchēmata*) (1388a1–2), with the latter also said to be an object of envy in *Rhet*. I.5 (1362a5–6). The inclusion of gifts of fortune as possible objects of envy may point in the direction of the broader notion of envy we found in *NE*, which extends over both the deserved and the undeserved doing-well of another. For gifts of fortune may naturally seem undeserved, or at least not deserved in the sense that they are brought about by one's own concerted efforts. (In *Rhet*. I.5 Aristotle claims: 'Good fortune (*eutuchia*) consists in the acquisition and possession of either all, most, or the most important of those goods of which luck (*tuchē*) is the cause' (1361b39–1362a2).) Of course, though, it is possible that Aristotle thinks that those experiencing envy nonetheless believe that both they and those they envy *deserve* such gifts of fortune, even if these goods do result from chance (cf. 'I deserve a lottery win too, not just you, after all the turmoil and toil we've both endured' or 'I deserve to have just as much power as you've fortuitously had bestowed on you, given that we're both equally impressive and accomplished'[32]). Indeed, after mentioning fame, honour, and gifts of fortune as things that can be envied in *Rhet*. II.10, Aristotle notes 'especially those that they themselves desire *and think they should have*' (1388a3–4; my emphasis). The 'think they should have' implies a notion of desert, but it only directly refers to it appearing to envious people that *they* deserve the goods in question, not to whether they construe the envied person as such as well (see also emulation below). Equally, the gloss does not seem to be indicating that all cases must be like this.

At any rate, it does seem clear that Aristotle thinks that envy at least *includes* cases in which the subject takes the doing-well of the other to be deserved (and that he restricts envy to such cases in *EE*), even if he also has a notion of it extending beyond this (most unequivocally in *NE*). With this in mind, we might characterize envy as follows:

Distress at the (deserved) doing-well of another; *qua* the other doing-well, not *qua* my not doing as well.[33]

---

[32] With Aristotelian envy these would be accompanied by the thought that it would (therefore) be best if those others were *to lose* their wealth/power. This is insofar as envy is focused on the undesirability of the other having the good, rather than (as with emulation) on the desirability of oneself gaining it. See 7.5 and **Cat.14**.

[33] In *Rhet*. II.9 Aristotle emphasizes that distress at the prospect of something happening *to me* owing to the good fortune of another (e.g. someone suddenly becoming rich and powerful) is *fear* (1386b20–4). Such a fear differs from both envy and indignation, which involve distress *at another's* doing-well. Cf. also the distress connected to hating (**Cat.4**).

At the end of his discussion of envy in *Rhet.* II.10, Aristotle mentions a pleasure-based emotion he associates with envy, which involves 'being pleased at the contrary things' (1388a26–7). Presumably, he means something like:

> Pleasure at another not doing-well (even though the other (in fact) deserved to do so); *qua* the other not doing as well as anticipated.[34]

For more on envy, see **3.5**, **7.5**, and **Cat.14**.

14. Emulation (*zēlos*) (*Rhet.* II.11)

In *Rhet.* II.11 Aristotle defines emulation as follows:

> emulation is a sort of distress at the apparent presence, in the case of others who are by nature like the person himself, of good things that are honoured and possible for someone to acquire, not owing to the fact that another has them but rather owing to the fact he himself does not. (1388a32–5)

In the account that follows he notes that if there are goods 'we think we deserve but do not have', we will be prone to emulation (1388a38–b1).[35] This refers to subjects of this emotion construing themselves as deserving the goods that have been achieved by the doing-well other, but it does not explicitly comment on whether emulation involves construing the other that is doing-well as deserving the goods too (cf. **Cat.13** on envy). Nonetheless, it is quite likely that Aristotle would envisage at least many cases of emulation as directed at the deserved doing-well of another. He appears to think that the emotion typically prompts a desire or motivation to attain the good things one experiences emulation about (see below and **7.5**), which is surely more natural if one construes such goods as both achievable and achieved in the other through purposeful human agency, rather than (say) by chance or luck. As examples of 'honoured goods' we experience emulation about, Aristotle mentions wealth, many friends, public office (1388b5), the virtues, and whatever is a source of advantage and benefit to others (1388b11–12). But he also mentions beauty (*kallos*: 1388b14), which may seem more out of the subject's control. However, according to the definition quoted above, to experience emulation about another's good, we must view that good as

---

[34] Cf. schadenfreude, **Cat.18** below, which (at least in *EE* III.7.1233b18–23) explicitly concerns enjoying someone's *undeserved* misfortune.

[35] We might think we deserve such things because our ancestors, relatives, friends, or countrymen are specially honoured for them and so we view them as things that are ours (1388b8–10).

'possible to acquire'. So whatever Aristotle intends by 'beauty', here, must, it seems, also be construed as such.

Emulation is similar to, but importantly different from, envy. Let us specify it as follows:

> Distress at the (deserved) doing-well of another; *qua* my not doing so well, not *qua* the person doing so.

Reeve (2018a: *ad loc.*) translates *zēlos* by 'jealousy'. It is worthwhile noting why this is inappropriate. Jealously is typically understood to involve distress at someone else possessing a good *at one's expense*. Think, for example, of straightforward (monogamous) romantic jealousy. Noel is jealous of Eric insofar as Eric's being with Amber entails that Noel cannot be. But, concerning *zēlos*, we are explicitly told that (i) it is my not having the good that is the crucial factor, not the fact that the other does, and (ii) it is nonetheless *possible* for me to acquire the good. It is clear that our case of romantic jealously fails on both counts: Eric's being with Amber (the 'good') *is* crucial (contra (i)) and it is so because it is his being with Amber that prevents Noel from being so (contra (ii)).[36] Envy and emulation, for Aristotle, are closely related to each other, but the distinction between them is not well captured by the distinction between envy and jealousy. Both envy and emulation, on his account, concern the doing-well of another, which involves the other possessing a good we want. But with envy the distress is focused on *the other possessing the good* (rather than on our not having it), whereas with emulation the distress is focused on *our not possessing the good* (rather than the other having it) (see also 3.5).[37] This contrast allows Aristotle to maintain that there is an important ethical difference between the two emotions:

> Emulation is a decent thing (*epieikes*) characteristic of decent people (*epieikoi*), whereas envy is a base one (*phaulon*) characteristic of base people (*phauloi*)— for the decent person, because of emulation (*dia ton zēlon*), is ready to attain the good things (*paraskeuazei tunchanein tōn agathōn*), whereas the base person, because of envy (*dia ton phthonon*), is ready for his neighbour not to have them. (II.11.1388a35–b1)

See 7.5 for more discussion of this passage.

---

[36] For more on the relation between jealousy and envy, see Purshouse (2004).
[37] Compare the following. Monty has a new tennis racket. Bert might be upset (i) because *Monty has got the racket and he wants to keep up with Monty* or (ii) because Monty *has got the racket that he (Bert) has wanted for ages*. In neither case does Monty get the good at Bert's expense (Monty's having the racket does not prevent Bert from having another such racket) and so in neither case does jealousy quite fit. Both might, in fact, be considered types of envy.

15. Disdain (*kataphronēsis*) (*Rhet*. II.11)

Aristotle does not provide a definition of this emotion in *Rhet*., but at the end of II.11 he tells us that disdain (or 'contempt': *kataphronēsis*) is the contrary of emulation:

> Disdain is the contrary of emulation, and to feel disdain of someone is the contrary of feeling emulous of him. And those who are so disposed that they feel emulous of others or others feel emulous of them are inclined to feel disdain for those who have the bad contraries of the goods that people feel emulous of, and to do so because of these. That is why they often feel disdain for those who are fortunate, whenever luck comes to them but without their having the good things that are honoured. (1388b22–9)

Aristotle also used the same word, *kataphronēsis*, as the label for one of the three kinds of offence or belittling (*oligōria*) he specifies in his discussion of anger in *Rhet*. II.2. He writes:

> For the one who disdains is offensive (*ho te gar kataphronōn oligōrei*) (for the things that people disdain are the ones they think are worth nothing, and the ones they think are worth nothing they are offensive about (*tōn de mēdenos axiōn oligōrousin*)). (1378b15–17)

Since someone's disdain, here, is construed, by the subject who experiences anger, as a slight, the disdain must appear to be *manifested* in some way. So this would be disdainful behaviour, or some such.[38] But in *Rhet*. II.11 disdain appears to qualify as an emotion in its own right (it is explicitly said to be the contrary of emulation). We can link the two notions if we envisage the disdainful behaviour alluded to in *Rhet*. II.2 to flow from the disdainful emotion mentioned in II.11. Perhaps some behaviour or comment or look is taken as an indication that the other possesses such an emotion directed at you. As an emotion disdain seems to be a negative state, which serves as a contrary to emulation not by being a representational pleasure about the same things emulation involves being distressed about, but by being a representational distress directed at the opposed state. Perhaps it could be characterized as:

> Disdain is a sort of distress at the presence (in the case of others who are by nature like oneself) of bad things that are dishonoured, whereby one looks down on the person insofar as they are dishonoured.

---

[38] In *Rhet*. II.3 Aristotle claims that behaving shamelessly (in front of another, by denying evident facts) displays *kataphronēsis*, 'at any rate, we feel no shame before those we deeply disdain (*kataphronein*)' (1380a20–1). See also *Pol*. V.3.1302b25–33, V.10.1311b40–1312a20.

Note that in specifying the emotion as a distress, we are not implying that the subject is *saddened* by the state of the other. Rather, the emotion seems to be a representational distress or pain in the sense that it involves experiencing contempt or disgust at the other. Hence, 'disdain'.[39]

16. Pleasure-based indignation (specified without a name in *Rhet.* II.9; linked to *nemesis* in *EE* III.7)

Besides the emotions discussed so far, which consist of those that received separate treatment in *Rhet.* II and their contraries, some other emotions are mentioned in the opening of *Rhet.* II.9.[40] The first of these Aristotle does not give a name. Just as he contrasts pity (distress at undeserved doing-badly) with (what we called) distress-based indignation (distress at undeserved doing-well), so too he claims that one who is distressed at undeserved doing-badly will take pleasure (*hēsthēsetai*) or be un-pained (*alupos*) at *deserved* doing-badly (1386b27–8).[41] This specifies a distinct representational pleasure:[42]

Being pleased at the deserved doing-badly of another.

Aristotle provides the following example:

no good person would be distressed when parricides and bloodthirsty murderers meet punishment; for it is right to experience joy (*chairein*) at (*epi* + dative) such things... (1386b28–30)

We saw in the discussion of distress-based indignation (Cat.12) that in *EE* III.7 (1233b23–5) Aristotle treats experiencing joy at deserved doing-badly as a kind of *nemesis*, even though in the official account of indignation (*to nemesan*) in *Rhet.* II.9 (also seen in *NE*) he appears to reserve 'indignation' for distress at undeserved doing-well alone. I think we can see how being pleased at deserved doing-badly might also be thought of as a kind of indignation. Distress at underserved doing-well and pleasure at deserved doing-badly seem to be two sides of the same coin: the sense of *injustice* in someone undeservedly doing-well is matched by the sense of *justice* of someone deservedly doing-badly. In the background, of course, is that in Greek mythology *Nemesis* was a Goddess of

---

[39] Cf. *EE* III.7, where we are told that that disdainful person (*kataphronētikos*) 'lives without regard for others' (1233b35–6).
[40] Aristotle is here considering what we should say the opposite of pity is and ends up specifying several emotions. I chart the overall picture in the Appendix.
[41] 'Deserved' (*axiōs*) is specified by 'in the contrary way' (*enantiōs*): *epi tois enantiōs kakopragousin* (1386b27–8); contrary to *epi tois anaxiōs kakopragousin* (1386b26–7).
[42] The 'unpained' variant may provide yet another privation-emotion (see 10.6).

retribution, bringing about just deserts to those who show excessive hubris (cf. *EE* III.7.1233b25–6). With our current emotion we have a hedonic response to the world being *righted*—justice being meted out—namely, pleasure or joy at deserved doing-badly. To distinguish this kind of indignation from the distress-based version (**Cat.12**), we might call it 'pleasure-based indignation'.

17. Pride-in-another (specified without a name in *Rhet.* II.9)

There is also another emotion mentioned in passing in *Rhet.* II.9, which again does not there receive a name. This is:

> joy…at deserved doing-well (*chairein…epi tois eu prattousi kat' axian*). (1386b30–1)[43]

Aristotle does not provide an example, but a case might be when someone has worked incredibly hard for something and subsequently achieves success with it. We might then experience pleasure at the other's deserved success: 'we are all extremely *proud* of you', we might say. This seems to be a kind of pride, but pride that is essentially other-directed. One experiences joy in the other's deserved success. As we have seen (**Cat.12**), *EE* III.7 also groups this under the term *nemesis* (along with distress-based and pleasure-based indignation, and pity), but we may more naturally view it as a kind of pride, pride-in-another. We might also think of it as some kind of 'admiration'. As a representational pleasure, the emotion is:

> Pleasure at the deserved doing-well of another.

18. Schadenfreude (*epichairekakia*) (*Rhet.* II.9; properly named in *NE* II.7)

The last of our additional emotions from the opening of *Rhet.* II.9 is schadenfreude. Aristotle links someone who is envious of another doing-well with someone who enjoys another's doing-badly. He writes:

> All these [sc. the emotions just discussed: pity, pleasure-based indignation, pride-in-another] belong to the same moral character, and the opposite [emotions] to the opposite; for the person who enjoys another's misfortune (*ho epichairekakos*) is the same as the envious person (*phthoneros*); for when someone

---

[43] Once again Aristotle indicates the formal object with *epi* + dative. See **2.3**.

is distressed at (*epi* + dative) the acquisition or possession of something [= envy], necessarily he takes joy (*charein*) at (*epi* + dative) its deprivation or destruction. (1386b33–1387a3)

This is all we get on the emotion in *Rhet*.[44] Although, strictly speaking, English has no word for taking joy in another's misfortune, the German 'schadenfreude' is now often used (and is in English dictionaries as such). And it makes good sense to use it.[45]

Interestingly, in his discussions of the means connected to the emotions in his ethical works, Aristotle views envy and schadenfreude as two vicious emotions either side of the mean *nemesis* (which, in the *EE*, is itself said to have multiple forms; see **Cat.12, 16**). In the *EE*, before turning to *nemesis*, he contrasts the vicious cases as follows:

Take, for example, the envious person (*ho phthoneros*) and the person who enjoys another's misfortune (*epichairekakos*). In terms of the states after which these are named, envy (*phthonos*) is distress at (*epi* + dative) those who deservedly do well (*to lupeisthai epi tois kat' axian eu prattousin*), whereas the emotion belonging to one who enjoys another's misfortune (*to de tou epichairekakou pathos*) does not have a name, but the person who possesses this is manifested in taking pleasure in undeserved doing-badly (*ho echōn dēlos esti tō(i) chairein tais para tēn axian kakopragiais*). (III.7.1233b18–22)

According to this, despite Aristotle being able to refer to the *person* disposed to manifest schadenfreude—an *epichairekakos*—he does not have a word for the emotion itself. However, by the time he wrote *NE* he seems to have found one. Indeed, he perhaps here *coins* one—for it does not seem to be attested before him and, as we have seen, in *EE* he claims that one does not exist.[46] He writes:

Nemesis is a mean between envy (*phthonos*) and schadenfreude (*epichairekakia*), and these are concerned with the distress (*lupē*) and pleasure (*hēdonē*) at (*epi* + dative) the fortunes of our neighbours: the person characterized by *nemesis* is distressed at (*epi* + dative) undeserved doing-well, the envious person, going

---

[44] Although see *Rhet*. II.2.1379b17–18.
[45] For the *Rhet*. passage just quoted, Kennedy (1991) translates 'malicious', Reeve (2018) employs 'spiteful'. With regard to the *NE* II.7 passage quoted below, Ross (1980, and still in the *ROT*), Irwin (1985), Crisp (2000) and Reeve (2014) all use 'spite', Broadie and Rowe (2002) 'malice'. But given that schadenfreude has now entered into English and preserves the etymology of *epichairekakia*, we should surely use it. Rackham (1934), in the *NE* Loeb, while translating 'malice', at least adds in a note: 'The word means "delight at another's misfortune", *Schadenfreude*' (96a).
[46] It is on the basis of detail like this that one may seek to establish that the *EE* is the earlier work, even if the two works share the three common books. (*MM* has the word (I.27.1192b18), but I take this to be a later work, and not by Aristotle himself.)

beyond him, is distressed at (*epi* + dative) all doing-well, and the person prone to schadenfreude falls so far short of being distressed that he even rejoices (*ho epichairekakos tosouton elleipei tou lupeisthai hōste kai chairein*).[47] (II.7.1108a35–b6)

Indeed, he had used his coinage (if that is what it was) a little earlier in *NE* as well. When he provided examples of emotions that do not admit of a mean because their very names imply badness, it joined envy (*phthonos*) and shamelessness (*anaischuntia*) as part of an unholy trinity (II.6.1107a9–11).

Pooling from the different sources, then, we can see that the definition of schadenfreude (*epichairekakia*) is:

Pleasure (or joy: *chairein*) at undeserved doing-badly.[48]

19. *Epithumia* (appetite) (*NE* II.5, *EE* II.2, *De an.* I.1 lists)

As we saw in **8.1** *epithumia* not only appears on the lists of emotions in *NE* II.5, *EE* II.2, and *De an.* I.1, it is also said to be an emotion just after Aristotle's official discussion of the individual emotions in *Rhet.* II concludes (II.12.1388b32–4), and is mentioned in the opening of *Rhet.* II.1, when Aristotle introduces the idea that emotions bear on a subject's judgements (*kriseis*) (1378a3–5). However, *epithumia* is one of Aristotle's two non-rational desires and, paradigmatically, picks out a desire for a bodily pleasure in response to a painful bodily state (see **8.2** and my 2012: ch. 4). In **8.3** I suggested that there could nonetheless be a sense in which at least a significant class of *epithumiai* could be said to include an emotion (i.e. a representational distress). *Epithumia*, in this sense, would amount to:

A desire for a (rectifying) pleasure accompanied by distress at a bodily pain, or discomfort, or bodily lack, or other lack or absence.

Structurally, this makes such *epithumiai* parallel to anger, consisting of a desire alongside a representational distress. In this case, the representational distress is:

---

[47] This is the passage with the broad notion of envy we flagged in **Cat.13**. The text continues: 'There will be an opportunity to discuss these issues later' (1108b5–6). But, sadly, the 'later' discussion does not appear in our edition of *NE* (although we have the parallel noted in *EE*). The discussion finishes at shame (*aidōs*) in IV.9, which was mentioned just before the *nemesis*-triad in the list in II.7 (and discussed in **Cat.7**).

[48] Contrast Ben-Ze'ev (2003: 116), who fails to see that Aristotle is attempting to characterize the same emotion, schadenfreude, in both the *EE* III.7 and *NE* II.7 passages quoted.

Distress at a bodily pain, or discomfort, or bodily lack, or other lack or absence.[49]

See Chapter 8 for more discussion.

20. *Chara* (joy) (*NE* II.5 and *De an.* I.1 lists)

Chara (joy) appears on the *NE* II.5 (1105b22) and *De an.* I.1 (403a18) lists of emotions. It is worth emphasizing that Aristotle sometimes characterizes pleasure-based emotions in terms of *chairein* ('joy'), rather than *hēdonē* ('pleasure'). Although I have generally stuck to specifying emotions in terms of representational *pleasures*, 'joy' can sound appropriate in some cases in English too (e.g. schadenfreude as joy at someone's undeserved misfortune) and I have no problem in such cases of thinking of emotions as 'representational joys' (see 2.4). Relatedly, in *Top.* II.6—echoing Plato's *Protagoras* (358a6–b3)—Aristotle claims that Prodicus used to divide pleasures (*hēdonai*) into joy (*chara*), delight (*terpsis*), and good cheer (*euphrosunē*); which, he tells us, are in fact all names for the same thing, viz. pleasure (112b22–4).

But insofar as *NE* II.5 and *De an.* I.1 place *chara* alongside other specific emotions, it would seem to be treated as an emotion in its own right, not simply marking a genus (or determinable). Indeed, in the *NE* list Aristotle places it alongside other emotions all of which together are characterized as 'accompanied by pleasure or distress' (1105b21–3). He can hardly place one of the genera (or determinables) of emotions on a list of some of its species (or determinates).[50] Interestingly, though, the other uses of *chara* we find in Aristotle go in two different directions, both concerning sensory pleasure. First, in *Gen. an.* we get the *chara* of male (I.18.724a1) and female (I.20.727b35) ejaculation. This would seem to amount to the pleasure one gets at the satisfaction of a sexual *epithumia*. Second, in *Pol.* VIII.7, by contrast, we get purifying[51] melodies providing a harmless *chara* to human beings (1342a15–16). On either use, it is not clear that we are going to get a *representational* pleasure *as such*, though representational pleasures can clearly be bound up with such experiences.

However, I have another suggestion. As we have seen, Aristotle employs *chairein* in characterizing the pleasures of some of his pleasure-based emotions (schadenfreude, pride-in-another). Perhaps he placed *chara* on his lists of emotions as a subgenus of pleasure-based emotions aiming to pick out these various joys?

---

[49] *Erōs*, erotic love or desire, is said to be type of *epithumia* in *Rhet.* II.7 (1385a23). Cf. *EE* VII.12.1245a24–6; *NE* IX.12.1171b29–32.
[50] Cf. *De an.* I.4: 'we say that the soul is distressed (*lupeisthai*), joyed (*chairein*), confident (*tharrein*) and afraid (*phobeisthai*), and further that it is angry (*orgizesthai*)' (408b1–2).
[51] Or 'action-involving' if we read *praktika* with the OCT, rather than *kathartika* with the MSS.

21. *Pothos* (longing or regret) (*NE* II.5 list)

This only appears on the *NE* II.5 list of emotions and there are in fact very few references to it in Aristotle at all.[52] In Plato's *Philebus* it appears on lists of emotions (47e1–2, 50b7–c1) and is said to be a kind of pain (47e3). But it is also said, along with the other emotions, to be 'mixed with pleasure' (48a1–4). In the *Cratylus* Socrates claims that it is a desire for something when that thing is absent or elsewhere (*pou*) (hence 'longing') rather than when present (desire for what is present, he calls '*himeros*') (420a3–7; cf. also e.g. *Republic* IX.573a7, *Phaedrus* 252a7, 253e6, *Symposium* 197d7). This chimes with one passage where Aristotle elaborates on *pothos* himself. In *NE* IX.5 he writes (I quote with some surrounding context):

> [Goodwill] seems, then, to be a beginning of friendship, as the pleasure of the eye is the beginning of love. For no one loves if he has not first been delighted by the form of the beloved, but he who delights in the form of another does not, for all that, love him, but only does when he *longs* for him when absent and has an appetite for his presence (ὅταν καὶ ἀπόντα ποθῇ καὶ τῆς παρουσίας ἐπιθυμῇ)...(1167a3–7)

This notion of *pothos* as pertaining to longing for a loved one when absent is echoed in the following passage from *Rhet.* I.11, which does not explicitly mention *pothos*:

> there is a certain pleasure that attaches to mourning and lamentation for a departed one, since there is distress at (*epi* + dative) his not being there and pleasure in remembering and, in a way, seeing him, the actions he was doing, and what he was like. That is why it made perfect sense to say: 'Thus he spoke, and stirred in all of them a deep desire for weeping'.[53] (1370b25–9)

So far as there is a representational distress bound up with such a desire, it would seem to be:

Distress at the absence of a loved one.[54]

---

[52] It is also on the list of emotions in *MM* I.7 (1186a14), but (on my view) this is a later work and not by Aristotle. In *PA* I.5 he uses a first-person plural verbal form: '... for as regard both those things on the basis of which one would examine them and those things about them which *we long to* (*pothoumen*) know, the perceptual phenomena are altogether few' (644b25–8). Cf. also *NE* I.7.1097b23.
[53] A quotation from Homer's *Iliad* (23: 108).
[54] Cf. Cooper (1996: 251) who characterizes it (without citing anything else in Aristotle, bar its mention on the *NE* II.5 list) as 'yearning for an absent or lost loved one'.

The passage from *Rhet.* I.11 also nicely illustrates the suggestion in the *Philebus* that *pothos* would be 'mixed' with pleasure. That too could be construed as an emotion:

Pleasure at remembering and visualizing a lost loved one.

Pothos, *qua* emotional, will also obviously be closely related to a desire that the lost loved one still be around. But Aristotle can keep both the emotions I have specified and this desire at least conceptually distinct from each other, even if the desire and the distress typically come together and some episodes may include all three.

Appendix: Tree diagram of emotions connected to (un)deserved doing-well or -badly

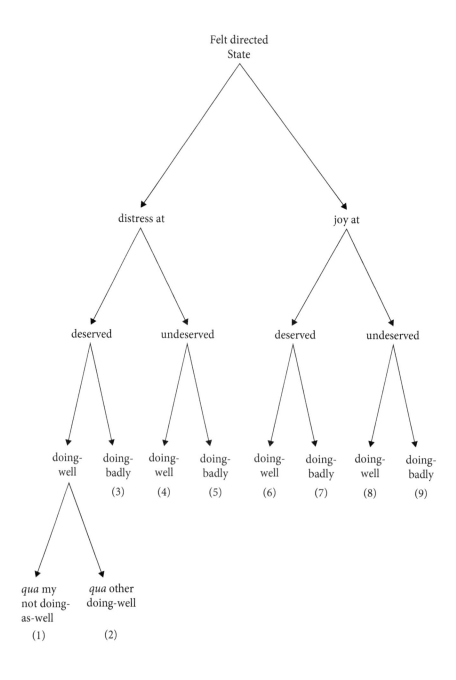

(1) = emulation* (**Cat.14**)
(2) = envy* (**Cat.13**)
(3) = disdain* (**Cat.15**)
(4) = distress-based indignation (**Cat.12**)
(5) = pity (**Cat.11**)
(6) = pride-in-another (**Cat.17**)
(7) = pleasure-based indignation (**Cat.16**)
(8) = [not mentioned]. For (8) consider: those who are unexpectedly gifted some fortune, through no good work of their own. If I do not view them as bad, I may still be happy for them.
(9) = schadenfreude (**Cat.18**)

Grouped in opposed distresses/pleasures:

Pleasure at undeserved doing-badly [schadenfreude] (9)	Distress at undeserved doing-badly [pity] (5)
Pleasure at deserved doing-badly [pleasure-based indignation] (7)	Distress at deserved doing-badly [disdain] (3) (i.e. contempt-at/looking-down-on-others insofar as they have brought dishonour upon themselves; *not*: sadness at their doing-badly)
Pleasure at deserved doing-well (pride-in-another) (6)	(i) Distress at deserved doing-well (*qua* the other doing-well) (envy) (2) (ii) Distress at deserved doing-well (*qua* my not doing-well) (emulation) (1)
Pleasure at undeserved doing-well [not mentioned] (8)	Distress at undeserved doing-well (distress-based indignation) (4)

* At least to the extent that these emotions concern *deserved* doing-well. See **Cat.13** and **Cat. 14** for more discussion.

Bibliography

Achtenberg, D. (2002). *Cognition of Value in Aristotle's Ethics*, Albany, State University of New York Press.
Allen, D. (2002). *The World of Prometheus: The Politics of Punishing in Democratic Athens*, Princeton, Princeton University Press.
Altham, J. E. J. (1986). 'The Legacy of Emotivism', in *Fact, Science and Morality: Essays on A.J. Ayer's Language, Truth and Logic*, G. F. Macdonald and C. Wright (eds.), Oxford, Basil Blackwell, 275–88.
Anscombe, G. E. M. (1965). 'The Intentionality of Sensation: A Grammatical Feature', in *Analytic Philosophy*, R. J. Butler (ed.), Oxford, Blackwell, 158–80.
Archer, A. (2015). 'Reconceiving Direction of Fit', *Thought: A Journal of Philosophy*, 4(3): 171–80.
Armstrong, D. M. (1968). *A Materialist Theory of the Mind*, London, Routledge and Kegan Paul.
Arnim, H. von (1903–5). *Stoicorum veterum fragmenta*, Vols. I–III, Leipzig, Teubner.
Arpaly, N. (2003). *Unprincipled Virtue*, Oxford, Oxford University Press.
Arpaly, N. and Schroeder, T. (1999). 'Praise, Blame and the Whole Self', *Philosophical Studies*, 93(2): 161–88.
Atkins, P. and Robertson Ishii, T. (2020). 'Essential vs. Accidental Properties', in *The Stanford Encyclopedia of Philosophy* (winter 2020 edn), E. N. Zalta (ed.), <https://plato.stanford.edu/archives/win2020/entries/essential-accidental/>.
Audi, R. (1990). 'Weakness of Will and Rational Action', *Australasian Journal of Philosophy*, 68(3): 270–81.
Aufderheide, J. (2016). 'Aristotle Against Delos: Pleasure in *Nicomachean Ethics* X', *Phronesis*, 61(3): 284–306.
Bain, D. (2003). 'Intentionalism and Pain', *Philosophical Quarterly*, 53(213): 502–23.
Barnes, J. (1971–2). 'Aristotle's Concept of Mind', *Proceedings of the Aristotelian Society*, 72: 101–14.
Barnes, J. (1984) (ed.). *The Complete Words of Aristotle: The Revised Oxford Translation*, Princeton, Princeton University Press.
Bedford, E. (1956–57). 'Emotions', *Proceedings of the Aristotelian Society*, 57: 281–304.
Bekker, I. (1831). *Aristotelis Opera*, Berlin, G. Reimer.
Benbaji, H. (2013). 'How Is Recalcitrant Emotion Possible?', *Australasian Journal of Philosophy*, 91(3): 577–99.
Bennett, J. (1974). 'The Conscience of Huckleberry Finn', *Philosophy*, 49(188): 123–34.
Ben-Ze'ev, A. (2003). 'Aristotle on Emotions Towards the Fortune of Others', in *Envy, Spite, and Jealousy: The Rivalrous Emotions in Ancient Greece*, D. Konstan and N. K. Rutter (eds.), Edinburgh, Edinburgh University Press, 99–121.
Block, I. (1960). 'Aristotle and the Physical Object', *Philosophy and Phenomenological Research*, 21(1): 93–101.
Bonitz, H. (1870). *Index Aristotelicus*, Graz., Akadmische Druck- u. Verlagsanstalt Graz. (1955 facsimile of the 1870 orig.).
Bostock, D. (2000). *Aristotle's Ethics*, Oxford, Oxford University Press.
Brady, M. E. (2005). 'The Fearlessness of Courage', *Southern Journal of Philosophy*, 43(2): 189–211.

Brady, M. S. (2007). 'Recalcitrant Emotions and Visual Illusions', *American Philosophical Quarterly*, 44(3): 273–84.
Brady, M. S. (2009). 'The Irrationality of Recalcitrant Emotions', *Philosophical Studies*, 145(3): 413–30.
Brady, M. S. (2013). *Emotional Insight: The Epistemic Role of Emotional Experience*, Oxford, Oxford University Press.
Broadie, S. and Rowe, C. (2002). *Aristotle: Nicomachean Ethics*, Oxford, Oxford University Press.
Broome, J. (2010). 'Rationality', in *A Companion to the Philosophy of Action*, T. O'Connor and C. Sandis (eds.), Malden, MA, Wiley-Blackwell, 285–92.
Broome, J. (2013a). *Rationality through Reasoning*, Malden, MA, Wiley-Blackwell.
Broome, J. (2013b). 'Enkrasia', *Organon F. Medzinárodný Časopis Pre Analytickú Filozofiu*, 20(4):425–36.
Burnet, J. (1900). *The Ethics of Aristotle*, London, Methuen and Co.
Burnyeat, M. (1992). 'Is an Aristotelian Philosophy of Mind Still Credible (a Draft)', in *Essays on Aristotle's* De anima, M. C. Nussbaum and A. O. Rorty (eds.), Oxford, Clarendon Press, 15–26.
Burnyeat, M. (1995). 'How Much Happens When Aristotle Sees Red and Hears Middle C? Remarks on *De anima* 2. 7–8', in *Essays on Aristotle's* De Anima, M. C. Nussbaum and A. O. Rorty (eds.), Oxford, Clarendon Press, 421–34 (suppl. essay in orig. vol. 1992).
Burnyeat, M. (2001). 'Aquinas on "Spiritual Change" in Perception', in *Ancient and Medieval Theories of Intentionality*, D. Perler (ed.), Leiden, Brill, 129–53.
Burnyeat, M. (2002). '*De anima* II.5', *Phronesis*, 47(1): 28–90.
Cairns, D. L. (1993). *Aidōs: The Psychology and Ethics of Honour and Shame in Ancient Greek Literature*, Oxford, Clarendon Press.
Cashdollar, S. (1973). 'Aristotle's Account of Incidental Perception', *Phronesis*, 18(2): 156–75.
Cassam, Q. (2010). 'Judging, Believing and Thinking', *Philosophical Issues*, 20(1): 80–95.
Castelli, L. M. (2015). '$Φθόνος$: $πάθος$, $ἦθος$, Perception of Desert and the Place of Envy in Rhet. II', in *La Retorica di Aristotele e la dottrina delle passioni*, B. Centrone (ed.), Pisa, Pisa University Press, 221–48.
Caston, V. (1996). 'Why Aristotle Needs Imagination', *Phronesis*, 41(1): 20–55.
Caston, V. (1998). 'Aristotle and the Problem of Intentionality', *Philosophy and Phenomenological Research*, 58(2): 249–98.
Caston, V. (2005). 'The Spirit and the Letter: Aristotle on Perception', in *Metaphysics, Soul and Ethics: Themes From the Work of Richard Sorabji*, R. Salles (ed.), Oxford, Oxford University Press, 245–320.
Caston, V. (2006). 'Aristotle's Psychology', in *The Blackwell Companion to Ancient Philosophy*, M. L. Gill and P. Pellegrin (eds.), Oxford, Blackwell, 316–46.
Caston, V. (2009). 'Commentary on Charles', *Proceedings of the Boston Area Colloquium of Ancient Philosophy*, 24(1): 30–49.
Caston, V. (2021). 'Aristotle and the Cartesian Theatre', in *Encounters with Aristotelian Philosophy of Mind*, J. Fink and P. Gregoric (eds.), London, Routledge, 169–220.
Caston, V. (unpublished). 'Aristotle on Perceptual Content'.
Cates, D. F. (2003). 'Conceiving Emotions: Martha Nussbaum's *Upheavals of Thought*', *Journal of Religious Ethics*, 31(2): 325–41.
Centrone, B. (2015). '$φόβος$ nella *Retorica* di Aristotele. Tra emozione istintiva e cognizione complessa', in *La Retorica di Aristotele e la dottrina delle passioni*, B. Centrone (ed.), Pisa, Pisa University Press, 143–70.

Chalmers, D. (2004). 'The Representational Character of Experience', in *The Future for Philosophy*, B. Leiter (ed.), Oxford, Oxford University Press, 153–81.
Charles, D. (1995). 'Aristotle and Modern Realism' in *Aristotle and Moral Realism*, R. Heinaman (ed.), Boulder and San Francisco, Westview Press, 135–72.
Charles, D. (2006). 'Aristotle's Desire', in *Mind and Modality: Studies in the History of Philosophy in Honour of Simo Knuuttila*, V. Hirvonen, T. Holopainen, and M. Tuominen (eds.), Leiden, Brill, 19–40.
Charles, D. (2009). 'Aristotle's Psychological Theory', *Proceedings of the Boston Area Colloquium of Ancient Philosophy*, 24(1): 1–29.
Charles, D. (2011). 'Desire in Action: Aristotle's Move', in *Moral Psychology and Human Action in Aristotle*, M. Pakaluk and G. Pearson (eds.), Oxford, Oxford University Press, 75–93.
Charles, D. (2015). 'Aristotle on Practical and Theoretical Knowledge', in *Bridging the Gap between Aristotle's Science and Ethics*, D. Henry and K. Nielsen (eds.), Cambridge, Cambridge University Press, 71–93.
Charles, D. (2021). *The Undivided Self: Aristotle and the 'Mind-Body Problem'*, Oxford, Oxford University Press.
Cheng, W. (2019). 'Aristotle's Vocabulary of Pain', *Philologus*, 163(1): 47–71.
Code, A. and Moravcsik, J. (1992). 'Explaining Various Forms of Living', in *Essays on Aristotle's De anima*, M. Nussbaum and A. O. Rorty (eds.), Oxford, Clarendon Press, 129–45.
Cooper, J. M. (1996). 'An Aristotelian Theory of the Emotions', in *Essays on Aristotle's Rhetoric*, A. O. Rorty (ed.), Berkeley, CA, University of California Press, 238–57.
Cope, E. (1877). *The Rhetoric of Aristotle, with a Commentary*, rev. and ed. J. Sandys, Cambridge, Cambridge University Press.
Corcilius, K. (2008). *Streben und Bewegen. Aristoteles' Theorie der Animalischen Ortsbewegung*, Berlin, Walter de Gruyter.
Corcilius, K. (2011). 'Aristotle's Definition of Non-Rational Pleasure and Pain and Desire', in *Aristotle's Nicomachean Ethics: A Critical Guide*, J. Miller (ed.), Cambridge, Cambridge University Press, 117–43.
Crane, T. (1998). 'Intentionality as the Mark of the Mental', in *Contemporary Issues in the Philosophy of Mind*, A. O'Hear (ed.), Cambridge, Cambridge University Press, 229–52.
Crane, T. (2001a). *Elements of Mind*, Oxford, Oxford University Press.
Crane, T. (2001b). 'Intentional Objects', *Ratio*, 14(4): 336–49.
Crane, T. (2003). 'The Intentional Structure of Consciousness', in *Consciousness: New Philosophical Perspectives*, A. Jokic and Q. Smith (eds.), Oxford, Oxford University Press, 33–56.
Crane, T. (2006). 'Intentionality and Emotion', in *Radical Enactivism: Intentionality, Phenomenology, Narrative*, R. Menary (ed.), Amsterdam, John Benjamins Publishing Company, 107–19.
Crane, T. (2009). 'Intentionalism', in *The Oxford Handbook of Philosophy of Mind*, A. Beckermann, B. P. McLaughlin, and S. Walter (eds.), Oxford, Oxford University Press, 474–93.
Crane, T. (2013). *The Objects of Thought*, Oxford, Oxford University Press.
Crisp, R. (2000). *Aristotle Nicomachean Ethics*, Cambridge, Cambridge University Press.
Curzer, H. (2012). *Aristotle and the Virtues*, Oxford, Oxford University Press.
Dalgliesh, T. (1997). 'An Anti-Anti-Essentialist View of the Emotions: A Reply to Kupperman', *Philosophical Psychology*, 10(1): 85–90.

D'Arms, J. and Jacobson, D. (2003). 'The Significance of Recalcitrant Emotion (or, Anti-Quasijudgmentalism)', *Royal Institute of Philosophy Supplement*, 52: 127–45.
Davidson, D. (1973-4). 'On the Very Idea of a Conceptual Scheme, *Proceedings and Addresses of the American Philosophical Association*, 47: 5–20.
Davidson, D. (1980). 'How Is Weakness of the Will Possible', *Essays on Actions and Events*, Oxford, Clarendon Press, 21–42.
Deigh, J. (1994). 'Cognitivism in the Theory of Emotions', *Ethics*, 104(4): 824–54.
Deonna, J. A. (2006). 'Emotion, Perception, and Perspective', *Dialectica*, 60(1): 29–46.
Deonna, J. A. and Teroni, F. (2012). *The Emotions: A Philosophical Introduction*, London, Routledge.
Deonna, J. A. and Teroni, F. (2014). 'In What Sense Are Emotions Evaluations?', in *Emotion and Value*, C. Todd and S. Roeser (eds.), Oxford, Oxford University Press, 15–31.
Deonna, J. A. and Teroni, F. (2015). 'Emotions as Attitudes', *Dialectica*, 69(3): 293–311.
de Sousa, R. (1987). *The Rationality of Emotions*, Cambridge, MA, and London, MIT Press.
de Sousa, R. (2007). 'Truth, Authenticity, and Rationality', *Dialectica*, 61(3), 323–45.
de Sousa, R. and Scarantino, A. (2018). 'Emotion', *The Stanford Encyclopedia of Philosophy* (winter 2018 edn), E. N. Zalta (ed.), <https://plato.stanford.edu/archives/win2018/entries/emotion/>.
Destrée, P. (2016). 'La poétique', in *Lire Aristote*, E. Berti and M. Crubellier (eds.), Paris, Presses Universitaires de France, 219–29.
Dewey, J. (1894). 'The Theory of Emotion: (1) Emotional Attitudes', *Psychological Review*, 1(6): 553–69.
Dewey, J. (1895). 'The Theory of Emotion: (2) The Significance of Emotions', *Psychological Review*, 2(1): 13–32.
Dietz, C. H. (2018). 'Reasons and Factive Emotions', *Philosophical Studies*, 175(7): 1681–91.
Diggle, J. (ed.-in-chief) (2021). *The Cambridge Greek Lexicon*, Cambridge, Cambridge University Press.
Dimas, P. (2019). 'Two Ways in Which Pleasures Can Be False: *Philebus* 36c–42c', in *Plato's Philebus, A Philsophical Discussion*, P. Dimas, R. E. Jones, and G. R. Lear (eds.), Oxford, Oxford University Press, 124–40.
Döring, S. A. (2003). 'Explaining action by emotion', *Philosophical Quarterly* 53(211): 214–30.
Döring, S. A. (2007). 'Seeing What to Do: Affective Perception and Rational Motivation', *Dialectica*, 61(3): 363–94.
Döring, S. A. (2009a). 'The Logic of Emotional Experience: Noninferentiality and the Problem of Conflict without Contradiction', *Emotion Review*, 1(3): 240–7.
Döring, S. A. (2009b). 'Why Be Emotional?' in *The Oxford Handbook of Philosophy of Emotion*, P. Goldie (ed.), Oxford, Oxford University Press, 283–302.
Döring, S. A. (2014). 'Why Recalcitrant Emotions Are Not Irrational', in *Emotion and Value*, S. Roeser, and C. Todd (eds.), Oxford, Oxford University Press, 124–36.
Döring, S. A. (2015). 'What's Wrong with Recalcitrant Emotions? From Irrationality to Challenge of Agential Identity', *Dialectica*, 69(3): 381–402.
Doris, J. M. (2002). *Lack of Character: Personality and Moral Behavior*, Cambridge, Cambridge University Press.
Dow, J. (2009). 'Feeling Fantastic? Emotions and Appearances in Aristotle', *Oxford Studies in Ancient Philosophy*, 37: 143–75.
Dow, J. (2011). 'Aristotle's Theory of the Emotions: Emotions as Pleasures and Pains', in *Moral Psychology and Human Action in Aristotle*, M. Pakaluk and G. Pearson (eds.), Oxford, Oxford University Press, 47–74.

Dow, J. (2014). 'Feeling Fantastic Again: Passions, Appearances, and Beliefs in Aristotle', *Oxford Studies in Ancient Philosophy*, 46: 213–51.
Dow, J. (2015). *Passions and Persuasion in Aristotle's Rhetoric*, Oxford, Oxford University Press.
Dretske, F. I. (1981). *Knowledge and the Flow of Information*, Cambridge, MA, MIT Press.
Dretske, F. I. (1986). 'Misrepresentation', in *Belief: Form, Content, and Function*, R. Bogdan (ed.), Oxford, Oxford University Press, 17–36.
Dretske, F. I. (2000). 'Reply to Lopes', *Philosophy and Phenomenological Research*, 60(2): 455–9.
Engberg-Pedersen, T. (1983). *Aristotle's Theory of Moral Insight*, Oxford, Oxford University Press.
Fine, K. (1994). 'Essence and Modality: The Second Philosophical Perspectives Lecture', *Philosophical Perspectives*, 8: 1–16.
Ford, A. (2015). 'The Purpose of Aristotle's *Poetics*', *Classical Philology*, 110(1): 1–21.
Fortenbaugh, W. W. (1970). 'Aristotle's *Rhetoric* on Emotions', *Archiv für Geschichte der Philosophie*, 52(1): 40–70.
Fortenbaugh, W. W. (1975). *Aristotle on Emotion*, London, Duckworth.
Fortenbaugh, W. W. (2002). *Aristotle on Emotion*, Second Edition, London, Duckworth.
Fortenbaugh, W. W. (2006). 'Aristotle and Theophrastus on the Emotions', *Aristotle's Practical Side: On His Psychology, Ethics, Politics and Rhetoric, Philosophia Antiqua, v. 101*, Leiden, Brill, 69–103.
Frede, D. (1993). *Plato Philebus, Translated with Introduction & Notes*, Indianapolis and Cambridge, Hackett Publishing.
Frede, D. (1996). 'Mixed Feelings in Aristotle's *Rhetoric*', in *Essays on Aristotle's Rhetoric*, A. O. Rorty (ed.), Berkeley, CA, University of California Press, 268–83.
Frijda, N. H. (1986). *The Emotions*, Cambridge, Cambridge University Press.
Frijda, N. H. (1994). 'Varieties of Affect: Emotions and Episodes, Moods and Sentiments', in *The Nature of Emotion: Fundamental Questions*, P. Ekman and R. J. Davidson (eds.), New York, Oxford University Press, 59–67.
Frijda, N. H. (2006). *The Laws of Emotion*, Mahwah, NJ, Lawrence Erlbaum Associates.
Frost, K. (2014). 'On the Very Idea of Direction of Fit', *Philosophical Review*, 123(4): 429–84.
Fussi, A. (2015). 'Aristotle on Shame', *Ancient Philosophy*, 35: 113–35.
Gastaldi, S. (2015). 'L'analisi aristotelica dell'ἔλεος nel cap. 8 del libro II della *Retorica* e il ruolo dell'ἐλεεινολογία nel discorso pubblico ateniese', in B. Centrone (ed.), *La Retorica di Aristotele e la dottrina delle passioni*, Pisa, Pisa University Press, 201–19.
Gaus, G. F. (1990). *Value and Justification: The Foundations of Liberal Theory*, Cambridge, Cambridge University Press.
Gaut, B. (2007). *Art, Emotion and Ethics*, Oxford, Oxford University Press.
Gautier, R. A. and Jolif, J. Y. (1970). *L'éthique a Nicomaque, introduction, traduction et Commentaire*, Vol. II. Commentaire, Louvain and Paris, Publications Universitaires.
Gendler, T. and Liao, S. (2019). 'Imagination', in *The Stanford Encyclopedia of Philosophy* (summer 2020 edn), Edward N. Zalta (ed.), <https://plato.stanford.edu/archives/sum2020/entries/imagination/>.
Goldie, P. (2000). *The Emotions: A Philosophical Exploration*, Oxford, Oxford University Press.
Goldie, P. (2009). 'Getting Feelings into Emotion Experience in the Right Way', *Emotion Review*, 1(3): 232–9.
Goldstein, I. (2002). 'Are Emotions Feelings? A Further Look at Hedonic Theories of Emotions', *Consciousness and Emotion*, 3(1): 21–32.

Gosling, J. C. B. and Taylor, C. C. W. (1982). *The Greeks on Pleasure*, Oxford, Clarendon Press.
Gottlieb, P. (2021). *Aristotle on Thought and Feeling*, Cambridge, Cambridge University Press.
Granger, E. H. (1984). 'Aristotle on Genus and Differentia', *Journal of the History of Philosophy*, 22(1): 1–23.
Graver, M. (2007). *Stoicism and Emotion*, Chicago, University of Chicago Press.
Green, O. H. (1992). *The Emotions: A Philosophical Theory*, Dordrecht, Kluwer Academic Publishers.
Greenspan, P. S. (1980). 'Emotions, Reasons, and "Self-Involvement"', *Philosophical Studies*, 38(2): 161–8.
Greenspan, P. S. (1981). 'Emotions as Evaluations', *Pacific Philosophical Quarterly*, 62(2): 158–69.
Greenspan, P. S. (1988). *Emotions and Reasons: An Inquiry into Emotional Justification*, New York and London, Routledge.
Grimaldi, W. M. A. (1988). *Aristotle, Rhetoric II: A Commentary*, New York, Fordham University Press.
Grzankowski, A. (2012). 'Not All Attitudes Are Propositional', *European Journal of Philosophy*, 23(3): 374–91.
Grzankowski, A. (2013). 'Non-Propositional Attitudes', *Philosophy Compass*, 8(12): 1123–37.
Grzankowski, A. (2016a). 'Attitudes towards Objects', *Noûs*, 50(2): 314–28.
Grzankowski, A. (2016b). 'Limits of Propositionalism', *Inquiry: An Interdisciplinary Journal of Philosophy*, 59(7–8): 819–38.
Grzankowski, A. (2017). 'The Real Trouble with Recalcitrant Emotions', *Erkenntnis*, 82(3): 641–51.
Grzankowski, A. (2020). 'Navigating Recalcitrant Emotions', *The Journal of Philosophy*, 117(9): 501–19.
Guthrie, W. K. C. (1981). *A History of Greek Philosophy*, Vol. VI: *Aristotle an Encounter*, Cambridge, Cambridge University Press.
Hackforth, R. (1972). *Plato's Philebus: Translated with an Introduction and Commentary*, Cambridge, Cambridge University Press.
Hamlyn, D. W. (1993). *Aristotle* De Anima *Books II and III (with Passages from Book I)*, Oxford, Clarendon Press (with a report on recent work and a revised bibliography by Christopher Shields; rev. edn of 1968 orig.).
Harris, W. V. (2001). *Restraining Rage: The Ideology of Anger Control in Classical Antiquity*, Cambridge, MA, Harvard University Press.
Harte, V. (2004). 'The *Philebus* on Pleasure: The Good, the Bad, and the False', *Proceedings of the Aristotelian Society*, 104(1): 113–30.
Harte, V. (2014). 'The *Nicomachean Ethics* on Pleasure', in *The Cambridge Companion to Aristotle's Nicomachean Ethics*, R. Polansky (ed.), Cambridge, Cambridge, University Press, 288–318.
Heinaman, R. (1990). 'Aristotle and the Mind-Body Problem', *Phronesis*, 35(1): 83–102.
Heinaman, R. (2011). 'Pleasure as an Activity in the *Nicomachean Ethics*', in *Moral Psychology and Human Action in Aristotle*, M. Pakaluk and G. Pearson (eds.), Oxford, Oxford University Press, 7–45.
Helm, B. W. (2001). *Emotional Reason: Deliberation, Motivation, and the Nature of Value*, Cambridge, Cambridge University Press.

Helm, B. W. (2002). 'Felt Evaluations: A Theory of Pleasure and Pain', *American Philosophical Quarterly*, 39(1): 13–30.
Helm, B. W. (2009). 'Emotions as Evaluative Feelings', *Emotion Review*, 1(3): 248–55.
Helm, B. W. (2015). 'Emotions and Recalcitrance: Reevaluating the Perceptual Model', *Dialectica*, 69(3): 417–33.
Heylbut. G. (ed.) (1889). *Aspasii in Ethica Nicomachea quae supersunt commentaria*, Commentaria in Aristotelem Graeca 19.1, Berlin, Reimer.
Hicks, R. D. (1907). *Aristotle* De Anima, *with Translation, Introduction, and Notes*, Cambridge, Cambridge University Press.
Higgins, N. (2015). 'Shame on You: The Virtuous Use of Shame in Aristotle's *Nicomachean Ethics*', *Expositions*, 9(2): 1–15.
Hinchman, E. S. (2013). 'Rational Requirements and "Rational" Akrasia', *Philosophical Studies*, 166(3): 529–52.
Hocutt, M. (1974). 'Aristotle's Four Becauses', *Philosophy*, 49(190): 385–99.
Humberstone, I. L. (1992). 'Direction of Fit', *Mind*, 101(401): 59–83.
Inglis, K. (2014). 'Philosophical Virtue: In Defense of the Grand End', in *The Cambridge Companion to Aristotle's* Nicomachean Ethics, R. Polansky (ed.), Cambridge, Cambridge University Press, 263–87.
Inwood, B. and Woolf, R. (2013). *Aristotle* Eudemian Ethics, Cambridge, Cambridge University Press.
Irwin, T. (1985). *Aristotle* Nicomachean Ethics, Indianapolis and Cambridge, Hackett.
Jimenez, M. (2020). *Aristotle on Shame and Learning to Be Good*, Oxford, Oxford University Press.
Johansen, T. (2012). *The Powers of Aristotle's Soul*, Oxford, Oxford University Press.
Jones, K. (2003). 'Emotion, Weakness of Will, and the Normative Conception of Agency', in *Philosophy and the Emotions*, A. Hatzimoysis (ed.), Cambridge, Cambridge University Press, 181–200.
Kahn, C. (1966). 'Sensation and Consciousness in Aristotle's Psychology', *Archiv für Geschichte der Philosophie* 48(1–3): 43–81.
Kahn, C. (1995). 'Aristotle on Thinking', in *Essays on Aristotle's* De Anima, M. Nussbaum and A. O. Rorty (eds.), Oxford, Clarendon Press, 359–79.
Kassel, R. (1976). *Aristotelis* Ars rhetorica, Berlin, de Gruyter.
Kennedy, G. A. (1991). *Aristotle, On Rhetoric: A Theory of Civil Discourse*, Oxford, Oxford University Press.
Kenny, A. (1963). *Action, Emotion and Will*, London and Henley, Routledge.
Knuuttila, S. (2004). *Emotions in Ancient and Medieval Philosophy*, Oxford, Clarendon Press.
Konstan, D. (2006). *The Emotions of the Ancient Greeks: Studies and Aristotle and Classical Literature*, Toronto and Buffalo and London, University of Toronto Press.
Kraut, R. (1986). 'Love De Re', *Midwest Studies in Philosophy*, 10: 413–30.
Kripke, S. (1980). *Naming and Necessity*, Cambridge, MA, Harvard University Press.
Kupperman, J. J. (1995). 'An Anti-Essentialist View of the Emotions', *Philosophical Psychology*, 8(4): 341–51.
Lazarus, R. S. (1991). *Emotion and Adaptation*, New York and Oxford, Oxford University Press.
Leighton, S. R. (1984). '*Eudemian Ethics* 1220b11–13', *Classical Quarterly*, 34(1): 135–8.
Leighton, S. R. (1996). 'Aristotle and the Emotions', in *Essays on Aristotle's* Rhetoric, A. O. Rorty (ed.), Berkeley, CA, University of California Press, 206–37.
Lennox, J. G. (2001). *Aristotle* On the Parts of Animals I–IV, Oxford, Clarendon Press.

Little, M. O. (1997). 'Virtue as Knowledge: Objections from the Philosophy of Mind', *Noûs*, 31(1): 59–79.

Lorenz, H. (2006). *The Brute Within: Appetitive Desire in Plato and Aristotle*, Oxford, Clarendon Press.

Lovibond, S. (1989–90). 'True and False Pleasures', *Proceedings of the Aristotelian Society*, 90(1): 213–30.

Lyons, W. (1980). *Emotion*, Cambridge, Cambridge University Press.

Machek, D. (2022). 'Aristotle on How Pleasure Perfects Activity (*Nicomachean Ethics* X.5 1175a29–b14): The Optimising-View', *Archiv für Geschichte der Philosophie*, 104(3): 448–67.

Maiese, M. (2011). *Embodiment, Emotion and Cognition*, Basingstoke, Palgrave MacMillan.

Majeed, R. (2022). 'What Not to Make of Recalcitrant Emotions', *Erkenntnis*, 87(2), 747–65.

Marks, J. (1982). 'A Theory of Emotion', *Philosophical Studies*, 42(2): 227–42.

Martin, M. G. G. (1993). 'Sense Modalities and Spatial Properties', in *Spatial Representation*, B. Brewer, N. Eilan, and R. McCarthy (eds.), Oxford, Blackwell, 206–18.

Martin, M. G. G. (1995). 'Bodily Awareness: A Sense of Ownership', in *The Body and the Self*, J. L. Bermúdez, N. Eilan, and A. Marcel (eds.), Cambridge, MA, MIT Press, 267–89.

McCready-Flora, I. (2014). 'Aristotle's Cognitive Science: Belief, Affect and Rationality', *Philosophy and Phenomenological Research*, 89(2): 394–435.

McDowell, J. (1978). 'Are Moral Requirements Hypothetical Imperatives?', *Proceedings of the Aristotelian Society*, 52: 13–29 (suppl. vol.).

McGinn, C. (1982). *Character of Mind*, Oxford, Oxford University Press.

McIntyre, A. (1990). 'Is Akratic Action Always Irrational?', in *Identity, Character, and Morality*, O. Flanagan and A. Rorty (eds.), Cambridge, MA, MIT Press, 379–400.

McIntyre, A. (2006). 'What Is Wrong with Weakness of Will?', *Journal of Philosophy*, 103(6): 284–311.

McLaughlin, B. and Bennett, K. (2018). 'Supervenience', in *The Stanford Encyclopedia of Philosophy* (winter 2018 edn), Edward N. Zalta (ed.), <https://plato.stanford.edu/archives/win2018/entries/supervenience/>.

McNaughton, D. (1988). *Moral Vision: An Introduction to Ethics*, Oxford, Blackwell.

Menn, S. (2010). 'In Memoriam Ian Mueller (1938–2010)', *Aestimatio* 7: 193–228.

Mills, M. J. (1985), 'ΦΘΟΝΟΣ and its related ΠΑΘΗ in Plato and Aristotle', *Phronesis*, 30(1), 1–12.

Montague, M. (2007). 'Against Propositionalism', *Noûs*, 41(3): 503–18.

Moraux, P. (1959). 'Aristotele *De motu animalium* a cura di Luigi Toracca', *L'Antiquité Classique*, 28: 363–6.

Morreall, J. (1985). 'Enjoying Negative Emotions in Fictions', *Philosophy and Literature*, 9(1): 95–103.

Moss, J. (2012a). *Aristotle on the Apparent Good: Perception, Phantasia, Thought, and Desire*, Oxford, Oxford University Press.

Moss, J. (2012b). 'Pictures and Passions in the *Timaeus* and *Philebus*', in *Plato and the Divided Self*, R. Barney, T. Brenna, and C. Brittain (eds.), Cambridge, Cambridge University Press, 259–80.

Mueller, I. (1970). 'Aristotle on Geometrical Objects', *Archiv für Geschichte der Philosophie*, 52(2): 156–71.

Müller, J. M. (2017). 'How (Not) to Think of Emotions as Evaluative Attitudes', *Dialectica*, 71(2): 281–308.

Müller, J. M. (2019). *The World-Directedness of Emotional Feeling: On Affect and Intentionality*, Cham, Palgrave Macmillan.

Naar, H. (2020). 'The Real Issue with Recalcitrant Emotions: Reply to Grzankowski', *Erkenntnis*, 85(5): 1035–40.
Nehamas, A. (1992). 'Pity and Fear in the *Rhetoric* and the *Poetics*', in *Essays on Aristotle's Poetics*, A. O. Rorty (ed.), Princeton, Princeton University Press, 291–314.
Neu, J. (1977). *Emotion, Thought and Therapy*, London, Routledge.
Neu, J. (2000). *A Tear is an Intellectual Thing: The Meanings of Emotion*, Oxford and New York, Oxford University Press.
Nieuwenburg, P. (2002). 'Emotion and Perception in Aristotle's *Rhetoric*', *Australasian Journal of Philosophy*, 80(1): 86–100.
Nussbaum, M. C. (1976). 'The Text of Aristotle's De Motu Animalium', *Harvard Studies in Classical Philology*, 80: 111–59.
Nussbaum, M. C. (1978). *Aristotle's De Motu Animalium*, Princeton, Princeton University Press.
Nussbaum, M. C. (1986). *The Fragility of Goodness, Luck and Ethics in Greek Tragedy and Philosophy*, Cambridge, Cambridge University Press.
Nussbaum, M. C. (1994). *The Therapy of Desire: Theory and Practice in Hellenistic Ethics*, Princeton, Princeton University Press.
Nussbaum, M. C. (1996). 'Aristotle on Emotions and Rational Persuasion', in *Essays on Aristotle's Rhetoric*, A. O. Rorty (ed.), Berkeley, CA, University of California Press, 303–23.
Nussbaum, M. C. (1999). 'Reply to Papers in Symposium on Nussbaum, *The Therapy of Desire*', *Philosophy and Phenomenological Research*, 59(3): 811–19.
Nussbaum, M. C. (2001). *Upheavals of Thought: The Intelligence of Emotions*, Cambridge, Cambridge University Press.
Nussbaum, M. C. (2004). 'Emotions as Judgments of Value and Importance', in *Thinking About Feeling: Contemporary Philosophers on Emotions*, R. C. Solomon (ed.), Oxford, Oxford University Press, 307–35.
Nussbaum, M. C. (2016). *Anger and Forgiveness: Resentment, Generosity, Justice*, Oxford, Oxford University Press.
Nussbaum, M. C. and Putnam, H. (1992). 'Changing Aristotle's Mind', in *Essays on Aristotle's De anima*, M. Nussbaum and A. O. Rorty (eds.), Oxford, Clarendon Press, 27–56.
Owen, G. E. L. (1971–2). 'Aristotelian Pleasures', *Proceedings of the Aristotelian Society*, 72: 135–52.
Pakaluk, M. (2005). *Aristotle's Nicomachean Ethics: An Introduction*, Cambridge, Cambridge University Press.
Pearson, G. (2006). 'Aristotle on Acting Unjustly without Being Unjust', *Oxford Studies in Ancient Philosophy*, 30: 211–33.
Pearson, G. (2009). 'Aristotle on the Role of Confidence in Courage', *Ancient Philosophy*, 29(1): 123–37.
Pearson, G. (2011). 'Non-Rational Desire and Aristotle's Moral Psychology', in *Aristotle's Nicomachean Ethics: A Critical Guide*, J. Miller (ed.), Cambridge, Cambridge University Press, 144–69.
Pearson, G. (2012). *Aristotle on Desire*, Cambridge, Cambridge University Press.
Pearson, G. (2014a). 'Aristotle and the Cognitive Component of Emotions', *Oxford Studies in Ancient Philosophy*, 46: 165–211.
Pearson, G. (2014b). 'Courage and Temperance', in *The Cambridge Companion to Aristotle's Nicomachean Ethics*, R. Polansky (ed.), Cambridge, Cambridge University Press, 110–34.

Pearson, G. (2018). 'Aristotle on Psychopathology', in *Evil in Aristotle*, P. Kontas (ed.), Cambridge, Cambridge University Press, 122–49.

Pearson, G. (2020). 'How to Argue about Aristotle about Practical Reason', *Proceedings of the Boston Area Colloquium in Ancient Philosophy*, 35(1): 31–58.

Pearson, G. (MS). *Aristotle on How We Grasp Objects of Emotion*.

Penner, T. (1970). 'False Anticipatory Pleasures: *Philebus* 36a3–41a6', *Phronesis*, 15(2): 166–78.

Peramatzis, M. (2011). *Priority in Aristotle's Metaphysics*, Oxford, Oxford University Press.

Pitcher, G. (1965). 'Emotion', *Mind* 74(295): 326–46.

Platts, M. (1979). *Ways of Meaning: An Introduction to a Philosophy of Language*, London, Routledge.

Price, A. W. (1995). *Mental Conflict*, London and New York, Routledge.

Price, A. W. (2009). 'Emotions in Plato and Aristotle', in *The Oxford Handbook of Philosophy of Emotion*, P. Goldie (ed.), Oxford, Oxford University Press, 121–42.

Price, A. W. (2011). *Virtue and Reason in Plato and Aristotle*, Oxford, Oxford University Press.

Price, A. W. (2017). 'Varieties of Pleasure in Plato and Aristotle', *Oxford Studies in Ancient Philosophy*, 52: 177–206.

Price, C. (2006). 'Affect without Object: Moods and Objectless Emotions', *European Journal of Analytic Philosophy*, 2(1): 49–68.

Prinz, J. (2004). *Gut Reactions: A Perceptual Theory of Emotion*, Oxford, Oxford University Press.

Prinz, J. (2010). 'For Valence', *Emotion Review*, 2(1): 5–13.

Purshouse, L. (2004). 'Jealousy in Relation to Envy', *Erkenntnis*, 60(2): 179–204.

Quine, W. V. O. (1961). 'Two Dogmas of Empiricism', *From a Logical Point of View*, New York, Harper and Row, 20–46.

Rackham, H. (1934). *Aristotle* Nicomachean Ethics, Cambridge, MA, Harvard University Press (rev. edn of 1926 orig.).

Rapp, C. (2002). *Aristoteles. Rhetorik. Übersetzung und Kommentar*, 2 vols., Berlin, Akademie Verlag (all refs. are to vol. 2).

Rapp, C. (2013). 'The Emotional Dimension of Friendship: Notes on Aristotle's Account of *Philia* in *Rhetoric* II.4', *Anuario Filosófico*, 46(1): 23–47.

Rapp, C. (2022). 'Aristotle's Rhetoric', in *The Stanford Encyclopedia of Philosophy* (spring 2022 edn), Edward N. Zalta (ed.), <https://plato.stanford.edu/archives/spr2022/entries/aristotle-rhetoric/>.

Rapp, C. and Primavesi, O. (eds.) (2020). *Aristotle's* De motu animalium: *Symposium Aristotelicum*, Oxford, Oxford University Press (with a new critical edn of the Greek text by Oliver Primavesi and an English trans. by Benjamin Morison).

Ratcliffe, M. (2019). 'Emotional Intentionality', *Royal Institute of Philosophy Supplement*, 85: 251–69.

Rawls, J. (1972). *A Theory of Justice*, Oxford, Oxford University Press.

Raymond, C. C. (2017). 'Shame and Virtue in Aristotle', *Oxford Studies in Ancient Philosophy*, 53: 111–61.

Reeve, C. D. C. (2014). *Aristotle* Nicomachean Ethics, Indianapolis and Cambridge, Hackett.

Reeve, C. D. C. (2017). *Aristotle* Politics, Indianapolis and Cambridge, Hackett.

Reeve, C. D. C. (2018). *Aristotle* Rhetoric, Indianapolis and Cambridge, Hackett.

Roberts, R. C. (1988). 'What an Emotion Is: A Sketch', *The Philosophical Review*, 97: 183–209.

Roberts, R. C. (1996). 'Propositions and Animal Emotion', *Philosophy*, 71: 147–56.
Roberts, R. C. (1999). 'Emotions as Judgments', *Philosophy and Phenomenological Research*, 59(3): 793–8.
Roberts, R. C. (2003). *Emotions: An Essay in Aid of Moral Psychology*, Cambridge, Cambridge University Press.
Rorty, A. O. (ed.) (1984). 'Aristotle on the Metaphysical Status of *Pathe*', *The Review of Metaphysics*, 37(3): 521–46.
Rorty, A. O. (1986). 'The Historicity of Psychological Attitudes: Love Is Not Love Which Alters Not When It Alteration Finds', *Midwest Studies in Philosophy*, 10: 399–412.
Ross, W. D. (1959). *Aristotelis Ars Rhetorica*, Oxford, Oxford University Press.
Ross, W. D. (1980). *Aristotle The Nicomachean Ethics*, trans. W. D. Ross, rev. J. L. Ackrill and J. O. Urmson, Oxford, Oxford University Press.
Rossi, M. and Tappolet, C. (2019). 'What Kind of Evaluative States Are Emotions? The Attitudinal Theory vs. the Perceptual Theory of Emotions', *Canadian Journal of Philosophy*, 49(4): 544–63.
Saenz, V. (2018). 'Shame and Honor: Aristotle's *Thumos* as a Basic Desire', *Apeiron*, 51(1): 73–95.
Sainsbury, R. M. (1999). 'Names, Fictional Names, and "Really"', *Aristotelian Society*, 73(1): 243–69 (suppl. vol.).
Salmela, M. (2011). 'Can Emotion be Modelled on Perception?', *Dialectica*, 65(1): 1–29.
Salmieri, G. (2008). *Aristotle and the Problem of Concepts*, PhD Dissertation, University of Pittsburgh, <http://d-scholarship.pitt.edu/8125/>.
Sanders, E. (2008). '*Pathos Phaulon*: Aristotle and the Rhetoric of *Phthonos*', in KAKOS: *Badness and Anti-Value in Classical Antiquity*, I. Sluiter and R. M. Rosen (eds.), Leiden, Brill, 255–81.
Sanders, E. (2014). *Envy and Jealousy in Classical Athens: A Socio-Psychological Approach. Emotions of the Past*. Oxford, Oxford University Press.
Scarantino, A. (2010). 'Insights and Blindspots of the Cognitivist Theory of Emotions', *British Journal for the Philosophy of Science*, 61(4): 729–68.
Scarantino, A. (2014). 'The Motivational Theory of Emotions', in *Moral Psychology and Human Agency*, J. D'Arms and D. Jacobson (eds.), Oxford, Oxford University Press, 156–85.
Scheiter, K. (2013). 'Giles Pearson: *Aristotle on Desire*', *Notre Dame Philosophical Reviews*, 2013.04.32, <https://ndpr.nd.edu/news/aristotle-on-desire/>.
Schlosser, M. (2019). 'Agency', in *The Stanford Encyclopedia of Philosophy* (winter 2019 edn), Edward N. Zalta (ed.), <https://plato.stanford.edu/archives/win2019/entries/agency/>.
Schofield, M. (2011). '*Phantasia* in *De Motu Animalium*', in *Moral Psychology and Human Action in Aristotle*, M. Pakaluk and and G. Pearson (eds.), Oxford, Oxford University Press, 119-134.
Schulte, P. and Neander, K. (2022). 'Teleological Theories of Mental Content', in *The Stanford Encyclopedia of Philosophy* (summer 2022 edn), Edward N. Zalta (ed.), <https://plato.stanford.edu/archives/sum2022/entries/content-teleological/>.
Searle, J. R. (1983). *Intentionality*, Cambridge, Cambridge University Press.
Sedley, D. (2005). 'Plato's Tsunami' *Hyperboreus*, 11(2): 205–14.
Sherman, N. (1993). 'The Role of Emotions in Aristotelian Virtue', *Proceedings of the Boston Area Colloquium in Ancient Philosophy*, 9: 1–33.
Sherman, N. (1997). *Making a Necessity of Virtue: Aristotle and Kant on Virtue*, Cambridge, Cambridge University Press.

Shields, C. (1988). 'Soul as Subject in Aristotle's *De Anima*', *Classical Quarterly*, 38(1): 140–9.
Shields, C. (2009). 'The Priority of Soul in Aristotle's *De Anima*: Mistaking Categories', in *Body and Soul in Ancient Philosophy*, D. Frede and B. Reis (eds.), Berlin, De Gruyter, 156–68.
Shields, C. (2011). 'Perfecting Pleasures: The Metaphysics of Pleasure in *Nicomachean Ethics* X', in *Aristotle's* Nicomachean Ethics, *A Critical Guide*, J. Miller (ed.), Cambridge, Cambridge University Press, 191–210.
Shields, C. (2016). *Aristotle*: De Anima, Oxford, Clarendon Press.
Sihvola, J. (1996). 'Emotional Animals: Do Aristotelian Emotions Require Beliefs?', *Apeiron*, 29(2): 105–44.
Sinhababu, N. (2009). 'The Humean Theory of Motivation Reformulated and Defended', *Philosophical Review*, 118(4): 465–500.
Sinhababu, N. (2015). 'Advantages of Propositionalism', *Pacific Philosophical Quarterly*, 96(1): 165–80.
Smith, M. (1994). *The Moral Problem*, Oxford, Blackwell.
Solomon, R. C. (1993). *The Passions*, Indianapolis and Cambridge, Hackett.
Solomon, R. C. (2003a). *Not Passions Slave: Emotions and Choice*, Oxford, Oxford University Press.
Solomon, R. C. (2003b). 'Against Valence ("Positive" and "Negative" Emotions)', *Not Passions's Slave: Emotions and Choice*, Oxford, Oxford University Press, 162–77.
Solomon, R. C. and Stone, L. D. (2002). 'On "Positive" and "Negative" Emotions', *Journal for the Theory of Social Behaviour*, 32(4): 417–35.
Sorabji, R. (1972). *Aristotle on Memory*, London, Duckworth.
Sorabji, R. (1993). *Animal Minds and Human Morals: The Origins of the Western Debate*, London, Duckworth.
Sorabji, R. (1999). 'Aspasius on Emotion', in *Aspasius: The Earliest Extant Commentary on Aristotle's* Ethics, A. Alberti and R. Sharples (eds.), Berlin and New York, De Gruyter, 96–106.
Sorabji, R. (2000). *Emotions and Peace of Mind*, Oxford, Oxford University Press.
Sorabji, R. (2001). 'Aristotle on Sensory Processes and Intentionality: A Reply to Burnyeat', in *Ancient and Medieval Theories of Intentionality*, D. Perler (ed.), Leiden, Brill, 49–61.
Spengel, L. (1867). *Aristotelis Ars Rhetorica*, Leipzig, Teubner.
Stephan, A. (2017). 'Moods in Layers', *Philosophia*, 45(4): 1481–95.
Stocker, M. (1979). 'Desiring the Bad: An Essay in Moral Psychology', *The Journal of Philosophy*, 76(12): 738–53.
Striker, G. (1996). 'Emotions in Context: Aristotle's Treatment of the Passions in the *Rhetoric* and His Moral Psychology', in *Essays on Aristotle's* Rhetoric, A. O. Rorty (ed.), Berkeley, CA, University of California Press, 286–302.
Strohl, M. (2011). 'Pleasure as Perfection: Nicomachean Ethics X.4–5', *Oxford Studies in Ancient Philosophy*, 41: 257–87.
Svavarsdottir, S. (1999). 'Moral Cognitivism and Motivation', *Philosophical Review*, 108(2): 161–219.
Swartzer, S. (2013). 'Appetitive Besires and the Fuss about Fit', *Philosophical Studies*, 165(3): 975–88.
Tappolet, C. (2000). *Emotions et valeurs*, Paris, Presses Universitaires de France.
Tappolet, C. (2003). 'Emotions and the Intelligibility of Akratic Action', in *Weakness of Will and Practical Irrationality*, S. Stroud and C. Tappolet (eds.), Oxford, Clarendon Press, 97–120.

Tappolet, C. (2009). 'Emotion, Motivation, and Action: The Case of Fear', in *The Oxford Handbook of Philosophy of Emotion*, P. Goldie (ed.), Oxford, Oxford University Press, 325–46.
Tappolet, C. (2012). 'Emotions, Perceptions, and Emotional Illusions', in *Perceptual Illusions: Philosophical and Psychological Essays*, C. Calabi (ed.), London, Palgrave Macmillan, 205–22.
Tappolet, C. (2016). *Emotions, Values, and Agency*, Oxford, Oxford University Press.
Taylor, C. C. W. (2003). 'Pleasure: Aristotle's Response to Plato', in *Plato and Aristotle's Ethics*, R. Heinaman (ed.), Aldershot, Ashgate Publishing, 1–20.
Taylor, C. C. W. (2006). *Aristotle:* Nicomachean Ethics, *Books II—IV*, Oxford, Clarendon Press.
Teroni, F. (2007). 'Emotions and Formal Objects', *Dialectica*, 61(3): 395–415.
Tuozzo, T. M. (1994). 'Conceptualized and Unconceptualized Desire in Aristotle', *Journal of the History of Philosophy*, 32(4): 525–49.
Tye, M. (1995). *Ten Problems of Consciousness: A Representational Theory of the Phenomenal Mind*, Cambridge, MA, MIT Press.
Tye, M. (2021). 'Qualia', *The Stanford Encyclopedia of Philosophy* (fall 2021 edn), E. N. Zalta (ed.) <https://plato.stanford.edu/archives/fall2021/entries/qualia/>.
Viano, C. (2010). 'Les passions comme causes dans la *Rhétorique* d'Aristote. Mobiles de l'action et instruments de la persuasion', *Journal of Ancient Philosophy*, 4(1): 1–31.
Viano, C. (2014). 'Le paradigme des passions. Aristote et les définitions non physiques de la colère', *Journal of Ancient Philosophy*, 8(1): 1–19.
Viano, C. (2021). *Aristotele* Retorica, Bari-Rome, Laterza.
Vigani, D. (2017). 'Aristotle's Account of Courage', *History of Philosophy Quarterly*, 34(4): 313–30.
Wall, D. (2009). 'Are There Passive Desires?', *Dialectica*, 63(2): 133–55.
Walton, K. L. (1978). 'Fearing Fictions', *Journal of Philosophy*, 75(1): 5–27.
Walton, K. L. (1990). *Mimesis as Make-Believe: On the Foundations of the Representational Arts*, Cambridge, MA, Harvard University Press.
Walton, K. L. (1997). 'Spelunking, Simulation, and Slime: On Being Moved by Fiction', in *Emotion and the Arts*, M. Hjort and S. Laver (eds.), Oxford, Oxford University Press, 37–49.
Warren, J. (2015). 'The Bloom of Youth', *Apeiron*, 48(3): 327–45.
Warren, J. (2021). *Regret: A Study in Ancient Moral Psychology*, Oxford, Oxford University Press.
Wedin, M. V. (1988). *Mind and Imagination in Aristotle*, New Haven, Yale University Press.
Wedin, M. V. (1995). 'Keeping the Matter in Mind: Aristotle on the Passions and the Soul', *Pacific Philosophical Quarterly*, 76(3–4), 183–221.
Wedin, M. V. (1996). 'Aristotle on How to Define a Psychological State', *Topoi*, 15(1): 11–24.
Whiting, D. (2011). 'The Feeling Theory of Emotion and the Object-Direct Emotions', *European Journal of Philosophy*, 19(2): 281–303.
Wilson, J. (2023). 'Determinables and Determinates', *The Stanford Encyclopedia of Philosophy* (spring 2023 edn), E. N. Zalta (ed.), <https://plato.stanford.edu/archives/spr2023/entries/determinate-determinables/>.
Wilson, J. R. S. (1972). *Emotion and Object*, Cambridge, Cambridge University Press.
Woods, M. (1982). *Aristotle* Eudemian Ethics *Books I, II, and VII*, Oxford, Clarendon Press.
Woods, M. (1992). *Aristotle* Eudemian Ethics *Books I, II, and VII*, Oxford, Clarendon Press, 2nd edn.

General Index

'accompanied by'. See *hepetai* ('accompanied by')
Achtenberg, D. 6n.17, 66–7, 67n.5, 76, 82, 100n.28, 251n.32, 289n.45
acting emotionally (= being motivated to act emotionally) 265–9
    Aristotle's view and 268–9
    Belief and Desire Cognitivism and 265–6
    Motivational theory of emotions and 266–9
action tendencies ((felt) states of action readiness)
    attitudinal theory and 271–2
    Motivational theory of emotions and. *See* Motivational theory of emotions, (in)action tendencies (states of action readiness, etc.) and
'add-on' theories of emotion 67–8, 68n.6
akrasia (akratic action, etc.) 151–2n.31, 175n.50, 210–11, 274n.30, 292. *See also* inverse *akrasia* (rational *akrasia*)
Allen, D. 152n.33
Altham, J. E. J. 271n.26
analysing emotions in terms of other intentional states 33–9
    constraints provided by the *fear + content* formulation 38–9
anger (*orgē*) 104–5, 105n.27, 137–53, 157–9, 276, 276n.6, 318
    desire of 144–6, 148–52, 154n.2
        brought about by *and* accompanied by the distress of anger 144–5, 215
        contrasted with desires of feeling-friendly-towards and hating 173
        formed in light of the distress of anger 215
        why Aristotle thinks essentially involves 148–52
    dialectical definition of 213–15
    distress of 141–6
    emotion, as a 145–6, 173, 183
    formal objects of 146n.18
    hating and 149–50, 150n.28, 171
    involving both a desire and an emotion 140–1, 145–6, 157
    pain as a background condition prompting 141–3, 176–7, 187, 233–4
    phainomenos in its definition 104–5, 105n.27
    picking out by just one of its components 157
    pleasure that arises from 105, 105n.38, 146–8, 173n.46
    schematic definition of. *See* schematic definition (of states such as anger)
    slighting and. *See* slight (= offence) (*oligōria*)
    thumos and 157–9, 157n.5, 177n.56
    Topics on the genus of 138–40
Anscombe, G. E. M. 17n.2, 18n.5
anxiety 255–6
'apparent' (*phainemonos*), use in Aristotle's formulations of emotions. See *phainomenos*, use of in Aristotle's formulations of emotions
appearance as/of truth (= assent of the subsystem) 31, 85–7, 86n.39, 283–6, 286–7n.38, 290
appetite
    bodily 179–80
    epithumia. See *epithumia* (= appetite)
Apprehender views of emotions 108–14
    response views, contrasted with 108–14
'apprehending' objects of emotion, notions of 24–5, 30–3
    epistemic access notion 30
    epistemic state notion 31
    not homunculi 24–5
    specifying notion 32
Archer, A. 269n.23
Armstrong, D. M. 59n.44
Arpaly, N. 308n.69
Arpaly, N. and Schroeder, T. 308n.69
Aspasius 45n.2, 50n.17, 250n.27
assent 285–9
    agential 286–7
    disclosive 286n.37
    inclinations to 288–9, 288nn.41–2, 289n.43
    of the subsystem. *See* appearance as/of truth (= assent of the subsystem)
    passive 286–8
Atkins, P. and Robertson Ishii, T. 131n.26
attitude. *See* intentional attitude (= mode, manner)
attitudinal theory of emotions 34–6, 36n.46, 271–2
'at what'. See *Rhet.* discussion of emotions under three heads, 'at what' (*epi poiois*)

'at whom'. See *Rhet.* discussion of emotions under three heads, 'at whom' (*tisin*)
Audi, R. 308n.69
Aufderheide, J. 120–2

background desiderative dispositions 176, 272–3, 292. *See also* character traits, as background to emotions
  motivational tendencies and 261, 268–9
Bain, D. 60n.46
Barnes, J. 25n.18
Bedford, E. 6n.19
being motivated to act emotionally. *See* acting emotionally (= being motivated to act emotionally)
being-put-out. *See* not-being-grateful-for (or being-put-out) (*ou charein echein*)
Belief and Desire Cognitivism 265–6, 270, 273
Benbaji, H. 277nn.7–8, 278n.11, 279nn.12–13, 288n.40, 291n.46, 296n.56, 303n.64
Bennett, J. 308n.71
Bennett, K. *See* McLaughlin, B. and Bennett, K.
Ben-Ze'ev, A. 329n.29, 330, 338n.48
besires 271n.26
Block, I. 23n.14
bodily appetites. *See* appetite, bodily; *epithumia* (= appetite)
bodily dimension of emotions. *See* material/physical/bodily dimension of emotions
Bonitz, H. 2n.5, 45n.3, 158n.6, 177n.57
Bostock, D. 117, 187n.23
boulēsis (wish, rational desire) 141n.6, 151n.31, 154n.2, 157, 163–4, 168–71, 170nn.36–7, 171n.43, 173, 187n.23, 261n.6
Brady, M. E. 165n.20
Brady, M. S. 6n.19, 6–7n.20, 277nn.7–8, 280n.16, 281n.21, 286, 286n.35, 288–9, 288nn.40–2, 289n.44, 291n.46, 296n.56, 298
Broadie, S. and Rowe, C. 206n.31, 337n.45
Broome, J. 277n.9, 292nn.48–50, 309–10
Burnet, J. 324n.14
Burnyeat, M. 2n.6, 197n.6, 233n.82

Cairns, D. L. 175n.51, 324nn.13–14
Cashdollar, S. 23n.14
Cassam, Q. 5n.14
Castelli, L. M. 329n.29, 330
Caston, V. 2n.6, 20n.9, 23n.14, 25n.18, 54n.29, 197n.3, 197n.6, 228n.72, 234n.83
Cates, D. F. 154n.1
causal reading of Aristotle on emotions. *See* individuation of emotions, causal view and; relation between intentional state that apprehends object of emotion and the emotion's pleasure or distress, causal view
cause 94–5, 102

Centrone, B. 154n.1
Chalmers, D. 19n.7
character traits, as background to emotions 95, 112–13, 125–9, 156–7, 173–7, 269, 273–4, 274n.30
charin echein. *See* feeling-grateful-for (*charin echein*)
charis. *See* favour (*charis*)
Charles, D. 2n.6, 27n.23, 173–4n.47, 195, 197, 197n.3, 197nn.5–6, 199–200, 199–200n.12, 201, 203–4n.25, 205n.29, 207, 207–8n.34, 209n.37, 213–19, 213nn.45–6, 214n.47, 216n.51, 217n.53, 221, 221n.63, 224–30, 224n.66, 225n.67, 227n.70, 228n.72, 231n.75, 233n.81, 234, 271n.26
Cheng, W. 61n.50
Chrysippus 276n.6
Code, A. and Moravcsik, J. 198–9n.9
'conditions under which'. *See Rhet.* discussion of emotions under three heads, 'conditions under which' (*pōs diakeimenoi*)
confidence (*tharsos*) 62, 164nn.18–19, 218, 248–50, 249nn.24–5, 322–3
  definition of 250
  fear, contrasted with 248–9
  phantasia and 248–9
  representational pleasure (positive state) in its own right (not simply privation-emotion) 249–50, 250n.27
Consistency principle. *See* Rational requirements, Consistency principle
Consistency principle2. *See* Rational requirements, Consistency principle2
content. *See* intentional content
Cooper, J. 4n.11, 6n.17, 45n.2, 91n.6, 100n.28, 105n.37, 137, 137n.1, 145n.17, 148, 154n.1, 168n.29, 168nn.31–2, 170n.36, 236, 236n.1, 239n.7, 249n.25, 250n.28, 289n.45, 340n.54
Cope, E. 105n.37, 236n.1, 243, 324n.14
Corcilius, K. 2n.6, 5n.13, 24n.16, 195
'core set' of emotions 8, 12, 51–2, 89, 99–100, 106n.41, 114
correctness conditions 25–6n.19, 35n.41, 86n.39, 271–2
courage (the courageous, etc.) and its coordinate vices (esp. cowardice) 26, 164–6, 165n.20, 165n.22, 165–6n.23, 202n.18, 232, 263, 269
  courageous person as undisturbed 166, 167n.26
  desire to flee and 164–5, 165n.21, 166n.24, 175–6
cowardice. *See* courage (the courageous, etc.) and its coordinate vices (esp. cowardice)

Crane, T. 8n.23, 17n.2, 18n.5, 18n.6, 19n.7, 24n.17, 35n.44, 59–60, 59–60n.45, 60n.46
Crisp, R. 29n.30, 337n.45
Curzer, H. 165n.22

Dalgliesh, T. 255n.41
D'Arms, J. and Jacobson, D. 6n.20, 71n.15, 277n.7
Davidson, D. 207n.33, 279n.12
Deigh, J. 27n.24
Deonna, J. A. 6n.19. *See also* Deonna, J. A. and Teroni, F.
Deonna, J. A. and Teroni, F. 2n.7, 3n.8, 6n.19, 19n.7, 31n.35, 34–9, 35n.41, 35n.44, 36n.46, 37n.47, 60n.47, 62, 73n.23, 108–9, 253–5, 271–2, 271n.27, 272n.28, 277nn.7–8, 278n.11, 280n.16
depression 255–6, 260
descriptive side/role of an emotion. *See* representational roles of emotions, descriptive
desiderative dispositions. *See* background desiderative dispositions
desire (in Aristotle) (*orexis*) 9, 151n.31, 154n.2, 157–9, 177, 185n.18
 anger and. *See* anger (*orgē*), desire of; anger, involving both a desire and an emotion
 background desiderative dispositions and. *See* background desiderative dispositions
 boulēsis. *See boulēsis* (wish, rational desire)
 cold desires for revenge. *See* material/physical/bodily dimension of emotions, cold desires for revenge and
 disturbance and. *See* disturbance (*tarachē*) and undisturbed (*atarachos*), in relation to emotions
 epithumia (appetite). *See epithumia* (= appetite)
 fear and. *See* fear, desire and
 feeling-friendly-towards and. *See* feeling-friendly-towards (*to philein*)
 hating and. *See* hating (*to misein*)
 motives for action in *Rhet*. I.10. *See* motives for action in *Rhet*. I.10
 non-rational contrasted with rational 157–9
 object of desire (*orekton*) 146, 186, 273n.29
  as an intentional object 24
 rational. *See boulēsis* (wish, rational desire)
 thumos. *See thumos*
 wish. *See boulēsis* (wish, rational desire)
desire/motivation and emotions (in contemporary philosophy) 259–70, 273, 291–6, 293n.52
 Motivational theory. *See* Motivational theory of emotions

Motivation principle. *See* Rational requirements, Motivation principle
Pointless motivation principle. *See* Rational requirements, Pointless motivation principle
recalcitrant emotions and. *See* recalcitrant emotions, practical irrationality and
de Sousa, R. 2n.7, 28n.28, 29n.32, 68n.7, 71n.15, 72n.18, 73n.23, 279n.12, 280n.16.
 See also de Sousa, R. and Scarantino, A.
de Sousa, R. and Scarantino, A. 25–6n.19, 28n.28, 205n.29, 291n.47, 315n.77
Destrée, P. 209n.38
determinate/determinable 50n.15, 63, 63n.54
deviant causal chains 92n.8
 Mere-Concurrence view and 90–1
 pure forms and 226–7
Dewey, J. 259n.1
dialectical definitions of emotions 198, 213–15
'dialectical' ('logical'), pejorative use of 200, 216–17, 217n.52
Dietz, C. H. 109n.46
Dimas, P. 58n.42, 162n.15
direction of fit 261, 269n.23, 271n.27
disdain (*kataphronēsis*)
 emotion, as a 334–5
 species of slight (*oligōria*). *See* slight (= offence) (*oligōria*), species of, disdain (*kataphronēsis*)
distress-based indignation 55, 80, 143, 160, 328–9
 'conditions under which' and 143
 disturbance and 160
'distress', use of 60–1
disturbance (*tarachē*) and undisturbed (*atarachos*), in relation to emotions 58n.41, 155, 160–3, 161n.11, 166–8, 167n.26
Döring, S. A. 6n.19, 6–7n.20, 31, 68n.7, 69n.11, 72n.18, 85, 85n.35, 86n.39, 277n.9, 280nn.16–18, 281nn.21–2, 281–2n.24, 282–3, 283n.28, 284n.31, 286–7, 286–7n.38, 288n.40, 289n.44, 291–4, 291n.47, 292nn.48–50, 299n.59, 300n.60, 308–14, 309n.72, 310n.74, 311n.75
Doris, J. M. 274n.30
Dow, J. 1n.2, 4n.11, 5n.15, 6n.18, 7n.21, 28n.29, 45–7, 45n.2, 54n.31, 56n.37, 67, 67n.5, 68, 69–70, 69n.11, 76–7, 81, 82, 93n.14, 96, 100n.28, 103n.34, 115n.1, 116, 116n.4–5, 117n.8, 118, 118n.9, 138n.2, 145n.17, 147–8, 161n.11, 168n.29, 168n.31, 172–3, 211n.42, 233, 236n.1, 240n.8, 246, 249n.25, 275–6n.3, 281n.21, 286, 289n.45, 317n.1
Dretske, F. I. 60n.46, 270–1n.25

Dual-component view of emotions (as a reading of Aristotle) 97–106
  non-representational pleasures/pains version 97–8
  representational pleasures/distresses version 98–104
    individuation of emotions and 99
    pain-at locutions and 99

EE specification of emotions, supplements in 250–3
  'for the most part' (*epi to polu*) 251–3
  'in their own right'/'intrinsically' (*kath' hauta*) 49, 49n.13, 252–3, 256
  'perceptible' 53–4, 251–2, 252n.25, 253n.36
emotional dispositions, training of 111–13
  apprehender views (perceptualism, judgementalism) and 111–12
  Aristotle's hedonic response view and 112–13
emotional responses to fiction 25, 84, 86, 272, 285, 303n.64
emotion(s) (For specific emotions, see under their own heads; e.g. anger, fear, etc.)
  'accompanied by' (*hepetai*) pleasure and pain. See *hepetai* ('accompanied by')
  analysing in terms of other intentional states. See analysing emotions in terms of other intentional states
  'apparent', Aristotle's use of in formulating. See *phainomenos*, use of in Aristotle's formulations of emotions
  bodily effects of 204–5, 204n.28, 205n.29
  change in 'judgement' (*krisis*: decision or verdict) and. See *kriseis* (= 'decisions or verdicts'); oratorical manipulation of decisions or verdicts (*kriseis*)
  composite nature, stemming from 204
  'core set' of. See 'core set' of emotions
  correctness conditions and. See correctness conditions
  desires/motivations and. See desire (in Aristotle) (*orexis*); desire/motivation and emotions (in contemporary philosophy)
  dialectical definitions of. See dialectical definitions of emotions
  directed at instantiations of the emotion's formal object 99–100. See also evaluative object of emotion (= formal object of emotion); pain-at locutions
  dispositional. See emotion(s), occurrent contrasted with dispositional
  distinct from the intentional state that apprehends its object (in Aristotle) 53, 69–70
  engendering or abating in an audience 200
  factive formulations of 100–1
  felt phenomenological dimension of. See felt phenomenological dimension of emotions (felt nature of emotions, etc.)
  genus/species and *differentia specifica* 148n.23. See also genus/species
  Identification view of. See Identification view of emotions
  individuation of. See individuation of emotions
  intentional state that apprehends its object and Aristotle 5–10, 216n.51
    identification view of 7–8. See Identification view of emotions, Aristotle, as a reading of
    response view of 7. See response view of emotions, Aristotle, as a reading of
  material/physical/bodily dimension of. See material/physical/bodily dimension of emotions
  'mixed feelings' 161n.12
  non-rational/belonging to non-rational part of soul 54n.30, 168, 168n.30
  occurrent contrasted with dispositional 3, 3n.10
  phenomenological dimension of. See felt phenomenological dimension of emotions (felt nature of emotions, etc.)
  pleasure and pain dimension of Aristotle's account of 8. See also pleasure and distress (or pain)
  praise and blame, in connection with 174–5, 175n.51
  proper (*pathē kuriōs*). See emotions proper (*pathē kuriōs*)
  representational roles and. See representational roles of emotions
  Response view of. See Response view of emotions
  Rhet. as providing an 'account' of 4–5, 4n.11
  use of term for *pathos/pathē* 2–3, 158–9, 159n.9, 177
emotions proper (*pathē kuriōs*) 247–8, 252–3, 254–6, 255n.40
emulation (*zēlos*) 55, 174–6, 332–3
  deserved/undeserved doing-well and 332–3
  disdain (*kataphronesis*), contrary of 334
  envy, contrasted with 77–9, 174–6, 174n.48, 333
  jealousy and 333
  virtuous background disposition and 174–6, 175n.51
Engberg-Pedersen, T. 154n.1
Enkratic principle. See Rational requirements, Enkratic principle

GENERAL INDEX   363

envy (*phthonos*) 55, 58, 80, 97n.19, 100, 112–13, 127, 174–6, 176n.53, 329–32, 333, 333n.37, 337–8
  deserved/undeserved doing-well and 80, 329–31
  disturbance and 160, 162, 167n.26
  emulation, contrasted with 77–9, 174–6, 174n.48, 333
  jealousy and 333
  pleasure-based emotion related to 332
  vicious background disposition and 112–13, 174–6, 175n.51, 176
epēreasmos. See slight (= offence) (*oligōria*), species of, spite (*epēreasmos*)
epi + dative. See pain-at locutions
epi poiois. See *Rhet*. discussions of emotions under three heads, 'at what' (*epi poiois*)
epithumia (= appetite) 60n.47, 109, 109n.47, 141n.6, 154n.2, 157–9, 159n.9, 173n.46, 177n.56, 179–91, 185n.18, 187n.23, 264n.15, 338–9
  accompanied by a representational distress 186–90, 187, 187n.23
  are all painful? 183–6
  does Aristotle consider to be an emotion in *Rhet.*? 179–83
  emotional (i.e. as involving a representational distress) 186–90
  formal object of 189
  for victory 187
  non-rational contrasted with involving reason 184–5
  oratorical manipulation of judgements (*kriseis*) and 181–2
  pain that serves as a background condition for anger and 187
  pleasure-based bodily desires 179–80, 184–5, 188–90
epi to polu. See *EE* specification of emotions, supplements in, 'for the most part' (*epi to polu*)
estō in definitions of emotions 201n.14
Ethics accounts of pleasure. See pleasure and distress (or pain), in the ethical works, as compatible with Aristotle's account of the emotions
evaluative object of emotion (= formal object of emotion) 25–7, 56–7, 71–3, 73n.23, 81, 99–100, 108–9, 216, 255, 260, 272, 280–1n.20, 302
  entering into the intentional content 34–9
  only providing necessary conditions for emotion-types 73n.23
  trivial and non-trivial specifications of 27, 71–3

favour (*charis*) 236–7, 237n.3, 243–4, 325–6
fear 26, 71–6, 80, 82–4, 105–6, 163–8, 201–6, 202n.18, 270, 271, 322
  chilling of the blood and 202–5
  confidence, contrasted with 248–9
  coward and the. See courage (the courageous, etc.) and its coordinate vices (esp. cowardice)
  definition not support *phantasia*-based view of emotions 106n.40
  desire and 163–8
    boulēsis to be saved and 163–4
  different motivational tendencies and 262–4, 266–9
  distinct from thrill 71–6, 82–4, 267–8
  distinct from thrilled panic 267–8
  disturbance and 160
  formal object of 71–3
  formulation of definition of 105–6
  motivational notion of 166–7
  recalcitrant emotions and. See Fido example; recalcitrant emotions, Dexter example and; recalcitrant emotions, Snarler example and
  shame and 324–5
feeling-friendly-towards (*to philein*) 57, 168–73, 252–3, 320–1
  boulēsis and 154n.2, 168–70
  desire of, contrasted with desire of anger 173
feeling-grateful-for (*charin echein*) 236–7, 243–4, 325–6
  definition of 237
  representational pleasure 237
felt phenomenological dimension of emotions (felt nature of emotions, etc.) 54, 54n.30, 61n.49, 63, 63n.55, 67–9, 110–11, 129–32, 205n.29
fiction, emotional responses to. See emotional response to fiction
Fido example 28, 85–6, 276, 277, 279, 280–5, 280n.20, 287–8, 288n.40, 289n.43, 290, 291, 293–302, 299n.58, 302n.62, 304, 306–7, 315
Fine, K. 131n.26
focus of the emotion. See particular object of the emotion, focus
Ford, A. 209n.38
formal object of emotion. See evaluative object of emotion
Fortenbaugh, W. W. 4n.11, 5n.15, 45n.2, 52–4, 56–8, 65, 76n.25, 90–3, 90n.3, 91nn.5–6, 96, 97–8, 98nn.21–3, 138n.2, 161n.12, 168n.29, 168n.31, 180n.4, 208n.35, 236n.1, 251n.31

'for the most part' (*epi to polu*). See *EE* specification of emotions, supplements in, 'for the most part' (*epi to polu*)
Frede, D. 5n.15, 46, 58n.42, 115n.1, 148n.23, 152n.32, 154n.1, 156, 158, 161nn.11–12, 182, 185, 289n.45
Frijda, N. H. 259n.1, 260n.2, 260n.4, 261n.7, 262, 270n.24
Frost, K. 269n.23
Fussi, A. 323n.12, 324n.16

Gastaldi, S. 105n.37
Gaus, G. F. 1n.2
Gaut, B. 261n.6, 295n.55, 297n.57, 305n.65, 314
Gautier, R. A. and Jolif, J. Y. 324n.14
Gendler, T. and Liao, S. 85n.38, 285n.32
genus/species 50n.15, 51n.19, 63n.54, 138–41, 141n.5, 147–8, 148n.23, 339
Goldie, P. 1n.2, 61n.49, 68n.6, 186n.20, 263n.10, 265n.17, 277n.8
Goldstein, I. 52n.23, 91n.6
Gosling, J. C. B. and Taylor, C. C. W. 115n.2, 118–19n.11, 119n.12, 130n.24, 161n.11, 211n.42, 240n.8
Gottlieb, P. 206n.32
Granger, E. H. 63n.54
Graver, M. 50n.17
Green, O. H. 6n.19, 87n.42, 259n.1
Greenspan, P. S. 6–7n.20, 28n.27, 61n.49, 85n.36, 276, 276n.5, 277n.7, 279, 280–1n.20, 284, 285nn.33–4, 303n.64
grief 55n.34, 186, 260–1, 261n.6
Grimaldi, W. M. A. 236n.1, 324n.14
Grzankowski, A. 18n.6, 277n.8, 279n.13, 279n.15, 286n.36
Guthrie, W. K. C. 324n.14

Hackforth, R. 58n.42
Hamlyn, D. W. 23n.14, 214n.47, 217n.53, 225
Harris, W. V. 142n.9, 151–2n.31, 152n.33
Harte, V. 58n.42, 63n.54, 118–19n.11, 119n.13
hating (*to misein*) 149, 168–9, 171–3, 251–3, 321
  contrasted with anger 149–50, 150n.28, 171, 173
Hedonic principle. *See* Rational requirements, Hedonic principle
'hedonic', use of 3, 43
Heinaman, R. 117, 233n.82
Helm, B. W. 6n.19, 6–7n.20, 29, 61n.49, 73n.23, 277nn.7–8, 278n.11, 279n.12, 280n.16, 281nn.21–2, 282, 283n.28, 285–8, 286–7nn.37–9, 288n.40, 289n.44, 290, 291n.47, 296n.56, 297–8, 303n.64, 306n.66
hepetai ('accompanied by') 44–52, 169n.33, 253n.37
  potential use of 46
  simultaneous use of 47–9
  subsequent use of 47–8, 48n.10, 319
Heraclitus 123n.14
Hicks, R. D. 23n.14
Higgins, N. 324n.16
Hinchman, E. S. 308n.70
Hocutt, M. 97n.19
holōs. See 'in general' (*holōs*) in specifications of emotions
Homer 151n.31, 165n.22, 186, 340n.53
hubris. *See* slight (= offence) (*oligōria*), species of, insult (*hubris*)
Huckleberry Finn 308–14
Humberstone, I. L. 269n.23

Identification view of emotions
  Aristotle, as reading of 7–8, 11, 33, 53, 65–70, 74–7, 94n.15, 98, 118, 118n.9, 126–7
    individuation of emotions and 74–7
    phenomenological dimension of emotions and 67–9
  contemporary views 82–7
    individuation of emotions and 82–3
    phenomenological dimension of emotions and 67–9
imperative side/role of an emotion. *See* representational role of emotions, imperative/prescriptive
indignation (*to nemesan, nemesis*)
  distress-based. *See* distress-based indignation
  pleasure-based. *See* pleasure-based indignation
individuation of emotions 57, 71–81, 93–4
  causal view and 93–4
  contemporary views and 82–3
  fear and thrill 71–3, 267–8
  how Aristotle individuates emotions 77–81
  identification view 74–7
Individuation problem, the 71–3
'in general' (*holōs*) in specifications of emotions 50, 50n.15
Inglis, K. 324n.14
'in light of' view. *See* relation between intentional state that apprehends object of emotion and the emotion's pleasure or distress, 'in light of' view
insult (*hubris*). *See* slight (= offence) (*oligōria*), species of, insult (*hubris*)
intentional attitude (= mode, manner) 19, 19n.7, 34–9, 35n.44, 60n.46, 74–7, 110
  in Aristotle 20–2, 77–81

intentional content 19–20, 19n.8, 34–9, 35nn.42–3, 60n.46, 74–7, 82–4, 110
   in Aristotle 20–2, 32n.38, 77–81
intentional object 18–20, 18nn.4–5, 19n.8, 35n.43, 74–7, 84–7, 110
   in Aristotle 22–4, 77–81
intentional state 17–20, 18n.3, 68
   as 'apprehending' objects of emotion. See 'apprehending' objects of emotion, notions of
   in Aristotle 20–2
   'in their own right'/intrinsically (*kath' hauta*) in *EE* specification of emotion. See *EE* specification of emotions, supplements in, 'in their own right'/intrinsically (*kath' hauta*)
inverse *akrasia* (rational *akrasia*) 308–10
   in Aristotle 308n.69
Inverse Enkratic principle. See Rational requirements, Inverse Enkratic principle
Inwood, B. and Woolf, R. 55n.35
'irrational', charge of 314–15. See also rationality; Rational requirements
Irwin, T. 45n.3, 50n.18, 324n.14, 337n.45

Jacobson, D. See D'Arms, J. and Jacobson, D.
Jimenez, M. 165n.22, 175n.51, 325n.19
Johansen, T. 197n.3, 207–8n.34, 223n.65
Jolif, J. Y. See Gautier, R. A. and Jolif, J. Y.
Jones, K. 286–7n.38, 308n.69
Joy 261–2
   in Aristotle (= *chara*) 262n.8, 339
Judgement 5n.12, 84
   assent, contrasted with 285–6
   belief and, used interchangeably 5n.14, 84
   representing an object as obtaining 84
   thought-based imaginations, contrasted with. See uncommitted thought (thought-based imaginations, etc.)
Judgementalism (judgementalists) 5–7, 27n.24, 31–3, 34–8, 67–9, 82–5, 110–13, 270, 277–9, 297
   contemporary account of emotions 6, 6n.19, 31, 34–7, 67–9, 82–5, 110–13. See also recalcitrant emotions, judgementalism and
   individuation of emotions and 82–7
   making an unwarranted representational addition 84–5, 87
   reading of Aristotle on emotion 5–7, 5n.15, 9n.24, 33, 289n.45
   recalcitrant emotions and. See recalcitrant emotions, judgementalism and

Kahn, C. 23n.14
Kassel, R. 184n.16, 187n.21, 237n.3, 264n.15
kataphronēsis. See disdain (*kataphronēsis*); slight (= offence) (*oligōria*), species of, disdain (*kataphronēsis*)
kath' hauta in *EE* specification. See *EE* specification of emotions, supplements in, 'in their own right' (*kath' hauta*)
Kennedy, G. A. 55n.35, 56n.36, 105n.37, 236n.1, 328n.24, 337n.45
Kenny, A. 27, 27n.24, 28n.26, 71, 72n.17, 73n.23
Knuuttila, S. 5n.15, 289n.45
Konstan, D. 149n.24, 151n.30, 152n.32–3, 168n.29, 168n.31, 236n.1, 237n.2, 242–3n.13, 244n.16, 245n.18, 324n.14
Kraut, R. 256n.42
Kripke, S. 131n.26
kriseis (= 'decisions or verdicts') 113, 113n.52, 181. See also oratorical manipulation of decisions or verdicts (*kriseis*)
Kupperman, J. J. 255n.41

Lazarus, R. S. 27n.24
Leighton, S. R. 5n.15, 44–5n.1, 45n.2, 52n.23, 90n.3, 91n.5, 91n.6, 97n.20, 168n.31, 180–2, 184, 251, 289n.45
Liao, S. See Gendler, T. and Liao, S.
Little, M. O. 271n.26
longing 55n.34, 187n.22, 340–1
Lorenz, H. 20n.9
love, romantic 189, 256, 340
Lovibond, S. 58n.42
Lyons, W. 3n.8, 72n.20, 72n.21, 82, 91n.6

Machek, D. 130n.24
Maiese, M. 259n.1
Majeed, R. 6n.20, 96n.18, 277n.8
Marks, J. 6n.19, 87n.42, 259n.1
Martin, M. G. G. 59n.44
material/physical/bodily dimension of emotions 195–234
   Aristotle's examples to show that emotions are in part bodily 230–4
   boiling of the blood around the heart 198, 217, 217n.53, 219, 232
   chilling of the blood in fear 202–5, 211
   cold desires for revenge and 200, 205, 213–15, 213n.46, 217n.53, 221, 226
   Enmattered form requirement [EFR] reading specified 197
   form-in-matter specification 198, 207–8, 207–8n.34

material/physical/bodily dimension
  of emotions (cont.)
  impure/pure forms 199, 221–3, 223n.65,
    226–7
  material component of a state such as anger
    198–9, 222–3
  Material component requirement [MCR]
    reading specified 196
  'material dimension of a specification',
    use of 199
  mathematical properties, contrasted
    with 227–30
  natural science (*phusikōs*) investigations
    and 207–12, 222–3
  principles involving matter/enmattered
    accounts 197, 197n.7
  Restricted Enmattered form requirement
    [REFR] reading specified 222
  Restricted Material component requirement
    [RMCR] reading specified 222
  Rhet. specifications of emotions as having
    indirect implications for 218
  schematic definition (of states such as anger)
    and. *See* schematic definition (of states
    such as anger)
  states of character and (= states of character as
    also realized in bodily states) 206n.31,
    232, 232n.80
McCready-Flora, I. 91n.6
McDowell, J. 271n.26
McGinn, C. 59–60
McIntyre, A. 308n.69
McLaughlin, B. and Bennett, K. 69n.10
McNaughton, D. 271n.26
Menn, S. 230
Mere-Concurrence view. *See* relation between
  intentional state that apprehends object
  of emotion and the emotion's pleasure or
  distress, Mere-Concurrence view
mild-manneredness (*praotēs*) in *NE* IV.5 (trait of
  character) 152n.33, 167, 167n.27,
    202n.20, 243n.14
  undisturbed and 167
mild-manneredness (*praotēs*) in *Rhet.* II.3
  (privation-emotion) 238–43,
    242–3n.13, 246, 319–20
  anger, contrary of 238–9
  'at-whom' section of discussion in
    Rhet. II.3 240–1
  'because of what' in *Rhet.* II.3 242n.12
  'conditions under what' section of discussion
    in *Rhet.* II.3 241
  defined 242
  privation-emotion, as 240, 242–3

  relation to becoming-mild-mannered
    (*praünsis*) 239, 240n.8
Mills, M. J. 329n.29
mono-state views/readings 7, 67n.3
Montague, M. 18n.6
Moore's paradox 281n.24
Moraux, P. 218n.55
Moravcsik, J. *See* Code, A. and Moravcsik, J.
Morreall, J. 268n.22
Moss, J. 6n.18, 7n.21, 45n.2, 48n.7, 58n.42,
  100n.28, 168n.29, 168n.31, 236n.1,
  249n.25, 251n.32, 271n.26, 275–6n.3,
  279n.12, 289n.45
Motivation principle. *See* Rational requirements,
  Motivation principle
'motivation', use of 293n.52
Motivational theory of emotions 259–69
  acting emotionally and 266–9
  fear and 262–4, 266–9
  grief and 261
  (in)action tendencies (states of action
    readiness, etc) and 259–65, 261n.7,
    267–9, 270–1
  joy and 261–2
  pride and 264–5
  relief and 265
  shame and 264
  teleosemantic theory of representation
    and 270–1
  thrilled panic and 267–8
motives for action in *Rhet.* I.10 156–60
Mueller, I. 230
Müller, J. M. 1n.3, 19n.7, 30, 30n.33, 95n.16,
  108n.43, 109n.46
Müller-Lyer illusion 280–2, 299, 301

Naar, H. 277n.8
Neander, K. *See* Schulte, P. and Neander, K.
Nehamas, A. 4n.11, 208n.35
Neu, J. 6n.19
Nieuwenburg, P. 4n.11, 6n.17, 100n.28, 289n.45
Nietzsche, F. 212, 212n.43
nostalgia 253–4
  as involving both pleasure and pain 253–4
not-being-grateful-for (or being-put-out) (*ou
  charein echein*) 243–4, 326
  privation-emotion as 243
  representational distress as 244
Nussbaum, M. C. 1n.2, 4n.11, 5n.15, 6n.19,
  26n.21, 30n.33, 52n.24, 54n.21, 66–7,
  66n.2, 68, 73n.22, 76, 82, 90n.3, 91n.6,
  92–3, 92n.11, 98–9, 98n.24, 100n.28,
  141n.7, 150n.29, 154n.1, 177n.58,
  179–80, 180nn.2–3, 202n.20,

218nn.54–5, 273, 278n.11, 279n.13, 289n.45, 318n.4, 328n.23
Nussbaum, M. C. and Putnam, H. 50n.15, 197n.3, 197n.6

object. *See* intentional object
offence. *See* slight (= offence) (*oligōria*)
'opposites of emotions', Aristotle's 238–48. *See also* privation-emotions (absence of an emotion, etc.)
oratorical manipulation of decisions or verdicts (*kriseis*) 113–14, 172, 181–2, 237, 242, 243, 246
orexis (desire). *See* desire (in Aristotle) (*orexis*)
ou charein echein. *See* not-being-grateful-for (or being-put-out) (*ou charein echein*)
Owen, G. E. L. 118–19n.11, 119n.13

pain-at locutions (*epi* + dative) 54–8, 79, 93, 99, 103
Pakaluk, M. 119n.13
particular object of emotion 25–6n.19, 28–9, 302
 focus 29, 29nn.31–2
 target 28–9, 28n.28, 35n.43, 255, 256
 and Aristotle 28–9, 28n.29, 143, 319n.6
pathē, pathos, paschein. *See* emotion(s), use of term for *pathos/pathē*
Pearson, G. 7n.21, 31n.36, 99n.25, 99n.26, 100n.28, 106n.40, 157n.5, 159n.7, 165nn.20–2, 170n.27, 171n.43, 173–4n.47, 175n.50, 177n.56, 177n.58, 179n.1, 181n.5, 184n.14, 187n.23, 232n.78, 249n.25, 263n.10, 271n.26, 274n.30, 275n.2, 275–6n.3, 289, 289n.45, 295, 338
Penner, T. 58n.42
Peramatzis, M. 197n.2, 199n.11, 224n.66, 228nn.72–3
'perceptible' in *EE* specification of emotions. *See* *EE* specification of emotions, supplements in, 'perceptible'
perception (*aisthēsis*) and perceptibles (*aisthēta*) 2, 2n.7, 20n.9, 21–2, 24–5, 25n.18, 54n.29, 66–7, 76, 109, 252n.35
 extrinsic (incidental) perceptibles 23–4, 23–4n.14, 54
 special perceptibles 23n.14, 54n.29
perception, use of in 'Perceptualism'. *See* Perceptualism (perceptualist theory of emotions, etc.), invoking notion of 'perception' that is only analogous to sense-perception
perceptual imagination 31–2, 85–6, 272, 284–5, 290, 304

Perceptualism (perceptualist theory of emotions, etc.) 5–6, 31–3, 34–8, 67–9, 82–3, 85–7, 111–12, 270, 279–85, 298–301
 appearance as/of truth and. *See* appearance as/of truth (= assent of the subsystem)
 contemporary account of emotions 6, 6n.19, 31, 34–8, 35n.42, 67–8, 82–3, 85–7, 111–12. *See also* recalcitrant emotions, perceptualism and
 'direct' contrasted with 'indirect' theories 6n.19, 280n.16
 individuation of emotions and 82–7
 invoking notion of 'perception' that is only analogous to sense-perception 279–80, 280–1n.20, 282, 284
 making unwarranted representational addition 85–7
 reading of Aristotle on emotion as 5–6, 6n.17, 9n.24, 33, 289n.45
 recalcitrant emotions and. *See* recalcitrant emotions, perceptualism and
 too restrictive 283–4
phainomenos, use of in Aristotle's formulations of emotions 56n.37. 99–105, 105n.27, 106–7, 318
phantasia 20n.9, 22, 24, 24n.15, 32n.38, 100, 106–7, 148n.23
phantasia-based view 5–8, 11n.29, 252n.35, 280n.19
 not supported by specification of fear 106n.40
phenomenological felt dimensions of emotions. *See* felt phenomenological dimension of emotions (felt nature of emotions, etc.)
physical dimension of emotions. *See* material/physical/bodily dimension of emotions
Pitcher, G. 3n.8
pity 55, 80–1, 110, 126–7, 327–8
 'conditions under which' and 143
 disturbance and 160
 schadenfreude and 81, 110
Plato (Platonic background, etc.) 4, 58, 115, 115n.2, 160–2, 162n.15, 171n.43, 177n.56, 180n.2, 185, 202n.18, 206n.30, 280n.19, 340. *See* Index Locorum for references to individual works
 process account of pleasure and 160–2
 representational pleasures/pains and 58
 tripartite division of emotions 177n.56
Platts, M. 269n.23
pleasure-based indignation. 55, 81, 335–6

pleasures and distress (or pain)
  activities, as 118–19
  bodily pains as representational 59–60, 59n.45, 60n.46
  chairein (joy) 61–2, 339
  consequent on the intentional state that apprehends its object 33, 53, 69–70
  defective pleasures 122–9
  'distress', use of 60–1
  genera of the emotions, as 147–8
  Hedonic principle. *See* Rational requirements, Hedonic principle
  in the ethical works, as compatible with Aristotle's account of the emotions 115–29
    'defective pleasures' worry 122–9
    'same-activity, same pleasure' worry 119–22, 129
  lupē 44, 61, 61n.48, 61n.50
  non-representational, reading of Aristotle 52–4
  pain-at locutions. *See* pain-at locutions
  perfecting activities, as 129–32
  philosophical objections to hedonic views 253–6
  Platonic notion of 115, 160–2
  process account of 115, 160–2
  representational 33, 54–63
    in Aristotle 54–8
    in contemporary discussions 59–63
  responses to intentional states that apprehend the emotion's object, as. *See* response view of emotions
  Rhet. I.11 account of 115–16, 115nn.1–2, 116nn.3–6
  usage of 44, 60–2
Pointless Motivation principle. *See* Rational requirements, Pointless Motivation principle
pothos (longing or regret) 187n.22, 340–1
praotēs. *See* mild-manneredness (*praotēs*) in *NE* IV.5 (trait of character); mild-manneredness (*praotēs*) in *Rhet*. II.3 (privation-emotion)
prescriptive role of emotions. *See* representational role of emotions, imperative/prescriptive
Price, A. W. 6n.18, 7n.21, 45, 45n.2, 49n.12, 62n.51, 99n.25, 100n.28, 105n.37, 115nn.1–2, 116, 116n.3, 116nn.5–6, 117, 117nn.7, 119nn.12–13, 121–2, 124–5, 125n.15, 127, 127n.18, 129, 129n.22, 131–2, 131n.27, 161n.11, 167, 167n.26, 168n.29, 168n.31, 180n.4, 236n.1, 240n.8, 251–2, 252n.34, 252n.35, 279n.12, 289n.45

pride 116, 264–5, 264n.15, 265n.16
  in-another 55, 78, 81, 101, 112, 161–2n.14, 265n.17, 336, 339
Primavesi, O. *See* Rapp, C. and Primavesi, O.
Prinz, J. 6n.19, 60n.47, 63n.53, 68n.7, 72n.19, 108n.44, 270–1n.25, 280n.16
privation-emotions (absence of an emotion, etc.) 182n.6, 238–48, 252–3, 254, 320, 325, 326, 335n.42
  contrasted with emotions 'proper' 247–8
  counting as emotions (*pathē*) 246–7
  positive states in their own right 247
Prodicus 62n.51, 339
Purshouse, L. 333n.36
Putnam, H. *See* Nussbaum, M. C. and Putnam, H.

quasi-judgmentalism, theory of emotions 6, 6n.19, 285–9, 297–8
  recalcitrant emotions and. *See* recalcitrant emotions, quasi-judgementalism and
  use of term 6, 6–7n.20
quasi-perceptualism, as a reading of Aristotle 6, 6n.18, 7, 33, 289n.45
  use of term 6
Quine, W. V. O. 49n.11

Rackham, H. 337n.45
Rapp, C. 2n.5, 2n.6, 7n.21, 44–5n.1, 45n.2, 51n.20, 101n.32, 115, 115n.1, 115n.2, 116n.6, 145n.17, 149n.26, 158n.6, 161n.11, 161n.13, 163n.16, 168n.29, 169n.33, 177n.57, 201n.14, 206n.32, 231n.76, 233n.82, 236n.1, 237n.2, 240n.8, 248n.23, 253n.37, 275–6n.3
Rapp, C. and Primavesi, O. 218n.55
Ratcliffe, M. 29n.31
rational desire. *See boulēsis* (wish, rational desire)
rationality 306–16, 307n.67. *See also* Rational requirements; recalcitrant emotions, irrationality of (when irrational)
  coherence, as 309–13
  responsiveness, as 310, 310n.74
  warrant, as 306–16, 310n.74
Rational requirements
  Consistency principle 277–8, 281–2, 290, 293, 300n.60, 309
    defined 277
  Consistency principle2 287, 290
    defined 287
  Enkratic principle 292–4, 300n.60, 309–11, 313
    defined 292
  Hedonic principle 302, 305n.65
    defined 302
  Inverse Enkratic principle 309–10
    defined 309

Motivation principle 293–4
   defined 293
   Pointless Motivation principle 294–5,
      300n.60, 305n.65
   defined 294
Rawls, J. 276–7n.6
Raymond, C. C. 165n.22, 201n.15, 206n.31,
   324n.13, 325n.19
reactive role of emotions. *See* representational
   role of emotions, reactive/responsive
recalcitrant emotions 84, 272, 275–316
   Aristotle's hedonic response view of emotions
      and 301–6
   Dexter example and 306–10, 307–8n.68,
      312, 315n.77
   examples of 276, 276–7n.6
   explaining the existence of on various
      theories 277–9, 280, 283–5, 287–90,
      297–8, 301
   Fido example and. *See* Fido example
   irrationality of (when irrational) 277,
      277n.8, 281–2, 282n.25, 283n.28, 289,
      289n.43, 290, 293, 298–306,
      302n.62, 305n.65
   judgementalism and 277–9, 297
   perceptualism and 279–285, 298–301
   practical irrationality and 290–6
   quasi-judgementalism and 285–9, 297–8
   rationality as warrant and 306–16
   response view of emotions and 301–6
   Scylla of judgementalism and the Charybdis
      of perceptualism and 286, 289,
      290, 301
   sensory illusions and 280–2, 281n.22,
      291, 291nn.46–7, 299, 300n.60,
      301–2
   Snarler example and 284, 288–9, 298–302,
      302n.62, 315
   view that allows objects of emotions to be
      apprehended by a variety of intentional
      states and 289–90
Reeve, C. D. C. 45n.3, 50n.18, 55n.35, 56n.36,
   77n.27, 101n.32, 105n.38, 115n.1,
   142n.8, 174nn.48–9, 182n.6, 185n.18,
   239n.6, 248, 249n.25, 317n.1, 319n.6,
   329n.27, 333, 337n.45
regret 201n.17, 241, 272, 318n.3, 340–1
relation between intentional state that
      apprehends object of emotion and its
      pleasure or distress 90–7
   causal view 52, 56, 70, 91–7, 97n.19,
      98, 98n.23
   'in light of' view 95–7, 272–3
   Mere-Concurrence view 90–1
relief 265, 272, 286n.37, 288n.40

representational roles of emotions 269–74
   descriptive 260–1, 269–73
   imperative/prescriptive 261, 269–73
   reactive/responsive 272–4
response view of emotions 7, 33, 95–7, 108–14,
      272–4, 301–6
   apprehender views of emotions, contrasted
      with 108–14
   felt nature of emotions and 110–11
   individuation of emotions and 110
   recalcitrant emotions and 301–6
Rhet. I.10 on motives for action. *See* motives for
   action in *Rhet.* I.10
Rhet. discussions of emotions under three
      heads 28n.29, 143, 319n.6
   'at what' (*epi poiois*) 56n.36, 143,
      319n.6, 329n.28
   'at whom' (*tisin*) 28n.29, 143
   'conditions under which' (*pōs
      diakeimenoi*) 143, 241–2, 249n.5
Rhet.-style definitions/specifications of
      emotions 196, 200–9, 211, 212–22,
      219n.57
   adequacy of 212–22
   explanatory power of 216–21
   picking out correct extension of
      emotions 200, 213–16
Roberts, R. C. 5n.14, 6n.19, 6–7n.20, 68n.7,
   73n.22, 85n.35, 280n.16–17, 282, 283,
   283n.29, 286, 286–7n.38, 287, 291,
   291n.46, 306n.66
Roberts, W. R. 56n.36, 105n.37
Robertson Ishii, T. *See* Atkins, P. and Robertson
   Ishii, T.
Rorty, A. O. 2n.5, 158n.6, 177n.57, 256n.42
Ross, W. D. 29n.30, 45n.3, 105n.37,
   237n.3, 337n.45
Rossi, M. and Tappolet, C. 36n.45
Rowe, C. *See* Broadie, S. and Rowe, C.

sadness 260, 261n.6, 272n.28
Saenz, V. 157n.5
Sainsbury, R. M. 28n.28
Salmela, M. 280n.16
Salmieri, G. 63n.54
Sanders, E. 329n.29, 330
Scarantino, A. 2n.7, 36n.46, 91n.6, 96n.18,
   259–74, 259n.1, 260n.4, 261n.5, 261n.7,
   262n.9, 263n.11, 267n.21, 270n.24,
   270–1n.25. *See also* de Sousa, R. and
   Scarantino, A.
schadenfreude (*epichairekakia*) 9–10, 55,
   58n.43, 62, 62n.51, 79, 81, 110, 126–7,
   273, 303–5, 330, 332n.34, 336–8,
   337n.45, 338n.48

schadenfreude *(epichairekakia) (cont.)*
  distress-based indignation and 328
  pity and 79n.30, 81, 110, 126–7
  pleasure-based indignation and 126–7
Scheiter, K. 157n.5, 170n.36
schematic definition (of states such as
  anger) 173–4n.47, 198–9, 198–9n.9,
  199–200n.12, 206, 208, 212, 222–3,
  226–7, 227n.71, 229
Schlosser, M. 92n.8
Schofield, M. 20n.9
Schroeder, T. *See* Arpaly, N. and Schroeder, T.
Schulte, P. and Neander, K. 270–1n.25
scorn 253–4
  involving both pleasure and pain 253–4
Searle, J. R. 6n.19, 19n.7, 87n.42,
  259n.1, 269n.23
Sedley, D. 29n.30
shame (as a disposition) 3, 206n.31, 324n.13
shame (as an emotion) (incl. both *aischunē* and
  aidōs) 3n.9, 27, 57–8, 71, 107, 204–6,
  244–5, 264, 264n.14, 323–5
  disturbance and 58n.41, 160, 162,
    163n.16, 167
  fear and 204–5, 204n.28, 206n.30, 324–5
  target of 28n.29
shamelessness *(anaischuntia)* 175, 175n.51,
  244–5, 246–7, 253, 324n.13, 325
  behaviour and 334n.38
  disdain *(kataphronēsis)* and 245
  disposition, as a 156n.4, 245n.19
  privation-emotion, as a 244–5, 246–7, 253
  unemotional, as 244–5
Sherman, N. 54n.31, 90n.3, 154n.1, 174n.49
Shields, C. 25n.18, 131n.27, 197n.3, 197n.7,
  209n.36, 214n.47, 217n.53
Sihvola, J. 4n.11, 6n.17, 100n.28, 289n.45
Sinhababu, N. 18n.6, 260n.3
slight (= offence) *(oligōria)* 27, 144, 149–50,
  240–1, 245, 318, 318n.4, 319n.6
  species of 318–19, 319n.6, 334
    disdain *(kataphronēsis)* 105n.37, 245, 319,
      334, 335n.19
    insult *(hubris)* 105n.37, 142, 213n.46, 319
    spite *(epēreasmos)* 105n.37, 149, 215n.48,
      319, 319n.5
Smith, M. 269n.23
Solomon, R. C. 6n.19, 63n.53, 68
Solomon, R. C. and Stone, L. D. 63n.53
Sorabji, R. 50n.17, 54n.29, 67n.5, 197n.6
Spengel, L. 105n.37
spite *(epēreasmos). See* slight (= offence)
  (oligōria), species of, spite *(epēreasmos)*
Stocker, M. 175n.50

Stoics the (Stoic notions, etc.) 30n.33,
  50n.17, 163n.17
Stone, L. D. *See* Solomon R. C and Stone, L. D.
Striker, G. 4n.11, 6n.17, 45n.2, 50n.17, 91n.6,
  100n.28, 138n.2, 145n.17, 148, 148n.23,
  156, 158–9, 159n.8, 161n.12, 168n.29,
  168n.31, 182–3, 183nn.10–11, 184–8,
  184n.13, 190, 211n.42, 236–7, 236n.1,
  238, 243n.15, 248–9, 254, 289n.45
Strohl, M. 129n.22, 130–2, 130n.24, 131n.25
supervenience 49, 68, 69n.10, 75, 119n.12,
  128–9, 130
supplements in the *EE* specification of emotions.
  See EE specification of emotions,
  supplements in
surprise 254–5
  hedonically neutral 254–5
  positive and negative 254
Svavarsdottir, S. 175n.50
Swartzer, S. 271n.26

Tappolet, C. 3n.8, 6n.19, 68n.7, 71n.15, 72n.19,
  85n.35, 86n.41, 280nn.16–18, 283n.28,
  289n.44, 296n.56, 308n.69. *See also*
  Rossi, M and Tappolet, C.
tarachē. See disturbance *(tarachē)* and undisturbed
  (ataraxos), in relation to emotions
target of the emotion. *See* particular object of the
  emotion, target
Taylor, C. C. W. 117, 154n.1, 324n.14. *See also*
  Gosling, J. C. B. and Taylor, C. C. W.
teleosemantic theory of representation 270–1,
  270–1n.25
Teroni, F. 71n.16, 72n.20, 73n.23, 109n.45.
  See also Deonna, J. A. and Teroni, F.
thought-based imaginations. *See* uncommitted
  thought (thought-based
  imaginations etc.)
thrill. *See* fear, distinct from thrill; fear, distinct
  from thrilled panic
thumos (spirit) 109, 109n.47, 151n.31, 154n.2,
  157–9, 177n.56
  preventing fear 203
  sometimes treated as synonymous with
    orgē 157–9, 157n.5, 177n.56,
    182, 182n.8
training of emotional dispositions. *See* emotional
  dispositions, training of
Tuozzo, T. M. 173–4n.47, 271n.26
Tye, M. 17n.2, 60n.46, 68n.9

uncommitted thought (thought-based
  imaginations, etc.) 31–2, 85, 272,
  285n.32, 290

undisturbed (*atarachos*). *See* disturbance (*tarachē*) and undisturbed (*atarachos*), in relation to emotions

Viano, C. 48n.8, 138n.2, 156, 159n.8
vice (vicious person, vicious response) 123–9, 129n.20, 131–2, 156–7, 337. *See also* courage (the courageous, etc.) and its coordinate vices (esp. cowardice); envy (*phthonos*), vicious background disposition and
Vigani, D. 165n.20, 165n.22, 166n.24
virtue (virtuous person, virtuous response, etc.) 121, 123–9, 129n.20, 131–2, 156, 328, 337. *See also* courage (the courageous, etc.) and its coordinate vices (esp. cowardice); emulation (*zēlos*), virtuous background disposition and

Wall, D. 261n.6
Walton, K. L. 285n.32
Warren, J. 130n.23, 318n.3
Wedin, M. V. 20n.9, 197n.3, 197n.7, 198n.9, 233n.82, 234
Whiting, D. 91n.6
Wilson, J. 63n.54
Wilson, J. R. S. 91n.6
wish. See *boulēsis* (wish, rational desire)
Woods, M. 251
Woolf, R. *See* Inwood, B. and Woolf, R.

Index Locorum

Aristotle

Categoriae
 8.9a36–9b9 2n.5
 8.9b11–33 204n.28
 8.9b28–10a11 2n.5

De interpretatione
 6.17a25–6 23
 6.17a33 23
 9.19a7–10 50

Analytica priora
 I.13.32b6–8 50
 I.13.32b11–13 50
 I.27.43b3 45
 I.27.43b17–19 45
 I.27.43b22 45
 I.27.43b29–31 45
 II.2.54b31 45
 II.3.56a27 45
 II.3.56a29 45

Topica
 I.1.100b23–101a4 102
 I.5.102a18–30 131
 I.12.105a14–16 50
 II.2.109b36–7 56, 100, 329n.30
 II.2.110a1–2 56, 100, 329n.30
 II.2.110a3 328n.25
 II.6.112b22–4 62n.51, 339
 III.2.117a5–15 46
 IV.1.121a30–9 115n.1
 IV.5.125b28–34 139
 IV.5.126a9–10 184n.12
 IV.5.126a13 168
 IV.6.127b30–2 138
 VI.1.139b12–17 211
 VI.3.140b27–8 183n.12
 VI.3.140b28 183n.12
 VI.5.142b27–9 141
 VI.8.146b2 141n.6, 170
 VI.8.146b5–6 170n.37
 VI.8.146b36–147a5 183–4n.12
 VI.8.146b37–147a1 170n.37
 VI.13.150b32–151a1 139, 144–5
 VI.13.151a14–15 144
 VI.13.151a15–16 139
 VI.13.151a16–19 139, 215n.49
 VIII.1.156a32–3 139

De sophisticis elenchis
 13.173a39 183n.12
 13.173a39–40 154n.2
 31.181b37–182a3 228n.72

Physica
 II.1.193b19–20 247n.22
 II.2 228n.72
 II.9 223n.65
 III.3.202b14–16 65n.1
 IV.3.210a15–24 50
 VII.3.247a17–18 54n.28
 VII.3.247b13–17 211n.41
 VII.3.247b17–248a6 211

De caelo
 II.7.289a11 45
 III.4.302b11 45

De generatione et corruption
 I.2.316a5–14 217n.52

De anima
 I.1 9n.25, 14, 196, 201–2, 206–7, 212, 218n.56, 222, 224, 338
 I.1.402b18–21 227
 I.1.402b20–1 229
 I.1.402b21–5 226
 I.1.402b25–403a2 200, 216–17
 I.1.402b25f 219
 I.1.403a1 218
 I.1.403a2 217
 I.1.403a3 2, 2n.6, 209
 I.1.403a3–5 197, 219
 I.1.403a3–7 211
 I.1.403a3–10 207–8
 I.1.403a7 2n.6, 50n.15, 173–4n.47, 177n.56, 179, 197n.6, 209n.37
 I.1.403a8–10 209n.36
 I.1.403a11–14 230
 I.1.403a11–16 227, 229, 230
 I.1.403a12–16 227
 I.1.403a16 2, 2n.6, 209, 246
 I.1.403a16–17 246
 I.1.403a16–18 169, 249, 253, 317, 338
 I.1.403a16–19 197, 230
 I.1.403a17 177n.56, 320n.7
 I.1.403a17–18 173–4n.47
 I.1.403a18 62n.51, 262n.8, 320n.8, 321n.9, 339

I.1.403a18–19 198–9n.9, 231n.75, 246
I.1.403a19–24 196, 197, 230–4
I.1.403a20ff 217
I.1.403a22–3 231n.75
I.1.403a22–4 276n.3
I.1.403a23 231n.75
I.1.403a23–4 234n.83
I.1.403a25 197, 199
I.1.403a25–7 173–4n.47, 195, 198, 226–7
I.1.403a26 227n.71
I.1.403a27–8 197–8
I.1.403a29 198
I.1.403a29–b3 224
I.1.403a29–b7 98n.23
I.1.403a29–b9 198
I.1.403a30–1 144n.14, 149, 173–4n.47, 198, 200, 214–16
I.1.403a31 214n.47
I.1.403a31–b1 150n.28, 198, 198–9n.9, 217n.53
I.1.403b1 198–9n.9
I.1.403b2 224
I.1.403b3 198, 224
I.1.403b3–7 213, 225
I.1.403b6–7 198
I.1.403b7 198, 207
I.1.403b7–10 225
I.1.403b8–9 224, 225
I.1.403b11–12 198
I.1.403b11–14 207–8n.34
I.1.403b13–14 207
I.1.403b14–15 207, 227, 229, 230
I.1.403b15–16 207
I.1.403b16–19 227, 230
I.4.408b1–2 339n.50
I.4.408b1–3 25n.18
I.4.408b7–8 203–4n.25
I.4.408b11–15 25n.18
II.1.412a19–20 25n.18
II.2.413b13–32 210n.40
II.2.413b23–4 184n.12
II.3.414b2 154n.2
II.3.414b5–6 183n.12
II.3.414b11–16 179n.1
II.6.418a11–12 23–4n.14
II.6.418a20–4 54, 54n.29
II.6.418a21 23
II.12.424a26–8 65n.1
III.1.425a24–7 54
III.3.427b7–8 175n.51
III.3.427b12–14 175n.51
III.3.427b24–6 32n.38, 139
III.3.428a12 21n.11
III.3.428a16–18 175n.51
III.3.428a19–21 46
III.3.428a24 175n.51

III.3.428b2 24
III.3.428b2–4 280n.19
III.3.428b3–4 24
III.3.428b4–9 21n.11
III.3.428b18–19 23–4n.14
III.3.428b21–2 23
III.3.428b25–30 24n.15
III.3.429a5 21n.11
III.7.431a8–14 67n.5
III.7.431a10–11 67n.5
III.8.432a10–12 24n.15
III.9.432a15–b7 210n.40
III.9.432a16 21
III.9.432b5 168
III.9.432b5–6 154n.2
III.9.432b29–433a1 166n.24, 234
III.10.433a11 21n.11
III.10.433a23–5 168
III.10.433a31–b13 210n.40
III.10.433b10–12 109n.47
III.10.433b11–12 24

De sensu
　1.436a9 50
　5.443b20–31 179n.1

De memoria et reminiscentia
　1.449b10–11 164n.18
　1.449b27–8 164n.18
　1.450a10–12 20n.9
　1.450a12–14 106n.40, 252n.35
　1.450a22–5 106n.40, 252n.35
　1.450a32–b11 20n.9

De somno
　3.456b17–28 211n.41

De insomniis
　2.460b11–16 234n.83
　2.460b18–20 24
　2.460b18–22 280n.19
　2.460b20–2 23–4

De respiratione
　20.479b20–6 203n.22, 204n.28

Historia animalium
　VI.18.571b8–10 179n.1
　VII.1.581b20–1 179n.1

De partibus animalium
　I.5.644b25–8 340n.52
　II.4 9n.25, 14, 195, 205n.29, 206n.31, 233
　II.4.650b27–30 203n.22, 203–4n.25
　II.4.650b27ff 219
　II.4.650b33–651a4 203–4n.25
　II.17.661a7–9 179n.1
　II.17.661a8 183n.12
　III.14.675b25–7 179n.1
　IV.11.692a23 203n.22

De motu animalium
  6.700b2 154n.2
  6.700b17–22 32n.38
  6.700b19–21 21, 22
  7 21n.11
  7.701a25–33 96n.18
  7.701a32 179n.1
  7.701a32–3 20, 20n.9
  7.701b28–32 205
  8.701b33–702a5 69n.12
  8.701b34 69n.12, 218n.54
  8.701b34–6 218n.54
  8.701b36–7 218n.55
  8.701b37–702a5 218, 249–50, 323
  8.702a1 69n.12
  8.702a4 69n.12
  8.702a5 218n.54
  8.702a5–7 218n.54
  11.703b6–8 234, 276n.3

De generatione animalium
  I.4.717a24 179n.1
  I.18.724a1 339
  I.20.727b35 339
  VII.1.774a3–6 179n.1

Problemata
  II.31.869b7 203n.22
  X.60.898a6 203n.22
  XI.36.903b12 203n.22
  XI.53.905a5–16 204n.28
  XXVII.1 203n.22
  XXX.1.954b13 203n.22
  XXX.1.954b39–955a18 203n.23

Metaphysica
  Γ.7.1011b23–9 23
  Δ.21 2n.5
  Δ.22 247n.22
  Δ.22.1022b28 247
  E.1.1025b18–28 208–9
  E.1.1025b28–1026a6 208n.35
  E.1.1025b30–4 228n.72
  E.1.1025b34–1026b2 50n.15
  E.1.1026a5–6 209
  E.1.1026a6 209n.36
  E.4.1027b18–19 23
  E.4.1027b20–3 23
  E.4.1027b28–31 23
  Z.3.1029a1–2 25n.18
  Z.5.1030b17–18 228n.72
  Z.5.1030b28–1031a1 154n.2
  Z.7.1032b2–5 247
  Z.7.1033a7–13 247
  Z.8 228n.72
  Z.10.1036a9–12 230
  Z.10–11 197n.5
  Z.11.1037a2–5 230
  Z.11.1037a5 25n.18
  Z.12.1037b14–18 23
  H.2.1043a12ff 226n.68
  Θ.3.1047a30–2 115n.1
  Θ.6 115n.1
  Θ.6.1048b24–5 47n.6
  Θ.10 23–4n.14
  Θ.10.1051b2–17 21n.11
  Θ.10.1051b30–1052a4 24n.17
  K.1.1059a14–16 230
  Λ.7 209n.36

Ethica Nicomachea
  I.3.1094b14–16 209n.39
  I.3.1094b20–1 209n.39
  I.3.1094b21–2 209n.39
  I.3.1094b23–7 209n.39
  I.4.1095b4–6 50
  I.7 209
  I.7.1097b23 340n.52
  I.8.1099a11–13 125n.15
  I.13 209n.39
  I.13.1102a5–6 209
  I.13.1102a16–17 209
  I.13.1102a18–19 209
  I.13.1102a23 209
  I.13.1102a23–6 209
  I.13.1102a25 210
  I.13.1102a26–8 209–10
  I.13.1102a28–32 210
  I.13.1102b28–1103a3 168n.30
  I.13.1103a3–7 168n.30
  II.2.1104a20–1 164
  II.3.1104b3–5 49
  II.3.1104b3–13 123
  II.3.1104b5–7 185n.19
  II.3.1104b7–8 202n.18
  II.3.1104b13–16 49, 51n.21
  II.3.1104b13–18 169n.33
  II.3.1104b14–15 46
  II.5.1105b21 185n.19
  II.5.1105b21–3 2, 10, 44, 50, 50n.16, 51n.21, 168n.30, 169, 177n.56, 179, 180, 247n.20, 249, 250–3, 253n.37, 317, 338, 339, 340, 340n.54
  II.5.1105b22 62n.51, 262n.8, 320n.8, 321n.9, 339
  II.5.1105b23–5 324n.13
  II.5.1105b25–8 168n.30
  II.5.1105b31–1106a2 175n.51
  II.5.1106a1 175n.51
  II.5.1106a4–5 3

II.5.1106a4–6 177
II.6.1106b16–20 247n.20
II.6.1106b16–23 50, 51n.19
II.6.1106b18–19 185n.19
II.6.1106b18–20 177n.56, 179, 180
II.6.1106b36–1107a2 246
II.6.1107a8–11 175, 325
II.6.1107a8–13 246–7, 253
II.6.1107a8–15 127
II.6.1107a9–11 55, 94, 101, 338
II.7.1107b1 166
II.7.1107b32 3
II.7.1108a30–b6 201n.16
II.7.1108a31 201
II.7.1108a31–5 3
II.7.1108a32 324n.13
II.7.1108a34–5 245n.17, 245n.19, 324n.13
II.7.1108a35–1108b1 328n.24
II.7.1108a35–1108b3 62n.51
II.7.1108a35–1108b6 55, 101, 337n.45, 337–8, 338n.48
II.7.1108b3 3
II.7.1108b3–4 201, 328
II.7.1108b3–5 329
II.7.1108b4–5 201, 330n.31
II.7.1108b5 3
II.7.1108b5–6 62n.51, 201, 338n.47
II.7.1108b6–7 201n.16
II.8.1108b19–26 125n.16
III.1.1110b18–24 201n.17, 318n.3
III.1.1110b32–1111a2 307n.67
III.1.1111a20–1 201n.17, 318n.3
III.1.1111a31 185n.19, 187
III.1.1111a32–3 183n.12
III.1.1111b1–2 159n.9
III.2.1111b5 45
III.2.1111b16–17 184n.12
III.2.1111b17 183n.12
III.2.1111b19–26 261n.6
III.2.1111b22–3 151–2n.31
III.2.1111b23–4 163
III.2.1111b26–9 163–4
III.2.1112a9 128n.19
III.2.1112a9–11 173–4n.47
III.2.1112a10–11 128n.19, 129n.21
III.3.1112a30–1 163
III.3.1113a11 146n19
III.4.1113a23–4 170n.37
III.5.1113b3 163–4
III.5.1113b27–30 180
III.6 165n.20
III.6.1115a7–12 201–2, 322n.11
III.6.1115a10 324
III.6.1115a10–11 29, 324

III.6.1115a10–12 27n.23
III.6.1115a12–14 165n.22
III.6.1115a16 166
III.6.1115a32–4 166
III.6–9 3, 250n.27
III.7 165n.20
III.7.1115b7 26
III.7.1115b7–10 164
III.7.1115b10–12 164
III.7.1115b10–13 165, 165n.20, 166
III.7.1115b13–14 164
III.7.1115b13–15 165n.20
III.7.1115b14–15 164–5
III.7.1115b15–19 250n.27
III.7.1115b17 164–5
III.7.1115b18 164
III.7.1115b24–8 29, 166, 232
III.7.1115b33–1116a2 250n.27
III.7.1115b34 26
III.7.1115b34–5 164
III.7.1116a1–2 165–6n.23
III.7.1116a2–3 164
III.7.1116a3 26
III.7.1116a12–15 164
III.8.1116a27–9 165n.22
III.8.1116b15–22 164
III.8.1116b22–3 165n.22
III.8.1116b24–30 323
III.8.1117a9–11 164n.19
III.8.1117a9–15 323
III.8.1117a15–16 164n.19
III.8.1117a18–19 166
III.8.1117a19 166
III.9.1117a29–30 250n.27
III.9.1117a30–2 166
III.9.1117a31 166
III.9.1117b3 250n.27
III.9.1117b9 250n.27
III.9.1117b11 202n.18
III.10–12 185, 185n.19
III.10.1118a1 187
III.11.1118b8–21 115
III.11.1118b8–27 179n.1
III.11.1118b9 184n.15
III.11.1118b15 184n.15
III.11.1118b19 184n.15
III.11.1118b30–2 189n.24
III.11.1119a3–4 189.24
III.11.1119a4 141n.6, 184n.12
III.12.1119a21–2 165–6n.23
III.12.1119a23–4 165–6n.23
III.12.1119b5–7 183n.12
IV.1.1120a14 45, 45n.3
IV.1.1120a26 45n.3

Ethica Nicomachea (*cont.*)
  IV.1.1120b32 45n.3, 45–6
  IV.1.1120b34 45–46
  IV.5 3, 3n.9, 150n.29, 177n.56, 245n.19
  IV.5.1125b26–9 167n.27
  IV.5.1125b27–8 152n.33
  IV.5.1125b27–9 152n.33, 243n.14
  IV.5.1125b33–1126a1 167
  IV.5.1125b34–1126a1 243n.14
  IV.5.1126a1 152n.33
  IV.5.1126a1–2 152n.33
  IV.5.1126a1–3 167n.27, 202n.20, 243n.14
  IV.5.1126a2 202
  IV.5.1126a2–3 152n.33
  IV.5.1126a4–8 26n.21, 150, 232n.80
  IV.5.1126a7 202
  IV.5.1126a7–8 202n.20
  IV.5.1126a9–11 26, 276n.3
  IV.5.1126a17 202
  IV.5.1126a19–22 156n.4
  IV.5.1126a21 202
  IV.5.1126a21–2 105n.38, 145, 173n.46
  IV.5.1126a22 202
  IV.5.1126a26–8 26
  IV.5.1126a28 202
  IV.5.1126a30 202
  IV.5.1126a36–b1 152n.33
  IV.9 165n.22, 201n.16, 220, 223, 324–5, 324n.14, 338n.47
  IV.9.1128b10–15 3n.9
  IV.9.1128b11 205
  IV.9.1128b11–12 324
  IV.9.1128b11–15 204, 206n.31, 234
  IV.9.1128b14 204
  IV.9.1128b18 264n.14, 324n.15
  IV.9.1128b19–21 324n.15
  IV.9.1128b29–30 324n.15
  IV.9.1128b31–2 264n.14, 324n.15
  V.1.1129b26–7 65n.1
  V.2.1130a18 164
  V.2.1130a30 164
  V.6.1134a17–23 112n.51, 175n.50
  V.8.1135b19–25 112n.51
  V.8.1135b28–9 105n.37, 149n.24
  V.9.1136b7–8 170n.37
  VI.2.1139a23 146n.19
  VI.2.1139b4–5 146n.19
  VI.13.1144b1–8 274n.30
  VII.2.1146a16–21 308n.69, 318n.3
  VII.3.1146b31–1147a24 210
  VII.3.1147a14–17 204n.26
  VII.3.1147a24–1147b3 21n.11
  VII.3.1147b6–9 210
  VII.3.1147b8–12 21n.11

VII.4.1148a21–2 184n.12
VII.4.1148a25 187
VII.4.1148a26 187
VII.4.1148b10–14 151–2n.31
VII.5.1149a7–8 26
VII.5.1149a8–9 26n.20
VII.6 151–2n.31
VII.6.1149a32–b1 20n.9, 21, 22n.13, 109, 273n.29
VII.6.1149a34–b1 181
VII.6.1149b20–1 145
VII.6.1149b27–1150a8 125n.15
VII.8.1151a10 175n.50
VII.8.1151b17–22 308n.69
VII.12 67n.5
VII.12.1152b33–1153a17 115, 161n.11
VII.12.1152b34–5 115
VII.12.1152b36 184n.12
VII.12.1153a7–17 118
VII.12.1153a9–10 117n.7
VII.12.1153a13–15 118
VII.12.1153a32–3 179n.1, 184n.12
VIII.1.1155a3 45
VIII.2.1155b31–4 169n.34
IX.4.1166b5 125n.15
IX.4.1166b5–25 125n.15
IX.4.1166b22–5 201n.17, 318n.3
IX.5.1167a3–7 340
IX.10.1171a6–8 327n.21
IX.12.1171b29–32 339n.49
IX.12.1172a4 117n.7
X.1.1172a19 45
X.3.1173a15 117n.7
X.3.1173a29–1173b20 115
X.3.1173b4–20 117n.7, 161n.11
X.3.1173b7–20 115
X.3.1173b29–31 117n.7
X.4 123
X.4.1174a6–8 117n.17
X.4.1174b13 119
X.4.1174b18–23 117, 119–20
X.4.1174b23–5 129–30
X.4.1174b23–33 119
X.4.1174b29–31 120
X.4.1174b31–3 129–30
X.4.1174b33–1175a3 120
X.4.1175a6–10 161–2n.14
X.5 127
X.5.1175a32–3 117, 117n.7
X.5.1175a34 117n.7
X.5.1175b3–6 117n.7
X.5.1175b16–17 122
X.5.1175b18–20 117n.7
X.5.1175b22–3 122

X.5.1175b24–8 122
X.5.1175b30 118
X.5.1175b30–5 67n.5
X.5.1175b32–5 118
X.5.1175b36–1176a3 122
X.5.1176a3–5 123
X.5.1176a5–9 123n.14
X.5.1176a10 123
X.5.1176a10–12 123
X.5.1176a12–24 123–4
X.6.1176b25–7 124
X.8.1178a14–16 204n.26
X.8.1178a20–1 204, 206n.31
X.9.1179b28–9 113

Magna moralia
I.7.1186a11–14 317n.2
I.7.1186a13 45n.2
I.7.1186a14 340n.52
I.12.1187b36–7 154n.2
I.12.1192b18 337n.46
II.6.1202b26–7 145

Ethica Eudemia
II.1.1219a26–32 168n.30
II.1.1219a32–3 210
II.1.1220a4–12 168n.30
II.2.1220b5–6 3, 177
II.2.1220b9–10 168n.30
II.2.1220b10–19 49n.14, 251n.33
II.2.1220b12–14 2, 10, 15, 44, 49–50, 168n.30, 169n.33, 177n.56, 179, 180, 235, 250, 317, 317n.2, 338
II.2.1220b12–18 3n.10
II.2.1220b14 53–4
II.2.1220b14–20 324n.13
II.2.1220b18–20 168n.30
II.3.1221a38–40 201, 329n.30
II.3.1221a38–b2 330n.31
II.4.1221b32–5 49n.14, 251n.33
II.4.1221b36–7 49, 251
II.5.1222b10–11 49n.14, 251n.33
II.7.1223a26–7 154n.2
II.7.1223a34 183n.12
II.7.1223b6–7 170n.37
II.7.1223b32–3 170n.37
II.8.1224a37 183n.12
II.8.1224b2 180
II.8.1225a20–33 112n.51, 263n.10
II.10.1225b24–6 154n.2
II.10.1225b30–1 184n.12
II.10.1225b32–4 151–2n.31
II.10.1226b16–20 146n.19
II.10.1227a3–5 146n.19
II.10.1227a18–31 170n.37
III.1 3

III.1.1228b17–29 165n.21
III.1.1228b23–4 26
III.1.1228b26–7 165n.20
III.1.1229a33–5 26, 27n.25, 71n.14, 202
III.1.1229a33–b1 105n.39, 322n.11, 325n.18
III.1.1229a39–b1 202
III.1.1229b31–2 145, 215
III.2 185
III.3 150n.29, 177n.56
III.7 201n.16, 220
III.7.1233b18–22 55, 101, 337, 338n.48
III.7.1233b18–23 332n.34
III.7.1233b19–20 48, 56, 89n.1, 100, 201, 329
III.7.1233b20–1 3
III.7.1233b21–2 201
III.7.1233b22 61
III.7.1233b23 3
III.7.1233b23–5 48, 55n.32, 89n.1, 101n.29, 126, 201, 328, 335–6
III.7.1233b24 328n.24
III.7.1233b25 61
III.7.1233b25–6 335–6
III.7.1233b26–9 3, 324n.13
III.7.1233b27–8 245n.19
III.7.1233b29 3
III.7.1233b35–6 335n.39
III.7.1234a23–33 274n.30
VII.2.1235b22 183n.12
VII.2.1235b23 170n.37
VII.2.1235b26–9 276n.3
VII.12.1245a24–6 339n.49

Politica
I.5.1254b8 7n.21, 54n.30, 168n.30
IV.11.1295b1–11 213n.46
V.3.1302b21–4 168n.28
V.3.1302b25–33 334n.38
V.8.1308a27–30 113n.53, 202, 220
V.10.1311a34–5 202
V.10.1311b36–40 168n.28
V.10.1311b40–1312a20 176n.52, 334n.38
V.10.1312b31–2 145, 215
V.10.1312b32–3 202
V.10.1312b32–4 171
V.11.1315a24–31 202
VI.5.1320a24–6 324n.17
VII.1.1323a29–30 276n.3
VII.7.1327b40–1238a1 170n.36
VII.17.1336a20–1 203n.23
VIII.7.1342a15–16 339

Rhetorica
I.1.1354a16–17 317n.1
I.2.1355b31–4 209n.38
I.2.1356a14–16 182
I.2.1356a15–16 169

Rhetorica (cont.)
  I.2.1356a22–5 104n.35
  I.2.1356a35–b6 101
  I.2.1356b16–18 101n.32
  I.2.1357b1–21 170n.38
  I.3.1358b3–5 44–5n.1, 113n.52, 181
  I.3.1358b4–7 182
  I.3.1358b9–10 44–5n.1, 113n.52, 181, 182
  I.5.1361b39–1362a2 331
  I.5.1362a5–6 331
  I.5–6 77n.27, 174n.48, 329n.27
  I.7.1363b28–33 46–8
  I.7.1363b30–1 50
  I.9 183n.11
  I.10 13, 155, 156, 159n.8, 160, 183n.9
  I.10.1368b12–14 156
  I.10.1368b14–15 156
  I.10.1368b16–18 156
  I.10.1368b18–20 156, 164, 165
  I.10.1368b20 156
  I.10.1368b21 156n.4
  I.10.1368b22–3 156n.4, 245n.19
  I.10.1368b23 156
  I.10.1368b23–4 156
  I.10.1368b25–6 156
  I.10.1368b32ff 157
  I.10.1368b37–1369a1 157
  I.10.1368b37–1369a4 182
  I.10.1369a1–2 157
  I.10.1369a1–4 168, 177n.56
  I.10.1369a2 158, 171n.43
  I.10.1369a2–3 158
  I.10.1369a2–4 157, 170n.36, 170n.37
  I.10.1369a3–4 171n.43
  I.10.1369a4 182n.8
  I.10.1369a6–7 171a43
  I.10.1369a7 157, 177n.56, 182n.8
  I.10.1369a7–31 158
  I.10.1369a9–18 158
  I.10.1369a12–13 187
  I.10.1369a18 159
  I.10.1369b7–11 158
  I.10.1369b7ff 182
  I.10.1369b11 182n.8
  I.10.1369b11–12 156n.4, 159
  I.10.1369b14–15 182–3
  I.10.1369b15–16 159, 182–3, 184n.13
  I.10.1369b23 183n.12
  I.10.1369b28–31 159
  I.10.1369b31–2 211
  I.11 12n.31, 115, 117, 159, 183
  I.11.1369b33–5 115, 115n.1, 160–1, 161n.11, 240n.8
  I.11.1370a5–6 116n.5

  I.11.1370a6–9 116n.5
  I.11.1370a10–11 61n.50
  I.11.1370a16–27 181, 184
  I.11.1370a17–18 183n.12, 184n.13
  I.11.1370b4–5 61n.50
  I.11.1370b9 61n.50
  I.11.1370b13 147n.21
  I.11.1370b13–14 151
  I.11.1370b15–16 186
  I.11.1370b25–6 261
  I.11.1370b25–8 62
  I.11.1370b25–9 55n.34, 186, 340, 341
  I.11.1370b26 55n.34
  I.11.1370b26–8 116
  I.11.1370b26–9 61n.50
  I.11.1370b31–2 116
  I.11.1370b32–4 116, 186–7, 264n.15
  I.11.1370b33–4 185–6
  I.11.1371a8–9 116
  I.13.1374b19–21 44–5n.1, 113n.52, 181
  II.1.1377b20–8 182
  II.1.1377b31 172
  II.1.1377b31–1378a3 169, 320n.8, 321n.9
  II.1.1377b31–1378a5 113
  II.1.1378a1–3 172
  II.1.1378a3–5 181–2, 247n.21, 338
  II.1.1378a4 183
  II.1.1378a16–19 183n.11
  II.1.1378a18 169n.34
  II.1.1378a19–21 4n.11, 113, 180
  II.1.1378a19–22 2, 10, 44, 47, 114, 169, 246, 250, 252–3
  II.1.1378a21–2 106n.41, 238
  II.1.1378a22 238
  II.1.1378a22–4 240n.9
  II.1.1378a22–6 28n.29, 143
  II.1.1378a22–9 319n.6
  II.1.1378a24 56n.36
  II.1.1378a24–6 319n.6
  II.1.1378a26 4n.11, 181, 200
  II.2 154n.2, 214–16, 215n.50, 218
  II.2.1378a30 2n.4, 13, 201n.14
  II.2.1378a30–1 53, 69, 92, 96, 214
  II.2.1378a30–2 27, 71, 104, 137, 140, 141, 144, 146n.20, 149, 318
  II.2.1378a30ff 214
  II.2.1378a31–b2 147
  II.2.1378a32 176
  II.2.1378a32f 220n.58
  II.2.1378b1–2 48n.10, 53, 69, 92, 96
  II.2.1378b1–3 105, 146–7, 319
  II.2.1378b1–4 147n.21, 151
  II.2.1378b2–3 48n.10
  II.2.1378b8 48n.10, 105, 147, 319

II.2.1378b8-9 151-2n.31
II.2.1378b11-1379a9 318
II.2.1378b14-15 245
II.2.1378b15-17 334
II.2.1378b18-20 149, 319n.5
II.2.1378b20 319n.5
II.2.1378b20-1 319n.5
II.2.1378b20-1379a9 319n.6
II.2.1378b21-3 319n.5
II.2.1378b23-5 142
II.2.1378b23-35 213n.46
II.2.1378b31-5 152n.32
II.2.1379a10-30 319n.6
II.2.1379a11-12 187
II.2.1379a11-24 142, 233
II.2.1379a12 161, 176
II.2.1379a16-17 176, 187, 233
II.2.1379a17-18 176
II.2.1379a18-19 176
II.2.1379a23-4 233-4
II.2.1379a24-6 143
II.2.1379a30-b37 319n.6
II.2.1379a34-8 28n.29
II.2.1379b17-18 337n.44
II.2.1380a1 56n.36
II.2.1380a2-5 220n.62
II.2-3 157n.5
II.3 3n.9, 152n.33, 242-3n.13
II.3.1380a6 239n.6
II.3.1380a6-9 319
II.3.1380a6-12 238-9
II.3.1380a8 56n.36, 201n.14, 239n.6
II.3.1380a9-16 240-1, 242-3n.13
II.3.1380a13-15 242
II.3.1380a14-16 201n.17, 318n.3
II.3.1380a15-18 149n.24
II.3.1380a20-1 334n.38
II.3.1380a22-30 241
II.3.1380a26-31 242-3n.13
II.3.1380a31-2 242n.12
II.3.1380a32-4 241
II.3.1380a33 241
II.3.1380a33-4 203n.24, 323
II.3.1380a34-b1 241
II.3.1380b1 145, 215
II.3.1380b2-3 241
II.3.1380b3-5 241
II.3.1380b5-6 242
II.3.1380b6-13 242
II.3.1380b10-13 149n.26, 231-2
II.3.1380b10-14 276n.3
II.3.1380b16-18 149n.24, 176
II.3.1380b16-20 242
II.3.1380b17-18 245

II.3.1380b19-21 245
II.3.1380b20-5 105n.37
II.3.1380b20-30 150, 242
II.3.1380b23-6 241n.10
II.3.1380b31-4 220n.62, 242
II.4 13, 106n.41, 137, 168-9
II.4.1380b35-1381a7 169-170
II.4.1380b36 201n.14
II.4.1380b36-1381a1 92n.10, 320
II.4.1380b37 170n.36
II.4.1380b37-1381a1 150n.27
II.4.1381a1-7 320
II.4.1381a3 170n.38, 173, 253
II.4.1381a3-5 57
II.4.1381a3f 220n.58
II.4.1381a5-10 57
II.4.1381a6 170n.38
II.4.1381a7 168
II.4.1381a7-10 170n.35
II.4.1381a7ff 170
II.4.1382a1-2 150n.27, 171, 220n.61, 319n.5
II.4.1382a1-3 321
II.4.1382a2 171n.42
II.4.1382a2-3 149, 215n.48
II.4.1382a3-15 149
II.4.1382a6-7 171n.40, 321n.10
II.4.1382a8 149
II.4.1382a8-12 171n.41
II.4.1382a9-12 150
II.4.1382a12-13 51, 114, 145, 149, 155, 169,
   171, 172, 215, 215n.48
II.4.1382a13 145
II.4.1382a16-19 220n.62
II.5 295
II.5.1382a21 48, 63, 89n.1, 201n.14
II.5.1382a21-2 11, 27, 53, 58n.41, 69, 71, 91,
   92, 96, 98, 99, 105, 160, 164, 166, 167n.26,
   168, 202, 249, 322
II.5.1382a22-7 322
II.5.1382a23-4 324-325
II.5.1382a24-7 202
II.5.1382a27-32 27, 71, 322
II.5.1382a27f 220n.58
II.5.1382a28 22
II.5.1382b10-12 28n.29
II.5.1382b14-16 28n.29
II.5.1382b26 22
II.5.1382b29-30 202n.18
II.5.1383a5-8 163
II.5.1383a8-12 220n.62
II.5.1383a13-15 220n.61
II.5.1383a13-19 248, 323
II.5.1383a15 56n.36
II.5.1383a17-18 164n.18

Rhetorica (cont.)
  II.5.1383a17–19 248
  II.5.1383a28 249n.25
  II.5.1383a28–9 249n.25
  II.5.1383b6 203n.24, 323
  II.6 3n.9, 325
  II.6.1383b11 56n.36
  II.6.1383b12 201n.14
  II.6.1383b12–13 48, 63, 89n.1
  II.6.1383b12–14 57, 264n.14, 323
  II.6.1383b13 160n.10
  II.6.1383b13–14 27, 71
  II.6.1383b14–15 244, 325
  II.6.1383b15f 220n.58
  II.6.1383b16 22
  II.6.1383b16–18 58
  II.6.1383b17–18 28n.29, 323–4
  II.6.1383b19 164
  II.6.1383b19–20 323n.12
  II.6.1383b22–4 107, 160
  II.6.1383b25 323n.12
  II.6.1383b29–30 323n.12
  II.6.1383b33–1384a2 323n.12
  II.6.1384a8–15 323n.12
  II.6.1384a15–20 323n.12
  II.6.1384a21–5 107
  II.6.1384a21–b26 28n.29
  II.6.1384a21f 220n.59
  II.6.1384a22 107
  II.6.1384b17–20 323n.12
  II.6.1384b27–1385a3 324
  II.6.1384b31 324
  II.6.1384b35–6 324
  II.6.1385a1–3 323–4
  II.6.1385a14–15 220n.61, 244
  II.7 14, 169, 235, 236, 244n.16
  II.7.1385a16 56n.36
  II.7.1385a16–17 220n.59
  II.7.1385a16–19 236, 325–6
  II.7.1385a17 201n.14
  II.7.1385a21–5 188, 189n.24
  II.7.1385a23 339n.49
  II.7.1385a29–33 220n.62
  II.7.1385b1–5 243
  II.7.1385b7–10 244, 326
  II.8.1385b11 56n.36, 237n.3, 243
  II.8.1385b13 48, 63, 89n.1, 201n.14
  II.8.1385b13–14 56, 99
  II.8.1385b13–16 27, 55, 71, 79n.30, 327
  II.8.1385b16–23 327n.22
  II.8.1385b23–6 143
  II.8.1386a4 22, 56n.36
  II.8.1386a4–5 220n.59
  II.8.1386a4–7 327
  II.8.1386a4–16 319n.6

  II.8.1386a5–11 202n.19
  II.8.1386a7–9 325
  II.8.1386a7–13 327
  II.8.1386a9–11 325
  II.8.1386a29–b7 327n.22
  II.9 317, 329, 335
  II.9.1386b8 248
  II.9.1386b8–15 80, 175n.51
  II.9.1386b8–1387a5 97n.19, 220n.60, 238
  II.9.1386b9 48, 56, 79, 89n.1, 100, 327
  II.9.1386b10–11 56, 100, 328n.25
  II.9.1386b11–13 94
  II.9.1386b12 56, 79, 100, 327
  II.9.1386b12–13 327n.21
  II.9.1386b13–15 328n.24
  II.9.1386b16–20 58n.41, 80, 160, 162, 330
  II.9.1386b20–4 80, 97n.19, 322n.11, 331n.33
  II.9.1386b22–4 105n.39
  II.9.1386b25–1387a3 80–81, 330
  II.9.1386b25–1387a5 94
  II.9.1386b26–7 48, 56, 61, 79, 89n.1, 100, 327, 335n.41
  II.9.1386b26–8 112
  II.9.1386b26–30 94
  II.9.1386b26–32 112–13, 126n.17
  II.9.1386b27 55n.32
  II.9.1386b27–8 55, 61, 100–101, 216n.51, 255n.40, 335, 335n.41
  II.9.1386b27–30 126
  II.9.1386b28–30 61, 335
  II.9.1386b30–1 48, 55, 61, 78, 89n.1, 101, 161–2n.14, 162, 163n.16, 336
  II.9.1386b33–1387a3 48, 55, 58n43, 61, 89n.1, 101, 112–13, 335–6
  II.9.1387a3–5 97n.19
  II.9.1387a6–23 77, 77n.27, 174n.48, 329n.27
  II.9.1387a7 56n.36
  II.9.1387a8–9 48, 55, 89n.1, 100, 328
  II.9.1387a9–10 201n.14
  II.9.1387a13 328
  II.9.1387b4 56n.36
  II.9.1387b5–8 143
  II.9.1387b9–11 143
  II.10.1387b22 56n.36, 329n.28
  II.10.1387b22–5 220n.59
  II.10.1387b23 48, 63, 89n.1, 201n.14
  II.10.1387b23–5 55, 77, 100, 174n.48, 329–30
  II.10.1387b35–1388a5 319n.6
  II.10.1388a1–2 331
  II.10.1388a1–5 176n.53
  II.10.1388a3–4 331
  II.10.1388a9–12 28n.29
  II.10.1388a26–7 332
  II.11.1388a31 56n.6
  II.11.1388a31f 220n.59

II.11.1388a32 48, 63, 89n.1, 201n.14
II.11.1388a32–5 55, 78, 174n.48, 332
II.11.1388a35–6 78n.28
II.11.1388a35–8 94
II.11.1388a35–b1 174, 332, 333
II.11.1388b5 332
II.11.1388b8–10 332n.35
II.11.1388b11–12 174, 332
II.11.1388b14 332
II.11.1388b22–9 334
II.11.1388b24–6 94
II.11.1388b29 4n.11, 181, 200
II.12 233
II.12.1388b31–2 181
II.12.1388b32–4 181, 338
II.12.1389a8 170n.36
II.12.1389a18–20 203, 323
II.12.1389a19 250n.27
II.12.1389a25–7 203
II.12.1389a25–8 250n.27
II.12.1389a27–8 323
II.12–13 206n.31
II.12–14 203
II.13 223
II.13.1389b29–30 203
II.13.1389b30–2 203
II.13.1389b32 250n.27
II.13.1390a1–3 245n.19
II.13.1390a11 213n.46
II.13.1390a15–16 213n.46
II.13.1390a15ff 213n.46
II.13.1390a17–18 213n.46
II.13.1390a18–21 327n.22
II.16.1390b32 45
II.21.1395a9 317n.1
II.23 102
II.24.1400b34–1401a1 102
II.24.1401a1 102
II.24.1401b3 317n.1
II.24.1401b12–14 102
II.24.1401b30–4 102
II.25.1402a33–4 102n.33
III.16.1417b1–2 205n.29
III.19.1419b25–6 317n.1

De arte poetica liber
13.1452b36–1453a4 220
13.1453a4 203, 220, 327

Plato

Euthyphro
12b–c

Apology
28c3–9

Cratylus
420a3–7 340

Philebus
31d4–9 160–1
31d5 162n.15
31d–32b 115
31e–32a 162n.15
32b2–3 162n.15
32b9–c5 162n.15
37a2–9 58
37e1–7 58
37e10 91n.5
42c9–d7 115
43c4–6 115
46a 51
46c–47b 51
47e1–2 340
47e3 340
48a1–4 340
48b8–9 58
48b11–12 58
50b7–c1 340

Symposium
197d7 340

Phaedrus
252a7 340
252e6 340

Protagoras
358a6–b3 62n.51, 339
358d6 202n.18

Gorgias
494c–e 51

Republic
III.390d 151–2n.31
IV.436a10–b1 180n.2
IV.436aff 177n.56
IV.437d–e 180n.2
IV.439c–441c 171n.43
IV.439d6–8 180n.2
IV.441b 151–2n.31
IX.573a7 340
X.602c10–11 280n.19

Timaeus
61c–68d 116n.4
64c7–d3 115
64c7–65b3 160–1
69b–70e 210n.40

Laws
646e4–647a6 324n.13

Definitions
416a9 206n.30